'This extraordinary state-of-the-art book distils the accumulated clinical and practical experience from the UK's pioneers of Early Intervention in Psychosis in Birmingham.

It is replete with varied and incisive case material covering all aspects of recovery; and does so combining science and evidence with compassion and amazing skill. This is a must-read for all practitioners working with psychosis.'

Max Birchwood, *Professor of Youth Mental Health, University of Warwick*

'This book reminds readers of the central purpose of early intervention services … to secure meaning to the lives of people experiencing psychosis for the first time.

Concepts of recovery are explored in a well-constructed manual that successfully blends evidence-based practice with practice-based evidence, informed by the experience of this book's authors in delivering these services over the last two decades.'

Dr David Shiers, OBE, *retired GP and former Joint National Lead for EIP*

'This excellent new book provides up-to-date evidence of how Early Intervention services have revolutionised the treatment of psychosis by providing a framework for the delivery of evidence-based interventions, embedded within a philosophy of hope and recovery. Moreover, this book challenges us to adjust our focus from early intervention to full, sustained, long-term recovery. It provides a compelling vision of an integrated system which engages effectively and enables rapid access to individualised treatment, without the need for compulsion. A vision worth pursuing.'

Stephen 'Moggie' McGowan, *Chair of IRIS (Initiative to Reduce the Impact of Schizophrenia) and Clinical Lead for Yorkshire and Humberside EIP and NHS England*

Recovering from a First Episode of Psychosis

Despite years of research, debate and changes in mental health policy, there is still a lack of consensus as to what recovery from psychosis actually means, how it should be measured and how it may ultimately be achieved. In *Recovering from a First Episode of Psychosis: An Integrated Approach to Early Intervention*, it is argued that recovery from a first episode of psychosis (FEP) is comprised of three core elements: symptomatic, social and personal. Moreover, all three types of recovery need to be the target of early intervention for psychosis programmes (EIP) which provide evidence-based, integrated, bio-psychosocial interventions delivered in the context of a value base offering hope, empowerment and a youth-focused approach.

Over the 12 chapters in this book, the authors, all experienced clinicians and researchers from multi-professional backgrounds, demonstrate that long-term *recovery* needs to replace short-term *remission* as the key target of early psychosis services and that, to achieve this, we need a change in the way we deliver EIP: one that takes account of the different stages of psychosis and the 'bespoke' targeting of integrated medical, psychological and social treatments during the 'critical period'.

Illustrated with a wealth of clinical examples, this book will be of great interest to clinical psychologists, psychiatrists, psychiatric nurses and other associated mental health professionals.

Chris Jackson is a consultant clinical psychologist and clinical lead for the Birmingham EIP service, Forward Thinking Birmingham. He has been involved in the development of psychological therapies for FEP for the last 25 years and has co-authored books on schizophrenia and early intervention approaches to first episode psychosis. His current interests include recovery, suicide prevention and emotional dysfunction following FEP, as well as refining the delivery of EIP services.

Eleanor Baggott is a UK-trained clinical psychologist. She worked at Birmingham and Solihull EIP for five years before emigrating to New Zealand. She is currently the senior clinical psychologist at Totara House, the EIP service in

Christchurch, and sits on the executive committee of the NZ EIP Society. She has a special interest in working with families and using mindfulness and acceptance-based approaches.

Mark Bernard is a principal clinical psychologist in the North Birmingham Early Intervention Psychosis Team within Forward Thinking Birmingham, UK. His current interests include the application of psychological approaches following first episode psychosis, the use of Routine Outcome Measures within Early Intervention Psychosis services, and the development of clinical pathways for At Risk Mental States.

Ruth Clutterbuck is a senior clinical psychologist in the East Birmingham Early Intervention for Psychosis Team, Forward Thinking Birmingham, UK. She has a special interest in social recovery following a first episode psychosis and leads on social recovery strategy for Birmingham EIP services.

Diane Ryles qualified as a mental health nurse in North Staffordshire 28 years ago. She was an original member of the West Midlands IRIS group and worked in Birmingham EIP for 14 years as a care co-ordinator, lead nurse and manager. She is now the matron for recovery services, and a trainer in family work and suicide prevention. She is also a carer for a relative with psychosis.

Erin Turner is a consultant psychiatrist in the Early Intervention for Psychosis Service, Solihull, UK, Co-chair of West Midlands EIP Expert Advisory Group and trustee of the mental health charity 'Beyond Shame, Beyond Stigma'. She led the development of the 'Silver Linings' app for young people recovering from psychosis and is a board member of HEARTH, Theatre Company. Her interests include promoting collaborative compassionate care and using the arts to reduce stigma and demystify psychosis.

Recovering from a First Episode of Psychosis

An Integrated Approach to Early Intervention

Chris Jackson, Eleanor Baggott, Mark Bernard, Ruth Clutterbuck, Diane Ryles and Erin Turner

Routledge
Taylor & Francis Group

LONDON AND NEW YORK

First published 2019
by Routledge
2 Park Square, Milton Park, Abingdon, Oxon OX14 4RN

and by Routledge
52 Vanderbilt Avenue, New York, NY 10017

Routledge is an imprint of the Taylor & Francis Group, an informa business

British Library Cataloguing-in-Publication Data
A catalogue record for this book is available from the British Library

Library of Congress Cataloging-in-Publication Data
A catalog record has been requested for this book

ISBN: 978-1-138-66919-2 (hbk)
ISBN: 978-1-138-66920-8 (pbk)
ISBN: 978-1-315-46073-4 (ebk)

Typeset in Times New Roman
by Wearset Ltd, Boldon, Tyne and Wear

To everyone past and present, who has touched, and been touched, by EIP. Most of all, to all those who are no longer with us, who never realised the contribution they made.

Contents

Figures

Tables

Foreword

From psychosis to politics[1]

Andrew Gordon

My name is Andrew Gordon. I'm a politician, a local councillor in a council with the collective responsibility for around 200,000 people, which manages a multi-million-pound budget and discharges a number of legal duties in the course of their business.

Not only am I a local councillor, but I was elected one of the youngest in the country at 18 in a seat that hadn't been won by my political party for around 20 years.

When I was on the election campaign trail, I remember having a conversation with one of my residents. I was telling them about my values, what I stand for and how I wanted my town to be run. He said I was crazy. I paused for a minute and responded, 'Yes I am', to which he shook my hand and told me I had his vote.

The title of this foreword implies that there is some sort of journey involved and I am going to deliver on that promise, which I can assure you is the most original political line in this piece. I am going to take you all on a journey. But before we do, I want to ponder the concept of 'if only' because in politics it's a question we ask quite a lot … if only Bernie Sanders was the democratic presidential candidate, if only Jeremy Corbyn had been an 8/10 instead of a 7/10 on the EU, if only Tony Blair hadn't invaded Iraq or if only Gordon Brown had triggered that early election.

For mental health, the Early Intervention in Psychosis service is the 'if only' for thousands. Ponder that a moment....

My journey of mental illness started in school; I was always a bit of an odd character but at 14, one day I just stopped attending. The reason I stopped attending is because I wanted to become a full-time hermit, run away to an island in the middle of nowhere and live off the land.

Now that didn't just happen out the blue, and clearly I never achieved my plan, but, in short, I was being bullied at school, and I started to dislike myself. I did not just hate myself, but I had an absolute disdain for myself. I thought I was the scum of the earth, some 'ugly', 'fat' 'worthless cretin'.

I began to harm myself. I would sometimes whip myself with a belt, I would sometimes punch myself, I stopped going out of the house and socially isolated myself for months on end. On top of all this, I started to hear voices.

Things became too much; my life had ceased to function and I was only 14. As I was approaching 15, I was placed in the Early Intervention in Psychosis Team but I think it was too late.

I ended up experiencing what I call a 'psychotic breakdown', in short, the voices told me Satan himself was going to come and send me to hell and that I was to run to escape. It started off with me pacing the room and then I jumped out the window, vaulted over the fence and started roaming the streets of Basildon.

Eventually the police came and picked me up, I guess because 15-year-old people wandering around thinking people were out to kill them is not exactly the safest situation in the world.

I was then faced with a Mental Health Act assessment, and you all thought managerial supervisions were traumatic. Try sitting in a room with two consultant psychiatrists and a social worker deciding whether or not you are to be sectioned under the Mental Health Act. It was then agreed that, assuming I was sent to an in-patient psychiatric unit willingly, that I did not need to be sectioned under the Mental Health Act.

I spent a year in an in-patient psychiatric unit, where I underwent intensive therapy and pharmacological interventions. I was pumped full of Risperdal by an inter-muscular injection. The impact this had on me was quite profound, I put on body mass (20 stone), I started hyper-salivating, I developed a twitch in my right leg and my mind became a prison.

That prison was a dark place to be, I couldn't think like Andrew and being only 16, I guess I didn't even know who Andrew was to begin with. The antipsychotic medication put a brake on my psychotic experiences. It gave my mind a chance to recover, which ultimately gave me an opportunity to take back control of my life. Without it, I would not be here today. The key with any medication is that it needs to be reviewed regularly and the person taking it needs to be educated as to the purpose of the medication and the alternatives, so they can make an informed choice.

I write this because, once I was discharged from hospital, I had a brilliant psychiatrist who worked with me to find a medication that suited my particular needs at the time. I transitioned from risperdal to abilify, fluoxamine and melatonin.

The psychiatrist took time to explain each medication, the effects on me and the other alternatives. He adjusted it depending on what I was experiencing at the time and helped me work through the side effects. I started to be able to make my recovery and I never missed a dose.

But, it didn't help me deal with the loss of my social and community networks or resolve the self-loathing, anxiety and obsessional thinking.

As the psychotic symptoms dissipated and I became more stable, I was eventually discharged from hospital back into the care of the Early Intervention in Psychosis team at 16, who, I guess, reflecting on it, helped me fight off the rest of the psychosis. However, during this period I started to become incredibly depressed. Ironically, this was the time I joined the Labour Party – but I would urge you not to read too much into that statement!

Given that I have been asked to write this foreword on a book about EIP (early intervention for psychosis) services, I wanted to dwell on my experience with an EIP team, in my own recovery. I want to draw upon three experiences here:

- walking in the woods: I loved walking and when I asked my nurse to walk with me, there were no barriers whatsoever.
- the therapist and whale music: for all you therapists out there.
- sitting in the back of a tiny car with the EIP support worker and four large psychotic guys.

I think that brings me on to what makes people who work in EIP the 'if only', what makes the EIP service so special, or at least what made it special for me was that you take a whole person. By doing something as simple as walking with me, you helped me get out the house, something at the time I probably hadn't done for ages. You also helped me trust nursing as a profession more because you treated me as an equal.

How often in therapy do we talk about building rapport? By introducing me to his house music and taking me to my Connexions appointment, the therapist did more rapport building than could ever come from just sitting in a room talking.

Taking me out bowling with other people, being taken to and from bowling in that 'diddy' three-door car. 'Damnit' guys, four in one, not only did you help me get out the house, confront my anxieties and build my social networks but you helped me do something I hadn't done in ages – laugh!

The list could go on but my point is what made EIP unique for me was its flexibility, it's a true person-centred approach, it's positive risk-taking. That's what makes EIP different, that's why I always say EIP saved my life.

In true political style, I think if you take anything away from this Foreword and the book, it's that you must fight hard to keep your unique approach, because it works and it transforms lives. It's so much more than just sessions of CBT or medication or BFT or even IPS. For me, EIP gave me the platform I needed to build my recovery. If only everyone who had emerging psychosis or who was experiencing psychosis for the first time had access to an EIP service like the one that saved my life.

I have given you a snapshot of my journey, and I have been through a lot. Would I change anything? No. No, because I wouldn't be the person I am today without my experiences.

My friends (the real cynics in life) aren't the ones who say 'life is tough', the real cynics in life are the ones who say 'everything will be alright!'. Life is tough, if it kicks you down, it will kick you, spit on you and keep kicking you until you force yourself to get back up, it is relentless and has no mercy.

It doesn't stop – if you fall behind, you have to run to catch up and keep running. But what life does do is create characters that have an indomitable will. People who have life, and just keep going. The most powerful asset you can have is the ability to learn from the unfortunate experiences and be able to come out and say things were tough, but I kept going in my recovery journey: from psychosis to politics.

I overcome things by constantly challenging my warped beliefs, I overcome things by meditation. I overcome things by sharing my experiences with the world. I overcome things by being brave. I overcome things by simply going to bed early or eating three square meals a day.

There is no silver bullet to prevention, but we can all do things to make a difference. Yes, I still feel quite lonely and isolated, yes, I have a tendency to be unsociable, yes, I can feel pretty damn depressed. Sometimes I even hate life and have thoughts of ending it all. The ultimate difference between when I was first referred to EIP and now is that, sometimes, just sometimes I can feel happy.

Hopefully by reading this book, it will help guide you, so you can help shape EIP services, whether in the UK or around the world, to make other people experiencing psychosis for the first time (and their families), a little bit happier too – to not accept the 'if only'

Note

1 This foreword was based on a speech given at the Early Intervention in Psychosis Network Annual Forum meeting, held at the Royal College of Psychiatrists, London, 7 March 2017.

Foreword

A carer's experience

Bernie Moraghan

Until three years ago, we, as parents, had never heard of Early Intervention Mental Health Services.

However, when our only son, 'Joe', then aged 24, was diagnosed with psychosis and sectioned under the Mental Health Act, there was a mixture of relief, at being able to access help for him, and also utter confusion, despair and sadness for his future and what it would hold. We knew from that day forward the lives of the whole family would change forever.

The hardest thing in the world is to hand your most precious loved one over to strangers who know nothing about him. They did not know he was smart, witty and funny with a great sense of humour, a talented piano player, which was handy at parties, sporty and healthy with his whole life ahead of him. They only knew the symptoms which Joe had developed. This illness had taken away his ability to maintain friendships, employment and he grew more isolated and beyond reach. We desperately hoped that Early Intervention had the magic words or pills to give us our son back.

The three years that Joe has been under the care and treatment of Early Intervention has included a spell in a Psychiatric Unit and six months in a Rehabilitation Hospital. During that time the skills and knowledge of all the team have had a tremendously positive effect on us all – it has been a life-saver.

The impact of having your loved one diagnosed with a mental illness is totally devastating. It is scary, you do not know what to do, where to go or what the future holds. Early Intervention services have helped and guided us through every step. The mental health seminars and support groups that were offered were invaluable, they provided us with the opportunity to meet the staff and support agencies, and gave us an insight into the illness, the types of medication, coping strategies and the importance of effective communication. It is good to listen and talk to other parents and carers, to compare your stories. One thing is certain: mental illness is not prejudiced. It can affect anybody from any walk of life. The team have encouraged us not to be afraid, but to be brave and talk to the staff when we are worried or concerned – they always listen, reassure and help. We have learnt how to work with the staff to achieve the best outcome and to realise that negatives can turn to positives – there is always a silver lining although sometimes you have to look really hard for it. Most importantly – to stay hopeful and healthy.

We discovered Early Intervention services do have the magic words and pills. They come in the form of the team's compassionate words and respectful, kind approach to Joe's needs. They have managed to build a really trusting, effective relationship with us all, and although Joe's progress has been measured and fluctuating, he has made huge strides in coping with his illness. With continued care, we are optimistic we shall see more of Joe's sense of humour, confidence and motivation as his recovery continues.

It has taken time to rebuild our relationship and to learn how to manage and cope with Joe's condition, but we have learnt to get the laughter and affection back – he even gives me a hug and pecks my cheek and says, 'Thanks, Mom', it is a simple gesture but means so much.

It has been a difficult and challenging journey but I am convinced that without the help and support of Early Intervention, we as a family would not exist today, we are so grateful.

Abbreviations

AASPIRE	Academic Autism Spectrum Partnership in Research and Education
ACT	Acceptance and Commitment Therapy
AD	antidepressant
ADOS	Autism Diagnostic Observation Schedule
ALT	autistic-like traits
AP	antipsychotic
ARMS	at risk mental states
ASD	Autistic Spectrum Disorder
AVH	auditory verbal hallucinations
BA	behavioural activation
BAVQ	Beliefs about Voices Questionnaire
BAVQ-R	Beliefs about Voices Questionnaire-Revised
BCSS	Brief Core Schema Scale
BDD	Body Dysmorphia Disorder (
BDI-II	Beck Depression Inventory-II
BFT	behavioural family therapy
BME	black and minority ethnic
BPD	borderline personality disorder
BPIQ-R	Personal Beliefs about Illness Questionnaire Revised
BPRS	Brief Psychiatric Rating Scale
CAARMS	Comprehensive Assessment of At Risk Mental States
CATIE	Clinical Antipsychotic Trials of Intervention Effectiveness
CB:IT	cognitive behavioural integrated therapy
CBD	cannabidol
CBQp	Cognitive Biases Questionnaire for Psychosis
CBT	cognitive behavioural therapy
CBTn	cognitive behavioural therapy for negative symptoms
CBTp	cognitive behavioural therapy for psychosis
CDS	Calgary Depression Scale
CHIME	Connectiveness, Hope, Identity, Meaning and Empowerment framework

CHR	clinical high risk
CKD	chronic kidney disease
CMHT	community mental health team
CMT	compassionate mind training
CQUIN	Commissioning for Quality and Innovation
CROMs	clinician reported outcome measures
CRT	cognitive remediation therapy
CSW	community support worker
CUtLASS 1	Cost Utility of the Latest Antipsychotic Drugs in Schizophrenia Study
CVD	cardiovascular disease
DIPT	delay in intensive psychosocial treatment
DISCO	diagnostic interview for social and communication disorders
DSH	deliberate self-harm
DUI	duration of untreated illness
DUP	duration of untreated psychosis
EET	enrolment in education
EIP	early intervention for psychosis
EMDR	eye movement desensitisation reprocessing
EPPIC	Early Psychosis Prevention and Intervention Centre
EPSE	extra-pyramidal side effect
ESM	event-sampling
EUFEST	European First Episode Schizophrenia Trial
EUPD/BPD	emotionally unstable/borderline PD
EWS	early warning signs
FEP	first episode of psychosis
FGA	first-generation antipsychotics
FI	family intervention
FMPS	Frost Multidimensional Perfectionism Scale
GABA	gamma-Aminobutyric acid
GAF-D	global assessment of functioning-disability
GASS	Glasgow Antipsychotic Side effect Scale
GMV	grey matter volume
GRIP	Graduated Recovery Intervention Program
GSDS	Groningen Social Disabilities Schedule
HDL	high density lipoprotein
HPA	hypothalamic-pituitary-adrenal
HTT	home treatment team
IAPT	improved access to psychological therapies
IMV	integrated motivational-volitional
INQ	Interpersonal Needs Questionnaire
IPS	individual placement and support
IRIS	Initiative to Reduce the Impact of Schizophrenia
IRT	individualised resiliency training

JBS	Joint British Societies
LD	learning disabilities
LUNSERS	Liverpool University Neuroleptic Side Effect Rating Scale
MBCT	mindfulness-based cognitive therapy
MDT	multi-disciplinary team
MI	motivational interviewing
NEET	not in education, employment or training
NPS	novel psychoactive substances
OCD	obsessive compulsive disorder
PANSS	Positive and Negative Syndrome Scale
PBCT	person-based cognitive therapy
PD	personality disorder
PDI	Peters Delusional Inventory
PIG	Policy Implementation Guide
PREM	patient reported experienced measure
PROM	patient reported outcome measure
PSI	psychosocial intervention
PTG	post-traumatic growth
PTSD	post-traumatic stress disorder
QoL	quality of life
QPR	Process of Recovery Questionnaire
RACS	Risk of Acting on Commands Scale
RBBs	restricted repetitive behaviours
RCT	randomised controlled trial
ROM	routine outcome measure
RRS	Ruminative Responses Scale
RSWG	Remission in Schizophrenia Working Group
rTMS	repetitive trans-cranial magnetic stimulation
RTT	referral to treatment
SA	suicide attempt
SaD	social anxiety disorder
SANS	Scale for the Assessment of Negative Symptoms
SAPS	Scale for the Assessment of Positive Symptoms
SAS	Social Adjustment Scale
SGA	second-generation of antipsychotic medications
SNRIs	serotonin-norepinephrine reuptake inhibitors
SR	social recovery
SRT	Social Recovery Therapy
SSD	schizophrenia spectrum disorders
SSRIs	selective serotonin reuptake inhibitors
SST	Social Skills Training
SUD	substance use disorder
TAU	treatment as usual
TC	total cholesterol

TD	tardive dyskinesia
TdP	Torsades de pointes
TEC	Trauma Experiences Checklist
TF-CBT	trauma-focused CBT
THC	9 tetrahydrocannabinol
TUS	Time Use Survey
UHR	ultra high risk
WSAS	Work and Social Adjustment Scale
YBOCI	Yale-Brown Obsessive Compulsive Inventory

Chapter 1

The first episode of psychosis and how EIP services have evolved to optimise adaptation and recovery

Mosi, a 21-year-old university student, was playing a football video game. He was playing as his favourite team Arsenal who were 1–0 up on West Ham with 10 minutes to play. Suddenly, without warning, he heard a voice telling him that he should finish the game and 'make a cup of tea'. He stopped, listened and assumed that it was his neighbour upstairs, fed up with the noise from his games console, shouting through the walls to get him to be quiet. The only problem was, he didn't have a neighbour. The man upstairs had moved out a month ago and the flat had been empty since. He began to get anxious and worried that his explanation might not be correct. In the days that followed the voice came back, usually in the evening, but sometimes during the day. The voice began to change. It was no longer advisory and pleasant but nasty and malevolent. Mosi began to think that he was merely hearing a spirit. However, he was becoming increasingly anxious that he had no influence over the voice but that it had 'control over him'. He was convinced that the voice had control of his heart and could 'shock' his body. He became anxious and depressed and stopped going to lectures. He didn't tell anyone about the voice because he was worried and ashamed about what people may think. Mosi was beginning to isolate himself, reluctant to go out as he became increasingly sensitive to what people were thinking about him on the street. He felt uncomfortable around them, aware that they 'may know something about what he was thinking'. He then 'split' with his girlfriend, unable to sustain a relationship, and thinking that it would save her from knowing the truth. It was only when his mother and father who lived 300 miles away came to see him that he was persuaded to see the GP at the university health centre who referred him to his local Early Intervention for Psychosis (EIP) service.

In this chapter we will attempt to explain what a first episode of psychosis (FEP) is, what causes it and who may develop it. Placing it in the context of the different stages of psychosis, we will briefly describe some of the possible antecedents to psychosis, who may be at risk of developing it, and the importance of getting people into services quickly in order to reduce the duration of untreated psychosis (DUP). We discuss how Early Intervention for Psychosis (EIP) services have emerged in different parts of the world, designed to help people with FEP during a 'critical period' of care which is formative, and crucial for long-term recovery.

Although Mosi's symptoms were relatively easy to spot, early psychosis rarely presents in 'neat parcels'. It is not always easy to diagnose quickly and may require a period of extended assessment to be sure that this is a FEP. Such a 'watching brief' allows symptoms to be assessed over a longer period of time and a pattern to emerge within the context of that person's life stage. That said, EIP services and trained mental health professionals have become increasingly adept at spotting the onset of psychosis, marked by the presence of a number of signs and symptoms (Box 1.1).

Box 1.1 Main symptoms of psychosis

- *Hallucinations:* 'Hearing voices speaking when no one else is there, or seeing, tasting, smelling or feeling things that other people do not' (Cooke, 2017, p. 10). 'Voices' sometimes talk to each other about the person or comment on his/her thoughts and/or actions in the third person.
- *Delusions:* 'Holding strong beliefs that others around you do not share' (Cooke, 2017, p. 10). Such personal beliefs about the world can take many forms (i.e. persecutory, grandiose, reference, etc.). For instance, delusions of reference are beliefs held by the person that the behaviour and remarks of others (in the street, on TV, on the radio, etc.) are meant for them.
- *Thought insertion, withdrawal and broadcast:* the feeling that thoughts have been inserted or withdrawn from the mind. In some cases the person may feel that their thoughts are being broadcast so that others can hear them, often over long distances.
- *Experiences of control:* the person may feel under the control of an alien force or power. They may also experience the feeling that an external force has penetrated their mind or body. This is often interpreted as the presence of spirits, X-rays or implanted radio transmitters. This may also be referred to as passivity phenomena.
- *Difficulties with thinking and concentrating:* an individual may experience difficulty concentrating or attending to everyday tasks and may appear distracted or preoccupied. Sometimes people talk in a way that other people find hard to understand, saying things that do not make sense or are not connected to each other.
- *Emotional and volitional changes:* emotions and feelings become blurred or less clear and are often described as becoming 'flat'. There may also be a loss of initiative or energy. Such changes are often referred to as 'negative symptoms'.

    Psychotic symptoms can emerge in different orders and with different timings depending on the biological, psychological and social influences at play. Low mood, anxiety and sleep abnormalities often precede the onset of psychosis as can a reduction in social functioning with associated loss of volition and drive (Rapado-Castro, McGorry, Yung, Calvo & Nelson, 2015). Occasionally, bizarre and/or aggressive behaviours may also be an early indication of an emerging psychotic illness (Hogins & Klein, 2017).

The first episode of psychosis marks a period in a journey of transition from a high risk of developing psychosis (e.g. presence of biomarkers) to an *ultra high risk* (UHR) stage (e.g. presence of sub-threshold symptoms of psychosis), through to FEP, where the course of the disorder is realised, with the person making either a 'good recovery', a 'poor recovery' or somewhere in between. That is, psychosis rarely just happens spontaneously. It develops over time, over a period that can be divided into stages. Some have argued that this maps neatly onto a clinical staging model (see Table 1.1) as applied in other branches of medicine where the different stages present different opportunities for a prevention-oriented approach to intervention (McGorry, Killackey & Yung, 2008), something we will return to throughout the book. For psychosis, this means having an awareness of the bio-psychosocial influences on transition from one stage to another and acting accordingly. For the earliest 'at risk' and UHR stages, this has so far not proved to be straightforward. For example, a recent meta-analysis (van der Gaag et al., 2013) reviewing the efficacy of interventions for ultra-high risk patients (UHR) concluded that while cognitive behavioural therapy-based (CBT) interventions can delay transition to a FEP in the short term (i.e. 12 months), this preventative effect was not evident over a longer period (i.e. over two years). In other words, delay of transition to 'full-blown' psychosis seemed to be 'delayed' as opposed to 'prevented'. It may also mean that we need to get better at reliably identifying UHR states in the first place (Fusar-Poli et al., 2012).

Given that there are still no efficacious interventions for the primary prevention of psychosis, secondary and tertiary prevention remains a focus point for intervention (Fusar-Poli et al., 2017). That is, a therapeutic focus on the period after the onset of 'full-blown' psychosis, the first episode (FEP). The FEP is often divided into two periods: *before* (also known as duration of untreated psychosis; DUP) and *after* adequate treatment with antipsychotic medication.

The reduction of DUP remains one of the primary goals of EIP. There is now a wealth of research to demonstrate that a long period of DUP (usually defined as over three months; Harris et al., 2005) is a robust predictor of poor general symptomatic outcome, more severe positive and negative symptoms, lower probability of remission and poor social functioning (Penttilä, Jääskeläinen, Hirvonen, Isohanni & Miettunen, 2014). Treatment delay for young people with psychosis throughout the world has been too high for too long and in developed countries, has often been associated with delays in secondary care as much as help seeking in primary care (Birchwood et al., 2013). It may also be influenced by variations in pathways to care among different ethnic groups (Anderson, Flora & McKenzie, 2014). That DUP is now seen as a potential modifiable predictor of outcome for psychosis has been one of the major drivers for the new Referral to Treatment (RTT) national quality standards introduced in the UK in 2016 (NICE, 2016). With a target of more than 50% of FEP referrals to EIP being picked up within 14 days (60% by 2021), this has become a proxy measure of DUP reduction in the NHS in England.

Although there is ongoing debate as to when the period of untreated psychosis begins and ends and how this should be measured, the second phase of the first episode marks the beginning of that period of time when adaptation and recovery are at their most important. DUP is an important and robust predictor of prognosis but one which accounts for only a small proportion in the outcome variance for psychosis (McGorry et al., 2008). Optimising bio-psychosocial treatment during the early stages of psychosis, within the context of a value-based mental health system prioritising hope, recovery and adaptation, remains essential.

The early intervention paradigm is partially predicated on the basis of the 'critical-period hypothesis' (Birchwood, Todd & Jackson, 1998). This argues that the early phase of psychosis (including the period of untreated psychosis) is a critical period in which long-term outcome is formative and that bio-psychosocial influences are at their most malleable and dynamic. It also predicts that there is a 'plateau effect' (McGlashan, 1988) two to three years after the onset of psychotic symptoms, where the most aggressive deterioration occurs, and the critical psychosocial influences, including family and psychological reactions, take place. It logically follows then that this presents vital opportunities for secondary prevention and recovery-based interventions that may ultimately affect the course of the psychotic illness. Although evidence for the hypothesis is relatively robust (Crumlish et al., 2009), there remains debate on how long the critical period lasts with implications for the length of time EIP should be offered (see Chapter 12).

At risk mental states (ARMS), ultra high risk (UHR) and clinical high risk (CHR)

In keeping with terminology from medicine and the study of physical diseases, such as cancer, mental health researchers in the 1980s and 1990s began studying the prodromes of people who developed schizophrenia spectrum disorders and affective psychoses. Since then, there has been an avalanche of studies of help-seeking individuals, displaying the early signs of a potentially emergent psychotic illness. Much of this early research was aimed at trying to identify, retrospectively, both the bio-markers of potential psychotic illnesses and the factors contributing to the transition to 'full-blown' or frank psychosis. One of the problems is that the term 'prodrome', in medicine, constitutes the antecedent signs and symptoms to an inevitable event, such as cancer. That is, those signs and symptoms that have been found, in hindsight, to have preceded the diagnosis of the disease. When translated to mental health, particularly early psychosis, this approach becomes problematic as transition to the threshold for a diagnosis of psychosis is not inevitable, even when numerous early markers for psychosis (e.g. sub-threshold psychotic symptoms, family history of psychosis, impairment in day-to-day functioning) are present (Conrad et al., 2017). Instead the term 'at risk mental state' (ARMS) in the

UK and 'ultra high risk'/'clinical high risk' (UHR/CHR) in other countries, has been adopted by clinicians and researchers to better capture the *potential* to reach threshold for a diagnosis of FEP. Subsequently, this has led to the development of instruments such as the CAARMS (the Comprehensive Assessment of At Risk Mental States; Yung et al., 2006), which can be used to test the predictive validity of prospectively defined ARMS and basic symptom criteria (Huber & Gross, 1989). Those whom these instruments assess to be at UHR/CHR have a significantly greater chance of making the transition to psychosis, with a recent meta-analysis showing, on average, an 18% transition risk at six months, 22% at one year, 29% at two years, 32% at three years and 36% after three years, irrespective of psychometric instrument used (Fusar-Poli et al., 2012). Most do not make a transition to psychosis. Non-self-selecting, non-help-seeking individuals with attenuated psychotic symptoms have an estimated transition rate of less than 1% (Kaymaz et al., 2012). Despite this, UHR/CHR groups tend to be composed of young people with high levels of distress and non-psychotic comorbid symptomatology. This indicates that these groups need help to reduce this distress, ideally, in a low-stigma, high hope, youth-oriented services (van Os & Guloksuz, 2017), examples of which already exist around the world (McGorry et al., 2013).

New NHS England/NICE recommendations and quality standards for EIP services in England (NICE, 2016) have proposed that all those referred to EIP services should be assessed for ARMS and responded to appropriately. However, recent results from a national audit of EIP services in the UK suggest that the number of individuals being assessed by EIP teams may still be quite low (5%) and variable (Adamson et al., 2018). It is likely that these cohorts will contain people with high levels of symptoms as they will be 'badged' as potential FEP cases (Yung, 2017). This approach appears to encourage a more integrated approach with EIP services, where transitioned cases can receive FEP intervention quicker. However, it opens up for debate the question of how and where such ARMS patients should be treated: in a wider generic youth mental health service or a specialist EIP service as sug-gested by new NHS England guidance? This also maps onto questions about what is the ultimate goal for services helping ARMS patients: to prevent 'transition' to frank psychosis or to facilitate a more person-centred holistic approach to help them with their current problems, whether that be anxiety, depression, addiction problems, poor social functioning or other issues (Stain et al., 2016)?

It is not the intention of this book to cover the ARMS/UHR/CHR literature or offer advice on how to assess, formulate and treat this group of people. Over the last 15 years there has been an explosion in academic papers, manuals and pro-tocols which we will not be able to do justice to. Instead we recommend the reader consults a number of very readable and well-written reviews and guides, such as French and Morrison (2004), Van der Gaag et al. (2013) and Fusar-Poli et al. (2015).

Diagnosis and the embracing of diagnostic uncertainty

Psychosis (and, by association, FEP) constitute an 'umbrella' term which takes into account a number of diagnoses, namely, schizophrenia, schizoaffective disorder, delusional disorder, drug-induced psychosis, psychotic depression, puerperal psychosis and bipolar disorder with psychotic features. Throughout this book we will use the term 'psychosis' predominantly as our preferred choice. However, at times, we will also use the term schizophrenia, and schizophrenia spectrum disorder, particularly when quoting literature and research studies which have used these terms.

Diagnosis has a long and controversial history in mental health (Bentall, 2009) but one that has provided the backbone for modern psychiatry (Lieberman, 2015). Although it is beyond the scope of this current book to provide arguments for and against the classification of psychiatric and psychological symptoms into discrete categorical groups (diagnoses), we hold the pragmatic position that, despite its problems, diagnosis remains a useful and common language by which clinicians and researchers can communicate with each other. Undoubtedly, tensions remain between different researchers, clinicians, professional groups and even countries as to how a diagnosis such as schizophrenia is used (Cooke, 2017) or whether psychotic symptoms, conceived of as lying on a continuum with normality, may provide a better fit with the data (Guloksuz & van Os, 2018).

The reliability and validity of traditional dichotomies (schizophrenia, bipolar disorder) based on neo-Kraepelin thinking, especially in the early stages of emerging symptoms, have been the subject of continuous scrutiny over the years (Bentall, 2009). It has been argued that the concept of schizophrenia is too narrow and pessimistic, accounting for the worst 30% of outcomes of a much broader spectrum of psychotic disorders (Perälä et al., 2007). This has led to a tautology for schizophrenia and recovery that suggests a diagnosis of schizophrenia is unlikely in those with a favourable recovery. Much of the literature on schizophrenia has perpetuated the erroneous idea that you cannot be diagnosed with schizophrenia and have a good outcome (Lally et al., 2017), or put another way: a good outcome would mean you never had schizophrenia in the first place (Robins & Guze, 1970). A diagnosis of schizophrenia also has an uncomfortable history of being inconsistently applied in different settings and countries across the world (Birchwood & Jackson, 2001). Although this has led to the increased use of diagnostic manuals, such as ICD and DSM, to improve reliability and accuracy (Spitzer, Andreasen & Endicott, 1978), for some, its validity remains problematic.

In addition, the concept of schizophrenia has met opposition from service user groups who often oppose the stigmatising nature of the diagnosis with its association to a chronic brain disease (Bentall, 2009). Many clinicians feel uncomfortable using the term and some countries, such as Japan and South

Korea, no longer refer to it (Takahashi et al., 2009). Yet despite this, the concept of schizophrenia continues to exert a powerful influence over research, treatment, psychiatric services and mental health policy throughout the world (Dutta, Greene, Addington, McKenzie, Phillips & Murray, 2007).

Questions have also been raised about the stability and trajectories of symptoms (psychotic and affective), and by association categorical diagnostic decisions, in young people in the early stages of psychosis (Heslin et al., 2015). This has led to most researchers and clinicians working with young FEP populations, choosing to delay a formal diagnosis (schizophrenia, bipolar disorder, drug-induced psychosis, etc.) in the first two to three years and instead opting to use the more ubiquitous term, first episode psychosis (FEP). This is underpinned by the concept of a psychosis continuum, or an extended phenotype (Howes & Kapur, 2009), and one that embraces 'diagnostic uncertainty' (Marwaha, Thompson, Upthegrove & Broome, 2016). Arguably, this also has the advantage of being significantly less stigmatising as it treats psychosis as more fluid and malleable (McGorry et al., 2008).

More recently, a number of researchers, particularly in Australia, have argued that a clinical staging model may provide a heuristic framework in which to understand the development and evolution of psychosis and other psychiatric disorders (McGorry, Hickie, Yung, Pantelis & Jackson, 2006). Set out as a more refined form of diagnosis, clinical staging differentiates the earlier and milder forms of psychosis from the more chronic aspects and defines where a person will lie on that continuum at a particular point in time. This has the advantage of allowing interventions to be better targeted with the least invasive treatment for that particular stage, lessening the chances that someone will be 'over-treated' and exposed to unnecessary 'side effects' (McGorry et al., 2008). Based on the recent work of Fusar-Poli et al. (2017), Table 1.1 shows a revised version of the 'clinical staging' model and the potential interventions which might be applied at each stage.

Stages 0–1c represent what happens before the FEP with the emphasis upon (mostly) psychosocial interventions rather than anti-psychotic medication (Van der Gaag et al., 2013). Stage 2 represents the acute stage of psychosis (psychotic symptoms of four weeks or more) followed by 'symptomatic remission' (see Chapter 2). Stages 3a through to 4 represent the various 'clinical recovery' trajectories that may follow. For example, in stage 3a, clinical recovery may be initially achieved but is followed by a relapse, in stage 3b, clinical recovery is followed by multiple relapses, and in clinical stage 3c, there is no return to pre-morbid levels of social functioning or symptoms. Ultimately these stages are also about adaptation, social recovery and personal recovery, topics defined in Chapter 2 and addressed throughout this book.

A 'clinical staging' model also reduces the chance that somebody's diagnosis will be needlessly changed during the early course of the illness. Hence, clinical staging and the embracing of diagnostic uncertainty allow the aforementioned 'watching brief' to prosper and the balance to be kept on the side of false

Table 1.1 Revised clinical staging model for psychosis and potential interventions

Clinical stage	Definition	Definition in clinical staging model	Potential intervention
0	Asymptomatic genetic risk	Premorbid	Selective primary prevention Mental health literacy Family psycho-education
1a	Negative and cognitive symptoms	ARMS/CHR	Indicated primary prevention Formal mental health literacy
1b	Attenuated psychotic symptoms	ARMS/CHR	Indicated primary prevention Family and individual psycho-education Active reduction of substance misuse
1c	Short-lived remitting psychotic episodes	ARMS/CHR	Indicated primary prevention As for 1b Close-in monitoring
2	Full-threshold FEP	Early 'clinical' recovery	Early intervention and secondary prevention Family and individual psycho-education Psychological therapies Active reduction of substance misuse Atypical anti-psychotics and other medications
3a	Single relapse of psychotic disorder	Late/incomplete 'clinical' recovery	Early intervention and tertiary prevention As for 2, but with emphasis on relapse prevention and staying well plans
3b	Multiple relapses	Late/incomplete 'clinical' recovery	Early intervention and tertiary prevention As for 2, but with emphasis on long-term stabilisation
3c	Incomplete 'clinical' recovery from FEP	Late/incomplete 'clinical' recovery	Early intervention and tertiary prevention As for 3a, clozapine in case of treatment resistance
4	Severe, persisting or unremitting illness	Chronicity	Maintenance intervention As for 3a–3c, but with emphasis on social recovery despite lack of symptomatic recovery

Source: Based on Fusar-Poli et al. (2017).

positives (people believed to have psychosis who turn out *not* to have) as opposed to false negatives (people who have psychosis but are denied the appropriate treatment). Cancer screening often has a high false positive rate especially when multiple tests are performed. Yet while trying to reduce obvious anxieties in patients, they operate on the basis that 'it is better to be safe than sorry'. Such an approach to early psychosis, of course, has to be backed by appropriate health care funding and mental health policy which allow 'false positives' to be embraced and not seen as an impediment to good patient care. Mental health services for young people have been slow to take up this challenge, but are slowly changing with a shift of paradigm from reactive to preventative mental health (McGorry, Bates & Birchwood, 2013).

Who will experience a FEP?

Incidence rates for psychosis vary widely across different countries (McGrath, Saha, Chant & Welham, 2008). So while the annual incidence rate for all psychoses in north-eastern Italy is 18 per 100,000 (Lasalvia et al., 2014), it is more than twice this (45 per 100,000) in East Anglia, UK, climbing to over 50 per 100,000 in more densely populated areas (Kirkbride et al., 2012b). In a systematic review of the incidence and prevalence of schizophrenia and other psychotic disorders in England, Kirkbride et al. (2012a) estimated that the average incidence for all psychotic disorders was 32 per 100,000. This roughly translates to a lifetime prevalence of over 3% (Perälä et al., 2007) with a specific diagnosis of schizophrenia accounting for nearly a third of all cases.

The incidence of psychosis is higher in young men than women up to the age of 45 but more equal after this age (Kirkbride, Stubbins & Jones, 2012a). For schizophrenia, the peak age of incidence is 20–29 for men and women but for women there is also another peak at the age of 30–39 (van der Werf et al., 2014).

Psychosis is more common in people who inhabit urban areas, belong to migrant and ethnic minority groups and those living in the most deprived environments (Castillejos, Martín-Pérez & Moreno-Küstner, 2018). Recent findings from a number of countries have suggested that those born, brought up and living in an urban environment are more likely to develop schizophrenia and other non-affective psychosis than those from more rural locations (Vassos, Pedersen, Murray, Collier & Lewis, 2012). These findings are unlikely to be the result of social drift alone (people moving into more urban environments *following* the onset of psychosis) and are more probably the *consequence* of being raised in an urban environment (Heinz, Deserno & Reininghaus, 2013).

When compared to the majority population, there is a two- to four-fold increase in the risk of developing psychosis among black and minority ethnic (BME) groups (Bourque, Van der Ven & Malla, 2011). Although this may be partially explained by the impact of simply living in an urban environment, (i.e. the vast majority of migrant and minority ethnic groups live in towns and cities), it has also been suggested that these groups are more likely to develop psychosis as a result of enduring racial discrimination, social marginalisation and other socio-economic disadvantage (Janssen et al., 2003).

The elevated risk among minority ethnic groups does not, however, appear to be an artefact of methodological or diagnostic bias (Tortelli et al., 2015), and has been observed in a wide variety of countries (Fearon et al., 2006). Recent evidence suggests that this phenomenon is also witnessed in minority ethnic groups in rural areas (Kirkbride et al., 2017).

People living in the most socially deprived environments will also be at a greater risk of developing psychosis (Morgan et al., 2017) and this has been mooted as a possible explanation for the high rates of psychosis in urban areas (Burns & Esterhuizen, 2008). Even among relatively wealthy populations, with low incidence rates, the onset of psychosis can be partially predicted by the relative social affluence of the cohort (Lasalvia et al., 2014). Social deprivation is likely to be greater in inner city areas where psychosis is at its highest and social and economic resources are low (Giggs, 1986). Conversely, where 'social capital', defined as 'a collective resource that inheres the social ties and connections of local communities' (Putnam & Goss, 2002) is low, psychosis rates are likely to be increased (Kirkbride et al., 2008). In an intriguing test of this hypothesis, Lofors and Sundquist (2007) using voter turnout as a proxy for 'social capital', found that in areas of Sweden where voter turnout was poor, there was an increased incidence of non-affective psychosis.

Evidence that social factors influence the development of psychotic symptoms has inspired some academics and clinicians to propose a theory that psychosis is more evident in groups who feel marginalised from the majority population. Better known as the 'social defeat' hypothesis (Selten, van Os & Cantor-Graae, 2016), this has provided a framework to understand some of the epidemiological patterns observed for FEP.

Psychosis is more likely to develop in families where it has been experienced before. Genetic factors contribute significantly, but not exclusively, to the aetiology of psychosis. Twin studies suggest that schizophrenia has a heritability estimate of around 80% (compared, for instance, to 60% for osteoarthritis of the hip and 30–50% for hypertension; van Os & Kapur, 2009). Recent advances in genetic research suggest that psychosis and schizophrenia are highly polygenic (controlled by a number of genes) and associated with small effects from multiple genetic influences as opposed to large effects from a single source (Owen, Sawa & Mortensen, 2016). Moreover, single genes or alleles associated with schizophrenia appear to be associated with a number of other phenotypic traits (i.e. expression of a person's genetic code, genotype, and its interaction with the environment) and diagnoses such as bipolar disorder, major depressive disorder and autistic spectrum disorder (ASD) (Lee, R. S. C. et al., 2013). However, despite recent advances in molecular genetics, our understanding of the cause and development of schizophrenia and psychosis remains largely unknown (Henriksen, Nordgaard & Jansson, 2017). Thus, caution is still warranted when drawing conclusions about the size of the genetic contribution in the aetiology of FEP.

Why do people develop psychosis?

It is now agreed that psychosis develops due to an interaction between a number of biological, psychological and social factors occurring over a given period of time. Less clear, however, is *how* these three factors fuse together to produce what we now know as psychotic symptoms.

In this book we will argue, like others before us (van Os, Kenis & Rutten, 2010), that people with a 'psychosis diathesis' (a predispositional vulnerability), develop psychosis because they struggle, through no fault of their own, to adapt to the social context they find themselves in. This thwarted adaptation then gives rise to a number of gene–environment interactions which have an impact on a developing and sensitised brain, generating psychotic and non-psychotic symptoms, which may develop into a 'full-blown' psychotic disorder, depending upon the biological, psychological and social factors present in that person's life at the time.

Stress-vulnerability models and FEP

Most psychosis researchers now agree that stress-vulnerability or stress-diathesis models (Nuechterlein & Dawson, 1984) provide the best framework to explain how biological, social and psychological factors interact with each other prior to, and during, the course of psychosis. According to this framework, psychiatric symptoms express themselves when stress, or a number of stressors, exceed the person's vulnerability level. Vulnerability in this context is seen as stable, intrinsic and usually biological (i.e. genetic). Thus, those described as having a 'high' vulnerability to psychosis require significantly less stress to trigger symptoms than those with 'lower' levels of vulnerability. Although the stress-vulnerability model has provided a useful framework for understanding how stressors impact on vulnerable individuals, researchers are still grappling with the mechanisms by which increased stress leads to psychosis (Millman et al., 2017).

One hypothesis which has been put forward is the idea that people who develop psychosis are more sensitive to the impact of *life events* (Mansueto & Faravelli, 2017), either positive or negative. Most researchers agree, however, rather than triggering psychotic symptoms and relapses, life events have a more cumulative effect, increasing the risk of psychosis the more they are experienced (Hirsch et al., 1996) or appraised as being less controllable (Horan et al., 2005).

Childhood trauma and FEP

That *childhood trauma* may be a precursor for psychosis has attracted a great deal of attention over recent years (Mansueto & Faravelli, 2017). Although reviews of this literature remain inconclusive and contradictory, most studies support the idea that people who have experienced physical, sexual, bullying and/or emotional abuse during childhood are at increased risk of a myriad of mental health disorders (Carr, Martins, Stingel, Lemgruber & Juruena, 2013), including psychosis. More up-to-date, better-designed, prospective studies, have tended to show that there is a dose-response association between childhood trauma and psychosis (van Os et al., 2010) and that this relationship is probably mediated by a number of connected paths, including anxiety, poor impulse control and motor retardation (Isvoranu et al., 2017). This points to the idea there may be an affective pathway to psychosis following exposure to childhood trauma, evidence for which comes from event-sampling (ESM) studies (Myin-Germeys & van Os, 2007). Other psychological and biological mechanisms that may mediate this relationship may include elevated sensitivity and lack of resilience to socio-environmental stress, enhanced threat anticipation (Reininghaus et al., 2016), instability of mood (Broome, Saunders, Harrison & Marwaha, 2015) and reactivity of the hypothalamic-pituitary-adrenal (HPA) axis (Ruby, Polito, McMahon, Gorovitz, Corcoran & Malaspina, 2014).

Neurobiology of psychosis

Overall, the *neurobiology* of psychosis remains poorly understood. Dopamine dysregulation along with aberrant assignment of salience to stimuli has been implicated as one possible causal biological mechanism (van Os & Kapur, 2009). Psychotic symptoms may subsequently occur when people attempt to make sense of these experiences (Kapur, 2004), leading to possible delusion formation when affective states and vulnerabilities in cognitive style (i.e. a 'jumping to conclusions' reasoning style) combine (Fine, Gardner, Craigie & Gold, 2007). Meanwhile, abnormalities in glutamate signalling may be more likely to account for cognitive and negative symptoms (Moghaddam & Javitt, 2012). Immune and inflammatory processes have now been implicated in a number of epidemiological, clinical and genetic studies of psychosis (Owen et al., 2016).

Cannabis and FEP

There is now overwhelming evidence that there is an association between *cannabis* use and the development of psychotic symptoms (Radhakrishnan, Wilkinson & D'Souza, 2014), especially where use is frequent as it is in FEP cohorts (Di Forti et al., 2015). Although there is some suggestion that cannabis may act as a *response* to psychotic symptoms (i.e. self-medication) most research appears to favour its aetiological role (i.e. cannabis leading to increased vulnerability to psychosis; Burns, 2013). Furthermore, those who continue to use cannabis after the onset of psychosis tend to have less favourable symptomatic recoveries, marked by higher relapse rates, longer hospital admissions, and more severe positive symptoms (Schoeler et al., 2016). Heavier use at a younger age, usually defined as mid to late teens, has also been shown to increase the risk of developing psychosis earlier (Helle et al., 2016). Cannabis use as a comorbidity and risk factor for FEP is discussed in more detail in Chapter 10.

Gene-environment interactions and FEP

Studies of wider *gene-environment interactions* to explain increased risk for psychosis remain in their infancy (Uher, 2014). However, it is feasible to suggest that they may hold the key as to why social and psychological adversity (e.g. growing up in an urban environment, child abuse, etc.), may lead to a FEP in only a minority of cases (van Winkel, Van Nierop, Myin-Germeys & van Os, 2013). Psychotic experiences which are more common in young people, often decline with age (Johns & van Os, 2001). These age-dependent transient and subclinical psychotic experiences often become more severe when there is repeated exposure to environmental risk factors (i.e. trauma, cannabis, etc.). In a relatively small number of people this can lead to the onset of a psychotic disorder (Dominguez, Wichers, Lieb, Wittchen & van Os, 2011). That is, the normal developmental expression of psychotic-like symptoms may become 'abnormally persistent' and more clinically relevant depending upon the amount of 'environmental load' the person is subjected to (Myin-Germeys & van Os, 2007). In such a developmental interactive model of psychosis, the genetic liability for psychotic disorders is partially mediated by 'differential sensitivity' to these adverse environments that have an impact during a critical period of development for the human brain (van Os et al., 2010).

Our understanding of the biological, psychological and social interactions in the aetiology of FEP has greatly progressed in the last 40 years. It is no longer viable to talk about a strictly 'biological diathesis' based on the notion proposed in the early stress diathesis models, that all vulnerability to developing psychosis is genetic in nature. Instead, it is reasonable to suggest that childhood and adult adversity, at both individual and societal levels, may not only sensitise the developing 'social' brain but also underpin the source of daily stressors, through, for example, the formation of negative beliefs, (Müller et al., 2017), that can then give rise to the onset of psychotic symptoms. These initial psychotic experiences are more likely to occur in people who struggle to adapt to psychosocial adversity when this adversity differentially interacts with liabilities created by genetic factors (van Os et al., 2010). In other words, the 'diathesis' in stress-diathesis models needs to be understood more as a form of bio-psychosocial vulnerability rather than as a purely biological or genetic entity (Longden, Sampson & Read, 2016). Overall, however, we still do not yet fully understand why some people who have such a bio-psychosocial predisposition for 'broad' psychosis spectrum syndromes go on to develop psychotic disorders such as schizophrenia, while others may only experience *non*-psychotic symptoms (e.g. anxiety, depression, trauma) or even make a full symptomatic and functional recovery. In the clinical staging model cited earlier (Table 1.1), research is ongoing to determine why some people progress to stages 3 and 4 whereas a minority only have a single episode and remain at stage 2.

EIP service provision

The treatment of psychosis has a variable history, often marked by long periods of negativity. More positive views gradually emerged towards the end of the last century, with rapid advances in medical, pharmacological, psychological and social treatments. Yet, probably the biggest advance in treating psychosis has been a shift of paradigm as a result of a scientific challenge to the neo-Kraepelinian pessimism. This has allowed researchers, clinicians, service users and families to change their philosophy and outlook towards one which embraces prevention, recovery and hope based on the principle of intervening as early as possible following a FEP (Jackson & Birchwood, 1996).

Early intervention for psychosis services began in Australia in the 1980s. Patrick McGorry, a psychiatrist, and his colleagues, noticed how young first episode patients differed from the older, multi-episode patients they were being treated alongside (McGorry, 2015). The drug and psychosocial treatments used for the latter did not necessarily translate to use with these young first episode patients. This led to the establishment of a 'Recovery Program' at Royal Park Hospital, Melbourne, using newly developed psychosocial approaches and new drug regimes (e.g. low doses of anti-psychotic medication). This eventually led to the setting up of EPPIC (Early Psychosis Prevention and Intervention Centre), a comprehensive programme for the treatment of young people with FEP.

Informed by these newly established EIP service improvements in Australia and the explosion of research papers pointing to the clinical benefits of early intervention with young people experiencing a FEP, Max Birchwood, a clinical psychologist, and colleagues set up the first EIP service in the UK, in Birmingham. This provided the 'blueprint' for subsequent EIP services based on an assertive community outreach model.

The first Birmingham team was based in the Archer Centre, a rehabilitation unit in a multi-ethnic part of inner-city Birmingham where incidence rates for psychosis were among some of the highest in the country. At the same time, a 'pressure group' called IRIS (Initiative to Reduce the Impact of Schizophrenia) was formed by professionals, family members (Jo Smith, David Shiers, Max Birchwood, Fiona MacMillan) and senior health managers (John Mahoney and Anthony Sheehan). Thanks to this group and the sympathetic and innovative political thinking around health reforms at the time, a national roll-out of EIP services occurred on the back of the Mental Health Policy Implementation Guide (PIG) for England and Wales (Department of Health, 2001). This proved to be one of the most comprehensive and successful mental health initiatives that had been witnessed anywhere in the world at that time.

Unfortunately, as the economic recession took hold, there followed a significant scaling-back of EIP services in the UK as health spending, especially in mental health, was reduced in real terms. Many EIP teams closed or were subsumed into community mental health teams (CMHTs) and other generic mental health teams, where fidelity to an EIP model was more difficult to achieve. A number of criticisms of mental health policy affecting EIP were made public (*Lost Generation*, Rethink Mental Illness, 2014) and members of the British Parliament such as Norman Lamb, IRIS, and a number of other influential people and organisations such as the mental health charity, Rethink, again took up the cause of EIP. This eventually resulted in the publication of a report (*A Five Year Forward View of Mental Health*, NHS England, 2016) in February 2016 by an independent mental health task force recommending, among other things, access for all to high quality mental health care and parity of esteem with physical illness.

Ultimately, this has led to the publication of an implementation guide setting out a set of quality standards which English NHS Mental Health Trusts were required to meet. The document, *Implementing the Early Intervention in Psychosis Access and Waiting Time Standard* (NICE, 2016) had three main aims:

1   The timely access to specialist early intervention services for more than 50% of people within two weeks.
2   Consistent access to a range of evidence-based biological, psychological and social interventions, as recommended by the NICE guidelines.
3   Equitable provision of care across groups who have traditionally found it difficult to access services (i.e. black and minority ethnic (BME) groups).

Developing the evidence base for EIP services

From its very beginnings, EIP has been founded on the principles of science and research. This has led to numerous service evaluation studies throughout the world that have compared EIP to traditional ways of intervening with early psychosis, often known ubiquitously as 'standard care'. Before considering these studies, we need to define what we actually mean by EIP, what its core components are, and how we measure fidelity to an EIP approach.

What are the key elements of an EIP team?

Following the roll-out of EIP across England at the beginning of the millennium, fidelity tools emerged in which EIP services were able to benchmark their teams against clear criteria. This was an attempt to measure the adherence to the EIP model so that teams were not simply 'rebadged' as EIP teams while continuing to roll out treatment as usual, ensuring that teams maintained fidelity to the model throughout austere financial times.

Fidelity tools have been developed in a number of western countries as services have looked to optimise and standardise the delivery of EIP. Such fidelity scales vary with regard to the number of items elicited and the methodologies used to extract them. For instance, in Denmark, Melau, Albert and Nordentoft (2017) used the Delphi Consensus method to develop an 18-point scale measuring both team structure and intervention content. In contrast, Radhakrishnan et al. (2017) evaluated a 64-item scale constructed from the original English Policy Implementation Guide (DoH, 2001) while Addington et al. (2016) published a fidelity tool containing 32 components supported by NICE guidelines, along with the need to provide physical health interventions.

One of the problems with multiple fidelity scales is the difficulty in comparing services, countries and evaluation studies to reach a consensus about how an EIP team should be constructed and what interventions it should be delivering. Box 1.2 lists the most frequently cited commonalities shared on these scales. In the UK, many of these are now measured as part of the new EIP quality standards (NICE, 2016).

Box 1.2 Commonalities across EIP fidelity tools

- the need for easy access
- embracing diagnostic uncertainty and therapeutic optimism
- assigning a care co-ordinator or case manager
- low caseloads (1:15; see Chapter 12)
- offering a range of bio-psychosocial interventions
- prescribing practice focusing on low-dose pharmacology
- access to specialist beds in crisis
- provision of CBT and psychological interventions
- psychoeducational family intervention
- measurement of DUP with the aim of reducing it to less than three months
- interventions for vocational and social recovery
- provision of services for substance misuse and other comorbidities

---

Does EIP work?

Fusar-Poli et al. (2017) reviewed the randomised controlled trials (RCTs) comparing EIP services providing most of the commonalities set out in Box 1.2. with various types of 'standard care'. In general, the largest and better powered of these trials have demonstrated positive results, at least in the short term (i.e. up to two years). There were benefits in improved positive symptoms (e.g. Srihari et al., 2015), negative symptoms (Petersen et al., 2005), total psychotic symptoms (e.g. Ruggeri et al., 2015;), reduced dosage of antipsychotic medication (Petersen et al., 2005) and admissions to hospital (e.g. Srihari et al., 2015). These larger, better-controlled, studies also highlighted benefits for improved clinical, social and personal recovery (Kane et al., 2016; see also Chapter 2) and improved adaptation of the family (Petersen et al., 2005). Such findings concur with other meta-analyses (Correll, Galling & Pawar, 2018) and non-RCT studies reporting high satisfaction with EIP services by service users and families alike (Lester et al., 2011). Lastly, there is now overwhelming evidence that EIP services, in the long term, save public money, usually as the result of reductions in hospital admissions, A&E costs and the increased advantage for EIP services of returning people to work (McCrone et al., 2013).

Overall, this book will explore which specific interventions and facets of EIP produce these benefits, with the hypothesis that it is an integrated, values-based team approach to EIP that is most likely responsible for these superior outcomes and cost savings (Radhakrishnan et al., 2017). Despite this, a number of challenges remain for the provision of EIP services. For instance, relapse of psychotic symptoms following an FEP remains unacceptably high with the majority of people experiencing a second episode within 10 years of the first (Fusar-Poli et al., 2017).

Relapse following psychosis

Falloon (1984) assimilated the early literature on relapse and proposed that relapse criteria should include a significant increase of positive symptoms, an appropriate duration of emerging clinical symptoms, and assessment of symptoms with objective and standardised measures. However, over the years there has been variation in how relapse has been conceptualised and measured (Fusar-Poli et al., 2017). Consequently, there is an urgent need to develop a standard and universally agreed set of criteria for psychotic relapse such as the criteria developed for remission by the Remission in Schizophrenia Working Group (RSWG; Andreasen, Carpenter, Kane, Lasser, Marder & Weinberger, 2005; see Chapters 2 and 3). A recent review indicates that the most commonly used criterion in published studies for psychotic relapse is readmission to hospital (Gleeson, Álvarez-Jiménez, Cotton, Parker & Hetrick, 2010). However, this is a narrow conceptualisation and in clinical services, relapse will often occur without readmission as there can be many reasons why a readmission may not occur in the advent of relapse. Therefore, for current purposes and throughout this book, we will define relapse as the re-emergence of significant positive symptoms using the remission criteria (e.g. scoring 4 and above on the Positive and Negative Syndrome Scale; PANSS; Andreasen et al., 2005) following a period of non-specific (e.g. increases in anxiety, depression, difficulties concentrating) and/or specific (e.g. attenuated positive symptoms) symptoms that require additional coping resources from service users, carers and clinical staff/services. Relapse, much like the FEP itself, can be viewed as the result of a complex interaction of vulnerability factors, stress, and (insufficient) protective factors located at the biological, psychological, environmental or social level.

Rates of relapse vary depending on how relapse has been operationalised, study type (RCT or epidemiological studies), treatment conditions (e.g. antipsychotics vs. placebo; intensive Early Intervention Psychosis (EIP) vs. Treatment as Usual (TAU)), and sample characteristics (first vs. multiple episode patients). Two studies (Álvarez-Jiménez et al., 2012c; Gaebel & Riesbeck, 2014) have reviewed relapse rates each year following a FEP. In year one, rates of relapse were between 20–30%, in year two, 43–45%, by year three, it was 55%, in year five, 75–80% and by follow up at year seven, 84% of patients had experienced relapse. Thus, by year seven, only 15% of FEP patients will not have relapsed, suggesting that only a small minority of patients (around 15–20%) will only have one episode. This raises the question of whether EIP services can somehow identify these people early in order to provide different levels and duration of care.

Fusar-Poli et al. (2017) recently reviewed 12 studies comparing the risk of relapse/admission for individuals receiving specialised Early Intervention Psychosis (EIP) vs. Treatment as Usual (TAU). The mean rates of relapse under TAU were 14% at nine months, 49% at 24 months, and 76% at more than 10 years, whereas for EIP the rates were 17%, 38%, and 54% for the same time periods. Despite the slightly lower mean rates of relapse under EIP, there was no meta-analytic evidence that EIP significantly improved the odds of relapse compared to TAU. Fusar-Poli et al. (2017) cite consistent evidence from naturalistic studies indicating that about 50% of FEP cases relapse at least once (clinical stage 3a), while 34% have multiple relapses (clinical stage 3b). The most robust predictors of the first relapse were non-concordance with medication (odds ratio 2.9) and having a diagnosis of schizophrenia (odds ratio 2.2) (Pelayo-Terán et al., 2017).

Other challenges for EIP: remission to recovery

Most gains made by EIP teams appear to be 'short-lived' (Secher et al., 2015). This finding, that EIP has changed short-term remission rates but not long-term clinical recovery, has recently been confirmed in a meta-analysis by Lally et al. (2017). Questions remain as what is the best way to deliver EIP (e.g. hub and spoke vs. specialist), how long EIP should be offered (Malla et al., 2017) and what happens after discharge from EIP services (Kam, Singh & Upthegrove, 2015). In the UK, specialised standalone EIP teams are recommended. Data from the recent national UK EIP audit indicates that 68% of EIP teams in the UK are classified as standalone, with only 2% being hub and spoke and 8% having an EI function within a CMHT.

It is also unclear whether NICE-recommended interventions that make up an 'EIP package' require better tailoring to an individual's needs (Smailes, Alderson-Day, Fernyhough McCarthy-Jones & Dodgson, 2015). Most of these issues we will endeavour to address throughout this book.

The structure of the book

That EIP services have been seen as the vehicle by which optimum care for FEP is delivered, is testament to the years of research, evaluation, clinical delivery and philosophy of care that this approach across the world has brought.

Yet, despite this, and as alluded to above, there remains large discrepancies in the way EIP is delivered, not only across the globe but within the same country and sometimes, within the same region (Fearon, 2013). Partly, as noted, this is to do with differences in the way teams and services are funded, the political status afforded to them and the social context in which they exist (rural vs. urban, ethnic make-up, etc.). There is, however, another reason. To date, there has never been a consistent view about how the different elements of EIP should be integrated. How should pharmacological treatments be used alongside psychosocial interventions, and to achieve what aim? There are very few evidence-based practice manuals of integrated EIP care giving guidance on how we may *integrate* care so that we can optimise recovery across all domains: symptomatic, social and personal. Quality standards can only direct us and provide the processes by which we achieve better outcomes for our service users and their families. On their own, however, they are not enough. They need to be placed in the context of a values-based EIP service which provides a framework for optimising care, which values the individual, their identity and the need for them and their family to adapt to the FEP and challenges that brings. This book is intended to be an evidence-based practice manual that will provide a template for an integrated bio-psychosocial approach to EIP.

Although it is argued that 'recovery' following FEP remains poorly defined (see Chapter 2), high quality medical, psychological and social approaches all play a vital role in the improvement of the long-term trajectories. While it is inevitable that some of these interventions will be seen by clinicians, service users and families as more important than others, it is proposed that it is the unique combination of all three approaches, tailored to each individual and their families, that is at the heart of optimising outcomes in EIP. Written by clinicians and researchers from multi-professional backgrounds in nursing, psychiatry and clinical psychology, this book presents the case that EIP is 'greater than the sum of its parts'.

In addition to its empirical roots and the importance that has been placed upon research and evaluation, the success of EIP also owes something to the values that have underpinned it from the beginning. As evidenced by the two Forewords to the book, the instillation of hope, the promotion of recovery, the emphasis upon prevention and an integrated bio-psychosocial approach to assessment, formulation and intervention are essential to this approach

In Chapter 2 we will attempt to define recovery from, and adaptation to, a FEP. Here we place emphasis upon the recovery triad: symptomatic, social and psychological and how young people with psychosis value each one differently during their recovery and adaptation. Chapters 3 and 4 are concerned with symptomatic recovery, the former evaluating evidence from a biomedical perspective while the latter is more concerned with a psychosocial approach. Chapters 5 and 6 focus on the optimisation of social recovery, from an assessment and intervention perspective. Personal and psychological recovery following a FEP is scrutinised in Chapter 7 while Chapter 8 is dedicated to what happens when psychological adaptation goes wrong and recovery is affected by emotional dysfunction, including anxiety, post-psychotic depression, post-traumatic stress disorder (PTSD) and shame. The theme of incomplete recovery and complexities in recovery and adaptation following a FEP is continued in Chapters 9 and 10 on suicidality and comorbidity respectively. Here, guidance on how these issues can be managed and placed on a more positive trajectory is also discussed. In Chapter 11, we set out the potential impact that a FEP can have on the family and how EIP services can help service users and their families optimise their recovery and adaptation following FEP. Chapter 12 integrates and 'brings together' the best way to optimise medical, psychological and social treatments under the banner of early intervention for psychosis. This hopefully will translate into 'operational' recommendations which can be set in the local and national socio-political context within which each EIP service and team needs to function. Finally, we will discuss the future of EIP and how it needs to adapt and change beyond outcomes measured by short-term remission to ones where long-term recovery is the goal for all young people and their families coming to terms with a FEP.

Chapter 2

Adapting, adjusting and recovering from a first episode of psychosis

The need for integration

Introduction

Much has been written about recovery from psychosis (Warner, 2009). Unfortunately many people remain confused as to how to define it, how to measure it and how it should be conceptualised so that it can make mental health services, such as EIP, more responsive to the needs of service users and their families. There is an argument because recovery in mental health has so many different meanings, it may no longer be useful as a concept and ought to be replaced by other more scientific concepts such as remission (Andreasen, Carpenter, Kane, Lasser, Marder & Weinberger, 2005). It could be argued that the term 'adaptation' may more accurately describe the bio-psychosocial process that people undergo following a FEP with the complex mix of pre- and post-psychotic factors determining how that person will fare, not only in the first 12 months of the illness but where they will end up 10, 20 and 30 years later. We still believe, however, that the concept of recovery is a relevant one, especially for young people adapting to the onset of psychosis, and it has a part to play in helping shape better EIP services. If this is to be achieved, a consensus needs to be reached by service users, families, clinicians, academics and policy-makers as to how the term should be used so that it is valid, standardised and measurable while also taking into account its highly individual nature.

In this chapter, we will attempt to define what we mean by recovery following a FEP, reflecting on concepts such as symptomatic recovery, functional recovery, social recovery and 'clinical recovery', and what we truly mean by 'full' recovery. We will then look at how people have come to view personal and psychological recovery (including psychological adaptation) as a process which is separate from other types of recovery but one that, we would argue, needs to be measured alongside symptomatic and social recovery. Finally, we will present an integrated approach to the three domains of recovery (symptomatic, social and personal) that follow a FEP and briefly discuss a potential framework for measurement that we will further build on throughout the book.

What do we mean by recovery from a FEP?

Recovery from mental health problems and, in particular, psychosis and schizophrenia, remains an appealing ideal. Unfortunately, despite a large and growing literature (Power, 2017), and adoption into mainstream thinking, we are no nearer a universal definition of what recovery from psychosis actually means, how we should measure it and how useful it is for patients, families, services and policy-makers. This is no less the case when applied to first episode psychosis (FEP) and early intervention for psychosis (EIP) services.

Bellack (2006) and others have pointed out that, to date, there have been two main approaches to the definition of recovery: one from a more scientific, psychiatric, biomedical perspective and the other from a more personal, humanistic, philosophical view with its roots mainly, but not solely, in socio-political campaigns (i.e. the consumer movement in the USA and other developed countries). More recently personal recovery has been used to reflect a more psychologically based recovery, defined by increased sense of hope, greater empowerment and reduced stigma (Wood & Alsawy, 2017).

From a scientific perspective, recovery is seen as an outcome, often, but not always, referring to the 'absence of disease' or 'cure'. This usually takes the form of remission in two key areas: (1) symptoms; and (2) social functioning, what some (Warner, 2009) refer to as 'complete' recovery (i.e. return to pre-illness levels of functioning) and others (Simonsen et al., 2017) call 'clinical' recovery. To add to this confusion, some researchers use the term 'clinical' recovery to refer to *only* symptomatic remission (e.g. Chan, Mak, Chio & Tong, 2017) while others have used the term 'functional' recovery to capture improvements in *both* symptoms and psychosocial functioning (Valencia, Caraveo, Colin, Verduzco & Corona, 2014). Over the years, the psychiatric scientific community has attempted to reach a consensus as to what is meant by remission of symptoms, what is adequate social functioning and over what length of time this needs to be demonstrated (Andreasen et al., 2005). In contrast, personalised definitions of recovery tend to place more emphasis on a *process* rather than an outcome that occurs over time in a non-linear fashion (Law & Morrison, 2014). Or in the case of personal recovery, *both* a process and an outcome (Slade & Hayward, 2007). It is also seen as highly individual (Slade, 2009b). All these approaches have their supporters and their detractors.

We, and others (Windell, Norman & Mall, 2012), believe that there are three main 'strands' of recovery following a FEP: (1) illness/symptomatic; (2) social/functional; and (3) personal/psychological and that these can be scrutinised and measured using a combination of patient reported outcome measures (PROMs) and clinician reported outcome measures (CROMs). We believe that EIP services should seek to optimise progress in all three of these areas of recovery. However, financial, clinical, personal, familial and political influences often dictate that one of these may unwittingly take precedence over the other two, with inputs being adjusted accordingly. For example, in an EIP service with low capacity and inadequate psychosocial resources, more emphasis may end up being placed on objective (and subjective) symptomatic recovery achieved through biomedical means. To a certain extent, in the UK, the new Referral to Treatment (RTT) standards (as discussed in Chapter 1) have been brought in to counteract such slippage into a uni-dimensional approach to recovery and help shape the way that care in EIP services is delivered. It remains to be seen whether these standards will be resourced to ensure adequate funding for psychosocial interventions. We will now consider the different types of recovery in more detail.

Symptomatic recovery and remission following a FEP

Symptomatic recovery refers to the reduction, amelioration and/or remission of positive psychotic symptoms (hallucinations, delusions and thought disorder) and negative symptoms (loss of pleasure, lack of drive, social withdrawal, etc.). For many years there was poor agreement as to how symptomatic recovery should be measured and the threshold criteria for when it had been achieved. This would often make it difficult to compare studies and cohorts with regard to the transferability of treatments and interventions. Psychiatric disorders such as schizophrenia and psychosis, it was believed, were also seen as different from medical conditions like leukaemia that could be potentially 'cured'. Here 'remission' was more easily defined as the complete *absence* of symptoms, and something relatively easy to measure due to the physical nature of the symptoms. Instead, it was argued that, like anxiety and mood disorders, people with schizophrenia and psychosis often continued to display mild symptoms, yet would still be considered 'remitted' (Andreasen et al., 2005). For such reasons, it was felt that the criteria for symptomatic remission needed to be better standardised.

In 2005, a consensus was reached by the Remission in Schizophrenia Working Group (RSWG) that specified that, in order to count as having symptomatic remission, a person needed to demonstrate two separate criteria: (1) *improvement* in symptoms; *and* (2) fulfilment of a *duration* criteria, namely, that they could demonstrate the presence of less than mild symptoms (<3) on the Positive and Negative Syndrome Scale (PANSS), the Scale for the Assessment of Positive Symptoms (SAPS)/Scale for the Assessment of Negative Symptoms (SANS) (<3) or the Brief Psychiatric Rating Scale (BPRS) (<3) for six months or less (Andreasen et al., 2005). Table 2.1 shows remission rates from longitudinal studies of adult FEP patients (since 2005) using the RSWG criteria. Here it can be seen that these rates varied between 37% and 78% with a mean average of 55%. Interestingly, when Lally et al. (2017), reviewing 60 studies measuring remission and 'clinical recovery' in FEP cohorts over three decades, used a 'broader' definition of remission (studies defining asymptomatic criteria but *not* duration), they found little difference in these rates (59% vs. 57%). This would indicate that symptomatic recovery will occur at different rates for different people and the time frame over which this happens for FEP may not be as relevant as it once was (Power, 2017).

Table 2.1 Longitudinal FEP studies using RSWG criteria to define symptomatic remission

Author	Country	Diagnosis	Study design	Length of follow up (years)	N at baseline	N at follow up	Remission (%)
Alaghband-Rad et al., 2006	Iran	FEP	Prospective	2	54	49	77.8
Clarke et al., 2006	UK	FEP	Prospective	4	166	132	57.6
Emsley et al., 2006	South Africa	FEP	Prospective	2	57	28	40
Naz et al., 2007	USA	FEAP	Retrospective	4	87	87	69
Addington & Addington, 2008	Canada	FEP	Prospective	3	240	147	36.7
De Haan et al., 2008	the Netherlands	FES	Prospective	5	110	104	37.5*
Gasquet et al., 2008	France	FES	Prospective	3	933	563	60.6
Whitty et al., 2008	UK	FES	Prospective	4	171	129	43
Boden et al., 2009	Sweden	FES	Prospective	5	124	76	52.6
Kurihara et al., 2011	Indonesia	FES	Prospective	17	59	43	44.2
Chang et al., 2012	Hong Kong	FEP	Retrospective	3	700	539	58.8
Tohen et al., 2012	USA	FEAP	Prospective	2	56	49	58.3
Verma et al., 2012	Singapore	FEP	Retrospective	2	1175	776	54.1
Morgan et al., 2014	UK	FEP	Retrospective	10	532	387	77

Source: based on Lally et al. (2017).

Note
* 9 months duration.

Of course, such a perspective assumes a syndromal approach to remission and symptomatic recovery, which is based on the idea that all positive symptoms of psychosis are correlated with each other and are indicative of the presence of a syndrome or cluster of symptoms. Measurement on generic psychosis scales such as the PANSS, which evaluates the degree to which psychotic symptoms are absent or present does not necessarily take account of adaptation to individual symptoms such as voices (Birchwood et al., 2018) or delusions (Freeman, 2016). As we will discuss in more detail in Chapter 4, positive symptoms such as hallucinations and delusions are often multidimensional (Haddock, Wood, Watts, Dunn, Morrison & Price, 2011) and personal to the individual (Greenwood et al., 2010). Thus, despite some people not always experiencing major changes in uni-dimensional scores, these service users may still experience, for instance, improvements such as reductions in distress and reduced compliance with malevolent voices. In turn, these may then be associated with improvements in social and personal recovery, topics discussed in more detail in Chapters 4, 5 and 7.

This then offers an alternative meaning to the concept of symptomatic *recovery*, one that is more subjective, person-centred and individualised (Haddock et al., 2011). This is in contrast to symptomatic *remission* which is defined solely on the basis of the severity of psychotic symptoms (mild or absent) and their duration (mild or absent symptoms for at least six months; Andreasen et al., 2005). 'Recovery', in this context, is then seen as comprising of an additional dimension, notably, improvements in economic (work, education, training, etc.) and non-economic *social* functioning (Lally et al., 2017) what we will refer to throughout this book as social recovery.

Social recovery: existing definitions and constructs

Social recovery, even more than symptomatic recovery, has suffered from vague and poorly defined outcome criteria (Lambert et al., 2010a). Despite widespread use of the term, it is important to acknowledge that 'social recovery' as a construct actually lacks an agreed definition and model. Different terms (e.g. 'functional' recovery), as well as different concepts have been used to reflect social recovery in the psychosis literature. Very broadly, they refer mostly to the difficulties with social and occupational functioning that can precede as well as follow psychosis. However, terms are often used interchangeably and can refer to a variety of similar and overlapping constructs such as 'social adjustment', 'social dysfunction', and 'social adaptation'. So what is social recovery? How can we best capture this for our patients? And why would we want to?

Returning to competitive employment or education has often been used to represent social recovery following psychosis (Mueser, Salyers & Mueser, 2001). However, to use this solely to define social recovery is restrictive, as it is clear that social recovery can include a return to functioning in a range of roles. Moreover, many young people with psychosis may never have worked since leaving school and would therefore, not be *returning*, as such (Fowler et al., 2018). It is also important to differentiate between those returning to positions of enhanced social recovery relative to others (e.g. and one commensurate with their pre-morbid levels of functioning) and those where there is no evidence of advancement in functioning (Tapfumaneyi et al., 2015).

The description of disrupted social functioning in schizophrenia provided in DSM-V (American Psychiatric Association, 2013) identifies three broad domains: work, interpersonal relations and self-care. The *Handbook of Social Functioning in Schizophrenia* (Mueser & Tarrier, 1998) defines impaired social recovery as an individual's inability to meet societal defined roles (e.g. home-maker, worker, student, spouse, family member, friend, etc.). Moreover, an individual's satisfaction with their ability to meet these roles, their ability to care for themselves and participation in leisure and recreational activities are also seen as an important component of social functioning. This recognises that social recovery has a social and cultural context that may vary from one country to another, and within different cultural groups, in the same country (Shrivastava, Johnston, Thakar, Stitt & Shah, 2011). Following a review of service-based definitions of 'clinical' recovery following psychosis, Liberman and Kopelowicz (2005) propose that the criteria should include (in addition to symptom remission and engagement in full or part-time activities in work or education); the ability to live independently without supervision, regular social networking, shared activities with friends, and sustained financial independence for at least two years (i.e. not fully dependent on financial support from disability insurance). In short, they assume that social recovery adopts a return to former or improved social and vocational functioning, but over a sustained period of time.

Álvarez-Jiménez et al. (2012b) define social (functional) recovery using four components derived from the ratings on the Quality of Life Scale (Heinrich, Hanlon & Carpenter, 1984). In addition to adequate vocational functioning (defined as paid employment, attending school or homemaking), these include appropriate interpersonal relationships with people outside the family, success in fulfilling the particular role that the person has chosen to attempt and regular participation in basic living tasks. Fowler et al. (2018) also advocate that social recovery be characterised multi-dimensionally. However, they place less emphasis on the acquisition of a job or studying as being representative of social recovery, arguing that being in employment should not be viewed as akin to being socially recovered, but as a potential part of the process towards social and economic participation. They advocate understanding occupation as *any* economically, socially or culturally valued activity, recognising these as important outcomes for people with psychosis in their own right.

Data from service user investigations also understand social recovery as going beyond symptom remission or engagement in employment or education (e.g. Windell & Norman, 2013). Subjective experiences of social recovery might include a sense of inclusion and social acceptance, and making a valued occupational contribution to others. Indeed, qualitative research with young people experiencing psychosis reflects the importance of a sense of belonging, connection, purpose and community involvement (Davidson, 2003), contribution (Anthony, 1993) and of objective participation in social and occupational activities (Eisenstadt, Monteiro, Diniz & Chaves, 2012). Indeed, Windell et al. (2012) conclude that participation in activity is central to the definition of recovery provided by FEP/EIP service users.

So, from a clinical, personal and service perspective, then, social recovery can mean everything required to function in society, including independent living skills, social/relationship capital and engagement in some meaningful, valued occupation/activity that may or may not be employment or study (Lecomte, Corbière, Ehmann, Addington, Abdel-Baki & MacEwan, 2014). However, these dimensions, within themselves, lack a consensus with regards definition. For example, studies might cluster together social integration and social inclusion variables and their constructs (e.g. social cohesion, social integration, social networks) alongside measures of occupational functioning and self-care, whereas others might make a distinction between optimum social network and other aspects of social functioning (Evert, Harvey, Trauer & Herrman, 2003). Finally, dimensions of social recovery may not be static. For example, Lecomte et al. (2014) call for any construct of social recovery to take into account the adaptations of modern culture on social factors, such as the potential influence of social media and communication technologies. In essence, as we will argue in Chapter 5, and consistent with Hodgekins et al. (2015b), social recovery should also include any valued activity that is defined by the service user as meaningful to them.

Yet despite the lack of consensus with regard to definition, social recovery goals are nonetheless reliably cited as important outcomes for the FEP population and efforts to measure them have had strong support (NICE, 2014; Warner, 2009). Chapter 5 will highlight how this has been approached by EIP services in the past and what may be the best way forward. Chapter 6 then sets out how we may optimise such social recovery goals through integrated bio-psychosocial interventions. The use of routine outcome measures (ROMs) to measure social recovery within an EIP service is shown in Appendix 2.

Complete/clinical recovery following a FEP

'Full', 'complete' or 'clinical' recovery from psychosis and schizophrenia remains the ultimate goal for most mental health clinicians and academics. Most reviews of the literature, as pointed out previously, have operationalised 'clinical recovery' (often simply referred to by some authors as 'recovery') as 'a multidimensional concept, incorporating *symptomatic and functional* improvement in social, occupational and educational domains with a necessary duration component' (Lally et al., 2017, p. 2) of two years or more.

For instance, Jääskeläinen et al. (2013) in a systematic review and meta-analysis of 50 studies reporting outcomes in individuals with a diagnosis of schizophrenia or related psychoses (i.e. not just FEP), claimed that 13.5% (range: 8–20%) had made improvements on *both* social and clinical measures and that improvements in one of these domains had persisted for at least two years. The authors concluded from these studies that despite major advances in treatments for psychosis over recent years, there had been little change in the total proportion of people with schizophrenia who could be considered 'completely recovered' from one year to the next. Likewise, Lally et al. (2017), in their recent review of 'clinical recovery' in *solely* adult FEP patients in longitudinal studies of more than one-year follow up, concluded that there was little evidence to suggest that this type of 'recovery' (unlike remission) had significantly improved over time. This was the case even when 'broader' criteria (sustained improvement of over one year as opposed to two) was applied. Unfortunately, studies of 'clinical recovery' (unlike remission) are often difficult to compare. This is because they fail to take account of the different definitions of, not so much symptomatic recovery, but social recovery that, as already discussed, besets the field of schizophrenia and psychosis research. Moreover, both the Lally et al. (2017) and Jääskeläinen et al. (2013) reviews measured 'clinical recovery' as endpoints which ranged from one to 25 years and not for the entire duration of follow-up, as this data is often unavailable. This makes it difficult to determine whether those considered 'clinically recovered' are different from that group of people (15–25%) who only ever have one episode in a decade or more (Fusar-Poli et al., 2017). In a recent study, Lappin et al. (2018), who followed a cohort of FEP patients from the AESOP trial up at 10 years, found that only 12.5% demonstrated 'sustained recovery' (defined as remission within six months and no further psychotic episodes over a 10-year follow-up). This group were more likely to be female, employed, in a relationship, have a short DUP and have a diagnosis other than schizophrenia, particularly mania or brief psychosis. More research is needed to determine whether 'clinical', 'full' and/or 'complete' recovery is just another way of framing a speedy remission followed by the absence of relapse. This is opposed to a definition of 'clinical' recovery that, in addition to symptomatic recovery and adaptation, also includes a return to a valued social role that has meaning for the person (Law & Morrison, 2014). This will be irrespective of whether they have relapsed or not.

Personal recovery following a FEP: definitions

Even with the best medical and psychosocial treatments and recent advances in service delivery (including EIP), only one in three people (38%), will achieve 'complete' clinical recovery following a FEP (Lally et al., 2017). Despite this, many young people still consider themselves 'recovered' despite living with ongoing symptoms or not returning to the levels of social functioning that they were at prior to their FEP (Davidson, 2003). Conversely, many young people make a very good recovery from their first episode of psychosis in terms of symptom and functional remission but still feel a sense of loss, hopelessness and entrapment (Birchwood, Jackson, Brunet, Holden & Barton, 2012) which can culminate in feelings of suicide and psychological crisis (Gajwani, Larkin & Jackson, 2017). Subjective feelings of personal recovery, which are more to do with the establishment of a fulfilling, meaningful life and a positive sense of identity founded on hopefulness and self-determination, can clearly not be ignored. It is argued that promoting a personal recovery approach helps to favour hope and creativity over disillusionment and defeat (Royal College of Psychiatrists, Care Services Improvement Partnership & Social Care Institute of Excellence, 2007). When EIP teams have adopted such an approach, they have found, that, according to both staff and service users, it has helped to promote resilience (Morton et al., 2010).

In the document, *A Common Purpose* (Royal College of Psychiatrists, et al., 2007), a joint position paper between the Care Services Improvement Partnership, the Royal College of Psychiatrists and the Social Care Institute of Excellence, it is argued that there are at least three different meanings of subjective personal recovery in mental health: (1) as a spontaneous and natural process; (2) as a response to effective treatments; and (3) as a way of growing with or despite continuing disability. Some service user definitions have acknowledged personal recovery to be a complex and idiosyncratic process involving: rebuilding life, rebuilding self and hope for a better future (Pitt, Kilbride, Nothard, Welford & Morrison, 2007). Andresen, Oades and Caputi (2003), on the other hand, argue that there are four key processes at play in personal recovery from psychosis and schizophrenia: (1) finding hope; (2) re-establishing identity; (3) finding meaning in life; and (4) taking responsibility for their own recovery. Law and Morrison (2014) pulled out eight main themes of personal recovery. These were: (1) improved knowledge of looking after self; (2) support from others, including services; (3) regaining control over one's life; (4) having a meaning and purpose to one's life; (5) having an acceptable quality of life; (6) having a positive and hopeful outlook on life; (7) being happy with who you are as a person; and (8) a living in a good and safe environment. Such themes have since been developed into a conceptual model known as the CHIME framework (Connectiveness, Hope, Identity, Meaning and Empowerment) by Bird, Leamy, Tew, Le Boutillier, Williams & Slade (2014) as part of the REFOCUS trial testing the validity of personal recovery concepts as well as providing a framework for measurement (e.g. QPR; see Appendix 2). Some of these themes are also picked up in the wider literature reviews that have gathered the opinions, not only of service users but also of health care providers and policymakers (e.g. Bonney & Stickley, 2008). Again, all these studies, reviews and trials emphasise the individual nature of the (personal) recovery process.

The view that personal recovery is a very individual process automatically implies that there is no one right or wrong way to experience it. Likewise, what helps a person at one time in their life may not at another (Slade, 2009b). This would naturally imply that there can never be a single way to enhance personal recovery for young people recovering from a FEP within EIP services (Windell et al., 2015).

Arguably, one of the most favoured definitions of personal recovery in the literature is that given by Anthony (1993):

> Recovery is a deeply personal, unique process of changing one's attitudes, values, feelings, goals, skills and/or roles. It is a way of living a satisfying, hopeful, and contributing life even with limitations caused by the illness. Recovery involves the development of new meaning and purpose in one's life as one grows beyond the catastrophic effects of mental illness.

Maybe a more succinct way of putting this, borrowing from a well-known phrase, is that personal recovery is about striving to be the best version of yourself that you can be. Living the best life that you can, despite, or maybe because of, a FEP remains the ultimate goal and marker of success for most young people with psychosis (Lam, Pearson, Ng, Chiu, Law & Chen, 2011). Recovering from a first episode of psychosis can, for some, be a very challenging experience while, for others, it can be a positive one (Jordan et al., 2017), which allows them to reflect, re-evaluate and set a new trajectory for themselves (Attard, Larkin, Boden & Jackson, 2017). Some people may even achieve what is referred to as post-traumatic growth (PTG), which is discussed in more detail in Chapter 7. Ultimately, however, as alluded to above, personal recovery is a subjective *process* and *outcome* that can be measured and evaluated in a number of different ways, including with a PROM (Patient Reported Outcome Measure) and PREM (Patient Reported Experienced Measure; see Appendix 2). In so doing, it can help shape the individual's goals and the way that EIP services are delivered (Harris, Collinson & das Nair, 2012).

Psychological adaptation following a FEP: definitions and meaning

While the term 'recovery' remains appealing because of its association with 'cure', 'return to normality' or 'getting back to where one was', for such reasons it also remains a problematic concept. Life events such as FEP change people in both challenging and positive ways at an individual, interpersonal and spiritual level (Bernard, Jackson & Birchwood, 2015; Jordan et al., 2018). Once you have experienced psychosis, as is also the case for other forms of mental or physical illness, you often need to change, adjust or adapt to your new 'world' or environment. By definition you do not remain the same person. The *Oxford English Dictionary* defines adaptation as 'the act or process of adapting or the state of being adapted' and that the verb adapt means: (1) 'To adjust (someone or something, especially oneself) to different conditions, a new environment (2) To fit, change or modify to suit a new or different purpose.'

The notion of psychological adaptation following psychosis may be conceptually broader than the term 'personal recovery'. The word 'recovery' may imply that someone needs to go back to how they used to be before an 'illness', however, this is contrary to those who do not see the need to 'recover' from something that has been a positive or 'normal' experience for them (Roberts & Wolfson, 2004). Moreover, as we have alluded to in Chapter 1, many young people with FEP have difficult and stressful pre-morbid experiences that they may not wish to 'recover' or return to. 'Recovery' is also typically focused on as an individual process that may place less emphasis on the social context, which as we will argue later, plays a huge part in someone's journey through psychosis.

These arguments seem particularly relevant when considering personal or psychological experiences following a first episode of psychosis where the concept of psychological adaptation may be more appropriate. Here, it may reflect more of the process of transformation into a new life and rarely just involves adjustment to a single experience or set of symptoms (Tan, Gould, Combes & Lehmann, 2014). More likely, it is a process that assimilates the experiences of psychosis through understanding and acceptance of the experiences (Attard et al., 2017). It may also be connected with coming to terms with the loss of the old self and 'strengthening' of the new post FEP self (Connell, Schweitzer & King, 2015). This may, or may not, occur in the presence of ongoing symptoms (Morrison et al., 2013; see Chapter 7 for further discussion).

Adaptation and adjustment following a FEP are rarely straightforward. Emotional dysfunction (Birchwood, 2003; see Chapter 8) is common and can express itself in terms of post-psychotic depression (Upthegrove, Ross, Brunet, McCollum & Jones, 2014), social anxiety (Michail & Birchwood, 2014) or post-psychotic trauma symptoms (Rodrigues & Anderson, 2017). Moreover, people may become suicidal and attempt to take their own lives if they feel defeated and entrapped by their illness and its psychosocial sequela (Gajwani et al., 2017). Part of this book (Chapters 8 and 9) is dedicated not only to understanding why this happens, but also to helping EIP services to assist young people to readjust and readapt to FEP. EIP services play a crucial role in supporting young people, and their families, with overcoming these effects and promoting processes of acceptance, integration and assimilation, through individual, family and social interventions. Throughout this book we will use the terms 'personal recovery', 'psychological recovery' and 'psychological adaptation' to describe a number of psychological *processes* and *outcomes* that occur following a FEP.

Interaction between symptomatic, social and personal recovery

Windell and colleagues (2012, 2013, 2015) used qualitative research methods and semi-structured interviews to explore how young people saw their own recovery three to five years after the initial treatment of an FEP in an EIP service in Canada. They found that the majority of individuals considered themselves to be 'recovered'. They also viewed their recovery during these early stages, as multi-dimensional, personalised and achievable. These young people defined 'recovery' as improvement in one or more of three domains: illness recovery, psychological and personal recovery, and social and functional recovery with variations in the emphasis that individuals placed on each one. For instance, there was variation in the extent to which individuals viewed recovery as involving a reduction in their symptoms. Overall, the findings from this study are consistent with the view that an individual's personal views of recovery during the early stages of psychosis tend to be overwhelmingly positive but also map onto what most people, whether researcher, clinician, policy-maker, family member or service user, consider to be the three pillars of recovery (symptomatic, social and personal/psychological). As illustrated in Figure 2.1, this would imply that the three types of recovery are both independent from each other but can also be overlapping, and that different people give different weights to the importance of each one. This would also have implications for redefining what is meant by 'complete' or 'full' recovery as current definitions shy away from the personal, psychological or subjective aspects of that. It would also suggest that while it may remain the ultimate goal for service providers (and perhaps families), 'clinical' recovery may not always be the ultimate goal for the individual at that particular stage of their life.

Towards an integrated approach to 'recovery' following a FEP

We have seen that different aspects of recovery following a FEP are not only difficult concepts to define, but, at times, seem at odds with each other. They may also become a cause of division and conflict within and between professional and service user groups (Morera, Pratt & Bucci, 2017). One illustration of

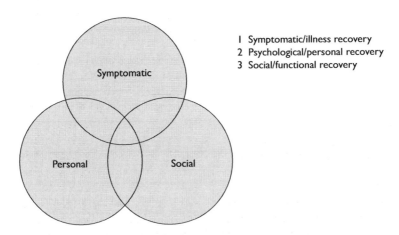

1 Symptomatic/illness recovery
2 Psychological/personal recovery
3 Social/functional recovery

Figure 2.1 The three domains of recovery following a first episode of psychosis.
Source: Windell, Norman, & Malla (2012).

this is the tension that exists between the idea of remission from positive symptoms of psychosis being seen as a marker of recovery, while, for some, recovery is viewed as a *process* or 'journey' which happens to the individual, irrespective of whether remission of psychotic symptoms takes place at all. Such thinking, we believe, is not only divisive but also counterproductive and fails to take account of the rich, complex, individual nature of what happens to people following a FEP from a biological, social and psychological perspective. As Power (2017) has argued:

> Recovery is more than simple remission of psychotic symptoms and return to premorbid functioning. It is not just a passive response to treatment. Nor is it just understanding one's prognosis and engaging with the treatments recommended. Recovery is a far more complex process. It demands change and adaptation.
>
> (p. 332)

Recovering from a first episode of psychosis, and therefore EIP service provision, need to take account of *all* three types of recovery: symptomatic, social and personal. As we have already seen in Chapter 1, there is now a growing consensus with regard to the commonalities of an EIP approach, as is reflected in the new EIP standards for England (NICE, 2016). There is less agreement about how they should be 'joined up' and how an integrated approach to EIP that enhances recovery in one domain, impacts on the other two. For example, in a recent study, MacDougal, Vandermeer and Norman (2017) found that reductions in positive symptoms of psychosis (symptomatic recovery) impacted directly upon self-esteem (personal and psychological recovery). Conversely, improving someone's overall self-concepts (psychological recovery), in particular their interpersonal self-concepts, may help with reductions in paranoid delusions; i.e. symptomatic recovery (Johnson, Jones, Lin, Wood, Heinze & Jackson, 2014; Lincoln, Mehl, Ziegler, Kesting, Exner & Rief, 2010). Finally, Norman et al. (2018) noted that social support, targeted at social and vocational recovery, had a significant impact upon symptomatic recovery from negative symptoms, five years later.

It is likely that the different components of EIP will have a symbiotic relationship with each other (Ruggeri et al., 2015). Moreover, these various elements will be experienced and valued by people, at the separate clinical stages of psychosis, in distinct ways As will be argued throughout this book, however, EIP service provision is founded on the idea that it should be 'greater than the sum of its parts', 'glued together' by a team approach and the formation of crucial therapeutic relationships (Tindall, Simmons, Allott & Hamilton, 2018). Indeed, when 20 young people recovering from a FEP in the north of England were asked what they most valued about their care from an EIP service, they described four main elements: (1) 'the therapeutic relationship'; (2) 'medical care'; (3) 'psychological interventions'; and (4) 'support, coping and recovery', with the therapeutic relationship being cited as the most important (Barr, Ormrod & Dudley, 2015).

Table 2.2 The meanings and measurement of recovery following an FEP (see Appendix 2)

	Symptomatic/illness	Social/functional	Personal/psychological
Meaning	Reduction in frequency, duration, intensity of positive and negative psychotic symptoms. Remission of psychotic symptoms over six months. Avoidance of relapse. Reduction in distress and interference in life due to symptoms, etc. Increase in more positive experiences of symptoms	Increase in time spent in meaningful economic and non-economic activity, living conditions (work, college, independent living, etc.) observable by others Increase in sense of well-being around activities consistent with roles and goals valued by self and others	An individualised view of recovery taking into account person's own values and goals and the process which they have been through (or are going through) to reach them. Outcomes may include reduction in emotional dysfunction and co-morbidity related to FEP (e.g., depression, anxiety, trauma, suicidality, etc.) and increases in self-efficacy, hopefulness and sense of worth

We believe, therefore, that symptomatic, social and personal/psychological recovery are ultimately measurable and influential to the development of 'optimum' mental health practice and the delivery of EIP services. Table 2.2 sets out a framework for understanding the meaning of recovery from a FEP across the three areas observed by Windell et al. (2012, 2013, 2015). Although recovery and adaptation are considered at both an objective and subjective level for two of the types of recovery, namely, the illness/symptomatic and social/functional domains, personal recovery and psychological adaptation are considered most measurable at a subjective level because of their individualised and internal nature. This is not to say that markers of personal recovery and psychological adaptation, such as anxiety, depression, PTSD, low self-esteem, etc. are not observable, only that they can only truly be evaluated through direct feedback from the service user (usually via a PROM; Patient Reported Outcome Measure). See Appendix 2 for guidance as to measuring recovery following a FEP.

Outcome measures used for the three different types of recovery will be discussed in the relevant chapters throughout the book. Here it can be seen, as in Table 2.2, that a mixture of CROMs (clinician reported outcome measures) PROMs (patient reported outcome measures), observation and personal accounts will be needed to reflect the true nature of recovery and adaptation to a FEP.

Measurement of recovery: an overview

Symptomatic recovery

As we have seen, symptomatic recovery can be measured from both an *objective* and *subjective* point of view. Objectively clinicians and researchers have often used global unidimensional CROMs, such as the PANSS (Kay et al., 1987) to measure changes in positive (hallucinations, delusions, conceptual disorganisation, etc.) and negative symptoms (blunted affect, social withdrawal, etc.). As noted previously, they can also be used to evaluate whether people have reached criteria for remission following medical (see Chapter 3) and psychosocial interventions (Chapter 4) or relapse (see Chapter 1). However, as argued in Chapter 4, these scales may not be sensitive enough to detect change for some people with FEP and other CROMs such as the PSYRATS (Haddock et al., 1999) may be more suited to reflect symptomatic recovery, especially following psychological interventions. Such CROMs, however, often fail to take into account the subjective nature of psychotic symptoms and what sense people make of them. Here PROMs such as the Beliefs about Voices Questionnaire-Revised (BAVQ-R; Chadwick, Less & Birchwood, 2000) and the Peters Delusional Inventory (PDI; Peters et al., 2004), are much better at tapping into the appraisals of the symptom that, with a CROM, will give a much better all-round measure of symptomatic recovery (see Appendix 2).

Social recovery

Social recovery can also be conceptualised as being measurable at both an objective and subjective level. Objective, and therefore observable, evaluations of social and functional recovery may include both economic and non-economic activity, including meaningful work in the case of the former and improvements in relationships, activities of daily living or hobbies in the latter. Objective measures of social recovery such as NEET status (not in education, employment or training) can be measured using criteria used in surveys of economic status (ONS, 2017). CROMs such as the GAF-D (Global Assessment of Functioning-Disability; Hall, 1995) are also a quick and useful tool. Alternatively, subjective measures of social recovery will be more of a reflection on the personal meaning of changes in social recovery for that person as they begin to move towards recovery of valued social roles and meeting their own individualised goals. Again, these can be measured on PROMs, such as the WSAS (Work and Social Adjustment Scale; Mundt, Marks, Shear & Greist, 2002) and the TUS (Time Use Survey; Short, 2006, and see Appendix 2). Both CROMs and PROMs and the objective and subjective evaluation of social recovery, are discussed in more detail in Chapter 5.

Personal recovery, psychological adaptation and emotional dysfunction

Personal recovery, as noted above, is only truly measurable at a subjective level (Law & Morrison, 2014). The process of personal recovery and psychological adaptation can be reflected in stories, narratives or other forms of artistic methods that service users can use to express their personal 'journey' or subjective experiences following a FEP (Attard et al., 2017). However, these not only make it difficult to make comparisons between service users and services, but also to quantify and demonstrate to individuals when they feel that they themselves, have made positive changes. The new Access and Waiting Time Standards (NICE, 2016) have recommended the routine use of PROMs, such as the QPR (Process of Recovery Questionnaire) (Neil et al., 2009) and DIALOG (Priebe et al., 2007), in EIP services in England to measure personal recovery (discussed in more detail in Chapter 12). Improvements in emotional dysfunction, such as post-psychotic trauma (Jackson et al., 2011), post-psychotic depression (Upthegrove et al., 2014) and social anxiety (Michail & Birchwood, 2014) may contribute to improved personal recovery (Morrison et al., 2013). The reduction of distress, on its own, however, may still not be sufficient for someone to feel that they have attained personal recovery. In Chapters 7 and 8, we discuss in more detail different approaches to the measurement of personal recovery, psychological adaptation and emotional dysfunction, and how they all need to be addressed and evaluated as part of recovering from a FEP. Suggestions for measures are provided in Appendix 2.

In summary, then, if we are to meet the challenge of improving long-term outcomes for the millions of people and their families throughout the world who have experienced, or are experiencing, a first episode of psychosis, we should consider, where possible, measuring outcomes in different ways across the relevant parts of the clinical staging model (see Table 2.1). For example, during stage 2 (FEP with early symptomatic and social recovery), more emphasis could be placed on the measurement of sustained symptomatic remission and objective measures of employment, training and pre-morbid role functioning. This may also be accompanied by measures of personal recovery and psychological adaptation to prevent issues of emotional dysfunction (Chapter 8) and comorbidity (Chapter 10). From stage 3 (incomplete clinical recovery), more emphasis would need to be placed on subjective measures of symptomatic recovery, objective and subjective measures of non-economic social recovery and subjective evaluation of personal recovery. Recovery from psychosis remains a multifaceted concept that needs to be evaluated across the three domains (symptomatic, social and personal) in different ways, at different times. Only then can we develop a true consensus about what it is to be 'recovered' and what bio-psychosocial interventions are required to achieve this (Chaterjee, 2017).

In the rest of this book we will attempt to give guidance as to how, on a clinical basis, people should outcome the three types of recovery, how they should intervene to promote each one and how an integrated EIP service should respond when a young person's recovery is 'thrown off course' following a FEP.

Learning points

- Despite its common use, there is still no one universal definition of what we mean by recovery from a FEP.
- Historically there has been a tension between a more scientific, clinical definition of recovery and one that is more personal and subjective.
- Symptomatic recovery often refers to the short-term remission of symptoms according to an agreed criteria based on the absence (or near absence) of psychotic symptoms over a set period of time (six months).
- Unlike symptomatic recovery, there has been no real consensus among clinicians and researchers as to how to define social recovery.
- This makes it difficult to compare studies that purport to measure 'clinical' recovery, defined as the remission of psychotic symptoms plus the return to meaningful role functioning (social recovery).
- Personal recovery and psychological adaptation describe a number of subjective psychological processes and outcomes that sometimes occur separately from symptomatic and social recovery, but can also be enhanced by it.
- Successful psychological adaptation following a FEP may move the person beyond personal recovery, towards post-traumatic growth (PTG).
- Symptomatic, social and personal recovery need to be measured alongside each other at different stages of FEP, using PROMs and CROMs to reflect differences in the subjective and objective nature of these three domains of recovery.

Chapter 3

Biological and medical approaches to symptomatic recovery and adaptation

Introduction

Compassionate patient-centred care, often involving the early judicial use of medication, lays the foundation for symptomatic recovery from FEP. Although antipsychotic (AP) medication is only one aspect of bio-psychosocial care, it is often the first component of treatment for a first episode psychosis (FEP) (Barnes, 2011; NICE, 2014) and the foundation upon which social and personal recovery is built. AP medication is highly valued by patients and their families, with 73% of 2,475 respondents rating it as the most helpful intervention (Schizophrenia Commission, 2012). Awareness of the evidence supporting AP use is imperative if EIP clinicians are to effectively reassure patients and their families, many of whom may be mistrustful of mental health services and psychiatric medications. Pharmacological treatments can play a role in all aspects of recovery but particularly so in symptomatic recovery and in minimising the risk of psychotic relapse (Leucht, 2012).

This chapter offers balanced, pragmatic, and evidence-based prescribing approaches in young first episode populations. We discuss how AP prescribing aids recovery from, and adaptation to, the distressing symptoms of psychosis, namely, hallucinations, delusions and thought disorder. We review current AP evidence regarding the efficacy of first- and second-generation APs, the optimal dose and length of treatment and the role of long-term maintenance therapy. Consideration is given to specific issues for young people taking APs for the first time, including medication concordance and the role of depots in FEP. Clozapine treatment and pharmacological strategies for individuals experiencing negative symptoms and/or cognitive dysfunction are reviewed. With the alarming backdrop of curtailed longevity for people with SMI (Reininghaus et al., 2014), we conclude by emphasising the importance of physical well-being in all aspects of recovery from FEP. This involves the need to regularly screen and intervene for AP side effects, many of which are explored alongside management strategies.

The initial treatment of FEP is critical as it shapes an individual's longer-term recovery prospects as well as their attitudes towards medication at a time when concordance rates are low (Miller et al., 2011). Psychiatrists can confidently offer evidence-based effective treatments in a climate of hope to counter the anti-medication rhetoric, at times influenced by inaccurate reporting of research. In order to maximise symptomatic recovery, clinicians should adopt a flexible and pragmatic approach to prescribing, empowering patients through compassionate care and collaborative decision-making. To reflect this and emphasise the therapeutic relationship between prescriber and patient, the term *concordance* rather than *adherence* or *compliance* is preferred.

The role of antipsychotics (APs) in recovery

The discovery of chlorpromazine's antipsychotic action in 1952 (Delay et al., 1959) transformed the outlook for sufferers of psychosis. Where previously patients were literally and metaphorically locked out of society in the 'asylums', the use of AP medication offered symptom control, a dramatic reduction in the use of physical restraint and the hope of discharge from overcrowded and under-staffed asylums (Eisensberg & Guttmacher, 2017). New optimism in the treatment of psychosis helped to lay the foundation for a recovery-focused approach which has the instillation of hope at its core.

Historically, however, medication was prescribed at unnecessarily high doses to sedate agitated patients, resulting in intolerable and stigmatising side effects. This, alongside aggressive marketing by pharmaceutical companies (Kallivayalil, 2008), led to controversy and a deep mistrust by many patients, their families and numerous mental health professionals. The 'Anti-Psychiatry' movement was founded in the 1950s alongside deepening divisions between 'biological' and 'psychoanalytic' psychiatrists, fuelled by the seminal thinking of Laing, Szasz and Cooper (Nasser, 1995). They challenged mainstream psychiatry and the use of APs, some arguing that mental illness is a myth (Szasz, 1974). Today the Critical Psychiatry Network continues to raise concerns about the perceived over-medicalisation of human struggles (Moncrieff, 2014) with many still decrying the use of APs to treat psychosis, despite the fact that medication is highly valued by patients and their families (Schizophrenia Commission, 2014).

While it is important to continually challenge psychiatric practice, unfortunately, at times, the arguments presented appear prejudiced and ill-informed, potentially perpetuating fear and stigma. Psychiatrists and those who work alongside them need 'broad shoulders' and sound evidence-based knowledge. They must weigh the benefits of APs against the potential side effects while maintaining a healthy scepticism of pharmaceutical companies' rhetoric (Tyrer & Kendall, 2009). Fear propagated by the 'anti-psychiatry' movement can be countered by building a trusting doctor-patient relationship, in which the patient and their family feel they are listened to and treated with dignity.

How do antipsychotics work? Addressing the role of dopamine

An important component of adaptation to psychosis is in 'making sense of' the experience. This can be enhanced by helping patients appreciate how and why medication is effective in treating psychotic symptoms.

Although we recognise that psychosis is the result of a complex interplay between neuroscience, psychological and environmental factors (Chapter 1), we focus here on the neurobiological aspect of psychosis and antipsychotics. Dopamine plays a pivotal role in regulating several aspects of basic brain function (Shen, Liao & Tseng, 2012). Neuroimaging studies reveal the association between hallucinations and delusions and dopamine hyperactivity in the mesolimbic area of the brain (Alves, Figee, van Amelsvoort, Veltman & de Haan, 2008). Dopamine over-activity alters the connectivity between the auditory cortex and speech and language areas of the brain (Boca's and Wernicke's), leading to difficulty distinguishing between internally and externally generated speech (Allen, Larøi, McGuire & Aleman, 2008). A hyper-dopaminergic brain mediates delusion formation by heightening the attention (over-salience) given to otherwise irrelevant environmental stimuli (Kapur, Arenovich, Agid, Zipursky, Lindborg & Jones, 2005). Delusions are thus created by the cognitive attempt to make sense of such novel and confusing experiences. Neurocognitive studies report dysfunction in the ability to discount or rationalise the mismatch (or prediction error) between expectation and experience (Corlett, Taylor, Wang, Fletcher & Krystal, 2010).

Further evidence that dopamine is implicated in the onset of psychosis is demonstrated by elevated striatal dopamine synthesis capacity and accentuated dopamine stress response in individuals *at risk of* psychosis (Howes, McCutcheon, Owen & Murray, 2017). Likewise, adversity in childhood (see Chapter 1) is linked to elevated striatal dopamine function in adulthood (Egerton et al., 2016).

APs dampen dopamine activity, thereby lessening the intensity of hallucinatory experiences and reducing attention given to irrelevant stimuli (Madras, 2013). As distress and sensory preoccupation lessen, so the ability to cognitively challenge unusual beliefs and experiences increases. Improvement in sleep, appetite and concentration are some of the direct and indirect effects of APs resulting in a less 'stressed' brain and mind (Krystal, Goforth & Roth, 2008). Although dopamine is viewed as the pharmacological keystone of psychotic states, progressive evidence indicates a role for other neurotransmitters, such as glutamate and serotonin (Rolland, Jardri, Amad, Thomas, Cottencin & Bordet, 2014).

AP treatment goals in FEP

The treatment goals of AP medication are reduction of distress, symptomatic remission, risk reduction and relapse prevention (see Chapter 4).

Reduction of distress

Recovery from psychosis cannot meaningfully begin until the distress experienced during the acute phase of psychosis is minimised. APs improve commonly associated sleep and appetite disturbances as biological functioning is restored. Reduction of distress by APs can occur rapidly, usually within the first week of treatment (Agid, Kapur, Arenovich & Zipursky, 2003) and often within 24 hours (Kapur et al., 2005).

Symptomatic reduction and remission

Treatment with APs helps alleviate the preoccupation with delusions and the intensity of the hallucinations alongside an improvement in maladaptive behaviour (Byrne, 2007). Thought perplexity and distractibility lessen and there is an awakening ability to concentrate on externally (rather than internally) generated stimuli (Menon, Mizrahi & Kapur, 2008). The evidence supporting APs' efficacy in treating psychotic symptoms is robust (Wunderink, Nienhuis, Sytema, Slooff, Knegtering & Wiersma, 2008) with reports of symptomatic response (reduction >20% PANSS (Positive and Negative Symptom Scale)) occurring in around 75% of FEP individuals (Češková, Radovan, Tomáš & Hana, 2007; Elmsley, 2006). Furthermore, medication concordance during the first year after FEP is the sole independent predictor of symptomatic recovery at the five-year follow-up (Norman et al., 2017).

Minimising the risk to self and others

Lifetime risk of suicide in schizophrenia and other psychotic disorders is estimated between 2% and 4% (Björkenstam, Björkenstam, Hjern, Bodén & Reutfors, 2014), is particularly high during the first year of contact with mental health services (Dutta, Murray, Hotopf, Allardyce, Jones & Boydell, 2010) and linked to a long DUP (Barrett et al., 2010). Command hallucinations, passivity experiences, hopelessness and substance misuse significantly heighten suicide risk in untreated psychosis (Mitter, Subramaniam, Abdin, Poon & Verma, 2013). Tiihonen (2006) reported mortality outcomes on an observational study cohort of 2,230 FEP patients. Those taking APs had significantly lower mortality with only one recorded suicide. In contrast, despite much lower overall numbers, 75 deaths were recorded in the untreated cohort, 26 of which were suicide.

Although extremely rare, if homicide occurs, it is significantly more likely during the untreated stage of FEP (Nielssen & Large, 2008). AP treatment in the first year of FEP significantly reduces aggressive acts from 12% to 2% (Leucht et al., 2012).

Relapse prevention

APs promote recovery by minimising risk of future relapses, a risk which remains high for five years following FEP (Robinson et al., 1999). Higher relapse rates are associated with poorer prognosis, compromising long-term recovery prospects. For some individuals, each relapse is associated with a greater delay in achieving symptom control and poorer probability of social recovery (Leucht & Heres, 2006). Meta-analyses of AP effectiveness one year following a FEP report a relapse rate reduction from 64% to 27% (Leucht, 2012). Over several years, continuing AP treatment reduces relapse by about two-thirds (Kissling, 1991). Indeed, the MESIFOS study (Wiersma, Wunderink, Nienhuis & Sytema, 2007) compared maintenance treatment with discontinuation in FEP and concluded that only small numbers can successfully be withdrawn from APs without relapse.

Practicalities of commencing medication in an individual recently diagnosed with FEP

Within the wider field of medicine, mental health professionals are unique in treating patients who sometimes do not recognise or accept that they are unwell, particularly in the early stages of the illness. Clearly, this will result in reluctance or unwillingness to commence medication.

Where a patient has capacity to make decisions about treatment choice, it is important to impart facts about medication clearly and realistically while, at the same time, instilling hope. In FEP, the initial assessment is pivotal in setting the foundations of recovery. If patients are treated with compassion and respect and feel they have been 'heard', they are more likely to engage in discussions about treatment. How psychiatrists and care co-ordinators broach the subject of medication with a patient is an important step in engagement and treatment concordance. Exploring an individual's beliefs about their 'symptoms' is a helpful starting point. Furthermore, an individual's account of how their experiences or beliefs make them feel can open up the conversation to treatment options. If rapport is building, they will often admit to feeling frightened, stressed and overwhelmed. Challenging delusional beliefs at this stage is not advisable and likely to be counterproductive (Freeman, 2016). Often individuals admit they are stressed but accepting psychosis may be 'a bridge too far'. It can be helpful to initially work within their attribution of the situation, e.g. their belief that unusual experiences are caused by demons, Djinns or black magic (Nelson, 2005) and it is advisable to discuss treatment in terms of reducing the distress associated with these experiences, rather than treating 'illness'.

A flexible approach to discussing medication is important, taking into account culture and previous health care experiences. Some fear that medication will cause personality changes. Others may experience persecutory delusions about the psychiatrist's intentions. On the other hand, many are relieved at the prospect of symptom relief. A brief description about how and why medication is prescribed may involve the role of dopamine over-activity in psychosis. Alternatively, medication can be described metaphorically, as a sponge soaking up stress, which in turn improves sleep, mood, appetite and concentration. It is helpful to provide patients and their families with information through leaflets or websites, such as 'Headmeds'.

What happens when a patient experiencing psychosis initially refuses medication?

Encouraging an acutely disturbed and paranoid patient to take medication without the use of the Mental Health Act (MHA) requires advanced skill. When a patient, despite our best efforts, refuses medication and there are significant risks associated, the use of the MHA is likely to be required. Having to take medication against one's will predictably provokes a profound sense of disempowerment and everything should be done to avoid this. Persuading a reluctant patient to take medication without use of the MHA is time-consuming and usually involves a tenacious and flexible approach. If risks to self and others are low, it is helpful to work with the young person, regularly monitoring their mental state. As engagement develops (Table 3.1) so too does trust and it is not uncommon for a young person who initially refused medication to agree a trial after a few weeks. This is time well spent, resulting in a patient who has not been forced to take medication against their will and who is significantly more invested in their recovery.

Table 3.1 Approaches to encourage commencement of AP in reluctant patients

Normalising	'Those voices sound scary. If I was hearing them I would feel stressed and probably wouldn't be able to sleep or concentrate ...' 'You may feel no one understands what you are going through but you are not alone-lots of people experience the same things that you have described.' 'Psychosis is much commoner than you think.'
Reassurance	'What you are experiencing is called psychosis. The good news is it is treatable. We will support you through your recovery. We use different types of treatments, one of which is medication. The medication is safe and effective. It won't take away your personality or make you feel "drugged" ...' 'You may not feel very hopeful at the moment; but I want to reassure you that we are going to help you get through this. I want to start you on a medication that usually begins working within days. You'll start thinking more clearly, begin to sleep better and feel more relaxed.... You should notice that the voices become quieter and less stressful ...'
Explanatory	'Stress isn't good for your body or mind. It can make you jumpy and irritable and prevent you sleeping properly. Toxic stress can affect your physical health and immune system. It can affect your ability to think rationally and may make you believe things that aren't true. It is really important to reduce the amount of stress in your body. That's where medication can be helpful. Think of it like a sponge, soaking up the stress ...'

First-, second- and third-generation APs

The choice of AP is ideally made jointly by the individual and clinician, based on an informed discussion of their relative benefits and side effect profiles. Prerequisite to helping patients and their carers reach an informed decision about medication choice is an understanding of the mode of action and side effect profiles of the different classes of medications.

First-generation AP

First-generation antipsychotics (FGA), or 'typicals', have high dopamine D2 receptor blockade. PET studies demonstrate response is optimised at 65–70% D2 occupancy, whereas exceeding 80% leads to substantial increase in side effects (Kapur, Remington & Jones, 1999). Nigrostriatal dopamine blockade results in movement disturbances, called extra-pyramidal side effects (EPSEs), commonly experienced at high doses. FGAs are divided into low potency (less propensity to EPSEs and more sedation), e.g. chlorpromazine, and high potency (more propensity to EPSEs and less sedation), e.g. haloperidol. Their side effects are discussed in greater detail later in the chapter.

Second-generation antipsychotics

Research in the 1980s challenged the simple dopamine D2 receptor blockade hypothesis (Jones, 2002), prompting further development of a new, second-generation of antipsychotic medications (SGA). These drugs are known also as 'atypicals' due to their mode of action on receptors additional to D2, including serotonin 5-HT2A/2C receptors, highlighting serotonin's role in the neurochemistry of psychosis. Lower levels of D2 antagonism and faster dissociation from dopamine receptors result in less EPSEs (Rummel-Kluge et al., 2010). However, SGAs commonly cause metabolic side effects and the management of these is discussed later in the chapter.

Clozapine, considered the first 'atypical' AP, produces activity on dopamine, serotonin (5HT2a, 5HT2c), GABA (gamma-Aminobutyric acid), histaminic and muscarinic receptors. This wide spectrum of activity appears to impart increased efficacy on both positive and negative symptoms, alongside a higher number of side effects. Clozapine is discussed in detail later in the chapter.

Third-generation antipsychotics

The prototype third-generation AP is aripiprazole (Mailman & Murthy, 2010), partial agonist of D2 and 5-HT1A receptors and antagonist at 5-HT2A. It binds to D2 receptors with the same affinity as dopamine but results in less intrinsic activity and therefore less EPSEs and hyperprolactinemia.

fatty tissue, it is slowly released with half-life of four to seven days. It is unlicensed in UK and therefore prescribed only under consultant supervision. Patients require monitoring for EPSEs.

Chlorpromazine is a useful FGA when psychotic symptoms are causing high levels of agitation, particularly in the acute phase and 'as required' (PRN). Fair-skinned individuals can develop photosensitivity and sunscreen is advised.

Haloperidol is a high potency FGA with less sedation than chlorpromazine and greater propensity to EPSEs. It is poorly tolerated and should therefore be avoided in FEP (Zhu et al., 2017).

What is the optimal AP dose and speed of titration to aid recovery in FEP?

AP doses have fallen significantly over the last 30 years (Fusar-Poli, Smieskova, Kempton, Ho, Andreasen & Borgwardt, 2013), informed by trials exhibiting limited clinical benefit at high doses alongside improved prescribing guidelines. Lower AP doses are required in FEP than for individuals with an established diagnosis of schizophrenia (Crespo-Facorro et al. 2006; Robinson et al. 1999). Young people's biological sensitivity to APs applies also to side effects, particularly EPSEs (Zhang et al., 2012). Furthermore, there is evidence of potential glial cell damage and brain structural changes at higher doses of AP medication (Fusar-Poli et al., 2013).

The short-term use of benzodiazepines can be helpful in the acute phase to reduce sedation, rather than increasing the AP dose.

APs' effects commonly occur during the first weeks of treatment (Leucht et al., 2005), often within days, debunking the myth that AP medication has delayed action (Agid et al., 2003). Some 90% of patients with suboptimal AP response at two weeks show no clinical improvement at six weeks (Samara et al., 2015), with treatment response in the first six weeks strongly predictive of symptomatic recovery (Emsley, Oosthuizen, Niehaus & Koen, 2007).

Implementing the evidence into practice

- EIP clinicians should use the lowest possible AP dose, balancing symptom control with both short- and long-term adverse effects (McGorry, Cocks, Power, Burnett, Harrigan & Lambert, 2011). If agitation and distress are significant, the addition of a short-term benzodiazepine is preferable to the use of high dose APs. Regular auditing of prescribing practices is recommended.
- Evidence suggests switching AP as soon as after two weeks and certainly by six weeks if no beneficial effect has been experienced and effective doses have been reached, in order to prevent unnecessary exposure to an ineffective AP.

Clozapine's role in FEP

Kane's (1988) seminal study, demonstrating the superior efficacy of clozapine for treatment resistance, has been replicated in various clinical trials (Lewis et al., 2005; Stroup et al., 2009) and meta-analyses (Wahlbeck, Cheine & Essali, 1999; Lieberman et al., 2005). Suboptimal response or 'treatment resistance' describes individuals who after two adequate AP trials (minimum 4–6 weeks), at least one of which is a SGA, continue to experience positive symptoms affecting their psychosocial functioning (Conley & Kelly, 2001). Symptomatic non-remission in FEP is relatively common, ranging from 17% to 25% (Lambert et al., 2008; Tang, Subramaniam, Ng, Abdin, Poon & Verma, 2016).

Clozapine benefits

About 75% of FEP patients with sub-optimal AP response experience an improvement on clozapine (Agid et al., 2007). The Phase 2 CATIE study compared clozapine to olanzapine, quetiapine and risperidone in treatment resistance (McEvoy, 2006), concluding that clozapine was significantly more effective than switching to another SGA and associated with longer time to treatment discontinuation. Patients receiving clozapine were less likely to discontinue treatment due to inadequate therapeutic response and, at 12 weeks, they reported their mental health was significantly better (Lewis et al., 2005). After seven years, more of the clozapine group were medication concordant (Guirgis et al., 2011), suggesting greater tolerability.

Clozapine confers additional benefits. It is associated with reduced suicide and self-harm rate (see Chapter 9), decreased impulsivity and aggressive behaviours (Spivak, Mester, Wittenberg, Maman & Weizman, 1997). Walker et al.'s (1997) retrospective analysis demonstrated an 83% reduction in suicide among current clozapine users, compared with those who had stopped.

Clozapine treatment results in lower hospitalisation rates (Doyle et al., 2017) and reduction in comorbid substance misuse (Brunette, Drake, Xie, McHugo & Green, 2005). Clozapine appears to improve cognitive functioning (Lee, 1999; Meltzer & McGurk, 1999), which is associated with employment and educational ability and therefore is a key consideration in social recovery (see Chapter 5). With low incidence of EPSEs, it is suitable for patients prone to EPSE and tardive dyskinesia (TD). Furthermore, clozapine use results in significant economic savings, estimated at £8.3 million for the UK alone (Duggan, 2003).

Given these facts, it is surprising that there is significant under-utilisation of clozapine (Tang et al., 2016) with a four- to seven-year delay to treatment commencement for potentially suitable patients (Doyle et al., 2017). More than half the patients receiving clozapine are prescribed three or more APs prior to commencing (NHS, 2014). This raises questions about potential avoidance and resistance to prescribing clozapine.

Tungaraza and Farooq (2015) surveyed 243 UK consultant psychiatrists to identify obstacles to clozapine prescribing. Their main concern was side effects, particularly weight gain and metabolic syndrome. A further barrier was the risk of neutropenia (3%) and agranulocytosis (0.8%) requiring regular blood tests, an active deterrent for those with needle phobia, as can the intensive monitoring requirement during initiation, particularly when patients require hospitalisation in a climate of scarce bed availability. Finally, under-confidence in prescribing clozapine contributes to under-utilisation by some psychiatrists. Further research is warranted to provide a better understanding of these barriers, given the implications for patients' quality of life and hospital admission rates. In order to optimise symptomatic, psychological and social recovery it is important to seize the opportunity to commence patients on clozapine during their EIP treatment (Yoshimura, Yada, So, Takaki & Yamada, 2017).

Implementing the evidence into practice

- Early identification of treatment resistance is aided by regular caseload audit.
- Pharmacy/IT systems can flag up patients who have been prescribed two or more APs.
- Barriers to clozapine initiation should be identified and discussed in EIP forums.
- Clozapine home initiation should be available by increasing EIP staff or via home treatment teams. The return on workforce investment more than compensates revenue spent.
- Home phlebotomy minimises the disruption of frequent blood-testing and improves overall tolerability.
- Resources for clozapine home initiation should be made available. It may help to remind commissioners that the return on workforce investment more than compensates the revenue spent. This includes home phlebotomy, which minimises the disruption of frequent blood-testing and improves overall patient tolerability. Access to gym sessions and dietary advice should be provided as it can help limit clozapine-induced weight gain.
- There are various augmenting strategies for sub-optimal response to clozapine, including lamotrigine, amisulpiride and aripiprazole (Mossaheb, 2012) with varying degrees of success.

How do we improve medication concordance? Should depots be prescribed more frequently in FEP?

Medication discontinuation is common in FEP (Miller et al., 2011). Some 50–75% of patients are partially medication non-concordant within one year (Lambert et al., 2010; Whale et al. 2016), due to lack of perceived benefits, intolerable side effects, forgetfulness and financial constraints (El-Mallakh & Findlay, 2015). AP discontinuation within the first year after psychosis remission is significantly associated with higher rates of relapse (Leucht, 2012) and AP concordance during the first year after FEP is the sole independent predictor of symptomatic recovery at five-year follow-up (Norman, 2017). Therapeutic alliance and insight are positively correlated with medication concordance (Tessier, Boyer, Husky, Baylé, Llorca & Misdrahi, 2017). Techniques to improve medication concordance include CBT, psychoeducation (El-Mallakh & Findlay, 2015), and MI (motivational interviewing) (Staring et al., 2010). Providing environmental cues, such as alarms and pillboxes can be effective (El-Mallakh & Findlay, 2015). Additionally digital technology can aid a young person's recovery from psychosis. Mobile phone apps, such as 'Silver Linings', developed by patients and clinicians, provide information about medication with a medication reminder alarm function (Jee, 2017).

Depots play a significant role in improved concordance and preventing relapse, yet are often overlooked in FEP (Whale et al., 2016), perhaps due to a misperception that they should be reserved for individuals with established schizophrenia (Table 3.4). Whale et al.'s (2016) naturalistic FEP cohort study over seven UK sites found that depots accounted for less than 1% APs prescribed in the first 12 months. Yet evidence suggests that long-acting injectable APs (along with clozapine) are the pharmacological treatments with the highest rates of relapse prevention in schizophrenia and lower rates of hospitalisation for FEP patients (Tiihonen et al., 2017).

Implementing the evidence into practice

*   In building trusting relationships with patients, EIP clinicians should have frank, honest, non-judgemental discussions about medication and risks involved with relapse.
*   Medication information imparted frequently in a format best suited to the young person is an important step in improving concordance. Consider the use of blister packs and pill boxes.

Table 3.4 Depots – doses and frequency

Trade name	Proper name	Dose/amount	How often
Modecate	Fluphenazine Decanoate	up to 100 mg	2–5 weekly
Depixol	Flupenthixol Decanoate	up to 400 mg	2–4 weekly
Haldol	Haloperidol Decanoate	up to 300 mg	2–4 weekly
Piportil	Pipothiazine palmitate	up to 200 mg	4 weekly
Clopixol	Zuclopenthixol Decanoate	up to 600 mg	1–4 weekly
Risperdal Consta	Risperidone	up to 50 mg	fortnightly
Xepilon	Paliperidone	up to 150 mg	monthly
ZypAdhera	Olanzapine	up to 405 mg	2–4 weekly
Abilify Maintena	Aripiprazole	up to 400 mg	monthly
Trivecta	Paliperidone palmitate	up to 525 mg	3 monthly

- Minimising side effects by regular screening and intervening is a key aspect of improved concordance.
- Providing environmental cues, such as alarms and pillboxes, can be effective (El-Mallakh & Findlay, 2015).
- Evidence of relapse and hospitalisation reduction suggests that depots, and long-acting oral preparations such as penfluridol, could be used with greater frequency in EIP. The choice of depot should be made collaboratively between clinician and patient. SGA depots are favourable due to their side-effect profile and positive effects on psychosocial functioning (Fu, Turkoz, Walling, Lindenmayer, Schooler & Alphs, 2018). The prospect of three-monthly depots (Trevicta-Paliperidone Palmitate) heralds significantly more palatable injection regimes. However, SGA depots are frustratingly expensive and, given the current economic climate, some mental health trusts insist on the use of FGA depots as the first line. Nonetheless, it is likely that very long-acting depots will play an increasing role in treating individuals with FEP in the future.

For how long should AP treatment continue after remission of FEP to maximise recovery?

Evidence linking relapse prevention with AP continuation in the short term is robust (Kissling, 1991; Leucht, 2012), with a recommended length of continuation following a FEP of 12–24 months (Barnes, 2011). Following symptomatic remission from FEP, around two-thirds of individuals relapse in the 12 months after AP discontinuation (Di Capite, Upthegrove & Mallikarjun, 2016).

Implementing the evidence into practice

- Patients frequently ask, 'How long do I have to be on this medication?' A collaborative decision about AP discontinuation following treatment for 12–24 months should only be arrived at after honest discussions with patients about the high relapse rate and associated risks of doing so.
- For patients with good prognostic factors (stage 2, Fusar-Poli model; see Chapter 1, Table 1.1), acute-onset positive symptoms, early functional recovery, high pre-morbid functioning, no substance misuse and a supportive family (Álvarez-Jiménez et al., 2016), it is reasonable to gradually (over several months) withdraw AP medication 12–24 months following symptomatic recovery. Identifying early warning signs and timely medication recommencement is of paramount importance to prevent a full-blown relapse and minimise residual cognitive deficits. Completing a 'staying well/ relapse prevention plan' prior to stopping APs is advisable (examined in more detail in Chapter 4).
- If one or more relapses are experienced with incomplete (stage 3) or delayed (stage 4) recovery, then long-term APs may be required.

Maintenance therapy versus discontinuation versus intermittent dosing

AP maintenance treatment halves the relapse risk in the three years following FEP (Mayoral-van Son et al., 2015; Wunderink et al., 2013). However, evidence supporting continued use beyond this period after a single psychotic episode is less compelling (Murray et al., 2016). Wunderink et al. (2013) compared maintenance treatment with reduction/discontinuation in more than 100 individuals with FEP. After six months of symptomatic remission, patients were randomly assigned to either maintenance treatment or reduction/discontinuation and followed up for seven years Although the short-term risk of relapse in the reduction/discontinuation group was twice that of the maintenance group, at seven years the rate of relapse was comparable (69% maintenance group vs. 62% reduction/discontinuation group). Notably, by the end of the seven-year study, the discontinuation group had achieved more than twice the functional recovery rate of the medication maintenance group (40% vs. 18%). There are methodological flaws in the study and it should be highlighted that less than 1/5 patients were off all medication during the last two years of follow-up. However, these results suggest that APs *alone* do not improve functional/social recovery or indeed alter the long-term course of the illness, and may in fact be a hindrance to social and personal recovery for some.

Furthermore, there are growing concerns over the cumulative effects of long-term AP use on both the physical health of individuals and on brain structure. Fusar-Poli et al.'s (2013) meta-analysis of grey matter volume (GMV) studies found a correlation between reduced GMV and AP treatment, with higher doses linked to greater structural changes. Although it is recognised that more severe illness is likely to be treated with higher AP doses, and we currently lack clear evidence of a causative link, it does highlight the need for caution in the use of long-term AP medication, particularly at high doses, at least until the evidence becomes clearer.

Concern about use of long-term APs may lend weight to the practice of intermittent AP dosing. There is currently a lack of robust evidence supporting this practice, and what research has been done concludes that intermittent AP treatment is not as effective as continuous, maintained AP therapy in preventing relapse (Sampson, Mansour, Maayan, Soares-Weiser & Adams, 2013). Thus, for the majority of patients, intermittent treatment cannot be recommended. However, for patients with good insight, who recognise their early warning signs (EWS) and are motivated to prevent relapse, this could be an option.

Psychopharmacology has made significant advances, yet pharmacological treatments do not appear to alter the long-term course of the illness for individuals with multiple relapses. The future of psychopharmacology for psychosis perhaps lies in the increasing specificity of prescribing using a clinical staging model (Fusar-Poli et al., 2017; Chapter 1, Table 1.1) alongside early identification and prediction of individuals' response to different APs (Wimberley, Støvring, Sørensen, Horsdal, MacCabe & Gasse, 2016). Clearly, a challenge for EIP moving forward is to identify early on those patients who will benefit from AP discontinuation and those who require longer-term treatments, including clozapine.

Implementing the evidence into practice

- Psychiatrists should make the decision to continue, discontinue or recommend intermittent dosing on a case-by-case basis, taking into account the patient's views, the severity of the illness, the prognostic factors, the resource availability and side effects.
- A chaotic lifestyle, heavy drug use, unstable accommodation and risky behaviour increase the likelihood of ongoing maintenance therapy.
- AP intermittent dosing can be attempted with individuals who have been in remission for 12 months, are highly motivated and engaged in their recovery. This should take place during their time with EIP where intensive treatment and regular monitoring can be provided to screen and intervene promptly if EWS develop. It is reassuring for individuals and their mental health team if early symptoms are recognised and treated promptly, preventing a full relapse.

Pharmacological approaches to negative symptoms and cognitive deficits

Rapidly growing interest in the 'negative symptoms' of psychosis over recent years underscores their importance in social recovery (Remington et al., 2016; Chapter 5). Negative symptoms are so named because they result in a deficit of functioning and include lack of drive and motivation, flattening of emotion, and poverty of thought and speech. They are symptoms which, arguably, confer the most long-term disability after FEP, placing heavy burdens on carers and society. The concept of negative symptoms has broadened to include cognitive impairments, encompassing deficits of attention, processing speed, problem solving and working memory (Schulz & Murray, 2016).

Cognitive deficits and negative symptoms are more predictive of social recovery than positive symptoms (Green, 2016), yet the currently available AP treatments primarily address the latter with poor impact on the former (Buckley & Stahl, 2007). Indeed, a meta-analysis of 168 RCTs on negative symptom-targeted pharmacological interventions revealed no significantly consistent benefits, with the exception of clozapine (Fusar-Poli et al., 2014).

The lack of responsiveness of negative symptoms to APs is a source of significant frustration for both patients and the clinicians treating them. To address this critical gap in our current care, clinicians should stay informed about new treatment developments involving a more sophisticated understanding of the relevant neurobiology underlying negative symptoms and cognitive deficits in psychosis (Walker et al., 2017).

Meta-analyses show small beneficial effects on negative symptoms when an antidepressant (AD) is used in addition to AP treatment (Helfer et al., 2016).

However, these results have not been consistently replicated and therefore ADs are not universally recommended in the absence of depressive symptoms.

Although cholinesterase inhibitors, rivastigmine, galantamine and donepezil, do show some promise in treating cognitive impairments (Singh, Kour & Jayaram, 2012), there is a lack of consistent evidence supporting their general use in the treatment of negative symptoms (Remington et al., 2016). Negative symptom improvement with psychostimulants, including methylphenidate has been reported (Lindenmayer, Nasrallah, Pucci, James & Citrome, 2013), but only in small numbers of carefully selected patients stabilised on APs.

The role of inflammation and immunology in psychosis has generated much interest (Khandaker, Cousins, Deakin, Lennox, Yolken & Jones, 2015; Lennox et al., 2017). Early trials involving minocycline, a broad spectrum tetracyclic antibiotic with neuroprotective properties, showed some promise in treating negative symptoms (Chaudhry et al., 2012; Levkovitz et al., 2009), yet a large-scale RCT showed no significant effect (Deakin et al., 2018).

The prefrontal cortex D1 dopamine receptor plays a critical role in cognitive dysfunction (Walker, Spring & Travis, 2017) and is thus an area for future research. Meta-analysis measuring the effect size of repetitive trans-cranial magnetic stimulation (rTMS) on negative symptoms reported clinically significant results (Dlabač-de Lange, Knegtering & Aleman, 2010), yet this finding was not replicated by a multi-centre RCT (Wobrock et al., 2015). There is considerable interest in the glutamatergic model of psychosis (Kantrowitz & Javitt, 2010), in particular, in NMDA receptor enhancement. Despite inconsistent effectiveness data, Goff (2015) argues that targeting glutamatergic transmission with greater receptor specificity remains one of the most promising future strategies in treating negative symptoms, particularly early in the course of illness.

Implementing the evidence into practice

- Clinicians should regularly screen for negative symptoms and cognitive dysfunction due to their toll on individuals recovering from psychosis. 'Negative symptoms' may in fact be secondary to ongoing positive symptoms, in which case, AP dose increase may be effective.
- Medication side effects, such as EPSEs or sedation, can mimic negative symptoms. The GASS (Glasgow Antipsychotic Side effect Scale) or LUNSARS (Liverpool University Neuroleptic Side Effect Rating Scale) are helpful at differentiating side effects from negative symptoms. If side effects are affecting social recovery, then a switch to an alternative AP with less sedation or EPSEs is recommended. A dose reduction should be considered if symptomatic recovery has been achieved.
- If negative symptoms persist, despite the above changes, a trial of clozapine should be considered (Meltzer & McGurk, 1999).
- If depressive symptoms are present, consider commencing an AD (Gregory, Mallikarjun & Upthegrove, 2017). Improvements in comorbid depression and

psychosis have been reported with many ADs, including SSRIs, trazodone and mirtazapine (Singh et al., 2010; Vidal, Mallikarjun & Upthegrove, 2015).

• With increasing emphasis on neuroscientific research, there is hope that one day biological treatments targeting negative and cognitive symptoms will be available. However, the current limitations of current pharmacological treatments in treating negative symptoms should result in the intensification of psychosocial strategies (Kendall, 2012).

Physical health and recovery

For too long, mental health services have focused on symptomatic recovery from psychosis without due consideration to physical health care. The fact that life expectancy remains 15–20 years less for individuals with schizophrenia (Reininghaus et al., 2014) is a modern health care scandal. *Risk reduction*, in mental health care, typically focuses on suicide and self-harm, rather than the *risk of lowered life expectancy* due to poor physical health. If we are to improve the life expectancy of individuals with FEP, we require a radical re-evaluation of our approach to physical health.

What causes premature death in patients with psychosis?

Increased mortality in psychosis is largely caused by cardiovascular risks (Hennekens, Hennekens, Hollar & Casey, 2005). Cigarette smoking is highly prevalent in FEP (Myles, Newall, Curtis, Nielssen, Shiers & Large, 2012), and a significant cause of premature death in the UK and worldwide (David, Johnstone, Churchman, Aveyard, Murphy & Munafò, 2011). This risk is further heightened by APs, poor diet, minimal exercise and metabolic syndrome (Laursen, Nordentoft & Mortensen, 2014). Metabolic syndrome is commoner in multi-episode schizophrenia compared with FEP (Vancampfort et al., 2015b). The period when medication is first prescribed in FEP is therefore a key opportunity for intervention.

Don't just screen, intervene (Lester, 2014)

In February 2016, NHS England published the *Five Year Forward View for Mental Health* with physical health a key part of that vision. The report recommends a national reduction in premature mortality among people with SMI by ensuring that their physical health needs are met by early detection and improved access to evidence-based interventions. Unfortunately reduced access to appropriate health care is notable for many individuals with psychosis. This is described as the 'inverse care law': those whose physical health needs are greatest receive sub-optimal treatment. The National Audit of Schizophrenia (2014) revealed <21% of people with psychosis and schizophrenia had all health parameters checked. Yet the majority viewed their health care as adequate, pointing to disappointingly low expectations. Furthermore preventable illness can go unrecognised and untreated if GPs assume that psychiatrists are monitoring their patients' physical health and vice versa. This is well articulated by Michael Balint's 'collusion of anonymity' (Edgcumbe, 2010) hindering both GPs and psychiatrists from taking responsibility for their patients' physical health care, resulting in undetected physical health risks. It is, therefore, imperative that primary and secondary care share results of investigations and decisions about the physical health care of their patients. The ability of IT systems to facilitate communication between professionals is crucial, allowing data sharing between primary and secondary care.

Despite concerted attempts by the UK DoH (Department of Health) and NICE to implement regular physical health monitoring in SMI, wide variations (25–70%) in the rates of physical health monitoring persist (Mitchell, Delaffon, Vancampfort, Correll & De Hert, 2011). In the UK, in 2014, the Commissioning for Quality and Innovation (CQUIN) payment was introduced as a financial incentive to improve physical health monitoring and intervention, with a goal of 80% EIP patients achieving full concordance with physical health assessment and relevant interventions. EIP teams failed to meet these targets, with an average score of 42% (National EIPN CCQI audit 2017), highlighting the difficulty in achieving this outcome without adequate investment and training. To aid implementation of the five-year forward plan for physical health in SMI, NHS England have produced a toolkit informed by findings from four different pilot sites, available at: www.england.nhs.uk/mentalhealth/wp-content/uploads/sites/29/2016/05/serious-mental-hlth-toolkit-may16.pdf. Poor physical health is perpetuated by AP side effects which we will now discuss.

Antipsychotic side effects and physical health

Minimising the adverse effects of medication is particularly important in the early stages of FEP treatment, given that they are a significant disincentive to concordance. Intolerable side effects can evoke long-term negative attitudes towards medication and mental health care, hampering recovery. Importantly APs, particularly SGAs, can worsen physical health risks as a result of metabolic syndrome.

Physical health monitoring should be most frequent when AP medication is initiated, as this offers a uniquely important opportunity for early detection and prevention. Side effect scales are helpful in identifying and quantifying side effects, particularly those which patients find embarrassing to discuss. The two most commonly used are the 22-item GASS (Glasgow Antipsychotic Side effect Scale) and 51-item LUNSERS (Liverpool University Neuroleptic Side Effect Rating Scale). The Lester (2013) Cardio-metabolic Health Resource tool (see Appendix 2) is an invaluable resource highlighting thresholds for intervention alongside treatment recommendations.

APs have characteristic side effect profiles. Table 3.5 presents these side effect profiles and now we will discuss them and their management. Broadly speaking, FGAs cause movement disorders whereas SGAs have a propensity to metabolic disorders.

Table 3.5 AP side effects and interventions

Side effect	Intervention
Weight gain (metabolic syndrome)	Lifestyle, e.g., Low carbohydrate diet and increased physical activity Switch to AP with less propensity to weight gain (see Table 3.7) Pharmacological – metformin, aripiprazole or orlistat
Dyslipidaemia (metabolic syndrome)	Lifestyle, e.g., fat lowering diet and physical activity Statins if Q-risk > 10%
Insulin resistance/diabetes (metabolic syndrome)	Lifestyle, e.g., reduced carbohydrate diet and increase physical activity Switch to AP with less propensity to insulin resistance, e.g., aripiprazole, amisulpiride Metformin
Hypertension (metabolic syndrome)	Lifestyle, e.g., weight loss, regular exercise, smoking cessation, reduction in alcohol consumption, stress management strategies, Pharmacological (e.g., ACE inhibitors, calcium channel blockers, diuretics according to NICE guidance)
EPSEs	Dose reduction Switch to alternative AP with less D2 blockade (e.g., olanzapine, aripiprazole, clozapine, quetiapine) Pharmacological – anticholinergics, beta blockers, benzodiazepines (short term)
Sedation	Change dose to evening Dose reduction Switch to less sedative AP (see Table 3.8)
Sexual dysfunction	Dose reduction Switch to aripiprazole, olanzapine, quetiapine, clozapine Pharmacological – sildenafil (Viagra), tadalafil (Cialis)

I Metabolic syndrome

Metabolic syndrome encompasses obesity, hypertension, dyslipidaemia and insulin resistance, and accelerates cardiovascular disease.

I(a) Weight gain/obesity

AP-induced weight gain is a major health concern for young people recovering from psychosis and can have a deleterious effect on recovery, intensifying shame and resulting in social anxiety and avoidance (Michail & Birchwood, 2012). It is caused by increased appetite, decreased satiety and altered energy homeostasis (Correll & Malhotra, 2004). AP-induced weight gain is common and rapid in FEP (Tarricone, Ferrari Gozzi, Serretti, Grieco & Berardi, 2009), affecting around 60% of treatment-naïve patients by 2–4 months (Álvarez-Jiménez, Hetrick, González-Blanch, Gleeson & McGorry, 2008). Body Mass Index (BMI), a measure of weight in relation to height, is a good risk indicator of phys-ical health (Table 3.6). Obesity is defined as BMI>30 and significantly linked to diabetes, dyslipidaemia and hypertension (Bays, Chapman & Grandy, 2007).

Weight gain can result in medication non-concordance and subsequent relapse (Weiden, Mackell & McDonnell, 2004). Thus, it is of particular concern to young people recovering from FEP, who are most sensitive to weight gain (Kahn et al., 2008). Although weight gain can occur with any AP medication, large-scale trials (CATIE, CUtLASS, EUFEST) report that olanzapine and clozapine have the greatest propensity (Table 3.7) (Jones et al., 2006, Kahn et al., 2008; Lieberman et al., 2005).

Table 3.6 Body mass index linked to weight

Weight category	Body Mass Index
Underweight	<18.5
Healthy weight	18.5–24.9
Overweight	25–29.9
Obese	30–39.9
Morbidly obese	>40

Table 3.7 APs ranked in order of liability for weight gain

High	Medium	Low
Olanzapine	Chlorpromazine	Aripiprazole
Clozapine	Quetiapine	Haloperidol
–	Risperidone	Amisulpride
–	Paliperidone	Lurasidone
–	–	Ziprasidone

Management of AP-induced weight gain

Frequent weight monitoring is important in the early stages of AP treatment enabling prompt recognition and intervention when BMI>25 (Greenwood & Shiers, 2016). NICE's (2014) recommendation of weekly weight measurements during the first three months of AP treatment is potentially an engagement disincentive and a pragmatic approach of monthly weight measurements may be preferable.

Where there is more than 5 kg weight gain, BMI>25 and symptomatic stability, an AP switch to one with lower propensity to weight gain should be considered.

Lifestyle approaches are effective, acceptable and cost-efficient (Álvarez-Jiménez et al., 2008), producing on average 3 kg weight loss (Cooper et al., 2016). Even small increases in activity in inactive individuals result in significant benefits.

RCTs show modest weight loss (around 2 kg) when aripiprazole is added to olanzapine or clozapine treatment (Fan et al., 2012; Mizuno et al., 2014). Metformin produces weight loss in AP-induced weight gain (Praharaj, Jana, Goyal & Sinha, 2011) and should be considered if BMI>35 alongside deteriorating glucose control (NICE, 2017). Orlistat reduces intestinal fat absorption; however, it is poorly tolerated due to troublesome side effects of bloating and steatorrhea, resulting in high discontinuation rates (Padwal, Kezouh, Levine & Etminan, 2007).

I(b) Dyslipidaemia

Dyslipidaemia is a broad term describing elevated total cholesterol (TC), or high density lipoprotein (HDL)-cholesterol concentrations below the 10th centile.

Management of dyslipidaemia

EIP teams should encourage lifestyle changes, including diet, increased physical activity and reduction in alcohol consumption. Statins are recommended for the primary prevention of cardiovascular disease (CVD) for adults who have a 10% or greater 10-year risk of developing CVD (NICE, 2014). The risk should be estimated using an appropriate calculator, such as Q-risk 3, which has been adapted for SGAs. However, these are likely to underestimate future risk in a young FEP population. The Joint British Societies (JBS 3) tool shows promise for better lifetime risk prediction (www.jbs3risk.com/pages/lifetime_risk.htm).

I(c) Insulin resistance and diabetes

Insulin resistance, the central characteristic of metabolic syndrome, leads to an increased risk of mortality from coronary heart disease (Khunti, 2005). FEP is independently associated with insulin resistance and abnormal glycaemic control

(Perry & Singh, 2017), an association first recognised by the Victorian psychiatrist, Henry Maudsley, in 1879. The risk of developing diabetes is further increased in patients treated with APs, in particular, SGAs. Pre-diabetes, a combination of excess body fat and insulin resistance, is identified by raised glycosylated haemoglobin (HbA1c)>42. Screening and regular monitoring at baseline, three months and annually allow early detection of dysfunction, and prompt intervention to prevent the onset of diabetes.

Management of insulin resistance and pre-diabetes

Clinical guidelines (NICE, 2017) suggest that the rate of progression from pre-diabetes to diabetes can be decreased significantly with radical lifestyle changes. Low and ultralow carbohydrate diets produce promising results (Lean et al., 2017).

AP switch is recommended if clinically appropriate to do so with amisulpiride and aripiprazole having the lowest propensity to diabetes. Metformin can prevent the onset of diabetes for those at particularly high risk (HbA1c 42–47) (NICE, 2017) if lifestyle modifications have been unsuccessful (Johansen, 1999).

1(d) Hypertension

Although rare in a young FEP population, AP-induced hypertension should be identified as early as possible to prevent complications, such as chronic kidney disease (CKD), diabetes and heart failure (Kennard & O'Shaughnessy, 2016). A reliable diagnosis of hypertension (BP>140/90 mmHg) requires multiple measurements, allowing for the 'white coat effect'. A single elevated BP entered into electronic records will flag the requirement for audited hypertension interventions, which can be circumvented by entering a high BP once three separate high readings have been confirmed.

Management of AP-induced hypertension

Lifestyle advice, including reducing salt, alcohol and fat intake, weight loss, smoking cessation and increasing physical activity levels, are recommended (NICE, 2016) alongside stress management strategies. If antihypertensive medication is required, choices will depend on the patient's age, ethnicity and associated comorbidity (Kennard & O'Shaughnessy, 2016).

2 Extra-pyramidal side effects (EPSEs)

EPSEs are common with FGAs. They are caused by excessive dopamine blockade in the basal ganglia of the substantia nigra and encompass the following features:

- *akathisia* – unpleasant feeling of restlessness, accompanied by difficulty sitting still for prolonged periods with an urge to constantly be on the move.
- *dystonia* – continuous muscle spasms, commonly involving the neck, extremities, back, tongue and eyes (oculogyric crises).
- *pseudo-Parkinsonism* – tremor, joint rigidity and bradykinesia.
- *tardive dyskinesia* (TD) – repetitive involuntary orofacial movements. This should be identified early to prevent irreversibility.

Management of EPSEs

Regular EPSE and TD screening during clinical reviews allows prompt intervention, such as lowering the AP dose or switching to an alternative AP. Anticholinergic medications, such as procyclidine and benztropine, counter dopamine blockade in the basal ganglia, effectively reducing EPSEs. Side effects of anticholinergic medication include dry mouth, urinary retention and blurred vision, with the potential to cause stimulating effects and should therefore be avoided near bedtime. Akathisia is more difficult to treat, is often unresponsive to anticholinergic medication, and beta blockers or benzodiazepines in the short term may be helpful if an AP change is inadvisable.

3 Sedation

Sedation is common with both SGAs and FGAs (Kahn, 2008) (Table 3.8). It is mediated through histamine, dopamine and adrenergic receptors. Sedation can be a beneficial side effect in the initial treatment of FEP, reducing agitation and distress. Patients should be reassured that tolerance to sedation often develops after days with continued treatment. Persistent daytime sedation and increased sleep time should, however, be avoided as they interfere with an individual's psychological and social recovery.

Management of AP-induced sedation

Sedation can be minimised by decreasing the dose, changing to a single bedtime dose, or switching to a less sedating AP.

Table 3.8 APs' sedative potential

Highly sedative	Moderately sedative	Mildly sedative
Clozapine	Olanzapine	Aripiprazole
	Quetiapine	Risperidone
	Chlorpromazine	Haloperidol
	Amisulpiride	Ziprasidone

4 Hyperprolactinemia

Prolactin, secreted by the pituitary gland, stimulates milk production in breast tissue. AP-induced hyperprolactinemia, defined as prolactin > 424 mIU/L in men and >530 mIU/L in women, is caused by D2-receptor blockade in the anterior pituitary gland (Holt & Peveler, 2010). Hyperprolactinemia is usually asymptomatic, but may be associated with irregular periods, male gynaecomastia, galactorrhoea and sexual dysfunction (Miyamoto, Galecki & Francois, 2015) due to its effects on oestrogen and testosterone. It may also reduce fertility and cause osteoporosis (De Hert, Detraux & Stubbs, 2016), the latter being linked to length of treatment (O'Keane, 2008). Notably schizophrenia itself is an independent risk factor for osteoporosis, possibly mediated by stress, leading to an increase in bone fractures (Kishimoto, De Hert, Carlson, Manu & Correll, 2012). The relative contribution of AP-induced hyperprolactinaemia in bone mineral loss in individuals with psychosis, however, remains unclear (De Hert et al., 2016). FGAs are more commonly associated with hyperprolactinaemia due to D2 blockade. Of the SGAs, risperidone and amisulpiride have the highest propensity to raise prolactin.

Management of hyperprolactinaemia

Hyperprolactinaemia has, to date, been under-researched and as such there is no consensus on how best to monitor and treat it. Gupta et al.'s (2017) helpful guidance recommends measuring prolactin at baseline and three months. If prolactin is raised >2,000 mIU/L or if associated symptoms are present, do the following:

- *Consider and exclude organic causes.* Hyperprolactinaemia, with headache, visual field defects and diplopia, requires further investigations, including an MRI and endocrinologist referral to exclude pituitary adenoma. Adenomas can be reduced in size by dopaminergic drugs or surgical resection.
- *If clinically appropriate, attempt AP dose reduction and repeat prolactin level.* The decision to do so should be weighed up, balancing the risk of potential relapse against that of hyperprolactinaemia.
- *Switch to an AP with less potential to cause hyperprolactinaemia,* such as aripiprazole, olanzapine, quetiapine and clozapine. Of these, aripiprazole has the least propensity due to its partial agonistic effect on dopamine receptors, lowering prolactin in >70% patients (Li, Tang & Wang, 2013). It can be an adjunctive treatment if an AP switch is unadvised.

5 Sexual dysfunction

Sexual dysfunction encompasses reduced libido, impotence, difficulty maintaining an erection and anorgasmia. It affects around 50% of individuals with schizophrenia (Dossenbach et al., 2005) and is a common cause of AP non-concordance in young sexually active FEP populations (Cutler, 2003). Sexual dysfunction affects up to 80% of individuals on AP medication (Park, Kim & Lee, 2012). Its cause is multifactorial: hyperprolactinaemia decreases libido, antimuscarinic and antihistaminic effects reduce sexual arousal and alpha1-adrenoceptor blockade causes erection and ejaculation problems in men by reducing peripheral vasodilation.

Management of sexual dysfunction

AP-induced sexual dysfunction is managed by dose reduction or switching medication. SGAs (other than risperidone) have lower incidence of sexual dysfunction than FGAs (Mahmoud, Hayhurst, Drake & Lewis, 2011). Pharmacological measures such as sildenafil (Viagra) or the longer-acting tadalafil (Cialis) are effective (Park et al., 2012) and safe to prescribe alongside APs.

6 Cardiac side effects

Some APs are associated with cardiac side effects, such as tachycardia, arrhythmias, and hypotension (De Hert et al., 2011). Orthostatic hypotension is the commonest adverse autonomic side effect of APs, mediated by anticholinergic or alpha-1 adrenoceptor blockade (Montastruc, Laborie, Bagheri & Senard, 1997), and the risk is highest with clozapine (Mackin, 2007).

QT interval prolongation is a surrogate marker for assessing the risk of ventricular tachycardia. Torsades de pointes (TdP), a polymorphic ventricular tachycardia associated with a prolonged QTc, can cause ventricular fibrillation and sudden death (Leenhardt, Glaser, Burguera, Nurnberg, Maison-Blanche & Coumel, 1994). The mean QTc length is roughly 400 ms, with an upper limit of 460 ms for females, and 450 ms for males. QTc intervals longer than 500 ms are a major risk factor for TdP. QT interval prolongation is commoner with FGAs, combinations of APs and doses exceeding the recommended maximum (Nielsen, Graff, Kanters, Toft, Taylor & Meyer, 2011). SSRIs, particularly citalopram, in combination with APs are associated with a modest but statistically significant increase in QTc (Beach et al., 2014), although to a lesser extent than TCAs (Vieweg, 2003).

Management of cardiac risks

A comprehensive medical and family history is important prior to AP commencement. A baseline ECG should be obtained when initiating high-risk agents, particularly if doses exceed the recommended maximum or more than one AP is prescribed, although polypharmacy should be avoided if possible. If QTc >450/460, consider changing the AP to one with less QTc prolongation. If prescribing antidepressants along with AP, consider SSRIs other than citalopram in individuals with cardiac risks.

Smoking and young people with FEP

Some 15.5% UK adults smoke tobacco (Statistics on Smoking, England, 2017), rising to a staggering 60% for FEP (Myles et al., 2012), many of whom smoke heavily (Kelly, 2000). Smoking reduces life expectancy and is therefore a significant cause of premature death in patients with psychosis (Kelly, 2000). Tobacco smoking causes a wide range of medical conditions (cancers, respiratory and cardiovascular disease) with negative effects on mental health, requiring higher doses of APs (Wium-Andersen, Orsted & Nordestgaard, 2015) and lengthier hospital admissions (Kobayashi, Ito, Okumura, Mayahara, Matsumoto & Hirakawa, 2010). Supporting young people with FEP to stop smoking is arguably the largest positive impact we can make on their physical health, yet it is an often over-looked component of recovery. The fact that early smoking cessation can significantly increase expectancy and quality of life should motivate EIP teams and services to ensure programmes and treatments are in place to aid this foundational aspect of recovery.

Nicotine replacement (patches, lozenges and gum) is an effective treatment (Cahill, Stevens, Perera & Lancaster, 2013) and the use of e-cigarettes causes a reduction in the toxic effects of tar and carbon monoxide (E-cigarettes: an evidence update – GOV.UK, 2015). Like any addiction treatment programme, perseverance and a long-term damage limitation view are necessary. Where once smoking was used as an 'engagement strategy', EIP staff now should reinforce the health benefits of giving up smoking, including potential AP dose reduction (Tsuda, Saruwatari & Yasui-Furukori, 2014). Some argue that smoking enhances cognitive functioning, yet the evidence in FEP suggests otherwise (Hickling et al., 2017).

EIP role in physical health prevention

All EIP clinicians have a role in physical health improvement and should receive adequate training to ensure skills and confidence in this area. EIP can extend the prevention paradigm by adopting an integrated approach to physical health, promoting a healthy lifestyle, screening for modifiable risk factors and AP side effects, ensuring low dose AP is prescribed where possible, and sharing health concerns with GPs. The late Professor Helen Lester, a Birmingham GP, eloquently articulated this in her inspiring Mackenzie lecture, 'Being bothered about Billy', available at: www.ncbi.nlm.nih.gov/pmc/articles/PMC3582983/. She extolled GPs and psychiatrists to work proactively and collaboratively to ensure better care for patients with psychosis.

If the disparity in mortality rates were affecting a large segment of the population with a less stigmatised characteristic, we would witness a public outcry. Now is the time for action (Shiers et al., 2015) requiring a radical approach. EIP teams need access to health trainers who are able to motivate young people with inertia, poor diets and sedentary lifestyles. Helping patients exercise for short periods (high intensity training) each week, adopt a healthy diet and stop smoking are arguably as important interventions as treating their symptoms of psychosis. Addressing the poor physical health experienced by people with psychosis is perhaps the defining challenge for modern-day psychiatry.

Learning points

- Initial AP treatment is critical in shaping longer-term recovery. Prescribing should involve collaborative decision making in a climate of hope.
- AP response often occurs rapidly in FEP, resulting in symptomatic reduction in 75% of people.
- APs significantly reduce the risk of harm to self and others.
- APs reduce relapse after FEP from 64% to 27%.
- APs have similar efficacy (except clozapine). EPSE sensitivity in FEP results in SGA improved tolerability. Lowest dose AP should be used to prevent side effects hampering recovery. Short-term benzodiazepines are preferable to high dose APs to reduce distress in the acute phase.
- Clozapine is underutilised and its use is delayed. EIP teams should ensure clozapine is offered to suitable patients.
- Concordance rates in FEP are low (25%). Concordance is improved by therapeutic relationship, education, depots and long-acting oral agents.
- AP treatment should continue for a minimum of 12–24 months after symptomatic recovery to reduce relapse risk.
- Research into the neurobiology of negative symptoms and cognitive deficits has failed to produce significantly successful pharmacological treatments. With the exception of clozapine, APs have minimal effect on these potentially disabling symptoms.
- The future of pharmacology for psychosis may use a clinical staging model alongside pharmacogenomics.
- Risk reduction in EIP should include reducing the risk of premature death, most frequently due to cardiovascular causes.
- Medication side effects perpetuate poor physical health. Early screening and intervening can be aided by the Lester cardiometabolic screening tool.
- EIP is an opportunity to effect sustainable physical health improvements, requiring an integrated mind-body whole team approach – encouraging the adoption of lifestyle changes, such as a low carbohydrate diet, regular exercise and smoking cessation – and significantly improves well-being and life expectancy.

Chapter 4

Psychosocial approaches to symptomatic recovery and adaptation

Introduction

Symptomatic recovery following a FEP, as evidenced from the previous chapters, is an important part of the adaptation and recovery process. Relapse occurs within five years for the majority of people as only 15–20% will experience a single psychotic episode (Álvarez-Jiménez et al., 2012b; Fusar-Poli, McGorry.& Kane, 2017). Persistent or relapsing symptoms are associated with negative consequences (Álvarez-Jiménez et al., 2012b) including more admissions, poor psychosocial functioning, and progression to a more chronic stage of psychosis. Therefore, sustaining symptomatic remission and recovery is a key part of EIP. As indicated in Chapter 3, anti-psychotic medication (AP) is recommended as the first line treatment for psychotic symptoms in FEP (NICE, 2014) and adhering to AP in the first year after onset of FEP is the sole predictor of symptomatic recovery at five years (Norman et al., 2017). However, APs are less effective with negative symptoms (Fusar-Poli et al., 2015), functional outcomes (Fusar-Poli et al., 2017), and on chronic presentations (Fusar-Poli et al., 2017; Lally et al., 2017). Although AP medication is highly valued by service users (Barr, Ormrod & Dudley, 2015) and carers (Schizophrenia Commission, 2012), many service users stop APs for different reasons, including intolerable side effects (Burns, Erikson & Brenner, 2013). Consequently, medication alone is not adequate to facilitate and maintain recovery from FEP (Fusar-Poli et al., 2017; Lally et al., 2017; Lecomte et al., 2014b) and service users, carers and practitioners highly value psychosocial interventions (PSIs) alongside medication (Schizophrenia Commission, 2012).

This chapter will consider the impact of PSIs on symptomatic recovery following a FEP. It will primarily focus on cognitive behavioural therapy (CBT) as it is recommended in clinical guidelines (Kreyenbuhl, Buchanan, Dickerson, Dixon & Schizophrenia Patient Outcomes Team, 2010; NICE, 2014) and is one of the most widely researched and practised PSIs for psychosis, with over 40 randomised controlled trials (RCTs) in the last three decades (Mueser et al., 2013). Family interventions (FIs) for psychosis (Claxton, Onwumere & Fornelly-Ambrojo, 2017) are also recommended in the clinical guidelines (Kreyenbuhl et al., 2010; NICE, 2014) and have been investigated in over 50 RCTs (Pharoah, Mari, Rathbone & Wong, 2010). FIs are covered in more detail in Chapter 11, so this chapter will just review their effect on symptomatic recovery. The impact of other PSIs, including social skills training, psychoeducation, and neurocognitive interventions such as cognitive remediation therapy (CRT), on symptomatic recovery will be briefly reviewed. Early Signs and Relapse Prevention Plans (ESRPP) will be considered, as this is one of the most widely used interventions aimed at sustaining symptomatic recovery in EIP, although it often incorporates medical interventions. Finally, we will consider how PSIs can be optimised within EIP services to facilitate and sustain symptomatic recovery and adaptation following a FEP.

Cognitive behavioural therapy for psychosis (CBTp)

CBTp developed in the UK in the early 1990s when it was applied to delusions, voices and paranoia (Chadwick, Birchwood & Trower, 1996). There are different approaches to CBTp (e.g. Birchwood et al., 2014b; Chadwick, 2006; Fowler et al., 2018; Gumley & Schwannauer, 2006; Morrison, 2017; Nelson, 2005), which share common elements, including psychoeducation about psychosis, the conceptualisation of psychotic experiences using a cognitive model, the development of a therapeutic alliance through collaborative empiricism, modifying distressing beliefs about delusions and hallucinations, and relapse prevention. Morrison (2017) argues CBTp effectiveness will be enhanced through adherence to manualised protocols, clinical guidelines, competency frameworks and CBT fidelity scales. In this chapter, we will focus on cognitive models of positive and negative symptoms.

CBTp typically involves up to 30 hours of therapy, encompassing 25 sessions in the first 6–9 months and five booster sessions over the subsequent 6–12 months (Gumley & Schwannauer, 2006; Morrison, 2017; Nelson, 2005). However, the number of CBTp sessions required to facilitate and sustain symptomatic recovery will vary, depending on need and other factors. NICE (2014) suggests a minimum of 16 sessions but clinicians report benefits from fewer (Nelson, 2005), which has been verified in RCTs examining low intensity CBTp (Hazell, Hayward, Cavanagh & Strauss, 2016). Alternatively, others may require more sessions for a range of reasons, including engagement difficulties based on problematic pre-morbid attachment (Gumley & Schwannauer, 2006), persistent positive symptoms (Nelson, 2005), or their recovery style (McGlashan, 1987). Irrespective of the duration of CBTp, there are usually four phases: (1) assessment and engagement; (2) development of change strategies; (3) longitudinal formulation; and (4) consolidation and relapse prevention. Morrison (2017) has provided a detailed overview of these phases based on an established model of cognitive therapy. We will now use a case study to demonstrate these phases.

Evidence into practice

Case study 4.1 David: FEP and CBTp therapy phases

David was 17-year-old young man referred to EIP with a FEP. He had not left his house unaccompanied in over two years due to worries that people were looking at and talking about him. He had developed a belief that there were cameras in his house monitoring him, that people on TV were looking at him, and that people were driving by his house to see him, which resulted in him feeling like a character in the film, *The Truman Show*. Despite starting antipsychotic medication, these experiences, along with believing that he was saying his thoughts out loud, persisted.

Stage 1 Assessment and engagement

David had had a good childhood with supportive parents and siblings. He had done well at school and had friends. He began smoking cannabis when he was 12 years old, which increased over time along with using ecstasy at the weekends. He became paranoid when he was 15 years old, which resulted in him dropping out of school and increasing his cannabis use. He became worried that he was verbalising socially inappropriate thoughts, which had resulted in further social withdrawal. He was depressed and pessimistic about his future. Although David still felt like he was in a *Truman Show*-like scenario, he had some doubts about this as he had recently jumped at the TV while watching a live programme and did not see any of the audience react to his sudden and unexpected movement. This indicated that David was willing to reconsider his existing beliefs and that he was psychologically minded and resourceful, which can be good indicators for engagement with CBT. Similarly, individuals who hold their delusional beliefs with less conviction and involvement (Nelson, 2005) and have an integrative recovery style (McGlashan, 1987) may also find it easier to benefit from CBT.

Following the assessment, an overview of the cognitive model was presented using the ABC (Beck, Rush, Shaw & Emery, 1979) and 5-area (Wright, Williams & Garland, 2002) models using examples from the first session. It was discussed that when David saw people on TV looking at him (Activating Event: A), his previous belief (Belief 1: B1) was usually, 'They are looking at me because I am famous. I am in some sort of *Truman Show*' (Conviction=100%), which was associated with a negative emotional Consequence (C1) (anxiety; intensity=100%). To demonstrate the association between David's thoughts and emotions, this belief was compared with his more recently developed belief (B2) 'After jumping at the TV none of the audience moved so it does not seem like they are looking at me ... maybe I am not in a *Truman Show* scenario', which was associated with less anxiety (C2: 40%). The positive impact of his behaviour on eliciting evidence against his *Truman Show* belief was emphasised to demonstrate how evidence gathering in CBT is often based on behaviour change alongside Socratic questioning. The role of attention and thinking processes such as Jumping to Conclusions (Garety, Freeman, Jolley, Ross, Waller & Dunn, 2011) and the Thinking and Feeling Brain (Nelson, 2005) were discussed to demonstrate how David had been jumping to conclusions in the absence of concrete evidence. This tendency to jump to conclusions was potentially more likely when he was experiencing a threat-based emotional state, under the influence of cannabis and in a psychotic state. Appendix 2 lists the Cognitive Biases Questionnaire for Psychosis (CBQp) (Peters et al., 2013), which identifies these unhelpful thinking processes and other measures for assessing, formulating and measuring symptomatic change in CBTp. Finally, David's psychotic experiences were discussed in the context of his life history and substance misuse as normalising is highly valued by service users of EIP and a key factor in establishing therapeutic alliance (Barr et al., 2015).

Stage 2 Development of change strategies

In this phase, a range of interventions (e.g. coping strategy enhancement, evidence gathering, graded exposure, attention training, behavioural experiments, cognitive restructuring) are covered. Goals and homework tasks are used to implement effective change. This phase is based on a cognitive formulation, which in this case was the model developed by Paul French and Tony Morrison (French & Morrison, 2004; see Figure 4.1). David's most important goal was to establish whether he was verbalising his thoughts aloud when people looked at him or became quiet, which was associated with distress and behavioural strategies (humming, holding his breath, avoiding and leaving public situations). Although these strategies were helping him to temporarily reduce his distress, they were functioning as safety behaviours as they were associated with unintended consequences, including social

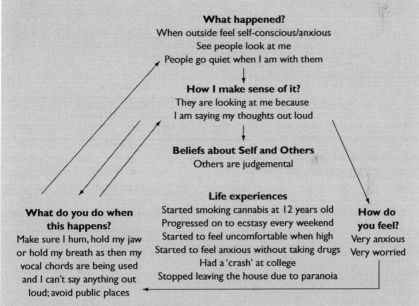

Figure 4.1 Cognitive formulation.

Source: Based on French and Morrison (2004).

isolation, low mood, cannabis use, and maintenance of his belief about verbalising his thoughts as he was not remaining in situations to test out his fears. Socratic questioning, evidence gathering, and behavioural experiments where David recorded himself with his mobile phone while dropping his safety behaviours helped him reality test this distressing belief. He consistently found that even when he had not hummed or held his breath and felt like he had verbalised inappropriate thoughts, there was never any evidence of this on the recordings he made. The therapy then focused on his cannabis use drawing on elements of Cognitive Behavioural Integrated Therapy (CB:IT) (Copello, Graham & Birchwood, 2001), which is discussed in Chapter 10.

Stage 3   Longitudinal historical formulation

For some individuals, the first two phases may be sufficient to modify unhelpful cognitive, emotional, and behavioural responses during psychotic experiences, which may then facilitate further symptomatic recovery. Others may benefit from a third phase, which develops a longitudinal formulation highlighting links between separate maintenance formulations (Morrison, 2017) and contextualising psychotic and emotional experiences within key life experiences (Gumley & Schwannauer, 2006), including childhood adversity (Read, Van Os, Morrison & Ross, 2005). This longitudinal formulation phase is illustrated in a second case study (Jake) later in this chapter. As David had no major developmental adversity and was making good progress with the existing intervention, stage 3 was not required, so the therapy moved to stage 4.

Stage 4   Consolidation/relapse prevention

This final phase consolidates effective change strategies, develops relapse prevention plans, monitors progress, and boosts self-efficacy. For David, this involved summarising and reflecting on the cumulative evidence against his concern that he was verbalising inappropriate thoughts and ensuring he did not hum or hold his breath when these concerns returned. During this phase, David gradually reduced his cannabis use and found part-time employment after receiving vocational support in the form of individual placement and support (IPS; see Chapter 6). His improved social and vocational functioning, abstinence from cannabis, and reductions in distress left him feeling more hopeful and optimistic about his future, which are key features of personal recovery (see Chapter 7).

Summary

This case study demonstrates how CBTp can facilitate symptomatic recovery and influence social and personal recovery. The therapy took many months to complete and David benefited from additional interventions, including family work, CBT-based exposure with his care co-ordinator, vocational support, and help with substance misuse. David received care co-ordination throughout this period, involving regular support to him and his parents, including psychoeducation about psychosis and cannabis. Finally, David was taking prescribed antipsychotic medication throughout this period. This illustrates the wide range of bio-psychosocial interventions that are often required to facilitate recovery from a FEP. This is why multi-component psychosocial interventions are recommended in clinical guidelines for a FEP (NICE, 2014, 2016) and increasingly feature in FEP care packages, such as NAVIGATE (Mueser et al., 2015).

Application of CBTP to different psychotic experiences

Before considering the evolving evidence base for CBTp, we will review the application of CBT to positive and negative symptoms.

CBT and positive symptoms

Hallucinations occur in 73% of individuals diagnosed with a FEP (Rajapakse Garcia-Rosales, Weerawardene, Cotton & Fraser, 2011). Some individuals (21%) experience visual hallucinations but auditory hallucinations are more common (36%) (Rajapakse et al., 2011). Some 22% of a FEP sample experienced commanding voices with 50% of these hearing commanding voices to hurt themselves and 31% hearing voices to harm others (Rajapakse et al., 2011). CBT for voices aims to change people's relationship with their voices and integrate emotional and psychotic experiences within the context of valued goals (Thomas et al., 2014), consistent with the CBT model above (Morrison, 2017). CBT for voices departs from traditional CBT by identifying that voices in themselves are not necessarily problematic or distressing but that the beliefs individuals hold about their voices' identity, power, intent, and control result in distress and problematic responses to voices (Chadwick, Birchwood & Trower, 1996). The Beliefs about Voices Questionnaire-Revised (BAVQ-R) (Chadwick, Less & Birchwood, 2000) is a 35-item measure that enables the development of formulation-based interventions to change beliefs about voices and an individual's unhelpful response to voices.[1]

Birchwood and colleagues demonstrated that compliance or appeasement behaviours can occur when the hearer believes the voice have malevolent intent and the power to deliver a threat. CBT for command hallucinations aims to weaken and challenge beliefs about the power of voices, enabling the individual to break free of the need to comply or appease, thereby reducing harmful compliance behaviour and distress. A proof of principle trial (Trower, Birchwood, Meaden, Byrne, Nelson & Ross, 2004) and a follow-up single blind RCT (COMMAND) (Birchwood et al., 2014b) demonstrated that CBT reduced harmful compliance with command hallucinations. The changes in compliance were consistent with changes in the voices' perceived power to deliver a supposed threat to the individual (Birchwood et al., 2018). CBT for commanding voices was highly acceptable to service users as shown by the high rate of completion (>80%) (Birchwood et al., 2014b). However, some participants remained depressed and distressed by their voices. Consequently, additional interventions focused at improving other aspects of symptomatic (e.g. see Chapter 8), social (see Chapters 5 and 6) and personal (see Chapter 7) recovery may still be required.

Alternative psychosocial interventions (PSIs) for voices

There are other PSIs for voices (and other psychotic experiences) in FEP samples with an evolving evidence base including Acceptance and Commitment Therapy (ACT) and mindfulness, which are considered in Chapter 7. A recent review of therapies for voice hearing (Thomas et al., 2014) highlights additional approaches, which focus on involving carer and social networks in therapeutic approaches, interpersonal relating, and the relationship between voices and past experiences. These approaches are consistent with evidence that many voice hearers, especially those who have suffered traumatic events (Read et al., 2005) can hold beliefs about their voices, which reflect broader schemas about self and others and one's place in the social world (Trower et al., 2004). Thus, CBT for voices typically involves a longitudinal formulation and schema level interventions (stage 3 outlined above). We will now illustrate this with a second case study to demonstrate the clinical application of the COMMAND approach.

Implementing the evidence into practice

Case study 4.2 Jake: CBTp with commanding voices

Jake, a 28-year-old man, experienced a FEP a year following the birth of his second child. He was admitted to hospital after becoming paranoid that people were targeting him and his family. He heard a voice telling him that he should harm himself, which he had acted on by cutting himself superficially. The voice was echoing his paranoid belief that something bad was going to happen to his young children, which resulted in Jake missing work and keeping his eldest son from going to nursery.

Stage 1 Assessment and engagement

Jake was commenced on antipsychotic medication in hospital. Upon discharge, he was more settled but was still hearing a critical male voice calling him 'useless' and threatening his children. Jake felt that the voice and threats towards his son were based in reality as he interpreted his recent episodes of self-harm as evidence that the voice could harm him and consequently his children. He felt useless as he could not financially support his family, which further contributed to his depression. He had thoughts of harming himself, which were echoed by the voice. Table 4.1 indicates his high score on the Calgary Depression Scale and moderate level of positive and

Table 4.1 Scores for case study 4.2: Jake FEP and CBTp for commanding voices

Measure	Baseline score level		Follow-up score level	
Psychosis (PANSS)				
Positive	21	High	11	Low
Negative	7	Absent	7	Absent
General	38	Moderate	26	Low
Total	66	Moderate	44	Moderate
Appraisals-BAVQ-R*				
Persecution	17	Moderate	6	Low
Benevolence	0	Low	3	Low
Engagement	0	Low	0	Absent
Resistance	21	Low	9	Moderate
Depression				
CDS	12	High	5	Low
Brief Core Schema Scale				
Positive Self	8	Low		
Negative Self	13	Medium		
Positive Other	10	Medium		
Negative Other	14	High		

Notes

1 PANSS = Positive and Negative Symptom Scale; BAVQ-R = Beliefs about Voices Questionnaire-Revised; CDS = Calgary Depression Scale.

2 *The scoring on the BAVQ-R reflects a recent factor analysis (Strauss et al., 2018).

general symptoms on the PANSS. On the BAVQ-R, Jake reported high levels of Persecution associated with his voice as he felt it was evil for threatening his children, it could make him do bad things that he did not want to do (e.g. cut himself), and it ruled his life. Jake did not hold any Benevolent beliefs about his voice as he did *not* feel it was trying to protect him nor help him achieve his goals, and he was *not* grateful for the voice. He reported low levels of Engagement with the voice as it did not reassure him, make him happy, and he did not seek advice from it. In contrast, he reported high levels of Resistance as the voice frightened him, made him feel down and angry, and he sometimes did things (self-harm) to stop it and told the voice to leave him alone, with little success.

Stage 2 Development of change strategies

Jake's therapeutic goals were to get rid of the voices, feel less anxious about his son going to nursery, return to work, and improve his relationship with his wife. It was discussed that the voices might not completely go following CBT, but the therapy could establish whether the voice had the power to harm his children. Anxiety management helped Jake develop more effective ways of managing his distress when he thought about his son leaving for the nursery and when he heard the voice. Thought diaries and behavioural experiments helped him establish that the voice's threats towards his children never materialised. After joining some sessions, Jake's wife gained an understanding of the formulation and reminded him of the lack of evidence supporting the voice's threats when he was distressed about letting his son attend nursery.

Stage 3   Longitudinal formulation

Once Jake felt the voice had less power over him and his behaviour, he agreed it would be helpful to understand the origin of the voice. This involved the development of a replacement belief for his experiences, a key part of CBT with voices (Nelson, 2005). Associations between Jake's fears for his son's well-being due to his son's long-standing physical health issues and the voice content were developed. Jake considered the possibility that the voice (despite its sense of persecution) might be originating from his own mind, reflecting his concerns about his son. The impact of Jake's early life experiences was considered. Jake had left home when he was 15 years old to escape persistent paternal physical and emotional abuse. This resulted in him developing negative beliefs about himself and others, assessed with the Brief Core Schema Scale (BCSS) (Fowler, Freeman, Smith, Kuipers, Bebbington & Bashforth, 2006) (see Table 4.1; Appendix 2). Sessions with his wife reassured him of his value and importance to her and their children. Jake acknowledged that, despite his early adversity, he had made progress in his life including gaining a degree, meeting his partner and having children. He accepted that, despite his lack of an appropriate male role model, he was a warm, loving and attentive father.

Stage 4   Consolidation and relapse prevention

At the end of therapy, Jake's voice had reduced to a moderate level. He still held Persecutory beliefs about the voice on the BAVQ-R but less than before and he accepted that the voice was potentially highlighting his worries about his son, which was associated with a slight change in his Benevolent beliefs about the voice (see Table 4.1). Jake found it hard to reconcile this new perspective with his old feelings about the voice and he never initiated contact with the voice. The voice was still not associated with any positive feelings so there were no changes in his Engagement with the voice. However, Jake experienced reductions in suspiciousness, anxiety, tension, depression, and social avoidance on the PANSS. He returned to work but accepted his vulnerability to stress and used more effective coping strategies. The development of an Early Signs and Relapse Prevention Plan (ESRPP) helped him maintain his recovery and reduced concerns (for both Jake and his family) about a relapse. This is outlined below.

CBT with delusional beliefs

We will now briefly discuss CBT-based approaches with delusional beliefs. As mentioned in Chapter 1, delusions are fixed false beliefs and have been documented in 74% of FEP individuals, including delusions of reference (25%), grandiosity

(13%), thought broadcast (9%), control (8%), and others (1–2%; sexual themes, somatic, nihilistic, and guilt) (Rajapakse et al., 2011). The most commonly held delusional beliefs in FEP are persecutory, with rates between 53% (Rajapakse et al., 2011) to 71% (Paolini, Moretti & Compton, 2016). In persecutory delusions, two distressing beliefs are usually present: (1) harm is going to occur; and (2) others intend it (Freeman & Garety, 2014). Consequently, feeling unsafe is the defining experience underlying persecutory delusions (Freeman, 2016). Persecutory beliefs are associated with high levels of distress and negative consequences, they are the most likely delusional belief to be acted upon and often result in hospitalisation (Freeman & Garety, 2014). Consequently, persecutory beliefs have received more empirical attention than other types of delusional beliefs.

Intervening clinically with delusions

Delusions are not discrete continuous entities but are complex and multidimensional, so it is important to consider their content, degree of conviction, resistance to change, distress, interference with social functioning, and personal reference (Freeman & Garety, 2014). These issues are important in CBT when discussing service users' goals (Nelson, 2005) and formulating the part of the delusional experiences they are hoping to change. Initial CBT-based approaches to delusional beliefs and paranoia (Chadwick et al., 1996) used the traditional change techniques outlined earlier in the chapter to help individuals review evidence for and against their beliefs. Nelson (2005) provides a detailed CBT-based treatment manual approach, which emphasises the importance of helping individuals develop alternative beliefs about their anomalous experience and a step-by-step process of modifying delusional beliefs. A more recent approach with persecutory beliefs does not explicitly focus on disproving past perceptions but helps individuals to establish that they are currently safe from harm (Freeman, 2016). This approach aims to reduce the feelings of threat underlying persecutory experiences by systematically removing factors associated with the onset and maintenance of persecutory beliefs, including a worrying thinking style, negative beliefs about self and others, interpersonal sensitivity, sleep disturbance, anomalous internal experience, and reasoning biases. Following distress tolerance and anxiety management, individuals are supported to enter threat-laden situations to establish for themselves that internal distressing sensations are not evidence of an objective threat and the harm they are concerned about will not materialise. This empirically based approach has culminated in the 'Feeling Safe Programme' (Freeman, Bradley, Waite, Sheaves, DeWeever, Bourke, et al., 2017), a focused CBT-based manualised treatment targeting the maintenance variables mentioned above.

Negative symptoms, FEP, and psychosocial interventions

As discussed in Chapters 1, 2 and 3, the term 'negative symptoms' refers to an absence or deficits in emotions, communication, and motivation (Elis et al.,

2013). When intervening clinically, it is important to distinguish between persistent negative symptoms, which are directly related to psychosis and transitory or secondary negative symptoms, which may be related to medication side effects or depression (Lutgens, Gariepy & Malla, 2017). An initial study found that 27% of a FEP sample had negative symptoms not confounded by depression or side effects (Malla, Norman, Jakhar & Ahmed, 2002) but more recent studies found only 5% (Gee et al., 2016a) to 11% (Ho, Chang, Tang, Hui & Chan, 2018) had persistently high negative symptoms. Baseline negative symptoms are one of the strongest predictors of poor outcomes following a FEP (Fusar-Poli et al., 2017) (see Chapter 5).

The need for psychosocial interventions (PSIs) for negative symptoms

As discussed in Chapter 3, a meta-analysis of pharmacological interventions found no consistent benefits (with the exception of clozapine) on negative symptoms (Fusar-Poli et al., 2014). Negative symptoms are twice as likely to be non-responsive to interventions compared to positive symptoms (Austin et al., 2015) and medication may contribute or exacerbate secondary negative symptoms (Leucht et al., 2009a). The notion that negative symptoms can be changed is relatively new as they have historically been regarded as a result of hedonic deficits (Velthorst et al., 2015) but PSIs, as an adjunct to medications, are now accepted as the best treatment (Elis, Caponigro & Kring, 2013; NICE, 2014).

Existing meta-analytic evidence (Elis et al., 2013; Fusar-Poli et al., 2014; Lutgens et al., 2017) provides different perspectives on the effectiveness of PSIs in reducing negative symptoms in non-FEP samples. Elis et al. (2013) reviewed the impact of three interventions: CBT, Social Skills Training (SST), and combined treatments (e.g. involving two more interventions used together) on negative symptoms with at least 10 RCTs. Most support was found for CBT followed by SST, although CBT was more effective at maintaining therapeutic gains. Negative symptom improvement was also associated with a combination of interventions (e.g. SST and family interventions). There was inadequate support for psychoeducation. The majority of studies reviewed did not include follow-up assessments so it is unclear whether symptom improvements persisted over time but there was evidence of benefits following longer interventions. Finally, many studies made claims about negative symptoms but used a measure of social functioning rather than negative symptoms, which do not necessarily capture or indicate improvement in negative symptoms (Elis et al., 2013).

Fusar-Poli et al. (2014) concluded that although PSIs produced small statistical reductions in negative symptoms, these were too small to translate into meaningful clinical improvements. This meta-analysis incorporated 27 different 'psychological interventions' which included 14 CBTp trials and a diverse range of other interventions (e.g. cognitive remediation therapy, psychoeducation, yoga, and physical exercise). Given the variation in these studies, it is debatable whether this meta-analysis was a meaningful evaluation of the impact of individual PSIs (including CBT) on negative symptoms, particularly as the majority of the trials did not target negative symptoms directly. We will return to this issue below, as many CBTp trials face similar problems (Thomas, 2015).

In contrast, Lutgens et al. (2017) examined the impact of seven separate groups of psychosocial interventions on negative symptoms. There was moderate meta-analytic evidence in support of CBT, skills-based, exercise, and music interventions compared to treatment as usual. In contrast, neurocognitive (including CRT) and family-based interventions were not effective in reducing negative symptoms. Interventions incorporating skills enhancement, behavioural activation, and more frequent intensity (>45 minutes per week) were more effective in reducing negative symptoms. However, the positive impact of the above interventions on negative symptoms was not significant when compared to 'active controls' where the treatment group was compared to another intervention instead of just treatment as usual (TAU). The vast majority of studies included samples with enduring psychosis and any positive impact on negative symptoms reduced once the intervention ceased. Consequently, there is a need for studies examining the impact of psychosocial interventions in FEP.

Fusar-Poli et al. (2014) argue that treatment for negative symptoms has been hampered by the lack of established cognitive models of negative compared to positive symptoms. To some degree, this is true as cognitive models of positive symptoms (Garety, Kuipers, Fowler, Freeman & Bebbington, 2001) have been more influential in both research and clinical practice. However, cognitive models of negative symptoms have been developed, which suggest that negative beliefs about social abilities, performance and lower expectancies for pleasure and success contribute to the maintenance of negative symptoms (Recto, Beck & Stolar, 2005; Grant & Beck, 2009). Two recent CBT trials have found that targeting beliefs (e.g. 'there is no point trying to make new friends'; 'I got damaged by my psychotic episode and I cannot enjoy things any more') resulted in reductions in some negative symptoms (Grant, Huh, Perivoliotis, Stolar & Beck, 2012; Staring, TerHuurne & van der Gaag, 2013). Although both trials had small samples and methodological problems, they are promising due to their focus on negative symptoms and use of a cognitive model of negative symptoms (Rector et al., 2005). Thus, these studies may be the origins of cognitive behavioural therapy for negative symptoms (CBTn). Chapters 5 and 6 consider the impact of negative symptoms on social recovery and outline additional approaches to reduce their impact on recovery.

Current evidence base for CBT for positive and negative symptoms

To date, there have been 12 meta-analyses reviewing up to 50 randomised controlled trials, which indicate that CBTp has small to moderate effect sizes, depending on trials included and outcomes evaluated (Peters et al., 2015). Two of the largest meta-analyses (Jauhar et al., 2015; Wykes et al., 2008) reported an inverse relationship between effect sizes and methodology, particularly blinding, suggesting caution in interpreting previous positive outcomes of CBTp as earlier trials were not as rigorous. In the majority of CBT trials, the impact on negative symptoms is considered a secondary outcome at the expense of positive symptoms (Velthorst et al., 2015). Wykes et al. (2008) reported a beneficial impact of CBTp on negative symptoms but a subsequent meta-analysis (Jauhar et al., 2015) concluded that CBTp (e.g. focused on positive symptoms) had no significant impact on negative symptoms. Velthorst et al. (2015) reviewed 30 RCTs published from 1993 to 2013 that reported on the impact of CBT on negative symptoms in people with a diagnosis of schizophrenia. The overall impact on symptom alleviation and reduction was small and heterogeneous and regression analysis indicated stronger treatment effects were found with earlier year of publication, lower study quality, and individual CBT vs. group CBT. Velthorst et al. (2015) conclude that the positive impact of CBTp on negative symptoms reported by Wykes do not generalise to more recent studies. However, a trend suggested that studies with more behavioural techniques were slightly more effective in reducing negative symptoms. So, it is also possible that older studies may have had more of a behavioural focus and an exclusive focus on cognitions may be less effective than exposure to pleasure and success experiences that might result from participating in social activities (see Chapter 6). Importantly, few of these studies were focused on FEP samples.

The most recent meta-analysis of CBTp on symptomatic recovery has attempted to address methodological issues in previous studies by using a more sophisticated method known as a network meta-analysis. Bighelli et al. (2018) only included individuals with at least moderate positive symptoms and a relative long duration of illness (median = 12 years) as network meta-analysis requires a homogeneous sample. Results indicated that CBTp (40 studies) was more effective on positive symptoms than treatment as usual, waiting list controls, and supportive therapy. In contrast to Jauhar et al. (2015), the impact of CBT on positive symptoms remained in blinded studies. CBT was also associated with greater reduction on overall symptoms, negative symptoms and quality of life and functioning. The effect size of CBT on positive symptoms was in the lower to medium range.

Despite the small but consistent effect sizes, the effectiveness of CBTp as an evidence-based practice has been questioned (Lynch, Laws & McKenna, 2010; Jauhar et al., 2015), which triggered a debate over whether CBTp has been 'oversold' (Mueser & Glyn, 2014; Peters, 2014; Tarrier, 2014). Thomas (2015) argues that this debate has provided much-needed critical thinking but it has overlooked some fundamental limitations of what CBTp provides as an intervention in clinical practice. At the point of development in the 1990s, CBT was helpful in grouping together approaches united by a pragmatic focus on reducing the impact of symptoms through effective use of coping skills and restructuring distress-related appraisals. However, over time, the concept of CBTp has become problematic due to its multi-component nature and application to a wide range of samples (Thomas, 2015) resulting in us not knowing what works for whom (Peters, 2014).

It has also been argued that global positive symptom severity as the primary outcome variable in CBTp trials provides an insufficient measure of adaption to psychosis (Birchwood & Trower, 2006; Thomas et al., 2014), as CBT was originally conceived as a therapy for distress (depression and anxiety), with the assumption that an individual's unhelpful emotional and behavioural responses to adverse life events were influenced by cognitive appraisals. In addition, even statistically significant changes in global symptom measures, such as the PANSS, do not necessarily translate into meaningful clinical improvements until there is at least a 30–50% change in such scores (Fusar-Poli et al., 2014). Thus, CBTp should focus on relieving distress and note that resolution of positive symptoms should be a secondary outcome (Birchwood & Trower, 2006). However, few CBTp trials have used distress and emotional dysfunction as either a primary or secondary outcome. Consistent with this reasoning, there is stronger evidence for effects on specific symptom measures (Birchwood et al., 2014a; Peters, 2014; Van der Gaag, Valmaggia & Smit, 2014).

The future of CBTp and FEP

CBT is not a panacea but neither is it ineffective (Birchwood et al., 2014a) as demonstrated in the most recent meta-analysis (Bighelli et al., 2018). The question going forward is, how it can become more effective when used in clinical service delivery? There are a number of possibilities. First, more recent CBTp studies have demonstrated the benefits of individually formulated CBTp (Van der Gaag et al., 2014) with specific protocols and outcome measures for command hallucinations (Birchwood et al., 2014a), delusions (Freeman, 2016) negative symptoms (Staring et al., 2013; Grant et al., 2012), and poor social functioning (Fowler et al., 2018). The more focused protocols and outcome measures used in these studies may lead them to be viewed as the first of 2nd generation CBTp studies, which aim to optimise outcomes with an established evidenced based intervention (first generation) (Thomas, 2015).

Second, there may be benefits from focusing on what patients need or want from CBTp by considering consumer-defined ideas of personal recovery (Byrne & Morrison, 2014; Thomas, 2015). Qualitative research suggests that service users value increased understanding of psychosis, the development of coping strategies, reappraisal of distressing beliefs, and normalisation (Berry & Hayward, 2011). Consistent with arguments made above regarding the aim of CBTp (Birchwood & Trower, 2006), service users did not always report or want full psychotic symptom remission but wanted to learn to accommodate and live with their psychotic experiences (Berry & Hayward, 2011). This was sufficient for them to feel they had attained personal recovery. These issues are explored in more detail in Chapter 7.

Third, using more focused outcome measures in CBTp trials will likely lead to larger effect sizes (Birchwood et al., 2014a; Thomas et al., 2014) but additional measures are required to examine the mediators of therapeutic change (Thomas et al., 2014) such as recently used in the COMMAND trial (Birchwood et al., 2018). In addition, trials of CBTp and clinical applications of CBTp need to ensure that Patient Reported Outcome Measures (PROMs) are used to capture changes in psychotic experiences important to service users (see Appendix 2).

Fourth, clinical guidelines (NICE, 2014, 2016) recommend that CBTp should be offered to everyone with a psychotic disorder, which should be delivered by qualified staff in an individual format and consist of a minimum of 16 sessions. However, services may need to focus on what they can actually deliver and recent meta-analytic evidence suggests that some individuals may benefit from less than 16 sessions of CBTp (Hazell et al., 2016).

Fifth, despite the fact that the evidence base for CBTn is still evolving (Grant et al., 2012; Staring et al. 2013), people experiencing negative symptoms consider the reduction of apathy or lack of initiative as one of their most important treatment goals (Sterk, van Rossum, Muis & De Haan, 2013). Given the association between negative symptoms and longer-term outcomes in FEP samples (Fusar-Poli et al., 2017), there is a need to offer interventions for negative symptoms alongside developing the evidence base underlying interventions (see Chapters 5 and 6).

Finally, although the most recent meta-analysis of CBTp shows the benefits of CBT on positive symptoms in a homogeneous sample with a long illness duration (Bighelli et al., 2018), it highlights the need for more studies with FEP samples. Bighelli et al. (2018) also found that few CBT (and other psychological interventions) collect data on relapse and adverse events. Consequently, they recommend that CBTp should routinely collect information on adverse events to establish that psychological interventions cause no harm.

Cognitive remediation therapy (CRT) and cognitive dysfunction

As mentioned in Chapter 1, impaired cognitive functioning is common in psychosis (O'Donnell & Martin, 2016) and is associated with poor psychosocial functioning, poor responses to PSIs and overall severity of symptoms, especially negative symptoms (Mueser et al., 2013). Furthermore, antipsychotic medications do not typically produce significant improvements in cognitive functioning (O'Donnell & Martin, 2016). Consequently, cognitive remediation therapy (CRT) was developed with the specific aim of improving cognitive functioning following severe and enduring mental health difficulties such as psychosis. There have been over 40 published RCTs of CRT (Mueser et al., 2013) and moderate meta-analytic evidence on cognitive symptoms (Wykes et al., 2011). However, concerns about methodological quality and delivery of CRT mean that larger-scale studies with systematic assessment of dose, task generalisation, changes in everyday behaviour, and individual differences in response are needed to establish standard implementations for dissemination (O'Donnell & Martin, 2016). Nonetheless, the results of cognitive remediation on improving cognitive functioning are more promising than any current pharmacological intervention and are not associated with known side effects. CRT is discussed in more detail in Chapter 6 due to the overlap between cognitive functioning and social functioning and recovery.

Impact of family interventions on symptomatic recovery

As family interventions (FIs) are covered in Chapter 11, we will only consider their impact on symptomatic recovery in this chapter. Carers often have limited information about psychosis and elevated rates of stress, burden, and distress, which can lead to high levels of unhelpful emotional expression. High levels of emotional expression are one of the most robust predictors of psychosis outcome and relapse (Álvarez-Jiménez et al., 2012b). Consequently, it is reasoned that family interventions could help reduce positive symptoms by improving the quality of the family environment (see Chapter 11).

FIs may also help with negative symptoms as providing support to the family network could enable them to help the young person engage in social activities and facilitate feelings of connectedness and emotional expression (Elis et al., 2013). Consistent with this, two studies looking at family therapy alone found improvements in negative symptoms. Eight of the 11 studies that Elis et al. (2013) reviewed, which included some type of family component, demonstrated improvements in negative symptoms. However, service users with family members who are willing to engage in family therapy may represent a subgroup that are more amenable to PSIs and have a greater support network to assist with treatment (Elis et al., 2013).

Despite the potential for family work to facilitate symptomatic recovery, the most recent meta-analysis of 14 trials of FIs in psychosis found no association between FIs and reductions in psychotic symptoms following completion of therapy but there was a delayed effect at a two-year follow-up (Claxton et al., 2017). In contrast, FIs were associated with reduced relapse rates but these were not sustained at follow-up. FIs were also not associated with reductions in the number of hospital admissions. However, FI was associated with other improvements (e.g. communication, carer burden), which are discussed in more detail in Chapter 11. Finally, the other meta-analysis discussed above also found no impact of FI on negative symptoms (Lutgens et al., 2017).

Impact of other PSIs on symptomatic recovery

In order to provide some clarity on the relative effectiveness of different PSIs, a meta-analysis of 48 outcome trials ($n=3,295$) compared the impact of six common PSIs including befriending, CBT, CRT, psychoeducation, social skills training (SST), and supportive counselling on positive, negative, and overall symptoms (Turner, van der Gaag, Karyotaki & Cuijpers, 2014). Results indicated that CBT was more effective (small effect size) in reducing positive symptoms compared to all the other interventions. However, SST was more effective in reducing negative symptoms compared to all other interventions. Befriending was less effective than other interventions in reducing overall symptoms. CBT was more effective than befriending for overall symptoms and more effective than supportive counselling for positive symptoms. However, the actual differences were small in terms of clinical significance, so therapeutic benefits of different interventions may reflect common factors and the fact that many participants were most likely taking medication (Turner et al., 2014). Nonetheless, it is probably not a coincidence that CBT appears more effective for positive symptoms whereas SST is more effective for negative symptoms as these outcomes are the targets of the different therapies (see Chapter 6). As mentioned above, a recent meta-analysis also found support for the efficacy of CBT on positive, negative and overall symptoms (Bighelli et al., 2018). However, this meta-analysis failed to find similar support for other PSIs (e.g. meta-cognitive training; mindfulness; ACT), which was most likely due to the small number of non-CBT-intervention-based studies (Bighelli et al., 2018).

Sustaining symptomatic recovery

The final part of this chapter will consider how symptomatic recovery can be sustained, that is, how the chances of a relapse of psychotic symptoms can be reduced (Birchwood, Iqbal., Chadwick & Trower, 2000) and how people can be supported to stay well following FEP (Gumley & Schwannauer, 2006). Sustaining symptomatic recovery following FEP is important given that the vast majority (80–85%) relapse within five years of a FEP (Álvarez-Jiménez et al., 2012b; Fusar-Poli et al., 2017). Relapse has significant consequences for service users, carers, service providers and the wider society. The re-emergence of positive symptoms of psychosis can be distressing for service users and their carers. Risks to self and others can be increased and relapsing psychosis costs four times more than stable psychosis (Álvarez-Jiménez et al., 2012b) often due to hospital admissions, which is the principal source of schizophrenia's annual cost to the UK NHS of over £3.9 billion (Schizophrenia Commission, 2012). Relapse can impact on identity formation, the development of peer and intimate relationships (Álvarez-Jiménez et al., 2012b; Gumley & Schwannauer, 2006), and on social recovery, which can impact significantly on longer-term symptomatic recovery (Álvarez-Jiménez et al., 2011). Consequently, sustaining symptomatic recovery, reducing relapse rates, and preventing progression from clinical stage 2 to a more enduring illness such as stages 3 and 4 (McGorry, Hickie, Yung, Pantelis & Jackson, 2006) are key objectives of EIP services (Fusar-Poli et al., 2017; NICE, 2014, 2016).

Table 4.2 Staying well and early signs relapse prevention plan

	What can I do to stay well?	Support I need?
Signs of being well • Mood is stable • I enjoy my work • I play with my children • I see my friends regularly • If I hear voices, I can manage them	Daily • Get enough sleep • Eat healthily • Take prescribed medication Regularly • Exercise, gym and play football • Make time for me • Make time to see my friends	• Encouragement from my wife • Regular contact with EIP • Attend medical reviews

	Managing triggers	Professionals involved
Potential triggers • Lack of money • Working too much • Losing sleep • My son's health	• Discuss worries with my wife • Take a short break from work • Manage any problems with sleep as soon as they arise	• Care Co-ordinator: • Consultant: • Psychologist

	How can I manage these?	Support I need?
First signs of difficulties • Become anxious • Poor sleep • Worrying about my son • I become self-critical • Feel low	• Follow my staying well plan • Discuss worries with my wife and father in law • CBT Strategies: Is there evidence to support my worries?	• Emotional support • Practical support from in laws • See care co-ordinator

	How can I manage these?	Support I need?
Middle signs of difficulties • Feel others are thinking badly of me • Want to keep son at home • Worries turn into voices • Feel paranoid	• Get as much sleep as I can • CBT: Is there evidence to support my worries/voices? • Remember the voices cannot harm my children • Time off work	• More visits from EIP • See psychologist again • Medical review

	How can I manage these?	Support I need?
Late signs of difficulties • Emotional distress increases • Cannot sleep at night • Start to act on voices (e.g., keep son at home) • Believe myself and my family are in danger	• Take prescribed medication • Discuss my concerns • CBT: The voices often lie • I felt paranoid before but no harm came to me or family • Longer break from work	• More visits from EIP • Regular medical review • Consider a hospital admission if my wife thinks this will help

Early Signs and Relapse Prevention Plans (ESRPPs)

The development of individualised Early Signs and Relapse Prevention Plans (ESRPPs) became a key part of clinical care in the original EIP services in the UK (Birchwood et al., 2000) and clinical guidelines (NICE, 2014). An ESRPP is based on the idea that anticipation of a relapse will enable preventative action to reduce relapse and sustain symptomatic recovery. These approaches often use trigger, early signs and coping cards to elicit and structure conversations between clinicians, service users and their carers with the aim of developing an Early Signs Relapse Prevention Plan (ESRPP) (see Table 4.2 for an example). Before starting this work, it is helpful to have an understanding of the young person's experiences and willingness to engage with ESRPP. In the Birmingham EIP service, we incorporate a staying well plan with the aim of promoting and sustaining a state of well-being while the early signs section differentiates strategies for service users/carers and the service. Although some service users value early signs more than a staying well plan (Barr et al., 2015), the participants in this study were all working or in education, so it is possible their good recovery status meant that a staying well plan was less of a priority than the threat from a potential relapse. In our experience, many individuals engage well with this approach as the positive focus of the staying well section provides a balance to the threat associated with a potential relapse. Case study 4.3 outlines the development of a staying well plan and an ESRPP with Jake (see case study 4.2).

Evidence into practice

Case study 4.3 Jake: staying well and Early Signs Relapse and Prevention Plan (ESSRP)

The top row in Table 4.2 summarises the staying well plan that Jake developed. The left-hand column illustrates the cognitive, emotional, and behavioural signs that Jake associated with being well. To the right are the activities and the support, which can maintain this state of wellness. The row below contains the triggers that could potentially be a source of stress for him and how he could manage these. The remainder of the plan summarises the early warning signs that could be indicative of an emerging relapse and the ways Jake can manage these himself or with support from others. The plan divides his early signs into three categories: early, middle, and late, which are somewhat arbitrary as relapse often involves a series of distressing cognitive, emotional, and behavioural changes, which merge seamlessly. However, the aim of an ESRPP is to help service users, carers, and staff identify the stage of a potential relapse and use helpful resources and coping strategies in an effective way at the right time. This approach encourages service users to take control and responsibility for their own mental well-being, use their own resources, and reduce dependency on services. It can enable the identification of support that service users and their carers will find helpful and acceptable in the event of an imminent or actual relapse. The template can be adapted to individual service users and can incorporate their own words to document their psychotic experiences and plans to remain well.

Effectiveness of ESRPPs

ESRPPs are recommended in clinical guidelines (NICE, 2014) and will feature in many service users' care plans. However, the original evidence for this emphasis on relapse prevention was based on only two studies (Birchwood, Todd & Jackson, 1989; Herz & Melville, 1980), which cited retrospective reports that the majority of service users experienced non-specific (e.g. anxiety, low mood, poor concentration, insomnia) and specific (e.g. low-level positive symptoms) changes in their thoughts, feelings, and behaviours preceding a relapse. Subsequent studies suggest that identifiable early signs appear in the weeks preceding relapse for the majority (70–93%) of service users (Van Meijel, van der Gaag, Kahn & Grypdonck, 2004) and they have modest predictive validity for relapse (Eisner, Drake & Barrowclough, 2013). A review of the effectiveness of ESRPPs found that multi-component early signs interventions were associated with 50% fewer relapses and fewer admissions but it was difficult to isolate the specific effects of the early signs component in the wide range of interventions provided (Eisner et al., 2013). Short-term intermittent targeted medication dependent on the emergence of early symptoms was less effective than moderate dose maintenance medication (see Chapter 3). However, early signs assessment was poor in most of the studies, assessment of relapse was not robust and study samples were highly selected (e.g. drug users and uncooperative patients were excluded) so the results may not generalise to generic clinical samples (Eisner et al. 2013). Studies with a wide variety of possible early signs that were monitored frequently achieved the most sensitive assessment of relapse risk (Eisner et al., 2013).

Improving the effectiveness of ESRPPs

In addition to more frequent monitoring of early signs, the effectiveness of ESRPP interventions could be improved by the addition of other hypothesised predictors of relapse, such as basic symptoms (Eisner, Barrowclough, Lobban & Drake, 2014), which are subtle clinical disturbances (see Chapter 1) and are identifiable by service users but rarely documented in case notes (Eisner, Drake, Lobban, Bucci, Emsley & Barrowclough, 2018). Qualitative research has found that service users with psychosis vary in the attention they pay to potential risk factors associated with relapse and early signs of relapse (Eisner et al., 2014). This study identified that residual psychotic symptoms, cognitive difficulties, infrequent clinician appointments, social isolation, and speed of deterioration (either very rapid or gradual) can all be significant barriers to effective use of early signs interventions. In contrast, having a supportive family member or friend facilitates more effective use of early signs interventions.

Consistent with the approach advocated throughout this book a review focused on preventing relapse following a FEP concluded that intensive psychosocial interventions (primarily CBT and FI) and low-dose medication strategies were the most effective in reducing relapse (Álvarez-Jiménez et al., 2011). However, the majority of these studies did not have an explicit focus on ESRPP and there was a lack of well-conducted FEP relapse prevention trials. Consequently, there remains a large discrepancy between the current evidence base (Álvarez-Jiménez et al., 2011; Eisner et al., 2013) and the widespread use and policy recommendations of ESRPPs (NICE, 2014).

Relapse is an individualised multi-dimensional process based on multiple interacting risk and protective factors (Power, 2017; Chapter 1) so prediction of relapse is challenging (Gaebel & Riesbeck, 2014) with no reliable predictive models following psychosis (Sullivan et al., 2017; Chapter 1). Nonetheless, emerging evidence indicates that individuals who only experience one psychotic episode (Stage 2) differ on clinical and demographic variables compared to those who relapse (Stage 3) (see Table 4.3). These studies suggest that ESRPPs may be particularly important for service users (e.g. males with poorer pre-morbid functioning) with specific bio-psychosocial factors (e.g. non-concordance with medication, substance misuse; carer's critical comments) that are associated with relapse (Álvarez-Jiménez et al., 2010, 2011, 2012b; Reveulta et al., 2017; Rosen & Garety, 2005). In contrast, ESRPPs may not be as critical for service users with protective factors, such as good pre-morbid functioning and social support as these may buffer environmental stress and confer lower vulnerability to relapse.

Individuals who appear at high risk of relapse could receive ESRPP alongside targeted formulation-driven CBTp for any positive (Birchwood et al. 2014a; Freeman et al., 2016; Thomas et al., 2014) and negative (Grant et al., 2012; Staring et al., 2014) psychotic symptoms and additional bio-psychosocial interventions, which provide social support, reduce critical comments in the family environment, discuss planned withdrawal of medication (instead of service users suddenly stopping) and address problematic substance misuse. This would be dependent on an individualised formulation aimed at identifying the presence of

Table 4.3 Variables associated with sustained symptomatic recovery and relapse following FEP

Sustained recovery (clinical stage 2)*	Relapse (clinical stage 3)
• Shorter DUP	• Male gender
• Better premorbid functioning	• Poorer premorbid functioning
• Less baseline negative symptoms	• More baseline negative symptoms
• More social support	• Carer's critical comments
• Rapid onset of psychotic symptoms	• Poor insight
• Favourable response to treatment	• Non-adherence to medication
• Diagnosis of affective psychosis	• Diagnosis of schizophrenia
	• Substance and cannabis misuse

Note
* Clinical stage refers to clinical staging model (McGorry et al., 2006; see Table 1.1).

these variables and the service user's motivation and ability to engage with interventions aimed at facilitating and sustaining symptomatic recovery. Operationalising this within an EIP MDT is discussed in Chapters 6 and 12.

Optimising PSIs to facilitate symptomatic recovery

This chapter has reviewed the potential of PSIs to facilitate and sustain symptomatic recovery following a FEP. We have focused on CBTp due to its strong evidence base, widespread delivery, and recommendations in clinical guidelines. However, it is unlikely that CBTp alone will be sufficient to meet the needs of young people with FEP. The majority of people who develop FEP are usually in their teens or early twenties with a range of developmental needs and challenges, which may be beyond the scope of a traditional CBTp intervention (Mueser et al., 2017). Consequently, clinical guidelines recommend a range of other interventions, such as work and education interventions (see Chapter 6) and FIs (see Chapter 11) (NICE, 2016). However, this issue is relevant to the delivery of CBT itself, particularly the second-generation CBTp approaches discussed above. Individualised Resiliency Training (IRT) in the NAVIGATE program (Mueser et al., 2015) incorporates a range of CBT-based interventions, including developing resilience and illness self-management skills, emotionally processing the FEP, social skills training, substance misuse, and wellness promotion, aimed at facilitating adaptation to FEP, which may be beneficial to many young service users.

The organisational setting of EIP that can support the delivery of PSIs also requires consideration. It has been argued that EIP teams achieve good outcomes as they are better suited than standard care in supporting the delivery of PSIs (Brabban & Dodgson, 2010) as smaller care co-ordinator caseloads facilitate engagement and a working alliance (Barr et al., 2015). As mentioned in Chapter 1, the current average caseload for a care co-ordinator in the UK is 17 cases, which is just over the recommended number (15) in clinical guidelines (NICE, 2014). However, many teams have much higher caseloads (e.g. at the time of writing, Birmingham EIP teams have caseloads of +25). Nonetheless, service users value a close and supportive relationship with their care co-ordinators above many other factors (Barr et al., 2015; see also Chapters 2 and 12) and this is likely to facilitate the delivery of psychosocial interventions.

Breitborde et al. (2017) highlight that the duration of untreated psychosis (DUP) has rightfully received widespread attention in EIP (see Chapter 1) but that the delay in intensive psychosocial treatment (DIPT) has attracted far less scrutiny despite a 16-year-old study finding that the mean DIPT (19 months) was nearly twice as long as DUP (8.6 months) (de Haan, Linszen, Lenior, de Win & Gorsira, 2003). More importantly although both DUP and DIPT were associated with negative symptoms, only DIPT statistically predicted negative symptoms (de Haan et al., 2003). This finding is consistent with evidence that interventions delivered in earlier clinical stages are likely to be more effective than ones delivered later (Breitborde, Moe, Ered, Ellman & Bell, 2017; McGorry et al., 2006). Despite the importance of this finding, DIPT does not appear to have been investigated in any subsequent studies. To some degree, the new Access and Waiting Time Standards in the UK (NICE, 2016) help address this issue as they mandate all new FEP cases should have access to evidence-based PSIs. However, as seen in Chapter 1, the delivery of PSIs within UK EIP remains low as only 34% received CBTp, 18% received FIs, and 22% received a vocational intervention. There is likely widespread variability in how EIP teams are resourced to deliver these interventions and EIP teams may not record delays in providing PSIs. Thus, measuring and monitoring DIPT may be important to improve the provision of psychosocial interventions in EIP services and facilitating and sustaining symptomatic recovery.

Sustaining longer-term symptomatic recovery

This chapter has reviewed evidence that PSIs can facilitate and potentially sustain symptomatic recovery following a FEP, with the strongest current evidence for the impact of CBT on positive symptoms and emerging evidence for negative symptoms. Other interventions such as FIs may have longer-term benefits on symptomatic recovery. The multi-component nature of PSIs has both advantages and disadvantages in facilitating and sustaining symptomatic recovery. The evidence base for multi-component early signs and relapse prevention interventions need to be developed. However, relapse prevention and sustained recovery following FEP remain key aims of FEP (Fusar-Poli et al., 2017; Sullivan et al., 2017). In Chapters 5 and 6, we will see that interactions between symptomatic and social recovery indicate that although symptomatic recovery is necessary for later recovery, it is not in itself sufficient (Álvarez-Jiménez et al., 2012b). Consequently, the best of way of sustaining symptomatic recovery over time may be to ensure that initial symptomatic remission is followed by social (Álvarez-Jiménez et al., 2012b) and personal (Lally et al., 2017) recovery, which are the focus of the next three chapters. We will return to the important interaction between symptomatic, social, and personal recovery in Chapter 12 when we consider how EIP teams aim to facilitate all three types of recovery.

Learning points

- Psychosocial interventions are important for facilitating recovery following FEP.
- CBT following FEP will be more effective with targeted assessments, formulations, interventions, and outcome measures but wider (non-symptomatic) goals following FEP also require addressing.
- There is less robust evidence for CBT on negative symptoms in FEP samples but cognitive models and more focused approaches (CBTn) are developing.

- The impact of family interventions (FIs) on symptoms is less robust but FIs can improve the quality of the home environment, which may have longer-term benefits on symptoms.
- Other PSIs, particularly skills-based ones, can reduce negative symptoms.
- The effectiveness of Early Signs Relapse Prevention Plans (ESRPPs) may be improved by identifying a wide range of early signs of relapse for each individual and monitoring these regularly.
- ESRPPs may be particularly important for service users who have clinical and demographic variables associated with a higher risk of relapse.
- Measuring delays in intensive psychosocial interventions (DIPT) could influence the delivery of PSIs and the recovery rates.
- Ultimately the most effective way of ensuring longer-term symptomatic recovery may be transforming initial remission into social and personal recovery.

Note

1 On the BVAQ-R, three subscales measure Omnipotent (perceived power of voices), Malevolent (negative intent) and Benevolent (positive intent) beliefs, and two subscales assess Engagement and Resistance with voices at the behavioural and emotional levels. A recent factor analysis suggests reducing the scale to 29 items by joining the Malevolent and Omnipotent subscales to one Persecutory Subscale (nine items), retaining the Benevolent Subscale (five items) and removing the division between emotional and behavioural responses on the Engagement (six items) and the Resistance (nine items) subscales (Strauss et al., 2018). Case study 4.2 and the ones in Chapter 8 reflect these recommendations.

Chapter 5

Social recovery in first episode psychosis

Introduction

In 1974, unemployment and poor social relationships were defined as characteristics of longer-term unfavourable outcomes in schizophrenia (Strauss & Carpenter, 1974). In 1980, observations of the link between social disability and psychosis prompted the formal inclusion of social recovery (SR) in the *Diagnostic and Statistical Manual of Mental Disorders* (DSM-III) classification of schizophrenia (Spitzer et al. 1978). Although rates of symptomatic recovery after psychosis have improved since this time, despite this early recognition, the same cannot be said for full functional recovery (Lally et al., 2017; Chapter 2). This chapter will focus on the impact of a FEP on social and occupational functioning and argue the case as to why interventions aimed at promoting SR after psychosis are crucial, if not essential, for longer-term outcome.

The impact of psychosis on social and occupational functioning

Social and occupational functioning can be negatively affected by a FEP (e.g. Cotton et al., 2017). This is universally agreed among EIP clinicians, patients and their families. However, there is a lack of consistency as to the precise nature and impact of psychosis on associated SR. This is unsurprising given the methodological variations in assessment, definitions of the concept, sampling and how patient variables are reported at data entry and follow-up (Silverstein & Bellack, 2008). What is accepted is that rates of SR remain consistently low for some people. Wunderink et al. (2009) report SR rates of 26.4% after two years (as measured by the Groningen Social Disabilities Schedule[1] (GSDS; WHO, 2001). Similarly, Robinson et al. (2004) report SR rates of 25.5% at five years (as measured by the Social Adjustment Scale[2] (SAS; Schooler, Weissman, Hogarty, Hargreaves, Attkisson & Sorenson, 1979).

Typical investigations of SR in FEP will often report vocational status alongside some measure of functioning, such as living arrangements, meaningful activity, self-care and relationships (e.g. Álvarez-Jiménez et al., 2012b), but compared to studies measuring symptomatic recovery, there are few that include SR as a primary outcome after FEP. Nevertheless, the consensus is that all aspects of social functioning can be negatively affected during a FEP, and in the short- to long-term stages of recovery. Individuals can experience significant difficulties developing and maintaining their social network (e.g. Thorup et al., 2006) and already report significantly smaller social networks than their peers when they present to services (e.g. Minor et al., 2015). Patients experiencing FEP demonstrate lower social functioning than non-clinical control samples and at levels equivalent to individuals with a more enduring course of the illness (Addington, Young & Addington, 2003).

On average, individuals aged between 16–36 years spend 63.5 hours per week engaged in structured activity such as work, education, housework, childcare, leisure and hobbies (Short, 2006). Significantly less time spent in meaningful activity (as measured by the Time Use Questionnaire (TUS; Short, 2006)) is reported by individuals after a FEP compared to the general population, with most reporting less than 45 hours a week (Hodgekins et al., 2015b).

Rates of unemployment among FEP groups range from 13% to 55% (e.g. Rinaldi, Killackey, Smith, Shepherd, Singh & Craig, 2010), despite many patients saying that they want to work (Iyer, Mangala, Anitha, Thara & Malla, 2011). Around 50% of people with psychosis are unemployed by the time they present to services (e.g. Cotton et al., 2017). Recent UK EIPN Access and Waiting Time Standard data (2017–2018) report 58% of individuals are not in education, employment or training (NEET) at initial EIP service assessment and only 22% receive a vocational intervention while in the care of EIP services. Estimates suggest that only 10–20% will return to competitive employment (e.g. Fowler et al., 2009a). Unsurprisingly, the impact on the economy as a consequence is considerable, with a significant proportion of individuals remaining financially dependent on the state for years following a FEP (e.g. Rosenheck et al., 2017a).

Social disability observed after a FEP can risk becoming stable and enduring (clinical stages 3c and 4; see Fusar-Poli et al., 2017; see Table 1.1) with initial poor social outcomes being closely associated with long-term social disability (e.g. Carpenter & Strauss, 1991). Indeed, many individuals will continue to struggle to achieve life milestones, suffer disruption in social roles and remain dependent on their parents (Lenior et al., 2001; Wiersma et al., 2000).

Despite such concerning findings, treatment approaches to psychosis have primarily focused on reducing symptoms; based on assumptions that once symptoms have resolved, SR will naturally improve. However, this is not as straightforward as originally was thought.

The relationship between social and symptomatic recovery after psychosis

Chapter 2 argued that symptomatic, social and personal recovery are measurable concepts, and only by understanding their distinct and relative influence on adjustment and adaptation to psychosis can we deliver the best EIP care. Given the rich and complex nature of this interaction (Windell, Norman & Mall, 2012), emphasis on any one domain without consideration of the others seems counter-productive to intervention.

When levels of social functioning are included alongside symptomatic outcomes, rates of (clinical) recovery rarely reach above 40% (Lally et al., 2017) and can be as low as 13% (Jääskeläinen et al., 2013). Whereas remission criteria is often met at increased rates (58%; Lally et al., 2017), SR is often more delayed and difficult to achieve (Álvarez-Jiménez et al., 2012b). Symptomatic recovery and associated positive outcomes (e.g. reduced hospitalisations and relapses) are not necessarily translated into SR. Symptom remission is more easily attainable than SR, but achieving both is more difficult again (Wunderink, Sytema, Nienhuis & Wiersma, 2009). Conversely, many individuals can retain the ability to function while still symptomatic (Albert et al., 2011), suggesting that these outcomes have a degree of independence. Albert et al. (2011) note that almost a third of their FEP sample were studying or employed after five years. Interestingly, almost a quarter of these individuals continued to experience symptoms. Assessment of symptoms without acknowledging social and occupational functioning, then, may not be a reliable indicator of recovery at any given point in time. Although long-term remission and recovery rates in FEP are more favourable than previously assumed (Lally et al., 2017), increased focus on SR may be particularly important for individuals experiencing psychosis in the long term.

Álvarez-Jiménez et al. (2012b) provide strong evidence for a bi-directional relationship between symptomatic and functional (social) recovery. Patients were assessed at eight months, 14 months and 7.5 years following a FEP. After 7.5 years, 26% of the sample met the criteria for full functional recovery.[3] Analysis of predictors at baseline and thereon yielded a crucial finding. Symptom remission at eight months predicted full functional recovery at 14 months. However, symptom remission at 14 months *did not* predict full functional recovery at 7.5 years. Instead, it was *only* social and vocational recovery at 14 months that predicted full functional recovery at 7.5 years, alongside remission of negative symptoms. Furthermore, 61% of the patients attaining full recovery had not been taking antipsychotics for two years preceding the 7.5 year follow-up. This suggests that SR alone may be able to support full recovery after initial antipsychotic treatment. It also has important implications for EIP in that the 'critical period' (Birchwood, Todd & Jackson, 1998) is perhaps even more 'critical' than originally thought in terms of sustaining long-term recovery. Interventions aimed at early SR (see Chapter 6) may prove crucial in ameliorating or even preventing chronic psychosis and long-term disability.

That SR can be attained for some in the absence of symptom improvements suggests adequate social and occupational functioning has a protective role and that only with SR can 'full' (i.e. symptomatic and functional) recovery be achieved. It is argued therefore, that SR outcomes could be a core indicator, if not *the* indicator, of the success of any form of treatment for psychosis (Priebe, 2007). Optimising SR following a FEP and monitoring engagement in meaningful social and occupational activity may prove to be a better indicator of a 'good outcome' than symptoms alone. Moreover, attention to SR has been identified as a primary aim of UK mental health policy (Department of Health, 2001) and a new key National Standard in EIP (NICE, 2016).

Understanding the factors that might underlie, predict and influence the process of SR following FEP, particularly those factors that are malleable, may enhance targeted psychosocial and vocational interventions and improve outcomes (Griffiths et al., 2018). The remainder of this chapter will explore risk factors associated with poor SR, the routes to social disability following FEP, and discuss why some individuals demonstrate good social outcomes while others do not. Guidance as to how EIP clinicians can apply this understanding to better identify individuals at higher risk of delayed, or arrested SR, will then be provided.

Factors determining SR

Why do some people recover after a FEP when others do not? What determines a better outcome? To answer these questions, researchers have used statistical methods to explore the variance in outcome after psychosis. Findings have helped pinpoint key predictors of recovery. We anticipate that these predictors can be used in EIP services to better identify those individuals who might be at a higher risk of poor SR following FEP.

Despite wide variations in definitions, methodology, measurement, and follow-up periods, studies attempting to identify predictors of clinical recovery in FEP have revealed strong predictors of SR too (e.g. Albert et al., 2011; Austin et al., 2013; Verma, Subramaniam, Abdin, Poon & Chong, 2012). For brevity, we have focused on those that have attempted to identify predictors of SR as the primary outcome of interest (see Table 5.1). Variables are categorised as demographic, pre-morbid,[4] baseline and clinical and organised in terms of how they relate to favourable and unfavourable SR outcomes and with reference to clinical stage of recovery (Fusar-Poli et al., 2017).

Factors that relate the strongest and most consistently to poor SR are poor pre-morbid functioning, longer DUP and negative symptoms. Studies demonstrated that these variables remain influential even when controlling for other factors (e.g. cognitive functioning). Aspects of neuropsychological functioning have also been tested as predictors of SR, but outcomes are varied. Interpretation is difficult due to extensive methodological variability, cognitive domains tested and possible effects of symptoms and medication on performance (Állott, Liu, Proffitt & Killackey, 2011). It may be more useful to examine and measure separate and specific cognitive domains, as different areas of SR may be associated with different cognitive factors (Fett, Viechtbauer, Penn, van Os & Krabbendam, 2011).

Table 5.1 Variables that are predictive or strongly associated with SR outcomes in FEP

SR outcome	Clinical stage	Demographic	Variables		
			Premorbid	Baseline	Clinical
Favourable	2	Female (Santesteban-Echarri et al., 2017)	Good educational attainment (Santesteban-Echarri et al., 2017; Siegel et al., 2006) Adjustment/better general functioning (Santesteban-Echarri et al., 2017) Work history (Santesteban-Echarri et al. 2017) Higher IQ (Leeson et al., 2009; Lucas et al., 2008)	Lower levels of negative symptoms (Lucas et al., 2008; Meng et al., 2006; Milev et al., 2005; Gee et al., 2016a)	Shorter DUP (Santesteban-Echarri et al., 2017; Cotton et al., 2017) Early remission of positive and negative symptoms (Santesteban-Echarri et al., 2017) Early reduction of negative symptoms (Cassidy et al. 2010; Gee et al., 2016a) Adherent to treatment (Cotton et al., 2017) Increased attention (Milev et al., 2005; Keshavan et al., 2003; Santesteban-Echarri et al., 2017) Processing speed and verbal fluency/language (Santesteban-Echarri et al., 2017) Better verbal and working memory (Keshavan et al., 2003; Lucas et al., 2008; Santesteban-Echarri et al., 2017)

Less favourable	3a or 3b	Male (e.g., Hodgekins et al. 2015a; Ayesa-Arriola et al. 2013; Gee et al., 2016a).	Poor functioning (Simonsen et al., 2007; Lucas et al., 2008, Cotton et al., 2006, Cotton et al., 2017; Hodgekins et al., 2015a; González-Blanch et al., 2010) Fewer years in education (Ayesa-Arriola et al., 2013; Cotton et al., 2017) Poor social functioning (Ayesa-Arriola et al., 2013) Forensic history (Cotton et al., 2017) Childhood trauma (Stain et al., 2013)	Poor functioning (Cotton et al., 2017) Higher levels of negative symptoms (Gee et al., 2016a; Hodgekins et al., 2015a; Siegel et al., 2006) Substance use (Cotton et al., 2017) Less insight (Cotton et al., 2017)	Younger age of onset (Hodgekins et al., 2015a) Longer DUP (Keshavan et al., 2003; Saravanan et al., 2010; Harrigan et al., 2003; Barnes et al., 2008, Cotton et al., 2017; González-Blanch et al., 2010; Norman et al., 2007) Longer DUI (Santesteban-Echarri et al., 2017) Longer duration of active psychotic symptoms after treatment initiation (Pelayo-Terán et al., 2018) Positive and negative symptoms (González-Blanch et al., 2010) Slower processing speed (Ayesa-Arriola et al., 2013) Cognitive (dys)function (e.g., Ayesa-Arriola et al., 2013; González-Blanch et al., 2010; Milev et al., 2005; Yamazawa et al., 2008)
Unfavourable	3c or 4	Male	Psychosocial disability (e.g., Häfner et al., 1999)	Psychosocial disability (Tandberg et al., 2012)	High levels of stable, severe negative symptoms (Gee et al., 2016a) Apathy (Evensen et al., 2012a)

Implementing the evidence into practice

Table 5.1 indicates that in practice, there are individuals who, due to the presence of specific socio-demographic and clinical characteristics, are already at a disadvantage in terms of making social and occupational gains. Collating a detailed social, educational and occupational history as soon as possible to identify risk factors for social disability is important. Table 5.2 has been developed from data presented in Table 5.1 to provide a checklist of variables that may place an individual at higher risk of impaired SR following a FEP at baseline, and after 12–18 months. The latter time point is selected, given evidence that SR at 14 months is predictive of longer-term functioning (Álvarez-Jiménez et al., 2012b). Specific asessment tools may be administered at this stage (see Appendix 2) and some useful examples are provided.

Using this checklist, or similar, in EIP services may promote earlier identification of high-risk individuals and offer increased opportunity for long-term treatment planning and tailored SR interventions. Raising awareness of the above factors with all clinicians involved in receiving and assessing new EIP referrals will aid this process.

Caution is advised regarding the risk of making false negatives or false positives in prognostic prediction. Factors associated with favourable outcome cannot always guarantee a good SR and it should not be assumed that the presence of protective baseline indicators negates the need for SR interventions. Likewise, it may be easier to predict unfavourable over favourable outcomes (Díaz et al., 2013). However, there may well be other unknown, directly and indirectly associated protective factors exhibited by high-risk individuals which will affect prognosis. Moreover, the level of risk is not 'set in stone' and fostering a sense of hope, mastery and agency over change is vitally important. Finally, SR is not a stable process, and so timing and initiation of any interventions must reflect this.

Trajectories of SR

EIP clinicians recognise that psychosis is unique to each individual (Chapter 1). This is acknowledged in the early literature, with studies dating back to the 1970s already identifying subgroups of individuals exhibiting different symptom profiles (Strauss & Carpenter, 1977). Indeed, in Lappin et al.'s (2018) 10-year follow-up study, one in eight individuals with FEP (12.5%) recovered early and did not experience a recurrent psychotic episode. Consequently, different types of symptomatic outcome have prompted more targeted interventions for symptomatic recovery (e.g. Gaynor, Dooley, Lawlor, Lawoyin & O'Callaghan, 2011). In contrast, SR following a FEP still tends to be conceptualised as a homogeneous construct. For example, studies have compared patient groups with non-patient samples as an entirety or identified predictors by calculating group means of scores on measures of social functioning. This approach assumes that

Table 5.2 Checklist of factors associated with poor SR following FEP

At baseline/initial EIP assessment	Example(s) of assessment tool (see Appendix 2)	Present (yes/no?) or score
Male	–	
Young age of onset	–	
Longer DUP: (>6-months) (>12-months) (>24-months)	–	
Poor premorbid educational functioning (e.g., did not finish/do well in secondary school)	PAS	
Poor premorbid social functioning (e.g., few friends)	PAS	
Poor premorbid occupational functioning (e.g., did not work/study following school)	PAS	
Lower baseline levels of functioning (e.g., not working or studying)	GAF:D/WASAS/SOFAS/FESFS/TUS	
Poor current social support (e.g., few friends)	FESFS	
High levels of negative symptoms	PANSS	
AT 12–14 MONTHS AFTER ENTRY TO EIP		
Persistent symptoms (especially negative symptoms)	PANSS	
Poor concordance	–	
Poor response to medication	–	
Persistently poor social and occupational functioning	GAF:D/WASAS/SOFAS/FESFS	
Limited time spent in meaningful activity (weekly)	TUS	

individuals come from a single population, and that predictor variables influence each member of the population in the same way.

Table 5.1 highlights how the FEP population comprises subgroups reporting different symptom profiles, who present to EIP services with different baseline levels of social and occupational functioning. Additional evidence suggests that some predictor variables then impact in different ways to influence recovery pathways. This is usefully illustrated by the findings of three studies reporting trajectories of SR following FEP (Albert et al., 2011; Cotton et al., 2017; Hodgekins et al., 2015a). Despite variations in measures, definitions of SR and the length of the follow-up period, there is an overlap between the SR outcome pathways identified in each study (see Table 5.3). We have tentatively attempted to map outcome onto hypothetical clinical stage to define three broad trajectories of SR after psychosis to inform our ability to identify those most in need in EIP services.

1 Good/favourable outcome: low risk of social disability

First, there appears to be a group of individuals who will not experience a decline in social/occupational functioning following a FEP, or, if they do, this will be brief (clinical stage 2). Indeed, recent studies report around 12–15% of FEP patients will only have one episode (Álvarez-Jiménez et al., 2012b; Gaebel & Riesbeck, 2014; Lappin et al., 2018). Albert et al. defined this group as achieving 'early stable' recovery, Hodgekins et al. (2015a) characterised this as attaining ≥45 hours week engaged in meaningful activity, and by Cotton et al. it was categorised as acquiring good vocational/occupational status. Albert et al. (2011) report predictors for good outcome as including female sex, younger age, growing up with both parents, pre-morbid social skills and less severe negative symptoms at baseline. Apparently, outcomes reported for these individuals were so distinctly better that the authors suggest it should have been obvious who these individuals were from the outset.

2 Less favourable outcome: moderate risk of social disability

The second group may experience 'early unstable' or 'late' SR after a FEP (Albert et al., 2011). SR might be delayed, or changeable and fluctuating, with individuals obtaining good SR at some time points after FEP but not at others (clinical stage 3a or 3b).

3 Unfavourable outcome: high risk of social disability

Finally, there seems to be a third cohort of individuals who do not achieve SR after a FEP (clinical stage 3c or 4). For this group, functioning might decline after FEP and not be regained and/or they might present as moderately or

Table 5.3 Studies reporting trajectories of SR following FEP

Study	Sample	Definition of SR	Length of follow-up	% of patients categorised at follow-up according to clinical stage		
				2	3a and 3b	3, 3c and 4
Albert et al., (2011)	N = 255	Stable remission for 2 years; not hospitalised/lived in a supported housing facility during previous 2 years; GAF-D >60; employed/studying	5 years	4	13.7*	–
Hodgekins et al. (2015a)	N = 764	Average weekly hours of structured activity over preceding month >45 hours indicative of poor social recovery	12 months	33.6**	–	66.3
Cotton et al. (2017)	N = 661	Vocational/occupational status categorised as 'good' (employed, homemaker, volunteering or studying), or 'poor' (on psychiatric leave or unemployed) through retrospective audit of medical files	18 months	30.4	–	55.6***

Notes
* Early unstable recovery' group + 'Late recovery' group.
** 'High decreasing' activity group + 'Moderate increasing activity' group.
*** 'Stable poor status' group + 'Decline in functional status' group.

severely socially disabled at baseline or before (clinical stage 1) at levels that then remain stable over time. Factors predicting the latter echo those found previously in the literature, namely, lower pre-morbid levels of education, lower pre-morbid scores on the Global Assessment of Functioning Scale (GAF; Hall, 1995), longer DUP (Cotton et al., 2017), male gender, poor adolescent pre-morbid functioning and high baseline negative symptoms (Hodgekins et al., 2015a). Further evidence for the influence of negative symptoms on recovery trajectory is reported by Gee et al. (2016a). Those in their sample who followed a trajectory characterised by high negative symptoms at baseline, regardless of subsequent remission or not, were less likely to have achieved SR at 12 months. These findings emphasise the importance of screening (Table 5.2) for negative symptoms early as a potential risk factor for poor SR.

Observations of heterogeneity in SR outcome raise important issues for treating FEP, in that delivering a 'one-size-fits-all' approach seems a clumsy response. Calls for more exploration of SR pathways are furthering our understanding of the factors shaping SR (Malla & Payne, 2005). Indeed, as the body of research evaluating the effectiveness of EIP increases (see Chapter 1), there is growing consensus to adopt clinically stratified treatment approaches according to the factors that are more strongly associated with relapse and treatment resistance (McGorry, 2011). This is with a view to offering co-ordinated, evidence-based, pre-emptive interventions to those at higher risk early on, as indicated by Fusar-Poli et al.'s (2017) staging model of treatment (see Table 1.1). We propose that this idea can be explicitly applied to SR, whereby patients are initially identified, and streamed according to risk of social disability. Mueser et al. (2017) recognise the importance of identifying psychosocial interventions within such a model, presumably as tailored interventions can then be offered with an assertiveness and intensity appropriate to the level of need. We will return to this recommendation in Chapter 6.

The following two case studies illustrate how, without an awareness of the evidence base, clinicians might risk adopting a generic approach to SR in FEP. We will return to the case studies later in the chapter to describe how we might understand on an individualised level, both patients' struggle to obtain 'good' SR after FEP.

Case study 5.1 Jade

Jade is withdrawn and isolative. Activity is limited to surfing the internet. She has gained excessive weight since being commenced on medication and her self-care can be poor. She avoids others, struggles to make eye contact, doesn't talk much, and conversations are ended quickly. She refuses to meet other members of the team or talk about her experiences of psychosis. She is reluctant to help around the house and on the rare occasions she does go out, is reliant on family accompanying her. Her time engaged in meaningful activity is less than 30 hours a week.

Background

Jade has always been shy. She grew up in rural community, was in the top sets at school and had a close group of friends. Her family moved to the city when she was 17 and she felt under pressure to form relationships with new peers. Another student seemed friendly and he became her first boyfriend. After a few months she discovered on social media that he had been unfaithful. She felt humiliated. She became depressed, withdrawn and assignments became a struggle. She stopped socialising and had little to occupy her spare time. She became increasingly preoc-cupied with her ex and began following him and his new girlfriend online, using aliases to make contact. She started stalking him and harassing his family. Her behaviour became increasingly erratic and disinhibited. She engaged in impulsive sexual encounters with men she had only just met. She became highly elated in mood, rude and irritable towards her family. She struggled to sleep and lost weight. She started publishing bizarre, grandiose blogs about herself online which people at college read. She experienced ideas of reference from the computer and music channels. She applied for several credit cards and spent large amounts of money over a short space of time. She eventually had a brief admission to hospital after becoming aggressive towards her younger brother.

Progress with EIP services

Jade's symptoms remitted swiftly, but she seemed flat in mood, lacked energy, motivation and described little enjoyment in activity. After discharge from hospital, her parents were keen for her to return to her studies or get a job to help them pay back the debts she had accumulated. They encouraged her to attend family events, and she felt pressurised to socialise. Her mother often invited people over to the house without telling her in order to 'get her used to making friends again'. Jade used her phone in company as a means of avoiding interaction which annoyed her mother. She was embarrassed at the thought of bumping into anyone from college. Medication calmed her but she felt 'slowed down' and feared others noticed this when she talked. She imagined herself looking twitchy and awkward, and assumed others would judge this to be strange and feel uncomfortable with her. Her parents' believed that if she was not 'back to normal soon' she would be judged as 'crazy' or 'slow'. She refused to contact old friends from home, saying that they had 'all moved on' and she was too embarrassed about experiencing a FEP.

Case study 5.2 Alex

Alex plays mostly on his games console, and occasionally goes out at night, although he avoids saying where to and what he does. His conversation is restricted and lacking in spontaneity, he gives minimal responses to most questions and rarely initiates conversation. His responses are short, conveying little information. Visits from his CPN are brief. Alex demonstrates little insight into his experiences.

His mother takes responsibility for many aspects of his routine activities (e.g. preparing meals, managing his finances, washing his clothes, etc.) but he says he can take his medication without prompting. He doesn't want any help from the team. His time engaged in meaningful activity is less than 20 hours a week.

Background

According to his parents, Alex was a 'disruptive and naughty' child with few friends. He struggled at school. A teacher reported that he had 'behavioural issues' and possibly a mild learning difficulty. He was arrested by police for buying cannabis at age 13 and reported that his dad 'beat him up' when he found out. Alex was expelled from school with no qualifications. He had contact with the police for minor offences throughout his teens and they would regularly come to the house. This was difficult for his mother, who often suspected the family was 'talked about' by the local community. His cannabis use gradually increased over time and he became more withdrawn and less motivated. After a fight with a local drug dealer, he began carrying knives in self-defence. He stopped watching TV, slept less and started washing and bathing excessively without explanation. He only trusted his family. He developed paranoid, persecutory ideas about being watched and feared the police were conspiring to frame him, abduct and harm him. He started experiencing vicious, commanding voices and was terrified. Due to concerns he might hurt himself, he eventually had to be restrained and admitted to a psychiatric intensive care unit with police support out of area. He initially developed severe side effects to antipsychotic medication. This was changed a number of times and it took some time for him to recover symptomatically enough to be discharged home.

Progress with EIP services

Alex immediately stopped using cannabis and stated he would never use it again. Over the next two years he presented as mostly withdrawn, flat in mood and engaged superficially with the team. When asked, he always said he felt 'fine'. He interacted little with his family, never communicated his needs, tended not to initiate conversation with staff or disclose much detail of his experiences even when prompted. He sometimes muttered to himself. He did not express any particular motivation to work or resume education. On one occasion, he said he intended to go to college at some point in the future but made no progress towards this. Due to his restricted communication it was difficult to ascertain how he spent his time. Although his CPN was frustrated, Alex's parents denied any concerns as long as he was 'not mixing with the wrong crowd', and Alex himself never seemed distressed, anxious or low.

Both Alex and Jade are experiencing delayed SR. Following psychosis, both present with a significant reduction in the quality and quantity of meaningful activity they engage in. They demonstrate limited functioning and a dependency on family to support them. Both are highly avoidant. Social networks are severely limited and they are reluctant to engage with services. Given the similarities between how Jade and Alex present, it would seem reasonable, on face value, to adopt a similar approach with both to address SR. However, detailed consideration of the individual factors that might underlie the *reasons* for SR delay may actually call for very different interventions.

Exploring causes of social disability following psychosis is important to identify mechanisms of change and develop effective interventions. Identification of predictors of SR following FEP does not explain why or how they exert their impact. Research suggests that different factors present both before and after the onset of psychosis might obstruct or facilitate SR in different ways for different individuals. Findings are summarised in Table 5.4. Gaining an understanding of the routes to social disability in this way provides opportunity for focused intervention which may well then have a favourable impact on outcome.

Implementing the evidence into practice

To develop an integrated package of intervention for SR, the entire MDT should be involved in the process of understanding what needs to be targeted and why. We emphasise a patient-centred approach to this (see also Chapter 12).

Fowler et al. (2013) suggest that it is important to consider the meaning of psychosis to the person in the context of their personal recovery (Chapter 7). Naturally, people will have developed idiosyncratic understandings about what it means to have experienced psychosis, take medication, undergo hospitalisation and be under the care of mental health services. Such ideas can elicit a range of emotions. For example, an individual who believes people with psychosis are violent may avoid social situations in case they become angry. Or, for those who fear relapse, beliefs may develop about factors associated with the risk of becoming unwell; such as particular environments, or internal states and images (Clark & Beck, 2011). Behavioural avoidance might be obvious, but there may also be avoidance of cognition, emotional states and feelings. Fowler et al. (2013) explicitly propose that presentations defining social disability (e.g. low motivation, avolition, anhedonia) actually arise as cognitive and emotional experiential avoidance. In short, avoidant behaviour and withdrawal are conceptualised as safety behaviours to manage anxiety and psychotic symptoms. Initially protective patterns of social avoidance may well have longer-term negative consequences for SR.

In summary, patients experiencing delayed SR exhibit common presentations manifesting as social withdrawal, inactivity and superficial or minimal engagement in meaningful activity. However, the reasons for SR delay for any one individual arise from a complex interplay of factors that exert an influence before the onset of psychosis and at different stages of recovery. Although the outcome might look similar across patients who are struggling, the underlying drivers as to *why* each individual might be struggling are very different. This is important because homogeneity in clinical presentation risks homogeneity in treatment approach. We attempt to illustrate this further by returning to Jade and Alex as case examples.

Table 5.4 Routes to favourable/unfavourable SR after psychosis

Factor associated with SR outcomes	Direction of outcome	Proposed means of obstructing/facilitating SR
Male gender	Unfavourable	• Functioning lower before (Morgan et al., 2008) and at presentation to EIP services (Cotton et al., 2009). • Higher levels of negative symptoms and rates of substance misuse negatively affect social functioning (Thorup et al., 2007).
Female gender	Favourable	• Present with FEP later thus reducing disruption of social/occupational skill development. • Larger social networks, more likely to be in relationship so less vulnerable to social isolation (Thorup et al., 2007). • More likely to be diagnosed with affective psychosis (e.g., Køster et al., 2008) which is associated with better SR (Macmillan et al., 2007).
Younger age of onset (Häfiner & an der Heiden, 1999)	Unfavourable	• Disruption of critical developmental stage(s) (e.g., identity formation, development of relationships, beginning academic/work career) thus affecting social and interpersonal trajectories (McGorry et al., 2008)
Untreated psychosis (e.g., Penn et al., 2005)	Unfavourable	• Impairs cognitive ability by impacting on underlying neurological and psychological processes (Marshall et al., 2005). • Increases isolation, unemployment, stigma and depression in critical period following FEP.
Poor premorbid functioning (Table 1.1 clinical stage 1)	Unfavourable	• Adjusting to FEP or prodromal phase leads to further decline (Harvey & Bellack, 2009). • High levels of social exclusion already, therefore more challenging to engage in treatment.

		• Impaired development of important processes and unique social demands of adolescence (e.g., individuation, separation, development of interpersonal skills and formation of identity. Reduces resilience/increases vulnerability when FEP develops (Harrop & Trower, 2001). • Adaptation after FEP harder to cope with (Gumley & Schwannauer, 2006). • Associated with more negative symptoms (see below) (MacBeth & Gumley, 2008).
Good premorbid functioning	Favourable	• Protects against impact of psychosis through increased social competence (Mueser et al., 1990). • Academic achievement predicts good social recovery. Elicits sense of mastery that reduces negative impact of FEP on self-esteem/self-worth (Romm et al., 2011).
Cognitive deficits	Unfavourable	• Social difficulties before or after FEP linked to cognitive deficits (e.g., lower IQ; Leeson et al., 2009). • Reduce adaptive skills required for social/occupational functioning including attention, working memory, planning, problem-solving and social cognition (Green, 1996).
Early adverse life experiences (e.g., abuse, neglect, separation). See Chapter 8.	Unfavourable (Stain et al., 2013)	• Associated with attachment difficulties, brain development and mentalisation skills (MacBeth et al., 2011). Complex interaction occurs between neurological anomalies and interpersonal difficulties. Latter maintained by maladaptive coping strategies (e.g., avoidance) leading to subsequent social/occupational impairments.

continued

Table 5.4 Continued

Factor associated with SR outcomes	Direction of outcome	Proposed means of obstructing/facilitating SR
Positive symptoms	Potentially unfavourable. However, symptomatic and functional recovery relatively independent, (e.g., Albert et al., 2011) and rates of symptomatic recovery following a FEP reliably higher than rates of social recovery (Lally et al., 2017).	• Avoiding and withdrawing from work/education and others to cope with aversive states, environmental salience, anomalous experiences etc. (Fowler et al., 2013). • Increased activity increases symptoms (Hogarty et al., 1997) leading others to discourage engagement in activity for fear of this. • Side-effects of antipsychotic medication impact upon the physical ability to engage in more occupation (see Chapter 3).
Negative symptoms (see Ventura et al., 2009, for a review)	Unfavourable, major predictor of poor functioning in FEP (e.g., Galderisi et al., 2013), with poorer SR linked to more severe symptoms (e.g., Gee et al., 2016a).	• Apathy and flat affect (Evensen., et al., 2012a; 2012b) associated: • indirectly; as possible markers of a more profound and chronic psychotic illness. • directly; as flattened affect and impaired social communication impacts on forming/maintaining relationships while apathy reduces motivation and goal directed behaviour. Circular problem develops with latter; i.e., before any intervention a collaborative goal must be established (ideally with active involvement from the patient). Lack of goal-directed behaviour and amotivation then directly obstructs process of intervention from outset. • Patient awareness of amotivation may cause them to view life situation less favourably (Evensen et al., 2012a).
Psychological distress; e.g., depression (Sonmez et al., 2013), low self-esteem (Gureje et al., 2004) and social anxiety (Michail, 2013).	Unfavourable	• High rates of depression, social anxiety and trauma can occur following FEP (Birchwood, 2003; Michail, 2013). • Depression associated with lower functioning (Sonmez et al., 2013), lower levels of close friendships and engagement with recreational activities (Joseph et al., 2017) and impacts upon ability to recover social and vocational roles (Windell et al., 2012).

- Negative beliefs about oneself (e.g., 'I am mad/have failed'), others (e.g., 'will reject me/think I'm crazy'), psychosis (e.g., 'stress will cause voices') and the world (e.g., 'is dangerous') develop following FEP. Attempts to reduce associated negative emotions through behavioural patterns of social and occupational avoidance protects from confirming beliefs, but distress remains as disconfirmation prevented.
- FEP causes trauma (see Chapter 8) and includes social and occupational avoidance as a symptom.

Delayed social recovery regardless of presence or absence of positive symptoms (Álvarez-Jiménez et al., 2012b)

Unfavourable

- Work, daily reward, a sense of purpose and secure relationships identified as underlying resilience in mental health (Geschwind et al., 2010; Rutten et al., 2013) and may provide a buffer during periods of stress and vulnerability to relapse.
- Adverse incentives of disability payments, identified as a barrier to employment in schizophrenia (Rosenheck et al., 2006).
- Clinicians focus on resolving symptoms first in the acute stage of psychosis as may be more malleable to treatment.

Reduced social network (Evert et al., 2003).

Unfavourable

- Poorer occupational/vocational functioning may lead to a loss of supportive relationships, or more extensive social networks may allow better occupational and vocational adjustment.
- Individuals exhibiting high social disability harder to engage with and more likely to dis-engage from services. Staff struggle to build rapport with those who already feel socially excluded, thus reducing opportunity for timely intervention and increasing risk of further social decline.

continued

Table 5.4 Continued

Factor associated with SR outcomes	Direction of outcome	Proposed means of obstructing/facilitating SR
Criticism, hostility and emotional over-involvement in staff (e.g., Berry et al., 2011) and relatives (Leff & Vaughn, 1985).	Unfavourable	• Experiences perceived to be under patient's control evoke more hostility and criticism than those attributed to uncontrollable factors (Berry et al., 2011). Others less tolerant of inactivity because it is viewed as intentional, whereas behavioural excesses (e.g., responding to unseen stimuli) more easily recognised as symptoms of mental illness (Weisman et al., 1998). • Less-qualified staff express higher levels of criticism towards patients with schizophrenia than those more experienced (Van Humbeeck et al., 2002). Those with less knowledge of psychosis less likely to attribute poor SR to factors beyond the patient's control. • Stigma internalised after FEP leads to a sense of external shame, anger and anxiety (Birchwood, et al., 2007) and subsequent social avoidance.

Case study 5.3 Jade

Barriers to SR for Jade included anxiety-related avoidance following assumptions that she was, or would be, perceived negatively. She was ashamed about how she behaved when unwell so she avoided those who had been witness to this and any reminders of what happened. Monitoring her performance in social situations supported assumptions that others would judge or had judged her negatively. For example, focusing on the speed she thought she talked during conversations compromised her attention to content of discussions, thus confirming ideas that her thinking was delayed. The physical symptoms of anxiety seized her attention in a similar way and supported her predictions about appearing awkward. Weight gain added to fears about attracting negative attention from others, and her sedentary lifestyle offered little opportunity for her to address this through exercise.

Avoidance had begun as a means of coping, as it helped protect Jade from unpleasant feelings of anxiety. However, it prevented any disconfirmation of the unhelpful assumptions she had, thus perpetuating distress and low self-esteem. Jade's avoidant behaviour also offered diminished opportunity for pleasure, reward or sense of accomplishment which endorsed beliefs she held about failure and loss. This elevated her risk of developing depression and, in turn, the risk of functional decline. Continued avoidance reduced her general tolerance for anxiety and made it increasingly difficult for her to socialise as time went on. In addition, the presence of some early negative symptoms at the referral stage to EIP services were noted, which again predicted longer-term risk of poor SR.

Criticism expressed by Jade's parents increased her tendency to withdraw from others, including the team. Her parents sometimes viewed her inactivity as intentional and placed additional pressure on her to make changes. Psychosis occurred at a time when Jade was embarking on a new stage in her life. This included adjusting to urban living and higher education, and forming romantic relationships. Perceptions that she had failed to cope with these demands created doubts about any future ability to achieve, function independently and maintain relationships. Awareness of old friends making progress in their lives confirmed these negative views of herself. As a consequence, Jade had decided not to risk engaging with previously held goals again for fear of failure once more.

Case study 5.4 Alex

The delay in Alex's SR was linked to very different factors. First, there were a number of pre-morbid, prognostic indicators present that placed him at a higher risk of poor SR. Male gender, experiencing a FEP younger, delayed access to treatment and poor educational attainment and social/occupational functioning prior to becoming unwell were all highlighted. Excessive cannabis use in his teens had reduced the opportunity for him to develop the social, occupational and problem-solving skills that could have helped him adjust to a FEP. Age-appropriate opportunity to develop his daily living skills were further curtailed by the hospital admission, where much of his self-care was directed by ward staff. His mother then took on this role when he returned home. Poor problem-solving, in addition to reduced and restricted communication, were discussed by the team. It was acknowledged that an underlying impairment in communication could make it more difficult for Alex to articulate SR goals in that it was easier for him to verbally deny any needs than try to express them. Ideas as to causes included an underlying neurodevelopmental disorder (see Chapter 10) which could pose additional, pre-existing challenges for him in terms of functioning. Other ideas included the presence of negative symptoms and/or thought disorder. The team recognised the need for extended assessment and that negative symptoms were a major predictor of poor SR.

The experience of psychosis itself was also important to consider at an individual level for Alex. He had been highly distressed by his symptoms (that his life was in danger), and his experience of treatment. Trust had not extended beyond family when he was unwell, yet he had spent a considerable amount of time separated from them while in hospital. He had been highly traumatised by what happened, but had had little perceived access to the support he needed at this time. Lack of engagement in conversations about psychosis and minimisation of any problems indicated a fear of illness that was trauma-related (Chapter 8). Symptoms of trauma impeded the recovery process for Alex.

Alex experienced his environment as unpleasantly salient and still harboured some paranoid ideas. His willingness to only go out at night was due to beliefs he would encounter people who would harm him. He also worried that the stress of going out during the day, or restarting cannabis, would trigger hostile and commanding voices. Observations of him muttering to himself supported the idea he was still symptomatic. Given his unpleasant experiences of medication, the team questioned concordance.

Alex's parents were initially content with his situation. They shared his view that over-stimulation through more activity would cause relapse and preferred for him to remain socially isolated to reduce the risk of him engaging in anti-social behaviour. They worried about his safety but were also keen to avoid any external shame associated with a return to his former lifestyle. Absence of encouragement and positive reinforcement from those important to him lowered any sense of self-efficacy or confidence he had about making positive changes.

Finally, the frustration Alex's presentation elicited in staff was important in understanding his case. He asked for nothing from the team, expressed no goals in terms of his recovery, his parents denied any concerns and his situation had remained unchanged for over two years. Poor functioning at this point after a FEP is highly predictive of longer-term social disability. Worryingly, however, staff and the team had begun to withdraw, thus creating a potential prognostic barrier to SR for Alex in the future.

In both case examples, avoidance operated as a barrier to SR but the function it served was actually very different for each. In Jade's case, avoidance was an indirect consequence of psychosis, specifically in response to the psychological processes implicated in depression and social anxiety that had arisen secondary to her becoming unwell. SR for Jade was closely related to her personal recovery (see Chapter 7). Conversely, for Alex, avoidance was a direct coping response to psychosis, either through attempts to manage anomalous experiences or reduce the risk of triggering or exacerbating them. SR for Alex was more aligned with symptomatic recovery (Chapters 3 and 4). Exploration of the system and context also revealed a variety of factors that influenced SR for Jade and Alex in very different ways. We will return to these cases in Chapter 6 when we consider intervention.

Monitoring SR outcomes

As discussed in Chapter 2, there is an absence of an absolute definition of SR following psychosis in the literature. However, irrespective of this lack of consensus we still require a workable definition in EIP to guide and effectively implement SR interventions, measure progress and evaluate outcome.

Qualifying SR

Identifying indicators of SR that have already been quantified in the field may help us to settle on our own definition. Obvious objective indicators include employment status, size of social network, relationship status and whether or not the individual lives independently. As outcomes, these can be unequivocally assessed and are relevant and easy to interpret. Employment-related outcomes in particular appeal at service, organisational, public and political levels. However, there are a number of reasons why we should not stop the search here for SR outcomes in FEP.

As discussed in Chapter 1, EIP teams work with people who have experienced a FEP within the three-year 'critical' period (Birchwood et al., 1998). It may be ambitious to anticipate improvement on one or more of these criteria within this time, particularly as SR takes longer (Crumlish et al., 2009) and is harder (Lally et al., 2017). Second, as already discussed, SR following FEP is not a homogeneous construct. A proportion of this population will already be working and living without support, thus making this an indicator for SR meaningless. In contrast, due to young age or poor pre-morbid functioning, some individuals experiencing a FEP may never have worked or lived independently, so attaining these outcomes within the 'critical' period will be more challenging. Finally, objective indicators cannot take into account cultural factors (Chapter 12), or individual goals and values. For personal or cultural reasons, gaining employment or a partner may be undesired, or even inappropriate for some people. Subjective indicators go some way to address this. However, the range of aspirations, expectations and views of SR from service user perspectives are nuanced, extensive and therefore impossible to fully capture using existing assessment tools.

In summary, although formal vocational activity (e.g. employment) is a key component of SR, there is a need to reflect a broader understanding of occupation (e.g. meaningful economically, culturally or socially valued activity) when establishing outcome (Fowler et al., 2009b). Observable, quantifiable efforts on behalf of the service user to engage, increase and sustain time in meaningful activity (including self-care, social and leisure activity) in line with their goals and values following a FEP seems a better indicator of SR and one promoted by researchers and clinicians within EIP (e.g. Fowler et al., 2018). This serves as our working definition of SR in EIP following FEP.[5]

A working definition of SR permits the opportunity for measurement. Popular objective and subjective indicators of the concept of SR have formed the basis for outcome measurement scales, and there are hundreds for psychosis (Burns & Patrick, 2007). Considering how SR has been measured by others will help to guide our own approach to quantifying SR in EIP.

Quantifying SR

From a scientific perspective, absence of a well-defined theoretical model or consistent construct of SR means any psychometric claiming to measure it will always defy assumptions of validity, reliability, objectivity and sensitivity to change. Indeed, there is an absence of adequate assessment of the psychometric properties of many of the SR scales in psychosis (Burns & Patrick, 2007). Strictly speaking, then, one cannot assume that SR outcomes can be truly tested and findings generalised. However, these caveats do not render SR outcome measures as defunct within EIP services. The importance of assessing and optimising SR for a FEP cannot be emphasised enough, regardless of problems with definition and measurement. Consistent, regular means of assessment are essential to monitor the stability of indicators of SR for patients in the absence of fluctuations in symptoms over time.

An overview of popular measures of SR is provided in Appendix 2. Assuming measures are universally agreed within the service, collected as standard practice, and used consistently to allow comparison over time, no one measure is advised over any other and we advise readers to decide which measures of SR might be most useful for their service.

Learning points

- Up to 80% of individuals can experience social disability after a FEP, with only 10–20% returning to competitive employment.
- SR can occur independently of symptomatic recovery but is harder to achieve.
- If symptoms do remit, this must be translated into functional gains otherwise long-term recovery is less likely to occur.
- SR after a FEP is best defined as time spent in meaningful economically, culturally or socially valued activity.
- We can identify who might be at higher risk of poor SR at baseline.

- The way poor SR manifests can seem on a surface level homogeneous across individuals.
- Developing an individualised understanding as to the factors underlying the potential function of inactivity and avoidance of social and occupational pursuits can reveal a far richer and diverse picture.
- Understanding the barriers to SR after a FEP for each individual is key to effective intervention.
- Making efforts to develop a team understanding as to what might be challenging SR on an individual level is not just key in opening avenues for intervention, it fosters empathy alongside hope and optimism for change.

Notes

1 Social roles on the GSDS include: self-care, housekeeping, family relationships, partner relationships, community integration, relationships with peers and vocational role.
2 Components of the SAS include: appropriate role function (e.g. paid employment/ school/homemaker), ability to perform day-to-day tasks unsupervised, reasonable personal appearance and grooming, adequate performance on chores and weekly social interactions with peer(s) outside of family.
3 Comprised of four components: (a) appropriate interpersonal relationships with people outside of family; (b) adequate vocational functioning (paid employment/attending school/efficient homemaker); (c) adequate accomplishment (success in fulfilling chosen role); and (d) regular participation in basic living tasks.
4 Pre-morbid functioning refers to performance in social, interpersonal, school and work domains prior to the onset of psychotic symptoms.
5 Quality of life (QoL) is often included in measures of SR in a FEP and is often measured subjectively. Some definitions of QoL might include levels of functioning and social and material conditions in addition to satisfaction appraisals. In pursuit of our own definition of SR following a FEP, we have chosen not to include experiences of recovery such QoL. We recognise there is considerable overlap (see Chapter 2), however, we suggest such subjective constructs are better encapsulated within the domains of personal recovery (see Chapter 7).

Chapter 6

Treatment approaches to social recovery in first episode psychosis

Introduction

EIP has yielded gains in SR on a range of outcomes compared to treatment as usual in community or stepped down care (Fusar-Poli et al., 2017). But some individuals continue to encounter problems with SR following discharge (Hodgekins et al., 2015a). Rates of 60% of patients not in education, employment or training (NEET) have been reported (Kam, Singh, & Upthegrove, 2015). Even if functioning does improve after EIP, this remains low relative to the general population. For example, EIP patients in Ruggeri et al.'s (2015) study provided a mean Global Assessment of Functioning Scale (GAF; see Appendix 2) score of 63 at follow-up, barely out of the low functioning range of <60. Furthermore, gains made under EIP services diminish in the longer term (Fusar-Poli et al., 2017), with NEET status increasing after discharge (Kam et al., 2015). As already pointed out in Chapter 2, Lally et al. (2017) conclude that although rates of symptomatic recovery have improved over time in the FEP population, rates of 'clinical' or 'full' recovery have not, suggesting that EIP services are potentially failing patients in this regard. New and adapted interventions targeting SR are needed in EIP services to address these shortcomings.

Employment and education

In addition to improved financial standing, work provides a range of benefits following a FEP, including a sense that one is valued and improved self-esteem (Torrey, Mueser, McHugo & Drake, 2000). Disruption to work or leaving education due to a FEP may elicit a sense of demoralisation or shame through unfavourable comparisons with peers (Rooke & Birchwood, 1998). Gaining employment, training or enrolment in education (EET) may protect against self-stigma and raise self-confidence. Work offers a sense of purpose, routine, structure and stimulation possibly missing or lost following a FEP and the working environment provides social opportunities and a way of re-establishing friendships. Work can also have an effect on reducing symptoms (Bond et al., 2001), and FEP patients who are students and/or employed report higher global and social functioning and less depression (Tandberg, Ueland, Andreassen, Sundet & Melle, 2012) than those NEET. Consequently, interventions supporting individuals back into employment after psychosis have received attention.

Historically, vocational rehabilitation for individuals with psychosis involved skills training in settings such as sheltered workshops or units. These initiatives, known as train-place schemes (Corrigan, Mueser, Bond, Drake & Solomon, 2008), taught service users a set of workplace-relevant skills to increase their chances of joining the competitive, employed workforce. However, due to limited success (Bond, 1992), train-place approaches have been superseded by alternative, place-train schemes where functioning in a working role is preferred over employment preparation or developing roles according to ability.

The most empirically validated model of supported employment to date for FEP is Individual Placement and Support (IPS). The approach is fully inclusive; the only requirement is that competitive employment is desired. A further seven key principles are then adhered to (rapid job search, service user choice, integration with employers and mental health teams, delivery by employment specialists, ongoing follow-up support, benefits counselling provision and competitive employment as the primary outcome; see Drake, Bond & Becker, 2012).

Reviews and randomised controlled trials (RCTs) of IPS consistently find that the model increases employment rates significantly from baseline to follow-up compared to standard care in FEP populations (Bond, Drake & Luciano, 2015), and the higher the fidelity to the model, the better the outcomes (Bond et al., 2012).

FEP often occurs between the ages of 16 and 25 so goals of this population often include a wish to complete education in conjunction with employment or as preparation for employment. The IPS model has been adapted to include supported education, in additional to supported employment (Nuechterlein, Subotnik, Turner, Ventura, Becker & Drake, 2008). IPS principles are still adhered to, but focus shifts to enrolment in mainstream education programmes if desired. The impact of IPS-type approaches on education outcomes in FEP is inconsistent. Some studies report no effect (Killackey et al., 2018), whereas others demonstrate success in engaging more individuals in education compared to standard care (Rosenheck et al., 2017b).

Implementing the evidence into practice

We recommend vocational interventions to be routinely offered within EIP and identify IPS as the preferred model, albeit with a number of caveats. Evidence for IPS is likely drawn from samples of highly motivated patients who not only want to work but are prepared to consent to research participation too. Implementing IPS as part of routine care may prove far more challenging (Craig et al., 2014). For example, known social factors can impede employment in individuals with psychosis, such as receipt of disability payments, and the fact that BME patients are less likely to be competitively employed than 'white' patients

(Rosenheck et al., 2006). There is little guidance in the IPS literature as to how teams address these additional challenges to employment.

IPS may help secure employment, but whether it helps people retain jobs has been a more contentious issue (Mueser, Gingerich, Salyers, McGuire, Reyes & Cunningham, 2005) as high drop-out rates have been noted (Bond et al., 1997). Extended follow-up, better reporting of attrition rates and standardisation of the follow-up period is required. Furthermore, many younger patients with FEP may prioritise education over employment, but the evidence base for supported education is less robust and the field currently lacks an agreed model.

IPS is not offered to those uninterested in working. Bond et al. (2008) advise care to achieve a balance between assertively outreaching individuals to encourage work, while respecting the importance of informed and shared decision-making and the right to choose. Interest in work may increase if attention is paid to developing more meaningful career pathways that are not limited to the low paid service sector placements that seem typical of IPS in the UK currently. However, even if this were achieved, IPS may remain most successful for those who are 'clinically recovered' and ready for work. This is only the case for a proportion of patients within a typical EIP service. Moreover, even within the group of IPS-eligible patients, there exists different needs requiring different approaches. Some individuals will be able to obtain employment with little external assistance. For the remainder, employment may be much desired but the individual may have low expectations of success. Accurate identification of who will benefit most from IPS is required. Lower global psychosocial functioning, lower educational attainment and reduced information processing efficiency have been found to indicate need for employment assistance in individuals with psychosis (Waghorn, Hielscher, Saha & McGrath, 2016). Assessing this objectively is important, as often judgements as to suitability for IPS may be made on the client's behalf, frequently by those involved in their care.

Exclusion from IPS due to lack of interest in paid work, or perceptions that the client may not be able to manage should not end efforts to source other job opportunities. Patients can often work in unpaid voluntary positions, acquire short-term 'cash in hand' jobs, be employed unofficially in family businesses or recruited into time-limited, 'one-off' roles, such as assisting at an event. In our experience, it is increasingly common for patients to become involved in work experience or service user movement opportunities offered by the mental health service providing their care. Whether or not such positions provide a stepping-stone to paid employment is unclear, they might nevertheless be valued alternatives to paid work while facilitating confidence and self-perceptions that they are work-ready.

We define SR as observable, quantifiable efforts to engage, increase and sustain time in economically, culturally or socially valued activity (including self-care and leisure) following a FEP (Fowler et al., 2009b). In line with this, patients may have other equally valid goals of SR not associated with work, such as making new friends or going on holiday. Mueser et al. (2017) advise more attention be paid to specific, personal goals related to role functioning as a means of harnessing motivation for vocation. They suggest that the success of IPS could be enhanced by acknowledging the confusion and ambivalence often present following a FEP alongside instilling hope and permitting time for early recovery. Importantly, it must be recognised that clients may also have other, ongoing problems with social functioning that require intervention before they are ready for employment.

Pharmacological interventions

An obvious impediment to SR is the enduring symptoms of psychosis. Antipsychotic medication (AP) remains the mainstay in reducing symptom severity and relapse in FEP (NICE, 2014; Chapter 3). However, there are a limited number of pharmacological trials that report SR outcomes after treatment. They indicate that APs alone fail to improve rates of SR in the long term (Wunderink, Nieboer, Wiersma, Sytema & Nienhuis, 2013).

AP side effects can be a barrier to activity and impede SR. As they are addressed more effectively by second-generation atypical APs (Crossley, Constante, McGuire & Power, 2010), one would expect greater gains in functioning than with conventional medication. However, findings from the schizophrenia literature are variable with regard to the impact of second- versus first-generation APs on quality of life (Jones et al., 2006). Second-generation APs for FEP may be superior to older medications in terms of lower discontinuation rates, improved tolerability (Boter et al., 2009) and side effect profiles (Crossley, et al., 2010), but these benefits do not translate into significant SR (Milev, Ho, Arndt & Andreasen, 2005). There have been some positive effects on psychosocial functioning reported for second-generation depots compared to oral preparations, however (Fu, Turkoz, Walling, Lindenmayer, Schooler & Alphs, 2018). In general, comparison studies measuring the SR benefits of one second-generation AP over another are equivocal (Swartz et al., 2007).

The limited effects of APs on SR may be due to fluctuations in functioning occurring independent of positive symptoms. Reductions in positive symptoms do not necessarily translate into SR and this relationship operates more independently than once assumed (see Chapter 5). Negative symptoms, however, are closely associated and significantly predicative of poorer SR in FEP (Ventura, Hellemann, Thames, Koellner & Nuechterlein, 2009). Unlike positive symptoms, they are not improved substantially by APs (Fusar-Poli et al., 2014; see Chapter 3). In fact, they are the least responsive to medication compared to all other psychotic symptoms (Leucht et al., 1999). Clozapine is the most effective AP in improving negative symptoms and in treatment-resistant psychosis (Fusar-Poli et al., 2014). Clozapine is recommended after two adequate trials of APs, including second-generation ones (Lieberman et al., 2005; see Chapter 3).

Interest has grown in other medications that might better target negative symptoms to improve SR. Correlations between negative symptoms and DUP have led to suggestions that negative symptoms are caused by a neuropathic process that progresses with DUP. Neuroprotection during the early stages of FEP has thus emerged as a treatment target. Minocycline is a broad spectrum tetracyclic antibiotic possessing neuroprotective properties and its use can reduce negative symptoms compared to placebo when added to standard treatment (Chaudhry et al., 2012). Although early trials suggested minocycline had the potential to improve SR outcomes for individuals (Lisiecka et al., 2015), more recent data has shown no effect (Deakin et al., 2018; see Chapter 3).

RCTs of APs may not be of sufficient duration to detect changes in SR domains such as sustained employment, or differences in SR gains between treatment groups. The PSP Scale (see Appendix 2) has been identified as a means of assessing changes in SR due to medication (Burns & Patrick, 2007). However, there remains a need to further develop measures in SR that are appropriate for FEP populations sensitive to the impact of pharmacological treatment.

Precise and sensitive diagnosis of other symptoms in addition to those related to psychosis is important because treatable conditions, such as depression, and AP side effects may underlie problems, such as lack of motivation, and be more of a risk factor for persistent social disability. Reducing extrapyramidal symptoms is associated with gains in quality of life (Swartz et al., 2007) and side effects such as weight gain, daytime sedation and increased sleep may easily be addressed through a review of treatment to reduce interference with functioning (see Chapter 3).

Psychosocial interventions (PSIs)

Social skills training (SST)

Psychosocial difficulties experienced by some individuals with psychosis are posited to relate to reduced social skills. This problem may impact upon SR by undermining patient autonomy, limiting opportunity to achieve personal goals and increasing social withdrawal and risk of isolation; hence they have become popular targets for intervention in schizophrenia. SST aims to improve SR through enhancing social competence, which is based on a distinct set of component skills roughly divided into two sets: expressive skills and receptive skills. SST varies between settings in terms of length of intervention, content and focus but most programmes implement behavioural techniques (e.g. role modelling, positive reinforcement, corrective feedback) on social performance. Skills are then practised in the 'real-life' environment to generalise gains made within the community (see Bellack, Mueser, Gingerich & Agresta, 2013, for a guide).

Although some studies provide support for the effectiveness of SST on SR outcomes in schizophrenia, other findings have not found an advantage of SST over standard care and note limited generalisability to everyday living (see NICE, 2014). The larger effects demonstrated by SST seem to be on skill measures more proximal to the locus of the particular intervention, e.g. assertiveness

(Pfammatter, Junghan & Brenner, 2006) or on reducing negative symptoms (Turner, McGlanaghy, Cuijpers, van der Gaag, Karyotaki & MacBeth, 2018). SST has a weaker impact on general SR outcomes and the evidence base for FEP is yet to be established. However, the fact that social competence is a target of intervention in SST may have particular relevance for FEP as this been promoted as a factor common to predictors of SR in this population (Hodgekins et al., 2015a).

Cognitive remediation therapy (CRT)

Impaired cognitive functioning has long been associated with psychosocial functioning (Mueser et al., 2013) and SR interventions after psychosis are less successful when cognitive functioning is impaired, including SST (Smith et al., 1999) and IPS (McGurk & Mueser, 2004). Consequently, improving cognitive functioning through remediation has been a popular focus for intervention.

CRT helps people develop the underlying cognitive skills to better perform daily tasks, reach recovery goals and improve role functioning. Programmes vary in length and focus but most combine teaching strategies with cognitive exercises providing practice across the range of cognitive functions (e.g. memory, attention, executive functioning) that are impaired (Wykes & Reeder, 2005). Exercises are often performed using computer software packages providing scores of accuracy and speed after participation to reinforce performance progress. Difficulty is then gradually increased over time. Additional strategies not directly remediative but designed to help patients cope, compensate for or adapt to the day-to-day impact of cognitive impairment might also be taught (e.g. the use of aide-mémoires).

Meta-analyses report significant effect sizes on CRT improving psychosocial functioning (Mueser et al., 2013) and employment outcomes (Chan, Hirai & Tsoi, 2015) in schizophrenia. Effects are maximised when CRT is integrated with other rehabilitative interventions such as social cognitive group work (Hogarty et al., 2004), SST (Silverstein et al., 2008) and supported employment (Bell, Choi, Dyer & Wexler, 2014). However, findings suggest that the 'boost' CRT offers SR seems to only benefit those with poorer initial functioning at baseline (Bell et al., 2014).

Cognitive impairments often appear early within the course of psychosis (Galderisi et al., 2009) but data on CRT is mostly drawn from older patients with schizophrenia. There is, however, increasing acknowledgement that the approach can benefit SR in FEP patients (Barlati, De Peri, Deste, Fusar-Poli & Vita, 2012). Indeed, some evidence suggests that CRT received at an earlier stage of schizophrenia (Bowie, Grossman, Gupta, Oyewumi & Harvey, 2014), and FEP (Lee, Redoblado-Hodge, Naismith, Hermens, Porter & Hickie, 2013) has a greater impact on SR compared to when received by older individuals, but this is not universally agreed (Revell, Neill, Harte, Khan & Drake, 2015). As in schizophrenia, however, the effects of CRT in FEP are enhanced when combined with other rehabilitative interventions (e.g. vocational skills training) (Revell et al., 2015).

Just how CRT improves SR is unclear. Gains have been linked to improvements in social cognition (Schmidt, Mueller & Roder, 2011), working memory (Lee, R. S. C. et al., 2013), planning (Wykes et al., 2012) and executive functioning (Reeder, Newton, Frangou & Wykes, 2004). Ventura et al. (2017) suggest improved attention and focus following CRT enhance the ability to track conversations, thus permitting a greater range, quality and quantity of social responses. CRT has a small to moderate effect on reducing negative symptoms in FEP (Ventura et al., 2017). If asociality is included in this, then one might expect an increase in social engagement and subsequent social functioning. Finally, the process of CRT could improve SR independently of neurocognitive factors. For example, increased social support, opportunities for work and increases in perceptions of self-efficacy as a consequence of positive feedback during CRT may all moderate SR.

Although the concepts and rationales of CRT are similar across delivery settings, differences occur in strategies used to transfer skills. CRT delivered as part of, or alongside, ongoing rehabilitation could better allow the patient to translate any cognitive improvements directly to 'real-world' functioning but it remains unclear which components of adjunctive programmes mediate the benefits of CRT. Once known, these could be combined with CRT in other settings to achieve similar gains. Applying or practising CRT with others might enhance SR (Revell et al., 2015). However, those willing to join a group are perhaps more socially skilled in the first place and more likely to make gains.

Younger populations who develop psychosis may retain more neural plasticity compared to older individuals and therefore may benefit more from cognitive training. When levels of cognitive impairment are equally high at baseline, individuals with FEP demonstrate more functional gains after CRT than those with established schizophrenia (Bowie et al., 2014). Although the level of benefit for younger groups has been doubted (Revell et al., 2015), CRT remains plausible as an intervention for FEP given the shared acknowledgment of its efficacy in combination with other rehabilitative programmes.

In EIP, screening individuals for cognitive impairment is indicated when functioning is deemed low and SR delayed. If impairments are detected, CRT might be useful alongside rehabilitation programmes, such as IPS. For others, cognitive exercises (e.g. practising recalling information or strategic planning) might still be useful if provided with opportunities for generalisation and practice as part of meaningful activity in 'real-world' environments.

Cognitive behavioural therapies (CBT)

CBT is guided by the premise that attitudes, beliefs and expectations influence emotions and behaviours. If poor SR after a FEP is defined as a reduction in economically, culturally and/or socially valued meaningful behaviours, it follows that the driving attitudes and expectations of the patient may be valid targets of CBT for psychosis (CBTp).

Historically, CBTp interventions aimed to reduce severity of psychotic symptoms to limit impact on functioning. The patient learns to question evidence supporting dysfunctional beliefs (such as persecutory ideation) and develop alternatives. CBTp is moderately effective in reducing psychotic symptoms (see Chapter 4). Effect sizes for functional improvement have been comparable to that for positive symptoms and negative symptoms, with most trials demonstrating gains in social functioning after CBTp (Wykes et al., 2008).

Cognitive models conceptualise negative symptoms as negative self-beliefs (Grant & Beck, 2008) where the individual implements ultimately unhelpful strategies to avoid distress associated with engaging in constructive activity. The strength of the relationship between SR and negative symptoms (Ventura et al., 2009), and their limited responsiveness to pharmacological treatment compared to positive symptoms have received attention from CBT practitioners. Although meta-analysis confirms the effectiveness of CBTp for negative symptoms (Lutgens, Gariepy & Malla, 2017), benefits are still less convincing than CBTp for positive symptoms (Velthorst et al., 2015; see Chapter 4). That there are more pathways to negative symptoms (Liemburg et al., 2013) which may require different treatment approaches may explain this. For SR, CBTp might be better indicated for 'secondary' negative symptoms, i.e. those related to dysfunctional expectancies about one's social and cognitive abilities (Oorschot et al., 2011). For some, the psychological and/or neurocognitive correlates and consequences of psychosis yield lived experiences characterised by failure and difficulties in functioning. Subsequent development of dysfunctional attitudes and negative appraisals about self and self-efficacy then increases the likelihood of negative symptoms which then manifest as lack of engagement in activity and goal-directed tasks.

Evidence from the FEP population supports a tailored approach when negative symptoms present as barriers to SR. Higher levels of negative symptoms at onset are linked to a higher risk of longer-term social disability (Gee et al., 2016a) with apathy and flat affect highlighted as contributors to poor SR (Evensen et al., 2012a, 2012b). Indeed, patients nominate apathy as the most distressing negative symptom (Selten, Wiersma & van den Bosch, 2000) and apathy reduction as the most important goal of treatment (Sterk, van Rossum, Muis & De Haan, 2013). Close monitoring of SR in individuals presenting with elevated negative symptoms on entry to EIP services is therefore warranted. Given the multi-dimensional nature of negative symptoms, there may be additional need for specific rehabilitative efforts for patients where specific symptoms (especially apathy) are delaying SR. Targeted CBTp at this point may prove useful. Indeed, recent small trials demonstrate some reduction in negative symptoms when associated beliefs are directly targeted (e.g. Staring, TerHuurne & Van der Gaag, 2013).

Few FEP studies target SR as a primary outcome of CBTp approaches but encouragingly, interest is growing. In the USA, Waldheter et al. (2008) designed a

Graduated Recovery Intervention Program (GRIP) to facilitate SR following a FEP. This emphasises goal pursuit, optimism and self-esteem to target malleable factors hindering SR, specifically, substance use and distress associated with residual symptoms. Treatment modules aim to address core areas of functioning, including social skills and social support, role functioning, recreational activity, and self-esteem/stigma. Engagement in GRIP is maximised by drawing on the external social support surrounding the patient. GRIP has been well received, with improvements in social functioning and goal attainment noted for those who engage more fully. Increased social competence and ratings of work productivity following GRIP have also been reported (Penn et al., 2011).

In the UK, Fowler and colleagues have explored the efficacy of another adapted form of CBTp to improve SR in psychosis (Fowler et al., 2009b). Social Recovery Therapy (SRT) combines CBTp techniques with assertive case management and a focus on meaningful, value-driven goals linked to increased activity. Activity is promoted through 'in vivo' behavioural experiments, graded exposure and other behavioural strategies. Barriers to activity, such as low-level symptoms or anxiety, are managed alongside. Cognitive therapy is used in conjunction with experiments to promote a sense of agency, optimism and hope, to reduce stigma and build positive beliefs about self and others (Fowler et al., 2013).

SRT was initially trialled with young people reporting social disability acquired up to eight years following a FEP (Fowler et al., 2009b). Those with non-affective psychosis benefited more from SRT, reporting more hours per week in structured activity, increased hope, fewer symptoms and more engagement in paid employment compared to treatment as usual. In addition to health, economic benefits (Barton, Hodgekins, Mugford, Jones, Croudace & Fowler, 2009), SRT is experienced by patients as an acceptable and satisfactory therapy for SR (Notley, Christopher, Hodgekins, Byrne, French & Fowler, 2015).

SRT offered in EIP services has had a positive impact on increasing activity levels for people with delayed SR (Fowler et al., 2018) and highlights that, despite emphasis on psychosocial interventions in EIP (NICE, 2016), a targeted approach to SR is required. Although the evidence base for SRT is still developing, it intuitively appeals as an intervention for a FEP within EIP teams. Where other interventions focus on specific limiters of SR (e.g. symptoms, cognitive impairments, reduced social skills), SRT demands that all barriers to activity are understood and targeted on an individual level. Factors previously seen as exclusion criteria for psychosocial therapies, such as ambivalence, comorbidity and disengagement, are instead reconceptualised as barriers to SR and become legitimate targets for SR intervention in their own right.

Implementing the evidence into practice

Specific cognitions might be more relevant for SR than others. Defeatist performance beliefs refer to a tendency to overgeneralise from past failures to future performance (e.g. 'Why try? I always fail') and so restructuring is associated with improving social and occupational functioning (Granholm, Holden, Link, McQuaid & Jeste, 2013). Beliefs about self-efficacy relate to negative symptoms and social functioning (Cardenas et al., 2013) and may reduce motivation and effort to meet goals when SR seems difficult (Grant & Beck, 2008; see Chapter 4). Negative expectancies of experiencing pleasure (e.g. 'I will not be able to enjoy this') (Oorschot et al., 2011) and social disinterest attitudes (e.g. 'having close friends is not as important as most people say') have also been predictive of low social functioning (Granholm, Ben-Zeev & Link, 2009) and may serve as further candidates for cognitive intervention.

Individuals with psychosis have described personal resilience, self-esteem, and hope as important components of SR (Davidson, 2003). Hodgekins and Fowler (2010) targeted beliefs associated with these concepts using SRT in FEP and found hope and positive identity mediated the effects of intervention on SR. Cognitive elements of the approach aimed to deliberately foster positive self-esteem, suggesting that promoting positive self-concept could be a key target of CBTp interventions for SR. This is in contrast to other CBTp approaches, particularly those targeting symptoms, which tend to focus on negative, self-defeating cognitions.

As the problem of delayed SR after a FEP concerns reduced activity, CBT approaches with a strong behavioural element, such as behavioural activation (BA), have appeal. BA is successfully used in the treatment of depression. Patients are exposed to pleasurable activities to elicit a sense of reward which positively reinforces desired behaviours and reduces negative affect (Kanter, Manos, Bowe, Baruch, Busch & Rusch, 2010). BA has developed to form a package of interventions involving assessment of goals and values, activity monitoring, activity scheduling, contingency management of environmental responses, targeted avoidance and skills training. BA could prove useful for individuals affected by psychosis who doubt their agency or functional capability to increase or take on meaningful activity, or who express negative predictions as to the benefits of such.

The amount of pleasure reported by individuals with schizophrenia after engaging in activity is no different to that expressed by non-clinical groups. However, *anticipating* pleasure is reportedly more difficult, hence they are less likely to initiate potentially enjoyable activity (Gard et al., 2007). BA techniques may be useful in revealing dissociation between anticipated and actual pleasure and raise patient awareness as to how withdrawal may impair SR. Interventions for negative symptoms (Lutgens, Gariepy & Malla, 2017) and a recent case study (Hasson-Ohayon, Arnon-Ribenfeld, Hamm & Lysaker, 2017) advocates BA as an effective intervention for psychosis. Interestingly, in their meta-analysis of CBTp for negative symptoms, Velthorst et al. (2015) report that behavioural techniques were slightly more effective than those with an exclusively cognitive focus.

Chapter 4 described how historically, psychological interventions targeting positive symptoms typically involved conversations with the client about challenging delusional ideas. Newer CBTp approaches emphasise the importance of tackling delusional ideas in context and demonstrate that 'in vivo' behavioural interventions can promote symptomatic recovery in a way that cannot be achieved just in the therapy room (Freeman, 2016). Can this 'in vivo' approach also be applied to unhelpful cognitions mediating the relationship between psychosis and SR? Drawing assertively on the systems surrounding the patient (e.g. employment partners, community programmes) offers a way to harness activity, and opportunity to collaboratively challenge beliefs that might be a barrier to SR. These are practices in which EIP clinicians are already well placed and experienced to provide.

Strengths and limitations of CBTp for psychotic symptoms are discussed in Chapter 4. Similar conclusions apply to its effectiveness for SR. The range of approaches makes generalisation to practical implementation difficult, as it is hard to ascertain which specific element is improving outcome (Thomas, 2015). Interventions differ with regard to relative emphasis on cognitive or behavioural components of treatment and there are qualitative differences within these components across trials. Some rely to a greater or lesser extent on adjunctive interventions, thus making it even more difficult to isolate the active components of therapy. Finally, non-specific social factors of some approaches may exert an influence. Sometimes, CBTp is delivered in groups, or alongside opportunities for increased social contact (e.g. an IPS). Such environments offer a means of extending social support systems and making connections with others sharing similar problems while providing an opportunity for developing social communication skills. This alone may affect a change in functioning separate to, in conjunction with, or even instead of, deliberate attempts to modify beliefs.

Consistent with the points made in Chapter 4, solutions may include increased use of individually formulated CBTp approaches (Van der Gaag, Valmaggia & Smit, 2014) with specific protocols and outcome measures for poor SR (Fowler et al., 2018). Using more focused SR outcome measures in trials may help yield larger effect sizes (Birchwood et al., 2014a). Finally, focusing on what patients need or want from CBTp (Thomas, 2015) by eliciting individual SR goals, alongside appropriate outcome measures (see Appendix 2) may more effectively capture gains in SR over time.

Other interventions for SR

Other interventions offer promise for SR after a FEP. These are not yet established practice or fully evidence-based, but may help facilitate SR in FEP populations.

Peer support and social support

Peer support programmes vary according to the activities offered and relationships between the individuals involved. Modes of delivery include groups, consumer-run services and peers collaborating with mental health clinicians (Davidson, Bellamy, Guy & Miller, 2012). Common to all is that those delivering the support have a 'lived experience' of mental illness (see Chapter 7). Goals are individualised but common themes include reducing social isolation, improving quality of life and increasing self-advocacy (Mead & Copeland, 2000). Outcomes include increased hopefulness (Cook et al., 2012), reduced hospitalisations (Sledge, Lawless, Sells, Wieland, O'Connell & Davidson, 2011) and greater improvements in social networks, quality of life and social support (Castelein et al., 2008). Online moderated peer-supported forums can help foster a sense of community and social connectedness among individuals with a FEP (Álvarez-Jiménez et al., 2013; see Box 7.2). Peers may compensate for the deficiencies in desired support and social relations often seen as a consequence of psychosis. They may also help reduce stigma, a factor found to adversely affect SR outcomes (Yanos, Roe, Markus & Lysaker, 2008). See also Phil's story (Box 7.1).

Social factors are a powerful predictor of long-term social and occupational functioning. Larger social networks and more active interactions with others have been associated with better SR after psychosis (Howard, Leese & Thornicroft, 2000), and social support targeted at improving SR can reduce negative symptoms in the long term (Norman, MacDougall, Manchanda & Harricharan, 2018). Family networks may offer longer-term support (see Chapter 11), while friends can provide help with personal problems and engagement in peer-related activities (Randolph, 1998). Some research suggests that social networks comprised of friends are associated with better SR than networks composed of relatives (Erickson et al., 1998). Conversely, positive relationships have been reported between the size of family networks and SR outcomes (Evert, Harvey, Trauer & Herrman, 2003). Some of this discrepancy might link to duration of illness and diagnosis, as different types of social network have been found to influence SR outcomes differently for FEP compared to schizophrenia (Erickson, Beiser & Iacono, 1998).

The direction of causal relationship between social networks and SR remains unclear. It is possible that more supportive and/or extensive social networks facilitate SR, just as much as the converse idea is plausible; that poorer SR leads to the loss of supportive relationships. Regardless of the nature of the association, people experiencing psychosis require supportive, meaningful relationships and patients' functioning may improve with interventions that help maintain and improve social networks outside of the family. Supporting patients to join schemes held in the local community is one recommendation.

Physical activity and healthy lifestyle interventions

In FEP, increased exercise has been linked to independent living skills (Nuechterlein, Ventura, McEwen, Gretchen-Doorly, Vinogradov & Subotnik, 2016) and improvements in negative symptoms, cognitive performance and social functioning (Firth et al., 2016a). Activity levels may decrease over time at follow up but early improvements in social functioning can be maintained, with social support deemed an important maintenance factor (Firth et al., 2016a). Physical activity can also counteract AP-induced weight gain (see Chapter 3), which may be impeding SR in various ways, including social avoidance.

In addition to lack of social support, poor motivation has been identified as a barrier to exercise among individuals with a FEP. However, low motivation is cited as a general obstruction to any activity even if valued and enjoyable (Firth et al., 2016a). Motivation therefore may be relevant to maintaining engagement in any new active lifestyle change that could promote SR (Vancampfort et al., 2015a), and prove another valid target for intervention.

Motivational interviewing (MI)

Motivational interviewing (MI) helps people commit to change by combining supportive and empathic counselling with directive methods for resolving ambivalence in the direction of change (Rollnick & Miller, 1995). MI has been implemented in psychosis, including as a way to address conflict with regard to concordance to medication (Kemp, Hayward, Applewhaite, Everitt & David, 1996) and substance use (Westra, Aviram & Doell, 2011; see Chapter 10). Velligan et al. (2006) hypothesise that even after factors such as symptoms, stigma and cognitive impairment are accounted for, there remains a 'compromise in motivation' component responsible for a proportion of functional disability observed in schizophrenia. They consequently name motivation as a critical treatment target in optimizing SR.

Training EIP clinicians in MI (in teams that already provide IPS) to focus on ambivalence related to employment and readiness to change can increase employment rates (Craig et al., 2014). For those with a high risk of social disability in EIP services, MI techniques could be implemented for patients who struggle to develop SR goals. Because it is the client rather than the clinician who makes the arguments for change, MI may particularly appeal to those who resist more directive therapeutic approaches. It may be implemented as a prelude to engagement in treatment or therapy, or as a standalone intervention to facilitate conversations about goals.

Eliciting goals and values

One way of identifying collaborative goals of SR is by using the SMART paradigm. Developed in the 1980s and adapted for use in mental health, this popular approach involves a conversation aimed to generate goals according to five main principles (that SMART goals are: Specific, Measurable, Achievable, Relevant and Time-limited). In our experience, the SMART method is a useful way to set targets for SR. However, goal-setting is harder for clients experiencing severe social disability. Those struggling to reach goals are often not new to the experience, and the exercise in itself can trigger a sense of vulnerability, possibly because it requires admittance that something is important to the person. This can open up the potential for failure, loss and disappointment. For some, the risk involved in attempting to achieve a worthwhile goal might not be worth taking.

When individuals struggle to identify SR goals in this way, a shift in focus towards their values may be useful. Values can be defined as principles, ideals, morals and standards that give life meaning. Rediscovering values to drive and guide goal-directed behaviour is endorsed by the acceptance and commitment therapy (ACT) approach. In ACT, the term 'values' refers to a chosen quality of purposive action that can never actually be obtained or reached but can be put into action moment to moment (Hayes, Strosahl & Wilson, 1999). In contrast, concrete goals and actions are specific, obtainable achievements carried out in service of a value. Increased awareness as to what an individual truly values may increase motivation towards purpose and intent. What is attractive about the approach is that defining or quantifying a point of achievement or 'goal' is not necessary, as values are not finite, thus reducing any anxiety associated with the risk of setting targets that might not be met. For example, a person might identify a particular relationship as important, such as their role as son or daughter. Behaviours can then be shaped purposefully so the individual lives more in line with this value. There will never be an end-point of 'achievement'; rather, it is a process of ongoing work in progress. Working alongside values can help the patient live a richer, fuller life according to how they define this. An important message to convey is that this can occur even in the face of symptoms and other ongoing problems (see also Chapter 7).

A modified version of the Personal Values Card Sorting Task (Miller et al., 2001) has been used in combination with MI to address substance use in individuals with schizophrenia (Graeber, Moyers, Griffith, Guajardo & Tonigan, 2003). The purpose of this task is to develop a discrepancy between a deeply held belief (or value) and a current behaviour. MI can then be used in an attempt to resolve this discrepancy and help the client move forward (see Moyers & Martino, 2006, for details). We promote this tool[1] as a viable method for exploring values with patients who might struggle to generate goals.

Staff training

The mechanisms of action of MI are not well understood. Clinician factors may play a role in influencing outcome, specifically empathy (Marcus, Westra, Angus & Kertes, 2011) and their own ambivalence to change (Craig et al., 2014). This is important, because is often EIP clinicians who serve as the conduit between SR interventions and the client. For example, decisions as to whether clients are work-ready may be heavily influenced by their care team and others. Clinicians can hold pessimistic views of patients' ability to return to work, characterised by lack of encouragement and low expectations (Marwaha, Balachandra & Johnson, 2009). This is important for SR, as positive expectations of outcome have found to predict better employment outcomes for patients with schizophrenia (O'Connell & Stein, 2011).

Employment may be discouraged for fear of work-related stress worsening symptoms and triggering relapse (Rinaldi, Killackey, Smith, Shepherd, Singh & Craig, 2010). In fact, prolonged inactivity may create more problems such as reduced confidence, low self-esteem and dependence on benefits over and above the demands of work causing relapse (Burns et al., 2007). Raising awareness of the risks of inactivity may reduce anxiety about the patient's ability to cope with work. Team-wide training and discussion are therefore advocated as part of the preparation for SR interventions (e.g. IPS).

Research indicates a link between poor staff-patient relationships and poor SR after psychosis (Berry, Barrowclough & Haddock, 2011). Levels of expressed criticism, hostility and emotional over-involvement from staff are presumed to impact upon engagement and the individual's ability and willingness to access SR opportunities. Levels of criticism are reportedly higher in less-qualified staff (Van Humbeeck et al., 2002). Staff with less knowledge of psychosis may be less likely to attribute poor SR to illness-related factors beyond the patient's control. However, robust effects have not been found for interventions that increase staff knowledge of psychosis on levels of staff criticism and patient functioning (Finnema, Louwerens, Slooff & Bosch, 1996).

Patient inactivity may be viewed as intentional and elicit intolerance, criticism and frustration (Weisman, Nuechterlein, Goldstein & Snyder, 1998). Re-appraising reasons for inactivity can reduce such negative views (Willetts & Leff, 2003). In EIP, training staff to reattribute delays in SR by identifying barriers to inactivity may prove to be an effective method of reducing negative feelings, increasing empathy, improving relationship quality, building engagement and may instigate prompting, encouragement and support (see Chapter 12). This could prove particularly useful for newer or less qualified staff.

Berry and Greenwood (2015) discovered that the quality of the therapeutic relationship and expectancies held by staff regarding the ability of patients with psychosis to perform social and community activities predicted social inclusion and vocational activity and this was mediated by patient hopefulness. Findings emphasise the power that professionals have in influencing SR outcomes and vote hopefulness as a mechanism by which teams can begin to facilitate SR interventions.

Implementing the evidence into practice

The remainder of this chapter provides further suggestions for how the SR interventions described above can be applied within EIP services. We follow up the case example of Jade (introduced in Chapter 5) to begin to illustrate an example of applying evidence-based SR interventions in practice.

Case study 6.1 Jade

Jade and her CPN completed the Work and Social Adjustment Scale (see Appendix 2). Jade scored 23, noting that her mental health difficulties impacted most on 'social leisure activities' and 'family relationships'. This then facilitated a conversation about goals towards making changes. Jade identified two goals: (1) to meet people who had had similar experiences to her and help them; and (2) to get on better with her mother.

Jade and her CPN selected the goal they thought might be easiest for Jade to achieve (Goal 1). This minimised the risk of confirmation of assumptions about failure. Under supervision of the team clinical psychologist, Jade's CPN used elements of the SRT approach to facilitate goal achievement. Cognitive restructuring helped challenge Jade's beliefs about being judged and she recognised that this might be less likely with people who had also had psychosis. The CPN then introduced more 'in vivo', interventions. Jade agreed to meet her in the clinic and they reflected on how others had responded to her in the waiting room. Afterwards, Jade agreed to joint meetings with her CPN and other members of the team. A peer support worker talked to Jade about her own lived experience of psychosis and introduced her to projects raising awareness of mental health difficulties in schools. Jade agreed to use her IT skills to help develop flyers. This helped to reduce the shame and stigma Jade felt about psychosis.

At her next care review, Jade was reportedly now spending 40 hours in meaningful activity a week. A new goal included volunteering at a school she had been making flyers for. Relationships at home had improved but Jade still tended to avoid her parents. Family work was offered to reduce levels of criticism and promote encouragement (see Chapter 11). After this, Jade's mother was able to better acknowledge Jade's struggle and both were more able to communicate feelings in a more helpful way. Jade spent less time in her room, and responded more frequently to her mother's positive requests to help around the house.

Jade's example illustrates the importance of assessing how past hopes and goals have been disrupted as a consequence of psychosis, and the barriers to SR that need to be understood and removed in order to navigate the patient back towards what is meaningful to them (see Chapter 7). However, to limit social disability effectively after FEP in this way we need first to develop an understanding as a team of exactly what best to offer, when to offer it and for whom it will be most effective.

Formulation of SR in teams

Team formulation provides a framework to draw together factors that contribute to the development and maintenance of social disability (Kinderman, 2005). Formulation meetings involving all those who work with the patient can be incorporated into any EIP multi-disciplinary team (MDT) schedule as part of routine reviews of care (see Chapter 12). Aims include identifying and understanding external and internal blockages to SR while taking into account patients' values, hopes, expectations and level of motivation to carry out future roles.

We know the risk of social disability and SR trajectories vary between individuals and this can be understood using a clinical staging approach (see Chapter 1, Table 1.1). Formulation guides an individualised plan of care (Meaden & Hacker, 2011) that can be tailored to facilitate SR and reduce risk of social disability. Negotiation with the wider system is often required (e.g. recovery partners, family, training/employment/education providers) as is identifying the availability of other social opportunities. Without these supports, there is limited scope for SR. Chapter 12 provides a useful operational framework of formulation (see Figure 12.1) and offers fuller discussion as to how to implement this in teams.

As a process, team formulation benefits understanding, care planning, relationships with patients and the team (Summers, 2006). It can also shift staff appraisals of patient behaviour by reducing blame and promoting appreciation as to the challenges of SR, while increasing optimism, positive feelings and promoting hope (Berry et al., 2009). The effectiveness of team formulation is illustrated in our case example of Alex (introduced in Chapter 5), and demonstrates why multi-component psychosocial interventions are recommended in clinical guidelines for a FEP (NICE, 2014, 2016).

Case study 6.2 Alex

Scheduling a formulation meeting as soon as possible allowed the team to develop a more integrated understanding of Alex's difficulties. This prevented the significance of Alex's case from being overlooked and support reduced or withdrawn. Input from the MDT helped Alex's care co-ordinator by reducing frustration associated with perceived lack of progress.

Alex and his care co-ordinator completed the Personal Values Card Sorting Task which helped identify what was important to Alex. Alex missed being active outdoors but this was difficult due to paranoia. Alex and his parents met with the EIP consultant psychiatrist. Alex and his mother confirmed Alex did not take APs regularly because he often forgot, and didn't think they helped. They talked about changing treatment and offered more assertive input to support him to take medication regularly (see Chapter 3). Alex then met with the team clinical psychologist for a neuropsychological assessment. This revealed the presence of an underlying neurodevelopmental disorder (see Chapter 10) which helped explain his communication difficulties.

Paranoia reduced with medication adherence and one day Alex agreed to walk to the park with a support worker from the team. This engagement continued alongside a reduction in symptoms and Alex started to talk about how frightened he had been by voices. This then permitted careful assessment of trauma by the team psychologist (see Chapter 8). Finally, family work with a psychoeducational component was offered to Alex and his family. A session devoted to relapse prevention (see Chapter 4) helped allay fears his parents had about relapse and stigma and raised awareness as to the importance of optimising Alex's SR. They began to encourage him to get up in the mornings and join them visiting extended family and friends.

As in Alex's case, it is often more junior or non-clinical staff who are recruited to support individuals with the greatest social need. Typical tasks include 'getting people out of the house', to encourage activity. Ironically, this means those who are less qualified and least informed become responsible for arguably the most important work with the most difficult to engage and complex of patients. This issue was addressed in the design of trials evaluating SRT (Fowler et al., 2018), where only trained and experienced clinicians were recruited to deliver the intervention. If not overtly psychotic, it may be easy for the rest of the team to miss need in these individuals. It is essential that all staff involved in an individual's SR plan are informed and included at every stage of the formulation process. Support staff should be aware that the SR work they do is vital; it must be underpinned and guided by a clear clinical formulation that they have been involved in developing. They are well placed to assess aspects of client functioning that other clinicians cannot, or are not privy to. For example, observing clients taking part in community activities might reveal previously unknown barriers to SR such as social anxiety. Good supervision and regular MDT reviews allow the formulation to be revised accordingly, and invite input from other disciplines to intervene.

Streaming SR interventions

The clinical staging model (Fusar-Poli et al., 2017; McGorry, Killackey & Yung, 2008) presents different opportunities for a prevention-oriented approach to care. Given the FEP population is not homogeneous when it comes to rates and trajectories of SR (Hodgekins et al., 2015a), we have proposed that this approach can also guide SR interventions. Thorough assessment and formulation help define the SR trajectory or 'stream' and determine the level of risk of social disability (see Chapter 5). Table 6.1 provides guidance for EIP teams as to how SR interventions might then be applied according to the stream.

Implementing a streaming protocol has the potential to increase efficiency by directing resources relevant to need and tailoring input. All streams should focus on SR as soon as symptoms are resolved, better managed (Pelayo-Terán et al., 2018) or less of a barrier to engagement in SR interventions (Fowler et al., 2009). Typically, symptom resolution and clinical stabilisation take place at an earlier stage followed by gradual functional improvement which occurs later and requires substantially longer to achieve. However, the assumption that complete symptom remission is necessary before SR can be addressed has been disproven (see Chapter 2). Symptoms can remain moderate, or moderated, alongside SR. Sole focus on remission risks the client and others becoming socialised into thinking that the symptom is 'the problem', thus further delaying SR interventions. This is important, because early SR is critical in sustaining progress in the longer term, even if the symptoms do not initially remit (Álvarez-Jiménez et al., 2012b). Be that as it may, the potential for improving SR through simply timing interventions sooner is likely to be limited unless an integrated, formulation-driven

Table 6.1 Streaming SR interventions

SR outcome	Clinical stage	Identification (see Appendix 2)	Interventions	Considerations
Favourable	2	• No/few risk factors (see Table 5.2) • GAF-D: 60≥ • WASAS: ≥10 • TUS: ≤45 hours a week • PANSS (neg symptoms): Absent/Low • Scores on above remain within non-clinical range • Engaged with SR goals	• Facilitate uptake of goal-led educational, social/vocational opportunities • IPS	• May not require as intense approach to SR as Stages 3 and 4. • Following period of symptom stability and SR, interventions could be reduced. • If SR sustained consider early discharge. • May need less input than Stages 3 and 4, but could attract more given willingness/ability to engage. • Aligning resources to better reflect need here recommended.
Less favourable	3a or 3b	• Some risk factors (see Table 5.2) • GAF-D >60. • WASAS 10–20, at times may >20. • TUS 30–45 hours a week • PANSS (negative symptoms): Moderate • Will demonstrate fluctuations in SR.	• Personal Values Card Sorting Task • IPS • Joined up working with recovery partners and psychoeducation necessary to prevent disengagement. • CRT may improve functioning when added to other programmes (e.g., IPS).	• Time interventions according to fluctuations in recovery. IPS sometimes not possible/ineffective/offered too soon. • Work opportunities provided within statutory/voluntary sectors may exclude individuals >25 years. Mental health problems operating as barriers to activity may be missed by external partners.

- More withdrawn/avoidant at times.
- Ongoing, careful assessment of psychopathology, including cognitive impairment to rule out/identify any barriers to readiness to work or vocational activity.

- SRT
- Cognitive restructuring to target beliefs associated with defeat/poor self-efficacy/negative expectancies of pleasure
- BA/behavioural experiments to tackle beliefs in context wherever possible. Implemented as an adjunct to above or standalone intervention.
- Healthy lifestyle/exercise programmes to facilitate community engagement
- Regular, consistent assessment of SR.

- Vocational interventions with group focus may increase social anxiety. This may need to be addressed through CBTp first.
- Patterns of avoidance initially protective and easy to miss. Overlook may increase risk of progression to Stage 3c/4.
- Poor SR evident at 12–14 months may indicate higher risk of clinical Stage 3c/4.

continued

Table 6.1 Continued

SR outcome	Clinical stage	Identification (see Appendix 2)	Interventions	Considerations
Unfavourable	3c or 4	• Majority/all risk factors (see Table 5.2) • GAF-D <60. • WASAS >20. • TUS <30 hours a week • PANSS (negative symptoms): high and include apathy • Unmotivated, low mood, loss of hope, substance misuse, anxiety, trauma, social withdrawal. • Presentation may resemble ARMS (e.g., attenuated psychotic symptoms/anomalies of experience)	• Establish collaborative goal (what client wants to do) • TUS can be a more sensitive way of monitoring/measuring outcome than goal setting. • Cognitive restructuring • MI • BA • Peers to support behavioural approaches/increase intensity and frequency of social contact/help staff to engage unmotivated clients. • Staff training and family work (see Chapter 11) to support change in narrative to reframe symptoms (e.g., depression) as barriers preventing progress • Regular, consistent assessment of SR and co-morbid psychopathology (see Chapters 8 and 10)	• Standard interventions often unsuccessful and attempted extensively/frequently so conveyance of hope and agency important. • Lack of goal-directed behaviour/amotivation is problem itself. All involved may struggle to obtain a focus for SR so risk of disengagement high. • Lasting change may depend on patient experiencing real changes day to day. Easily demonstrated by TUS. • Cognitive work important for clients with early negative symptoms/poor premorbid functioning as they may never have held a positive sense of self/self-efficacy, even prior to FEP. • However, they may be less able to take advantage of formal interventions.

- Conceptualise barriers to recovery within a system/context not located 'within' the individual. Support then be recruited from wider system.

- Caution advised with regard to implementing interventions too didactically/prescriptively as may confirm ideas about limited personal agency/strengthen stigma about mental illness and imply reduced competence.
- Peers can help promote a sense of hope and recovery, positive self-concept, reduce stigma and help counter pessimism or low expectations.
- Re-appraising negative attitudes toward delays in SR helps instigate hope, encouragement and practical support.
- Relapse is likely to be spotted over social decline and inadvertently prioritised so clients risk getting missed if teams become busy and overburdened.
- Comorbid psychopathologies (e.g., depression) risk being missed/marginalised following remission of positive symptoms and/or poor engagement. These associated problems may still be delaying SR.

approach has been developed that is tailored to the individual. Integrating SR goals within the context of personal recovery is useful here. Fostering a recognition that a value-driven and purposeful life can be lived even in the face of symptoms and other problems, is essential (see Chapter 7). Resilience, positive expectations and hope are core components and mediators of SR (Hodgekins & Fowler, 2010) and should be instilled into any intervention.

Future research may determine whether individuals attaining good, sustained and stable SR after FEP benefit from an EIP approach over and above that conferred by naturally occurring protective factors. Conversely, for those at higher risk, longer-term EIP services may be crucial to consolidation and sustained improvement of initial functional gains. This aligns with stage-specific processes regarding the course of psychosis.

Learning points

- EIP improves work outcomes after a FEP when IPS is included.
- The higher the fidelity to the IPS model, the better the outcomes.
- Younger patients may prioritise education over employment but comparable benefits of supported employment on education rates have not been as consistent.
- It is important to assess who will benefit most from IPS. Exclusion should not end efforts to source other work opportunities.
- Goals of SR may not be work-related.
- SST yields better outcomes when specific skills are targeted. Its effectiveness in improving SR in FEP is not yet established.
- Screening for cognitive impairment following a FEP is advised if SR is delayed.
- CRT can enhance SR in a FEP when combined with other interventions (e.g. IPS).
- Reviews of traditional CBTp demonstrate moderate effect size improvements in SR as a secondary outcome. These trials have predominantly studied participants with long-standing disorders. Fewer identify SR as a primary outcome of interest.
- Adapted CBTp approaches for SR can be effective, and challenging attitudes associated with defeat and self-efficacy alongside fostering hope and positive self-concept is important.
- The BA components of CBTp may be useful in targeting withdrawal from meaningful activity.
- Early identification and streaming those at risk of poor SR offer an opportunity to target specific interventions at the most optimum time to promote a favourable longer-term outcome.
- Targeting a wider construct of SR than work alone to include all meaningful activity is necessary for those at moderate to severe risk. This should be driven by the values of the client.

- Some individuals may never reach a point in their recovery to engage in interventions such as CBTp. They require a tailored, intensive approach to SR and if this is not delivered early on, longer-term social disability is a risk.
- Individualised formulations and in-vivo multi-systemic assertive outreach are necessary for the SR of individuals, who are less engaged, ambivalent about change, and who present with comorbidities.
- Those at high risk of social disability may present as difficult to engage but deemed as having responded to treatment. However, they may be experiencing other problems that impact on SR. Reduced ability combined with poor engagement risks this group being overlooked or 'falling through the net' completely.
- Positive expectations and hope are core to SR and should be instilled into any intervention.

Note

1 Available at https://casaa.unm.edu/Instruments.

Chapter 7

Optimising personal recovery and promoting psychological adaptation following first episode psychosis

Introduction

> Psychosis had a huge impact on me and my life. Essentially it came in and disrupted everything that was normal and good in my life. It affected my social life, my passion for music, my dreams and ambitions, what was going on in my head and my general outlook on life. To have something come and do that for you can be a really scary thing, and for me it was really tough to get past. There were times when it felt like the whole world was against me. Times when I felt like I had nothing to live for. It really impacts you in quite a surreal way.

Sam's story, above, highlights the personal impact of a FEP. We return to Sam's story later in this chapter (Box 7.3) and discuss how early intervention for psychosis (EIP) and psychological therapy helped support his personal recovery. A lot is involved in this process and the stakes are high, for if we cannot support someone through this type of recovery, they could be more vulnerable to outcomes such as anxiety, trauma, depression and suicide (see Chapters 8 and 9). This chapter focuses on ways EIP can specifically promote personal recovery and facilitate the processes of psychological adaptation, rather than it simply being a 'side effect' of interventions targeting symptomatic and social recovery.

As noted in Chapter 2, there have been many attempts to define personal recovery with a number of recurrent themes emerging. Many of these are summarised in Table 7.1. Collated from international studies, sampling a range of opinions from individuals who have experienced psychosis (although not all FEP samples), it can be seen that several common themes feature in people's views of their personal recoveries and psychological adaptation. These include surviving the experiences; beginning the process of integration and assimilation; hope and optimism; rebuilding; developing social roles and a sense of belonging; making sense of experiences; and transforming the self through new outlooks and values. Anthony's (1993) definition quoted in Chapter 2, remains, we believe, probably the most succinct summary of personal recovery following a FEP.

Table 7.1 Personal recovery and psychological adaptation following psychosis: Themes from the literature

Theme summary
Surviving the experiences and overcoming adversity and stigma 1, 2, 4, 5
Early recovery processes which help facilitate later processes of integration and assimilation e.g. engaging in/accepting treatment, regaining control over experiences, understanding and normalising experiences 1, 2, 4, 5, 6, 7, 8
Maintaining hope for a better life and holding an optimistic view about the future with a desire to progress in life and achieve goals 1, 2, 9, 10, 11
Re-building life, returning to life, and working towards goals 2, 4, 5, 7, 10
Re-engaging with the social world, gaining a sense of belonging to a community/network, and having a valued social role 1, 2, 3, 8, 12, 13, 14
Integrating the experiences of psychosis, constructing a meaning from these experiences and recognising personal growth arising from these experiences, which could include using experiences to help others 1, 2, 4, 7, 8, 9, 12, 15
Transformation of the self, which could include developing a new outlook and values in life and relationships, with a sense of agency, self-acceptance, and fulfilment, which may include spiritual growth 1, 4, 8, 9, 12

Notes

1 Lam et al. (2011);	9 Bird et al. (2014);
2 Baggott (2010);	10 Dunkley & Bates (2015);
3 Eisenstadt et al. (2012);	11 Jordan et al. (2018);
4 Windell et al. (2012);	12 Hagen & Nixon (2010);
5 Bjornestad et al. (2016);	13 Subandi (2015);
6 Gumley & Clark (2012);	14 Windell & Norman (2012);
7 Windell et al. (2015);	15 Tan et al. (2014).
8 Connell et al. (2015);	

Psychological adaptation and personal recovery following FEP: what are the key ingredients?

As argued in Chapter 2, the notion of 'psychological adaptation' following psychosis may be conceptually broader than the term 'personal recovery'. The word 'recovery' may imply someone going back to how they used to be before an 'illness', whereas 'psychological adaptation' reflects more of a process of 'transformation' into a new self or life. This process assimilates the experiences of psychosis, through understanding and being connected with this new life, which may or may not include the presence of ongoing symptoms. The concept of psychological adaptation may capture the process of assimilating the potentially 'catastrophic effects' (Anthony, 1993) that a FEP can have on them, such as loss, threat to social rank, decreased acceptance by others, shame, humiliation, exclusion, subordination and lowered self-esteem. These are difficult issues from which to 'recover' and need an ongoing process of psychological adaptation, compassionate self-acceptance and the development of subjective self-agency to help someone move forward with their life, despite these challenges. Some of the key ingredients needed for this to take place are, again, highlighted in Table 7.1 If a person can achieve some of these, this could also help them to continually adapt and respond to the challenges that life may bring following a FEP.

Of course, not everyone will go through *all* these processes, nor in the same order, and a person's 'recovery style' may influence their willingness to talk about their FEP experiences (Thompson, McGorry & Harrigan, 2003). If, however, EIP services are set up to support personal recovery and psychological adaptation, they may enable the person to move towards acceptance, resilience and even post-traumatic growth (Dunkley & Bates, 2015), themes that are expanded on below.

The social context is also important, and having social support and valued relationships can help buffer against stigma, and foster hope and a sense of social worth (Windell & Norman, 2013). 'Acceptance' by others may in turn help the person process their own experiences and develop meaningful frameworks to make sense of their FEP. Of course, the social context prior to FEP is also important (e.g. trauma, social deprivation, family relationships, etc.) and can impact on psychological adaptation and personal recovery (see Chapter 8).

Acceptance and recovery style

'Acceptance' following psychosis has been described as a process of 'integrating the experience of psychosis into self-identity' (Windell & Norman, 2013, p. 498). This is complex and involves a variety of interacting factors, including the person's experience of psychosis itself and the social consequences that follow FEP.

This is similar to the concept of an 'integrative' as opposed to a 'sealing over' recovery style (McGlashan, 1987). Those with an 'integrated' recovery style are more likely to acknowledge the significance of their psychosis, be more curious about it and more likely to take active steps to cope and seek help and advice about it. Those who 'seal over' are more likely to avoid experiences related to psychosis and diagnosis (Tait, Birchwood & Trower, 2003). Integrative recovery styles have been linked to improved outcomes, including engagement with services, symptom recovery and overall functioning (Thompson et al., 2003). 'Integrators' also demonstrate increased willingness to emotionally process the traumatic aspects of FEP (Jackson et al., 2004), which can be important for psychological adaptation. Recovery style may change during the recovery process. For example, as symptoms and insight improve, people may 'seal over' as a way of dealing with the negative consequences of psychosis (Tait, Birchwood & Trower, 2004). Recovery style and post-psychotic trauma are discussed further in Chapter 8.

Resilience

Resilience has been defined as 'the process of adapting well in the face of adversity, trauma, threats or significant sources of stress' (American Psychological

Association, 2014, para. 4). Despite its application in other areas of mental health (Johnson, J. et al., 2011), resilience has been less well studied in psychosis. In an exception to this, Gooding et al. (2017) explored resilience in people who had been diagnosed with schizophrenia and experienced suicidal thoughts and found that they often engaged in a range of 'psychological mechanisms', including passive acceptance, resistance, emotional coping approaches, and strategies to actively counteract stressors. Individual traits (e.g. optimism) can also play a part in someone's resilience (Lepore & Revenson, 2006). In early psychosis, family resilience can provide social support, encourage help seeking and enable more functional, adaptive responses (Mo'tamedi, Rezaiemaram, Aguilar-Vafaie, Tavallaie, Azimian & Shemshadi, 2014; Chapter 11). EIP can help foster resilience by promoting positive changes in the person's life (Jordan, MacDonald, Pope, Schorr, Malla & Iyer, 2018), supporting post-traumatic growth (Dunkley & Bates, 2015) and provide a safe environment to help facilitate disclosure and develop coping skills (Lepore & Revenson, 2006). This can be provided in different ways through, for instance, the case manager relationship, psychological therapy, group work and peer support.

Post-traumatic growth (PTG)

Post-traumatic growth (PTG) is based on the observation that some people can experience positive changes following a traumatic experience, something that has also been observed following a FEP (Jordan et al., 2018). This may include: positive lifestyle changes, new possibilities and new perspectives; positive character traits and stronger sense of self, which integrates the episode; improved connections and relationships; greater religiosity; and appreciating life more. Indicators of PTG can be seen in studies exploring the general processes of recovery following FEP (see Table 7.1).

Although the concept of PTG is important for personal recovery, PTG on its own is not sufficient, nor is it required for people to progress in their psychological adaptation following a FEP. Many people are focused on their symptomatic and social recovery, and do not set out to specifically achieve PTG. The perception that the person has grown through their experiences, and may be in a 'better place' following a FEP, can be helpful for their personal recovery, but growth also needs to be reflected in changes to behaviour and functioning (Attard, Larkin, Boden & Jackson, 2017).

Measuring personal recovery and psychological adaptation following psychosis

Measuring personal recovery and psychological adaptation alongside symptom and social recovery is important to demonstrate outcomes and can help clients reflect on their own recovery journeys. However, the objective measurement of personal recovery is less clear than for social and symptomatic recovery, and many personal recovery measures are understandably subjective in nature (PROMs).

Slade et al. (2008) suggest that psychometric properties are less important in user-orientated measures of recovery, and what is measured must be significant and meaningful to the person (Williams, 2015). Personal recovery processes are individual, so it is useful for measures to represent personal goals, and place more emphasis on hearing the stories of those with lived experience of psychosis and their 'journey of recovery'. This highlights the conceptual difference between personal recovery and clinical recovery (discussed in Chapter 2) and raises key questions as to the function of these measures.

Law, Morrison, Byrne and Hoson (2012) acknowledge that it is inherently difficult to measure the unique concept of personal recovery, and that it is feasible and valid only when service users and clinicians work collaboratively and that there is no 'gold standard' measure. Nonetheless, the Process of Recovery Measure, which is a service user-based measure of recovery, is currently recommended as part of the new standards for EIP in the UK (NICE, 2016).

Appendix 2 summarises some of the main personal recovery measures which feature in the literature. Many of these measures assess personal recovery from a subjective level, given that it is a highly individual process of personal recovery. They are tools which have broader utility than just measuring outcomes, and can be used to explore and reflect on an individual's personal recovery journey.

In addition, it may be useful to consider the role for non-psychosis specific measures which tap into different aspects of personal recovery and psychological adaptation. These are beyond the scope of this chapter, but could include measures in areas of acceptance, resilience and PTG; general well-being and quality of life; and a person's values, strengths and goals.

Factors and interventions that support the process of personal recovery and psychological adaptation following a FEP

Alongside the usual EIP foundations which promote engagement and meaningful relationships, such as accessible, youth-friendly and non-stigmatising services; a fundamental ingredient of personal recovery, in the context of EIP, is the instillation of hope (Bertolote & McGorry, 2005; Lam, Pearson, Ng, Chiu, Law & Chen, 2011). Hope that you can move beyond FEP has the potential to help individuals and their families in their adaptation following FEP, and can help counter stigma. This could include promoting stories of recovery through peer support and online resources, as well as support from EIP clinicians, to see that there is hope for life beyond FEP.

Choice, empowerment and consumer participation

Chapter 2 raises the importance of choice, empowerment and consumer participation to personal recovery and psychological adaptation following a FEP. EIP interventions need to be individually tailored and formulation-driven to suit the specific needs of the individual and, where possible, offer a range of different options to choose from (see Chapter 12). Choice is a way of empowering a young person in their recovery from FEP in order to counteract the often disempowering and traumatic experiences that young people can have in the acute phases of FEP (see Chapter 8). Therefore, it is important that treatment plans should be driven by the individual's priorities (Bjornestad et al., 2016). Clinicians can support service users' psychological adaptation following a FEP by empowering them, treating them as autonomous individuals, giving them agency, focusing on strengths, and demonstrating that their views are valued. This can provide the message that they are the expert on their own life and their own agent of change, Grealish et al. (2013) conceptualise empowerment as 'being listened to, being understood, taking control and making decisions for themselves' (p. 136). Consequently, one of the goals for EIP is to have a range of interventions and treatments available, to help empower young people to make choices about which interventions they would find helpful for their recovery goals (Bjornestad et al., 2016). This can lead to more accessible and supportive services, which can provide better quality and more empowering care.

The role of social support

Caring relationships are important for personal recovery, as they can provide the sense of being loved and valued despite psychosis; show faith in the person's ability to recover; provide a sense of continuity between life before and following psychosis; and provide social support. These messages of value and acceptance from others can increase someone's sense of social worth and promote hope, and in turn help buffer against negative effects of psychosis and barriers to personal recovery, such as stigma (Connell, Schweitzer & King, 2015).

The role of medication

From Chapter 3, it is clear that medication plays a vital role in symptomatic recovery in FEP and is valued by service users and carers (Schizophrenia Commission, 2012). For medication to be most helpful, it is important to minimise adverse effects, give the lowest doses possible, and give people as much choice as possible. By providing choice, empowerment and involvement in decision-making regarding medication, services will increase the likelihood of people being concordant with their medical treatment, as well as promoting themes important to personal recovery (see also the Foreword to this book, 'From psychosis to politics'). Chapter 3 also raises the potential role of medication in helping promote empowerment, through self-management of early warning signs to help prevent relapse (see also Chapter 4).

The role of metacognition

Metacognition refers to the capacity someone has to think about their own thinking, and the thinking of others (Flavell, 1979). In psychosis, it can be helpful for people to develop metacognitive skills, e.g. increasing awareness of their cognitive biases, such as jumping to conclusions or ignoring dis-confirmatory information (Lysaker, Hamm, Hasson-Ohayon, Pattison & Leonhardt, 2018). Kukla et al. (2013) found that people with better metacognitive skills held stronger subjective perceptions of recovery, beyond the symptoms of psychosis, suggesting that being able to reflect on oneself and integrate ideas about oneself and others within the larger world could help the person to progress in their personal recovery. Lysaker et al. (2008) highlight links between metacognition and internalised stigma, showing how personal narratives of people who have experienced psychosis can be adversely affected by internalised stigma and deficits in metacognition. Metacognitive skills can often be developed through psychological therapies, discussed later in this chapter (see also Chapter 4).

Case manager interventions

The therapeutic relationship between the case manager and the service user is of central importance in supporting symptomatic, social and personal recovery (see Chapter 12). For psychological adaptation specifically, case managers can use the relationship to instil hope, help clients build their sense of self and identity, work collaboratively, explore values and goals, help them discover where to find meaning in life, and maintain enthusiasm even when the client is struggling (Tindall, Francey & Hamilton, 2015).

In addition, core case manager interventions, such as psychoeducation and relapse prevention, can give opportunities to promote personal recovery, such as helping people make sense of their experiences (Hagen & Nixon, 2010) through self-reflection, shared formulations, increasing understanding and integration of experiences, processing loss, normalising, validating and instilling hope for self-management and recovery. Relapse prevention work is particularly important, given relapse can lead to demoralisation, entrapment, shame, stigma, guilt, embarrassment or self-blame and lead to experiences of marginalisation and a lack of control (see Chapter 4), which are clearly counter-productive to a person's psychological adaptation and personal recovery. As discussed in Chapter 4, focusing on 'staying well' rather than relapse can help promote empowerment, self-efficacy and hope for recovery, e.g. Wellness Recovery Action Planning (WRAP; Copeland, 2015). This kind of work can bring up the pain and grief of the experience of psychosis as well as the pain that can arise from the process of recovery itself (Buck et al., 2013). When case managers return to these interventions over time, they can be a tool for acceptance-based work, grief processing and integration of experiences.

The role of peers

Peer support providers, with personal experience of recovery from mental health issues, receive training and supervision to help them guide and support others going through similar issues (International Association of Peer Supporters, www.inaops.org). Chapter 6 discusses the role for peer support in promoting social recovery. However, there is less literature on the role of peer support in promoting personal recovery, particularly in FEP (White, Price & Barker, 2017). One peer worker explains:

> I wanted to be able to show people that however low you go down, there is a way up, and there is a way out.... The thing I try to instil is, no matter where you are, if you want to get somewhere else you can, there's always a route to get to where you want to be.
>
> (Repper, 2013, p. 4)

There are also benefits to the peer workers themselves to help them find meaning in their experiences and feel socially relevant (Windell & Norman, 2013). Box 7.1 presents Phil's journey to becoming a peer support worker following his experiences of FEP. Peers can be brought together though group work, social activities and joint appointments. More formal peer support could include structured peer interventions, such as Intentional Peer Support (Mead, 2014), which can be delivered in a group (O'Donoghue, Morris, Oliver, Johns & Jolley, 2018) or on a one-to-one basis, or by training peer workers to provide psychosocial interventions (Dent-Pearce, Daya, Karagounis & Thomas, 2014).

Box 7.1 Phil's story: a journey through psychosis and into peer support

At age 19, a traumatic brain injury after a snowboard accident, trouble sleeping and alcohol/drugs triggered symptoms of psychosis. The identity I had constructed tentatively during adolescence was thrown into crisis. I felt grief over the loss of the life I had chosen, leaving behind my past friends and lifestyle. Learning how to make sense of these experiences will be lifelong – as is personal recovery. In my experience, therapeutic engagement and trust are difficult to achieve when the system is oppressive, leading to stigma and discrimination. Thankfully this cycle of poor health was broken by some incredible services and practitioners. I fully owe my life to some parts of the system that have taken it as their mission to be recovery-focused.

My diagnosis is no longer a life sentence for me. I made a commitment to integrate into a recovery community of like-minded people who are empowered to accept a new identity. This whole-person view of health and recovery has included a spiritual aspect, as well as physical body, mental, and social community connections. I can now admit that my life had become unmanageable. Moving towards creative and hopeful possibilities has gone hand in hand with the acceptance of my symptoms – I live well regardless of the presence or absence of them. As I continue to experience psychotic features day by day, I am also learning to listen and observe without judgement. Acknowledge, and move on.

Peer support started for me while I was staying in the psychiatric wards. From day one I was forming relationships with other survivors of the system. These peer relationships were fluid and organic, based on hope and learning, and so purposeful. Those peer relationships broke down the isolating barriers of stigma, discrimination and oppression; and they were able to give me a sense of humanity again.

When studying to become a Community Support Worker (CSW), I began to examine my values and experiences, and learned about what had happened to me, a journey of rediscovery. I find, through my current role as a peer support worker, there is greater opportunity for satisfaction than if I had ignored a huge aspect of myself. My perspective of life is richer and broader, thanks to supporting others who are on similar journeys. I have a deeper understanding of myself, and a deeper understanding of how I can be with another human.

Creative interventions

Although art therapies have been used in EIP settings (e.g. Parkinson & Whiter, 2016), there are mixed findings on their effectiveness for symptomatic recovery (Attard & Larkin, 2016). Art therapies may, however, prove more useful in promoting personal recovery, although there remains little research, as yet, investigating this. Creative interventions can be positive tools for promoting psychological well-being and may aid personal recovery journeys (Darewych & Bowers, 2017). Engaging with FEP clients in artistic ways can help them gain insights into their world by helping them communicate and process their experiences (Attard et al., 2017). EIP services can help promote creative interventions in different ways, e.g. providing specialist art or music therapists; collaborating with local arts organisations; engaging individuals or groups in artistic activities (Lutgens, Gariepy & Malla, 2017); or holding groups at art galleries, away from the demands and stigma of mental health services. One young person who attended an EIP art group run by a local community arts organisation describes how this helped his personal recovery:

It has been very up and down for me, but one thing that has truly helped has been being creative. I had the opportunity to go to a local art group and produce some art together with like-minded individuals, in a very supportive, encouraging environment. I learnt various techniques which opened my eyes to how positive it can be when dealing with a mental illness to have freedom of artistic expression. The art group brought out the best in me. It has fuelled my creativity and empowered me, and many others, to do something constructive and it has improved my sense of well-being massively.

The role of music therapy in personal recovery following psychosis has also been explored (McCaffrey, Carr, Petter, Solli & Hense, 2018), although less specifically with FEP clients. Music can be incorporated into EIP through helping people access music spaces or groups where they can explore personal and creative interests and gain a sense of achievement and pleasure. In Birmingham EIP, we have found this helps with service engagement. In Christchurch, New Zealand, the music group helps people engage when they may otherwise find social situations difficult, provides informal peer support, and creates a sense of togetherness and belonging through the experience of playing and creating music together. This helps people increase confidence, gain a sense of achievement and help create collaborative relationships between clients and the service.

Family interventions (FIs)

Key roles for families in promoting personal recovery following a FEP are loving, valuing and empowering their relative and inspiring hope for recovery (Onwumere, Grice, & Kuipers, 2016). For instance, Behavioural Family Therapy (BFT) can help promote personal recovery by increasing family understanding and improving communication, which can help individuals feel more 'attached' to their families again (see Chapter 11).

Lifestyle interventions

While lifestyle interventions in EIP would usually be associated with promoting physical health and well-being (see Chapter 3), these may have a positive impact on someone's personal recovery too. Meaningful leisure activities and lifestyle strategies to improve sleep, self-care, stress management and substance use reduction, can help enhance a person's sense of control, hope and agency. Even a lifestyle activity like yoga, widely used in the general population to promote well-being, has begun to attract attention for its utility with people experiencing psychosis (e.g. Pradhan & Pinninti, 2016).

Cultural approaches

EIP services work with people from a wide range of different backgrounds. For instance, 35% of UK EIP service users are from non-white ethnic minorities (National Audit data, Royal College of Psychiatry, 2018). Cultural differences exist in the presentation and interpretation of psychotic symptoms (Whaley & Geller, 2003) and cultural factors may influence the course of illness and recovery (Rosenfarb, Bellack, Aziz, Kratz & Sayers, 2004). As mentioned in Chapter 1, it is important to work closely and sensitively with ethnic minority groups and adapt EIP to ensure services and interventions are accessible, promote health equality and reduce the potential for stigma and aversive mental health treatment (Islam, Rabiee & Singh, 2015; see Chapter 12).

Spirituality is one area of importance for personal recovery. Although symptoms of psychosis can have religious themes, for many people, a spiritual or religious interest can be a 'healthy expression of healing and recovery' (Hagen & Nixon, 2010, p. 725). Religiousness and spirituality have been linked with self-perceived well-being (Corrigan. McCorkle, Schell & Kidder, 2003) and quality of life; can promote hope and a sense of community (Bellamy, Jarrett, Mowbray, MacFarlane, Mowbray & Holter, 2007); help with meaning-making and provide a sense of fulfilment and connectedness (Ho, Lo, Chan & Chen, 2014); and bring someone joy and purpose (Anderson-Clarke & Warner, 2016). It may also help people overcome loss and despair, which are common following a FEP, by giving someone positive meaning and hope for recovery, forgiveness, social support and spiritual coping skills (Young, 2015; see also Chapter 9).

In Birmingham EIP, we may work with local religious leaders, such as Imams and chaplains, when individuals or families require some guidance from a spiritual or cultural perspective, while also working alongside the more traditional mental health team. This is in line with recommendations that EIP includes the person's religious and spiritual experiences in assessment and therapy (Islam, Rabiee & Singh, 2015). In NZ, cultural workers, such as Pūkenga Atawhai (Māori Mental Health Workers) use cultural models to understand a person's difficulties and guide interventions. For example, the Te Whare Tapa Whā model of Māori health (Durie, 1994) provides a holistic model of wellness, where alongside physical health (Taha Tinana) and mental health (Taha Hinengaro), the family health (Taha Whānau) and spiritual health (Taha Wairua) are of equal importance. This links to a broader concept of 'recovery' than symptoms and social functioning alone. EIP team approaches to working with people from diverse cultural and ethnic backgrounds are also discussed in Chapter 12.

Group approaches

Group work in EIP can help promote symptomatic and social recovery (see Chapters 4 and 6); give opportunities to interact with peers (as mentioned previously); and can provide a sense of belonging, autonomy, responsibility and self-esteem (Yalom & Leszcz, 2008). Group work in some EIP services has attempted to address the three different aspects of recovery (e.g. Malla, McLean & Norman, 2004) by covering medication and early warning signs (symptom recovery), relationships and social skills (social recovery) and identity issues and coping with stigma (personal recovery). There are also groups using therapy models with inherent processes relevant to symptom, social and personal recovery (e.g. ACT for Recovery groups; O'Donoghue et al., 2018).

In Birmingham EIP, we developed a Personal Recovery Group, following a qualitative investigation of recovery in FEP (Baggott, 2010). The aim of the group is to provide a space for sharing stories of hope and recovery; meeting others who have been through similar experiences to help understand, normalise and de-stigmatise them; help people integrate their experiences; discuss stigma and disclosure; increase self-management of difficulties (beyond just symptoms); acknowledge fears along with hopes for the future and set recovery goals.

The group is delivered in a closed-group format and consists of six two-hour sessions, held weekly. It is interactive and uses videos of people talking about their experiences of psychosis and recovery, with different activities and exercises including artwork. The videos used are a combination of clips available online (see Box 7.1) and clips from video interviews with previous group members. The groups are held away from mental health service premises, at various youth-friendly and non-stigmatising locations around the city. Run by two EIP facilitators, where possible, they also involve a previous 'graduate' of the group as a peer facilitator. These peer facilitators are highly valued by group members, and use their own experiences of psychosis and recovery to help others reflect on their experiences and promote hope for the future. Peer facilitators are supported by the other group facilitators and remunerated for their time and expenses, an important part of valuing the role that they have.

Group attendees have shown improvements in their self-ratings of recovery, as measured by the Recovery Star, Recovery Assessment Scale and CHOICE questionnaire (see Appendix 2) and qualitative feedback is positive with themes including positivity for the future, reduced isolation and value in meeting others, understanding more about psychosis, and confidence in recovery.

Psychological therapies

As mentioned previously, psychological therapies have a key role in promoting aspects of psychological adaptation, such as acceptance, resilience and the processes of transformation and PTG. Just having the space to talk about experiences can be helpful, as self-disclosure is often associated with higher PTG and improved personal recovery (Pietruch & Jobson, 2012). As mentioned in Chapter 4, one major premise of psychological therapies for psychosis is that an individual's FEP is conceptualised as understandable in relation to their life story and experiences. This is a fundamental step in supporting someone to psychologically adapt to their experiences. Understanding that there is meaning in these experiences, and using therapeutic conversations and interventions to help someone change their relationship to them, can be an important stage in acceptance and PTG.

The process of personal recovery can be challenging. Psychological therapy can help people become aware of the concrete things they have lost while being unwell and the need to come to terms with themselves as an 'ordinary' person in an ordinary world who has agency within their lives (Buck et al., 2013). As such, along with gains and progress, we need to support people with their simultaneous pain and grief. This relates to the concept of acceptance, which is important for personal recovery, and is an important component of some psychological therapies, such as ACT, discussed further below.

Rufus May, a clinical psychologist with lived experience of psychosis, gives a useful account of the role of therapy to help make sense of experiences and move towards recovery (May, 2004). Stephanie Allan also reports personal experiences of psychological therapy following FEP:

I was given a mixture of cognitive behavioural therapy and 'third-wave' therapies such as mindfulness in addition to being allowed to vent! My resilience increased throughout the sessions and by the time they finished I had a better opinion of myself and was able to understand that psychosis was an illness that could be treated and not some kind of supernatural punishment.

(Allan, 2017, p. 235)

Cognitive behavioural therapy for psychosis (CBTp)

CBT for psychosis (CBTp) is discussed in Chapters 4 and 6 with regard to symptom and social recovery. CBTp aims to reduce distress associated with psychotic experiences and improve functioning, through helping people achieve their personal goals. Focusing on personal goals is also vital for personal recovery. Chapter 4 highlights some of the ways CBTp, targeting symptomatic and/or social recovery, can also impact on personal recovery, or where someone's delayed personal recovery may be a maintaining factor in their ongoing symptoms. For example, the CBT model of negative symptoms (Grant, Huh, Perivoliotis, Stolar & Beck, 2012) outlined in Chapter 4, highlights how cognitions, such as 'I got damaged by my psychotic breakdown and I can't enjoy things any more', can contribute to avoidance, withdrawal, negative symptoms and reduced cognitive, behavioural and emotional competencies, which consequently block goal attainment. By targeting these cognitions, CBTp could facilitate personal recovery. Likewise targeting these unhelpful beliefs in a personal recovery intervention could also facilitate social and symptomatic recovery. Finally, CBT helps young people process the traumatic aspects of FEP (Jackson et al., 2009; see Chapter 8), which in turn can play a role in promoting personal recovery and psychological adaptation.

Acceptance, mindfulness and compassion-focused approaches ('third-wave')

'Third-wave' cognitive-behavioural interventions are a group of therapy approaches that focus more on a person's relationship with thoughts and emotions rather than their content. These approaches emphasise mindfulness, acceptance, values and meta-cognition (Hayes & Hofmann, 2017). Some of these interventions have been developed or adapted specifically for psychosis, including Acceptance and Commitment Therapy (ACT; Bach & Hayes, 2002), Mindfulness-Based Cognitive Therapy (MBCT; Segal, Williams & Teasdale, 2002), Person-Based Cognitive Therapy (PBCT; Chadwick, 2006), and Compassionate Mind Training (CMT; Gilbert, 2010), which we discuss below. While they have distinct characteristics and techniques and are often delivered and researched independently, there is often an overlap between them that can be used integratively for people experiencing psychosis (Wright, Turkington, Kelly, Davies, Jacobs & Hopton, 2014).

The main aim of these therapies is to increase a person's willingness to embrace a wide range of experiences (e.g. thoughts, feelings, sensations, memories, voices), as they occur in the present moment, instead of avoiding or suppressing them (Khoury, Lecomte, Gaudiano & Paquin, 2013). These skills can be helpful in changing how someone relates and responds to their experiences of psychosis and help reduce the distress associated with symptoms, rather than aiming to reduce the symptoms themselves. The importance of acceptance in the process of psychological adaptation following FEP, as discussed previously, is a central tenet of these approaches.

Meta-analytic evidence from 13 studies of FEP found that third-wave interventions for psychosis, (e.g. mindfulness, acceptance and compassion approaches) were moderately effective, with a greater effect on negative than positive symptoms (Khoury et al., 2013). With regards to personal recovery, these approaches can increase self-efficacy and reduce internalised stigma (Davis & Kurzban, 2012). Learning mindful responses to psychotic experiences can help the person understand that they are transient experiences and do not define the person, which can help them to accept the experiences and ultimately themselves (Abba, Chadwick & Stevenson, 2008). Mindfulness approaches may therefore help people develop a transformative experience of psychosis and promote psychological adaptation (Hagen & Nixon, 2010). In FEP specifically, these kinds of interventions have been shown to increase self-understanding and acceptance (Ashcroft, Barrow, Lee & MacKinnon, 2012), and predict lower self-stigma (Mersh, Jones & Oliver, 2015).

A number of recent useful books provide the rationale, evidence and interventions for acceptance, compassion and mindfulness-based approaches for psychosis (e.g. O'Donoghue et al., 2018). We will now briefly discuss some of these.

Compassion-focused approaches

Following a FEP and subsequent episodes, people can feel shamed, marginalised and stigmatised by their experiences, which can lead to avoidance of the social world (Turner, Bernard, Birchwood, Jackson & Jones, 2013). In turn, this can restrict their ability to generate positive emotions, and impact on their personal or psychological adaptation to the experiences of psychosis (see Chapter 8). Increasing a person's compassion towards themselves can play a part in psychological adaptation following psychosis. Current evidence suggests that compassion-focused therapy (CFT; Gilbert, 2010) can have a positive impact on the well-being of individuals with psychosis (Mayhew, 2015) (see case study 8.4, Josie, in Chapter 8).

Johnson, D. et al. (2011) report on an intervention using loving-kindness meditation. Although they were primarily targeting negative symptoms, they noted the impact this also had on people's psychological recovery in terms of improvements in environmental mastery (i.e. feeling in control of life), self-acceptance and satisfaction with life.

Mindfulness-based approaches

Mindfulness-based Cognitive Therapy (MBCT; Segal et al., 2002) was originally developed for relapse prevention following depression. It uses traditional CBT methods and incorporates mindfulness and meditation to help people 'decentre' from their experiences, that is, become more accepting of them without attaching or reacting to them (Hofmann, Sawyer, Witt & Oh, 2010). MBCT has been adapted for people experiencing psychosis and has been shown to help change the way people construe themselves, others, and their experience of psychosis; it can also increase self-understanding and the ability to act with awareness (Randal, Bucci, Morera, Barrett & Pratt, 2016).

Person-Based Cognitive Therapy (PBCT) for distressing psychosis (Chadwick, 2006) combines mindfulness with cognitive therapy and acceptance approaches. The aim of PBCT is to understand and reduce a person's distress as well as promoting their strengths and well-being. Ellett (2013) provides an overview of PBCT for distressing psychosis while Strauss and Hayward (2013) demonstrate how this can be used in a group format. PBCT can facilitate psychological adaptation, through helping people develop new meanings, accept present-moment experiences, promote positive self-schemas and increase metacognitive awareness within the context of collaborative learning and promoting acceptance.

Acceptance and commitment therapy

As mentioned previously in this book (in Chapters 4 and 6), a number of studies have applied acceptance and commitment therapy to psychotic experiences (ACTp) (Butler et al., 2016). In terms of psychological adaptation and PR, ACTp does not focus on symptoms themselves, but rather the person's psychological relationship with these symptoms. For example, Shawyer et al. (2007) found that people who were more accepting of voices had lower depression and more confidence in coping with their symptoms (voices), and better self-rated quality of life.

As well as helping people with their relationship to symptoms, this approach extends to helping people adapt their relationship to their FEP as a whole. This can include helping people to identify their values and take actions in line with these despite the experiences of psychosis; helping people to step back ('defuse') from the unhelpful 'stories' they hold about themselves following a FEP; and using mindfulness skills to help them respond more flexibly to the experiences of psychosis and other challenges faced in life. Existing evidence indicates that ACT is a promising adjunctive therapy for people with psychosis, particularly for changes in negative symptoms and reduced re-hospitalisation (Tonarelli, Pasillas, Alvarado, Dwivedi & Cancellare, 2016) but further research is warranted.

Psychological treatments like ACT, which promote acceptance of distress in the service of valued goals and target the believability of psychotic symptoms, can be a useful adjunct to pharmacological strategies that aim to directly reduce symptoms (Gaudiano, 2015). When team members are consistent with each other, this can reduce conflicting or confusing messages to the person and their family, i.e. one aim is to reduce or take away the symptoms with medication, and a simultaneous aim is to help the person learn ways of living a meaningful life even with ongoing symptoms. By normalising and validating the person's desire to get rid of the symptoms and return to their 'normal' life while finding ways to help them get out and live the life they want anyway, even with ongoing symptoms, the person may feel more empowered in their recovery process, instead of passively waiting for trials of different medication to take effect. This can be an important part of integrating and adapting to these experiences.

Another strength of ACT is the normalising stance of humanness, i.e. we are all 'swimming in the same soup' (Bach & Moran, 2008, p. 83). We are not separating out psychosis as different or 'mad'. Practitioners often use these approaches in their own lives, so there is a genuineness and shared experience of these approaches and tools, which can be a helpful part of supporting someone in their journey of adaptation following psychosis. Facilitator self-disclosure has also been found to be helpful in group contexts (O'Donoghue et al., 2018), as it helps illustrate the common humanness of struggling with experiences, especially when moving towards something of value; a useful message to convey when supporting someone in their personal recovery following FEP.

Other psychological interventions to promote personal recovery

Other types of psychological therapy could be helpful in supporting people in their process of psychological adaptation, although there is little applied specifically to FEP groups. Hamm et al. (2013) discuss five integrative therapy approaches for people affected by psychosis, demonstrating how these frameworks are consistent with personal recovery. They all emphasise interpersonal attachment, personal narratives, metacognitive processes and the importance of the therapeutic relationship. Other therapies that could play a role in promoting psychological adaptation following FEP include Cognitive Interpersonal Therapy (e.g. Gumley & Schwannauer, 2006), Metacognitive Therapy (e.g. Kukla, Lysaker & Salyers, 2013); Narrative CBT for Psychosis (e.g. Rhodes & Jakes, 2009); and Open Dialogue (Seikkula, Aaltonen, Alakare, Haarakangas, Keränen & Lehtinen, 2006). Undoubtedly there is overlap between different therapeutic approaches, in terms of targeting the core processes of personal recovery. Regardless of which specific therapies are used, it is important that the therapeutic relationship is strong, and that adequate time is given for the person to progress. This often does not occur in a linear fashion, takes time and requires a willingness from the practitioner to sit with fluctuations in personal recovery and the process of psychological adaptation.

Using technology to enhance personal recovery

Increasingly, technological resources are available to help support people in their recovery following psychosis and can provide a useful platform for interventions designed to enhance personal recovery and as a supplement to existing care (Álvarez-Jiménez, Aaltonen, Alakare, Haarakangas, Keränen & Lehtinen, 2014). Most of the research has looked into the use of the internet or mobile device-based interventions for people with psychosis, which has included e-interventions to promote recovery (Gucci & Marmo, 2016), deliver peer support (Baumel, Correll & Birnbaum, 2016), reduce stigma (Ladea, Bran & Claudiu 2016) and cope with voices (Gottlieb, Harper Romeo, Penn, Mueser & Chiko, 2013). Thomas et al. (2016) used a digital intervention to support personal recovery specifically, by helping clinicians structure therapeutic discussions about personal recovery using video interviews of people with psychosis talking about how they managed issues in their own recovery.

Technology may help optimise psychosocial interventions in FEP (Breitborde, Moe, Ered, Ellman & Bell, 2017) by peer-to-peer social networking and enhancing social connectedness and empowerment as illustrated by the Silver Linings App, developed in Birmingham (see Box 7.2). In addition, websites that provide information, videos and blogs where people who have experienced psychosis talk about their experiences can help people learn more about their own psychosis, provide normalisation, and help them create more meaning from their experiences. Opportunities to share their experiences of psychosis with others online can, for some, be a way of creating meaning from their experiences, by using them to help others who may be going through something similar. Box 7.2 provides some useful website links, which could be recommended to young people and their families, and can be used individually or in group contexts.

Box 7.2 Useful online resources for promoting personal recovery/ psychological adaptation

- www.talkingminds.co.nz: a website on psychosis co-designed with FEP clients.
- www.attitudelive.com: a documentary, In My Mind: Psychosis, about young peoples experiences of FEP and recovery.
- www.time-to-change.org.uk: an anti-stigma organisation with personal stories of people with mental health experiences, including psychosis, aimed at promoting awareness and understanding.
- Silver Linings App: an app developed with EIP clients and clinicians in Birmingham, with useful tools for recovery, e.g. goal setting, coping strategies.
- www.youtube.com: videos by Rufus May and Eleanor Longden (clinicians) and Jonny Benjamin (campaigner) with lived experience of psychosis symptoms.

Implementing the evidence into practice

Case study 7.1 Sam: supporting personal recovery following FEP using third-wave CBT approaches

Some of Sam's personal challenges following FEP were highlighted at the start of this chapter. This case example presents Sam's story (Box 7.3) and some of the ways EIP helped facilitate his personal recovery following FEP.

Sam had achieved well at school, had a good network of friends, and a supportive family. Although he had dabbled in recreational cannabis use in his late teens, this did not impact negatively on his functioning. Sam was confident and well liked, positive about his future and looking forward to pursuing a career in the music industry after his degree. However, Sam became unwell soon after he moved to a different city to start university. The transition to university was difficult for him, his sleep pattern was poor, and in the first few months he used increasing amounts of alcohol and cannabis. He began missing lectures, and then began to worry that he was getting behind, comparing himself unfavourably to his peers. He became suspicious and withdrew even more. Using more cannabis to try and help him cope with his stresses only exacerbated his symptoms. He started to experience some unusual perceptual experiences, such as hearing things that weren't there, and his behaviour became more erratic. This alerted his flat mates, and he was assessed by the university medical service.

He was admitted voluntarily to hospital and diagnosed with a first episode of psychosis and prescribed antipsychotic (AP) medication, initially risperidone, that was later changed to aripiprazole due to side effects. Sam responded well to AP medication and his symptoms resolved relatively quickly. After discharge, he withdrew from university and returned to live with his parents. Sam was referred to the EIP service in his local area, and with the support of the team and his family, was able to maintain his symptomatic recovery. Sam also made some progress in aspects of his social recovery, picked up some part-time modules at his local university, and continued to socialise with his friends. He abstained from cannabis, recognising that this was unhelpful for his mental health, and engaged well with his case manager, the team psychologist and his psychiatrist.

On the outside, Sam seemed to be making a good symptomatic and social recovery. However, Sam was struggling with his personal recovery, his psychological adaptation to his experience and receiving a diagnosis of psychosis. For Sam, the social changes in his life and disappointment of university not turning out the way he hoped had a big impact. Insight into his psychosis was good but made him vulnerable to experiencing internalised stigma and fear for the future. Some of the issues that Sam was struggling with included:

- Comparing himself to friends who 'have their life sorted', and comparisons to his previous self. He felt like a different person, had lower self-esteem and confidence, and was experiencing some social anxiety in contrast to his previous 'breezy' personality. He saw himself previously as a positive person, but now held a more negative outlook, feeling pessimistic about what the future would hold, unlike his previous 'glass half-full' self.

- He felt a little lost, disconnected from his previous valued activities, including music and his university band, which elicited strong feelings of loss. He attempted to manage these painful feelings of loss by avoiding music which unintentionally increased his disconnection from it.
- Struggling to talk to friends about psychosis and worrying what they would think of him, he developed self-limiting and self-stigmatising beliefs about his future.

Sam received a number of different interventions during the first 6–12 months with EIP. In addition to approaches which targeted symptoms and social functioning, Sam engaged with one-to-one psychological therapy, which predominantly focused on his personal recovery and integrated a number of CBT and mindfulness-based approaches.

ACT approaches included values exploration and supporting his reconnection with music by setting goals and actions and using a 'passengers-on-the-bus' metaphor to help him understand more about the nature of thoughts and feelings and promote acceptance of them, Sam also practised defusion skills to step back from unhelpful thoughts, developed mindfulness skills to observe internal experiences without getting caught up in judgements, e.g. focusing on inter-actions with friends rather than making comparisons with them. He used everyday mindfulness to spot moments of connection and enjoyment rather than just focusing on the thoughts that things had changed from before. Finally, self-as-context interventions helped him see that psychosis is a part of his life but not the whole of him.

Compassionate approaches included normalising his experiences, relating to himself with kindness, thinking about what other people would say or what he would say to them; giving himself time for recovery and acknowledging the suffer-ing he had been through; watching videos of other people talking about their experiences of psychosis and recovery, and bringing compassion to them, to help him bring it to himself.

CBT approaches included identifying common unhelpful thinking patterns, and bringing compassionate rationalisations to these; attention shift experiments, to help him practise focusing outward on his social interactions rather than being caught up in his head; focusing on behavioural actions and engaging in activities that brought closeness, achievement and enjoyment as well as bringing him in touch with his values.

Sam also took part in a peer support group, a Personal Recovery Group and was offered creative groups, such as the music and art group. All of these added further opportunities to promote his personal recovery and psychological adaptation. In supporting Sam, we worked patiently and flexibly, anticipating fluctuations in his overall progress (Box 7.3). There were times when he seemed to 'turn a corner' in his personal recovery, but there were also 'down days', and so 'the door' for support remained open.

Box 7.3 Sam's account of his journey through FEP and into personal recovery

This year has been a bit of a rollercoaster. I started off looking to start my university degree in a different city studying music. Then something I never expected happened, I had a psychotic episode. At the time, I had no idea what was going on. I was fearful for my life, paranoid, on edge, couldn't sleep.

Psychosis had a huge impact on me and my life. Essentially it came in and disrupted everything that was normal and good in my life. It affected my social life, my passion for music, my dreams and ambitions, what was going on in my head and my general outlook on life. To have something come and do that for you can be a really scary thing, and, for me, it was really tough to get past. There were times when it felt like the whole world was against me. Times when I felt like I had nothing to live for. It really impacts you in quite a surreal way. And it's a really personal thing to go through as well. No one else knows what's going on. Some people might know bits and pieces, and some might know a good deal but it feels like no one knows what it's like to go through it. I think something I've come to realise is that you're not alone. There are a lot of people out there going through similar things to you and I think that's a real comforting thing to know.

Throughout the recovery process, there were definitely ups and downs, with a lot of them being downs. I think an important thing I learned was that it's one big process. It takes time and you can't rush it. It really tests your patience. One of the big challenges I faced was the conflict with self. There was a constant battle going on in my head, one which was really hard to fight. Negative thinking absorbs you, thinking 'why aren't I the same person I used to be?' or 'why is everyone doing better than me right now?'. These thoughts become really hard to deal with, especially when you're dealing with them all the time. It can turn quite quickly into a downward spiral, where nothing looks good or hopeful. When you're in that position, everything looks grim and you're left thinking 'will things ever get better?'

I began to really connect with music about six months in. I had been trying other things like poetry, writing, reading and running as well. But having this connection really helped me on my recovery. It was something I became able to do and enjoy, kind of like an outlet, a constant that was always there. I think being able to express yourself is another important aspect of recovery. For me, I kept a journal of my recovery which I would try to write in fairly regularly. There I could express the highs, the lows and everything in between. It really became something that I enjoyed doing, keeping a record of my journey.

Sam's story highlights how different aspects of recovery interlink, and how integrated treatments can help support someone in their journey of adaptation following psychosis, in the symptom, social and psychological realms. A range of interventions are useful, to empower the person to find the approaches that work for them, and at different stages of their recovery. The process of psychological adaptation takes time, even beyond symptomatic recovery, and of course this process may take longer when someone is still experiencing delays in their symptom or social recovery. Chapter 12 reinforces that the team approach of EIP is crucial, working together (and with the client) to ensure progress in all three aspects of recovery.

Optimising personal recovery and psychological adaptation following FEP: the relationship between the three domains of recovery

This chapter has focused on the ways in which EIP can support someone in their psychological adaption and personal recovery following FEP. A range of interventions are suggested, within the context of promoting hope, providing choice and opportunities for empowerment and establishing good therapeutic relationships with clients. As we have proposed throughout this book (see Figure 2.1), it is important that EIP services, where indicated, address personal recovery *alongside* symptomatic and social recovery (see Chapter 12). Social and symptomatic recovery are intrinsically linked with personal recovery and influence the process of each other in a reciprocal way (Windell, Norman, Lal & Malla, 2015). However, they are also important individual processes, e.g. symptomatic recovery does not mean a person will experience personal recovery, nor must symptoms be eradicated for someone to experience psychological adaptation following a FEP.

There is a complex relationship between personal and symptomatic recovery (Rossi et al., 2017). Personal recovery can be enhanced by the remission of psychotic symptoms as well as a more integrated attitude towards the experiences of psychosis (Wciórka, Switaj & Anczewska, 2015). For example, symptom levels and emotional discomfort have been linked with self-reported recovery, personal confidence, hope, goal orientation and sense of domination by symptoms (Jørgensen et al., 2015). Similarly, ongoing psychotic symptoms can be a barrier to the way someone makes sense of their experiences and their development of coping self-efficacy (Mazor, Gelkopf, Mueser & Roe, 2016). At the same time, negative interpersonal self-concepts and believing that others don't accept them can mediate symptoms such as paranoia (Lincoln, Mehl, Ziegler, Kesting, Exner & Rief, 2010). Windell and Norman (2013) report how medication is seen by some as an important turning point in the acceptance of being unwell or needing assistance, yet, for others, medication side effects can negatively impact on sense of self, which in turn may impact on personal recovery. Therefore, it is important that EIP services work collaboratively with service users and strive to empower them and promote their choice and agency.

Social recovery can provide key opportunities for personal recovery, as social activities and connections can provide an important sense of meaning, purpose and worth, enhance the person's perceived social value and help them discover or re-discover their strengths, talents and abilities (Windell & Norman, 2013). Subjective experiences of social recovery can include a sense of inclusion and social acceptance, belonging, connection and purpose (Subandi, 2015). These place emphasis on values, connection and meaning, all important to someone's psychological recovery. Social support and valued relationships can help with their sense of self, control, acceptance of illness and engagement in treatment, buffering against stigma and promoting positive expectations, hope and perceived social worth (see Chapters 5 and 6). These factors, gained from participation in social relationships and occupational activities, are viewed by many people as a sign of their personal recovery, and not just their social recovery (Connell et al., 2015).

Learning points

- The processes of personal recovery following FEP are intrinsically interlinked with symptom and social recovery, although there are specific features of personal recovery.
- Themes of personal recovery include: overcoming adversity and stigma; regaining control and accepting help; hope and optimism; rebuilding one's life and working towards valued goals; establishing a sense of belonging and valued social roles; integrating the experience of psychosis; and reconstructing the self.
- There are a number of PROMs that can be useful to measure personal recovery following a FEP, and promote conversations about recovery.
- There are a multitude of approaches, ranging from the service ethos (e.g. inspiring hope) through to individual psychosocial interventions, which can help people on their journey through the challenging personal effects of FEP.
- One core task of supporting someone in their psychological adaptation is to help them make sense of, and integrate, their experiences of psychosis and the social challenges they may face.
- Psychological therapies, particularly third-wave cognitive-behavioural therapies, can have an important role in promoting psychological adaptation.
- Opportunities for people to hear from others about their experiences are invaluable, which can be provided through group work, peer support and online resources.

Chapter 8

When psychological adaptation and recovery go wrong

Emotional distress and recovery from psychosis

This chapter considers the impact of emotional dysfunction on recovery in FEP. Emotional dysfunction is often unhelpfully referred to as 'comorbidity' (Hartley, Barrowclough & Haddock, 2013) and in this book we draw a distinction between emotional dysfunction in FEP and comorbidities (e.g. ASD, Personality Disorders), which are considered in Chapter 10. Emotional dysfunction is pervasive in non-affective FEP (Birchwood, 2003) and implicated in the development (Freeman & Garety, 2003; Hartley et al., 2013), persistence (Hartley et al., 2013; Myin-Germeys & van Os, 2007) and relapse (Birchwood, 2003; Gumley & Schwannauer, 2006; Hartley et al., 2013) of psychosis. However, the causal relationships between emotional experiences and psychosis remain to be established (Hartley et al., 2013). Emotional dysfunction often persists after the resolution of positive symptoms (Birchwood, 2003) and contributes to delays in recovery (Achim, Maziade, Raymond, Olivier, Merette & Roy, 2011) due to association with hospital admissions, negative appraisals of psychosis, suicide, self-harm, substance misuse and social avoidance (Birchwood, 2003; Hartley et al., 2013; Mueser, Lu, Rosenberg, & Wolfe, 2010). We will now discuss depression, anxiety, trauma, and shame following a FEP. The association between emotional dysfunction and suicide is considered in Chapter 9.

Depression and psychosis

Experiencing depression following a FEP can contribute to delayed recovery in different ways. The impact of depression cannot be underestimated, as for service users and their carers it can negate any sense of personal recovery, as outlined in Chapter 7. Positive and negative symptoms of psychosis may have abated but post-psychotic depression can elicit a sense of overwhelming loss, an absence of hope, disempowerment (Sandhu, Ives, Birchwood & Upthegrove, 2013), entrapment (Birchwood, McGorven & Spencer, 2000) and suicidality (Upthegrove et al., 2010). Consequently, individuals may struggle to engage with bio-psychosocial interventions, which not only could ease their depression, but also facilitate their recovery. Individuals experiencing depression following remission of psychotic symptoms value supportive social networks to facilitate their recovery from FEP but report a lack of empathy from friends and family due to perceptions that they are now 'recovered' and should be getting on with their lives (Sandhu et al., 2013). Depression following psychosis is associated with lower levels of friendships and recreational engagement (Joseph et al., 2017), which may contribute to poor social recovery. Finally, recovery, as has been argued consistently throughout this book, entails not only an absence of psychotic symptoms but also a sense of regaining independence, social and vocational roles (Windell, Norman & Mall, 2012) and control over one's life and one's mind, including an absence of psychotic depression (Sandhu et al., 2013). Consequently, symptomatic recovery may not be sufficient to invoke 'full' recovery in the presence of depression in the post-psychotic phase due to its negative impact on social and personal recovery.

Depression in FEP: prevalence, course, associates and insight

The prevalence of depression in FEP typically ranges from 15–83% (Chang et al., 2015; Sonmez, Romm, Andreassen, Melle & Rossberg, 2013; Upthegrove, Birchwood, Ross, Brunett, McCallum & Jones, 2010) depending on the stage of illness considered, heterogeneity in the samples, the assessment tools used, and the definitions of depression used. In the *acute phase*, prevalence rates vary from 15–35% (Chang et al., 2015; Sonmez et al., 2013; Upthegrove et al., 2010) and is associated with more severe and distressing positive symptoms (Hartley et al., 2013), including malevolent voices (Upthegrove, Ross, Brunet, McCollum & Jones, 2014) and impaired social and personal recovery (Cotton et al., 2012; Chang et al., 2015; Joseph et al., 2017). In the *post-psychotic phase*, rates of depression vary between 5–54% (Sonmez et al., 2013; Upthegrove, 2009) and is associated with more baseline positive (Upthegrove et al., 2010) and negative (Sonmez et al., 2013) symptoms, poorer social recovery (Sonmez et al., 2013), loss, shame, and entrapment (Birchwood et al., 2000) and higher suicidality at follow-up (Sonmez et al., 2013). Finally, FEP patients with depression are more likely to have been depressed *before the onset* of their psychosis (Cotton et al., 2012; Upthegrove et al., 2010), and to have had a past diagnosis of personality disorder and suicide attempts (Cotton et al., 2012), longer DUP (Sonmez et al., 2013; Upthegrove et al., 2014), exposure to stressful life events (Chang et al., 2015), and a family history of psychiatric diagnosis (Cotton et al., 2012). Therefore, a detailed pre-morbid and developmental assessment is important with post-psychotic depression (and other types of emotional dysfunction), which can be informed by standardised measures (see Appendix 2).

Depression is often associated with increased insight following psychosis (Birchwood et al., 2000; Cotton et al., 2012), which may reflect an accurate awareness of the challenges associated with psychosis (e.g. loss of social roles and relationships, hospital admissions, residual symptoms, and relapses) (Rooke & Birchwood, 1998). In contrast, a lack of insight may represent a 'sealing over' psychological defence mechanism (McGlashan, 1987; see Chapter 7) and may protect against depression and poor psychological well-being (Jackson, Knott, Skeate & Birchwood, 2005; Tait, Birchwood & Trower, 2003). A meta-analysis found that global insight was weakly, but significantly, associated with depression (Murri et al., 2015) but this relationship was moderated by the phase and duration of psychosis. In the acute phase, depression was associated with lower levels of insight but with more insight in samples with longer illness duration. Thus, longer duration of illness may lead to more depression, due to an increased awareness of psychosis and its associated negative consequences. However, insight is not a unitary concept (see also Chapter 9) and different aspects of insight (e.g. the need for treatment vs. the awareness of illness) may be differentially associated with depression in different phases (acute vs. post-psychotic) of psychosis (Upthegrove et al., 2014).

Assessing and monitoring post-psychotic depression

Given the negative outcomes associated with depression, it is not surprising that guidelines recommend that depression following psychosis is routinely monitored (NICE, 2014). Following a review of 48 studies, Lako et al. (2012a) recommended using the Calgary Depression Scale (CDS) (Addington, Addington, & Maticka-Tyndale, 1993), as it has been designed to assess depression in samples diagnosed with psychosis, it can differentiate depression from negative symptoms and extrapyramidal side effects, and it had the best predictive validity. A score of 6 or more is usually accepted as the criterion for post-psychotic depression. The CDS is completed by clinicians so it is primarily a measure of observed depression. Consequently, it can be useful to augment it with a measure of self-reported depression as health care providers often miss depression in FEP (Cotton et al., 2012; Sandhu et al., 2013). The Beck Depression Inventory-II (BDI-II) (Beck, Steer & Brown, 1996) is reliable in assessing depression in people with schizophrenia but it has poorer predictive validity compared to the CDS (Lako et al., 2012a) and is not suitable for use in the acute phase of psychosis (Upthegrove et al., 2010). However, in the absence of significant extrapyramidal side effects, negative symptoms, and acute positive symptoms, the BDI-II can be used with service users to assess depression and trigger discussions about their levels of sadness, pessimism, past failure, self-dislike, self-criticism, and worthlessness. These conversations can reveal the personal impact of FEP, which can inform formulations and guide interventions. This is illustrated in the case study 8.1 (Shazia). Post-psychotic depression is associated with appraisals of entrapment, shame, humiliation, and isolation (Birchwood et al., 2000; Rooke & Birchwood, 1998), which can be assessed with the Personal Beliefs about Illness Questionnaire Revised (BPIQ-R) (Birchwood, Jackson, Brunet, Holden & Barton, 2012). These appraisals can persist over time despite individuals experiencing symptomatic recovery (Upthegrove et al., 2014).

Bio-psychosocial interventions for depression

Medication

In the acute phase, depression sometimes reduces with medical treatment of positive symptoms alone (Birchwood et al., 2000). However, when depression persists after the resolution of positive symptoms, the potential benefits (e.g. reducing risk of suicide, relapse, improving functioning) of introducing an anti-depressant need to be weighed against the potential negative side effects (Upthegrove, 2009). In clinical practice, there is evidence of both over- and under-prescribing of anti-depressants (Lako et al., 2012b), which may reflect a lack of detailed prescribing advice in clinical guidelines (Gregory, Mallikarjun & Upthegrove, 2017; Lako et al., 2012b; Upthegrove, 2009) and the lack of historical robust evidence on the potential effectiveness of anti-depressant medication in schizophrenia spectrum disorders (Gregory et al., 2017; van Rooijen, Vermeulen, Ruhe & de Haan, 2017). An initial meta-analysis concluded there may be some benefits of anti-depressant medication following psychosis (Whitehead, Moss, Cardno & Lewis, 2003) but the majority of these trials focused mainly on tricyclic anti-depressants, which would no longer be the first-line pharmacological therapy for depression (Gregory et al., 2017). A more recent meta-analysis of 26 moderate to low quality studies concluded that anti-depressants are effective for the treatment of depression in samples meeting the criteria for schizophrenia (Gregory et al., 2017). Anti-depressants displayed a moderate effect size (over placebo), which is similar to effect sizes reported in Chapter 4 for CBTp but there were significant methodological problems in the studies analysed by Gregory et al. (2017) and few studies used FEP samples. Nonetheless, when depression in FEP has been identified, clinicians are recommended to offer a trial of anti-depressants (Gregory et al., 2017). Additional medical strategies for managing depression in FEP include reducing the dose of AP medication or switching to an alternative AP, as there is some evidence that some antipsychotics (e.g. aripiprazole, quetiapine, clozapine, olanzapine) are slightly more effective in reducing depression (van Rooijen et al., 2017).

Psychological

The potential benefits of CBT in facilitating symptomatic recovery were considered in Chapter 4. In terms of the efficacy of CBT for depression following psychosis, progress in this area has been hampered by randomised control trials (RCTs) not directly targeting depression. As concluded in Chapter 4, in order for CBTp to be more effective, future trials will need to be more focused in their approach. Thus, although depression in the acute phase can recede in response to medical treatment of positive symptoms (Birchwood et al., 2000), it is also predicted by voice malevolence, safety behaviours and entrapment (Upthegrove et al., 2014), which can all be addressed by CBTp (Trower, Birchwood, Meaden, Byrne, Nelson & Ross, 2004). In terms of improving post-psychotic depression, there is consensus that CBTp will be more effective when it is able to reduce the perceived psychological threat from receiving a diagnosis of psychosis and the associated experiences of shame, entrapment, and isolation that often accompany it (Upthegrove et al., 2014). This is illustrated in the case study 8.1.

Implementing the evidence into practice

Case study 8.1 Shazia: FEP and post-psychotic depression

Shazia was a 22-year-old woman who had had a short hospital admission after developing FEP. She had been prescribed antipsychotic medication but her care co-ordinator and psychiatrist remained concerned about her low mood and hope-lessness and referred her for psychological input.

1 Assessment and engagement. Shazia met the criteria for post-psychotic depression as she was largely free of positive symptoms on the PANSS but scored high on both measures of depression (see Table 8.1). On the BDI-II,

Table 8.1 Score for case study 8.1: FEP and post-psychotic depression

Measures	Baseline score level		Follow-up score level	
Psychosis (PANSS)				
Positive	9	Low	7	Absent
Negative	18	Moderate	9	Low
General	35	Moderate	19	Low
Total	62	Moderate	35	Low
Depression				
CDS	12	Severe	2	Low
BDI-II	32	Severe	9	Low
Personal Beliefs About Illness-R				
Loss	10	High	5	Low
Control	12	High	7	Low
Entrapment	12	High	6	Low
Group Fit	7	Low	4	Low
Shame	11	High	6	Low
Brief Core Schema Scale				
Positive Self	4	Low	–	
Negative Self	5	Low	–	
Positive Other	22	High	–	
Negative Other	0	Low	–	

Note
PANSS = Positive and Negative Symptom Scale; CDS = Calgary Depression Scale; BDI-II = Beck Depression Scale.

she reported high levels of sadness, pessimism, and worthlessness, which she attributed to her current lack of employment, loss of motivation, and uncertainty about how to move forward in her life. She reported high levels of self-criticism and guilt due to blaming herself for her breakdown, feeling dependent on her parents and siblings, her inability to get out of bed and engage with her environment, and her lack of enjoyment and pleasure when family members made an effort to socialise with her. She reported high levels of loss, entrapment, shame, and low perceived control on the PBIQ-R. She was experiencing confusion over the onset of her psychosis and her admission but denied any significant intrusive (traumatic) re-experiencing about her time in hospital. Her early environment was warm and supportive, which was consistent with scores on the Brief Core Schema Scale (BCSS). Although she scored low on the Positive Self subscale, she agreed that she was 'good', and 'respected' but she denied feeling 'valuable', 'talented', 'successful', or 'interesting'.

2 Development of change strategies. Shazia's goals were to feel less depressed, less negative in her thinking, more engaged with her environment, and more optimistic about her future. Behavioural activation helped her establish a more consistent daily and social routine. Initially, she was dependent on her mum for this and she benefited from reappraising her negative thoughts about there being no point engaging in social activities and her previous interests. Shazia required persistent CBT-based work to help her acknowledge the small achievements she was making. Her hopelessness and suicidal ideation resulted in her being prescribed an anti-depressant. Joint sessions with her mum revealed a range of triggers in the build-up to her episode, which helped Shazia appreciate her vulnerability to stress and how these experiences had contributed to her FEP.

3 Longitudinal formulation. It became apparent that vocational progress was crucial for Shazia's feelings of recovery but this was blocked by strong feelings of shame due to a work-based incident in the build-up to her FEP. Shazia had been avoiding contact with her colleagues and was not keen on returning to work when the opportunity arose. CBT helped her review evidence against her concerns and, on her return to work, she was welcomed back warmly by her colleagues, which helped her realise that her negative beliefs and expectations were not always accurate. Ultimately she decided on a different vocational direction and eventually enrolled on a college course. Although her levels of depression and negative appraisals dropped during the 12 months of therapy, it was only when she started to make progress on her course and found a new relationship that her mood significantly improved.

4 Consolidation and relapse prevention. At follow-up (see Table 8.1), Shazia had less observed (CDS) and self-reported (BDI-II) depression and lower appraisals of loss, control, entrapment, and shame on the PBIQ-R. She had continued to take anti-depressant medication, complete regular thought diaries and felt optimistic about her relationship and course.

Anxiety disorders and psychosis

Between 38% (Achim et al., 2011) and 45% (Cosoff & Hafner, 1998) of individuals who receive a diagnosis of psychosis also meet the criteria for an anxiety disorder. An anxiety disorder alongside psychosis is associated with more severe psychopathology (Achim et al., 2011), including delusions and voices (Hartley et al., 2013), more hospital admissions (Cosoff & Hafner, 1998), and poorer quality of life, recovery, and functioning (Achim et al., 2011). Achim et al. (2011) report lower rates of anxiety disorders in FEP compared to cases with multiple relapses but the number of FEP studies was extremely small, often only two or three for a particular disorder. Anxiety disorders may be more frequent in outpatient samples than in-patients, but this may be because anxiety disorders are more easily differentiated from psychotic symptoms following discharge when individuals have entered a post-psychotic phase (Achim et al., 2011). During the acute psychotic phase, it can be challenging to differentiate symptoms of anxiety from positive symptoms due to phenomenological similarity and overlap. Consequently, standardised measures can improve the identification of the source of anxiety following FEP, associations with distress and poor functioning (see Appendix 2).

Social anxiety

Some 25–32% of FEP samples meet the criteria for Social anxiety Disorder (SaD) and an additional 12%, who do not reach the full criteria for SaD, experience distress and avoidance-related behaviours directly due to social anxiety (Michail, 2013). These figures will not surprise clinicians working within EIP services as problems with social anxiety are extremely common. In FEP, social anxiety is associated with depression, poorer social functioning, worse quality of life, and earlier relapse (Michail, 2013). Rates of social anxiety are higher in FEP samples (25%) than in general populations (12%) (Buckley, Miller, Lehrer & Castle, 2009), which suggests that the experience of psychosis itself may be driving this social anxiety. Birchwood and colleagues (Birchwood et al., 2007; Michail, 2013; Michail, Birchwood & Tait, 2017) have identified that social anxiety following psychosis is associated with internalised shame and stigma associated with having a psychotic illness, fear of this stigmatised identity being uncovered, concealment behaviours (e.g. not discussing mental health difficulties with others; avoiding informing potential partners and employers), and social marginalisation. Social anxiety can occur independently of positive symptoms of psychosis in FEP but consistent with the other types of emotional dysfunction discussed in this chapter, there may be different pathways to social anxiety in psychosis (Michail, 2013). Thus, when intervening, it is important to identify the source, duration and consequences of social anxiety. Although there is a good evidence base for intervening with social anxiety without psychosis using CBT, there are only two studies with FEP samples (Halperin, Nathan, Drummon &

Castle, 2000; Kingsep. Nathan & Castle, 2003). Both found improvements in social anxiety, depression, and quality of life (Michail et al., 2017). However, methodological problems with these studies indicate a need for CBT trials based on the model of social anxiety in FEP outlined above (Birchwood, Cassidy, Brunet, Gilbert, Iqbal & Jackson, 2007).

Panic

Panic is common in samples with psychosis spectrum disorders with a mean prevalence of 10% (Achim et al., 2011) to 25% (Buckley et al., 2009), which is higher than the lifetime prevalence (2–5%) in the general population. Few studies have investigated panic in FEP. Buckley et al. (2009) identified two studies with FEP samples that found rates of 6% and 11%. Individuals who experience panic alongside psychosis have more severe psychopathology, suicidality, and substance misuse (Buckley et al., 2009). Consistent with the approach advocated throughout this book, it is important to identify idiosyncratic triggers for an individual's panic prior to intervening. During the acute psychotic phase, panic may be triggered by a range of psychotically related concerns, such as feeling overwhelmed by a threatening voice and perceived persecution or in the post-psychotic phase by fear of one's identity as an individual with psychosis being uncovered (Birchwood et al., 2007) or by the prospect of relapse (Gumley & Schwannauer, 2006).

Obsessive-compulsive disorder (OCD)

Mean prevalence rates in psychosis samples suggest that nearly one in four (23%) can experience symptoms indicative of OCD (Buckley et al., 2009). The rates within FEP samples are slightly lower and range between 10% (Hagen, Hansen, Inge & Larsen, 2013) and 15% (Buckley et al., 2009). Within EIP services, young people present with a range of experiences indicative of OCD. Often these experiences can precede the onset of psychosis by a number of years (Buckley et al., 2009), beginning in early adolescence. These experiences can be classic OCD-type presentations where an individual has fears of contamination and avoidance behaviours (Clark, 2007) or obsessive concerns about their appearance such as Body Dysmorphia Disorder (BDD), which can cause significant depression, anxiety, and loss of functioning (Veale, 2001). Young people may experience obsessional ruminations and fears about sexual identity, which can be addressed with provision of normative information regarding their prevalence followed by CBT for obsessions (Clark, 2007). In addition, traumatic intrusive re-experiences of psychosis-related themes can also take on an obsessional quality. OCD alongside psychosis is associated with more severe psychopathology, neuropsychological impairments and poorer prognosis, due to more disability, increased admissions, and less likelihood of being married and employed (Buckley et al., 2009). OCD in the context of psychosis can be associated with depression (Buckley et al., 2009;

de Haan, Sterk, Wouters & Linszen, 2013; Hagen et al., 2013), earlier age of psychosis onset (Buckley et al., 2009; Hagen et al., 2013), poorer functioning before and after FEP, and more suicidal plans and attempts (de Haan et al., 2013). This highlights the importance of identifying the presence of OCD in FEP presentations as early as possible and intervening.

Implementing the evidence into practice

Case study 8.2 Rachel: FEP and OCD

Rachel was a 17-year-old woman referred to EIP after developing critical voices and beliefs that others could read her mind. She was diagnosed with an Autistic Spectrum Disorder (ASD) (Asperger's Syndrome) (see Chapter 10) at 12 years old and had a five-year history of OCD. Rachel lived with her parents and younger sister. She was commenced on medication for her psychotic and obsessive experiences but she was still struggling with voices and OCD.

  1 Assessment, engagement, and formulation. Rachel scored moderately on the PANSS (see Table 8.2). She was preoccupied by a voice, which told her that she was useless and that she was going to become infected with a disease, which would result in her developing a potentially fatal illness. This voice echoed her obsessive concerns and commanded her to avoid

Table 8.2 Scores for case study 8.2: FEP and OCD

Measure	Baseline score level		Follow-up score level	
Psychosis (PANSS)				
Positive	14	Low	12	Low
Negative	11	Low	9	Low
General	42	Moderate	31	Low
Total	67	Moderate	52	Moderate
Beliefs About Voices Revised (BAV-R)				
Persecution	20	High	10	Moderate
Benevolence	5	Low	1	Low
Engagement	4	Low	0	Absent
Resistance	13	High	4	Low
(Y-BOCS)				
Time spent	6	Severe	4	Moderate
Interference	5	Severe	3	Moderate
Distress	8	Severe	3	Moderate
Resistance	6	Severe	3	Moderate
Control	6	Severe	3	Moderate
Total	31	Severe	16	Moderate

Note
PANSS = Positive and Negative Symptom Scale; Yale-Brown Obsessive Compulsive Scale (Y-BOCS).

certain objects, wash her hands for specific durations, and repeat associated behaviours a number of times. Assessment with the BAVQ-R indicated that Rachel held Persecutory beliefs about her voice as she was worried that if she did not do what the voice told her (e.g. wash her hands continually, avoid touching certain objects), something bad would happen to her, which resulted in her performing these behaviours more frequently and for longer duration than she wanted. She sometimes felt the voice was trying to protect her from contaminated objects (moderate Benevolence), which resulted in her Engaging with the voice. Rachel's obsessions were triggered by situations (e.g. dirty and stained objects in public places) where she perceived a potential threat of contamination and new and unfamiliar situations (e.g. starting at a new college, going on holiday to a new place), which may have been partly related to her ASD. ASD is discussed in more detail in Chapter 10. When distressed, her voice repeated her fears of contamination and her worry that something catastrophic was going to occur, which would drive her compulsive avoidance and her repetitive (including hand washing) behaviours. Since hearing the voice Rachel rarely resisted her compulsive urges due to the extra sense of threat it evoked. Consequently, she rarely tested out her underlying obsessional belief that she would contract a contaminated related illness. Assessment with the Yale-Brown Obsessive Compulsive Inventory (YBOCI) (Goodman et al., 1989) revealed that Rachel performed compulsions for between three and eight hours each day, which caused severe distress and disruption to her life and her family's routines (e.g. Rachel and her sister were frequently late for school in the morning).

2 *Development of change strategies.* Rachel's therapeutic goals were to feel less distressed by her voice and to reduce the amount of time she was engaging in compulsive behaviours and the negative impact they were having on her daily routines. Socratic questioning, thought diaries, and behavioural experiments based on models of OCD (Clark, 2007) and command hallucinations (Trower et al., 2004) supported Rachel establishing that after dropping her safety behaviours she would not become sick with a contaminated illness.

3 *Longitudinal formulation.* There was no significant childhood adversity so the formulation focused on the interaction between her previous OCD and subsequent psychosis (see above).

4 *Consolidation and relapse prevention.* At Rachel's request, her mum joined some sessions and supported her implementing and maintaining the CBT-based strategies above. Consistent with recent models of CBTp (Trower et al., 2004), Rachel did not experience much of a reduction in the severity of her voice according to her scores on the PANSS, but 12 months after starting therapy, her Persecutory beliefs about the voices reduced and her Resistance towards them increased (see Table 8.2). Her OCD-related difficulties dropped from the extreme level to the moderate category on the YBOCI so they now preoccupied her between one and three hours a day. She remained focused on completing her A-levels with the hope of going to university.

Trauma and post-traumatic stress disorder (PTSD)

Consistent with the central tenet of this book, psychosis can be conceptualised as a challenging and traumatic life event, which requires psychological adjustment and adaptation (Jackson, Knott, Skeate & Birchwood, 2005; Jackson et al., 2009). Indeed, some individuals can meet the criteria for PTSD due to the traumatic nature of their experiences.

Prevalence and impact of PTSD in FEP

Rates of PTSD in psychosis samples range from 11–67% (Berry, Ford, Jellicoe-Jones & Haddock, 2013) with pooled prevalence rates of PTSD symptoms being 42% and those for PTSD diagnosis being 30% (Rodrigues & Anderson, 2017). For FEP samples who have just experienced one psychotic episode (clinical stage 2; see Table 1.1), rates of PTSD varied from 31–46% with a median rate of 39% and for those with multiple episodes (clinical stages 3 and 4), rates varied from 31–67% with a median rate of 51% (Berry et al., 2013).This suggests higher rates of PTSD following relapse. However, when recent onset and multiple episode samples were assessed with identical assessment processes, similar rates of PTSD were reported, with slightly higher rates in the recent onset sample (39%) vs. the multiple episode sample (31%) (Mueser et al., 2010). The prevalence rates are consistent with suggestions that approximately one in three individuals with a diagnosis of FEP reach criteria for PTSD (Buckley et al., 2009; Jackson et al., 2005, 2009; Mueser et al., 2010). Experiencing PTSD following psychosis is associated with more severe psychopathology, suicidality and admissions (Buckley et al., 2009), more depression (Rodrigues & Anderson, 2017; Turner et al., 2013) and reduced quality of life and increased dependency on services (Grubaugh, Zinzow, Paul, Egede & Freuh, 2011). Consequently, clinical guidelines (NICE, 2014) recommend that all FEP cases are screened for post-traumatic stress disorder symptoms. Potential measures for screening PTSD (and childhood trauma) are in Appendix 2.

Sources of PTSD in FEP

PTSD can arise in FEP due to stressful in-patient admissions, acute psychotic symptoms, and adverse life events experienced prior to the development of psychosis (Morrison, Frame & Larkin, 2003). Many studies do not separate the traumatic impact of psychotic experiences and treatment experiences but two studies with recent onset samples (Mueser et al., 2010) and multiple onset (Lu et al., 2017) suggest that psychosis-related experiences are associated with higher rates of PTSD (approximately 47%) than treatment experiences (approximately 30%).

- *Traumatic impact of treatment experiences* Experiencing restraint, seclusion, sedation, and being forced to take medication and the side effects of medication most frequently elicited distress after FEP (Berry et al., 2013; Lu et al., 2017). Threats and acts of physical and sexual assault by others, involuntary admissions involving the police, isolation from family members and separation from normal routines, and a perceived lack of fairness, respect and empathy from support staff were also distressing. One in four service users reported that the most traumatic aspect of their treatment was a long stay in hospital without any explanation (Lu et al., 2017). These experiences elicited a range of negative emotions including anger, sadness, shock, fear, distrust and numbness.

- *Traumatic impact of psychotic symptoms.* The most distressing symptoms reported by services users in a quantitative review (Berry et al., 2013) and a qualitative study (Lu et al., 2017) were paranoid delusions, threatening, commanding or critical voices and losing touch with reality. These symptoms were associated with loss, disruption to life, physical harassment, violence and problems in relationships (Berry et al., 2013). Thoughts and attempts to harm self and others and suicidal acts were also associated with high levels of distress (Berry et al., 2013; Lu et al., 2017). These traumatic psychotic symptoms elicited anger, shock, anxiety, numbness, shame and helplessness (Lu et al. 2017). Other common emotions in the post-psychotic phase were sadness due to the overall impact of psychosis-related experiences and relief that acute psychotic experiences had stopped (Lu et al., 2017).

- *Traumatic impact of childhood experiences.* As alluded to in Chapter 1, individuals who develop psychosis have often experienced high rates of trauma earlier in their lives, including childhood sexual (13–64%) and physical (22–66%) abuse (Grubaugh et al., 2011). Meta-analysis has found that childhood trauma is associated with nearly a threefold increased risk of psychosis in adulthood (Varese et al., 2012) and the severity of hallucinations and delusions (Bailey, Álvarez-Jiménez, Garcia-Sanchez, Hulbert, Barlow & Bendell, 2018). Experiencing childhood trauma also increases vulnerability to experiencing emotional dysfunction following FEP including depression (Sitko, Bentall, Shevlin, O'Sullivan & Sellwood, 2014), social anxiety (Michail & Birchwood, 2014), and PTSD symptoms in reaction to a psychotic episode (Bendell et al., 2012). Childhood trauma is associated with more severe symptoms at baseline and follow-up (Aas et al., 2016), poorer psychosocial functioning (Lysaker, Meyer, Evans, Clements & Marks, 2001), and higher rates of problematic substance misuse (Tomassi et al., 2017). Consequently, individuals who have experienced childhood trauma may be a subgroup within FEP who are vulnerable to slower or delayed recovery (Aas et al., 2016). Thus, individuals who progress from stage 2 to stages 3 and 4 in the clinical staging model may be more likely to have a history of childhood trauma. However, this information may not always be known to FEP clinicians as victims of childhood abuse are often reluctant to disclose abuse (Read, Hammersley & Rudegeair, 2007). Thus, where the presence of childhood trauma (especially childhood sexual abuse) is suspected, developing a trusting therapeutic relationship is crucial. Screening measures for childhood trauma are listed in Appendix 2. The Trauma Experiences Checklist (TEC) (Cristofaro et al., 2013) has been developed specifically for use with FEP samples.

Other variables associated with PTSD symptoms

There are no consistent associations between treatment experiences (including the number and duration of admissions) and rates of PTSD symptoms (Berry et al., 2013) but subjective stressfulness of psychosis-related experiences (including admissions) is associated with increased risk of PTSD following FEP (Jackson et al., 2005). Thus, consistent with models of PTSD (Ehlers & Clark, 2000), psychosis-related appraisals, such as lack of control and perceived lack of crisis support (Chisholm, Freeman & Cooke, 2006) and shame (Turner, Bernard, Birchwood, Jackson & Jones, 2013), are associated with post-psychotic trauma. In addition, individuals with a history of physical or sexual abuse experience higher levels of distress associated with admissions following the onset of psychosis (Berry et al., 2013). Finally, while there is inconsistent evidence regarding links between the severity of psychotic symptoms and psychosis-related PTSD, there are more consistent associations between psychosis-related PTSD and distress (anxiety and depression) (Berry et al., 2013). This robust association between emotional dysfunction and PTSD is consistent with findings in traumatised samples without psychosis (Grubaugh et al., 2011).

The nature of trauma and PTSD following FEP

There has been a debate about whether FEP meets the DSM-IV criteria for PTSD (Jackson et al., 2005), which specifies that a traumatic event needs to pose a threat to physical integrity (Criteria A1) and elicit feelings of fear, helplessness, or horror (Criteria A2) (APA, 2000). This debate has now evolved as traumatic FEP experiences meeting Criteria A do not necessarily produce increased traumatic symptoms, comorbidity, or functional impairment more than those not meeting Criteria A (Mueser et al., 2010). More importantly, DSM-V (American Psychiatric Association, 2013) has now removed Criteria A2, which inadequately captured the emotional impact of a psychotic episode. We have seen above that traumatised psychotic samples report a wider range of emotions (e.g. sadness, anger, shame, mistrust) (Berry et al., 2013; Lu et al., 2017) than listed in Criteria A2. In addition, PTSD following a FEP is often accompanied by depression (Berry et al., 2013; Turner et al., 2014), which, as seen above, is typically associated with feelings of shame, loss and entrapment (Birchwood et al., 2000; Rooke & Birchwood, 1998). Consequently, there is an increasing awareness that traditional diagnostic criteria for PTSD may not translate well to psychotically derived PTSD (Dunkley et al., 2015; Jackson, Bernard & Birchwood, 2011), which will likely lead to the re-conceptualisation of trauma following FEP and new interventions.

Reducing the traumatic impact of FEP and levels of PTSD following psychosis

Given the high rate of associations between stressful in-patient experiences and PTSD in samples with psychosis, and associations between traumatic in-patient experiences and poor engagement with subsequent treatments (Grubaugh et al., 2011), it may be possible to reduce rates of PTSD by improving the experiences of individuals hospitalised for psychosis. This could occur by redesigning in-patient environments to reduce the incidence of potentially traumatic experiences (e.g. use of restraints, being forced to take medication; threats and assaults) (Berry et al., 2013; Lu et al., 2017) and ensuring wards are more validating and recovery-focused (Lu et al., 2017). Given that some of the most traumatic treatment experiences are admissions involving the police (Berry et al., 2013) and admissions without adequate explanations (Lu et al., 2017), consistent communication with service users about their admission and reducing use of the police are important. These strategies will most likely be easier to implement when a young person is already known to services as careful monitoring of early signs of relapse may alert the service user, carers, and professional to the possibility of an imminent relapse (see Chapter 4). However, this will be more challenging when a young person is presenting to services for the first time or is not actively engaged with services. In these situations, liaising with street triage teams may help as it can reduce use of Section 136 in the UK Mental Health Act (1983) and ensure that police officers are accompanied by a mental health professional (Keown et al., 2016). Consistent communication, street triage, and other efforts to reduce the traumatic impact of admissions may be even more important for members of black and minority ethnic (BME) groups. As we pointed out in Chapter 1, people from BME groups tend to have more adverse pathways into mental health services via the police and are still admitted compulsorily at very high rates in the UK (Morgan et al., 2017).

Psychological interventions for PTSD following psychosis

Trauma-focused CBT (TF-CBT) and Eye Movement Desensitisation Reprocessing (EMDR) aim to facilitate the disclosure and processing of thoughts, memories, feelings and behaviours associated with traumatic events. Trauma-focused interventions are recommended in clinical guidelines (NICE, 2014) and can help reduce symptoms of PTSD in psychosis samples but are less effective on secondary outcomes, such as anxiety, depression and social functioning (Swan, Keen, Reynolds & Onwumere, 2017). Exposure-based reprocessing is most likely the effective ingredient in psychological interventions for PTSD (Van den Berg et al., 2015). Consequently, a new CBT-based intervention integrates this strategy with trauma-focused CBT to treat both traumatic and psychotic symptoms (if present) within the same intervention (Keen, Hunter & Peters, 2017). Consistent with the models of CBTp outlined in Chapter 4, the therapy consists of different phases including assessment, engagement, and goal-setting (Phase 1), stabilisation and coping strategy enhancement (Phase 2), trauma-focused formulation (Phase 3), integrated psychosis and trauma-focused interventions including cognitive restructuring, reliving and/or re-scripting (Phase 4), and relapse prevention (Phase 5). In a case series involving 10 participants, the therapy was well received, appeared safe despite the frequent presence of positive symptoms and was associated with improvements in traumatic and psychotic symptoms, depression, anxiety, and well-being (Keen et al., 2017b). This integrated approach reflects the reality of intervening clinically in an EIP service, as individuals recovering from FEP often present with overlapping symptoms of psychosis and trauma.

Implementing the evidence into practice

Case study 8.3 Daniel: FEP and psychosis-related PTSD

Daniel was referred to EIP after developing paranoia and distressing visual hallucinations. After his wife became pregnant, Daniel became worried about their lack of finances and increased his hours at work. This resulted in long absences from the family home and he became suspicious that his wife was having an affair with a neighbour. He became stressed and tired and began using stimulants while working and then cannabis to help him relax and sleep. These substances fuelled his suspicious concerns and he left a recording device in the bedroom he shared with his wife. One night after working a 12-hour shift and ruminating on his suspicions, he became intoxicated and confronted and assaulted his wife. The police were called and Daniel was admitted to an acute psychiatric ward under a Section 2 of the Mental Health Act.

1 Assessment and engagement. Upon discharge, Daniel was no longer experiencing visual hallucinations but he scored slightly on the PANSS (see Table 8.3) as he was still mildly suspicious about his wife and their neighbour. These suspicions reduced after Daniel and his wife moved to a new house due to negative memories associated with their previous house. Daniel was experiencing high levels of depression, moderate levels of anxiety, and met the criteria for PTSD on the Impact of Event Scale-Revised (Weiss & Marmar, 1997) (see Table 8.3). Daniel had high levels of intrusive re-experiences about the night he had interrogated and assaulted his wife. These intrusions were being maintained by negative appraisals that he could have seriously harmed his wife and their unborn baby. He believed that he deserved to feel guilty, depressed, and anxious as an absence of distress meant he did not care for his wife. Cognitive, emotional, and behavioural avoidance was not alleviating his distress and intrusions. He spent his days watching television, avoiding interacting with his wife and baby, ruminating on past events, and relying on zopiclone to sleep at night.

Table 8.3 Scores for case study 8.3: FEP and psychosis-related PTSD

Measure	Baseline score level		Follow-up score level	
PANSS				
Positive	10	Mild	8	Mild
Negative	9	Mild	7	Absent
General	34	Moderate	22	Mild
Total	53	Moderate	35	Mild
Distress				
Depression (CDS)	7	Moderate	3	Mild
Depression (BDI-II)	19	Moderate	7	Mild
Anxiety (BAI-II)	18	Moderate	6	Mild
Impact of Event Scale-IES-R				
Intrusions	16	High	8	Low
Avoidance	22	High	6	Low
Hyperarousal	16	High	5	Low
Total	54	Severe	19	Low

Note
PANSS = Positive and Negative Syndrome Scale; CDS = Calgary Depression Scale; BDI-II = Beck Depression Inventory II; BAI-II = Beck Anxiety Inventory.

2 *Development of change strategies.* Daniel wanted to spend time with his wife and baby without feeling distressed and have less thoughts and nightmares about the night he assaulted his wife. He reviewed evidence for and against his suspicious beliefs about the affair, which included listening back to the audio recording he had made. Trauma-focused CBT based on cognitive (Ehlers & Clark, 2000) and guilt-based (Lee, Scragg & Turner, 2001) models of PTSD developed a trauma-based narrative of the night he assaulted his wife. Hot-spots were identified, cognitive and affective updates were developed, and reliving using these updates aimed to reduce the guilt and emotional distress associated with his intrusive re-experiences. Consistent with clinical recommendations (Keen et al., 2017b; Lee & James, 2011) anxiety management and grounding work occurred before the development of the trauma narrative and reliving.

3 *Longitudinal formulation.* This was not necessary as Daniel's distress was derived from the events above and there were no significant previous life events impacting on him in a negative way.

4 *Consolidation and relapse prevention.* Additional cognitive restructuring helped Daniel review evidence for and against his belief that he did not deserve to be married to his wife, be a father, or move on with his life. Over time, this helped reduce his sense of guilt and negative self-beliefs. He became more relaxed, spending time with his wife and baby and considered returning to work. These improvements were associated with reductions in depression and PTSD (see Table 8.3).

Shame and stigma following psychosis

Shame is part of a social threat detection system, which warns us that significant others are viewing us negatively and that we are at risk of being excluded from a valued social group (Gilbert, 2003). Shame compromises innate human needs to be seen as attractive and belong in social groups (Baumeister & Leary, 1995) and is triggered by significant changes in personal identity and social status (Gilbert, 2003), such as receiving a diagnosis of a stigmatised identity like psychosis (Birchwood et al., 2007). Psychosis is associated with higher rates of shame than non-mental health illnesses (Keen et al., 2017a) and most individuals (87%) with FEP report being subject to stigma and discrimination because of mental health difficulties (The Schizophrenia Commission, 2012). Stigma and external shame can be internalised (Gilbert, 2003) and can compromise recovery from a FEP due to associations with positive symptoms (Vass et al., 2015), social anxiety and marginalisation (Birchwood et al., 2007), post-psychotic depression (Birchwood et al., 2000; Turner et al., 2013) and psychosis-related trauma (Dunkley et al., 2015; Turner et al., 2013). Individuals experiencing a FEP may also experience shame due to critical voices (Trower, Birchwood, Meaden, Byrne, Nelson & Ross, 2004) and a perceived inability to live up to social and personal goals (Rooke & Birchwood, 1998). Finally, FEP samples may be vulnerable to shame due to negative experiences prior to psychosis, as shame is associated with childhood trauma and adversity in different samples (Andrews & Hunter, 1997) including those with psychosis (Connor & Birchwood, 2011) and many individuals with psychosis have elevated rates of childhood adversity (Read et al., 2005; Varese et al., 2012). Case study 8.4 (Josie) illustrates the impact of childhood trauma on the development of shame in an individual recovering from a FEP.

Interventions for shame and stigma

Interventions to reduce shame and stigma can be divided into those aimed at reducing shame based appraisals and those aimed at changing negative societal attitudes towards mental illness. In terms of psychological interventions, Birchwood et al. (2012) report positive reductions in shame (and related appraisals) following CBT for trauma associated with psychosis (Jackson et al., 2009) but only at 6-month follow-up. Changes in shame appraisals were not maintained at 12 months consistent with other evidence that shame-based appraisals of psychosis can be stable, persist over time and be associated with depression (Upthegrove et al., 2014). As mentioned above, individuals with psychosis who report high levels of childhood trauma may require a different therapeutic approach such as compassion focused therapy (CFT) (Gilbert, 2010). CFT aims to help shame-prone individuals with overdeveloped threat-based affect systems and underdeveloped soothing affect systems, which have their origins in developmental adversity, such as childhood trauma and poor attachments (Gilbert, 2010; see Chapter 1). Case study 8.4 uses elements of CFT.

In terms of anti-stigma programmes, poor knowledge about mental health problems, negative attitudes and discriminatory behaviour may have negative consequences for people experiencing mental health difficulties (Evans-Lacko et al., 2012). We have already highlighted how the internalisation of negative stereotypes of mental illness can be associated with negative outcomes, including emotional distress (Birchwood et al., 2007), and positive symptoms (Vass et al., 2015). Individuals with mental illness living in communities with higher levels of public stigma, have greater self-stigma, lower empowerment chances of employment and greater risk of mortality (Evans-Lacko et al., 2012). Population-level anti-stigma programmes, such as Time to Change in England (Henderson et al., 2017), have the potential to develop less negative attitudes towards individuals with mental illness (Evans-Lacko et al., 2018). However, it remains to be seen whether such interventions will also be associated with reductions in the internalisation of stigmatising attitudes among people with mental difficulties, including FEP.

Implementing the evidence into practice

Case study 8.4 Josie: FEP, shame, trauma and childhood sexual abuse

Josie, a 20-year-old woman, was referred to EIP after developing fluctuations in mood, paranoia, and critical voices following a period of poor sleep. Her positive symptoms quickly resolved in response to antipsychotic medication but she informed her care co-ordinator that she had been feeling depressed and anxious for many years and wanted to talk to a psychologist.

1 Assessment and engagement. Josie disclosed that she had been sexually and emotionally abused from the age of 11 to 15 years by a male relative. She had managed to stop the sexual abuse five years ago. Standardised assessments indicated that she was free of positive and negative symptoms of psychosis but that she was experiencing high levels of traumatic intrusions, avoidance, and hyperarousal in relation to her abuse, which met the criteria for PTSD (see Table 8.4). She was severely depressed and anxious and was commenced on anti-depressant medication. Josie denied having any traumatic intrusions in relation to her psychosis and had good insight into her psychotic episode, viewing it as the cumulative effect of dealing with the stress of the sexual and emotional abuse.

2 Formulation. Given the long-standing nature of her abuse and her high levels of PTSD and distress, a longitudinal formulation was produced before the start of any interventions. Josie's main source of distress was the sexual and emotional abuse she had experienced. This abuse was often unpredictable, manipulative, threatening and associated with a deep sense of shame and self-blame. She was constantly questioning herself why she had let it happen, whether she had encouraged it, and why she had not disclosed it to someone.

Table 8.4 Scores for case study 8.4: FEP, shame, trauma and childhood
        sexual abuse

Measure	Baseline score level		Follow-up score level	
PANSS				
Positive	7	Absent	7	Absent
Negative	7	Absent	7	Absent
General	20	Moderate	10	Mild
Total	34	Moderate	20	Mild
Distress				
Depression (CDS)	12	Severe	3	Mild
Depression (BDI-II)	33	Severe	14	Mild
Anxiety (BAI-II)	26	Moderate	5	Mild
Impact of Event Scale-IES-R				
Intrusions	22	High	10	Low
Avoidance	20	High	6	Low
Hyperarousal	14	High	6	Low
Total	56	Severe	22	Low
Shame				
Internal Shame (ISS)	65	High	19	Low
External Shame (OAS)	36	Moderate	20	Low

Note
ISS = Internalised Shame Scale (Cook, 1996); OAS = Other As Shame Scale (Goss
et al., 1994).

She had high levels of external and internal shame and self-criticism. Her ability
to self-reassure and emotionally regulate her distress was underdeveloped. Josie
had some fear-based appraisals that this male relative could still cause her harm
and she continued to experience occasional emotional abuse and manipulation
by him. This was understandably associated with hypervigilance and a sense of
threat. Due to the nature of the abuse, she had felt unable to seek support from
her immediate family, so felt alone and powerless. From a protective point, she
had experienced some positive attachment experiences, had some close friends
and a good awareness of her own and other's emotional states. Given her high
levels of shame and self-criticism, a formulation using a compassion-focused
approach (Gilbert, 2010) and shame-based PTSD (Lee et al., 2001) focused on
the consequences of her sexual abuse and its internal (negative views of self)
and external (abuse being discovered) threats. This included her ways of managing these threats (cognitive avoidance, secrecy) and the unintended consequences of these strategies including her persistent depression, intrusive
re-experiences, shame, isolation, and lack of emotional and practical support in
managing her situation.

   3 Development of change strategies. Josie's goals were to feel less depressed,
anxious and ashamed, move on from the abuse, and find a job. She was uncertain
how to achieve her goals and was extremely ambivalent about disclosing the

abuse or informing the police. In the first part of therapy, Josie learnt more effective ways of regulating her emotions and re-appraised her feelings of self-blame. She was still hypervigilant due to occasional contact (in the company of other relatives) with the male relative who had abused her, so it did not feel appropriate to proceed with reliving at this point or turn off her hyper-vigilance as it is likely the threat-focused part of her mind was still keeping her safe (Keen et al., 2017b; Lee & James, 2011) from potential threats from her abuser. After reflecting on the advantages and disadvantages of disclosing the abuse, she informed her parents who immediately sided with her, confronted the male relative, and ensured that Josie did not have any further contact with him. Her parents supported her with making a statement to the police and to press charges. Following this, Josie's anxiety and depression improved. She then engaged in trauma-focused CBT (Ehlers & Clark, 2000) tailored for shame-based memories using compassion-focused therapy-based updates (Lee & James, 2011) for specific 'hot-spots' of sexual and emotional abuse. This helped lower her levels of trauma and external shame (see Table 8.4) as she reflected that, contrary to her expectations, her immediate family had not thought any less of her following her disclosure.

4 Consolidation and relapse prevention. Josie required many months of therapy. She still had days when she felt low and her internal shame was more resistant to change. However, she became less self-critical and more capable of self-reassurance in relation to the abuse but required support with using these new and unfamiliar ways of relating to herself.

Pathways to emotional dysfunction and recovery following FEP

This chapter has considered how emotional dysfunction can impact negatively on recovery and how intervening to reduce emotional dysfunction can promote psychological adaptation and facilitate recovery. We will now consider an over-reaching framework that can inform this approach. Birchwood (2003) identified three potential pathways to emotional dysfunction following psychosis, including positive symptoms of psychosis (the first pathway), psychological reactions to psychosis (the second pathway) and developmental trauma (the third pathway). These pathways can be helpful when identifying the origin and source of emotional distress and dysfunction following psychosis and associated poor recovery. For example, if an assessment and formulation indicate that an individual is experiencing emotional distress in association with specific positive psychotic symptoms (first pathway), then medical (outlined in Chapter 3) and psychological interventions could target positive symptoms, drawing on specific models outlined in Chapter 4 and different case studies (4.1 and 4.2 in Chapter 4; and 8.2, in this chapter).

In contrast, if an individual is now largely free of psychotic symptoms but still experiencing depression, anxiety, trauma or shame, then the assessment and formulation could examine the association between the distress and psychological appraisals (the second pathway). The key at this point is formulating the particular type of emotional dysfunction and understanding how this may relate or overlap with the individual's psychotic experiences. Interventions, at this point, will most likely be psychological with an emphasis on using evidence-based CBT approaches outlined in this chapter and Chapter 4. However, as we have discussed throughout this book, medical (see Chapter 3 and this chapter) and social/vocational (see Chapter 6), and other psychological (see Chapters 7, 9, and 12) interventions aimed at specific types of emotional distress, such as depression or anxiety, may also be helpful.

Finally, in the third pathway, emotional dysfunction arises following psychosis due to childhood and developmental adversity. This pathway can interact with the other two pathways as more adversity in childhood may result in more severe positive symptoms (Aas et al., 2016), which in turn may result in more severe emotional dysfunction in the acute phase (Hartley et al., 2013) (the first pathway). In addition, individuals with a history of childhood trauma are more likely to experience delayed recovery following a FEP (Aas et al., 2016) and different types of emotional dysfunction following a FEP including PTSD (Bendall et al., 2014), social anxiety (Michail, 2013), and depression (Aas et al., 2016), which implicates the second pathway. Birchwood's (2003) framework also allows the possibility that emotional dysfunction may precede the onset of psychosis. This pre-existing emotional dysfunction may persist following a FEP and impact recovery negatively. Consequently, such emotional dysfunction may require the same range of medical, social and psychological interventions covered throughout this book.

Other issues to consider when recovery is delayed or incomplete

Engagement, recovery style and attachment

Engagement with EIP and psychological therapy may depend on a range of variables, such as recovery style (McGlashan, 1987), as individuals who integrate their psychosis can have better engagement with services (Tait et al., 2003) and superior outcomes and functioning (Thompson, McGorry & Harrigan, 2003) than those who deny or 'seal over' their psychosis. As alluded to in Chapter 7, recovery style is associated with attachment (Drayton, Birchwood & Trower, 1998), which is now regarded as an important mediator between childhood trauma and recovery following a FEP (Read & Gumley, 2008). Thus, assessing an individual's attachment style may help guide engagement and inform interventions when working with someone who is experiencing delayed or incomplete recovery. For example, service users with an insecure attachment style may require more or less intensive engagement and their care co-ordinators may benefit from additional clinical supervision to manage ruptures in therapeutic relationships and engagement difficulties.

Emotional regulation

Childhood adversity and early attachments can impact on an individual's ability to regulate their emotions following a FEP (see Chapter 1). Emotional dysfunction across a range of different types of psychopathology, including those with psychosis (Bernard et al., 2015; Khoury & Lecomte, 2012) are associated with a style of emotional regulation characterised by rumination, avoidance and low levels of re-appraisal (Aldao, Nolen-Hoeksema & Sweizer, 2011). These findings may be particularly relevant to people who have experienced psychosis due to an increased sensitivity to stress in FEP samples (Myin-Germeys & Van Os, 2007; see Chapter 1), which is heightened for those who have experienced childhood trauma (Lardinois et al., 2011). Given the high rates of childhood trauma (Varese et al., 2012) and emotional dysfunction (Birchwood, 2003) in FEP, the presence of maladaptive emotional strategies may result in vicious cycles of distress, persistent psychotic symptoms, and relapses. Consequently, the effectiveness of psychological interventions for emotional dysfunction following psychosis may be enhanced by placing more emphasis on the development of emotional regulatory strategies (Bernard et al., 2015; Gumley & Schwannauer, 2006; Khoury & Lecomte, 2012).

Recovery after relapse

Finally, given that this chapter has focused on the recovery period following a FEP, it has mainly focused on stage 2 from the clinical staging perspective (McGorry, Hickie, Yung, Pantelis & Jackson, 2006). However, the different types of emotional dysfunction considered in this chapter can be experienced at stages 3 and 4 in the clinical staging model and we have seen evidence above that certain difficulties, such as depression, may become more entrenched in stages 3 and 4, potentially due to increased insight about the negative impact of having numerous psychotic relapses (Murri et al., 2015). At the same time, if an individual has progressed to stage 3 and is experiencing delayed or incomplete recovery, and is at high risk of further relapses, then a broader range of interventions will be required to improve the chances of adaptation and recovery (see Chapter 12).

Learning points

- When intervening with emotional dysfunction following a FEP, the effectiveness of bio-psychosocial interventions will depend on a number of variables, including phase of psychosis, how people are making sense of their psychosis, their social support network, their attachment and recovery style, engagement with services and emotional regulation.
- The effectiveness of interventions will depend on identifying and assessing emotional dysfunction as early as possible using standardised measures.

- As discussed throughout this book, recovery from psychosis does not occur in a social vacuum and social and environmental variables may facilitate or hinder recovery.
- Bio-psychosocial interventions may ameliorate adverse social and environmental situations, but, as seen in the case studies above, objective changes in vocational roles and relationships (case study 8.1 Shazia), accommodation (case study 8.3 Daniel), and threats from abusers (case study 8.4 Josie) are sometimes necessary for recovery to progress.
- Finally, direct support from family members in implementing psychological strategies (e.g. Shazia and Rachel), providing emotional support (Daniel), and increasing personal safety (Josie) can be instrumental in facilitating recovery. The impact and importance of family and carer networks are covered in more detail in Chapter 11.

Chapter 9

Identifying and managing suicidality following a first episode of psychosis

Introduction

From Chapters 7 and 8 it can be seen that sometimes, and often despite progress in symptomatic and social recovery, people with psychosis sometimes fail to psychologically adapt and adjust to the onset of psychosis. At the extreme, this may lead to thoughts, feelings and behaviours consistent with the idea of ending their lives (Gajwani, Larkin & Jackson, 2017). In this chapter we will look at suicidality following a FEP; how often people think about it, act on it and the numbers of people who unfortunately will take their life because of it. We will then attempt to explain through predictive and theoretical approaches why people feel this way following a FEP. Then, and most importantly, we will try to show how we can predict who is most at risk and how we may be able to reduce, not only the unacceptably high rates of premature deaths in young people with psychosis, but also the suffering and distress that can be present in people who are contemplating suicide.

Prevalence of suicide and suicidality in FEP

Psychiatric textbooks from the 1980s and 1990s have suggested that the lifetime risk for suicide in people diagnosed with schizophrenia is between 5% and 10% (Palmer, Pankratz & Bostwick, 2005) depending on whether that is calculated as proportionate morbidity[1] or case fatality.[2] The former usually gives the higher estimate. Recent cohort studies of FEP, however, have suggested that even older case fatality studies may have given estimates at the top end of the true figure which is more likely to be between 1.9% and 4.3% (Björkenstam, Björkenstam, Hjern, Bodén & Reutfors, 2014). Although these figures are lower than was initially predicted, and give some cause for optimism, they still represent a figure up to 12 times higher than the suicide rates observed in the general population of England and Wales (Dutta, Murray, Hotopf, Allardyce, Jones & Boydell, 2010).

The increased risk for FEP patients tends to be at the beginning, at the onset and during the first year of the illness. However, this risk is likely to persist for a number of years (Dutta et al., 2010), with the people at greatest risk of future suicide being those who have self-harmed or attempted suicide previously (Björkenstam et al., 2014). Aside from an elevated risk of self-inflicted death, suicidal behaviour during the early stages of psychosis can bring other complications, most notably increased hospital admission, interpersonal issues and social problems.

Defining and classifying suicidal ideations, communications and self-injurious behaviours are, however, notoriously difficult and, to date, there is no agreed taxonomy that incorporates the full range of what clinicians and researchers think of as suicide-related behaviours. For example, clinically, deliberate self-harm (DSH) is differentiated from suicide attempts by the presence (or absence) of intent to die. In reality, absence of intent is difficult to prove as many patients after the event may deny they wanted to die despite evidence to the contrary (e.g. high levels of lethality in the attempt, etc.).

Despite such shortcomings, attempts have been made to measure the incidence and prevalence of suicidal behaviours in first episode samples. Rates vary widely depending on the length of the follow-up period, methodology, attrition rates and country studied. For instance, while Addington et al. (2004) reported that only 2.9% of their Canadian FEP cohort attempted suicide during the first year of treatment, Robinson et al. (2010) noted a much higher figure (21.6%) when those treated in an Australian EIP service were followed up over a longer seven-year period. This makes it difficult to compare studies and establish the true rate of attempted suicide following a FEP.

Accurate figures for suicidal *ideation* in FEP cohorts is no less difficult to estimate but seems to consistently produce rates 25–33% higher than that for suicidal behaviours (attempts and DSH) alone (Barrett et al., 2015). That is, suicidal ideation following the onset of psychosis seems to be very common and may be a consequence of adaptation to a stressful event at a transitional period of life.

For *completed* suicides, this ratio can be over 300 times higher, depending on the time period studied. A recent multi-site study in the UK (Birchwood et al., 2014a) looked at the prevalence of suicidality in FEP during the first 12 months of inception into an early intervention service. Only one death across all sites (0.1%) was recorded as being the result of suicide (Jackson, Birchwood & the UK NEDEN Group, 2012). In terms of prevalence of *suicide attempts* and deliberate self-harm, for those for whom data was available, 18% reported making at least one attempt at deliberate self-harm or a suicide attempt (SA) in the year following inception into an EI service. Of these, 34% were admitted to hospital because of their suicidal or deliberate self-harming behaviour. During the first year of receiving an early intervention service, 31.1% reported experiencing *suicidal ideation* (Calgary Depression Scale; CDS, question 8) when asked. Of the 219 who admitted to suicidal ideation, 61% could be classified as 'mild' (score of 1 on CDS). Studies that have followed FEP patients up over a longer period of time have shown that suicidal ideation during the first year of early intervention may be predictive of suicidality later on. Madsen et al. (2016), in a longitudinal study of suicidal thinking and behaviour in FEP patients, noted that those with frequent suicidal ideation at baseline were four and a half times more likely to have frequent persistent suicidal ideation up to 10 years later. Suicidal ideation in the first year of EIP also predicted suicide attempts at five years, but not number of completed suicides. This would indicate that the relationship between suicidal ideation, suicide behaviour and suicide is complex and mitigated by a number of factors in young people with psychosis.

Predictors of suicidality in FEP

In view of the fact that *thinking* about taking your own life does not always lead to *attempted* or *completed* suicide, efforts have been made to identify which distal and proximal factors, following a FEP, put people at most risk during the three stages of the suicide process (Power & McGowan, 2011). These will be considered separately below:

Predictors of suicidal ideation in FEP

As pointed out above, not all studies of FEP and suicidality reliably separate out suicidal thinking from suicidal behaviour as the dependent variable or outcome of interest. This makes it difficult to differentiate between those factors that influence the early stages of the suicidal process and those that take it to a much more potentially serious level (Pompili et al., 2011). From the studies of FEP populations that have been published, we know that insight, trauma and depressive symptomatology may increase the likelihood that someone will start contemplating ending their life.

Some have argued that insight (the extent to which a person understands the nature, significance and severity of his/her psychotic symptoms) may be a risk factor for hopelessness and suicidal ideation during and following a FEP. However, the relationship between suicidal ideation and insight is complex and may change during the adaptation and recovery period. Barrett et al. (2015), for instance, have shown that if insight during the first year following a FEP increases from baseline, the risk of suicidal *thinking* tends to decrease. Conversely, if insight reduces over time, the risk of suicidal *thinking* generally increases. If it remains stable, so does suicidal ideation. These findings may be an indication that suicidal thinking is inextricably linked with psychotic symptoms. As we will see later, this is contrary to what is found for *completed* suicides which may have other bio-psychosocial drivers.

Unsurprisingly, suicidal *ideation* in FEP cohorts is also predicted by the presence of depressive symptoms. Moreover, the ability of depressive symptoms to predict suicidal ideation also tends to be independent of other variables (Chang, Chen, Hui, Chan, Lee & Chen, 2014).

Finally, the experience of trauma (but not the severity) prior to the onset of psychosis has also been shown to be associated with suicidal ideation in FEP samples

(Tarrier, Khan, Cater & Picken, 2007). Clinically, taken together, pre-psychosis trauma, depression, hopelessness, poor insight and past suicide attempts put FEP patients at elevated risk of suicidal ideation during treatment by an EIP team.

Predictors of suicidal behaviours in FEP

Suicide attempts in FEP are most common just prior to, and soon after, entry to mental health services. In a study of 607 people entering a specialist EIP service in Australia, almost half of the suicide attempts (48.2%) occurred after six months of treatment (Fedyszyn, Harris, Robinson, Edwards & Paxton, 2011) with very few people (27.4%) going on to attempt more than once.

Nordentoft et al. (2002) found that in their 'OPUS' Danish/Norwegian FEP cohort, *attempted* suicide was predicted by female gender, hopelessness and hallucinations. Levine et al. (2010) also noted that college-educated, unmarried female FEP patients were the most likely to be admitted to hospital for a suicide attempt while Bertelsen et al. (2007) noted that female gender predicted suicide attempts in the second year of treatment. Conversely, early suicide attempters in a Spanish FEP cohort were more likely to be males, living in urban areas, with poorer pre-morbid adjustment, higher anxiety and unusual thought content (Ayesa-Arriola et al., 2015).

Bertelsen et al. (2007), like Nordentoft et al. (2002), noted that depressive and psychotic symptoms (especially hallucinations) at baseline predicted suicidal behaviour one year later. Similarly, Canal-Rivero et al. (2016) found that the severity of psychotic symptoms at the onset of FEP predicted earlier and later suicide attempts. Finally, in a recent meta-analysis and systematic review of longitudinal studies (McGinty et al., 2018), depressive symptoms during FEP were shown to be associated with longer-term risk of suicidal behaviour. More specifically, being depressed for more than 50% of the first episode can increase the risk of suicidal behaviour up to seven years later (Robinson et al., 2010). On the other hand, it is likely that the more *psychological* depressive symptoms such as hopelessness and suicidal ideation, at the start of treatment, will confer a greater risk of suicidal behaviour during the first year of EIP (Jackson et al., 2012). Using other measures that document recent negative events and a history of self-harm, may further improve the predictive power of a diagnosis of depression alone.

PTSD, trauma and exposure to sexual and/or physical abuse have also been shown to be associated with suicide attempts in FEP patients (Tarrier et al., 2007). Although further research is needed to disentangle the contributory mechanisms by which traumatic events increase the risk of suicidal behaviours, trauma may also lead to drug and alcohol abuse which is also known to confer a risk for suicidal behaviours following a FEP (Robinson et al., 2010).

Length of the duration of untreated psychosis (DUP) has also been found to be related to suicidal behaviour (Addington et al., 2004) and may be indicative of the sense of entrapment and defeat that people often experience as a result of psychotic symptoms. Very little research, however, has differentiated between the predictive value of DUI (the duration of untreated illness) and DUP. This would be important, as DUP is likely to be preceded by a period of emotional dysregulation (Van Os & Kapur, 2009) and may, therefore, confer an additional risk period for suicidal behaviour prior to the onset of psychotic symptoms (Jackson et al., 2012).

Of course, vulnerability to suicidal behaviours during long periods of DUI and DUP may simply be a reflection of poor pre-morbid functioning. That is, those who are less willing and/or able to seek help prior to their FEP (and who will, therefore, have greater levels of DUP and DUI), are more likely to have been functioning cognitively and socially at a lower level.

Bakst et al. (2010) reported that worse pre-morbid functioning was associated not only with a suicide attempt prior to first hospital admission, but also with an increased likelihood of further attempts in the four years following first admission. Less research has studied the impact of current functioning on the likelihood of suicidal behaviour although some markers of social recovery such as employment may not have the same predictive power in people with psychosis as they do in the general population.

Other correlates of suicidal behaviour in FEP include the number of psychiatric admissions a person has had (Haw, Hawton, Sutton, Sinclair & Deeks, 2005), younger age (Bertelsen et al., 2007) and increased insight (Crumlish et al., 2005).

There is relatively little research in first episode and older psychosis samples into protective factors for suicidal behaviour. In the wider suicide literature, religion has often been mooted as a moderating factor, reducing the risk of both suicidal behaviour and completed suicides (Stack & Kposowa, 2011). In one of the few studies that have studied the link between suicidal behaviour and religiousness, Huguelet et al. (2007) found no evidence of an association. In contrast, Jackson et al. (2012) presented evidence from the NEDEN study to suggest that the absence of a faith (irrespective of what that faith was) did confer a greater risk of attempted suicide and self-harm in FEP patients. In other words, having a faith acted as a buffer against suicidality.

In summary, the first three years of early intervention is a highly risky period for suicidal behaviours. A number of risk and protective factors may increase or decrease the probability of such behaviour although we still know little about their predictive utility in multi-factorial models.

Predictors of completed suicides in FEP

Predicting who will die by suicide, whether having experienced an FEP or not, remains a notoriously difficult science. One reason for this is that, despite the unacceptably high numbers of people who die by suicide each year, suicide, fortunately, remains a relatively rare event, accounting for approximately 1.5% of all deaths worldwide (Hawton & van Heeringen, 2009). Even among high risk populations, such as those experiencing the onset of psychosis, as noted previously, case fatality due to suicide may be less than 2%. Therefore, many adequate predictors of suicidal thinking and suicidal behaviour do not necessarily turn out to be good predictors of death by suicide.

Despite the high ratio of suicide attempts and self-harming to completed suicides, it is now well established that previous episodes of DSH and SAs are among the best predictors of completed suicides in FEP cohorts (Robinson et al., 2010).

Nordentoft et al. (2004), in a nested case control design, found an increased mortality rate due to suicide in the first year of treatment among younger FEP patients, with the highest rates occurring just after being discharged from hospital. Mitter et al. (2013), on the other hand, found older patients with a longer DUP, worse symptomatic recovery but better social recovery, to be at greater risk of completed suicide. Cohorts from these two studies, however, were ethnically and socially different, with the former Nordentoft study analysing data from a Scandinavian population sampled from Denmark and Norway, while the Mitter study looked at the records of 1,397 patients from an EIP Programme in Singapore.

In line with this, there have been inconsistent findings as to whether somebody's ethnicity acts as a protective factor against suicide. In the general population, age-standardised suicide rates in England and Wales are lower for South Asian men when compared with White men. Women of South Asian origin, on the other hand, have slightly elevated rates compared to their White peers (Bhui & McKenzie, 2008). For people with psychosis, the influence of ethnicity on completed suicides may have been under-estimated. Hunt et al. (2003), for instance, in the national confidential enquiry into suicide in England and Wales in people with mental health issues, noted that Black Caribbean patients who died by suicide were far more likely to have a diagnosis of schizophrenia (74%) than White or other ethnic groups. They also had a greater probability of other multiple risk factors, such as being unemployed, living alone, with a history of violence and drug misuse, and it is likely that perceived preventability (through the treatment of psychosis) maybe highest among Black Caribbean people.

In conclusion, predicting suicidal risk in FEP populations is a complex and dynamic process that changes at different stages of recovery (Power & McGowan, 2011) and may vary for different ethnic and social groups. Ultimately, this may point to the need for a more theoretical approach to suicidality or one based on machine learning (Suvisaari et al., 2018) than one which relies solely on traditional statistical prediction.

Assessing risk of suicide in FEP using the O'Connors model and an integrated bio-psychosocial formulation approach

Working in EIP teams with potentially high levels of suicidality, we have found that Rory O'Connor's Integrated Motivational-Volitional (IMV) model (O'Connor, 2011) allows a more integrated and dynamic bio-psychosocial approach to formulating risk and suicide prevention plans. In essence, these follow the model set out in Figure 9.1.

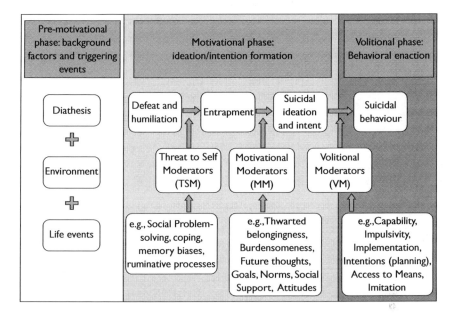

Figure 9.1 Integrated motivational-volitional model.
Source: O'Connor (2011).

I Assessing the stress-diathesis in suicidal FEP patients (pre-motivational stage)

All suicide risk assessments in EIP need to establish the background factors and triggering events that may have contributed to the current feelings of defeat, humiliation, entrapment and suicidality in people adapting to a FEP. That is:

> a) … what has contributed to that person's vulnerability (diathesis) and
> b) what in that person's environment and/or what recent events have triggered that vulnerability to produce these appraisals and feelings? Clinicians should be aware of genetic and biological factors that may increase this risk, for example, a family history of mood disorders and suicide.

It would also be desirable to assess sensitivity to social stress, pessimism and impulsivity, all of which may be related to mood regulation and decision-making involving neurobiological processes. Information regarding these could be sought through careful and detailed history-taking (e.g. past impulsive behaviours, details of responses to past stressful situations, etc.). Sexual abuse and other forms of childhood trauma and adversity may also have an epigenetic effect on suicide risk through the diathesis and gene-environment interaction (van Heeringen & Mann, 2014) and should be enquired about as a matter of routine in any good risk assessment. Questionnaires such as the Childhood Trauma Questionnaire (CTQ; Bernstein et al., 1994) may help where shame is high and the person finds it easier to fill in a self-report questionnaire than talk about the trauma openly. Personality traits such as perfectionism (particularly socially prescribed perfectionism) should also be enquired about in this part of the risk assessment, as they may confer personal vulnerability to suicidal behaviour and its antecedents. While careful clinical questioning may tease out such perfectionistic traits, questionnaires such as the Frost Multidimensional Perfectionism Scale (FMPS; Stober, 1998) may provide useful supplementary information. Perfectionism may have resulted from the consequences of early experiences or inconsistent parenting (Miller & Vaillancourt, 2007) and the interpersonal aspects of the service user's early life should be asked about where possible.

As we noted in Chapter 1, life events and daily hassles are experienced frequently by FEP patients. Differential activation theory (Williams, Barnhofer, Crane & Beck, 2005) would predict that even small events (e.g. an argument with a family member) would lead to an increase in suicidal thinking if such ideation had been experienced in previous episodes of low mood. In other words, suicidal thoughts in FEP patients can become reactivated, despite disappearing when mood returns to normal, after low mood is triggered again (Back, 2013). This points to a clear interaction between diathesis and stress in suicidal FEP patients and reinforces the need to take a thorough history, not only of suicide behaviours and attempts, but also of episodes of depressive and suicidal thinking prior to, during, and after the onset of psychosis (McGinty et al., 2018). This also highlights the dynamic nature of risk that demands continuous assessment beyond an initial clinical interview (often limited to just upon entry to EIP). Thus, even though background risk factors are often static and not malleable to change, daily events that arise (e.g. arguments) can still interact with them to increase or decrease this risk.

2 Assessing defeat and entrapment following a FEP

Entrapment and defeat following a FEP can be assessed through careful interviewing and the use of standardised scales. During an assessment, experiences of the loss of valued roles and goals brought about by the onset of psychosis, as well as experiences and perceptions of relapse, should be carefully noted.

In terms of questionnaires, the entrapment scale (Gilbert & Allen, 1998) is a 16-item self-report scale (PROM) that measures both internal ('I feel powerless to change myself') and external entrapment ('I feel powerless to change things') on a five-point rating scale. Entrapment can also be measured using the PBIQ-R (Birchwood, Jackson, Brunet, Holden & Barton, 2012), a scale especially designed to measure service users' appraisals of recovery following a FEP. 'Defeat' on the other hand, can be measured using the defeat scale (Gilbert &

Allen, 1998), a 16-item patient reported outcome measure (PROM) measuring low social rank and perceptions of failure to fulfil one's goals ('I feel that I am one of life's losers').

It may also be useful at this stage, consistent with the framework set out in Figure 9.1, to enquire about ruminative processes (i.e. 'brooding'), problem-solving and coping. Although poor problem-solving and coping are most likely accounted for by the presence of low mood (Speckens & Hawton, 2005), 'brooding' ruminative processes, where the person dwells on their symptoms or situation, may interact with impaired problem-solving to heighten feelings of entrapment and defeat and subsequent suicidality. The Ruminative Responses Scale (RRS; Treynor et al., 2003) is a useful PROM, with good psychometric properties, which can be used to supplement clinical interviewing.

3 Assessing suicidal thinking following a FEP

Suicidal thinking is a generic term given to the thoughts, images and hallucinations that relate to someone wanting to take their own life. This may include: reasons for living, the wish to die, wish not to live, frequency of ideation, intensity of ideation, desire for an attempt and talk of suicide/death. Hallucinations may come in the form of command hallucinations where there is a direct and explicit instruction to harm or die by suicide (Byrne, Birchwood, Trower & Meaden, 2006), often naming the means by which they should do it. Other suicidal hallucinations may be more vague, simply implying that things would be better if that person was not around. Although the relationship between suicidal behaviour and command hallucinations remains unclear (Haddock, Eisner, Davies, Coupe & Barrowclough, 2013), and is undoubtedly mediated by other variables such as omnipotence (Bucci, Birchwood, Twist, Tarrier, Emsley & Haddock, 2013), enquiring about the risk of acting on the command may provide a useful measure of whether this form of suicidal ideation is more likely to lead to someone acting on it. This can be directly measured by the RACS (Risk of Acting on Commands Scale; Trower, Birchwood, Meaden, Byrne, Nelson & Ross, 2004).

The International Suicide Prevention Trial (InterSePT) Scale for Suicidal Thinking (ISST), a 12-item clinician outcome reported measure (CROM) designed to be used with suicidal patients with schizophrenia and schizoaffective disorders (Ayer, Jayathilake & Meltzer, 2008), also allows clinicians to assess the extent to which suicidal thinking is influenced by hallucinations and delusions. In addition, it also allows the clinician to rate other aspects of a person's suicidal thinking, including their wish to die, the frequency of their suicidal ideation, the control they think they have over their suicidal thoughts, possible methods and their reasons for contemplating an attempt. This could be used alongside Power and McGowan's (2011) 'Early Intervention Suicide Risk Factor Check-list' which divides risk factors into 'Current Risk Factors' (e.g. preoccupation with morbid/suicidal thoughts), 'Historical Risk Factors' (e.g. previous suicidal ideation) and 'Future Potential Risk Factors' (e.g. service transitions).

Another useful questionnaire to supplement clinical questioning about suicidal thinking is the Calgary Depression Scale (CDS; Addington, Addington, Maticka-Tyndale & Joyce, 1992). As mentioned in Chapter 8, the CDS is a nine-item semi-structured interview specifically developed to assess depression in people with schizophrenia. It has a specific question about suicidal thinking and reported behaviour (Question 8; Have you felt that life wasn't worth living? Did you ever feel like ending it all? What did you think you might do? Did you actually try?), which could be responded to by acknowledging 'Frequent thoughts of being better off dead, or occasional thoughts of suicide'. See Appendix 2.

To supplement direct questions about suicidal thinking, and, according to O'Connor's framework, the service user could also be asked about: a sense of hopelessness, their perceptions of social support, whether they feel they belong or not and their view of themselves as a burden. All these can be asked directly in an interview but can also be supplemented by PROMs and CROMs such as the Interpersonal Needs Questionnaire (INQ; Van Orden, 2012) and the Revised UCLA Loneliness Scale (Russell, Peplau & Cutrona, 1980).

4 Assessing factors that increase the volition to act on suicidal thoughts (from thinking to behaviour)

Having access to means of suicide, having the capability to attempt suicide and knowing others who have engaged in suicidal behaviour are all examples of factors that make the likelihood of acting on suicidal desires and thoughts more likely; the so-called volitional moderators in O'Connor's IMV model (O'Connor, 2011).

Central to the link between intention and acting are suicide plans. The how, when and where will need to be established if someone does admit to planning to die by suicide. Some people will have a very specific plan while others will be more vague (i.e. 'take some pills'). Obtaining as much detail about not only the current plan but other plans in the past is essential. Research in non-psychosis examples has found that it is the most severe suicide plan in a person's past which is more likely to be a better predictor of completed suicide and number of attempts than the current plan alone (Beck, Brown, Steer, Dahlsgaard & Grisham, 1999)

As noted previously, another major theoretical advance in linking suicidal behaviour with intention and desire has been Joiner's concept of acquired capability (Joiner, 2005). Clinicians should always be mindful of the patient's courage or sense of competence to make an attempt. Engagement in painful self-injury in the past may be a marker of this. Therefore, in addition to taking a thorough history of past suicidal attempts, the risk assessment should include details of past behaviours that may indicate increased pain tolerance (e.g. multiple tattoos, intravenous drug use, etc.). Exposure to painful and provocative events is likely to be more common in FEP populations (Heelis, Graham & Jackson, 2016).

The management of suicidal risk following a first episode of psychosis: psychological, social and medical interventions

A number of reviews now exist to aid clinicians in finding the best way of helping people considered to be at risk of suicide (Riblet, Shiner, Young-Xu & Watts, 2017). Although some clinicians and researchers have attempted to develop specifically tailored protocols for suicidal service users in generic psychosis services (Tarrier, Gooding, Pratt, Kelly, Maxwell & Awenet, 2013), less guidance has been given on how to intervene with younger, first episode psychosis patients, struggling to adapt to the onset of psychosis. Even fewer have considered integrated team approaches to the prevention and management of suicidality in this group.

Pharmacotherapy

There is now growing evidence to suggest that pharmacological treatment with modern antipsychotic medication can help reduce suicidality in people with psychosis (see Chapter 3). This seems to be especially the case for clozapine, which can lead to a reduction in death by suicide, suicide attempts, depressive symptoms, helplessness and suicidal ideation in neuroleptic resistant patients (Hennen & Baldessarini, 2005). Such anti-suicide properties are, to a lesser extent, also evident in other second-generation, atypical anti-psychotics, particularly when compared with the older anti0psychotics, such as haloperidol (Ringbäck, Berglund, Lindström Nilsson, Salmi. & Rosén, 2014). There is, however, little data on how the new atypicals impact on suicidality in young FEP patients in the early stages of the illness. In general, there is a poor understanding of the mechanisms by which these drugs render their anti-suicidal effect (Pompili et al., 2016). The risk of akathisia and other side effects (i.e. metabolic) may also need to be taken into account as they can also add to a growing sense of hopelessness, defeat and entrapment.

Anti-depressants in the form of SSRIs (selective serotonin reuptake inhibitors) and SNRIs (serotonin-norepinephrine reuptake inhibitors) remain an important tool for the treatment of depression and suicidality in young people with psychosis. They are, however, not without their risks and the paucity of research on the treatment of suicidal thoughts and behaviours in young people with psychosis does not always help clinicians make informed choices about optimal treatment. This research, like all research into suicide, is dogged with the problems of low base rates that limit the power of RCTs. Moreover, as mentioned in Chapter 8, despite growing evidence of the safety and efficacy of anti-depressants in schizophrenia (Gregory, Mallikarjun & Upthegrove, 2017), there are currently no clear guidelines for the pharmacological management of depression during FEP (McGinty et al., 2018). Trials in non-psychotic populations, despite evidence that younger patients may have an increased risk of suicidality with SSRIs and SNRIs (Sharma, Guski, Freund & Gøtzsche, 2016), suggest that there does appear to be increasing protection from these drugs as age increases (Goldney, 2011). There also seems to be a differential effect for the various types of SSRIs, with sertraline offering the best tolerability and efficacy and the lowest risk of suicidal behaviour (Geddes, Barbui & Cipriani, 2009).

Lithium may also have some anti-suicidal properties, with evidence suggesting that it can reduce the risk of suicide and non-fatal suicidal behaviour independent of its effectiveness as a mood stabiliser, although the evidence is contradictory (Riblet et al., 2017) and there is a scarcity of research into its management of suicidal behaviour in FEP populations.

Psychological interventions

CBT may have an increasing role to play in helping people who are struggling with suicidal thoughts, feelings and behaviours, although its ability to prevent actual death by suicide has yet to be proven (Riblet et al., 2017). While most of the CBT for suicide literature tends to be applicable to non-psychosis populations, there is some evidence that it may also reduce suicidal ideation in psychosis and schizophrenia. Recent work undertaken by Tarrier and colleagues has successfully applied a specially adapted CBT suicide prevention in psychosis protocol (CBSPp) (Tarrier et al., 2013). Moreover, Mewton and Andrews (2016) reviewed 15 RCT studies of CBT for adults (18+) with various psychiatric diagnoses (including psychosis) who also had suicidal tendencies. They concluded that although there was little evidence that CBT focusing on aspects of psychosis and mental illness was effective, even for recent onset schizophrenia, CBT which targeted suicidal thinking and behaviour may be.

In this vein, Power et al. (2003) cautioned against the routine use of CBT to increase insight in patients with a FEP in the hope of reducing suicidal tendencies. It has been noted previously in this chapter that there is a complex relationship between insight and suicidal desire in FEP patients but these latest therapeutic reviews would point, at the very least, to prioritising the management of suicidal symptoms over the improvement of insight. Likewise, the long-term reduction of depression on its own without concomitant reductions in suicidal thoughts and behaviours over time may not be enough.

One of the earliest psychological interventions targeted specifically at suicidality in FEPs was the LifeSPAN trial in Australia (Power et al., 2003) which compared a CBT-based therapy group with a control group receiving standard care only. Although both groups demonstrated reductions on measures of suicidal ideation, suicide attempts and general psychopathology, being in the therapy arm conferred no advantage, in terms of reduced suicidality, over standard care alone.

More recently, however, Tarrier et al. (2014) have demonstrated that CBSPp was superior to TAU (treatment as usual) in reducing suicidal ideation. It also had a more positive effect on secondary measures, such as hopelessness, depression, self-esteem, functioning and psychotic symptoms. Despite this, it is not yet known whether CBSPp reduces suicide attempts or completed suicides in young, risky FEP patients.

The evidence base for family approaches to suicidal first episode patients is less well established (Napa, Tungpunkom & Pothimas, 2017). However, families often feel excluded from conversations about their relative's suicidal risk and prevention plans to mitigate it. This is because the young person with psychosis often feels ashamed, or more commonly, does not want to worry or burden their families. Many clinicians and teams are then reluctant to break confidentiality. While there are some occasions when telling the family may make the situation worse (particular if there is a history of familial abuse or a catastrophic breakdown in relationships), these tend to be rare and EIP services should work towards bringing the family 'on board', as soon as possible. While this should be done with the agreement of the service user if possible, there may be occasions where speaking to the family is necessary without consent (see also Chapter 11).

Safety plans for FEP patients 'at risk' of suicide

Safety plans, also known as 'crisis' plans, are now a common feature of the management of suicide and suicidality across a number of diagnostic groups. Although there is no universally agreed method of constructing a suicide safety plan, evidence for their effectiveness is beginning to emerge (Stanley & Brown, 2012). These authors have proposed that a suicide prevention safety plan should be comprised of six steps or components, completed collaboratively by clinician and patient. These are:

1   The identification of early warning signs of suicidal thinking and behaviour.
2   Agreeing on, and learning to employ, internal coping strategies.
3   Learning distraction with social engagement or a change of environment.
4   Accessing suicide-protective social support.
5   Seeking help through crisis resources.
6   Restricting access to lethal means.

It remains unclear, however, despite clinical recommendations, how effective these safety plans are when applied to young people with psychosis. Despite their growing popularity, they should not be seen as a 'quick fix' but need to be carefully constructed by skilled clinicians over a number of sessions.

We have found that safety plans based on the O'Connor IMV framework (Figure 9.1) provide a useful template to help young FEP patients to manage their suicidal feelings and behaviours. At each stage, a plan can be collaboratively constructed with the patient, to help them identify the triggers, emotions and appraisals that are contributing to their suicidal thinking and behaviours at that time. For example, moderators identified from the IMV model such as 'brooding', social alienation and burdensomeness can be identified here, with an appropriate plan to tackle them agreed by the EIP team. In this case, social contact with more than one member of the team, increased meaningful group-based activities, peer support, social recovery interventions (see Chapter 6) and family work (see Chapter 11) may all address burdensomeness in young FEP patients. Such a plan can also help identify means and possible methods by which the person would undertake if things became too much for them. This allows the management of means safety by which the access to lethal means is restricted. An example of a safety plan will be provided using a clinical case study (case study 9.1, Justin). Here we will demonstrate how this can be developed using the framework given in Figure 9.1.

An integrated team approach for FEP patients 'at risk' of suicide

As indicated above, not only can prevention safety planning take place at an individual patient-clinician level, but also at an integrated team level too. For example, many EIP teams adopt a *zoning system* at multidisciplinary team (MDT) meetings that allows everyone in the team to become aware of particular patients who may be at short-, medium- or long-term risk of suicide. It also allows more shared responsibility of risk so that it does not fall unfavourably on one or two individuals within the team. There are a number of versions of these types of zoning systems of care and each team will have its own way of doing it. However, some of the general principles set out to 'enhance operational management and ensure the effective targeting of case management' (Ryrie, Hellard, Kearns, Robinson, Pathmanathan & O'Sullivan, 1997, p. 515) include the idea of 'real-time' feedback so that the EIP team is aware of which service user is at risk at any one time. Risk is 'RAG' rated so that red comprises the greatest risk, amber is considered moderate risk and green is low risk. All these risk categories are supplemented by continuous risk assessment using structured risk assessments, such as the InterSePT scale, suicide risk factor checklists or a more semi-structured clinical interview, as highlighted in this chapter. Patients at risk are written onto 'boards' where the team is based, or more likely nowadays, on a computer spreadsheet projected onto the wall in clinical team meetings. An action plan to reduce suicide risk is then agreed by the team. The EIP team decide whether the person should move in and out of the risk zone and at what level. This approach has been used by a number of EIP teams, including Birmingham and Solihull, where we have used a more 'stripped-down' version of Ryrie et al.'s original approach placing the person at risk of suicide in a 'worries' or 'high intensity' support section on a 'virtual board' (i.e. Excel spreadsheet). Such integrated team approaches are discussed in more detail in Chapter 12.

Implementing the evidence into practice

Case study 9.1 Justin

Justin is 25. His father and older brother are doctors, his mother is an accountant. He describes a constant pressure from his parents to do well academically. They always made the important decisions in his life. Around the time of his AS Level exams, he took an overdose. He reported feeling like a 'failure'.

Justin left home at 18 to study medicine. For the first time, he began drinking alcohol and partying. His friends, good-naturedly, teased him the morning after, accusing him of engaging in drunken pranks. Justin himself never had any recollection of these events but felt incredibly shamed at the thought he might have behaved disrespectfully. He had an idea that his friends could be involved in a conspiracy against him and began to suspect the university was also involved. Over time, these ideas became more delusional. He believed he was somehow spiritually chosen by God as a perfect human. He described voices, along with a localised feeling of pressure in the top of his head, and believed these were evidence of God communicating with him. He believed that the government was threatened by his supernatural presence. He feared he would be kidnapped by the secret service, and possibly killed. He withdrew from university, returned home and was referred to his local EIP service.

Justin made a good symptomatic and social recovery. He enrolled to study locally, requesting only minimal contact with the team, wanting to 'get on with his life'. Taking medication was an 'embarrassing reminder' of what happened. After two years, a medication-free trial was started. After six weeks, Justin reported early warning signs, including the pressure sensation in the top of his head. He recommenced treatment to good effect, but this symptom remained. This did not feel particularly unpleasant and he had insight into the experience. Despite this, Justin became increasingly hyper-vigilant to the feeling. He noticed it more when he was alone, or not engaging in physical (distracting) activity. Thinking about the feeling made it difficult for him to concentrate and increasingly anxious to the point he found it difficult to travel on public transport. Its presence led to a realisation that he might have a long-term psychotic illness, for Justin, this meant he would always be 'crazy', never be 'normal' and was 'not good enough' compared to others. He became more and more preoccupied and distracted by its presence, his anxiety meant he was less able to study, so he began to worry that he would fail his exams and when alone revising, or sitting in lectures, he spent time monitoring for its presence.

Justin felt increasingly unable to cope with studying. He was desperate to take 'time out' but believed he would be viewed as a 'failed doctor'. He tentatively suggested taking a break to his mother. She stated that the only reason she had delayed her retirement was so she could fund his studies. He felt 'guilty' about being an 'inconvenience'. For Justin, 'giving up was not an option' as the alternative to not qualifying was to be 'unemployed and on benefits and a complete, embarrassing failure'. He could see no way out and he did not know what to do.

Rumination prevented Justin from concentrating on work. He would say 'I must be really mad', 'why is this happening to me?', 'I'll never get better', 'there will always be something wrong with me'. He felt trapped. Sometimes he would bang his head in frustration until it bruised. He sometimes held on to the hope that his course was almost over and that he had 'come this far', that he could always retake exams, and that lots of people, including successful doctors had mental health problems. He became upset thinking about how 'devastated' his brother would be if he hurt himself.

As Justin's final exams approached, he became preoccupied with ways he could escape, and avoid taking them. He stated that he would rather die than 'fail and amount to nothing'. He experienced intrusive thoughts about behaving 'recklessly' (e.g. fantasising about pulling the emergency cord on the train, running in front of cars). One evening after university he came close to jumping in front of a train and one night he lay awake considering gaps in his timetable the following day and potential ligature points around his flat.

Further assessment of the stress-diathesis (i.e. pre-motivational stage in the IMV model, Figure 9.1) revealed that there was a family history of affective disorders. His grandmother, although not formally diagnosed, had symptoms consistent with a bipolar II disorder and his father had had episodes of depression (although none had required hospitalisation). Upon further enquiry, it transpired that Justin's father had been quite strict with Justin and his siblings when they were young, partially reflecting his own emotionally confused upbringing. Justin felt that his father was only able to express his affection for him by showing concern about his academic achievements, often becoming angry if Justin's schoolwork fell below standard. As a consequence, and with a desire to please his parents, Justin developed an internalised perfectionistic approach to his career and achievements. At a relatively young age, he began to set high standards to motivate himself to succeed, at both his schoolwork and hobbies. For instance, he became a very good cricketer, representing both his school and county. Further assessment also revealed that he had had a very brief period of self-harming in his late teens, usually preceded by low mood and feelings of failure. He felt particularly vulnerable during periods of high stress, such as exams or after arguments with his girlfriend.

During the assessment, Justin completed the PBIQ-R, scoring 11 on the entrapment subscale. This indicated that he felt his psychosis had become a burden, holding him back from achieving his goals. He initially became frustrated and then despairing, at his inability to concentrate on his work. He felt he had little control over the situation and could do little to change it. As there was no evidence of command hallucinations, assessment for suicide risk concentrated on his ambivalence for living. Although these were often just fleeting thoughts that lasted a few minutes at a time, on some days they became more frequent and more intense. Their duration also lengthened to well over two hours. This was confirmed by the CDS, with answers to question 8 indicating that on some occasions he had been contemplating a plan to kill himself. He had started to scope out possible high buildings or drops around his home city where he jump off to his death. To a certain extent, these plans were thwarted by his perceived inability to travel on public transport because of his anxiety. However, more information was gathered about these plans and those from the past that included thoughts about overdosing on his prescribed medication. Justin admitted, for instance, that he would consider stockpiling medication and fetching a rope from his father's garage so that he could use it to kill himself. He had previously scoped out a tree in a local park that was strong enough to support his weight but concealed from view. As a result, plans were put in place to make sure that Justin was given only small amounts of his anti-psychotic and anti-depressant medication at a time. There was careful scrutiny by his EIP team to make sure that he was also not stockpiling this medication. Given his history of self-harming in the past, this was also enquired about and carefully monitored. Special attention was given to antecedents, triggers and accompanying changes in mood. Justin's 'acquired capability' to kill himself was taken into account. His pharmacological knowledge as a medical student was considered to put him at increased risk.

All things considered, Justin was placed in the 'worries/high intensity' section on the team board in order to make sure that he was seen two or three times a week in normal working hours and referred to the home treatment team (HTT) out of hours. Justin was very reluctant to tell his parents about how he felt and was adamant at first that he did not want the team to discuss this with them either. The formulation of Justin's suicidal behaviour using the IMV framework is shown in Figure 9.2.

Justin was referred to the team's psychologist for CBTp who, with the help of the formulation in Figure 9.2, developed a 'safety plan'. The safety plan (Figure 9.3), again based on the IMV architecture of O'Connor, focused not only on his suicidal thinking, but also his sources of entrapment and defeat. These were exacerbated by the unrelenting high standards that he set for himself and the other self-beliefs that he thought his parents held about him (i.e. that he was a failure and would never make anything of his life). He also felt entrapped by his poor concentration and inability to work effectively.

The plan gave Justin and his EIP team a number of bio-psychosocial strategies at each stage to help thwart the suicide process from the pre-motivational stage, through the motivational stage, to the volitional stage by targeting the relevant moderating influences at each juncture. For example, during the pre-motivational stage (in Figure 9.3 labelled 'Background factors and triggers'), schema work addressing Justin's perfectionism and unrelenting standards ('diathesis') was carried out by the team psychologist. This was supplemented by family work by Justin's care co-ordinator targeting the 'expression of feelings' within the family and advice to take a break from university to help reduce environmental stressors. Lastly, psychoeducation about psychosis, relapse prevention work and interventions to reduce shame and stigma associated with developing psychosis for the first time ('Life Events') were also introduced.

CBTp, CBSPp and Compassionate Mind Therapy were used to address Justin's beliefs on defeat, humiliation and entrapment during the 'motivation' stage (labelled in Figures 9.2 and 9.3 as 'ideation/intention formation'). In addition, Justin was encouraged to use coping strategies that would better help him to manage his anxiety and stress with the help of short-term 'pro re nata' medication prescribed by the team's psychiatrist. Rumination was targeted in his CBT sessions through the use of behavioural experiments and getting him to generate problem-solving strategies as described in the CBSPp manual (Tarrier et al., 2013).

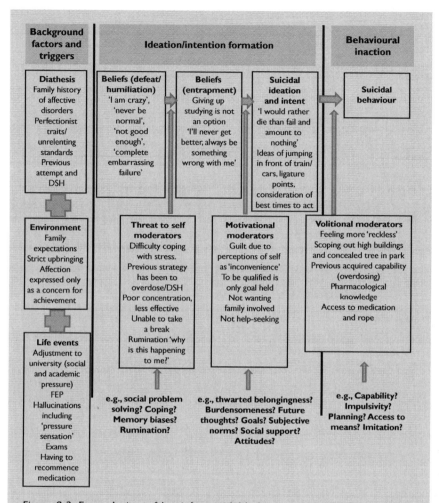

Figure 9.2 Formulation of Justin's suicidal behaviour.

Interventions used to reduce the transition from feelings of defeat/entrapment to suicidal ideation, included placing Justin on the team's 'zoning board' and increasing the amount of contact that he received from the team. This was in order to monitor and continually assess the frequency and intensity of his suicidal thinking. Family work, discouraging withdrawal and isolation, increasing emotional and social support through his trusted friends and structured team activities (e.g. cricket) were also encouraged. Working with the university through student support was also seen as important to allow him to gain support for disengaging from his overvalued goal of academic achievement and feeling of being a burden to his family. Details for crisis numbers were also given at this point to reassure him and his family 'out of hours'.

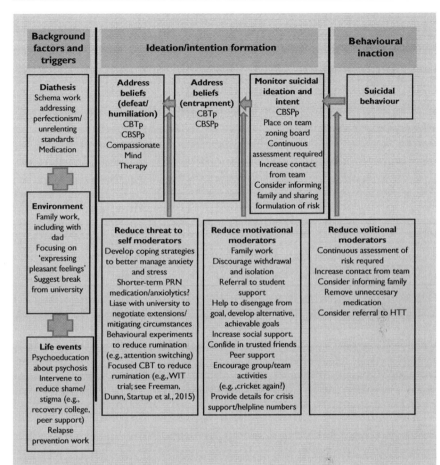

Figure 9.3 Justin's safety plan.

During the 'ideation/intention' formation stage Justin believed that he would not be able to handle the stress of the exams and therefore devised a plan to hang himself during one of the gaps in his timetable. Following discussion with the psychologist and his care co-ordinator, Justin agreed that if he got to this point he would not feel 'safe' and would need to confide in someone he trusted. He named a couple of friends who knew about his mental health issues. In addition to increasing a sense of connectedness to potential 'rescuers', it also helped him to recognise that it would be unwise for him to be on his own at this time. Justin and his psychologist discussed other strategies to keep him busy, including playing table tennis with his friends in the student canteen.

He said that he would not write a suicide note to his parents because he did not want to upset them further. It was agreed with Justin, as part of the plan, that the EIP team would ask him on a regular basis about detailed arrangements to kill himself (including stockpiling medication and getting hold of a rope) and that he would help to manage this by handing them over. At this point, because of Justin's acquired capability through his knowledge of pharmacology and physiology, it was predicted that any attempt at suicide would be highly lethal and that he would not seek help or assistance to stop him once he had made up his mind. For such reasons it was negotiated as part of the plan, that the team should be allowed to share their concerns with the family. It was also hoped that this might also reduce feelings of guilt and burdensomeness if the family were able to empathise and reassure. At first, Justin was not happy about this and refused this request. However, he did agree to family work to address broader issues of communication, problem-solving and how they felt towards each other.

Working directly within this framework and with his suicidal appraisals, beliefs and emotions through Socratic questioning, behavioural experiments and compassion-focused techniques allowed Justin to eventually reduce his 'brooding' and increase his sense of self-efficacy. For example, behavioural experiments such as the 'attention switch' (Renner et al., 2017), allowed him to test out what it would be like to reduce his hypervigilance to the pressure sensation in his head and thereby reduce his anxiety.

This therapeutic work was integrated with pharmacological management of his suicidal ideation with anti-depressant medication and ongoing management of his psychotic symptoms with anti-psychotic medication. Eventually, with the help of the family meetings, and other support from the EIP team and student services, Justin felt ready to tell his family how he had been feeling. Justin eventually made a good 'psychological' recovery after a number of months (see Chapter 7), confirmed by post-intervention results on the PBIQ-R and CDS, that allowed him to continue with his studies and pursue a career in medicine.

FEP and suicidality: the role of the EIP services

Of course, in practice, many suicides in young people with psychosis can be difficult to predict. Firm evidence for the role of EIP in suicide reduction still remains inconclusive with some retrospective studies showing a positive effect (Chan et al., 2018) while others demonstrate no significant advantage over standard care (Anderson et al., 2018). Clearly, better-designed prospective, longitudinal studies are needed to clarify the role of EIP in suicide and suicidality. The case of Justin highlights the successful management of someone who is suicidal but willing to engage and talk about their suicidal feelings and intentions. Many other service users do not. In our experience of working in an EIP service over many years, many of the completed suicides appeared to have been unpredictable and, only with the 'benefit of hindsight', were we able to identify signs that might have alerted us and their families to an increased risk. As alluded to earlier, suicide prediction remains an inexact science with the majority of serious suicidal attempts in EIP being classified as 'impulsive' (Fedyszyn et al., 2011). This is not to say, however, that we should give up on the idea of striving, through the symbiotic relationship between research and clinical practice, to improve models, theories, interventions and policies (e.g. the 'Zero Suicide' ambition recently launched in England) that will help us reduce the unacceptably high rates of suicide and suicidal behaviour in young people with psychosis. When suicides in EIP services do occur, it is vital that the whole team, and not just the clinicians who have the most contact with the person, are supported. How to support teams and individuals following a suicide is described in more detail in Chapter 12.

The emphasis that EIP teams place on high levels of scrutiny and engagement during the first three years of EIP may be crucial to help recognise and manage people when they reactivate the 'suicidal mode' (Back, 2013). It may also be that such high levels of support, and the relationships that patients often have with their care co-ordinators and other professionals in EIP, increase a 'sense of belonging' (see Chapters 7 and 12) that protects people with early psychosis from feeling entrapped and suicidal. We know from research (Joiner, 2005) and anecdotal evidence, that the mere presence of a compassionate human relationship, even at the point of actual suicide completion, may avert death. This is illustrated in the case of Jonny Benjamin, a British mental health campaigner recovering from psychosis, in a now well-publicised story (Benjamin, 2018).

Jonny writes about how a stranger (Neil Laybourn) showed kindness and spoke to him at the point he was about to end his life by jumping from Waterloo Bridge in London. Neil, having changed Jonny's mind about ending his life, then disappeared into the crowd of commuters on their way to work. Six years later a campaign by Jonny, with the help of Rethink (UK mental health charity) and social media, gave Jonny the opportunity to thank Neil, the 'stranger on the bridge'. This act of compassion and kindness on the bridge, emphasising the importance of connecting and positive human relationships, even within the space of 30 minutes, had a profound and long-lasting effect on both men. In particular, it has changed the way that Jonny manages his psychosis, his personal recovery and adaptation, and the way he views his future. Both men remain good friends and now campaign together to promote awareness of ways to prevent suicide.

The importance of integrated and sustained recovery to prevent suicidality

We have written about how thoughts, feelings and suicidal behaviours can influence, and be influenced by, someone's personal recovery and psychological adaptation following a FEP and the role that EIP can play in offering a sense of hope and fostering a sense of belonging (Gajwani et al., 2018). Moreover, the increased risk of suicide that seems to occur during the period (4–12 years) following discharge from EIP services appears to be associated with poor premorbid occupational functioning, the number of relapses and inadequate adherence to anti-psychotic medication during the first three years of EIP (Chan et al., 2018). This would indicate that early and sustained symptomatic, social and personal recovery may not just change the long-term trajectories of young people with psychosis but could save lives as well.

Learning points

- The number of people with FEP who go on to die by suicide (2–4%) is lower than was initially thought.
- This is still significantly higher than would be found in the UK general population.
- Most suicides occur during the early stages of psychosis.
- Although completed suicides in FEP are relatively rare, suicidal ideation and behaviour are not.
- A number of bio-psychosocial mediating and moderating factors will determine whether psychological states of defeat and entrapment transition to self-inflicted death in a complex and dynamic process.
- These moderating factors may be used as the basis for a comprehensive risk assessment, safety prevention plan and medical, psychosocial and team-based interventions to prevent death by suicide in people with early psychosis.

Notes

1 Proportionate mortality describes the percentage of deaths over a specified period of time, attributable to suicide.
2 Case fatality is the proportion of the original cohort, expressed as a percentage, who have died as a result of suicide

Chapter 10

Working with comorbidity and diagnostic uncertainty

Introduction

EIP is not exclusively a 'psychosis' service (Marwaha, Thompson, Upthegrove & Broome, 2016). Comorbidity is common in psychosis (Austin et al., 2013) and should be considered the norm. Mood and anxiety disorders, post-traumatic stress disorder (PTSD) and negative symptoms have already been discussed at various points throughout the book. This chapter focuses instead on lesser-understood comorbidities, illustrating the clinical challenges of embracing diagnostic uncertainty and managing complexity. The comorbidities creating some of the greatest challenges in EIP are autism spectrum disorder (ASD), personality disorder (PD) and substance use disorder (SUD).

There is increasing awareness of the overlap of ASD and psychosis (Chisholm, Lin, Abu-Akel & Wood, 2015; King & Lord, 2011), yet, until recently, ASD has been largely ignored in EIP literature. Although ASD awareness is increasing, EIP services are ill-equipped to sufficiently diagnose ASD in FEP. Thus, there are many individuals with undiagnosed comorbid ASD-psychosis who experience difficulty in achieving symptomatic, social and personal recovery due to care not adequately tailored to their needs. Similarly, more could be done to improve the recognition and diagnostic reliability of psychosis in those with an existing diagnosis of ASD. Specific training on diagnosis and management of ASD in FEP populations are a vital prerequisite for this. Person-centred interventions for ASD-P in EIP should be a priority for future research and urgent action at a procedural and policy level (Larson et al., 2017).

FEP and PD, particularly emotionally unstable/borderline PD (EUPD/BPD) are common comorbidities. We explore similarities and differences in psychotic symptoms, including voice hearing, between BPD and schizophreniform psychotic disorders. Individuals with BPD who experience voices and/or paranoia may benefit from an extended assessment where this is diagnostic uncertainty. When FEP is excluded, these individuals should be promptly referred to an appropriate team to minimise dependency risk and inappropriate labelling. Individuals with FEP and comorbid BPD are likely to benefit from treatment combinations, which may involve trauma-focused psychotherapy. EIP assertive engagement and rapid crisis response can be adapted for this patient group as this may actually hinder recovery in some individuals and result in 'burn-out' for EIP clinicians.

SUD, a common comorbidity in FEP, creates management challenges. Diagnosing 'drug-induced psychosis' in FEP can delay referral to EIP, lengthening DUP. Cannabis, an independent risk factor for psychosis (see Chapter 1), is associated with worsened prognosis and delayed recovery. Its use is prevalent in FEP and EIP teams should acquire 'in-house' SUD skills to better manage this group of patients, particularly given the current UK climate of SUD service provision predominantly outside the NHS.

Autism spectrum disorder (ASD)

Prevalence rates of ASD are rising as a result of broadening diagnostic boundaries and increasing awareness (Neggers, 2014), rather than a spontaneous epidemiological phenomenon (Bertelli et al., 2015). There is significant overlap between psychosis and ASD, with ASD increasingly recognised as an important comorbidity in psychosis (Larson et al., 2017). Yet, despite this knowledge, ASD may be poorly understood among EIP clinicians. If we are to enable patients with comorbid ASD and FEP to maximise their recovery potential across all three domains, we should examine the latest concepts and management for this subgroup of individuals. We focus primarily on high functioning (or high ability) ASD, the subgroup most likely to be encountered in an EIP setting. Until recently, high ability individuals with social and communication difficulties were diagnosed with 'Asperger's syndrome', classified separately from autism under the umbrella term 'pervasive developmental disorders'. The DSM-V (APA, 2013 revised) classifies Asperger's syndrome and autism together as ASD and the latest ICD11 classification system will mirror these changes (Lord & Jones, 2012).

What is ASD?

ASD, a neuro-developmental disorder, encompasses a wide-ranging spectrum of characteristics with differing degrees of disability across multiple contexts (APA, 2013). There are two core features:

> Social and communication deficits (Matson et al., 2012). Individuals with ASD often respond atypically to expressions of emotion. Social-emotional reciprocity deficits include difficulties engaging in two-way conversation and initiating or responding to social interactions. Reduced speech prosody, echolalia (repeating phrases from others) and neologisms (Volden & Lord, 1991) are common. Nonverbal communication difficulties include poor eye contact and reduced facial expressions.

Individuals with ASD commonly display restricted repetitive behaviours (RBBs) with limited interests and an obsessional, all-encompassing 'hobby' (Szatmari et al., 2006). Low tolerance for uncertainty results in avoidance and preference of structure and routine.

Sensory stimuli over-sensitivity to loud noises, itchy clothes and textured food can cause distress. Although behaviours typically present in early childhood, high ability individuals may not fully manifest difficulties until later in life when social demands exceed capacity, such as during the transition from primary to secondary school or during adolescence. There are many who believe ASD should not be considered or classified a disorder (Baron-Cohen, 2002), proposing instead that the difficulties that ASD individuals experience are borne out of an education system, health service and wider society not being able to fully appreciate the talents and accommodate the difficulties that people with ASD experience. Society's failure to adapt adequately to the needs of individuals with ASD perpetuates already high levels of distress, increasing vulnerability to mental disorders such as psychosis.

Prevalence of ASD and psychosis

In the UK, it is estimated that 700,000 individuals live with a diagnosis of ASD (NAS, 2018), a prevalence of 1% of the general population (Brugha et al., 2011). Clinical and research interest in the confluence between ASD and psychosis, in symptoms, aetiology and genetics is growing (Pinto et al., 2014; Wood, 2017).

Given the increased vulnerability to psychosis and high levels of social stress that many individuals with ASD experience, it is unsurprising to find increased prevalence of individuals with ASD on an EIP caseload. Mouridsen et al.'s (2008) 32-year cohort autism study reported psychosis in 6.6% compared with 0.9% matched control. Stahlberg et al.'s (2004) study had higher psychosis prevalence (14.8%), interestingly, half of which were affective in presentation. Davidson et al.'s (2013) EIP survey reported 3.6% prevalence of ASD, four times that of the general population but lower than expected given the previous studies. When autistic-like traits (ALT) are included, the figure is significantly higher (Kincaid et al., 2017), although study rates vary enormously, reflecting ASD heterogeneity.

Notably psychosis in comorbid ASD (ASD-P) is more commonly affective in presentation (Mouridsen et al., 2008). Larson et al.'s (2017) study of 116 individuals with ASD-P reported more diagnoses of atypical psychosis with affective features and fewer of schizophrenia compared with individuals with psychosis only. Those with ASD-P had fewer stereotyped interests/behaviours compared with ASD alone. This data may point towards a specific subtype of ASD-P. Identified shared risk factors for ASD and psychosis include birth trauma and adverse childhood events (Chisholm et al., 2015). Increased family history of mood disorders (Smalley et al., 1995) and association with depression, hopelessness and suicidality (Upthegrove et al., 2017) in FEP and ASD suggest shared heritability.

Diagnostic challenges

ASD is often undiagnosed due to inflexibility in both educational and health systems. To improve recognition and diagnostic reliability, clinicians require an understanding of abnormal perceptions and cognitions in both ASD and psychosis.

Identifying ASD in individuals with FEP

Individuals with high ability ASD who never receive a formal diagnosis are described by Lai and Baron-Cohen (2015) as a 'lost generation of people'. An ASD diagnosis can help individuals develop better coping strategies to reduce distress (Murphy et al., 2016). An improved understanding of why certain situations are anxiety-provoking and why they may have been subject to teasing and bullying can help an individual battling with a sense of failure. An ASD diagnosis helps families by providing an understanding of the disorder, and improved communication strategies and may provide a gateway to social and financial support (NAS, 2018).

EIP clinicians face challenges when encountering individuals with undiagnosed ASD. Questions may be raised about the value of referring the young person for an ASD assessment and, given the scarcity of adult ASD services, many EIP clinicians are unsure what to do, and are reluctant to carry out an assessment themselves. An ASD assessment may also be avoided to circumvent further 'labelling', mistakenly believing there is no added advantage to an ASD diagnosis.

Practicalities of diagnosing ASD

NICE (2016) recommends a multidisciplinary assessment, involving a family member or other informant and previous school reports. Clinical diagnosis of ASD has 93% inter-rater trained clinician reliability (Baird et al., 2006) and ASD assessment training is readily available for all clinicians. 'In-house' ASD assessments combine patient and economic advantages and gaining ASD expertise allows knowledge and skills to be disseminated within teams.

ASD diagnostic instruments

Identification of a broader spectrum of ASD has resulted in the extension of diagnostic instrument content and form (Stabel et al., 2013). A great number of validated autism screening and diagnostic tools exist with good sensitivity and specificity. Table 10.1 lists the screening tools that could be used in an EIP clinical setting.

Table 10.1 ASD assessment screening and diagnostic tools

Tool	Description	Advantages
AQ 50 (Baron-Cohen, 2011)	50 question self-administered questionnaire Screening tool – score of 33 or above suggests ASD traits and fuller assessment may be required	Quick, Easy to use Simple to score. Can be done online with instant results
Autism Diagnostic Observation Schedule (ADOS) (Luyster et al., 2009)	Semi-structured assessment of communication and social interaction Four modules, each suited to developmental needs	Module 4 developed specifically for adolescents and young adults with verbal fluency(Bastiaansen et al., 2010)
The Diagnostic Interview guide ASD (Berney, 2011)	Semi-structured guided assessment	Online training available alongside face-to-face provided by RCPsych
The Diagnostic Interview for Social and Communication Disorders (DISCO) (Wing et al., 2002)	Developed as both clinical and research instrument for use with children and adults of any age	It takes wider perspective of social and communication difficulties to capture females with ASD who are often missed by ICD and DSM criteria

Identifying psychosis in individuals with ASD

We have discussed complexities in encountering undiagnosed *ASD* in individuals with FEP. We now consider difficulties diagnosing and managing psychosis in individuals with already established ASD, as illustrated by the case study 10.1.

Case study 10.1 Mo

Mo, aged 19 years, was diagnosed with high ability ASD at the age of 12, following a lengthy wait and prolonged assessment period. On leaving college with three reasonable 'A' levels, he started a decorating apprenticeship. This lasted only two weeks due to a dispute with his manager. Around the same time, he became increasingly isolated, rarely leaving his bedroom. His mum's concerns about his mental health heightened when he developed a conspiracy theories preoccupation and began accusing her of filming him while he slept. His GP referred him for an EIP assessment which took place at his home.

The assessment was time-consuming due to Mo's seeming insistence on repeatedly returning the discussion to conspiracy theories. His speech was pressured with pedantic language, and he strongly resisted interruptions. He answered many questions, particularly about mood and feelings, with difficulty. He denied experiencing heightened or abnormal perceptions, although reported hating bright lights and described the sound of the hoover as 'deafening'. He also denied thought insertion, withdrawal, broadcast and other passivity experiences; although the interviewer was not convinced he fully understood her questioning.

Unable to elucidate definitive psychotic symptoms, the psychiatrist interviewed his mum, who described Mo's fixed belief that she enters his room to film him and adds rat poison to his food. She also described a significant change in his behaviour and functioning over the previous year, particularly the last three months, now rarely leaving his bedroom, refusing to eat meals cooked by her and having difficulty sleeping.

The collateral history helped establish the delusional content of Mo's unusual beliefs. The significant behaviour change, sleep disturbance, social withdrawal, irritability and hostility at an age when psychosis typically emerges, enabled the psychiatrist to conclude that Mo was experiencing FEP, a diagnosis likely to have been missed had the assessment not involved his mum. He was taken on by EIP and allocated to Gary, a CPN care co-ordinator.

Progress was slow, hampered by poor engagement with Gary. Mo remained in his bedroom when Gary visited and refused the prescribed risperidone, despite repeated reassurances of its safety and effectiveness. Hospital admission was considered and decided against, due to the risk of worsening symptoms in what would be a hugely stressful environment for Mo. After three months, Gary presented Mo's formulation (using the 5 Ps format; Table 10.2), highlighting difficulties and

Table 10.2 Team formulation: 5 Ps

Presentation
Mo has an established diagnosis of ASD and FEP, with persecutory and referential delusions, social withdrawal, severe anxiety and seep disturbance.

Predisposing
High levels of social anxiety and the cumulative stress from years of difficulties managing social relationships. Mo experienced a number of adverse childhood experiences – his parents separated when he was aged 8 and he was the victim of repeated bullying throughout school.

Precipitating
Managing the social environment and relationships in work and leaving work under stressful circumstances heightened his sense of failure precipitating the onset of psychosis

Perpetuating
Increase in social isolation, resultant lack of structure, and increased time available to research conspiracy theories Non-concordance with medication and lack of engagement with EIP team

Protective
Supportive Mum, high academic achievements, interest in IT. Doesn't abuse substances.

progress since the initial assessment. A Learning Disabilities (LD) psychologist with expertise in ASD attended.

Concerns were expressed that EIP had been unable to 'engage' Mo in any social, psychological or biological therapies. The LD psychologist suggested effective communication and engagement strategies for young people with ASD, encouraging Gary to adopt a different approach. Recognising the importance of structure and time-keeping, he began visiting Mo on a set day and time each week, ensuring punctuality. Rather than avoiding the subject of conspiracy theories due to fears of colluding in a delusion, he joined Mo in conspiracy theory research. Gradually Mo began trusting Gary and started playing computer games with him. Gary's improved understanding of ASD reduced his frustration and he started to enjoy visits with Mo. As Mo's trust in Gary developed, he reconsidered medication, particularly since Gary reassured him it would help with 'sleep' and 'stress'. Gary taught Mo anxiety management techniques, giving a written account of what they had done after each session and clear 'homework' instructions.

Gradually Mo's persecutory delusions lessened and he enrolled on a computer course at college. Gary accompanied him on enrolment day to meet the learning support team, who offered weekly mentoring sessions, digital technology assistance and a separate quiet room to take exams. On starting college, his anxiety levels increased, however, with support, he managed his anxiety with no psychotic symptom return. Social anxiety reduced further on an SSRI and after a year he successfully discontinued risperidone, choosing instead to remain on the SSRI. On discharge from EIP to primary care after three years with no psychotic relapse, the protective factors in his life had been greatly enhanced. His relationship with Mum had improved, he was enjoying his new job as a computer analyst with a manager who was encouraged to make allowances for his ASD and he had a better understanding of effective coping strategies for anxiety. Interestingly, he never knowingly accepted that he had experienced a psychotic episode.

Psychosis in ASD can be missed if it presents atypically, with high levels of anxiety and affective symptoms (Larson et al., 2017). Furthermore, the assessment process may inadequately accommodate the needs of ASD individuals. Questions to elicit psychosis may be misunderstood due to literal interpretations and misleading answers.

It is equally important that individuals with ASD are not incorrectly diagnosed with psychosis (Nylander & Gillberg, 2001), exposing them to unnecessary labels and treatments. Rigid fantastical beliefs expressed simply and concretely can be mistaken for delusions, sensory hypersensitivity or idiosyncratic sensory experiences for hallucinations (Woodbury-Smith, 2010). Communication and speech flow impairments, including neologisms and over-inclusivity, can mimic thought disorder. Lack of social reciprocity may be interpreted as blunted affect and social avoidance as negative symptoms. Theory of mind impairment increases the likelihood of individuals misjudging others' intent, easily mistaken for paranoia or referential delusions (Frith & Happé, 1994).

These diagnostic difficulties require a pragmatic, collateral and longitudinal approach in assessment. Individuals with ASD may benefit from lengthier assessment periods, allowing time for information gathering and a formulation-driven management plan.

Enhancing recovery for individuals with ASD-psychosis

ASD-related social and communication difficulties create engagement obstacles to psychological and social therapies. Clinicians may rely more heavily on biological treatments, thereby denying patients with ASD-psychosis an integrated service. To mitigate against this we suggest the following strategies.

Implementing the evidence into practice

Practical recovery strategies for FEP and comorbid ASD

- *Engagement* requires consistency and patience. The same clinician should aim to visit at the same time and day each week.
- *Communication* needs and preferences should be established at the outset by asking individuals whether they would prefer written rather than verbal information (Nicolaidis et al., 2016). Metaphors and irony cause confusion due to literal interpretations; language that is clear and to the point is preferable. Individuals with ASD often benefit from more time to answer questions. Picture boards with feelings and emotion symbols are helpful tools for individuals struggling to articulate their emotional difficulties. Technology aids, for example, the Silver Linings Psychosis app (Jee, 2017), uses symptom rating graphs, a less stressful way for some to communicate with clinicians.
- *Employment and education support*. Routine and structure aid recovery and EIP teams should actively support a return to employment or education, where possible. However, social and communication difficulties result in higher unemployment rates and unnecessary job losses, and only 16% of autistic adults are in full-time work (NAS, 2018). Liaising with employers about difficulties associated with ASD and psychosis encourages workplace adaptations to be made. High ability individuals with ASD bring strengths to the workplace, including attention to detail, ability to maintain focus, and reliability (Lorenz & Heinitz, 2014). A manager who appreciates and understands the social difficulties their ASD employee will encounter in the workplace and who makes necessary adjustments is likely to be rewarded with a reliable staff member.
- *Housing*. Given the poor employment figures, it is unsurprising that many individuals with ASD live in social housing (Koyama, Kamio, Inada & Kurita, 2008). Accessing appropriate accommodation with adequate support is an essential component of the treatment plan requiring integrated social care.

- *Pharmacological treatment.* Antipsychotic medication remains the mainstay treatment for psychosis in individuals with ASD (see Chapter 3). However, given the frequently high levels of anxiety, the addition of an SSRI can be helpful. Beta blockers are a useful addition for treating the physical symptoms associated with anxiety (tachycardia, hyperventilation, dizziness). Reduction in anxiety is likely to improve psychotic symptoms, thereby enabling lower doses and potential discontinuation of anti-psychotic medication.
- *Psychological treatment.* Individual CBTp can be adapted for ASD-P (Cooper, Loades & Russell, 2018)
- *Resources.* There are many resources for individuals with ASD, their friends, families and team members. The AASPIRE (Academic Autism Spectrum Partnership in Research and Education) Healthcare Toolkit provides information to improve care for patients, their families and healthcare providers for adults with ASD (https://autismandhealth.org/).

Borderline personality disorder (BPD)

Borderline personality disorder (BPD) diagnosis attracts controversy (Myers, 2017), not least because it is a reductionist concept (individuals often experience difficulties across different domains of personality types), poorly understood, and viewed by some as stigmatising (Gunderson, 2010). The authors endorse treating an individual rather than a 'diagnosis', yet recognise EUPD/BPD as short-hand concepts understood by mental health professionals and many patients. EUPD and BPD are interchangeable terms, however, we choose BPD in this chapter due to its more frequent use in literature and patient information. BPD is frequently encountered in EIP settings, presenting diagnostic and management challenges to EIP clinicians. Although we refer primarily to BPD, our discussion extends to individuals diagnosed with complex PTSD, typically associated with chronic and repeated traumas (Matheson, 2016).

BPD prevalence studies are handicapped by poor diagnostic reliability and temporal instability of personality disorder (Zimmerman, 1994), however, it is generally accepted that BPD is a condition affecting around 1% of the population (Coid, Yang, Tyrer, Roberts & Ullrich, 2006; Torgersen, Kringlen & Cramer, 2001), the core features of which include intense fear of abandonment and chronic feelings of emptiness. It is largely characterised by inconsistent self-identity, changeable moods that result in unstable relationships, explosive anger and impulsive, reckless behaviour. Self-harm and suicide attempts are common.

BPD is so named as it is thought to occupy the *border* between neurotic and psychotic disorders (although these boundaries are not as discrete as traditionally thought; Kelleher & Cannon., 2014). Around 20–50% of individuals with BPD report psychotic symptoms (Schroeder, Fisher & Schäfer, 2013), auditory verbal hallucinations (AVH) being particularly common (Merrett, Rossell & Castle, 2016).

Aetiology of comorbid BPD, complex trauma and FEP

As discussed in Chapter 1, the 'stress vulnerability' model (Nuechterlein & Dawson, 1984) is a framework to describe why psychotic symptoms present when life stressors exceed an individual's vulnerability threshold. Childhood trauma is associated with both BPD and psychosis (Coughlan & Cannon, 2017; Read, Os, Morrison & Ross, 2005), the relationship likely to be mediated by mood instability (Broome, Saunders, Harrison & Marwaha, 2015), poor impulse control and anxiety (Isvoranu et al., 2017).

BPD comorbidity in FEP is a complex subject, to which we cannot do justice in this short section. However, because of the significant overlap of symptoms and aetiology between BPD and FEP, we will focus on two important clinical issues: the diagnostic challenges in attempting to differentiate BPD from FEP at initial assessment and the management challenges in treating comorbid PD and FEP.

Diagnostic uncertainty

It is important that individuals with BPD are not incorrectly diagnosed with a schizophreniform psychotic disorder. On the other hand, it is crucial that individuals experiencing psychosis are not excluded from EIP simply because they display features of emotional instability and challenging behaviour. To aid diagnostics, we examine the nature of the psychotic symptoms typically experienced in BPD, attempting to differentiate these from schizophrenia spectrum disorders.

If the entry criteria to EIP depend on the presence of auditory verbal hallucinations (AVHs) (Marwaha et al., 2016), this creates difficulties as they are present in approximately 50% of individuals with BPD (Merrett et al., 2016). Furthermore, there is increasing acceptance that 'voice hearing' is relatively common in the general population (Beavan, Read & Cartwright, 2011; Woods et al., 2015), particularly in adolescents and young adults (Yung et al., 2009). While the vast majority of voice hearers (84%) are not seeking help (Kråkvik et al., 2015), for those referred to secondary care, a thorough assessment is required.

It follows, therefore, that the mere presence of AVHs is of limited value diagnostically. So are there differentiating factors in the AVHs experienced in functional psychosis compared to BPD and other trauma-related disorders? According to Schroeder et al. (2013), AVHs experienced in BPD are similar to those in schizophrenia spectrum disorders (SSD) in terms of phenomenology, emotional impact, and persistence over time. Kingdon et al. (2010) found many similarities in experiences of AVH between the two groups, however, they differed in frequency of paranoid delusions, which were less frequent in the BPD subgroup. In addition, Niemantsverdriet et al. (2017) report longevity of AVH in BPD, with mean duration of 18 years.

Given the many similarities between AVHs in FEP and BPD, it is important to consider phenomenological differences to aid diagnosis and inform treatment. It is generally accepted that a core feature of psychosis is a dysfunction in reality testing. Hearing voices in internal or external space is not a sufficiently specific diagnostic feature, however, perceived attribution of the voice is. A systematic review of studies comparing voice hearing in psychosis compared to BPD revealed that the 'BPD voices' tended to be more derogatory and self-critical in nature and the voice-hearers' response to the voices more emotionally resistive (Merrett et al., 2016). Conversely, AVHs in SSD were more frequently accompanied by delusional beliefs and a subjective sense of lack of control. Kurt Schneider made significant advances in our understanding of psychosis and schizophrenia. His 'first rank' symptoms traditionally informed our classification of schizophrenia and remain a core component of the mental state examination of suspected psychosis. Yet these 'symptoms' are not pathognomonic of schizophrenia (Tschöke, Uhlmann & Steinert, 2011) or, indeed, any type of psychosis and are therefore of limited diagnostic value. Oliva et al. (2014) studied prevalence and characteristics of thoughts and perceptions in individuals with BPD and found that Schneiderian first rank symptoms, such as passivity of thought were present in 46% of their sample. When psychotic symptoms were present, they were, however, more likely to be atypical and transient. Tschöke et al. (2014)

Table 10.3 Phenomenological and other differences between BPD psychotic experiences and FEP/SSD

BPD	FEP/SSD
Psychotic experiences more likely to be atypical and transient (Oliva et al., 2014)	Delusions if present more likely to be bizarre (Tschöke et al., 2014)
Psychotic experiences less frequent (Kingdon et al., 2010)	Psychotic experiences more likely to be daily occurrence (Kingdon et al. 2010)
More derogatory/self-critical (Merrett et al., 2016)	Asociated with delusional perception (Tschöke et al., 2014)
More often associated with resistance (Merrett et al., 2016)	Associated with subjective lack of control (Merrett et al., 2016)
Less associated functional impairment (Tschöke et al., 2014)	Associated with greater functional impairment (Tschöke et al., 2014)
Symptoms (particularly AVHs) likely to have been present since childhood (Niemantsverdriet et al., 2017)	Psychotic symptoms likely to commence late adolescence/early adulthood
More likely to be female (Niemantsverdriet et al., 2017)	More likely to be male (Koester et al., 2007)
Negative symptoms and cognitive disorganisation absent (Niemantsverdriet et al., 2017)	Associated with thought disorder, negative symptoms and cognitive disorganisation (Niemantsverdriet et al., 2017; Tschöke et al., 2014)

found that thought disorder and bizarre delusions, including delusional perception, are commoner in SSD than BPD. In addition, the psychotic symptoms in SSD are more likely to be present on a daily basis and associated with more functional impairment, cognitive decline and negative symptoms than in BPD. These findings are summarised in Table 10.3.

Implementing the evidence into practice

Case study 10.2 Sophie

Sophie, aged 21, was referred by her GP with low mood, suicidal behaviour and 'hearing voices'. The referral was triaged by 'single point of access' team as suspected FEP (due to voice hearing) and passed on to EIP. On assessment Sophie described mood instability, with extreme fluctuations throughout the day. She also described 'voice hearing' since the age of eight. The voice was experienced initially as a denigrating female and as years progressed the voices increased in number and intensity and were mostly persecutory in nature.

Sophie described seeing people others couldn't ,e.g. a hooded man standing in her room or outside in the garden. When she looked in the mirror, she saw a ghostly figure with red eyes standing behind her. She felt the presence of someone continually watching her, resulting in her showering in her underwear. She repeatedly looked over her shoulder when out due to the sense that a 'presence' was following her. Sophie had a history of superficial cutting and two previous impulsive overdoses. She had long-standing 'weight issues', was repeatedly on diets, and intermittently used laxatives to control her weight.

She had experienced a chaotic upbringing, being the youngest of six children. Following her birth, she was separated from her mum, who was suffering postnatal depression. She described her dad as a 'bully', who drank heavily, during which times he was repeatedly verbally and physically abusive towards her and her mum. Sophie's description of her mum suggested emotional unavailability.

She was suspended twice from school for behavioural problems. She had a history of intense attachments and volatile relationships, with impulsive overdoses following arguments. She tended to 'drink to get drunk', used sex 'to feel loved' and smoked high potency cannabis to help relax. She was unsuccessful in keeping jobs for longer than two months, usually due to 'fall-outs' with managers and work colleagues.

Sophie wore carefully applied make-up, and was warm in affect with reactive mood. She was articulate, her speech spontaneous and there was no evidence of underlying thought disorder. She reported intense fluctuations in mood with no perceived personal control over her emotions. She described hearing a number of voices in both internal and external space. She recognised that the voices were more intense and negative at times of heightened stress. The voices never conversed with each other or commented on her actions. She had never experienced thought echo. She denied experiencing olfactory, gustatory or somatic hallucinations, nor delusions of thought passivity (insertion, withdrawal, broadcast). On further exploration of the 'paranoia', it became clear that this was in fact more of a sensation of being watched rather than a fixed, firmly held belief. She had always been very sensitive to her surroundings and to other's perceptions of her. There was no evidence of any other delusional beliefs.

Given her history and presentation documented in the mental state examination, a formulation of her problems was shared with her. From an early age, Sophie had experienced attachment difficulties due to an emotionally unavailable mother and an abusive father. As long as she could remember, she experienced an over-whelming fear of rejection which fuelled her over-dosing behaviour when relation-ships were in danger of ending. Her capacity to regulate her emotions remained under-developed, tending to rely on external factors such as substances, food and relationships to maintain a sense of happiness. She therefore felt completely 'con-trolled' by her external environment.

Sophie enquired about her diagnosis, given that she was experiencing 'voices', and wondered if she was 'going mad'. It was explained that 'voice hearing' can be caused by a number of reasons. For some, 'voices' can be caused by an excess of dopamine in the brain. In her case, it is more likely that the 'voices' are a direct response to the trauma she experienced in childhood. In discussion about some of her other dif-ficulties, it was explained that the feeling of being watched is particularly common among people who are very self-conscious with heightened sensory sensitivity. It was also explained that many of Sophie's experiences, such as the fear of abandonment, impulsivity, emotional instability and formation of intense and unstable relationships, suggested a diagnosis of Borderline Personality Disorder.

Sophie found the sensitive discussion about her diagnosis helpful. She didn't find the diagnosis of BPD stigmatising, instead she found it empowering to hear someone validating her symptoms and linking them to her childhood experiences. She was interested to discover that many people had similar experiences and that there were techniques she could use to gain control of her mood and the 'voices'.

It was decided, and communicated to the GP, that Sophie did not at that time require an EIP service. Before she left, she was given written information on BPD and directed to websites such as Mind, RCPsych, and 'Hearing Voices Network'. In addition, she was encouraged to watch a short 5-minute film 'Compassion for voices' https://compassionatemind.co.uk/resources/videos/compassion-for-voices-a-tale-of-courage-and-hope

She received structured psychological input from IAPT (Improved Access to Psychological Therapies) and over time Sophie gradually started viewing the voices as less alienating and persecutory. She began to accept, rather than resist, their presence and started communicating with them with compassion (Corstens, Longden, McCarthy-Jones, Waddingham & Thomas, 2014).

Sophie's case highlights the importance of carrying out a thorough assess-ment, considering the aetiology and diagnostic category which best represents an individual's difficulties. In practice, many of the young people referred for an EIP assessment have experiences which are *borderline* between psychotic and non-psychotic and their symptoms cannot be neatly boxed into a diagnosis. Thus, it is an inexact science and not always an easy distinction to make during an initial assessment. Refraining from a simplistic reductionist approach to psychotic symptoms allows individuals with diagnostic uncertainty to have an extended assessment period, formulation and integrated bio-psychosocial management plan.

Management of individuals with diagnosed FEP and concurrent BPD

Prevalence of BPD comorbidity with FEP

Bahorik and Eack's (2010) study report an 18% prevalence of BPD comorbidity with schizophrenia. Similarly, an audit of 100 consecutive admissions to an early psychosis service found 22% of the FEP sample had co-occurring BPD (Francey, Jovev, Phassouliotis, Cotton & Chanen, 2017). This group were younger, more likely to have other comorbidities, and were at higher risk of suicide and aggression. Furthermore, these young people experienced greater difficulty accessing standard care for FEP and received relatively different treatments, including different pharmacotherapy. Mental health teams should be aware of unconsciously harbouring stigmatising attitudes towards patients with FEP and borderline traits by excluding them from EIP services. We should avoid adopting a polarised and reductionist view of an individual's difficulties, assuming the patient has *either* psychosis *or* BPD, rather than recognising that both can co-exist. Under-recognition of psychosis in individuals with challenging personality traits will result in a longer DUP and a potentially poorer subsequent symptomatic, social and psychological recovery.

Implementing the evidence into practice

Case study 10.3 highlights these diagnostic difficulties and the challenges an EIP team may face when treating an individual with comorbid FEP and BPD.

Case study 10.3 Pete

Pete grew up in foster care. With a flair for football, he gained a place at a football academy. His coach took a shine to him, delighting Pete who had rarely experienced positive adult role models. His coach's 'interest' quickly progressed to grooming and systematic sexual abuse lasting several years. Deeply traumatised with overwhelming feelings of shame and fear (his coach said he would kill him if he disclosed the abuse), he became increasingly anxious with insomnia. He began abusing drugs and was repeatedly arrested for petty theft. His mood became unstable, resulting in attempted suicide on a number of occasions. Pete had no friends, felt angry most of the time and 'hated everyone'. The only love he felt able to share was with his dog, to whom he was devoted.

At the age of 20, he began hearing the voice of his abuser. It began as a whisper gradually becoming louder. It yelled obscenities, calling him a 'paedo', stating it would be better for everyone if he were dead. He also heard a child screaming and a third voice arguing with the others about him. Pete became convinced that the voices were able to control his thoughts and, because he could hear his thoughts outside his head, he believed that others could as well. He socially withdrew. Other than walking his dog before sunrise, he rarely left his house.

He was admitted to hospital following a serious suicide attempt. On the ward, his challenging hostile behaviour caused 'splitting' of the nursing staff, most of whom believed his behaviour was caused by personality disorder. He refused to speak to the psychiatrist or psychologist and spent most of his time alone in his bedroom. Five days after he was admitted, the in-patient Consultant was told by the nurse in charge during ward review that Pete had exhibited no psychotic symptoms, just difficult and challenging behaviour. He was discharged to the community team with a diagnosis of BPD. He failed to attend his outpatient appointment and his mental health continued to deteriorate.

He was readmitted eight months later, having been picked up by the police after an alert by a member of the public due to suspicious behaviour near a railway bridge. During this admission he was assessed by EIP and diagnosed with FEP and comorbid BPD.

The bizarre delusions and disordered thoughts responded well to antipsychotic (AP) treatment. However, he continued to experience derogatory AVHs which were considered to be the result of the systematic abuse he had experienced as a child and he was therefore referred for a psychological assessment. He refused to meet the psychologist, stating he would only see Julie, his care co-ordinator. She had worked hard to build a therapeutic relationship with him; however, once he began building trust in her, dependency quickly developed and he refused to see any other members of the team. This became difficult to manage when he presented in crisis, particularly when Julie was unavailable. He was considered a high risk individual due to impulsive self-harm and repeated suicide attempts in the context of heavy drinking sessions. He frequently texted Julie late on a Friday afternoon threatening to end his life, giving her considerable cause for concern. Julie became increasingly stressed and called for a team meeting to discuss ways to better manage Pete. It was agreed that the dependency Pete had developed on her was hindering his recovery and a change of care co-ordinator to Dave was proposed. It was decided that Pete should use the office phone to communicate with the team rather than by text as his texts were becoming abusive when they weren't responded to immediately. Finally, it was agreed that every effort should be made to engage Pete in psychological therapy. The team manager met with Pete and explained the new management plan, much to Pete's annoyance.

Dave adopted a firm boundaried approach and, they slowly began to develop a therapeutic relationship. Aware that Pete had experienced serial sexual abuse as a child, resulting in extreme mistrust of others and likely to be perpetuating the psychotic symptoms, Dave gently explained the potential benefits of psychotherapy. Pete agreed to engage in a trial of Trauma Focused CBT, during which he explored feelings of guilt and shame. Pete found the sessions extremely difficult, yet he learnt techniques to better manage his anxiety and hypervigilance when in public. By the end of the three years with EIP, Pete was showing signs of recovery. Although he had many more goals to reach and remained symptomatic, his symptoms were less intense, less frequent and less distressing. His self-harm had significantly lessened, his alcohol consumption had reduced and he was now able to leave his house on his own to visit the local shops. He had built up a trusting relationship with the EIP team, who were aware that he would perceive his discharge from EIP as a rejection. As a result, they arranged a very gradual transfer to the local community team with several joint visits with the new care co-ordinator.

Pete's case illustrates important management strategies for patients with comorbid FEP and BPD/complex PTSD and highlights potential complications when using a standard EIP approach. There is a lack of research into the most effective treatment strategies for these vulnerable individuals. Gleeson et al.'s (2011) pilot study combined FEP treatment plus specialist intervention for BPD and found this to be an acceptable and safe treatment. Francey et al. (2017) suggest a need to develop new clinical guidelines and effective treatments for this specific subgroup of patients with FEP and co-occurring BPD. With this in mind, we suggest the following strategies

- A formulation-driven management plan (see Chapter 12), taking into account previous childhood traumas.
- Maintenance of clear professional roles and firm boundaries alongside a flexible approach to engagement and treatment.
- Awareness that assertive engagement techniques to build trust can create dependency in those with attachment difficulties. Practices adopted by EIP teams, such as texting patients, should be reviewed, since they can cause professional boundary blurring, resulting in care co-ordinators feeling overwhelmed, particularly when patients text repeatedly in crisis and outside working hours.
- A repeated rapid response to repeated self-harm behaviour or other crises can inadvertently reinforce unhealthy coping strategies and foster dependency.
- Childhood trauma predisposes to psychosis (Mansueto & Faravelli, 2017) creating heightened sensitivity to social stressors (Reininghaus et al., 2016), resulting in mistrust and social avoidance. Preparing a mistrustful individual for trauma-focused psychotherapy requires skill, patience and persistence and low grade CBT, such as simple anxiety management techniques, can be a helpful starting point (see Chapter 8). The addition of an anxiolytic, such as an SSRI, can lower anxiety levels and enhance resilience, allowing an individual to better engage in their social recovery (see Chapter 6).

- Sharing care co-ordination of these individuals reduces clinician burn-out. Psychotherapy supervision and reflective discussion for cases with high complexity can be helpful (see Chapter 12).
- Repeated team discussions with regularly updated care and 'crises' plans encourage shared understanding of the potential 'risks' and a consistent approach from all team members. (Chapter 12).

Substance use disorders (SUDS)

SUDs, an independent risk factor for the development of and delayed recovery from FEP, contribute to the symptoms and burden of disability (Seddon et al., 2015). Persistent substance misuse is associated with treatment non-concordance, disengagement and poor remission rates (Lambert et al., 2005). Despite this knowledge, many young people with FEP and comorbid SUDs continue receiving the misleading diagnosis of 'drug-induced' psychosis and are denied EIP as a result. Treatment of SUDs should be an integral part of EIP, given their frequency, effect on recovery, and difficulty accessing specialist services. SUD service scarcity is a worldwide problem (World Health Organisation, 2012), compounded in the UK due to their privatisation (Drummond, Day & Strang, 2018).

Cannabis prevalence

Despite upward trends in some regions (e.g. the USA), global cannabis consumption has remained stable in recent years (United Nations Office on Drugs and Crime, 2016). According to Home Office statistics on drug use in the UK (2017), cannabis is the most commonly used illegal drug, with 16% of younger adults aged 16–24 having used it in the previous year. Cannabis use increases significantly in an FEP population with prevalence rates as high as 75% (Myles, Myles & Large, 2015). EIP typically treats patients with multiple drug and alcohol use, however, in view of the frequency of use and its association with psychosis (see Chapter 1), we will focus primarily on cannabis.

There are several cannabis forms: resin, herb and oil. Cannabis resin, or hash, is a dried brown mass. Herbal cannabis, also called weed, marijuana or grass, is used most frequently, the commonest of which is skunk, aptly named due to its pungent smell. Skunk is produced from cannabis plant buds, grown indoors in a nutrient-rich liquid to enhance potency. Cannabis oil, a thick brown liquid, is used less frequently.

Cannabis contains many active ingredients, two of which have received the most attention: 9 tetrahydrocannabinol (THC) and cannabidol (CBD). The latter, with potentially protective and therapeutic effects (Iuvone et al., 2009), is largely absent from modern high potency cannabis. 'Skunk' contains extremely high levels of THC (16–30%) with less than 0.1 CBD. THC effects include sedation, relaxation, giggling and increased appetite. It alters and heightens perception, including perceived time passage. THC also causes nausea, dizziness, anxiety, suspicion and paranoia. Emerging evidence links heavy adolescent cannabis use with altered brain structure (Rigucci et al., 2015) and cognitive impairments (Camchong, Lim & Kumra, 2016).

Synthetic cannabis

There is a growing trend, particularly among the homeless and prison communities, of synthetic cannabinoid abuse (UK government, Statistics on Drug Misuse, England', 2017), a class of novel psychoactive substances (NPS) previously referred to as legal highs before the Psychoactive Substances Bill illegalised them (Home Office, 2016). Synthetic cannabinoids sprayed onto plants and packaged as scented herbs, are given names such as 'Spice', 'K2' and 'black mamba'. Their packaging looks harmless, the effects rarely are. Their high potency and lack of regulation render them dangerous, putting vulnerable young people at greater risk of developing psychosis (Murray et al., 2016).

The link between cannabis and psychosis

The public and political debate about cannabis use has become unnecessarily polarised between those who believe it is a harmless drug with therapeutic properties and those who view it as a significantly negative factor in young people's mental health. As a clinician working in EIP, it is hard to have a fully objective opinion; all too often we see young people thwarted in their struggle to recover from psychosis by the ongoing use of cannabis. It is difficult, therefore, to view cannabis as 'non-addictive' when we repeatedly observe young people with FEP return to cannabis use, having vowed 'never to touch the stuff again'. Difficult, too, to accept that cannabis is 'therapeutic' for mental distress when we know that THC can cause reality distortion and an accentuation of paranoia. And, finally, it is difficult to be persuaded by the argument that cannabis is 'harmless' when we see families at breaking point, wanting to support their son or daughter's recovery while being rendered powerless to do so in the face of its continued use.

We know from the abundance of evidence that cannabis is associated with an increased prevalence of psychosis (Arseneault, 2002; Di Forti et al., 2009; see Chapter 1) and younger age of onset (Large et al., 2011) by around three years (Helle et al., 2016). There is a dose response relationship between the quantity and strength of cannabis use and psychosis risk, with high potency cannabis and synthetic cannabinoids carrying the greatest risk (Murray et al. 2016). We know also that cannabis use in FEP is associated with poorer symptomatic recovery, greater number of anti-psychotics used (Patel et al., 2016), increased hospitalisation (Large et al., 2017; Patel et al., 2016) and higher relapse rates (Schoeler et al., 2016). Furthermore, comorbid cannabis use predicts reduced psychosocial functioning (Seddon et al., 2015). For these reasons, cannabis use is a hugely important comorbidity to be understood and managed by EIP clinicians if we are to improve the symptomatic and social recovery of our patients.

Challenging the concept of 'drug-induced psychosis'

Given the clear link between cannabis and psychosis, we suggest the term 'drug-induced psychosis' to describe cannabis use in FEP is both misleading and nosologically dubious. This diagnosis refers to short-lived psychotic symptoms caused by prolonged or heavy street-drug use, such as amphetamines, cocaine and ecstasy, resolving once the drug wears off. It is vitally important to differentiate this from comorbid cannabis use and FEP. The authors have frequently encountered patients with FEP and comorbid cannabis use being erroneously diagnosed as 'drug-induced psychosis' (often in a crisis presentation at A&E) and denied EIP referral. There is perhaps a misperception among some mental health professionals that if the young person abstains from cannabis, the psychotic symptoms will spontaneously resolve. However, cannabis is often used as 'self-medication' in FEP (Ferdinand et al., 2005) and given the evidence that its use worsens prognosis (Patel et al., 2016), these individuals should be referred to EIP to commence treatment immediately.

Implementing the evidence into practice

Case study 10.4 Yousof

Yousof is 21 years old. A heavy cannabis user since 15, he enjoyed the confidence it gave him alongside the social aspect of smoking with friends. However, he noticed that cannabis began causing suspiciousness and heightened sensitivity. At 18, he started experiencing auditory hallucinations. Initially he heard 'someone' call his name, while smoking with his mates. His friends denied hearing the voice, resulting in paranoia about them, believing they could read his thoughts through the TV and microwave. His behaviour became increasingly bizarre. He was picked up by police while trying to remove his neighbour's Christmas tree lights, believing they were transmitting his thoughts. He was brought to A&E on a Section 136, diagnosed with a 'drug-induced psychosis', given an appointment for the community mental health team (CMHT) and advised to refrain from cannabis use. He failed to attend the CMHT appointment and continued smoking cannabis. A further deterioration in his mental state resulted in a hospital admission and referral to EIP.

It took several weeks before a symptomatic response to anti-psychotic medication was experienced. There was a lessening in the intensity of hallucinations and delusions and he was eventually discharged after two months. Despite a reduction in positive symptoms, he continued to experience low-level paranoia and auditory hallucinations, believing he could hear his neighbours plotting against him. Furthermore, he had to contend with pronounced negative symptoms. He spent most of his days alone in his bedroom, continued to smoke cannabis and minimally engaged with the EIP team

After 18 months of poor psychosocial recovery and treatment with two different APs, he agreed to commence clozapine. This resulted in a significant symptomatic and social recovery over the next 12 months. His motivation improved and he began engaging in meaningful therapeutic activities with his care co-ordinator, who was trained in motivational interviewing (MI). They explored his reasons for continued cannabis use without judgement and Yousof considered positive aspects to quitting cannabis. One of the strongest motivators was his desire to return to work. His care co-ordinator helped him prepare for a job interview in a local car factory. Yousof knew he would be screened for drugs as part of the interview process and as a result he was determined to stop cannabis. He was given sleep hygiene information and three days of a hypnotic to overcome the temporary sleep disturbance he experienced. His support worker took him to the gym to help him manage his cravings. By the end of the three years with EIP, Yousof had achieved a good symptomatic, personal and social recovery, his family relationships had improved, he was in part-time work and he no longer used cannabis.

SUD treatments as a component of recovery from psychosis

Yousof's case highlights the risk of diagnosing 'drug-induced psychosis' in FEP, which can delay EIP treatment and lengthen DUP. Symptomatic, social and personal recovery following FEP is hampered by persistent substance misuse. Strategies are therefore required to engage and support this vulnerable group. Although we have primarily explored cannabis, the concepts and principles of drug rehabilitation apply to all substances. The aim of SUD treatment in FEP is to reduce risk, minimise substance use and enhance recovery.

Unfortunately, not all EIP teams have access to formal substance misuse services (Aydin, Tibbo & Ursuliak, 2016) and EIP teams should therefore be trained to deliver 'in-house' treatments, adopting a person-centred, non-judgemental approach, using psychoeducation, motivational interviewing (Rollnick et al., 2008), Cognitive Behavioural Integrated Therapy (C-BIT) (Copello, Graham & Birchwood, 2001), and family support (Mueser et al., 2009). A review of FEP substance misuse treatment programmes found that approximately half the patients became abstinent or significantly reduced their drug use after FEP (Wisdom, Manuel & Drake, 2011).

Components of effective substance misuse treatment strategies in FEP

- *Screening* to establish which substances are used, including quantity, frequency, route of administration, duration and pattern of use (NICE, 2011).
- *Psychoeducation* about the effect of cannabis and other substances. Helpful resources, such as Talk to Frank ('Drugs A–Z|FRANK', 2018), aimed specifically at adolescents are a useful starting point.
- Aim for *full symptomatic recovery*, taking care to enquire about latent/masked symptoms since effectively treating psychotic symptoms is associated with reductions in substance misuse (Lambert et al., 2005).

- *Motivational interviewing (MI)* has promising short-term results in reducing cannabis use in young people with psychosis (Bonsack et al., 2011). It has benefits in all aspects of health care and should be integrated into routine clinical practice (Rollnick et al., 2008). MI focuses on exploring and resolving ambivalence to behaviour change and supporting existing motivations to change and has already been discussed in Chapter 6.
- *Cognitive Behavioural Integrated Therapy (C-BIT)* (Copello et al., 2001) is based on the theory that people who believe substances help them better manage symptoms of psychosis develop distortions in their logical reasoning and minimise negative consequences of drug use, resulting in ambivalence. C-BIT has four stages: (1) engagement and building motivation to change; (2) negotiating behaviour change; (3) SUD relapse prevention; and (4) psychosis relapse prevention. Integrated C-BIT training for EIP services results in improved clinician confidence in treating substance misuse (Copello et al., 2001).
- SUD-related *family interventions* result in an improved rate of engagement and retention in drug misuse programmes (Mueser et al., 2009). Family MI and interaction skills training resulted in short-term reductions in patients' quantity and frequency of use and parental distress (Smeerdijk et al., 2015).
- Peer-based support such as *Alcoholics or Narcotics Anonymous* is helpful for people motivated to change, with evidence supporting its approach in youth addiction recovery (Kelly et al., 2008).
- The *social aspects of peer group belonging* motivate continued drug use and should be considered. Offering young people social activities, e.g. football as an alternative should be a core aspect of an EIP treatment package.
- *Contingency management (CM)* uses financial rewards as a motivator for behaviour change with limited evidence of its effectiveness in FEP (Johnson et al., 2016).
- *Pharmacological strategies.* There is no pharmacological substitute for cannabis, NPS or stimulants. When an individual quits substances, they are likely to experience withdrawal symptoms with sleep disturbance, and agitation. Although this is likely to be short-term, they may benefit from a short course of hypnotics or temporary increase in anti-psychotic medication. Clozapine is associated with a reduced number of substance use relapses in individuals with schizophrenia compared to other anti-psychotics (Arranz et al., 2017).

Learning points

- Comorbidity is the norm in EIP.
- ASD presents diagnostic challenges, both in identifying ASD in individuals with FEP and FEP in individuals with ASD.
- Mental health services are insufficiently resourced to assess and manage adult ASD. Training provision for EIP clinicians to undertake ASD screenings and best manage ASD-P should be a future priority for EIP teams.

- FEP and BPD have a number of symptomatic and aetiological similarities. AVHs alone are of minimal diagnostic value in differentiating FEP from BPD. EIP teams should consider an extended assessment where there is diagnostic uncertainty. Individuals with BPD and FEP excluded should be offered a formulation of their difficulties and directed to appropriate help.
- Managing comorbid FEP and BPD requires a compassionate, firm and boundaried whole team approach.
- Heavy cannabis use predisposes to FEP, resulting in worsened prognosis, delayed recovery, treatment failure, hospitalisation and increased relapse rate.
- Mental health services may require training to better understand that co-morbid cannabis use in FEP should not be labelled 'drug-induced psychosis', thereby denying patients EIP.
- Adequately treating symptoms (positive, negative and comorbidities) of psychosis can result in reduced substance misuse. Clozapine is the most effective AP in reducing SUD in psychosis.
- Management of cannabis and other SUDs in FEP is an integral role for EIP. Psychoeducation, MI, C-BIT, family work, social support, NA/AA, CM and short-term pharmacological support can all aid abstinence.

Chapter 11

Family adaptation and recovery following FEP

Introduction

Working with families is an integral part of supporting young people with FEP and remains a current topic of discussion and research (Onwumere, Jansen & Kuipers, 2018). As outlined in Chapter 1, the onset of FEP often occurs at a crucial time in a young person's development and can have a huge impact on family relationships. Supporting a relative through FEP and their subsequent recovery can be challenging, and families need support to help them adjust and adapt. Families who are supported to maximise adaptive functioning, minimise disruption to family life, manage stresses and cope more effectively are in a better position to promote recovery for their relative.

This chapter first considers ways families can support their relative's symptomatic, social and personal recovery. Second, the impact of FEP on the family is discussed and interventions to support family adaptation and recovery are presented. Finally, some barriers to implementing family interventions (FIs) are considered and ways of embedding family work in EIP are suggested, including a 'step and choice' pyramid model of FIs for FEP. The chapter concludes with a case example, illustrating a range of FIs useful for EIP families.

The term 'family' is used in this chapter, but this can also include the wider social networks of a person, e.g. important friendships or the other residents of their accommodation. The term 'carer' is used because it reflects a recognised role in the UK, although it must be noted that many family members do not choose this term for themselves.

The importance of involving families in EIP

The provision of family and carer support is an essential component of EIP delivery (NICE, 2014, 2016). Seventy per cent of UK EIP clients report having a carer, and 63% are living at home with family members (Birchwood et al., 2014a). These social networks can help support symptomatic, social and personal recovery following FEP. However, there can be a significant impact on these networks, e.g. high demands on caregivers (caregiver 'burden'), distress, grief and loss, high stress levels, stigma and shame, and impact on the quality of life (QOL), well-being and mental health of family members. Without attention, these issues could lead to long-term problems in relationships, as well as having a detrimental impact on the health and well-being of the family members themselves. If EIP only focuses on how families can help the young person's recovery, this risks ignoring the emotions of the carers, and reduces the likelihood of them seeking support for themselves (Lavis et al., 2015). Early intervention with families can help reduce longer-term negative outcomes for carers, including depression, stress and exhaustion (Kuipers 2008), can have a positive impact on the course of the young person's recovery and reduce the risk of ongoing disruption to family lives.

Family work in FEP: summary of the literature

There have been a number of FI reviews in FEP specifically, mostly demonstrating positive outcomes for families and service users. Bird et al. (2010) found that family work in FEP reduces hospitalisations and relapse, when it includes the young person with their family. However, Sadath et al. (2015) argued there was a dearth of such studies and so could not make reliable conclusions about the consistent efficacy of FIs in FEP. More recently, Ma et al. (2017) found that FIs improved outcomes for carers, e.g. reducing the negative impact of caring, improving the caregiving experience and improving family functioning. Claxton et al. (2017) found that FIs improved service user functioning, reduced the likelihood of relapse, and reduced symptoms at follow-up, although this was not found at the end of treatment. For carers, the negative impact of caring and well-being improved at the end of treatment, although these gains were not sustained at follow-up. There were also reductions in criticism and conflictual communication (i.e. reduced 'expressed emotion' (EE), see below). The authors conclude that FIs for FEP are effective for families and service users, although they recommend more research to identify which therapeutic components are most effective.

The role of families in promoting symptomatic, social and personal recovery

Family members can play an important role in recovery following a FEP (Day & Petrakis, 2016). Some of the ways families promote symptomatic, social and personal recovery are presented in Table 11.1. Baker and Martens (2010) have created a guide for FEP families, providing practical suggestions for them to support their relative's recovery, as well as suggestions for their own recovery/self-care.

Table 11.1 Role of families in promoting recovery

Family role	How?	Evidence
Supporting early recovery and crisis management	Help seeking	Dominguez et al., 2014
	Engagement with EIP	Stowkowy et al., 2012
	Responding when services unavailable	Worthington et al., 2013
	Manage self-harm and suicide risk	Addington et al., 2009 and see Chapter 9
Supporting symptomatic recovery	Linking with services	Onwumere et al., 2016
	Improving concordance, supervising and reminding patient to take medication, Providing practical support (e.g., collecting prescriptions)	Rabinovitch et al., 2013; Baker & Martens, 2010
	Promoting coping and self-management skills	Zou et al., 2013
	Helping directly with substance use interventions	Tantirangsee et al., 2015
	Better family functioning is associated with reduced cannabis use	González-Blanch et al., 2015
	FIs improve psychotic symptoms, functioning and reduce number of hospitalisations	Chien et al., 2016
	Relapse prevention interventions with family accelerates response to early warning signs	Gleeson et al., 2013
	High expressed emotion (EE), especially criticism, is associated with risk of relapse and shorter time to relapse. Behavioural Family Therapy can sustain symptomatic recovery by reducing EE. Helping families manage impact of caring improves, relapse outcomes	Koutra et al., 2015

continued

Table 11.1 Continued

Family role	How?	Evidence
Supporting social recovery	Encouraging patient to spend time in meaningful activity	See Chapter 5
	Help patient maintain meaningful social relationships	Zou et al., 2013
	Siblings help patient to engage in social activities and connect with peers	Randolph, 1998
	Help patient to identify goals and support them to achieve these	Tas et al., 2012; Gregory, 2009 and see Chapter 6
	High EE associated with perception that lack of activity is intentional. FIs may reduce EE to address this	Weisman et al., 1998
Supporting personal recovery	Help patient feel valued, which is important contributor to self-esteem	Norman et al., 2012
	Empower patient and promote hope	Windell & Norman, 2013
	High EE may impact negatively on patient's self-worth and self-esteem. FIs may reduce EE to improve this	
	FIs help families process feelings of loss and grief from impact of FEP and aid psychological adaptation by increasing compassion and acceptance	Gumley et al., 2010; Patterson et al., 2000
	FIs can help to reduce stigma which is barrier to personal recovery	Ngoc et al., 2016
	Increased knowledge, optimism and hope in families, promotes hope for patient and a belief that they can move beyond 'catastrophic effects' of psychosis	Anthony, 1993 see Chapter 7

The impact of FEP on families

Impact on mental health

Significant rates of psychiatric comorbidity have been found in FEP carers (Tennakoon et al., 2000), and often peak during the early phase of the illness (Sadath, Muralidhar, Varambally, Gangadhar & Jose, 2017). This highlights the importance of FIs being delivered early, to help families with stressors in life, alongside their caring role, and help shape their appraisals and subjective experiences of caring, which can be a key factor in their health and well-being (Kate et al., 2013b). Encouraging family members to write about events could be helpful for those experiencing trauma symptoms following their relative's FEP (Barton & Jackson, 2008), which may be particularly prevalent at this early stage.

Impact of caring and quality of life

Families supporting a loved one with psychosis can experience significant 'burden' and reduced quality of life (QOL; Kate, Grover, Kulhara & Nehra, 2014). The emotional impact on FEP families is often at similar levels to more chronic presentations (Sagut & Duman, 2016) and distress may actually be higher at the initial onset (Sadath, Muralidhar, Varambally, Jose & Gangadhar, 2015). This suggests that a FEP is an intensely emotional experience for families, with the risk of ongoing impact and stress on the caregivers, and the potential for developing chronic levels of grief and loss (Olwit, Musisi, Leshabari & Sanyu, 2015). This may be particularly the case if the person with psychosis is living with caregivers (Zhou et al., 2016), which is relatively common in EIP.

Increased load on carers is related to patient and carer factors, e.g. concordance (Kretchy, Osafo, Agyemang, Appiah & Nonvignon, 2018), symptoms and DUP (Jagannathan, Thirthalli, Hamza, Nagendra & Gangadhar, 2014), functioning (Kaya & Oz, 2015), disruptive or aggressive behaviour (Ahlem et al., 2017), and negative symptoms (Rabinovitch, Cassidy, Schmitz, Joober & Malla, 2013). Carer factors include appraisals of impact (Addington, Collins, McCleery & Addington, 2005), level of support from others (Caqueo-Urízar, Urzúa, Jamett & Irarrazaval, 2016), time spent caregiving (Kate et al., 2013a), stigma (Fernando, Deane, McLeod & Davis, 2017), and unhelpful coping strategies (Kate et al., 2014). Cultural differences can also affect the ways families can experience the impact of caregiving and the impact on their wellbeing (Caqueo-Urízar, Gutiérrez-Maldonado, Ferrer-García & Darrigrande-Molina, 2012).

The caring role can lead to poorer quality of life (QOL), spending less time working outside the home and missing workdays (Caqueo-Urízar et al., 2016). This in turn could contribute to poorer relationships between clients and caregivers (Caqueo-Urízar et al., 2016), and impaired care or support, contributing to increased risk of relapse or readmission (Floyd, Gemmell & Brown, 2014). EIP can help reduce carer 'burden' by supporting families to develop their own

Wellness Recovery Action Plan (WRAP), which may help to reduce isolation, increase coping ability, increase confidence and self-esteem, reduce feelings of guilt and improve relationships (Kelly, 2011). The Meriden Family Programme (Birmingham, UK) has developed a useful set of self-help workbooks called 'Caring for Yourself', with exercises and activities to help family members develop coping skills and promote carer self-care and well-being (www. meridenfamilyprogramme.com).

Stigma and shame in families

Stigma can intensify the negative impact of caregiving (Fernando et al., 2017), affect QOL (Allerby et al., 2015) increase shame, isolation and stress (Molavi, Karimollahi, Sadeghie-Ahary, Taghizadeh & Elhameh, 2015), and lead to discomfort in disclosing their relative's condition (Koschorke et al., 2017). Families sometimes stigmatise their own relative, or hold stigmatising views about others with those conditions (Ediriweera, Fernando & Pai, 2012).

Stigma can be particularly high in FEP families from ethnic minorities, who may experience higher levels of shame and be compelled to conceal the young person's illness (Wong et al., 2009). For example, some families have raised concerns about stigma and the impact on marriage prospects for their children (Islam, Rabiee & Singh, 2015). This may lead to increased stress for families and the young person or make engagement with services more difficult.

Stigma can impact on a family's response to their relative's experiences, including reduced help-seeking (Franz, Carter, Leiner, Bergner, Thompson & Compton, 2010). FIs can address some of these unhelpful beliefs, by giving families more understanding about psychosis, and helping them reach out for support. Koschorke et al. (2017) suggest that messages including 'recovery is possible' and 'no one is to blame' are more helpful than focusing on biomedical knowledge alone. Feelings of shame in caregivers can contribute to high expressed emotion (EE) (Cherry, Taylor, Brown, Rigby & Sellwood, 2017 and see below). FIs can help families with their appraisals and responses, e.g. by adapting CBTp for families (discussed later in this chapter).

Expressed emotion (EE)

EE refers to the pattern of interactions and nature of family relationships, reflected in the attitudes and communication styles of family members. EE itself is not pathological or unique to families affected by mental illness, however, it can contribute to relapse among people who have a vulnerability to stress. Communication patterns in 'high EE' families are often characterised by more intense and negative verbal exchanges, which can be oppositional or conflictual in nature and more rigid. There are two main maladaptive types of high EE: critical comments (CC) and emotional over-involvement (EOI). CC generally refers to verbal and non-verbal communications which convey feelings of anger, rejection, irritability, ignorance, blaming, or negligence. Family members may express frustration at non-concordance with treatment or complain to their relative or the EIP team about a perceived lack of improvement. They can often feel that their relatives are not trying hard enough. EOI refers to the behaviour of caregivers such as blaming themselves, sacrificing things, being over-protective/ excessively concerned, and neglecting their own personal needs (Venkatasu-bramanian & Amaresha, 2012). Parents may speak on behalf of their loved one or wish to accompany a young person on a social activity, rather than risk the discomfort of them struggling alone.

However, not all 'low EE' families demonstrate adaptive communication and relationship patterns either and families with poor coping skills may oscillate between low EE at times, and high EE when facing a crisis (Kuipers & Bebbing-ton, 1988). There may also be a subgroup of low EE families who are 'burnt out', and the low EE response may reflect apathy and indifference or hopeless-ness/helplessness, rather than demonstrating calm concern (Vaughn, 1986). This may be perceived as ambivalence or a lack of interest in the person.

In recent years there has been more focus on EE with FEP families (Domínguez-Martínez, Medina-Pradas, Kwapil & Barrantes-Vidal, 2017). CC and EOI are influenced by client and family/carer factors. These include level of symptoms, functioning (Hooley, 1987) and aggression (Sehlo, Youssef, Hussein & Elgohary, 2015) and relatives' attributions of blame towards the client and level of carer distress. So CC are associated with higher carer distress and attri-butions of blame to the young person, whereas EOI is associated with attribu-tions of control to the client and greater negative perceptions of psychosis (Domínguez-Martínez et al., 2017).

Carers' level of perceived stress can increase EE in FEP and levels of social support may have a limited impact on this (Sadath et al., 2017). Cherry et al. (2017) found that EOI and CC were associated with shame, EOI was also associ-ated with feelings of guilt. FIs in FEP can help to reduce high EE, especially criticism and conflictual communication (Claxton et al., 2017).

The Cognitive Model of Caregiving (Kuipers, Onwumere & Bebbington, 2010) considers the role of carer attributions, illness perceptions, coping behaviour, social support, distress and self-esteem, in the experience of care-giving. This model highlights the need for interventions (e.g. problem-solving) aimed at modifying factors which maintain EE. The goal is then to improve rela-tionship styles and promote therapeutic change for the young person (e.g. redu-cing relapse) and their carers.

In FEP, the most common form of EE is EOI. However, this may be develop-mentally appropriate. Patterson et al. (2005) suggest that high EOI in FEP carers appears to be related to feelings of loss, and may be an adaptive reaction to this experience. EE should not be used to label families as 'difficult' which can serve to invalidate the understandable levels of grief and distress within a family affected by a FEP. There may also be cultural differences to consider (Wüsten & Lincoln, 2017).

How families adapt and recover following FEP

In EIP, we often see families demonstrate tremendous patience, collaboration and flexibility in supporting their relatives, i.e. having 'strength to overcome considerable adversity' (Mizuno, Takataya, Kamizawa, Sakai & Yamazaki, 2013, p. 72). They often seek to understand more about psychosis and find ways of trying to make sense of this. Adaptation may be related to the family members' level of empowerment, coping strategies, social functioning and active participation in the family (Morin & St-Onge, 2015). In turn, level of empowerment, well-being and resilience in the family can influence recovery (Subandi, 2011). Some families may even experience personal growth (Floyd et al., 2014) and their own networks can grow (Jordan, Pope, Lambrou, Malla & Iyer, 2016). The following section highlights some adaptive processes which can help families move towards their own recovery, and ways to promote these.

Adaptive emotional expression and communication

As well as maladaptive, there can be adaptive types of EE (e.g. EOI may be a demonstration of concern; Koutra, Vgontzas, Lionis & Triliva, 2014). Adaptive EE interactions often convey warmth, tolerance and positive regard, and are non-critical. Families may demonstrate better metacognitive skills, and have less negative caregiver experiences (Jansen, Haahr, Lyse, Pedersen, Trauelsen & Simonsen, 2017). They cope by minimising the focus on disturbing behaviour, give clear guidelines on what is acceptable, see problems as isolated incidents, and attribute incidents to the illness rather than blaming the person directly (Leff & Vaughn, 1985). Adaptive EE families show concern for their family member, try to protect them, provide a positive nonverbal environment and focus on finding solutions to problems, all of which can help to improve family tensions (Hahlweg, Nuechterlein, Goldstein, Magana, Doane & Snyder, 1987). Supporting families with their coping, problem-solving, metacognitive skills, beliefs and attributions, could in turn help them to communicate more effectively.

Positive relationships are also considered in the Cognitive Model of Caregiving (Kuipers et al., 2010). Factors contributing to positive relationships include the family having had positive relationships prior to psychosis and carer appraisals that the person is not to blame but they recognise there are problems for which their relative needs support. They still see the person underneath the problems, access their own support network and keep their own interests and own life going. Kuipers et al. (2010) stress that these carers still require interventions, such as information, and help to integrate their caring role into the other demands of life. Carers still experience reactions such as stress, worry, sadness and grief, for which they need support, despite the fact they may seem to be coping well in comparison to other families.

Coping factors and social support

Self-talk, active problem-solving and positive re-framing can be antidotes to the avoidant coping strategies that can maintain psychological distress, per-petuate EOI and increase the negative impact of the caring role (Cotton, McCann, Gleeson, Crisp, Murphy & Lubman, 2013). When caregivers experi-ence more self-efficacy, they can experience a reduced 'burden' of care (Durmaz & Okanli, 2014). Psychological flexibility has also been found to buffer against caregiver distress in families affected by a FEP (Jansen, Haahr, Lyse, Pedersen, Trauelsen & Simonsen, 2017), which can be promoted though interventions such as acceptance and commitment therapy (ACT), which is discussed later in this chapter.

Perceived higher levels of social support can also reduce the 'burden' of care and increase well-being (Jagannathan et al., 2014). However, this can be nega-tively impacted by stigma. McCann et al. (2011) explored how FEP caregivers coped with stigma and found that some adopted an open approach to disclosure rather than being secretive, due to fears about stigma. This was associated with lower 'burden' of care and less need for clinical support.

Better management of symptoms by the young person can lead to less demand on caregivers (Kate et al., 2013a). However, it is not always possible to quickly reduce a person's symptoms (see Chapters 3 and 4) and, given that the impact of FIs on service user recovery may be inconsistent (Claxton et al., 2017), it is important that we also focus on carer and family member outcomes. This includes developing their coping skills, time management around caring, and self-care skills. Cotton et al. (2013) suggest that interventions which facilitate the use of adaptive problem-solving and positive re-appraisal can promote carer coping and reduce psychological distress.

Working through grief and loss

When a loved one experiences psychosis, family members commonly experi-ence feelings of grief and loss, including revising their hopes and expectations about their relative's life (Lafond, 2009). Initially, family members may be focused on practical support, but over time they may experience ongoing emo-tional discomfort, hopelessness, chronic sorrow or depression (Olwit et al., 2015). Level of grief in FEP caregivers is correlated with service users' social and global functioning, and leads to increased distress in caregivers, higher EE and greater caregiving needs (Mulligan, Sellwood, Reid, Riddell & Andy, 2012). In FEP families, appraisals of loss linked to EE, and CC or EOI could be understood as adaptive reactions to loss (Patterson, Birchwood & Cochrane, 2005). Therefore, working through grief and loss here can be considered an adaptive process for families.

Grieving is a normal process and can be a healthy and adaptive experience. Through this, families can rekindle hope, come to terms with the illness of their loved one, and move towards a better quality of life or even 'peacefulness' (Lafond, 2009, p. 168). Lafond's approach recommends supportive listening, educational information and cognitive-behavioural work. Adapted to suit a particular family's needs, it aims to meet families where they are, look compassionately at their situation and offer them guidance and tools to help them manage their grieving journey. Lafond highlights the utility of this model for FEP families, and recommends helping families acknowledge loss, learn to work with the grieving process, understand the different stages of grief, allow themselves to feel what they feel (e.g. denial, sadness, anger, fear) and move towards acceptance.

Family interventions to promote adaptation and recovery in families following FEP

Family work can reduce psychological distress and enhance personal recovery in all members of the family (McCann et al., 2013), improve the experiences of caregiving and increase opportunities to contribute positively to their relative's care (Claxton et al., 2017). EIP support can help families come to terms with their relative's experiences and help them identify and carry out their roles in supporting their loved one, even for families where no 'problem' has been identified. In addition, helping families recognise the progress that their relative is making and the new goals that they are formulating for themselves, could help family members do the same (Addington et al., 2009).

There are clear standards for involving families in EIP and a range of evidence-based FIs are recommended (NICE, 2014, 2016). The focus is on working collaboratively with families, empowering them to cope with the challenges they face, and helping them support their relative in their recovery, while acknowledging the potential trauma, loss and grief that they can experience following their relative's FEP.

Earliest interventions and engaging families

One early priority for EIP is to identify and meet the immediate needs of the family, and recognise the understandable distress they may be in. Their family member has experienced the onset of psychosis, they may have faced challenges in accessing services, had traumatic experiences of in-patient admissions (see Chapter 8) or experienced a long duration of untreated psychosis. Clinicians need to create a space for 'caring, non-blaming and respectful communication: to debrief the family and offer information, empathy and support' (Crisp et al., 2014, p. 12). If immediate needs (e.g. confusion, frustration or misinformation) can be addressed, this can reduce distress and improve the way families respond to their relative. Helping families understand more about psychosis and their relative's challenges, and re-appraise negative beliefs (e.g. attributions of blame) can help high EE levels to become less entrenched in FEP families

(Domínguez-Martínez et al., 2017), reduce the risk of criticism emerging, and improve carer outcomes (Koutra, Simos, Triliva, Lionis & Vgontzas, 2016). Other useful early interventions include:

- space for validation and support; caring, non-blaming, non-judgemental and respectful communication;
- clear and accurate information;
- reassurance about the illness;
- realistic expectations for prognosis;
- opportunities to express feelings associated with the onset of psychosis;
- access to family peer support when possible.

FEP families in first contact with services often have insufficient information on the illness, are concerned about their family member's future and so usually require early psychoeducation. Clients may enter EIP following a hospital admission, and psycho-education interventions have been developed for FEP families during the first admission (e.g. Petrakis & Laxton, 2017). Enhancing the social support available for family members is also important at this stage, to help them manage the impact of caring after their relative is discharged (Jagannathan et al., 2014).

Information often needs to be reinforced and repeated over time, as it can be hard for families to process and retain, especially at times of crisis and stress, and other needs may be identified later. Family-led, flexible and individually tailored FIs can ensure that they do not increase stress in the family. Families need time and opportunities to learn, understand, make room for uncertainties and to process grief and loss (Crisp et al., 2014). Early involvement that is collaborative and empowering can help lay the foundation for the ongoing involvement and empowerment of families.

Supporting families with the caregiving role

Families often want to focus on their relative's recovery and not their own well-being. Analogies can be helpful, e.g. 'place your own oxygen mask on first, before helping someone else' or 'you can't pour from an empty cup'. O'Donoghue et al. (2018) use the 'reservoir' metaphor (Kroeker, 2009) in their carer workshops to highlight how draining caring can be, and the need to 'replenish' one's reservoirs in order to continue caring. It is useful to continue revisiting self-care and support needs with families and offering them different avenues of support.

Psychoeducation

FEP psychoeducation programmes can help reduce the impact of caregiving (Sin, Gillard, Spain, Cornelius, Chen & Henderson, 2017) and have been found to reduce levels of stigma in families (Ngoc, Weiss & Trung, 2016). They can also increase insight and acceptance, provide knowledge about early warning signs, improve communication, planning and problem-solving skills, and lead to greater independence for the young person (Nilsen, Frich, Friis, Norheim & Røssberg, 2016). Psychoeducation may include: information about psychosis, crisis management, problem-solving skills, clarifying myths and misconceptions, and providing emotional support. Because diagnostic uncertainty is common in FEP, discussions with families can help them understand more about their relative's presentation, while acknowledging that uncertainty can be difficult. In addition, psychoeducation for families can be a tool to promote messages of hope, that recovery is possible and no one is to blame, which in turn could help reduce stigma (Koschorke et al., 2017).

Psychoeducation can be tailored to suit the needs of individual families, depending on factors such as cultural background and education level. Both the Meriden Family Programme, and Baker and Martens (2010) provide useful guidelines. An online 'Dealing with Psychosis Toolkit' is also available. This has a specific section for carers/supporters at www.earlypsychosis.ca. Services may decide to develop their own locally based resource/information pack for their FEP families, and in Birmingham we co-created one with a panel of EIP family members.

Relapse prevention work

As discussed in Chapter 4, relapse prevention is an important intervention for young people regarding their symptom management. This in turn can help them feel empowered to manage their symptoms/wellness more effectively. Involving families in relapse prevention work can be an opportunity for them, alongside their relative, to make more sense of psychosis and how this developed. As mentioned in Chapter 4, involving family members in relapse work can improve the service user's ability to notice early warning signs and put action plans into place (Eisner, Barrowclough, Lobban & Drake, 2014). All this is helpful in their adaptation and recovery. In addition, this work can provide opportunities to give further psychoeducation to the family, acknowledge feelings such as anxiety and grief, and promote hope for recovery.

Relapse prevention interventions can be adapted to work at a family level and FIs such as behavioural family therapy (BFT) (see below) include a relapse prevention component. The Meriden Programme 'Caring for Yourself' workbooks have a useful section on developing a staying well/relapse prevention plan for families, including distinguishing early warning signs (EWS) from 'off days', so these are not misinterpreted as EWS. Sessions could be held jointly or just with family members and then discussed altogether, depending on the family; and a focus on 'staying well' rather than just relapse prevention can be helpful.

Problem-solving interventions

Interventions which facilitate adaptive problem-solving and positive re-appraisal can promote carer coping and reduce psychological distress in FEP (Cotton et al., 2013). Problem-solving interventions for FEP families can help improve the negative impact of caregiving (Chien, Thompson, Lubman & McCann, 2016). McCann et al. (2017) developed a self-directed problem-solving intervention for FEP carers. This five-week 'self-help' programme led to improvements in carers' problem-solving skills when addressing problems related to the care and support of their relative with FEP. Problem-solving is also a core component of BFT (discussed below).

Behavioural family therapy (BFT)

BFT (Falloon & Liberman, 1983) is an evidence-based, psychoeducational FI integrating behavioural and CBT approaches. It has been used with FEP families (Burbach, Fadden & Smith, 2010) and is recommended by treatment guidelines for psychosis (NICE, 2014). It focuses on sharing information about psychosis and enhancing communication and problem-solving skills in the family. BFT is an approach with clear pathways for staff training and supervision with the Meriden Family Programme (Fadden, Heelis & Bisnauth, 2010) and is used worldwide.

BFT is a manualised approach, but individually tailored to suit different families' needs. It is usually offered for 10–12 sessions over 3–6 months, although it varies, depending on the family. The key components of BFT are:

- engagement
- assessment and goal-setting
- information-sharing and relapse-planning
- communication skills
  - expressing pleasant feelings
  - making positive requests
  - active listening
  - expressing unpleasant feelings
- problem-solving skills
- disengagement

The key principles of BFT are consistent with promoting family adaptation following a FEP. BFT takes a here-and-now approach, which can help families feel more comfortable engaging with it, because it is not perceived to be about attributing blame or 'uncovering family secrets'. The use of the stress-vulnerability model and psychoeducation component can be helpful for both family members and their relative, and the communication and problem-solving skills are introduced to families in a way that empowers them to use these skills in day-to-day life. These skills can help families manage stresses, discuss contentious issues and manage crises themselves as a family unit. It helps the family to identify EWS and therefore, as a family, play a role in relapse prevention. Stephanie Allan writes about her experiences of BFT with her EIP team:

> The sessions were once a week and in the evenings so that my mother could attend around work. My psychiatrist and support worker delivered all of the therapy. With retrospect, I can understand myself to be lucky that Behavioral Family Therapy (BFT) was delivered by those who knew me best. I was already seeing my support worker a couple of times a week and the psychiatrist at least once a month so we had already established trust. Indeed, I felt that I could rely on them being impartial, should the sessions get heated. The Meriden Family Programme website describes BFT as 'essential in all families where a member experiences serious mental health difficulties' due to the potential for relationship dysfunction. We met for around nine sessions which mostly focused on the development of effective communication skills, educating my mum on psychosis and developing a 'staying well' plan for me so that my family could tell if I was becoming unwell again. The sessions were never overly formal and my psychiatrist often made everyone a cup of tea to drink during them. Despite my initial cynicism, the benefits of better communication soon became apparent and I began to enjoy being around my family again and felt attached to them once more.
>
> (Allan, 2017)

Adapting one-to-one psychological therapy approaches to involve families

Traditionally, therapies for psychosis such as CBTp are delivered one-to-one with clients. As seen in the case studies in both Chapters 4 and 8, there can be benefits of involving families in this work or adapting the approaches to be delivered on a family level, resulting in greater gains for the person (Garety, Fowler, Freeman, Bebbington, Dunn & Kuipers, 2008) and improved social functioning and QOL (Kozhyna, Korostiy & Gaichuk, 2013). In addition, this work together could improve family functioning, equip family members with knowledge and skills, shape attributions and support the young person to implement therapy tools. If clinicians are already using these approaches with clients, it is an accessible way to provide family work rather than delivering a separate or new intervention. Examples of integrating families into therapy include:

- *Cognitive behavioural therapy (CBT)*. Lobban and Barrowclough (2016) present an interpersonal CBT framework for involving relatives in CBTp and the role they can play in recovery processes. The aim is to identify unhelpful interpersonal cycles and shift towards patterns that facilitate positive and supportive relationships. Specific strategies vary depending on the family and include behavioural strategies (e.g. doing more quality things together) and cognitive strategies (e.g. supporting each other to look at things in more helpful ways).

- *Compassion-focused therapy (CFT).* Compassion-focused FIs can play a role in helping families develop compassionate responses to their relative and their difficulties and understand their own threat-based reactions in non-blaming, empathic and accepting ways (Gumley, Braehler, Laithwaite, MacBeth & Gilbert, 2010).
- *Acceptance and commitment therapy (ACT).* The benefits of using ACT-based approaches with FEP families includes the positive impact on meta-cognitive skills, found to be important for recovery in people experiencing psychosis and their caregivers (Jansen et al., 2017). ACT skills can help family members respond differently to their own unwanted thoughts and feelings, which in turn could help improve interactions and reduce EE, given feelings, such as guilt and shame, have been linked to EE (Cherry et al., 2017). ACT also helps people behave consistently with their values rather than being 'dictated' by the thoughts or feelings they are experiencing. This could help family members reduce patterns of critical comments and behavioural control. ACT promotes adaptive rather than avoidant coping, which is also helpful, as avoidant coping strategies have been linked to family members' psychological distress, EOI and increased carer 'burden' in FEP (Cotton et al., 2013). The core aim of ACT is to increase psychological flexibility, which can buffer against caregiver distress in families affected by FEP (Jansen et al., 2017). ACT approaches can be combined with more traditional BFT approaches to meet a range of family needs, and has received positive feedback from families in our EIP work.

Other family approaches

Carers groups

A wide range of group programmes have been developed for family members of people affected by psychosis, providing psychoeducation, support, opportunities to meet other families, and promoting self-care. Family groups can also use components of communication skills and problem-solving skills training, e.g. 'Caring for Carers' by the Meriden Family Programme, an 11-week group programme which mirrors many of the principles and strategies of BFT. The hope is that information and skills can be taken away by group members and used at home, which could benefit the client and their recovery.

Some ACT groups have been developed for clients and families together (Butler et al., 2016) and for carers alone (Wutke, 2013). O'Donoghue et al. (2018) report on a series of 'ACT for Recovery' workshops, adapted to address the psychological needs of people caring for individuals with psychosis (including FEP). The focus is on strengthening motivation of family members to act on their values and step back from unwanted thoughts and feelings rather than getting caught up in them. This can help them be more present in daily life and improve their well-being.

Carer/family groups are often highly valued in FEP, especially meeting other families. This helps inspire hope for recovery, which is often a struggle for families (Klapheck, Lincoln & Bock, 2014). Other outcomes include increased understanding of relevant topics (Petrakis, Oxley & Bloom, 2013); less isolation and feeling supported (Riley, Gregory, Bellinger, Davies, Mabbott & Sabourin, 2011); reduced stigma (Day, Starbuck & Petrakis, 2017); improved experiences of caregiving (Smallwood et al., 2016); and improved relationships with the young person (Riley et al., 2011).

Family peer support

In formal family peer support, family members who have 'been there' are given training and support to provide assistance to families who are earlier in the process of supporting a relative through psychosis.

Although there is little research on family peer support in FEP specifically, peer approaches for carers/families in general have led to improvements in health, coping, functioning and social support (Bademli & Duman, 2014). Leggatt and Woodhead (2015) describe a family peer support programme in FEP, highlight the benefits for families and discuss ways to overcome challenges to implementation. There is a useful guide for training family peer support workers in EI (Leggatt, 2012), outlining six interactive sessions to help the trainee family peer supporter learn about using their experiences to help others and emphasises the importance of their own self-care and having access to ongoing support and supervision.

There can be challenges implementing family peer support in EIP and few teams have designated family peer support roles within the team. It may be more feasible to invite family members to speak to groups about their experiences of psychosis and recovery, and if this is not possible, it can be helpful to share stories from other family members via books (e.g. Chandler, Bradstreet & Hayward, 2013) or websites.

Online approaches

Online interventions for psychosis are generally well received by carers and can be a useful supplement to existing care (Álvarez-Jiménez et al., 2012a). Online interventions for FEP families include Chan et al. (2016), whose internet-based self-help psychoeducation programme helped overcome barriers such as service accessibility, high caseloads and self-stigma. In addition, Gleeson et al. (2017), who developed a moderated online social therapy (MOST) programme for FEP families, which integrates online therapy, social networking, support from peers and 'experts', and social problem-solving.

The Meriden Family Programme website is a useful online resource, and they launched the 'MyCare App' in 2016. This free app was developed in conjunction with families and carers and is designed to help carers take good care of themselves. There is a web-based version at www.mycareapp.co.uk.

Cultural approaches to family work

It is known that there are elevated rates of psychosis in immigrants and black and minority ethnic (BME) communities, and they can have different experiences of services and elevated admissions (see Chapters 1 and 12). There may also be differences in family functioning e.g. levels of family support may be greater in collectivist cultures (Mellor, Carne, Shen, McCabe & Wang, 2013), however, there may be greater levels of criticism in close-knit family structures (Wüsten & Lincoln, 2017), and families may view problems as the responsibility of the whole family (Wiguna, Ismail, Noorhana, Kaligis, Aji & Belfer, 2015). Families from minority groups may be even more vulnerable to experiencing stigma, which could be a further barrier to them accessing EIP and FIs (e.g. Islam et al., 2015).

There are some examples of culturally adapted FIs for psychosis (e.g. Lewis, Takala, Qaadir, Cowan, Borreggine & Rackley, 2017; Maura & Weisman de Mamani, 2017), and it remains a key target to increase engagement for BME youth and families and address specific barriers to accessing treatment. This is a particularly important issue that needs attention, given the under-representation of BME groups in research into FIs in FEP (Claxton et al., 2017). Cultural approaches which hold spiritual/cultural and medical perspectives together are useful to help families and services develop shared explanations around FEP and find opportunities to sensitively reshape family narratives about symptoms, to help reduce negative appraisals and stigma. For example, when families believe that their relative is being influenced by a 'Djinn' or spirit, this can lead to 'double stigma' due to the mental illness and spiritual affliction (Lewis et al., 2017). Useful practical strategies can include using interpreters to help facilitate family involvement, involving local spiritual leaders such as chaplains or Imams, or using specialist cultural workers where available.

Supporting FEP siblings

Siblings can play an important role in supporting recovery, as there may be times when a young person would rather be supported by a sibling than a parent, such as in social activities and relationships with peers.

Many FIs provide the opportunity to involve siblings too, such as BFT and relatives' groups. Adaptations may be needed, e.g. involving siblings who are living elsewhere or involving young siblings. Siblings have reported they would like accessible information, including sibling-specific information packs, websites, information on how to support their sibling, and contact with other siblings either online or through face-to-face support groups (Canning, 2006). Smith et al. (2010) give some practical suggestions for working with siblings including ways to identify siblings and acknowledge their role; helping siblings support their relative; promoting sibling self-care; and adaptations needed to meet the needs of siblings.

There are a number of resources that have been developed specifically for FEP siblings, including written resources (e.g. *A Sibling's Guide to Psychosis*, Mulder & Lines, 2005) and online interventions (Sin et al., 2013) and resources (e.g. www.rethink.org).

Children of FEP clients

Small but significant numbers of FEP clients have children or will have children during their time with EIP, although there is little research specifically into FEP parents. Engur (2017) conducted a systematic review of the effect of psychosis (in general) on parenting and parent-child relationships, and found disruption in communication; impairments in parenting abilities; parenting stress; disorganised parenting; maladjustment in relationships; a sense of 'burden' from the parenting role; and maladaptive parenting styles.

Being a parent can bring a sense of meaning, purpose, pride and pleasure, which can help motivate parents with psychosis towards change (Evenson, Rhodes, Feigenbaum & Solly, 2008). The more parents are supported to improve family functioning, the less negative outcomes and disorganisation may occur in parenting and the parent-child relationship (Engur, 2017). Evenson et al. (2008) recommend extra support during the first few months of fatherhood, parenting programmes and systemic approaches to help fathers with psychosis and their families. There are also helpful suggestions about supporting parents affected by postpartum psychosis, e.g. Doucet et al. (2012), who suggest parents often look for reassurance and information, and support groups can help normalise experiences and reduce isolation.

Assessments for families

A number of assessments for FEP families, across a range of domains, are now available (www.meridenfamilyprogramme.com). The domains reflect some of the issues that families affected by FEP can face (see Table 11.1), and provide some ideas for measuring the effectiveness of FIs delivered to target these different areas.

Implementing FIs in EIP

Despite the comprehensive evidence base for FIs in psychosis and their recommendation in national guidelines, a recent national audit in the UK found that only

18% of families of FEP patients received FI (RCP, 2016). There are long-standing challenges to implementing these in practice, at service user, family, clinician and organisational levels (Bucci, Berry, Barrowclough & Haddock, 2016; Onwumere et al., 2016; Selick, Durbin, Vu, O'Connor, Volpe & Lin, 2017). A summary of some of the main barriers to practicing FIs in EIP teams, alongside practical recommendations to address them are provided in Table 11.2.

A step and choice model of family interventions in EIP

We present a service model developed from our own experience of working with families in EIP. Figure 11.1 shows a pyramid model, influenced by a similar model in Mottaghipour and Bickerton (2005), which highlights the different aspects of family work we find useful and practical in an EIP setting, depending on the resources and opportunities available. Routine elements that are a core part of EIP staff skills are along the lower tiers of the pyramid, and with training, support and resources, practitioners could be delivering the higher tiers.

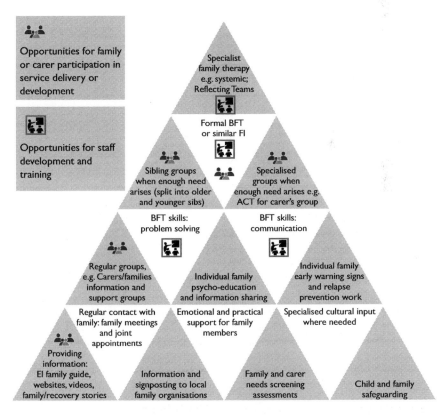

Figure 11.1 A step and choice model of FIs in EIP.

Table 11.2 Overcoming barriers to implementing FIs in EIP services

Level of barrier	Type	Recommendation for EIP services
Family	• Negative attitudes about FIs. • Discordant relationships with patient. • Previous difficult experiences with services. • Fear of criticism/blame (Fadden and Smith, 2009).	• Provide culture of family work and family-focused initiatives pitched at different levels, including family peer support. • Offer sessions for new relatives/carers, include an overview of service, other families lived experience of EIP, promotion of self-care, and opportunity to meet with local carer organisations. • See Crisp et al. (2014) for tips for engaging families in EIP.
Service user	• Patient unwilling to engage in FIs. • Patient willing to work therapeutically, but refuse family involvement.	• Deliver FI to family, but encourage patient to participate by leaving the door open (literally and figuratively) to increase curiosity. • Adapt traditional one-to-one interventions (e.g., CBT) to pay attention to family and social relationships (Kozhyna et al., 2013). • Review guidelines around navigating confidentiality e.g. the Common-sense Confidentiality guide (Northumberland Tyne and Wear NHS, 2016) and The Triangle of Care (Worthington et al., 2013).
Clinician	• Inadequate staff training in FIs, lack of access to supervision, preventing maintenance of learnt skills. • Self-doubt and lack of confidence hinder staff from offering FIs.	• Use team-based approach to staff training. Provide ongoing, team-based supervision (e.g., monthly family supervision groups), facilitating peer support between colleagues (e.g. joint working). Create a supportive environment for newly trained staff to begin using skills soon after training.

	• Fears about 'opening a can of worms' or waiting for the 'perfect family'. • Questioning of the effectiveness of family work. Newer staff to EIP may be more familiar with individual treatment approaches • High caseloads present challenges with prioritising family work over competing demands of the service. Staff seeing FIs as an optional extra/not seeing family work as being their role.	• Identify family champions and clinical leads for FIs. • Demystify family work; that family work doesn't have to be 'therapy'. • Implement Step & Choice Model (see Figure 11.3 and see below).
Organisational	• Lack of allowances made in terms of caseload demands, shortage of management support and dearth of high-quality training, supervision and support. • Crisis interventions prioritised over FIs.	• Invite managers and senior clinicians to training days. • Source organisational and commissioning level support to ring-fence time for FIs. • Develop local strategic plans for FI implementation. • Ensure job roles reflect family focus of EIP. • Integrate family workers into teams. • Discuss families at MDT meetings to identify families for FIs. • Foster shared culture of family work where it is seen as everyone's responsibility and families viewed as 'partners in care'. • Raise awareness that although FIs are initially more time intensive, they reduce crises longer-term.

All families will receive the bottom tier, and, where possible, be offered the next tier, and know that the following tier is available on a needs basis (e.g. when there are enough siblings identified for a sibling group). Finally, the top tier may require specialist input from a family worker in the team, or referral to a specialist family therapy practitioner or team, and would be for a few families in particular need. This may be for families where other FIs within the EIP team have been offered and tried, but problems continue to be evident in family functioning. The pyramid also highlights opportunities for family peer involvement and suggests opportunities for practitioner skill development.

Implementing the evidence into practice

Case study 11.1 Tom: a family's experience of FEP and recovery

Tom was becoming more withdrawn, increasingly bizarre in his conversations and behaviour, and aggressive towards family. However, they struggled to get him to see the GP, which led to delays in obtaining treatment. By the time he was admitted to hospital under the Mental Health Act, the family were already feeling let down, and unsure whether services would be able to help their son. Tom's uncle had been diagnosed with schizophrenia, but had not made a good recovery and tragically had died by suicide. This caused the family a great deal of distress about what the future would hold for Tom. The family were struggling with Tom's substance use, which he said helped him cope with the voices and slow down his thinking. However, the family could see that it made his symptoms worse, and there were frequent conflicts. Tom's younger sister, Amy, was beginning to struggle at school, with her final year exams approaching, and the stress of the situation at home was becoming very difficult. She felt unable to bring her friends round to the house and felt responsible for trying to support her parents. Mum was trying everything to help Tom, including taking his phone off him in an attempt to stop him contacting drug dealers. However, this just led to further conflict between them. Dad often got angry at Tom, and believed he was just being difficult, and upsetting his Mum on purpose. The family were concerned about Tom's lack of activity, and that he spent the majority of his time in his room playing computer games and using cannabis. They began to feel hopeless about his future.

The family were provided with psychoeducation about psychosis. This helped them understand more about Tom's symptoms and some of his responses to them, such as his social withdrawal and attempts to self-manage them through cannabis use. They were involved by the case manager in interventions to help Tom identify other strategies he could use to try and cope with the symptoms. Tom's family were then able to encourage Tom to practise these between sessions. Tom's family were included in the early warning signs and relapse prevention work. This helped them feel more confident that they could identify signs of his mental state deteriorating and follow an action plan to get Tom's care reviewed quickly. Tom's parents attended the EIP carers education and support group. They found this a helpful way to meet other families, and felt more hopeful when hearing about the progress that their relative had now made. This group also included teaching some communication skills and problem-solving skills from BFT. This helped them practise some more adaptive communication skills at home, and, in time, Tom agreed to have some sessions altogether. This seemed to help with situations that had been creating conflicts before. Tom's sister was invited to the family sessions as well although she was unable to attend regularly. She was also provided with some specific online resources for siblings and encouraged to contact the team if she wanted further information or support.

Tom's family appeared more able to support him in his symptom, social and personal recovery. They engaged him in activities, such as going for walks with Mum and doing some house painting with Dad. Communication improved, and less arguments and fewer crises arose. The family were more actively managing early warning signs, and family members were aware of their own stresses and the self-care strategies which could help them at those times. The family were trying to reinforce Tom's successes with positive communication, reinforcing the valued role he had in the family, and through engaging him in social activities. However, despite feeling more hopeful for the future, the family had concerns about Tom's upcoming discharge from EIP. The team were considerate of this and worked carefully with the family to prepare for this transition.

Learning points

- Working with families is a core part of EIP and there are many different opportunities and ways to work with families including support for families with or without the young person, structured FIs, such as BFT, that include the young person, and group programmes for relatives.
- FIs play a useful role in helping families with the challenges of caring, including helping them manage difficult feelings and work through grief and loss.
- FIs that target adaptive interactions and communication can help improve family relationships and recovery outcomes.
- Many routine aspects of EIP can involve families, such as psychoeducation and relapse prevention work.
- Having a range of FIs at different levels and following a stepped model, promoting choice and individualised treatment options, can be helpful.
- Peer support and opportunities to meet other family members can be invaluable.
- The Meriden Family Programme website has many resources for professionals and families (www.meridenfamilyprogramme.com).

Chapter 12

Integrating and operationalising symptomatic, social and personal recovery

Managing EIP and pathways of care

'The whole is more than the sum of its parts'
(Aristotle)

Introduction

Throughout this book we have argued that recovery from FEP is complex and multifaceted and needs to be approached from three broad but complementary perspectives: symptomatic, social and personal. This final chapter aims to demonstrate how this approach to recovery can be achieved through integrated working in an EIP team and is divided into four sections.

Section 1 reviews the previous chapters and discusses facilitators, barriers and potential interactions between symptomatic, social, and personal recovery, along with reviewing evidence based interventions and good practice.

Section 2 focuses on how these three types of recovery can be facilitated in EIP services by developing a strategic and operational framework that not only draws upon a comprehensive and developing evidence base, but also offers hope to young people and their families struggling to adapt to FEP. We revisit the primary goal of EIP services and discuss the pivotal role of sustained engagement during the critical period and the importance of youth-friendly and culturally accessible services. We consider the role of Routine Outcome Measures (ROMs) in improving and maintaining quality in EIP.

Section 3 considers a typical EIP care pathway from referral to discharge planning and the role of formulation driven care plans in facilitating recovery.

Section 4 considers what happens after EIP, the ideal length of the critical period and the need for continuous intensive input for some. Finally, the book ends by considering the future of EIP.

Section 1 Overview of the book: the importance and relevance of EIP

Chapter 1 proposed that psychosis develops as a result of poor bio-psychosocial adaptation to a stressful environment and is best treated and managed within a specialised EIP service as recommended in the clinical guidelines (NICE, 2016). It highlighted that personal and social recovery has historically been less well defined and has received less attention than symptomatic recovery (remission) and also outlined how the Clinical Staging Model (Fusar-Poli et al., 2017) can provide an overarching framework for conceptualising different recovery trajectories following a FEP and can inform interventions. Chapter 2 highlighted the tension between personal recovery as a process and symptomatic and social recovery (i.e. clinical recovery) as a scientific outcome, and differentiated between personal recovery and psychological adaptation following FEP.

We concluded that symptomatic, social and personal recovery need to be measured alongside each other at different stages of FEP. Chapters 1 and 2 also highlighted that although remission rates following a FEP are more favourable than previously thought (58%), rates of (clinical) recovery (38%) have not significantly improved over the last two decades (Lally et al., 2017).

Chapter 3 discussed the importance of prescribing medication in a collaborative and empowering decision-making process, highlighting the benefits of antipsychotics (APs) in symptomatic recovery, lower rates of relapse and risk reduction. We discussed the importance of low dose prescribing alongside regular medication reviews in a FEP population sensitive to side effects. We considered strategies to improve concordance, including depot use in this young population with notoriously poor concordance rates. We highlighted the benefits of clozapine in those with poor symptomatic and social recovery and emphasised the need for EIP to develop physical health care strategies to counter side effects and prevent longer-term debilitating physical health conditions. Since APs have a minimal effect on negative symptoms and social recovery, we highlighted the importance of prescribing alongside a range of psychosocial interventions to facilitate and sustain social, and thereby 'clinical', recovery following a FEP. The following chapters examined these psychosocial interventions in more detail.

Chapter 4 reviewed evidence that cognitive behavioural therapy (CBT) can facilitate positive symptomatic recovery more effectively with more targeted assessments, formulations and interventions. However, FEP samples have many other needs, which may require a broader approach. The evidence for CBT on negative (CBTn) symptoms in FEP samples is less established but interventions can be informed by models of negative symptoms and focused interventions developed with samples in more chronic presentations. Recent evidence indicates that family interventions (FIs) in FEP are associated with symptomatic recovery and lower relapse rates but these effects are not sustained over time. Early Signs and Relapse Prevention Plans require further evidence but remain a key part of EIP. It was concluded that the best way of sustaining symptomatic recovery may be ensuring that remission is translated into personal and social recovery.

Chapters 5 and 6 proposed that social recovery should be defined as time spent in meaningful economic, cultural or social valued activity. Translating initial remission into early social recovery after FEP is critical in sustaining longer-term functioning and can occur independently of symptomatic recovery, although is harder to achieve. Up to 80% of individuals can experience social disability after FEP, with only 10–20% returning to competitive employment. However, we are now better at identifying those at baseline who might be at higher risk of poor or delayed social recovery. This provides an opportunity to target specific interventions at the most optimum time to maximise the chances of early social recovery which potentially may facilitate a more favourable longer-term outcome. It is vital to understand the barriers to social recovery for each individual to devise an individualised formulation and plan; especially for those who are more ambivalent about change, those with comorbid issues and for those who may struggle with CBTp. Positive expectations and hope are core components and mediators of social recovery and should be instilled into interventions focused on improving social recovery.

Chapter 7 highlighted that personal recovery has been historically neglected at the expense of symptomatic and social recovery, although it has always been recognised as equally valued by service users. It reinforced the need for an integrated approach highlighting that the processes of personal recovery are intrinsically interlinked with those of symptomatic and social recovery. We argued that the service ethos (e.g. inspiring hope) as well as group work and individual level psychosocial interventions can help with psychological adaption and making sense of psychotic experiences.

Chapter 8 proposed that high levels of different types of emotional dysfunction following FEP pose different challenges for achieving symptomatic, social, and personal recovery. In particular, high levels of post-psychotic depression, anxiety, trauma, and shame can exacerbate positive symptoms, impact negatively on social recovery and associated interventions, and diminish feelings of hope and positive identity, which are key to personal recovery. We recommended that emotional dysfunction in FEP should be identified as early as possible using standardised measures to inform and guide interventions. The effectiveness of medical, social, and psychological interventions will depend on attachment and developmental history, social support, recovery style, engagement with services, emotional regulation, and stage of psychosis. Recovery from FEP does not occur in a social vacuum and environmental variables may facilitate or hinder recovery. The following two chapters explored additional factors (e.g. co-morbidity) that can impact or hinder recovery and what happens when recovery is significantly compromised.

Although Chapter 9 noted that the number of deaths by suicide for people with FEP is lower than initially thought (2–4%), most occurring during the early stages of psychosis, rates are still significantly higher than in the general population and suicidal ideation and behaviour are not rare. A number of bio-psychosocial mediating and moderating factors will determine whether psychological states of defeat and entrapment transition to death by suicide through a complex and dynamic process and these factors may be used as the basis for a comprehensive risk assessment and intervention to prevent suicide in people with early psychosis.

Chapter 10 emphasised that comorbidity in FEP should be considered the norm and the management of comorbidities is an integral component of EIP. This, however, can present both diagnostic and management difficulties for teams as illustrated by comorbid autism spectrum, borderline personality and substance use disorders. We highlight the benefits of an extended assessment period where there is diagnostic uncertainty and the need for specific training in diagnosis and management of these conditions, requiring a boundaried approach.

Finally, Chapter 11 described the importance of family and carer involvement in FEP. While a supportive and warm family environment can facilitate recovery, a critical and unsupportive environment with high levels of carer stress and burden can be a barrier to recovery. Consequently, providing carer support and FIs in FEP may not only improve the quality of the home environment but can also facilitate symptomatic recovery and reduce relapse. EIP teams should also support family members in understanding psychosis, working through their own grief to reduce carer stress and promote the recovery of the family unit.

Synergy between symptomatic, social and personal recovery

Throughout the book we have emphasised the synergy and inter-dependency between the three types of recovery (Windell, Norman & Mall, 2012). Although early remission is the sole predictor of symptomatic recovery at five years (Norman et al., 2017) translating initial remission into early social recovery is more likely to result in longer-term symptomatic *and* social and personal recovery than remission alone (Álvarez-Jiménez et al., 2012b). However, for some individuals, symptomatic recovery may not necessarily lead to social and personal recovery so psychosocial interventions to promote social and personal recovery may not only be necessary but also protect against longer-term disability and enduring negative symptoms. Although positive symptoms can be a barrier to social recovery if untreated, the assumption that complete symptom remission is necessary before social or personal recovery can be addressed is unfounded (Fowler et al., 2018). The previous chapters considered the facilitators and barriers to symptomatic (Chapters 3 and 4), social (Chapters 5 and 6) and personal (Chapter 7) recovery along with evidence-based interventions and good practice for the different types of recovery. The facilitators and barriers to symptomatic, social and personal recovery along with evidence-based interventions and good practice for the different types of recovery are summarised in Table 12.1.

Table 12.1 indicates that there is overlap between the factors that both facilitate and pose a barrier to the different types of recovery. Recovery is facilitated by having better pre-morbid functioning with evidence from Chapter 5 highlighting that good functioning in the pre-morbid phase, employment at baseline, and maintaining a vocational role during FEP facilitate longer-term recovery. Similarly, it is likely that translating early remission into social recovery not

Table 12.1 Recovery following FEP: facilitators, barriers and interventions

Recovery	Facilitators	Barriers	Interventions and good practice
Symptomatic	• Short DUP • Quick remission following medication • Low side effects • Good insight • Good engagement • Functional emotional regulation • Supportive carer network	• Longer DUP • Non-adherence • Substance misuse • Emotional dysfunction • Critical carers or high expressed emotion	• Antipsychotic medication • CBTp and CBTn • Family work • Identifying emotional dysfunction • Identifying high risk of relapse • Early signs and relapse prevention
Social	• Good premorbid functioning • Short DUP • Remission translated into early social recovery	• Poor pre-morbid functioning • Poor baseline functioning • High negative symptoms • High cognitive dysfunction • Lack of social support • Persistent psychotic symptoms	• CBTp • Individual placement support • Family work • Combing CRT and vocational interventions • Early identification of those at risk of poor social recovery
Personal	• Remission of symptoms • Integrative Recovery Style • Supportive carers • Good social support network	• Persistent psychotic symptoms • Persistent emotional dysfunction • Post-psychotic depression • High levels of trauma • Traumatic inpatient admissions • Sealing over recovery style	• CBT for emotional dysfunction • Acceptance, mindfulness and compassion-based interventions • Family work • Peer support
Overall recovery	• Good premorbid functioning • Quick remission translated into early social recovery • Good insight • Good engagement with service and bio-psychosocial interventions	• Poor premorbid functioning • Longer DUP • High baseline negative symptoms • Persistent psychotic symptoms • Persistent emotional dysfunction • Persistent substance misuse • Low adherence with medication • Unsupportive family environment • Delays in Intensive Psychosocial Treatments (DIPT)	• Early identification of those at risk of poor recovery • Persistent engagement and offering of bio-psychosocial interventions • Reducing Delays in Intensive Psychosocial Treatments (DIPT) • Reducing substance misuse • Extending critical period

only facilitates personal recovery, but that social and personal recovery is likely to be associated with longer-term symptomatic recovery. Longer-term symptomatic recovery should also make it easier for individuals to maintain their valued social and vocational roles (social recovery), which, in turn, should result in a sustained positive identity, and experiences of well-being and hope (personal recovery). Good engagement with the EIP service and bio-psychosocial interventions are likely to facilitate all three types of recovery. In contrast, a history of poor academic and social functioning and a longer DUP (Oliver et al., 2018) are associated with poor longer-term recovery. High levels of baseline negative symptoms, persistent psychotic symptoms, emotional dysfunction, substance use, poor concordance with anti-psychotic medication, delays in intensive psychosocial treatment (DIPT) (de Haan, Linszen, Lenior, de Win & Gorsira, 2003) and an unsupportive or critical family environment will more likely lead to poorer recovery and progress from stage 2 to stage 3 in the clinical staging model (McGorry, Edwards, Mihalopoulos, Harrigan & Jackson, 1996). A recent case note review has found that these facilitators and barriers to recovery are reflected in real-world EIP clinical practices. Jones et al. (2017) found that achievement of FEP treatment goals at discharge from EIP was associated with better motivation to engage with interventions, having vocational goals and social recovery at baseline, more individual and social strengths, and more family support. In contrast, not achieving any treatment goals at discharge was associated with more developmental adversity, poorer pre-morbid functioning, a longer treatment history prior to FEP, and limited insight. Jones et al. (2017) conclude that there are multiple individual, family and social factors that converge to facilitate either a positive or a negative engagement with EIP interventions, which impact on recovery trajectories and longer term outcomes.

Section 2 EIP: philosophy, goals, engagement, values and team work

Philosophy of EIP

Chapter 1 described the development of the EIP movement over the past 30 years, from pioneering specialist services in Australia and the UK to an accumulation of evidence to support the emergence of EIP services internationally and the development of frameworks and benchmarks which define an effective EIP service (NICE, 2016). The universal declaration EIP (Bertolote & McGorry, 2005) sought to embed the values, goals and standards of EIP into a document that articulated its universal principles while being cognisant of the local socio-economic delivery context.

The EIP declaration set out five key outcomes for EIP programmes throughout the world: (1) improving access and engagement; (2) raising community awareness; (3) promoting recovery; (4) family engagement and support; and

(5) practitioner training. This book maps onto these outcomes as its primary focus is on promoting recovery following FEP.

This clear set of objectives and values helped confirm that EIP services were 'more than the sum of its parts' as they transcended a set of interventions in clinical guidelines and placed them in a framework, which emphasised the optimisation of service user- and carer-focused outcomes.

Goal of EIP

The ideal goal of EIP is early and sustained remission along with social and personal recovery so individuals do not progress from stage 2 of the clinical staging model (McGorry et al., 2006; see Table 1.1), and do not experience relapses or hospital admissions. Currently this is not realistic for everyone who experiences a FEP, as the majority of people (80%) will at some point experience a relapse (Fusar-Poli et al., 2017). Hence the development of EIP services to provide input during the critical period for 2–5 years following a FEP with the aim of reducing relapse and altering the longer-term recovery course. Understanding why some FEP patients engage with services and some disengage is key (Tindall, Simmons, Allott & Hamilton, 2018).

Sustaining engagement and reducing risk of disengagement

Adolescents and young adults are at high risk of disengaging from mental health services (O'Brien, Fahmy & Singh. 2009). In addition, black and minority ethnic (BME) groups are disproportionally represented in FEP (Morgan, Charalambides, Hutchinson & Murray, 2010) and EIP caseloads (Royal College of Psychiatry, 2018) and are more likely to disengage from mental health services (Lal & Malla, 2015). Successful initial and sustained engagement is linked to both strategic and systems issues as well as the value base of the team members.

The importance of youth-friendly services

Having a community-based well-being setting away from traditional psychiatric services is important in providing a sense of hope and optimism and reducing concerns about stigma. McGorry et al. (2013) provide examples of youth-friendly and accessible service models, including examples from Australia (Headspace), Ireland (Jigsaw), and the UK (Pause). In Headspace, young people, aged 12–25 years, can access support for well-being, including psychosis, ensuring that young people receive support whatever their presenting problems, resulting in rapid access to specialist services. These models emphasise prevention, resilience, emotional well-being and accessing help, regardless of presenting symptoms and diagnosis.

However, since 2014, there has been increasing pressure in the UK to provide EIP for all FEP cases irrespective of age (NICE, 2016). This includes adults over the age of 35 who have historically not been seen by EIP and a small proportion of older adults who meet the criteria at age 60+. EIP for adults over 35 and older adults requires a different approach due to differences in aetiology of symptoms and needs, including social, vocational, psychological, and carer needs. It remains to be seen how EIP services in the UK respond to this challenge and also whether EIP produces the same improvements across different outcomes with older adults that are currently being achieved with younger adults recovering from FEP.

The importance of culturally accessible and responsive services

Engaging and understanding barriers to engagement in BME groups remains an issue for all mental health services. For BME groups engaging with EIP, there is no evidence that ethnicity is associated with engagement, but cultural beliefs and ethnicity may impact on beliefs about aetiology (Casey et al., 2016) and help seeking (Singh et al., 2015), supporting the need for flexible approaches and understanding of common cultural beliefs of illness and recovery.

Language barriers may require the use of interpreters and we advocate the importance of this, especially in taking histories and ensuring complex information is accurately relayed to service users and families. Family members should not be used as interpreters due to concerns of accuracy of information exchange and confidentiality issues, potentially placing them in compromising situations. However, care should be taken in ensuring that service users feel comfortable with the professionalism of interpreters, as in close-knit communities, there may be concerns that confidentiality may not be respected or preserved. Increasing levels of skill mix to engage African-Caribbean patients (Bhui & Bhugra, 2002) and employing BME staff who speak different languages may be beneficial.

BME groups with FEP often differ in their pathways to care (Anderson, Flora & McKenzie, 2014) and Black African and Caribbean patients have a decreased likelihood of GP involvement and increased likelihood of police involvement (Bhui, Ullrich, Kallis & Coid, 2015). Consequently, services need to consider more flexible and localised methods of engaging BME communities (Islam, Rabiee & Singh, 2015). Referral routes should not solely centre on traditional health settings, since there are multiple community pathways and resources, which may be more acceptable and accessible to potential service users and ethnic groups. Requests for support and advice from family, religious leaders, community and youth workers should be encouraged and team members should be willing to accept non-traditional pathway routes proactively. The Youthlink culturally informed conceptual framework in Western Australia reported success in engaging Aboriginal youth through building alliances with the community (Sabbioni et al., 2018). In Birmingham, the central mosque provides accommodation to young men with mental health problems, recognising the willingness of community leaders and cultures to embrace and support those with mental distress. Thus, EIP can improve its engagement with BME groups by improving the accessibility of youth-focused services in low stigma settings supported by local multi-agency strategies. The 300 Voices in Birmingham (Time to Change, 2016) used a co-production engagement model in a series of workshops, which resulted in service users becoming more hopeful and confident talking about their own mental health problems and improved relationships and understanding between service users and professionals. It challenged mental health stigma and discrimination, both within mainstream services and African and Caribbean communities. These programmes have the potential to reduce in-patient costs and increase savings in a range of front-line services. More importantly, by receiving help earlier, BME groups will not only have more positive engagement and experiences with mental health services, their longer-term recovery will also be improved. The 300 Voices Toolkit (Time to Change, 2016) is a 146-page overview on how to deliver a 300 voices project and has been used to improve personalisation of mental health care delivery in South London and Maudsley NHS Foundation Trust (SLaM).

Engagement/disengagement: definitions and associates

Engagement using assertive outreach principles is recognised as an intervention in its own right but its process remains poorly understood (Tindall et al., 2015, Tindall, Simmons, Allott & Hamilton, 2018). A systematic review of 10 studies with FEP samples found that disengagement rates range from 20.5% to 40% with around 30% of young people disengaging from specialist FEP services (Doyle et al., 2014). Recent reviews considered factors associated with non-concordance with bio-psychosocial interventions (Leclerc, Noto, Bressan & Brietzke, 2015) and disengagement from specialist FEP services (Doyle et al., 2014), which are summarised in Table 12.2. Both reviews concur that there is higher risk of disengagement following FEP for individuals who either do not live with family or have little family support, for individuals with persistent substance use, and for those with persistent positive symptoms. Casey et al. (2016) found that duration of untreated illness (DUI) but not DUP, predicted engagement in 103 FEP patients presenting to an EIP service. They also noted that those with higher levels of qualifications and those believing that mental illness was less likely to be caused by social stress or odd thoughts, also predicted poorer engagement. Many of these risk factors are potentially modifiable and services could use these factors to identify and then implement strategies to reduce risk of non-concordance and service disengagement.

Meta-analytic evidence suggests engagement can be facilitated by assessing service users' strengths and needs, making services accessible, providing education about the service, providing meaningful homework tasks, and assessing treatment barriers (Lindsey et al., 2014). Other facilitators of engagement include addressing recovery needs holistically and focusing on employment and education goals (Smith, Easter, Pollock, Pope, & Wisdom, 2013).

Table 12.2 Factors associated with non-concordance and disengagement from bio-psychosocial interventions and FEP services

Patient-related	Environment-related	Treatment-related	Illness-related
• Lower education level[1]	• Lack of family involvment[1,2]	• Rapid remission of negative symptoms*[1]	• Positive symptom severity[1,2]
• Persistent substance misuse[1,2]	• Not living with a family member[1]	• Therapeutic alliance[1]	• More relapses*[1]
• Forensic history[1]	• Social adjustment difficulties[1]	• Voluntary first admission*[1]	• Longer DUP*[1,2]
• Unemployment[1]			
• History of physical abuse[1]			
• Poor insight*[1]			

Notes
* = Just medication non-adherence.
1 = Leclerc et al. (2015).
2 = Doyle et al. (2014).

The role of EIP in engagement

Initial and flexible engagement in people's homes can be one of the defining characteristics of EIP which make it appealing to service users and families alike (Tait, Ryles & Sidwell, 2010). Windell and Norman (2013) note the importance of a warm, friendly and accessible atmosphere for all aspects of recovery and these are crucial in this initial engagement phase. Sensitive engagement incorporates not just the time or location of contacts and visits but practical considerations to reduce stigma. During home visits, it is helpful to establish who is in the house and how comfortable the service user feels talking in front of family friends or flatmates and how, and to whom, verbal messages are relayed. Similarly, during community activities, it is helpful to be aware of potentially stigmatising actions such as wearing professional ID badges or carrying professional equipment (e.g. medicine bags, files, etc.). Dressing appropriately for the environment may also be another important consideration.

A multi-faceted approach is helpful in engagement. The employment of youth workers, Individual Placement and Support (IPS), and recovery workers can be highly effective in maintaining a less stigmatising link with service users compared to mental health care professionals (see Chapters 6 and 7). In addition to facilitating care delivery, maintaining the positive ethos of the team and promoting social recovery, peer support workers can potentially reduce risks of disengagement. Involving family or carer networks in EIP care can significantly reduce the risks of disengagement (Tindall et al., 2018).

Respect for the family unit involves understanding the culture and beliefs of that family and what the family is requiring in terms of support. Chapter 11 discusses family intervention in detail, and structured family interventions should be seen as a natural extension of continuous family engagement which is practised by all team members. Since EIP services place high value on family involvement, family engagement should be the norm, or starting point, so that rather than asking a service user 'Is it OK if we speak with your family?', instead a team member might say, 'It's really important that we involve and support your family, who would be the best person to speak to first?'

In our experience, service users will state if they do not want family members involved. However, many young people will not object if there is a clear rationale, and many express relief that the model focuses on family support. Similarly, sensitive issues which have not yet been shared with families (e.g. the extent of substance use, personal/sexual relationships) can be initially addressed with service users separately, only involving the family when there is a need to.

Consideration should be given to who is in the family. In particular, with young people, romantic relationships may be transient, and so alliances with stable networks should be sought if possible. Smith et al. (2010) have promoted the needs of siblings and the awareness of the special relationships siblings have. Siblings may be worried about their own mental health while also being the main source of confidence and support within the household for the service user. Equally, maintaining the balance in the family and avoiding colluding with potentially humiliating practices is important. For example, care should be maintained to preserve the natural order in the family (e.g. role of older sibling) and avoid asking, for instance, a young sibling to 'check on' an older brother or sister's medication concordance or getting them to report on their substance use.

Value base

Regardless of professional background, a shared recovery-based philosophy which values young people and their families affected by psychosis as well as delivering early treatment is essential for the team to have a shared vision and promote the 'EIP brand'. It is important to promote compassion, hopefulness and recovery not just in clinical settings but also in the service's operational policy. The value base should be clearly observable in interactions from referral through to discharge from EIP teams so that service users and families feel supported throughout. This includes sensitive handling of telephone calls, recognising potential distress and anxiety when people ring for help and offering timely communication and resolutions. All staff need a genuine passion for working with young people, understanding that the experience of psychosis is often traumatic for the young person, family members and friends (see Chapter 8). Similarly, all staff should support the concept of a multimodal recovery from psychosis, as promoted throughout this book. Some awareness of youth culture and social norms is necessary, including current habits and practices around substance use. Staff attitudes to the inevitability of substance use should be reflected by asking routinely about alcohol and drug use and acknowledging the varied reasons they are used (see Chapters 1 and 10). We would argue that the age of the worker is not as important as the awareness of the current and changing youth culture.

We advocate focus on outcomes and goals defined by service users. We endorse Rethink's 100 ways to support recovery guidance (Slade, 2009), which suggests values, beliefs and behaviours for recovery-focused staff. Roberts et al. (2009) in Torbay produced a recovery guideline with reflections for staff following each visit, e.g. Did I actively help the service user to make sense of their mental health? Did I actively promote independent management of mental health? As well as personal reflection, these questions can become a core part of supervision and be used in the effective recruitment of staff. Positive attitudes not only help engagement but a pessimistic view and low expectations of patient's ability to return to work may impact on outcomes. For example, as described in Chapters 5 and 6, positive expectations of outcome expressed by care co-ordinators have been found to predict the number of days in employment for patients with schizophrenia.

Value-based recruitment (HEE England, 2016) into EIP clinical posts may be promoted, which incorporates the NHS core values and involves service users in the process. Traditional recruitment interviews may not be the most helpful method of choosing the best candidate or eliciting values and skills. It may be better in the longer term to employ some less experienced staff with the right 'mind set' or to carry a vacancy, than to recruit a 'safe pair of hands' where the common goal is not shared. The Birmingham and Solihull EIP teams enlist the help of young service users trained in recruitment to choose clinical posts. Applicants facilitate focus groups on set themes and service users feed back to the recruiting manager on the applicant's performance, including communication and language used. Young people also assess the ability of applicants to engage a young person in devising a collaborative treatment plan. This method offers the opportunity for rich feedback on potential staff member's engagement skills. Service users report that they prefer this method to participating in a formal interview process with other professionals.

In addition to the core values defined by the constitutions such as those adhered to in the English NHS, the following characteristics and beliefs of staff may be particularly useful in EIP:

- Recognise that their own engagement skills and communication will influence the attitude of the patient to recovery.
- Have a genuine belief in the multimodal approach and the need for teamwork.
- Understand that patient and family stress may present as hostility and frustration (see Chapter 11).

- Understand that families are significantly affected by psychosis, may have other stresses, have needs in their own right and know much more about their relative than you.
- Understand that recovery is individual, varied and multifactorial.
- Promote the possibility of overcoming difficulties, while acknowledging that recovery and adaptation may have setbacks and that the future is uncertain.
- Awareness of the prevalence and reasons for recreational drug and alcohol use and the need for integrated recovery.
- Desire to promote least restrictive practice, while understanding responsibility for personal and public safety.

EIP MDT staff and roles

Staff knowledge

Initial induction, mentoring and regular team training ensure that emerging knowledge is shared and that staff retain clarity about the service aims and philosophy. Of particular importance is the knowledge of negative symptoms, emotional dysfunction, safeguarding matters and substance misuse, which is likely to impact on value base and engagement. Chapters 5 and 6 on social recovery discuss the link between lack of understanding and critical comments in more detail and the importance of support staff, who may spend the most time with services users, understanding the vital role they play in promoting social recovery. Each staff member should be aware of early signs of a setback or vulnerabilities, such as a support worker understanding that a patient declining a social activity that they usually enjoy on several occasions may be a sign of social isolation and relapse and feel able to share that concern with the team.

Training

There are a number of EIP training modules available online (e.g. provided by Orygen in Australia), which focus on the key elements and interventions provided by teams. In the UK, the IRIS group and the Sainsbury Centre developed a training package based on the Australian training and courses are available nationally. Other services such as Camden and Islington and the Birmingham and Solihull EIP services have devised internal training programmes for clinicians, which include suicide prevention training, psychologically informed social recovery, psychoeducational family interventions and motivational interviewing. Staff are encouraged to ask for additional training on anything they feel would benefit their practice, in addition to core training and away days, they may provide workshops and refreshers on IPS and physical health interventions. There is a need for EIP clinicians to develop a broad skills base, particularly in the recognition and management of comorbidities, such as ASD, PD and SUD, which is likely to require specific tailored training (see Chapter 10).

Supervision

In light of the challenges facing care co-ordinators and the potential for stress and burnout, clinical and caseload supervision is vital. Supervision can help prevent unhelpful patient dependence and assist care co-ordinators to reflect on changes in engagement. In particular, transference is common in this service user group with staff often feeling protective and maternal/paternal towards particular service users. It is also important for staff to reflect on perceived non-engagement and also the reduction of contact owing to avoidance of difficult feelings (Martindale & Summers, 2013). We have already discussed the pivotal role of establishing and sustaining engagement but continually dwelling on engagement as a therapeutic tool, can lead to a lack of structure and unfocused visits without purpose.

A multi-professional team approach

The professional make-up of EIP teams can vary but services require a range of professionals to maintain fidelity to the EIP model (see Chapter 1), including medical, social recovery, and psychological experts, who can bring different approaches to sustaining engagement. In line with the value base, professionals in the team can demonstrate respect for their colleagues' strengths and roles by supporting an integrated approach. This in turn will support service users. For instance, a psychologist offering interventions for managing anxiety and carrying out CBT interventions will need to be aware of prescribed medication, which may impact on this. If the team psychiatrist is prescribing anxiolytic medication while the service user is undergoing a graded exposure plan with another professional, this should be formulated, shared and understood by the team, patient and their family. Medical reviews should be arranged outside of the young person's college commitments, reinforcing the importance of the three types of recovery.

Interventions by specialist team members require integration with the ongoing case management and regular team discussions, sharing of information and a working team formulation result in a genuine integrated care plan. Team formulations were briefly introduced in Chapter 6 and will be discussed later. The team manager plays a vital role in setting the tone of the team and ensuring a cohesive approach, while the care co-ordinator conveys this to the service user (Tindall et al., 2015). Previous chapters have focused on roles that have traditionally been associated with specific professionals. Care co-ordinators often deliver core interventions, including psychoeducation, substance use and family work. Table 12.3 summarises the new Access and Waiting Time Standards for EIP in the UK (NICE, 2016) and the potential role of EIP staff in this.

Table 12.3 EIP staff involvement in EIP access and waiting time standards (2016)

Standards	EIP staff involvement		
	Care co-ordinators	Psychiatrist	Psychologist
1 Referrals to EIP treated within two weeks	✓	✓	✓
2 Assessment and formulation inclusive of trauma and adversity from specialist EIP	✓	✓	✓
3 CBTp	✓		✓
4 FIp	✓		✓
5 Antipsychotic medication	✓	✓	
6 Physical health interventions and monitoring	✓	✓	
7 Supported employment	✓		
8 Carer-focused education and support program	✓	✓	✓
9 Care planning a Mental Health Care and Treatment b Provision of information about psychosis	✓		
10 Substance misuse-assessment and therapy	✓	✓	✓
11 Routine outcome measures (ROMs): HoNoS; QPR; DIALOG	✓	✓	✓

The importance of care co-ordination in EIP

Care co-ordination within EIP is an under-rated skill. As the main link between the EIP team and the service user and family, the care co-ordinator plays a central role in co-ordinating many, if not all, aspects of care. While many come from nursing backgrounds, social workers and other professionals may also fulfil this role. Good EIP care co-ordinators have flexible engagement and therapeutic skills, are knowledgeable and empathic, have excellent time management skills, can prioritise workload, and have capacity to manage stress and remain calm and focused in a crisis. Thus, the role of EIP care co-ordinators is multifaceted and demanding.

The care co-ordinator plays a fundamental role in engaging the service user and forming a therapeutic alliance, balancing the desire to assess needs with managing risk. They often see service users more frequently than others in the team which may mean they are the first to pick up on early warning signs of relapse, unhelpful substance use or other changes. Service user feedback and research support the importance of EIP care co-ordinators in facilitating a good therapeutic relationship following a FEP. As discussed previously in Chapter 2, when Barr et al. (2015) asked 20 young people with FEP about the most valuable aspect of their EIP care, most pointed to the need to have a good relationship with their EIP care co-ordinator. In particular, service users recovering from FEP reported that they had most valued having a care co-ordinator, who genuinely cared about them, listened to their concerns, valued them as a whole person, not just as someone who is ill, were non-judgemental, and stayed with them through their three-year period of care. Similarly, Lester et al. (2012) conducted semi-structured interviews with 21 young people who had been under the care of FEP over two time periods. These young people spoke favourably about their experience of care under EIP and that EIP staff had provided 'gold standard' care, which they felt that other services had failed to match. In particular, these young people valued their care co-ordinator as someone they had been able to easily access, talk to, and trust. They also stressed the importance of good interpersonal continuity of care.

Where possible, the personal characteristics and skills of the care co-ordinator, such as expertise in effectively managing those with negative symptoms or skills with working with young parents, should be considered when allocating caseloads. Similarly, shared hobbies and interests (e.g. music, TV shows, sports, etc.) can initially promote common ground. While some team members may have expertise, interest or skills in a particular area such as delayed social recovery, a varied caseload should be encouraged to prevent 'burnout'. Establishing trust in the care co-ordinator, along with talking about experiences and developing a routine outside the house, is a key factor influencing engagement (Tindall et al., 2015).

Role of care co-ordinator in delivering new standards of care for EIP in England

Although all EIP staff play unique and important roles in delivering the new NHS England standards (NICE, 2016) and providing bio-psychosocial interventions, EIP care co-ordinators are probably more likely to be either directly or indirectly involved in delivering more of the standards compared to other EIP staff. Specifically, the two-week waiting time standard is often met *only* when the care co-ordinator has accepted a new referral onto their caseload and begun the engagement process. As indicated in Table 12.3, care co-ordinators also play a crucial role in the second standard as they are expected to be skilled in working with a bio-psychosocial formulation and support people with their biological, psychological and social needs as well as be able to function as part of a multi-disciplinary team (NICE, 2016). Care co-ordinators may deliver psychosocial interventions like CBTp and FIs if they are trained and supervised in their delivery (NICE, 2016). In the past, care co-ordinators would often do this informally, or in a low-intensity way. However, since the Access and Waiting

Time Standards (NICE, 2016), many are availing themselves of training in CBTp and FIs provided by NHS England and are increasingly likely to have a more direct role in delivering these interventions. As outlined in Chapter 11, Meriden are based in Birmingham, UK, and are national and international trainers in Behavioural Family Therapy (BFT). The majority of EIP care co-ordinators within the Birmingham service are trained in BFT and are expected to provide these interventions as part of their care co-ordinator role.

Care co-ordinators, especially nurses, play a pivotal role in monitoring the impact of antipsychotic medication, including its effectiveness and side effects. They are often the first member of the team to pick up on non-concordance with AP medication, which as we have seen, can be a significant risk factor for relapse (Álvarez-Jiménez et al., 2012c). Conversely, care co-ordinators can play a key role in facilitating medication concordance, which is the sole independent predictor of symptomatic recovery at five-year follow up (Norman et al., 2017). They often play a key role in monitoring the physical health of service users, ensuring they are booked in for annual physical health assessments, and following up on recommended interventions to improve physical health. Given that many care co-ordinators are nurses, they also may have a role in leading service-level initiatives to improve physical health in FEP.

Care co-ordinators are often involved in supported employment interventions, ranging from assessing and identifying educational and employment needs, to referring to vocational organisations for specific interventions such as IPS (see Chapter 6), or providing more direct support by helping service users apply for jobs and college courses, supporting them with interviews, and often supporting them overcome barriers (e.g. anxiety, low mood) to access these opportunities. The care co-ordinator is directly responsible for recovery-based approaches to care planning (NICE, 2016). In the Access and Waiting Time Standard, care planning is made up of two separate components: (1) care planning and treatment; and (2) provision of information about psychosis.

Care co-ordinators often play a role in identifying problematic substance use, which, as we have seen in Table 12.1, is a significant barrier to different types of recovery and is associated with relapse (Álvarez-Jiménez et al., 2012c) and non-concordance with bio-psychosocial interventions (Leclerc et al., 2015) and disengagement from EIP services (Doyle et al., 2014). Care co-ordinators may also play a direct or indirect role in assessing and intervening with problematic substance use. For example, in Birmingham and Solihull Mental Health Trust, many EIP care co-ordinators completed CB:IT training for problematic substance use (Copello, Graham & Birchwood, 2001) (see Chapter 10 for a description) to improve assessments and interventions for FEP service users who use substances on their caseloads. Finally, care co-ordinators may play an important role in helping EIP services to collect Routine Outcome Measures (ROMs) that are mandated in the new Access and Waiting Time Standards (NICE, 2016).

Care co-ordinator caseloads

In the early 2000s, caseload numbers in the UK were recommended as between 10–15 per care co-ordinator (IRIS, 2000) with more recent guidance suggesting a limit of 15 (NICE, 2016). However, the recent EIPN audit (Royal College of Psychiatrists, 2018) found national rates of 17, with much higher ratios in many of the urban EIP services. As the role of care co-ordinator is so fundamental in addressing the three types of recovery, sustaining engagement and delivering the national standards, the quality of service is likely to be significantly compromised with higher caseloads. This may result in increased disengagement rates, potentially missing early signs of relapse and less time to develop bio-psychosocial assessments and formulations, impacting on outcomes. High caseloads have negative consequences for care co-ordinators themselves as they are likely to feel less engaged in psychosocial recovery-orientated work, which can lead to job dissatisfaction.

EIP team operations

EIP team manager

The EIP team manager also has an extremely important role. They set the recovery ethos and agenda for the whole team and are responsible for ensuring that systems are in place for supervising the entire caseload so that those service users who are most visible (e.g. those who present in crisis or seek help more assertively) do not take up resources at the expense of those with more covert symptomatic, social, or personal recovery needs. Thus, routine appointments with service users should only be cancelled in exceptional circumstances. Management of the service user journey and recovery goals needs to be reinforced constantly in team meetings, supporting the team through crisis, case management and clinical supervision, as well as regular clinical reviews.

EIP team meetings

Team meetings maintain the culture, cohesion and value base of the team. They also play a key role in ensuring the symptomatic, social, and personal recovery needs of service users and their carers are being met and that the impact of relapse and other crises is reduced. Senior team members can model respectful, recovery-focused language. The meetings require enough structure to enable staff to discuss and be aware of important clinical issues facing those service users at risk or those in a difficult phase of their life or care. To be effective, the meetings should be seen as a priority where possible and attended by all of the team. If all staff are not present, the value is lost and staff will cease to see the meeting as the primary decision-making vehicle. However, overly formal meetings may disinhibit staff, especially less experienced ones, from using the team as a source of guidance and support.

Weekly MDT meeting

The weekly multidisciplinary team meeting is an opportunity to discuss new referrals, ensure prompt initial assessments are organised and care co-ordinators have a plan to establish engagement. As discussed in Chapter 9, the 'zoning board' allows the team to increase support in a planned way to reduce the risk, or at least minimise, the impact of a relapse or other issues, such as elevated suicide risk, and operationalise the stress vulnerability model, noting those service users who are facing acute and chronic stressors. This will include acknowledging that a social recovery-focused goal (e.g. starting college) may be a vulnerable time for a service user who may feel pressure to succeed. Although they may not be displaying any current signs of relapse, their vulnerability to relapse is known by the team. Early recognition of non-concordance with medication, depressive symptoms, recreational drug use and other social concerns will enable the treatment plan to remain relevant and focused. Similarly, any behaviour changes, such as disengaging with visits/contacts, should be discussed. A section on 'problem-solving' where staff feel able to discuss concerns or 'stuckness' within the team should be encouraged and timetabled. For example, a care co-ordinator may be feeling that a young person is not progressing with a social programme as expected. Encouraging a reflective problem-solving discussion may elicit the need for a change of direction, or reinforce the need for patience, as well as creating a shared ownership of the team. If a service user is already showing early warning signs of potential relapse, the team can review the individual relapse signature and plan and consider increased support. This may include the need for help from other teams if required (e.g. crisis resolution teams).

Daily handover

A brief 15-minute meeting at the start of the working day can help ensure that intensive support plans, developed in the weekly MDT meeting, are followed up. This can also be an opportunity for staff to have a quick debrief on any crisis or concerns from the previous working day and think about additional crisis plans for the day ahead.

Weekly formulation CPA reviews

The routine, regular, review of patients, whether case reviews or Care Programme Approach (CPA) meetings should be timetabled differently, so that every service user's care is formally reviewed. This ensures that the 'forgotten settled' do not get overlooked, including those patients and families who rarely ask for help or do not present with behaviours likely to elicit interventions.

Managing relapse and crisis

If someone does relapse, the team would need to review interventions. Preferably this can be done at home but, if not, admission to hospital may need to be considered. Ideally, EIP teams could have their own crisis resolution team, respite houses and in-patient wards and crises and relapses would be managed by the EIP service. In practice, this is not always commissioned or viable. While some EIP services work flexibly, and over a seven-day service, there are likely to be times when generic crisis teams and acute mental health wards are required. The advantage of this may be that EIP teams do not become absorbed in crisis management at the expense of recovery. The disadvantages may be that the philosophy of care may be different and confusing for the service user and family and that service users are exposed to chronically ill patients, which may induce fear for the future.

If other teams supplement or lead on care during times of crisis, including hospital admission, a member of the EIP team maintaining contact with the patient throughout this period is essential to maintain continuity and reinforce the recovery journey and a sense of hope. Wherever possible, the EIP team should lead or advise on prescribing of medication and other aspects of care, reinforcing the over-arching staying well plan. Family work and psychological interventions should be continued whenever possible or, at least, the contact maintained to reduce anxiety and foster a sense of 'being with' the patient. Family members and service users rarely understand the differences between a home treatment team and EIP and, if care is not within the philosophy of EIP, this can feel confusing to people who may feel let down.

Admissions

Hospital should not necessarily be viewed as a 'failure', depending on the purpose of admission. Sometimes a stay in respite or hospital may offer family members a break from a caring role and enable a review of support required. In light of the role that unexplained admissions may have in post-traumatic symptoms following FEP (see Chapter 8), if someone needs to be admitted to hospital, team members should take time to explain the process and rationale, acknowledge fears and offer support and guidance. This might include accompanying the service user or family to the hospital, giving advice on what to pack, and helping out with organising lifts for visits. If a service user is being admitted a long way from home, the reason for this needs to be explained, including the process and likely timeframe for repatriation. This may require difficult discussions on lack of resources which often need to be shared with service users and families. Following admission, the team should offer an opportunity for the service user and family to talk through the process and consider if there was any learning for future potential relapses.

Supporting the team through crisis

The EIP population is a complex group and often, despite the best efforts of all professionals, there are times when the team face the challenge of team recovery after a difficult incident (e.g. suicide or serious assault). Following any serious event, the team is likely to face external scrutiny (e.g. coroner's inquest, serious incident review). Supporting the team is vital for the safe management of the service, promoting hope and examining values following the incident. Where a member of staff has been assaulted, there may be a need to continue a change in care co-ordinator or other key personnel in order to manage staff feelings alongside providing consistency. It is also an opportunity for the team to learn from what happened and potentially change their practice. For such reasons, the team may benefit from an independent facilitator with supportive sessions for individuals impacted by the event also being made available (Andriessen, 2009) Research with health care professionals in other mental health services has found that the most common feelings of mental health nursing staff following a patient suicide were surprise, shock, anger, concern, frustration, fear (Canning & Gournay, 2014), and feelings of blame, guilt, and shame (Pallin, 2004;). Staff have identified that talking as soon as possible after the event when the incident is still fresh in everyone mind is helpful (Bohan & Doyle, 2008).

Following serious incidents, it is preferable to hold a team debriefing meeting with all team members within one or two days. The manner in which staff are informed about a suicide can significantly impact on staff coping and, as expected, informing staff in a compassionate manner can reduce negative impact (Canning & Gournay, 2014). A debriefing meeting should be facilitated by senior clinicians or managers and used to provide concrete information on known details of the suicide. It can be an opportunity for staff to express their feelings (e.g. of shock, frustration, sadness) and have these validated and normalised. This can help reduce staff feelings of isolation and facilitate the start of the emotional processing of the suicide. Given that there is an association between the depth of staff involvement with patient and impact of their suicide (Joyce & Wallbridge, 2003), particular attention should be paid to those who had most contact with the service user, which has meant that they will often have established the strongest and deepest relationship with the service user and their family. Feelings of blame, guilt, shame and a pervasive sense of failure can lead staff to question their professional competence after a suicide (Pallin, 2004). Furthermore, staff may become increasingly risk-averse for all service users on their caseload and revisit all risk assessments following a patient suicide (Canning & Gournay, 2014). Thus, they will likely benefit from additional clinical and caseload supervision following a suicide. Others (up to 85% of clinical staff) find peer support from other clinicians helpful and perhaps even more helpful than a formal team debriefing (Bohan & Doyle, 2008).

Safeguarding

All professionals have a responsibility to identify and act on any safeguarding concerns. From practice, common issues that occur within EIP include management of money and finances, physical aggression towards siblings, specific risks relating to relapse and disclosures of past sexual abuse. Expressing concerns assertively, calmly and honestly involving the families promotes an open and collaborative dialogue and approach. This is likely to maintain the relationship after the risk is managed. Service users who are parents require special consideration especially if they live alone. The care co-ordinator may experience some transference. For example, they may feel protective of young mothers who have demonstrated considerable resilience in managing a young child while adapting to a psychotic illness. Extra support around long school holidays using local groups should be sought and safeguarding introduced from a supportive perspective. Engaging with the extended family is encouraged to support service users in maintaining parenting and building supportive networks.

Routine outcome measures (ROMs)

We recommend a mixture of clinician reported outcome measures (CROMs) and patient reported outcome measures (PROMs). Appendix 2 lists outcome measures for the three types of recovery including service or generic outcome measures. Such ROMs within EIP can help demonstrate quality of services to clinical staff, service users and their carers, referrers and commissioners. Using IT and informatics systems effectively can facilitate collection of ROMs and ensure that ROMs are integrated in a coherent and meaningful way that does not place too much additional burden on staff, patients or families. Patient reported experience measures (PREMs) enables the team to reflect on their customer care and user satisfaction. These include mandatory outcomes as part of the Minimum Mental Health Data Set (MMHDS) and the Access and Waiting Time Standards (NICE, 2016; see Table 12.3), but also additional measures owing to the limitations of broad measures on clinical understanding.

Section 3 EIP care pathways

Referrals

Given that EIP services should be designed to reduce delay, referrals should be managed proactively with flexibility for referral methods. If the team is reliant on referrals from an organisational Single Point of Access, the team need to ensure that those triaging referrals are aware of EIP principles, criteria, and targets and feel able to contact the team manager for discussion of ambiguous cases. This is equally true for people likely to pass through court diversion or crisis assessment teams. It may also help save time in referring young people to alternative services without the need for assessment. A friendly, approachable response to referrers and staff, impacts on acceptability to referrers as well as to service users and families.

Initial assessment

The new Access and Waiting Time Standards (NICE, 2016) propose that all FEP should receive an assessment and formulation (inclusive of trauma and adversity) from a specialist EIP team. Following referral, a clinician should try to contact the service user by telephone and arrange to see them at the earliest mutually convenient time. We advocate two professionals visit the service user at home if possible in the spirit of multi-professional collaboration, so that one can lead the assessment and another can provide information on the service and engagement 'hooks'. This is also likely to increase the likelihood of the continuity on the next visit when a care co-ordinator or other team member may be introduced. The assessors should give immediate verbal feedback on the outcome of the assessment and whether the EIP criteria has been met. If feasible, an initial intervention plan should also be discussed (e.g. whether the team will be working with the service user and the next planned visit).

Initial engagement

The engagement and assessment phase often overlap in practice and it may, in some cases, take up to three months to engage the service user and family in meaningful discussion, complete multimodal assessments and to plan an individually formulated plan of care. As described in Chapter 8, those service users with a trauma history may need a more measured and sensitive pace during the assessment (and treatment) phase.

Formulation and targeted care planning: one size does not fit all

After an initial engagement and assessment period (approximately three months), we recommend that a team formulation meeting is held. This detailed assessment and formulation can directly inform interventions aimed at facilitating symptomatic, social, and personal recovery forming the basis for an integrated care plan.

Although written care plans are part of the CPA process in England, they should not be a paper exercise, completed by one individual in isolation but be informed by a clear, multifaceted formulation (Meaden & Hacker, 2011). This may seem obvious, but formulated care should be based on the best possible evidence-based practice, coupled with the readiness and views of the service user and family. For example, if a service user is adamant that they do not like blood tests or needles and will not entertain the idea of taking regular tests, then the prescribing of drugs such as clozapine is unlikely to be successful or prag-matic. Similarly, service users with chaotic lifestyles may struggle taking split doses of medication and prefer a more simplified drug regime.

Engaging service users in developing a meaningful, realistic and paced indi-vidualised plan creates a more positive and collaborative treatment approach. Psychologists and occupational therapists in EIP teams, in particular, have an important role in understanding delays in social recovery and leading formula-tion discussions. While psychologists may lead on formulating psychosocial interventions, support workers and recovery workers have an important role in encouraging and supporting services users in developing social activities and networks.

Formulation template

Formulated care enables the team to focus on the most appropriate interventions at the most appropriate time. A team formulation can use a framework based on the 5 Ps model (Problem, Protective, Precipitating, Prolonging, and Protective factors) (Weerasekera, 1993), but can also incorporate other psychological and formulation frameworks. The key to managing complex cases is to prioritise and carry out a multi-professional formulation, which is reviewed and reformulated to make service users with delayed social and psychological recovery a priority. Figure 12.1 contains a template, which can be used in formulation and multi-disciplinary reviews when discussing a service user's developmental history, onset of psychosis, contact with EIP, and their subsequent recovery or relapse. Each review considers the current presentation and presenting problems from the service user's, carers' and EIP perspective. In addition, there is an explicit dis-cussion about recovery based on the tripartite model of recovery we have used throughout this book. In the ideal scenario the service user would always be present for this discussion but for various reasons, this is not always possible. However, the service user's voice can be present if PROMs have been completed prior to the CPA review.

Formulations, ROMs and symptomatic, social and personal recovery

When discussing symptomatic and social recovery, the staff can also use the different CROMs alongside the PROMs (see Figure 12.1 and Appendix 2) to inform their own clinical observations, as well as feedback from service users and their carers on current levels of symptoms. This triangulation facilitates a more accurate assessment of recovery, progress or deterioration between reviews. It ensures that personal recovery is given equal footing with sympto-matic and social recovery. Current levels of recovery and the service user's goals are then discussed alongside consideration of the current protective (e.g. rapid remission, good insight, recovery style; family support) and prolonging (e.g.

Predisposing Factors for FEP	Events and Experiences Since EIP
Precipitating Factors for FEP	
First Episode Psychosis (FEP) Presentation	Relevant Recent Factors (precipitating factors)
DUP:	

RECOVERY PROFILE

Perspectives	Symptomatic Recovery	Social Recovery	Personal Recovery
Service User	Feedback PROMs -Positive and Negative Symptoms	Feedback PROMs -Work and Social Adjustment -Time Use	Feedback PROMs -QPR: -DIALOG: -Goals:
Carer	Feedback	Feedback	Observations
EIP	Clinicians Observations CROMs -HONOS (items: 6-8) -GAF-S: -Positive and Negative Symptoms:	Clinicians Observations CROMs -GAF-D: -HONOS (items: 9-12): -NEET:	Clinicians Observations CROMs (Psychological Recovery) -Calgary Depression Scale -Impact of Event Scale

CLINICAL STAGE (McGorry et al., 2006)

Early Recovery	Late/Incomplete Recovery			No Recovery
Stage 2 Symptom and Functional Remission	Stage 3a Initial recovery then single relapse	Stage 3b Initial recovery then mulitple relapses	Stage 3c Premorbid functional or symptom level never reached	Stage 4 Severe, persistent, or unremitting illness

Longer Term Recovery and Service Engagement

Is there a high risk of relapse ?	YES	NO	Don't Know
Is there a high risk of poor social recovery?			
Is there a high risk of service disengagement ?			

Perpetuating Factors	Protective Factors

RECOVERY CARE PLANS		By Whom	By Date
Symptomatic			
Social			
Personal			
Others	(e.g., to reduce risk of relapse, poor social recovery, disengagement)		

Figure 12.1 FEP recovery formulation and care plan.

persistence substance use; poor concordance with medication and psychosocial interventions; social isolation and living alone) factors to directly guide and inform the care plan, which is also divided into interventions to facilitate symptomatic, social, and personal recovery.

Finally, it can also be seen from Figure 12.1 that the EIP Recovery Formulation and Care Plan can be used to trigger a discussion about many other important issues that we have covered in this and previous chapters. In particular, having a summary of the developmental history, onset of psychosis, progress since EIP including their clinical stage, their current symptomatic, social and personal recovery, and their protective and prolonging factors can be used alongside information summarised in the tables in this book to help answer questions about current risk of relapse (see Table 4.3), risk of unfavourable social recovery (see Tables 5.1 and 5.2), and the risk of disengagement (see Table 12.2).

Once the formulation and intervention plan is developed and agreed with the service user and their family, the next 3–12 months are spent implementing this plan. This plan is then regularly reviewed (with the service user and their family) and then formally reviewed by the team in the next team formulation meeting, which usually occurs 3–6 months later, depending on progress and clinical need. At this follow-up meeting, the formulation and care plan is reviewed and updated with new information including current symptomatic, social, and personal recovery, which again will be informed by the ROMs This is repeated at subsequent formulation meetings through the EIP period of care.

Section 4 Discharge and care post EIP

Although Lester et al. (2012) noted the abilities of EIP teams to assertively engage patients; they also highlighted the lack of effective disengagement strategies, including establishing links with general practitioners to facilitate effective discharge from secondary or specialist mental health care. Considering the longer-term pathway and preparing for discharge from EIP are an essential part of the recovery process as this can help sustain the benefits achieved in EIP.

The clinical staging model, alongside current levels of symptomatic, social, and personal recovery, risk, and the wishes of service users and their carers, can help inform discharge and subsequent service planning. The main discharge pathways following EIP are summarised in Table 12.4. As indicated, service users in clinical stage 2, with a lower risk of relapse and good social recovery, are less likely to require ongoing specialist mental health services and could be discharged to primary care services. However, in preparation, this requires a clear and comprehensive plan for both the GP and patient including medication, monitoring requirements, physical health concerns, early warning signs/staying well plan, and contingency planning in the event of relapse, including how to re-access help. Solihull EIP service offers a discharge planning meeting at the GP surgery which allows the psychiatrist or care co-ordinator to meet with the GP along with the patient, to answer any questions the GP may have about AP medication, monitoring requirements and contingency planning. This is appreciated by GPs, many of whom are under-confident in the ongoing care of patients with psychosis.

Table 12.4 Recovery, clinical stage and discharge planning

Recovery criteria	Clinical stage	Discharge pathway
• Sustained symptomatic, social, and personal recovery. • Low risk of relapse • Low risk of poor social recovery • Supportive networks • Likely to help seek	2	Primary Care (e.g., GP; Family Practitioner)
• Delayed or inconsistent symptomatic, social, and personal recovery • Higher risk of relapse • Higher risk of poorer social recovery • Higher risk of poor adherence with services and bio-psychosocial interventions • Persistent substance misuse more common	3a 3b 3c	Secondary Care (e.g., Community Mental Health Team)
• Incomplete or absence of symptomatic, social and personal recovery • Persistent or frequent relapse of psychotic symptoms • Comorbid substance misuse • Long history of poor functioning • Very poor help seeking • Poor support network	4	Specialist Secondary Care (e.g., Assertive Outreach; Rehab and Recovery)

Discharge to the generic adult services, for many, will mean the expectation that they will attend planned appointments, with busy community mental health teams (CMHTs) unlikely to be able to offer the same level of support, including follow-up for non-attendance. Preparation for adult services requires significant planning and is appreciated by service users (Lester et al; 2012). While many service users in the UK are managed under the Care Programme Approach when they are at EIP, there may not be capacity for such a robust approach when they are followed up. Care needs to be taken in order to articulate the specific needs of service users, especially those with a poor social recovery outcome and those who live alone. For instance, without a care co-ordinator, the young person may not be able to manage their mail, deal with changes in benefit systems, pre-empt relapse and follow their staying well plan. Similarly, discussion with family members around transition from EIP is essential so that family members do not feel abandoned by mental health services. Handover periods should be planned in proportion to the likely disruption in care.

Particular planning should be given to those young people who develop psychosis in their teenage years and may not be ready for the adult world while still in their early twenties. Similarly, it is likely that those service users who are already in clinical stage 3c or even stage 4 at service intake will need persistent intensive case management (ICM) following discharge from EIP.

Length of critical period and EIP care

Commissioned services need to be clear on the expected length of intervention in specialised teams. Birchwood et al. (1998) originally defined the 'critical period' as lasting between 3–5 years which has now been operationalised in many EIP services, despite concerns that this may be too short for some people (Lutgens et al., 2015) In Chapter 1, it was noted that relapse rates after 24 months of an EIP service intervention can vary between 14 and 66%, with an average of 38% (Fusar-Poli et al., 2017). A review of FEP cases discharged from EIP found 60% relapsed within the 3.5 year follow-up period (Kam, Singh & Upthegrove, 2015). Patients who relapsed following discharge from EIP were most likely to do so within the first year of discharge. The number of relapses occurring during EIP care predicted time to relapse post discharge. Kam et al. (2015) concluded that more emphasis is needed on relapse prevention and early post-discharge monitoring, especially within the first year for those who have experienced previous relapses. This raises the question about the ideal length of the critical period.

Thus, while it is feasible that those in stage 3b or 3c may benefit from extending the critical period with recent evidence of superior outcomes for those who had an additional two or three years of EIP (Malla, Shah & Lal, 2017), this is still not robust (Norman et al., 2017) and further research is required. As Lally et al. (2017) pointed out in their recent meta-analysis of remission and clinical recovery in FEP populations, psychosis is unlikely to be a deteriorating condition for most people. It plateaus relatively early, within the first two years. This should then allow EIP teams to predict and plan for discharge from the beginning, during the early stages of EIP. This will not only help the service user prepare for the future after EIP but also help manage the appropriate distribution of resources to optimise symptomatic, social and personal recovery for everyone (Ahmed, Peters & Chakraborty, 2018).

Learning points

- Although symptomatic, social and personal recovery following an FEP can be viewed and measured separately, they are usually inter-related.
- There are a number of facilitators and barriers for all three types of recovery and understanding and acting on these will be essential for better long-term outcomes.
- An integrated EIP service with a clear operational structure and vision, led by a well-trained and knowledgeable team with a strong value base, is likely to be more effective at achieving symptomatic, social and personal recovery following FEP.
- The team should be multidisciplinary with a recovery focus and sound value base, which is reflected in the operational practice and interactions with young people and their families.
- Care and interventions based on evidence-based knowledge, formulation and service user choice promoting social recovery is the primary aim.
- Initial and sustained engagement through the critical period and EIP care pathway is crucial, as approximately 30% disengage from EIP.
- EIP care co-ordinators play a pivotal role in establishing and sustaining engagement and the delivery of key evidence-based interventions.
- High EIP caseloads have a negative impact on the quality of care for service users and their families, on recovery, and the effectiveness of EIP.
- Using routine outcome measures (ROMs) within EIP can improve the quality of care.
- Formulated care, based on the clinical staging model, can inform interventions to facilitate symptomatic, social, and personal recovery.
- Effective partnerships with other agencies and care providers will ensure that transitions are well managed and that care is consistent during the recovery and discharge pathways.

Conclusion

Recovering from FEP and future challenges for EIP services

EIP has now been widely acknowledged as an effective and acceptable service model, supported by clinical evidence and promoted as the gold standard FEP treatment by the Department of Health in the UK and the WHO. It is popular with service users and families with evidence of lower detention rates for non-BME groups under the MHA, higher employment levels and lower rates of suicide than in generic services (Marwaha, Thompson, Upthegrove & Broome, 2016). Throughout this book we have continually provided up-to-date evidence of how EIP services have revolutionised the treatment of early and first episode psychosis (e.g. Correll, Galling & Pawar, 2018). Although the exact reasons for the success of EIP services are still unclear, some have argued that it is the attitude of staff and the model promoting the delivery of effective specialist psychosocial interventions that appear to be a key ingredient to its success (Brabban & Dodgson, 2010). Others have argued that EIP services have led to the reduction of DUP, and early and sustained treatment throughout the critical period (Cocchi, Meneghelli, Erlicher, Pisano, Cascio & Preti, 2013). We have put forward, throughout this book, the idea that it is the integrated, 'joined-up' nature of EIP, with a clear framework for the delivery of evidence-based interventions which are embedded in a philosophy of care offering hope and recovery, that lies behind its success (Bertolote & McGorry, 2005). Consequently, EIP has become reflective of the quote from Aristotle at the beginning of Chapter 12: 'the whole is more than the sum of its parts'.

Yet despite these triumphs, EIP will need to continually evolve and adapt if it is to further improve the delivery of care for FEP. In many ways we stand at the 'crossroads' of its development, at a time when resources for health care in general, and mental health care provision in particular, are coming under ever greater scrutiny to achieve 'more for less'. Lally et al. (2017) have recently drawn attention to the positive impact that specialist EIP services may have had on remission rates in FEP populations since they started over two decades ago. This has *not* been the case for rates of 'clinical' recovery.

This, with other studies quoted throughout this book, point to the focus of EIP services on short-term, over long-term, outcomes. Sustaining recovery across all three domains (symptomatic, social and personal) must now be seen as a priority. Using a staging framework (McGorry et al., 2006) may help with this as we move towards more stage-specific interventions. However, staging models are only as good as the interventions that can be provided at each stage. We need new medications other than APs, to help deal with the prognostic and recovery impeding effects of negative symptoms and the cognitive deficits that often accompany them (van Os & Kapur, 2009). When we do use APs, we need to use them better, quicker and more effectively to combat poor symptomatic recovery (i.e. earlier use of clozapine; Lally et al., 2016; Fusar-Poli et al., 2017) and ultimately help sustain longer-term recovery. This applies no less to psychosocial treatments, where delays in intensive psychosocial interventions (DIPT) may be as important as delays in medical treatments (DUP) (de Haan, Linszen, Lenior, de Win & Gorsira, 2003). Many of the improvements in psychological and social treatments for psychosis that have been made over the last two decades relate to their refinement and individualisation according to, not only the clinical stage where they are applied, but also the specific recovery needs of that person. This needs to continue with advances in theoretical models, better tailored assessments and interventions that target specific outcomes (e.g. Birchwood et al., 2018; Fowler et al., 2018; Jackson et al., 2009).

Knowledge about the engagement of FEP patients in psychosocial treatments and medical interventions has also been understated. In spite of high engagement rates for EIP compared with generic services (Dodgson, Ross, Tiffin, Mitford & Brabban, 2012), some young people with FEP are still failing to engage with services and outcomes for functional recovery remain poor. Although we know that families, illness beliefs and therapeutic rapport mediate engagement and disengagement from EIP services (Casey et al., 2016; Doyle et al., 2014; Leclerc et al., 2015), with the exception of a few studies (e.g. Tindall, Francey & Hamilton, 2015), we still know little about the *process* of engagement (and disengagement) with EIP clinicians and services. More qualitative research is needed to understand, and therefore optimise, these relationships in order to maximise all forms of long-term recovery.

Many people from BME backgrounds presenting with FEP still continue to experience adverse pathways to care at an unacceptably high rate which is not fully explained by clinical presentation alone (Bhui et al., 2015). This group also suffer from poorer outcomes across a number of recovery domains (Morgan et al., 2017) and much work still needs to be done by EIP services, not only on reducing adverse care pathways for this group (Mann et al., 2014), but also on improving long-term outcomes as well (Singh et al., 2013).

NEET status of BME groups with early psychosis remains high, as it does for the FEP population as a whole, which increases even further upon discharge from EIP services (Kam et al., 2015). Sustained recovery from FEP will not be realised until the national and local socio-economic, as well as the psychological factors that maintain this problem, are understood and acted upon (Jones, Godzikovskaya, Zhao, Vasquez, Gilbert & Davidson, 2017).

Formulations and personalised care plans remain key if EIP is to move into its next era and leave behind the 'one-size-fits-all' philosophy applied to the treatment of psychosis and schizophrenia in too many mental health settings (Power, 2017). Indeed, as we move into an age of personalised medicine (Demjaha, 2018) and 'big data' (Power, 2017), there has never been a better time to use the advances in technology and research methodology to treat people, not as a homogeneous group of FEP patients, but as individuals in their own right, with bespoke plans of care and tailored treatment 'packages'. This will also allow the relevant stakeholders (families, clinicians, managers, researchers, policy-makers, etc.) to recognise that people adapting to early psychosis have their own views about what recovery means to them (Windell, Norman & Mall, 2012) and how it should be ultimately measured and evaluated.

Although we have argued throughout this book that one of the strengths of EIP is its integrated approach to mental health care, one that takes into account the bio-psychosocial factors that underpin the aetiology of psychosis and its course, much more still needs to be done to build on this. Integrated formulations in EIP MDTs will only be effective if the workforce has the right skills and knowledge to use them. One of the welcomed features of the new RTT standards in the UK (NICE, 2016) is the manpower framework it recommends for the implementation of evidence-based interventions within EIP. Not all countries, and therefore not all EIP services, will be lucky enough to have such a template. More research is still needed as to what constitutes the staffing make-up of the 'optimum' EIP team, taking into account the social and geographical context in which they will need to deliver care to their FEP population.

Training and continuing professional development (CPD) remain essential, with regard to not only keeping abreast of new treatments and assessments, but also in equipping staff to deal with the proliferation of co-morbid issues and emotional dysfunction that are now common in EIP services. These not only represent proxy measures of poor psychological adaptation, but can also impede long-term progress and sustained recovery across symptomatic and functional domains.

Of course, all these improvements will require resources and investment. We now know much more about what kind of resources are required in EIP to optimise fidelity to the model (Radhakrishnan et al., 2017). We believe that the economic case has now been cogently made for increased and sustained investment for EIP services in order to save money in the short term (i.e. reducing hospital admissions). However, now is the time to make the case more strongly for the advantages of increases in long-term recovery across the three domains. Increased economic and non-economic activity, and the personal fulfilment of valued roles and goals, will ultimately lead to long-term benefits, not only for that individual and their families, but also for society as a whole. Only then, when joined-up, long-term thinking across government departments (in whatever country) is in place, and they can recognise the advantages of moving the 'goal-posts' from remission-based EIP services to ones that emphasise long-term recovery, will we truly see the investment that is needed.

In the Foreword to this book, Andrew Gordon talked about the 'if only', that it is important in mental health care for young people and their families that we do not accept the 'if only'. Sustaining long-term symptomatic, social and personal recovery following a FEP should now become the goal for the next generation of EIP services so that none of us (clinicians, researchers, managers, commissioners and policy-makers), upon our retirements, need to say 'if only'.

Appendix 1

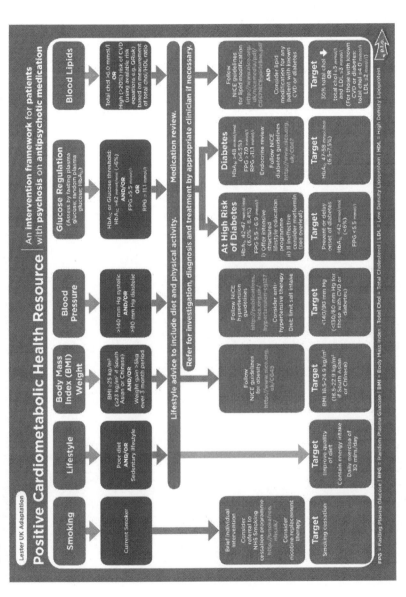

Figure A1.1 Positive Cardiometabolic Health Resource.

Although this clinical resource tool targets antipsychotic medication, many of the principles apply to other psychotropic medicines given to people with long term mental disorders.

The general practitioner and psychiatrist will work together to ensure appropriate monitoring and interventions are provided and communicated. The general practitioner will usually lead on supervising the provision of physical health interventions. The psychiatrist will usually lead on decisions to significantly change antipsychotic medicines.

Primary care's Quality and Outcomes Framework (QOF) includes four physical health indicators in the mental health domain: BMI (MH12); blood pressure (MH13); total to HDL cholesterol ratio (MH14); Blood glucose (MH15). Currently MH14 and MH15 are only for those aged over 40yrs.

History and examination following initiation or change of antipsychotic medication

Frequency: as a minimum review those prescribed a new antipsychotic at baseline and at least once after 3 months.

Ideally weight should be assessed 1-2 weekly in the first 8 weeks of taking a new antipsychotic as rapid early weight gain may predict severe weight gain in the longer term.

Subsequent review should take place annually unless an abnormality of physical health emerges, which should then prompt appropriate action and/or continuing review at least every 3 months.

At review

History: Seek history of substantial weight gain (e.g. 5kg) and particularly where this has been rapid (e.g. within 3 months). Also review smoking, exercise and diet. Ask about family history (diabetes, obesity, CVD) in first degree relatives <60 yrs) and gestational diabetes. Note ethnicity.

Examination: Weight, BMI, BP.

Investigations: Fasting estimates of plasma glucose (FPG), HbA$_{1c}$ and lipids (total cholesterol. LDL, HDL, triglycerides). If fasting samples are impractical then non-fasting samples are satisfactory for most measurements except for LDL or triglycerides.

ECG: include if history of CVD, family history of CVD, or if patient taking certain antipsychotics (see Summary of Product Characteristics) or other drugs known to cause ECG abnormalities (eg erythromycin, tricyclic anti-depressants, anti-arrythmics - see British National Formulary for further information).

interventions

Nutritional counselling: reduce take away and "junk" food, reduce energy intake to prevent weight gain, stop soft drinks and juices, increase fibre intake.

Physical activity: structured education-lifestyle intervention. Advise physical activity e.g. Advise a minimum of 150 minutes of 'moderate intensity' physical activity per week (http://bit.ly/Oe7DeS).

If unsuccessful after 3 months in reaching targets, then consider specific pharmacological interventions (see below).

Specific Pharmacological interventions

Anti-hypertensive therapy: Normally GP supervised. Follow NICE recommendations http://publications.nice.org.uk/hypertension-cg127.

Lipid lowering therapy: Normally GP supervised. Follow NICE recommendations http://www.nice.org.uk/nicemedia/pdf/CG67NICEguideline.pdf.

Treatment of Diabetes: Normally GP supervised. Follow NICE recommendations http://www.nice.org.uk/CG87.

Treatment of those at high risk of diabetes: FPG 5.5-6.9 mmol/L; HbA$_{1c}$ 42-47 mmol/mol (6.0-6.4%) Follow NICE guideline PH 38 *Preventing type 2 diabetes: risk identification and interventions for individuals at high risk* (recommendation 19) - http://guidance.nice.org.uk/PH38.

• Where intensive lifestyle intervention has failed **consider metformin trial** (this would normally be GP supervised).

• Please be advised that **off-label** use requires documented informed consent as described in the GMC guidelines. http://www.gmc-uk.org/static/documents/content/Good_Practice_in_Prescribing_Medicines_0911.pdf. These GMC guidelines are recommended by the MPS and MDU, and the use of metformin in this context has been agreed as a relevant example by the Defence Unions.

• Adhere to British National Formulary guidance on safe use (in particular ensure renal function is adequate). Start with a low dose e.g 500 mg once daily and build up, as tolerated, to 1500-2000 mg daily.

Review of antipsychotic medication: Normally psychiatrist supervised. Should be a priority if there is:

• Rapid weight gain (e.g. 5kg <3 months) following antipsychotic initiation.

• Rapid development (<3 months) of abnormal lipids, BP, or glucose.

The psychiatrist should consider whether the antipsychotic drug regimen has played a causative role in these abnormalities and, if so, whether an alternative regimen could be expected to offer less adverse effect:

• As a first step prescribed dosages should follow BNF recommendations; rationalise any polypharmacy.

• Changing antipsychotic requires careful clinical judgment to weigh benefits against risk of relapse of the psychosis.

• Benefit from changing antipsychotic for those on the drug for a long time (>1 year) is likely to be minimal.

• If clinical judgment and patient preference support continuing with the same treatment then ensure appropriate further monitoring and clinical considerations.

Don't just SCREEN – INTERVENE
for all patients in the "red zone"

RC PSYCH

Royal College of Physicians

RCGP Royal College of General Practitioners

Royal College of Nursing

DIABETES UK CARE. CONNECT. CAMPAIGN.

NHS CQC

HQIP

Download Lester UK Adaptation: www.rcpsych.ac.uk/quality/NAS/resources

Adapted for use by the RCGP/RCPsych. With permission from Curtis J, Newall H, Samaras K.© HETI 2011

Figure A1.1 Continued

Appendix 2

Table A2.1 Assessment measures for recovery following FEP

Recovery domain	Measure	Assesses	Type	Reference
Symptomatic	PANSS	Severity of 7 positive and negative symptoms	CROM	Kay et al., 1987
Symptomatic	PSYRATS	Dimensions of hallucinations and delusions	CROM PROM	Haddocks et al., 1995
Symptomatic	BPAS	Severity of 4 positive and negative symptoms	CROM	
Symptomatic	SAPS	Hallucinations, delusions, bizarre behaviour, thought content	CROM	Andreasen, 1985
Symptomatic	SANS	Affective flattening, alogia, avolition, anhendonia, inatttention	CROM	Andreasent,1984
Symptomatic	Negative Symptom Assessment Scale (NSA-4)	Reduced speech quality, range of motion, social drive, and intent	CROM	Alphs, 2010
Symptomatic	SEPS	Positive and Negative impact of experiences, support, and dimensions of psychosis	PROM	Haddock et al., 2010
Symptomatic	Choice of Outcome In CBT for PsychosEs; for psychosis (CHOICE)	Severity of psychotic experiences and satisfaction with therapy	PROM	Greenwood et al., 2010
Symptomatic	Peters Delusional Inventory	Distress, preoccupation, conviction of different beliefs	PROM	Peters et al., 1999
Symptomatic	Paranoia Checklist	Frequency, conviction, distress of paranoid beliefs	PROM	Freeman et al., 2006

continued

Table A2.1 Continued

Recovery domain	Measure	Assesses	Type	Reference
Symptomatic	Beliefs about Voices Questionnaire Revised (BAVQ-R)	Perceived power, engagement, and resistance	PROM	Chadwick et al., 2000
Social	PAS	Pre morbid social and school functioning	CROM	Cannon-Spoor et al., 1982
Social	GAF	Global functioning. Split version measures functional disability (GAF:D) separately to symptoms	CROM	Hall, 1995; Aas, 2010
Social	SOFAS	Social and occupational functioning	CROM	Goldman et al., 1992
Social	PSP	Changes in social functioning sensitive to symptoms	CROM	Morosini et al., 2000
Social	GFS	Quality and quantity of relationships	CROM	Cornblatt, 2011
Social	GFR	Performance level and support required in primary role	CROM	Cornblatt, 2011
Social	TUS	Time spent in constructive economic and structured social activity	PROM	adapted by Short 2006
Social	SFS	Social functioning across 5 domains	PROM	Birchwood et al., 1990
Social	WASAS	Impact of mental health difficulties on ability to carry out activity across 5 domains	PROM	Mundt et al. 2002
Social	FESFS	Performance and frequency of youth focussed behaviour across multiple domains of social functioning	PROM	Lecomte et al., 2014

Category	Measure	Description	Type	Citation
Personal	QPR	Process of Recovery Measure	PROM	Williams et al., 2015
Personal	DIALOG	Quality of Life and Treatment Satisfaction	PROM	Priebe et al., 2007
Personal	GOALS	Progress on goals identified by patient	PROM	Law and Jacob, 2015
Personal	Recovery Star	Progress across 12 domains	PROM	Dickins et al., 2012
Personal	Calgary Depression Scale (CDS)	Observed Depression	CROM	Addington et al., 1993
Personal	Beck Depression Scale-II (BDI-II)	Self-reported Depression	PROM	Beck et al., 1996
Personal	Beck Anxiety Inventory (BAI)	Self-reported anxiety	PROM	Beck & Steer, 1990
Personal	Y-BOCI	Obsessions and Compulsions	PROM	Goodman et al., 1989
Personal	IES-R	Intrusions, avoidance, and hyperarousal	PROM	Weiss & Marmar, 1997
Personal	Trauma Experiences Checklist	Interpersonal abuse and family stress, violence, death, and legal involvement	PROM	Cristofaro et al., 2013
Personal	PBIQ-R	Loss, shame, control, group fit, and entrapment	PROM	Birchwood et al., 2012
Personal	ERQ	Re-appraisal and Suppression	PROM	Gross & John, 2003
Personal	FFSC	Self-Criticism and Re-assurance	PROM	Gilbert et al., 2004
Recovery	HoNOS	Behavioural, Impairment, Symptoms, Social	CROM	Wing et al., 1996
Personal	RAS	Five aspects of recovery from consumer's perspective: confidence, help-seeking, goal orientation, reliance, lack of domination by symptoms	PREM	Giffort et al., 1995

continued

Table A2.1 Continued

Recovery domain	Measure	Assesses	Type	Reference
Personal	STORI	5 stages of personal recovery: moratorium, awareness, preparation, rebuilding, growth	PREM	Andresen et al., 2006
Personal	RPI	Anguish, connectedness, confidence, other's care/help, hope/cares for self	PREM	Jerrell et al., 2006
Personal	IMR	Aspects of illness management & recovery: Client/clinician versions	PROM CROM	Mueser et al., 2005
Personal	INSPIRE	Consumer experiences of support received from services	PREM	Williams et al., 2015
Personal	EWPSS	Visual analogue scale measuring sense of empowerment in relation to symptoms of psychosis	PROM	Martins et al., 2017
Personal	RSQ	'Integrated' or 'sealing over' recovery style (see also PROM version; Drayton et al., 1998)	CROM	McGlashan 1987

Notes

1 CROM = Clinician Reported Outcome Measure; PROM = Patient Reported Outcome Measure; PREM=Patient Rated Experience Measure.

2 PANSS = Positive and Negative Syndrome Scale; PSYRATS = Positive Symptoms Rating Scale; SAPS = Scale Assessment of Positive Symptoms & SANS = Scale Assessment of Negative Symptoms; BPNS = Brief Positive and Negative Rating Scale; SEPS = Subjective Experiences Psychosis Scale; PAS = Premorbid Adjustment Scale; GAF=Global Assessment of Functioning Scale; SOFAS = Social and Occupational Functioning Assessment Scale; PSP = Personal and Social Performance Scale; GFS = Global Functioning Scale: Social; GFR = Global Functioning Scale: Role; TUS; Time Use Survey; SFS = Social Functioning Scale; WASAS =Work & Social Adjustment Scale; FESFS = First Episode Social Functioning Scale; Y-BOCI = Yale Brown Obsessive Compulsive Inventory; PBIQ-R = Personal Beliefs about Illness Questionnaire; ERQ = Emotional Regulation Questionnaire; FFSC = Forms and Functions of Self-Criticism; RAS=Recovery Assessment Scale; STOR=Stages of Recovery Instrument; RPI=Recovery Process Inventory; IMR=Illness Management and Recovery Scales; INSPIRE=.

3 Some measures are focused on distress (e.g. Beck scale) and measure symptoms of depressions and anxiety but in keeping with the structure of the book we have categorised them here under the personal recovery domain (see chapter 8).

* Recovery = Measures different domains of recovery.

References

Aas, I. M. (2010) Global Assessment of Functioning (GAF): properties and frontier of current knowledge. *Annals of General Psychiatry, 9*, pp. 2095–2101. doi: 10.3371/CSRP.5.2.6.

Aas, M., Andreassen, O. A., Aminoff, S. R., Færden, A., Romm, K. L., Nesvåg, R., et al. (2016) A history of childhood trauma is associated with slower improvement rates: Findings from a one-year follow-up study of patients with a FEP. *BMC Psychiatry, 16*(1). doi: 10.1186/s12888-016-0827-4.

Abba, N., Chadwick, P. & Stevenson, C. (2008) Responding mindfully to distressing psychosis: A grounded theory analysis. *Psychotherapy Research, 18*(1), 77–87.

Achim, A. M., Maziade, M., Raymond, R., Olivier, D., Merette, C. & Roy, M.-A. (2011) How prevalent are anxiety disorders in schizophrenia? A meta-analysis and critical review on a significant association. *Schizophrenia Bulletin, 37*, 811–821. doi: 10.1093/schbul/sbsp148.

Adamson, V., Barrass, E., McConville, S., Irikok, C., Taylor, K., Pitt, S., et al. (2018) Implementing the access and waiting time standard for early intervention in psychosis in the United Kingdom: An evaluation of referrals and post-assessment outcomes over the first year of operation. *Early Intervention in Psychiatry, 26*. doi: 10.1111/eip.12548.

Addington, D., Addington, J. & Maticka-Tyndale, E. (1993) Assessing depression in schizophrenia: The Calgary Depression Scale. *British Journal of Psychiatry, 162*, 39–44.

Addington, D., Addington, J., Maticka-Tyndale, E. & Joyce, J. (1992) Reliability and validity of a depression rating scale for schizophrenics. *Schizophrenia Research, 6*(3), 201–208.

Addington, D., Norman, R., Bond, G., Sale, T., Melton, R., McKenzie, E. & Wang, J. (2016) Development and testing of the First-Episode Psychosis Services Fidelity Scale. *Psychiatric Services, 67*(9), 1023–1025. doi: 10.1176/appi.ps.201500398.

Addington, J. & Addington, D. (2008) Symptom remission in first episode patients. *Schizophrenia Research, 106*(2–3), 281–285. doi: 10.1016/j.schres.2008.09.014.

Addington, J., Collins, A., McCleery, A. & Addington, D. (2005) The role of family work in early psychosis. *Schizophrenia Research, 79*(1), 77–83. doi: 10.1016/j.schres.2005.01.013.

Addington, J., Collins, A., McCleery, A. & Baker, S. (2009) A model of family work in first-episode psychosis: managing self-harm. In F. Lobban & C. Barrowclough, *A Casebook of Family Interventions for Psychosis* (pp. 47–66). Chichester, Wiley.

Addington, J., Williams, J., Young, J. & Addington, D. (2004) Suicidal behaviour in early psychosis. *Acta Psychiatrica Scandinavica, 109*(2), 116–120.

Addington, J., Young, J. & Addington, D. (2003) Social outcome in early psychosis. *Psychological Medicine, 33*, 1119.

Agid, O., Kapur, S., Arenovich, T. & Zipursky, R. (2003) Delayed onset hypothesis of antipsychotic action: A hypothesis tested and rejected. *Schizophrenia Research, 60*(1), 309. doi: 10.1016/s0920-9964(03)80242-6.

Agid, O., Remington, G., Kapur, S., Arenovich, T. & Zipursky, R. (2007) Early use of clozapine for poorly responding first-episode psychosis. *Journal of Clinical Psychopharmacology, 27*(4), 369–373. doi: 10.1097/jcp.0b013e3180d0a6d4.

Ahlem, H., Zgueb, Y., Ouali, U., Laajili, Y., Alaya, S., Jomli, R., et al. (2017) Family burden in caregivers of schizophrenia patients. *European Psychiatry, 41*, 799–800. doi: 10.1016/j.eurpsy.2017.01.1541.

Ahmed, S., Peters, K. Z. & Chakraborty, N. (2018) Discharges from an early intervention in psychosis service: The effect of patient characteristics on discharge destination. *BJPsych Open, 4*(5): 368–374. doi: 10.1111/eip.12552.

Alaghband-Rad, J, Boroumand, M, Amini, H, Sharifi, V, Omid, A, Davari-Ashtiani, R, et al. (2006) Non-affective acute remitting psychosis: a preliminary report from Iran. *Acta Psychiatrica Scandinavica, 113*(2), 96–101.

Albert, N., Bertelsen, M., Thorup, A., Petersen, L., Jeppesen, P., Le Quack, P., et al. (2011) Predictors of recovery from psychosis: analyses of clinical and social factors associated with recovery among patients with first-episode psychosis after 5 years. *Schizophrenia Research, 125*, 257–266.

Aldao, A., Nolen-Hoeksema, S. & Schweizer, S. (2011) Emotional-regulation strategies across psychopathology: A meta-analytic review. *Clinical Psychology Review, 30*, 217–237.

Allan, S. (2017) Early intervention in first episode psychosis: A service user's experience. *Schizophrenia Bulletin, 43*(2), 234–235. doi: 10.1093/schbul/sbv227.

Allen, P., Larøi, F., McGuire, P. & Aleman, A. (2008) The hallucinating brain: A review of structural and functional neuroimaging studies of hallucinations. *Neuroscience & Biobehavioral Reviews, 32*(1), 175–191. doi: 10.1016/j.neubiorev.2007.07.012.

Allerby, K., Sameby, B., Brain, C., Joas, E., Quinlan, P., Sjöström, N., et al. (2015) Stigma and burden among relatives of persons with schizophrenia: Results from the Swedish COAST study. *Psychiatric Services, 66*(10), 1020–1026. doi: 10.1176/appi.ps.201400405.

Allott, K., Liu, P., Proffitt, T. M. & Killackey, E. (2011) Cognition at illness onset as a predictor of later functional outcome in early psychosis: Systematic review and methodological critique. *Schizophrenia Research, 125*, 221–235.

Álvarez-Jiménez, M., Alcazar-Corcoles, M. A., González-Blanch, C., Bendall, S., McGorry, P. D. & Gleeson, J. F. (2014) Online, social media and mobile technologies for psychosis treatment: A systematic review on novel user-led interventions. *Schizophrenia Research, 156*(1), 96–106.

Álvarez-Jiménez, M., Bendall, S., Lederman, R., Wadley, G., Chinnery, G., Vargas, S., et al. (2013) On the HORYZON: moderated online social therapy for long-term recovery in first episode psychosis. *Schizophrenia Research, 143*, 143–149.

Álvarez-Jiménez, M., Gleeson, J., Bendall, S., Lederman, R., Wadley, G., Killackey, E., et al. (2012a) Internet-based interventions for psychosis: A sneak-peek into the future. *Psychiatric Clinics, 35*(3), 735–747.

Álvarez-Jiménez, M., Gleeson, J. F., Henry, L. P., Harrigan, S. M., Harris, M. G., Killackey, E., et al. (2012b) Road to full recovery: Longitudinal relationship between symptomatic remission and psychosocial recovery in first-episode psychosis over 7.5 years. *Psychological Medicine, 42*, 595–606.

Álvarez-Jiménez, M., Gleeson, J. F., Henry, L. P., Harrigan, S. M., Harris, M. G., Amminger, G. P., et al. (2010) Prediction of a single psychotic episode: A 7.5 year prospective study in FEP. *Schizophrenia Research.* doi: 10.1016/j.schres.2010.10.020.

Álvarez-Jiménez, M., Hetrick, S., González-Blanch, C., Gleeson, J. & McGorry, P. (2008) Non-pharmacological management of antipsychotic-induced weight gain: systematic review and meta-analysis of randomised controlled trials. *The British Journal of Psychiatry, 193*(2), 101–107. doi: 10.1192/bjp.bp.107.042853.

Álvarez-Jiménez, M., O'Donoghue, B., Thompson, A., Gleeson, J., Bendall, S. & González-Blanch, C., et al. (2016) Beyond clinical remission in first episode psychosis: Thoughts on antipsychotic maintenance vs. guided discontinuation in the functional recovery era. *CNS Drugs, 30*(5), 357–368. doi: 10.1007/s40263-016-0331-x.

Álvarez-Jiménez, M., Parker, A. G., Hetrick, S. E., et al. (2011) Preventing the second episode: a systematic review and meta-analysis of psychosocial and pharmacological trials in first episode psychosis. *Schizophrenia Bulletin, 37*, 619–630.

Álvarez-Jiménez, M., Priede, A., Hatrick, S. E., Bendall, S., Killackey, E., Parker, A. G., et al. (2012c) Risk factor relapse following treatment for first episode psychosis: a systematic review and meta-analysis of longitudinal studies. *Schizophrenia Research, 139*, 116–128.

Alves, F., Figee, M., van Amelsvoort, T., Veltman, D. & de Haan, L. (2008) The revised dopamine hypothesis of schizophrenia: evidence from pharmacological MRI studies with atypical antipsychotic medication. *Schizophrenia Research, 102*(1–3), 96–97. doi: 10.1016/s0920-9964(08)70291-3.

American Psychiatric Association. (2000) *Diagnostic and statistical manual of mental disorders* (4th edn). Washington, DC: American Psychiatric Association.

American Psychiatric Association. (2013) *Diagnostic and statistical manual of mental disorders* (5th edn). Washington, DC: American Psychiatric Association.

American Psychological Association. (2014) *The road to resilience.* Retrieved from www.apa.org/helpcenter/road-resilience.aspx.

Anderson, K., Flora, N. & McKenzie, K. (2014) A meta-analysis of ethnic differences in pathways to care at the first episode of psychosis. *Acta Psychiatrica Scandinavica, 130*(4), 257–268.

Anderson, K. K., Norman, R., MacDougall, A., Edwards, J., Palaniyappan, L., Lau, C. & Kurdyak, P. (2018) Effectiveness of early psychosis intervention: Comparison of service users and nonusers in population-based health administrative data. *The American Journal of Psychiatry, 175*(5), 443–452. doi: 10.1176/appi.ajp.2017.17050480.

Anderson-Clarke, L. & Warner, B. (2016) Exploring recovery perspectives in individuals diagnosed with mental illness. *Occupational Therapy in Mental Health, 32*(4), 400–418.

Andreasen, N., Carpenter, W., Kane, J., Lasser, R., Marder, S. & Weinberger, D. (2005) Remission in schizophrenia: Proposed criteria and rationale for consensus. *The American Journal of Psychiatry, 162*(3), 441–449. doi: 10.1176/appi.ajp.162.3.441.

Andresen, R., Caputi, P. & Oades, L. (2006) Stages of recovery instrument: development of a measure of recovery from serious mental illness. *Australian and New Zealand Journal of Psychiatry, 40*(11–12), 972–980.

Andresen, R., Oades, L. & Caputi, P. (2003) The experience of recovery from schizophrenia: towards an empirically validated stage model. *Australian and New Zealand Journal of Psychiatry, 37*(5), 86–94.

Andrews, B. & Hunter, E. (1997) Shame, early abuse and course of depression in a clinical sample: A preliminary study. *Cognition & Emotion, 11*, 373–381. doi: 10.1080/026999397379845.

Andriessen, K. (2009) Can postvention be prevention? *Crisis, 30*(1), 43–47.

Aneesh, T., Sonal Sekar, M., Jose, A., Chandran, L. & Zachariaha, S. (2009) Pharmacogenomics: The right drug to the right person. *Journal of Clinical Medicine Research*, doi: 10.4021/jocmr2009.08.1255.

Anthony, W. (1993) Recovery from mental illness: The guiding vision of the mental health service system in the 1990s. *Psychosocial Rehabilitation Journal, 16*(4), pp. 11–23. doi: 10.1037/h0095655.

Arranz, B., Garriga, M., García-Rizo, C. & San, L. (2017). Clozapine use in patients with schizophrenia and a comorbid substance use disorder: A systematic review. *European Neuropsychopharmacology*. http://dx.doi.org/10.1016/j.euroneuro.2017.12.006

Arseneault, L. (2002). Cannabis use in adolescence and risk for adult psychosis: longitudinal prospective study. *BMJ, 325*(7374), 1212–1213. http://dx.doi.org/10.1136/bmj.325.7374.1212.

Ashcroft, K., Barrow, E., Lee, R. & MacKinnon, K. (2012) Mindfulness groups for early psychosis: A qualitative study. *Psychology and Psychotherapy, 85*(3), 327–334.

Attard, A. & Larkin, M. (2016) Art therapy for people with psychosis: A narrative review of the literature. *Lancet Psychiatry, 3*(11), 1067–1078.

Attard, A., Larkin, M., Boden, Z. & Jackson, C. (2017) Understanding adaptation to first episode psychosis through the creation of images. *Journal of Psychosocial Rehabilitation and Mental Health, 4*(1), 73–88. doi: https://doi.org/10.1007/s40737-017-0079-8.

Aust, T. & Bradshaw, T. (2017) Mindfulness interventions for psychosis: a systematic review of the literature. *Journal Psychosomatic and Mental Health Nursing, 24*(1), doi: org/10.111/jpm.12357.

Austin, S. F., Mors, O., Budtz-Jørgensen, E., Secher, R. G., Hjorthøj, C. R., Bertelsen, M., et al. (2015) Long term trajectories of positive and negative symptoms in first episode psychosis: a 10 year follow up study in the OPUS cohort. *Schizophrenia Research, 168*(1–2), 84–91.

Austin, S. F., Mors, O., Secher, R. G., Hjorthøj, C. R., Albert, N., Bertelsen, M., et al. (2013) Predictors of recovery in first episode psychosis: the OPUS cohort at 10 year follow-up. *Schizophrenia Research, 150*, 163–168.

Aydin, C., Tibbo, P. & Ursuliak, Z. (2016). Psychosocial interventions in reducing cannabis use in early phase psychosis. *The Canadian Journal of Psychiatry, 61*(6), 367–372. http://dx.doi.org/10.1177/0706743716639931.

Ayer, D. W., Jayathilake, K. & Meltzer, H. Y. (2008) The InterSePT suicide scale for prediction of imminent suicidal behaviors. *Psychiatry Research, 161*(1), 87–96. doi: 10.1016/j.psychres.2007.07.029.

Ayesa-Arriola, R., Alcaraz, E. G., Hernández, B. V., Pérez-Iglesias, R., López Moríñigo, J. D. L., Duta, R., et al. (2015) Suicidal behaviour in first-episode non-affective psychosis: Specific risk periods and stage-related factors. *European Neuropsychopharmacology, 25*(12), 2278–2288. doi: 10.1016/j.euroneuro.2015.09.008.

Ayesa-Arriola, R., Rodríguez-Sánchez, J. M., Pérez-Iglesias, R., González-Blanch, C., Pardo-García, G., Tabares-Seisdedos, R., et al. (2013) The relevance of cognitive, clinical and premorbid variables in predicting functional outcome for individuals with first-episode psychosis: A 3 year longitudinal study. *Psychiatry Research, 209*, 302–308.

Bach, P. & Hayes, S. (2002) The use of Acceptance and Commitment Therapy to prevent the rehospitalization of psychotic patients: A randomized controlled trial. *Journal of Consulting and Clinical Psychology, 70*, 1129–1139.

Bach, P. & Moran, D. (2008) *ACT in practice: Case conceptualization in Acceptance and Commitment Therapy*. Oakland, CA: New Harbinger.

Back, D. B. (2013) Understanding the suicidal mind: An ecological investigation of the differential activation hypothesis of suicidal relapse in first episode psychosis. Unpublished doctoral dissertation. University of Birmingham, UK.

Bademli, K. & Duman, Z. (2014) Effects of a family-to-family support program on the mental health and coping strategies of caregivers of adults with mental illness: A randomized controlled study. *Archives of Psychiatric Nursing, 28*(6), 392–398. doi: 10.1016/j.apnu.2014.08.011.

Baggott, E. (2010) Recovery from first-episode psychosis and the role for services beyond first-episode detection. Doctoral thesis, University of Warwick.

Bahorik, A. & Eack, S. (2010). Examining the course and outcome of individuals diagnosed with schizophrenia and comorbid borderline personality disorder. *Schizophrenia Research, 124*(1–3), 29–35. http://dx.doi.org/10.1016/j.schres.2010.09.005.

Bailey, T., Álvarez-Jiménez, M., Garcia-Sanchez, A. M., Hulbert, C., Barlow, E., Bendall, S. (2018) Childhood trauma is associated with severity of hallucinations and delusions in psychotic disorders: A systematic review and meta-analysis. *Schizophrenia Bulletin, 44*(5), 1111–1122, doi: https://doi.org/10.1093/schbul/sbx161.

Baker, S. & Martens, L. (2010) *Promoting recovery from first episode psychosis*. Toronto, ON: Centre for Addiction and Mental Health/Centre de toxicomanie et de santé mentale.

Bakst, S., Rabinowitz, J., Bromet, E. J. (2010) Is poor premorbid functioning a risk factor for suicide attempts in first admission psychosis? *Schizophrenia Research, 116*(2–3), 210–216.

Barlati, S., De Peri, L., Deste, G., Fusar-Poli, P. & Vita, A. (2012) Cognitive remediation in the early course of schizophrenia: A critical review. *Current Pharmaceutical Design, 18*, 534–541.

Barnes, T. (2011) Evidence-based guidelines for the pharmacological treatment of schizophrenia: recommendations from the British Association for Psychopharmacology. *Journal of Psychopharmacology, 25*(5), 567–620. doi: 10.1177/0269881110391123.

Barnes, T., Leeson, V. C., Mutsatsa, S. H., Watt, H. C., Hutton, S. B. & Joyce, E. M. (2008). Duration of untreated psychosis and social function: 1-year follow-up study of first-episode schizophrenia. *The British Journal of Psychiatry, 193*(3), 203–209.

Barnes, T. & Paton, C. (2011) Do antidepressants improve negative symptoms in schizophrenia? *British Medical Journal, 342*, 3371. doi: 10.1136/bmj.d3371.

Baron-Cohen, S. (2002). Is Asperger syndrome necessarily viewed as a disability? *Focus on Autism and Other Developmental Disabilities, 17*(3), 186–191. http://dx.doi.org/10.1177/10883576020170030801.

Barr, K., Ormrod, J. & Dudley, R. (2015) An exploration of what service users value about early intervention in psychosis services. *Psychology and Psychotherapy: Theory, Research and Practice, 88*, 468–480. doi: 10.1111/papt.12051.

Barrett, E., Mork, E., Færden, A., Nesvåg, R., Agartz, I., Andreassen, O. A., et al. (2015) The development of insight and its relationship with suicidality over one year follow-up in patients with first episode psychosis. *Schizophrenia Research, 162*(1), 97–102.

Barrett, E., Sundet, K., Faerden, A., Nesvåg, R., Agartz, I., Fosse, R., et al. (2010) Suicidality before and in the early phases of first episode psychosis. *Schizophrenia Research, 119*(1–3), 11–17. doi: 10.1016/j.schres.2010.03.022.

Barton, G. R., Hodgekins, J., Mugford, M., Jones, P. B., Croudace, T. & Fowler, D. (2009) Cognitive behaviour therapy for improving SR in psychosis: cost-effectiveness analysis. *Schizophrenia Research, 112*, 158–163.

Barton, K. & Jackson, C. (2008) Reducing symptoms of trauma among carers of people with psychosis: Pilot study examining the impact of writing about caregiving experiences. *Australian and New Zealand Journal of Psychiatry, 42*(8), 693–701. doi: 10.1080/00048670802203434.

Baumeister, R. F. & Leary, M. R. (1995) The need to belong: Desire for interpersonal attachments as a fundamental human motivation. *Psychological Bulletin, 117*, 497–529. doi: 10.1037/0033-2909.117.3.497.

Baumel, A., Correll, C. & Birnbaum, M. (2016) Adaptation of a peer based online emotional support program as an adjunct to treatment for people with schizophrenia-spectrum disorders. *Internet Interventions, 4*(1), 35–42.

Bays, H., Chapman, R. & Grandy, S. (2007) The relationship of body mass index to diabetes mellitus, hypertension and dyslipidaemia: comparison of data from two national surveys. *International Journal of Clinical Practice, 61*(5), 737–747. doi: 10.1111/j.1742-1241.2007.01336.x.

Beach, S., Kostis, W., Celano, C., Januzzi, J., Ruskin, J., Noseworthy, P., et al. (2014) Meta-analysis of selective serotonin reuptake inhibitor–associated QTC prolongation. *The Journal of Clinical Psychiatry, 75*(05), 441–449. doi: 10.4088/jcp.13r08672.

Beavan, V., Read, J. & Cartwright, C. (2011). The prevalence of voice-hearers in the general population: A literature review. *Journal of Mental Health, 20*(3), 281–292. http://dx.doi.org/10.3109/09638237.2011.562262.

Beazley, P. (2011) The Recovery Star: is it a valid tool? *The Psychiatrist, 35*(5), 196–197.

Beck, A. T., Brown, G. K., Steer, R. A., Dahlsgaard, K. K. & Grisham, J. R. (1999) Suicide ideation at its worst point: A predictor of eventual suicide in psychiatric outpatients. *Suicide & Life-threatening Behaviour, 29*(1), 1–9 doi: 10.1111/j.1943-278X.1999.tb00758.x.

Beck, A. T., Rush, A. J., Shaw, B. F. & Emery, G. (1979) *Cognitive therapy of depression.* New York: Guilford Press.

Beck, A. T. & Steer, R. A. (1990) *Manual for the Beck Anxiety Inventory.* San Antonio, TX: Psychological Corporation.

Beck, A. T., Steer, R. A. & Brown, G. B. (1996) *Manual for the Beck Depression Inventory-II.* San Antonio, TX: Psychological Corporation.

Bell, M. D., Choi, K. H., Dyer, C. & Wexler, B. E. (2014) Benefits of cognitive remediation and supported employment for schizophrenia patients with poor community functioning. *Psychiatric Services, 65*(4), 469–475.

Bellack, A. S. (2006) Scientific and consumer models of recovery in schizophrenia: concordance, contrasts, and implications. *Schizophrenia Bulletin, 32*(3), 432–442.

Bellack, A. S., Mueser, K. T., Gingerich, S. & Agresta, J. (2013) *Social skills training for schizophrenia: A step-by-step guide.* New York: Guilford Publications.

Bellamy, C., Jarrett, N., Mowbray, O., MacFarlane, P., Mowbray, C. & Holter, M. (2007) Relevance of spirituality for people with mental illness attending consumer-centred services. *Psychiatric Rehabilitation Journal, 30*(4), 287–294.

Bendall, S., Álvarez-Jiménez, M., Hulbert, C. A., McGorry, P. & Jackson, H. (2012) Childhood trauma increases the risk of post-traumatic stress disorder in response to FEP. *Australian and New Zealand Journal of Psychiatry, 46*, 35–39. doi: 10.1177/0004867411430877.

Benjamin, J. (2018) *The stranger on the bridge*. London: Palgrave Macmillan.

Bentall, R. P. (2009) *Doctoring the mind: Why psychiatric treatments fail*. London, Allan Lane.

Bernard, M., Jackson, C., Birchwood, M. (2015) Cognitive behaviour therapy for emotional dysfunction following psychosis: The role of emotional (dys)regulation. In A. Meaden & A. Fox (eds) *Innovations in psychosocial interventions for psychosis: Working with the hard to reach*. Hove: Routledge.

Bernstein, D. P., Fink, L., Handelsman, L., Foote, J., Lovejoy, M., Sapareto, E., et al. (1994) Initial reliability and validity of a new retrospective measure of child abuse and neglect. *The American Journal of Psychiatry, 151*(8), 1132. doi: 10.1176/ajp.151.8.1132.

Berry, C. & Greenwood, K. (2015) Hope-inspiring therapeutic relationships, professional expectations and social inclusion for young people with psychosis. *Schizophrenia Research, 168*, 153–160.

Berry, C. & Hayward, M. (2011) What can qualitative research tell us about service user perspectives of CBT for psychosis? A synthesis of current evidence. *Behavioural and Cognitive Psychotherapy, 39*(4), 487–494.

Berry, K., Barrowclough, C. & Haddock, G. (2011) The role of expressed emotion in relationships between psychiatric staff and people with a diagnosis of psychosis: a review of the literature. *Schizophrenia Bulletin, 37*, 958–972.

Berry, K., Barrowclough, C. & Wearden, A. (2009) A pilot study investigating the use of psychological formulations to modify psychiatric staff perceptions of service users with psychosis. *Behavioural and Cognitive Psychotherapy, 37*, 39–48.

Berry, K., Ford, S., Jellicoe-Jones, L. & Haddock, G. (2013) PTSD symptoms associated with the experiences of psychosis and hospitalisation: A review of the literature. *Clinical Psychology Review, 33*(4), 526–538. doi: 10.1016/j.cpr2013.01.011.

Bertelli, M., Piva Merli, M., Bradley, E., Keller, R., Varrucciu, N., Del Furia, C. & Panocchia, N. (2015). The diagnostic boundary between autism spectrum disorder, intellectual developmental disorder and schizophrenia spectrum disorders. *Advances In Mental Health And Intellectual Disabilities, 9*(5), 243–264. http://dx.doi.org/10.1108/amhid-05-2015-0024.

Bertelsen, M., Jeppesen, P., Petersen, L., Thorup, A., Ohlenschlaeger, J., le Quach, P. et al. (2007) Suicidal behaviour and mortality in first episode psychosis: the OPUS trial. *The British Journal of Psychiatry. Supplement, 51*, 140–146.

Bertolote, J., and McGorry, P. (2005) Early intervention and recovery for young people with early psychosis: Consensus statement. *The British Journal of Psychiatry Supplement, 48*, 116–119.

Bhui, K. & Bhugra, D. (2002) Mental Illness in Black and Asian ethnic minorities: pathways to care and outcomes. *Advances in Psychiatric Treatment, 8*, 26–33.

Bhui, K. & McKenzie, K. (2008) Rates and risk factors by ethnic group for suicides within a year of contact with mental health services in England and Wales. *Psychiatric Services, 59*(4), 414–420. doi: 10.1176/appi.ps.59.4.414.

Bhui, K., Ullrich, S., Kallis, C. & Coid, J. W. (2015) Criminal justice pathways to psychiatric care for psychosis. *The British Journal of Psychiatry, 207*(6), 523–529, doi: 10.1192/bjp.bp.114.153882.

Bighelli, I., Salanti, G., Huhn, M., Schneider-Thoma, J., Krause, M., Reitmeir, C., et al. (2018) Psychological interventions to reduce positive symptoms in schizophrenia: systematic review and network meta-analysis. *World Psychiatry, 17*, 316–329. doi: 10.1002/wps.20577.

Birchwood, M. (2003) Pathways to emotional dysfunction following psychosis in first episode psychosis. *British Journal of Psychiatry, 182*, 373–375.

Birchwood, M., Cassidy, P., Brunet, K., Gilbert, P., Iqbal, Z. & Jackson, C. (2007) Social anxiety and the shame of psychosis: a study in first episode psychosis. *Behaviour Research and Therapy, 45*, 1025–1037.

Birchwood, M., Connor, C., Lester, H., Patterson, P., Freemantle, N., Marshall, M., et al. (2013) Reducing duration of untreated psychosis: Care pathways to early intervention in psychosis services. *The British Journal of Psychiatry, 203*(1), 58–64. doi: 10.1192/bjp.bp.112.125500.

Birchwood, M., Dunn, G., Meaden, A., Tarrier, N., Wykes, T., Davies, L., et al. (2018) The COMMAND trial of cognitive therapy to prevent harmful compliance with command hallucinations: Predictors of outcome and mediators of change. *Psychological Medicine, 48*, 1966–1974. doi: https:doi//.org/10.1017/S0033291717003488.

Birchwood, M., Iqbal., Z., Chadwick, P. & Trower, P. (2000) Cognitive approach to depression and suicidal thinking in psychosis I: Ontogeny of post-psychotic depression. *British Journal of Psychiatry, 177*, 516–521. doi: 10.1192/bjp.177.6.522.

Birchwood, M. & Jackson, C. (2001) *Schizophrenia.* Hove: Psychology Press.

Birchwood, M., Jackson, C., Brunet, K., Holden, J. & Barton, K. (2012) Personal beliefs about illness questionnaire-revised (PBIQ-R): Reliability and validation in a first episode sample. *British Journal of Clinical Psychology, 51*(4), 448–458. doi: 10.1111/j.2044-8260.2012.02040.x.

Birchwood, M., Lester, H., McCarthy, L., Jones, P., Fowler, D., Amos, T., et al. (2014) The UK national evaluation of the development and impact of Early Intervention Services (the National EDEN studies): Study rationale, design and baseline characteristics. *Early Intervention in Psychiatry, 8*(1), 59–67. doi: 10.1111/eip.12007.

Birchwood, M., McGorven, D. & Spencer, E. (2000) Schizophrenia: early warning signs. *Advances in Psychiatric Treatment, 6*, 93–101.

Birchwood, M., Michail, M., Meaden, A., Tarrier, N., Lewis, S., Wykes, T., et al. (2014) Cognitive behaviour therapy to prevent harmful compliance with command hallucinations (COMMAND): A randomised controlled trial. *Lancet Psychiatry, 1*, 23–33.

Birchwood, M., Smith, J. O., Cochrane, R., Wetton, S. & Copestake, S. O. N. J. A. (1990) The Social Functioning Scale The development and validation of a new scale of social adjustment for use in family intervention programmes with schizophrenic patients. *The British Journal of Psychiatry, 157*, 853–859.

Birchwood, M., Smith, J., Macmillan, F., Hogg, B., Prasad, R., Harvey, C., et al. (1989) Predicting relapse in schizophrenia: the development and implementation of an early signs monitoring system using patients and families as observers. *Psychological Medicine, 19*, 649–656.

Birchwood, M., Todd, P. & Jackson, C. (1998) Early intervention in psychosis: the critical-period hypothesis. *International Clinical Psychopharmacology, 13*, 31–40.

Birchwood, M. & Trower, P. (2006) The future of cognitive behaviour therapy for psychosis: not a quasi-neuroleptic. *British Journal of Psychiatry, 188*, 107–108.

Birchwood, M., Trower, P., Brunet, K., Gilbert, P., Iqbal, Z. & Jackson, C. (2007) Social anxiety and the shame of psychosis: A study in first episode clients. *Behaviour Research and Therapy, 45*, 1025–1037.

Bird, V., Leamy, M., Tew, J., Le Boutillier, C., Williams, J. & Slade, M. (2014) Fit for purpose? Validation of a conceptual framework for personal recovery with current mental health consumers. *The Australian and New Zealand Journal of Psychiatry, 48*(7), 644–53. doi: 10.1177/0004867413520046.

Bird, V., Premkumar, P., Kendall, T., Whittington, C., Mitchell, J., Kuipers, E. (2010) Early intervention services, cognitive-behavioural therapy and family intervention in early psychosis: systematic review. *The British Journal of Psychiatry, 197*(5), 350–356.

Björkenstam, C., Björkenstam, E., Hjern, A., Bodén, R. & Reutfors, J. (2014) Suicide in first episode psychosis: A nationwide cohort study. *Schizophrenia Research, 157*(1–3), 1–7. doi: 10.1016/j.schres.2014.05.010.

Bjornestad, J., Bronnick, K., Davidson, Hegelstad, W. T. V., Joa, I., Kandal, O., et al. (2016) The central role of self-agency in clinical recovery from first episode psychosis. *Psychosis, Psychological, Social and Integrative Approaches*, 1–9.

Bodén, R., Sundström, J., Lindström, E. & Lindström, L. (2009) Association between symptomatic remission and functional outcome in first-episode schizophrenia. *Schizophrenia Research, 107(2–3)*, 232–237. doi: 10.1016/j.schres.2008.10.004.

Bond, G. R. (1992) Vocational rehabilitation. *Psychiatric Rehabilitation, 166*, 244–275.

Bond, G. R., Becker, D. R., Drake, R. E., Rapp, C. A., Meisler, N., Lehman, A. F., et al. (2001) Implementing supported employment as an evidence-based practice. *Psychiatric Services, 52*, 313–322.

Bond, G. R., Drake, R. E. & Becker, D. R. (2008) An update on randomized controlled trials of evidence-based supported employment. *Psychiatric Rehabilitation Journal, 31*, 280.

Bond, G. R., Drake, R. E. & Becker, D. R. (2012) Generalizability of the Individual Placement and Support (IPS) model of supported employment outside the US. *World Psychiatry, 11*, 32–39.

Bond, G. R., Drake, R. E. & Luciano, A. (2015) Employment and educational outcomes in early intervention programmes for early psychosis: A systematic review. *Epidemiology and Psychiatric Sciences, 24*, 446–457.

Bond, G. R., Drake, R. E., Mueser, K. T. & Becker, D. R. (1997). An update on supported employment for people with severe mental illness. *Psychiatric Services, 48*, 335–346.

Bond, G. R., Drake, R. E., Mueser, K. T. & Latimer, E. (2001) Assertive community treatment for people with severe mental illness. *Disease Management and Health Outcomes, 9*, 141–159.

Bonney, S. & Stickley, T. (2008) Recovery and mental health: a review of the British literature. *Journal of Psychiatric and Mental Health Nursing, 15*(2), 140–153. doi: 10.1111/j.1365-2850.2007.01185.x.

Bonsack, C., Gibellini Manetti, S., Favrod, J., Montagrin, Y., Besson, J., Bovet, P., et al. (2011). Motivational intervention to reduce cannabis use in young people with psychosis: a randomized controlled trial. *Psychotherapy and Psychosomatics, 80*(5), 287–297. http://dx.doi.org/10.1159/000323466.

Boter, H., Peuskens, J., Libiger, J., Fleischhacker, W. W., Davidson, M., Galderisi, S., et al. (2009) Effectiveness of antipsychotics in first-episode schizophrenia and schizophreniform disorder on response and remission: An open randomized clinical trial (EUFEST). *Schizophrenia Research, 115*, 97–103.

Bourque, F., Van der Ven, E. & Malla, A. (2011) A meta-analysis of the risk for psychotic disorders among first- and second-generation immigrants. *Psychological Medicine, 41*(5), 897–910. doi: 10.1017/S0033291710001406.

Bowie, C. R., Grossman, M., Gupta, M., Oyewumi, L. & Harvey, P. D. (2014) Cognitive remediation in schizophrenia: efficacy and effectiveness in patients with early versus long-term course of illness. *Early Intervention in Psychiatry, 8*, pp. 32–38.

Brabban, A. & Dodgson, G. (2010) What makes Early Intervention in Psychosis services effective? A case study. *Early Intervention in Psychiatry, 4*, 319–322.

Breitborde, N. J. K., Moe, A. M., Ered, A., Ellman, L. M. & Bell, E. K. (2017) Optimizing psychosocial interventions in first-episode psychosis: current perspectives and future directions. *Psychology Research and Behaviour Management, 10*, 119–128.

Broome, M. R., Saunders, K. E., Harrison, P. J. & Marwaha, S. (2015) Mood instability: significance, definition and measurement. *The British Journal of Psychiatry, 207*(4), 283–285.

Brugha, T., McManus, S., Bankart, J., Scott, F., Purdon, S. & Smith, J., et al. (2011). Epidemiology of autism spectrum disorders in adults in the community in England. *Archives of General Psychiatry, 68*(5), 459. http://dx.doi.org/10.1001/archgenpsychiatry.2011.38.

Brunette, M., Drake, R., Xie, H., McHugo, G. & Green, A. (2005) Clozapine use and relapses of substance use disorder among patients with co-occurring schizophrenia and substance use disorders. *Schizophrenia Bulletin, 32*(4), 637–643. doi: 10.1093/schbul/sbl003.

Bucci, S., Berry, K., Barrowclough, C. & Haddock, G. (2016) Family interventions in psychosis: a review of the evidence and barriers to implementation. *Australian Psychologist, 51*(1), 62–68. doi: 10.1111/ap.12172.

Bucci, S., Birchwood, M., Twist, L., Tarrier, N., Emsley, R. & Haddock, G. (2013) Predicting compliance with command hallucinations: Anger, impulsivity and appraisals of voices' power and intent. *Schizophrenia Research, 147*(1), 163–168. doi: https://doi.org/10.1016/j.schres.2013.02.037.

Buck, K., Roe, D., Yanos, P., Buck, B., Fogley, R., Grant, M., et al. (2013) Challenges to assisting with the recovery of personal identity and wellness for persons with serious mental illness: Considerations for mental health professionals. *Psychosis, 5*(2), 134–143.

Buckley, P., Miller, B. J., Lehrer, D. S. & Castle, D. J. (2009) Psychiatric comorbidities and schizophrenia. *Schizophrenic Bulletin, 35*(2), pp. 383–402.

Buckley, P. & Stahl, S. (2007) Pharmacological treatment of negative symptoms of schizophrenia: therapeutic opportunity or cul-de-sac? *Acta Psychiatrica Scandinavica, 115*(2), 93–100. doi: 10.1111/j.1600-0447.2007.00992.x.

Burbach, F., Fadden, G. & Smith, J. (2010) Family interventions for first-episode psychosis. In P. French, J. Smith, D. Shiers, M. Reed & M. Rayne, *Promoting recovery in early psychosis: A practice manual.* Oxford: Blackwell.

Burns, A. M., Erikson, D. H. & Brenner, C. A. (2013) CBT for medication resistant psychosis. Meta-analysis. *Psychiatric Services, 65*(7), 874–880. doi: 10.1176/appi.ps.201300213.

Burns, J. K. (2013) Pathways from cannabis to psychosis: A review of the evidence. *Frontiers in Psychiatry, 4*, 128. doi: http://doi.org/10.3389/fpsyt.2013.00128.

Burns, J. K. & Esterhuizen, T. (2008) Poverty, inequality and the treated incidence of first-episode psychosis. *Social Psychiatry and Psychiatric Epidemiology, 43*(4): 331–335.

Burns, T., Catty, J., Becker, T., Drake, R. E., Fioritti, A., EQOELISE Group, et al. (2007) The effectiveness of supported employment for people with severe mental illness: a randomised controlled trial. *The Lancet, 370*, 1146–1152.

Burns, T. & Patrick, D. (2007) Social functioning as an outcome measure in schizophrenia studies. *Acta Psychiatrica Scandinavica, 116*, 403–418.

Butler, L., Johns, L., Byrne, M., Joseph, C., O'Donoghue, E., Jolley, S., et al. (2016) Running acceptance and commitment therapy groups for psychosis in community settings. *Journal of Contextual Behavioral Science, 5*(1), 33–38. doi: 10.1016/j.jcbs.2015.12.001.

Byrne, P. (2007) Managing the acute psychotic episode. *British Medical Journal*, *334*(7595), 686–692. doi: 10.1136/bmj.39148.668160.80.

Byrne, R. & Morrison, A. (2014) Service users' priorities and preferences for treatment of psychosis: A user-led Delphi study. *Psychiatric Services*, *65*(9), 1167–1169.

Byrne, S., Birchwood, M., Trower, P. & Meaden, A. (2006) *A casebook of cognitive behavior therapy for command hallucinations: A social rank theory approach.* New York: Routledge.

Cahill, K., Stevens, S., Perera, R. & Lancaster, T. (2013) Pharmacological interventions for smoking cessation: An overview and network meta-analysis. *Cochrane Database of Systematic Reviews*. doi: 10.1002/14651858.cd009329.pub2.

Calhoun, L. G. & Tedeschi, R. G. (2004) The foundations of posttraumatic growth: New considerations. *Psychological Inquiry*, *15*(1), 193–102. doi: 10.1207/s15327965pli1501_03.

Camchong, J., Lim, K. & Kumra, S. (2016). Adverse effects of cannabis on adolescent brain development: A longitudinal study. *Cerebral Cortex.* http://dx.doi.org/10.1093/cercor/bhw015.

Canal-Rivero, M., Barrigón, M. L., Perona-Garcelán, S., Rodriguez-Testal, J. F., Giner, L., Obiols-Llandrich, J. E., et al. (2016) One-year follow-up study of first suicide attempts in first episode psychosis: Personality traits and temporal pattern. *Comprehensive Psychiatry*, *71*, 121–129. doi: 10.1016/j.comppsych.2016.08.014.

Canning, L. (2006) *Rethink sibling survey.* London, Rethink.

Canning, P. & Gournay, K. (2014) The impact of patient suicide on community mental health teams. *British Journal of Mental Health Nursing*, *3*(5), 235–240.

Cannon-Spoor, H. E., Potkin, S. G. & Wyatt, R. J. (1982) Measurement of premorbid adjustment in chronic schizophrenia. *Schizophrenia Bulletin*, *8*(3), 470.

Caqueo-Urízar, A., Gutiérrez-Maldonado, J., Ferrer-García, M. & Darrigrande-Molina, P. (2012) Burden of care in Aymara caregivers of patients with schizophrenia. *Revista de Psiquiatría y Salud Mental (English Edition)*, *5*(3),191–196. doi: 10.1016/j.rpsmen.2011.07.004.

Caqueo-Urízar, A., Urzúa, A., Jamett, P. & Irarrazaval, M. (2016) Objective and subjective burden in relatives of patients with schizophrenia and its influence on care relationships in Chile. *Psychiatry Research*, *237*, 361–365. doi: 10.1016/j.psychres.2016.01.013.

Cardenas, V., Abel, S., Bowie, C. R., Tiznado, D., Depp, C. A., Patterson, T. L. et al. (2013) When functional capacity and real-world functioning converge: the role of self-efficacy. *Schizophrenia Bulletin*, *39*, 908–916.

Carpenter, W. T. & Strauss, J. S. (1991) The prediction of outcome in schizophrenia IV: Eleven-year follow-up of the Washington IPSS Cohort. *The Journal of Nervous & Mental Disease*, *179*, 517–525.

Carr, C. P., Martins, C. M., Stingel, A. M., Lemgruber, V. B. & Juruena, M. F. (2013) The role of early life stress in adult psychiatric disorders: A systematic review according to childhood trauma subtypes. *The Journal of Nervous and Mental Disease*, *201*(12), 1007–1020. doi: 10.1097/NMD.0000000000000049.

Carver, C. S. (1998) Resilience and thriving: Issues, models, and linkages. *Journal of Social Issues*, *54*, 245–266. doi: http://dx.doi.org/10.1111/j.1540-4560.1998.tb01217.x.

Casey, D., Brown, L., Gajwani, R., Islam, Z., Jasani, R., Parsons, H., Tah, P., Birchwood, M. & Singh, S. (2016) Predictors of engagement in first-episode psychosis. *Schizophrenia Research*, *175*(1–3), 204–208.

Cassidy, C. M., Norman, R., Manchanda, R., Schmitz, N. & Malla, A. (2009) Testing definitions of symptom remission in first-episode psychosis for prediction of functional outcome at 2 years. *Schizophrenia Bulletin*, *36*(5), 1001–1008.

Castelein, S., Bruggeman, R., Van Busschbach, J. T., Van Der Gaag, M., Stant, A. D., Knegtering, H. & Wiersma, D. (2008) The effectiveness of peer support groups in psychosis: A
randomized controlled trial. *Acta Psychiatrica Scandinavica,* 118, pp. 64–72.

Castillejos, M. C., Martín-Pérez, C., Moreno-Küstner, B. (2018) A systematic review and
meta-analysis of the incidence of psychotic disorders: the distribution of rates and the
influence of gender, urbanicity, immigration and socio-economic level. *Psychological
Medicine, 22,* 1–15. doi: 10.1017/S0033291718000235.

Češková, E., Radovan, P., Tomáš, K. & Hana, K. (2007) One-year follow-up of patients with
first-episode schizophrenia (comparison between remitters and non-remitters). *Neuropsychiatric Disease and Treatment, 3*(1), 153–160. doi: 10.2147/nedt.2007.3.1.153.

Chadwick, P. (2006) *Person based cognitive therapy for distressing psychosis.* Chichester: John Wiley & Sons Ltd.

Chadwick, P., Birchwood, M. & Trower, P. (1996) *Cognitive behaviour therapy for delusions, voices, and paranoia.* Chichester: John Wiley & Sons Ltd.

Chadwick, P., Less, S. & Birchwood, M. (2000) The revised Beliefs about Voices Questionnaire (BAVQ-R). *The British Journal of Psychiatry, 177,* 229–232.

Chan, J. Y., Hirai, H. W. & Tsoi, K. K. (2015) Can computer-assisted cognitive remediation improve employment and productivity outcomes of patients with severe mental
illness? A meta-analysis of prospective controlled trials. *Journal of Psychiatric
Research, 68,* 293–300.

Chan, R. C. H., Mak, W. W. S., Chio, F. H. N. & Tong, A. C. Y. (2017) Flourishing with
psychosis: A prospective examination on the interactions between clinical, functional,
and personal recovery processes on well-being among individuals with schizophrenia
spectrum disorders. *Schizophrenia Bulletin, 44*(4), 784–786. doi: 10.1093/schbul/
sbx120.

Chan, S., Tse, S., Sin, H., Hui, C., Lee, E., Chang, W. & Chen, E. (2016) Web-based
psychoeducation program for caregivers of first-episode of psychosis: An experience
of Chinese population in Hong Kong. *Frontiers in Psychology, 7.* doi: 10.3389/
fpsyg.2016.02006.

Chan, S. K. W., Chan, S. W. Y., Pang, H. H., Yan, K. K., Hui, C. L. M., Chang, W. C.,
Lee, E. H. M. & Chen, E. Y. H. (2018) Association of an early intervention service for
psychosis with suicide rate among patients with first-episode schizophrenia-spectrum
disorders. *JAMA Psychiatry, 175*(5), 458–464.

Chandler, R., Bradstreet, S. & Hayward, M. (2013) *Voicing caregiver experiences: well-
being and recovery narratives for caregivers.* Lancing, West Sussex, Fairhall and
Bryant Ltd.

Chang, C. W., Cheung, R., Ming Hui, L. C., Lin, J., Kit Wa Chan, S., Ho Ming Lee, E.,
et al. (2015) Rate and risk factors of depressive symptoms in Chinese patients presenting with first-episode non-affective psychosis in Hong Kong. *Schizophrenia Research,
168*(1–2), 99–105.

Chang, W. C., Chen, E. S. M., Hui, C. L. M., Chan, S. K. W., Lee, E. H. M. & Chen,
E. Y. H. (2014) The relationships of suicidal ideation with symptoms, neurocognitive
function, and psychological factors in patients with first-episode psychosis. *Schizophrenia Research, 157*(1), 12–18. doi: 10.1016/j.schres.2014.06.009.

Chang, W. C., Tang, J. Y., Hui, C. L., Lam, M. M., Chan, S. K., Wong. G. H., et al.
(2012) Prediction of remission and recovery in young people presenting with first-
episode psychosis in Hong Kong: A 3-year follow-up study. *Australian and New
Zealand Journal of Psychiatry, 46*(2), 100–108. doi: 10.1177/0004867411428015.

Chatterjee, S. (2017) An international response to improving outcomes for first-episode psychosis is warranted, but more needs to be done to make it happen. *World Psychiatry, 16*(3), 271–272. doi: 10.1002/wps.20451.

Chaudhry, I., Hallak, J., Husain, N., Minhas, F., Stirling, J., Richardson, P., Dursun, S., Dunn, G. & Deakin, B. (2012) Minocycline benefits negative symptoms in early schizophrenia: A randomised double-blind placebo-controlled clinical trial in patients on standard treatment. *Journal of Psychopharmacology, 26*(9), 1185–1193. doi: 10.1177/0269881112444941.

Cherry, M., Taylor, P., Brown, S., Rigby, J. & Sellwood, W. (2017) Guilt, shame and expressed emotion in carers of people with long-term mental health difficulties: A systematic review. *Psychiatry Research, 249*, 139–151. doi: 10.1016/j.psychres.2016.12.056.

Chien, W., Thompson, D., Lubman, D. & McCann, T. (2016) A randomized controlled trial of clinician-supported problem-solving bibliotherapy for family caregivers of people with first-episode psychosis. *Schizophrenia Bulletin, 42*(6), 1457–1466. doi: 10.1093/schbul/sbw054.

Chisholm, B., Freeman, D. & Cooke, A. (2006) Identifying potential predictors of traumatic reactions to psychotic episodes. *British Journal of Clinical Psychology, 45*, 545–559. doi: 10.13481014466505X09136.

Chisholm, K., Lin, A., Abu-Akel, A. & Wood, S. (2015) The association between autism and schizophrenia spectrum disorders: A review of eight alternate models of co-occurrence. *Neuroscience & Biobehavioral Reviews, 55*, 173–183. http://dx.doi.org/10.1016/j.neubiorev.2015.04.012.

Clark, D. A. & Beck, A. T. (2011) *Cognitive therapy of anxiety disorders: Science and practice*. New York: Guilford Press.

Clark, D. M. (2007) *Cognitive behavioural therapy for OCD*. New York: Guildford Press.

Clarke, M., Whitty, P., Browne, S., McTigue, O., Kamali, M., Gervin, M., et al. (2006) Untreated illness and outcome of psychosis. *British Journal of Psychiatry, 189*, 235–240.

Claxton, M., Onwumere, J. & Fornelly-Ambrojo, M. (2017) Do family interventions improve outcomes in early psychosis? A systematic review and meta-analysis. *Frontiers in Psychology, 8*, 371. doi: 10.3389/fpsyg.2017.00371,

Cocchi, A., Meneghelli, A., Erlicher, A., Pisano, A., Cascio, M. T. & Preti, A. (2013) Patterns of referral in first-episode schizophrenia and ultra high-risk individuals: results from an early intervention program in Italy. *Social Psychiatry and Psychiatric Epidemiology, 48*(12), 1905–1916. doi: 10.1007/s00127-013-0736-5.

Coid, J., Yang, M., Tyrer, P., Roberts, A. & Ullrich, S. (2006) Prevalence and correlates of personality disorder in Great Britain. *British Journal of Psychiatry, 188*(05), 423–431. http://dx.doi.org/10.1192/bjp.188.5.423.

Conley, R. & Kelly, D. (2001) Management of treatment resistance in schizophrenia. *Biological Psychiatry, 50*(11), 898–911. doi: 10.1016/s0006-3223(01)01271-9.

Connell, M., Schweitzer, R. & King, R. (2015) Recovery from first-episode psychosis and recovering self: A qualitative study. *Psychiatric Rehabilitation Journal, 38*(4), 359–364.

Connor, C. & Birchwood, M. (2012) Abuse and dysfunctional affiliations in childhood: An exploration of their impact on voice-hearers' appraisals of power and expressed emotion. *Psychosis, 4*(1), 19–31. doi: 10.1080/17522439.2011.630745.

Conrad, A. M., Lewin, T. J., Sly, K. A., Schall, U., Halpin, S. A., Hunter, M., et al. (2017) Utility of risk-status for predicting psychosis and related outcomes: evaluation of a 10-year cohort of presenters to a specialised early psychosis community mental health service. *Psychiatry Research, 247*, 336–344.

Cook, D. R. (1996) *Empirical studies of shame and guilt: The internalised shame scale. In knowing feeling: Affect, script, and psychotherapy*, (ed.) D. L. Nathanson., (pp. 132–165). New York: Norton.

Cook, J. A., Steigman, P., Pickett, S., Diehl, S., Fox, A., Shipley, P., et al. (2012) Randomized controlled trial of peer-led recovery education using Building Recovery of Individual Dreams and Goals through Education and Support (BRIDGES). *Schizophrenia Research, 136*, 36–42.

Cooke, A. (ed.) (2017) *Understanding Psychosis and Schizophrenia: Why people sometimes hear voices, believe things that others find strange, or appear out of touch with reality, and what can help: Revised version.* London: British Psychological Society Division of Clinical Psychology.

Cooper, S., Reynolds, G., Barnes, T., England, E., Haddad, P., Heald, A., et al. (2016) BAP guidelines on the management of weight gain, metabolic disturbances and cardiovascular risk associated with psychosis and antipsychotic drug treatment. *Journal of Psychopharmacology, 30*(8), 717–748. doi: 10.1177/0269881116645254.

Copeland, M. E. (2015) *WRAP: Wellness Recovery Action Plan.* Massachusetts: Advocates for Human Potential.

Copello, A., Graham, H. & Birchwood, M. (2001) Evaluating substance misuse interventions in psychosis: The limitations of the RCT with 'patient' as the unit of analysis. *Journal of Mental Health, 10*(6), 585–587.

Corlett, P., Taylor, J., Wang, X., Fletcher, P. & Krystal, J. (2010) Toward a neurobiology of delusions. *Progress in Neurobiology, 92*(3), 345–369. doi: 10.1016/j.pneurobio.2010.06.007.

Cornblatt, B. A., Auther, A. M., Niendam, T., Smith, C. W., Zinberg, J., Bearden, C. E. & Cannon, T. D. (2007) Preliminary findings for two new measures of social and role functioning in the prodromal phase of schizophrenia. *Schizophrenia Bulletin, 33*(3), pp. 688–702.

Correll, C., Galling, B., Pawar, A. (2018) Comparison of early intervention services vs. treatment as usual for early phase-psychosis: A systematic review, meta-analysis, and meta-regression. *JAMA Psychiatry.* doi: 10.1001/jamapsychiatry.2018.062.

Correll, C. & Malhotra, A. (2004) Pharmacogenetics of antipsychotic-induced weight gain. *Psychopharmacology, 174*(4). doi: 10.1007/s00213-004-1949-9.

Corrigan, P., McCorkle, B., Schell, B. & Kidder, K. (2003) Religion and spirituality in the lives of people with serious mental illness. *Community Mental Health Journal, 39*(6), 487–499.

Corrigan, P. W., Mueser, K. T., Bond, G. R., Drake, R. E. & Solomon, P. (2008) *Principles and practice of psychiatric rehabilitation: An empirical approach.* New York: Guilford Press.

Corstens, D., Longden, E., McCarthy-Jones, S., Waddingham, R. & Thomas, N. (2014) Emerging perspectives from the hearing voices movement: implications for research and practice. *Schizophrenia Bulletin, 40*(Suppl. 4), S285–S294. http://dx.doi.org/10.1093/schbul/sbu007.

Cosoff, S. J. & Hafner, R. J. (1998) The prevalence of comorbid anxiety in schizophrenia, schizoaffective disorder, and bipolar disorder. *The Australian and New Zealand Journal of Psychiatry, 32*(1), 67–72.

Cotton, S., McCann, T., Gleeson, J., Crisp, K., Murphy, B. & Lubman, D. (2013) Coping strategies in carers of young people with a first episode of psychosis. *Schizophrenia Research, 146*(1–3), 118–124. doi: 10.1016/j.schres.2013.02.008.

Cotton, S. M., Lambert, M., Schimmelmann, B. G., Filia, K., Rayner, V., Hides, L., et al. (2017) Predictors of functional status at service entry and discharge among young people with first episode psychosis. *Social Psychiatry and Psychiatric Epidemiology, 52*, 575–585.

Cotton, S. M., Lambert, M., Schimmelmann, B. G., Foley, D. L., Morley, K. I., McGorry, P. D., et al. (2009) Gender differences in premorbid, entry, treatment, and outcome characteristics in a treated epidemiological sample of 661 patients with first episode psychosis. *Schizophrenia Research, 114*, 17–24.

Cotton, S. M., Lambert, M., Schimmelmann, B. G., Mackinnon, A., Gleeson, J. F. M., et al. (2012) Depressive symptoms in first episode schizophrenia spectrum disorder. *Schizophrenia Research, 134*, 20–26.

Coughlan, H. & Cannon, M. (2017). Does childhood trauma play a role in the aetiology of psychosis? A review of recent evidence. *Bjpsych Advances, 23*(05), 307–315. http://dx.doi.org/10.1192/apt.bp.116.015891.

Craig, T., Shepherd, G., Rinaldi, M., Smith, J., Carr, S., Preston, F. & Singh, S. (2014) Vocational rehabilitation in early psychosis: cluster randomised trial. *The British Journal of Psychiatry, 205*, 145–150.

Crespo-Facorro, B., Ortiz-Garcia de la Foz, V., Mata, I., Ayesa-Arriola, R., Suarez-Pinilla, P. & Valdizan, E., et al. (2013) Treatment of first-episode non-affective psychosis: a randomized comparison of aripiprazole, quetiapine and ziprasidone over 1 year. *Psychopharmacology, 231*(2), 357–366. doi: 10.1007/s00213-013-3241-3.

Crespo-Facorro, B., Perez-Iglesias, R., Ramirez, M., Pelayo-Terán, J., Martinez, O. & Vázquez-Barquero, J. (2006) FC4E A practical clinical trial comparing haloperidol, rispiridone and olanzapine for the acute treatment of first episode of non-affective psychosis. *Schizophrenia Research, 86*, 39. doi: 10.1016/s0920-9964(06)70117-7.

Crisp, K., Creek., R., Fraser, S., Stavely, H. & Woodhead, G. (2014) *In this together: Family work in early psychosis*. Orygen: Youth Health Research Centre.

Cristofaro, S. L., Clear, S. D., Wan, C. R., Broussard, B., Chapman, C., Haggard, P. J., et al. (2013) Measuring trauma and stressful events in childhood and adolescence among patients with first-episode psychosis: Initial factor structure, reliability, and validity of the Trauma Experiences Checklist. *Psychiatry Research, 201*, 618–625. doi: http://dx.doi.org/10.1016/j.psychres.2013.06.015.

Crossley, N., Constante, M., McGuire, P. & Power, P. (2010) Efficacy of atypical v. typical antipsychotics in the treatment of early psychosis: meta-analysis. *The British Journal of Psychiatry, 196*(6), 434–439. doi: 10.1192/bjp.bp.109.066217.

Crumlish. N., Whitty, P., Clarke, M., Browne, S., Kamali, M., Gervin, M., et al. (2009) Beyond the critical period: longitudinal study of 8-year outcome in first-episode non-affective psychosis. *The British Journal of Psychiatry, 194*(1), 18–24. doi: 10.1192/bjp.bp.107.048942.

Crumlish, N., Whitty, P., Kamali, M., Clarke, M., Browne, S., McTigue, O., et al. (2005) Early insight predicts depression and attempted suicide after 4 years in first-episode schizophrenia and schizophreniform disorder. *Acta Psychiatrica Scandinavica, 112*, 449–455. doi: 10.1111/j.1600-0447.2005.00620.x.

Cutler, A. (2003) Sexual dysfunction and antipsychotic treatment. *Psychoneuroendocrinology, 28*, 69–82. doi: 10.1016/s0306-4530(02)00113-.

Darewych, O. & Bowers, N. (2017) Positive arts interventions: Creative clinical tools promoting psychological well-being. *International Journal of Art Therapy, 23*(2).

David, S., Johnstone, E., Churchman, M., Aveyard, P., Murphy, M. & Munafò, M. (2011) Pharmacogenetics of smoking cessation in general practice: Results From the Patch II and Patch in Practice trials. *Nicotine & Tobacco Research, 13*(3), 157–167. doi: 10.1093/ntr/ntq246.

Davidson, C., Greenwood, N., Stansfield, A. & Wright, S. (2013) Prevalence of Asperger syndrome among patients of an Early Intervention in Psychosis team. *Early Intervention in Psychiatry, 8*(2), 138–146. http://dx.doi.org/10.1111/eip.12039.

Davidson, L. (2003) *Living outside mental illness: Qualitative studies of recovery in schizophrenia.* New York: New York University.

Davidson, L., Bellamy, C., Guy, K. & Miller, R. (2012) Peer support among persons with severe mental illnesses: a review of evidence and experience. *World Psychiatry, 11,* 123–128.

Davis, J., Chen, N. & Glick, I. (2003) A meta-analysis of the efficacy of second-generation antipsychotics. *Archives of General Psychiatry, 60*(6), 553. doi: 10.1001/archpsyc.60.6.553.

Davis, L. & Kurzban, S. (2012) Mindfulness-based treatment for people with severe mental illness: A literature review. *The American Journal of Psychiatric Rehabilitation, 15*(2), 202–232.

Day, K. & Petrakis, M. (2016) Family interventions in early psychosis service delivery: A systematized review. *Social Work in Mental Health, 15*(6), 632–650. doi: 10.1080/15332985.2016.1271381.

Day, K., Starbuck, R. & Petrakis, M. (2017) Family group interventions in an early psychosis program: A re-evaluation of practice after 10 years of service delivery. *International Journal Of Social Psychiatry, 63*(5), 433–438. doi: 10.1177/0020764017710301.

Deakin, B., Suckling, J., Barnes, T., Byrne, K., Chaudhry, I. & Dazzan, P., et al. (2018) The benefit of minocycline on negative symptoms of schizophrenia in patients with recent-onset psychosis (BeneMin): a randomised, double-blind, placebo-controlled trial. *The Lancet Psychiatry, 5*(11), 885–894. doi: 10.1016/s2215-0366(18)30345-6.

De Haan, L., Linszen, D. H., Lenior, M. E., de Win, E. D. & Gorsira, R. (2003) Duration of untreated psychosis and outcome of schizophrenia: Delay in intensive psychosocial treatment versus delay in treatment with antipsychotic medication. S*chizophrenia Bulletin, 29*(2), 341–348.

De Haan, L., Nimwegen, L., Amelsvoort, T., Dingemans, P. & Linszen, D. (2008) Improvement of subjective well-being and enduring symptomatic remission: A 5-year follow-up of first episode schizophrenia. *Pharmacopsychiatry, 41*(4): 125–128. doi: 10.1055/s-2008-1076729.

De Haan, L., Sterk, B., Wouters, L. & Linszen, D. H. (2013) The 5-year course of obsessive-compulsive symptoms and obsessive-compulsive disorder in first-episode schizophrenia and related disorders. *Schizophrenia Bulletin, 39*(1), 151–160. doi: http://doi.org/10.1093/schbul/sbr077.

De Hert, M., Detraux, J. & Stubbs, B. (2016) Relationship between antipsychotic medication, serum prolactin levels and osteoporosis/osteoporotic fractures in patients with schizophrenia: A critical literature review. *Expert Opinion on Drug Safety, 15*(6).

De Hert, M., Detraux, J., van Winkel, R., Yu, W. & Correll, C. (2011) Metabolic and cardiovascular adverse effects associated with antipsychotic drugs. *Nature Reviews Endocrinology, 8*(2), 114–126. doi: 10.1038/nrendo.2011.156.

Delay, J., Pichot, P., Nicolas-Charles, P. & Perse, J. (1959) Etude psychométrique des effets de l'amobarbital (amytal) et de la chlorpromazine sur des sujets normaux. *Psychopharmacologia, 1*(1), 48–58. doi: 10.1007/bf00408111.

Demjaha, A. (2018) On the brink of precision medicine for psychosis: Treating the patient, not the disease: A commentary on: Association between serum levels of glutamate and neurotrophic factors and response to clozapine treatment by Krivoy et al. 2017. *Schizophrenia Research, 193*, 487–488. doi: 10.1016/j.schres.2017.08.011.

Dent-Pearce, L., Daya, I., Karagounis, J. & Thomas, N. (2014) Integrating peer work with a specific therapeutic target: Experiences from the Voice Exchange program. In K. Kellehear, A. Lane, M. Cassaniti, B. Tooth, C. Chapman, S. Robertson, et al. (eds). *What we share makes us strong: Contemporary MHS in mental health services.* Balmain, NSW: The MHS.

Department of Health (2001) *The mental health policy implementation guide.* London: Department of Health.

Di Capite, S., Upthegrove, R. & Mallikarjun, P. (2016) The relapse rate and predictors of relapse in patients with first-episode psychosis following discontinuation of antipsychotic medication. *Early Intervention in Psychiatry.* doi: 10.1111/eip.12385.

Díaz, I., Pelayo-Terán, J. M., Pérez-Iglesias, R., Mata, I., Tabarés-Seisdedos, R., Suárez-Pinilla, P., Barquero, J. L., et al. (2013) Predictors of clinical remission following a first episode of non-affective psychosis: sociodemographics, premorbid and clinical variables. *Psychiatry Research, 206*, 81–187.

Dickins, G., Weleminsky, J., Onifade, Y. & Sugarman, P. (2012) Recovery Star: validating user recovery. *The Psychiatrist, 36*(2), 45–50.

Di Forti, M., Marconi, A., Carra, E., Fraietta, S., Trotta, A., Bonomo, M., et al. (2015) Proportion of patients in south London with first-episode psychosis attributable to use of high potency cannabis: A case-control study. *The Lancet Psychiatry, 2*(3), 233–238. doi: 10.1016/S2215-0366(14)00117-5. doi: 10.1192/bjp.bp.113.127753.

Di Forti, M., Morgan, C., Dazzan, P., Pariante, C., Mondelli, V., Marques, T., et al. (2009). High-potency cannabis and the risk of psychosis. *British Journal of Psychiatry, 195*(6), 488–491. http://dx.doi.org/10.1192/bjp.bp.109.064220.

Dlabač-de Lange, J., Knegtering, R. & Aleman, A. (2010) Repetitive transcranial magnetic stimulation for negative symptoms of schizophrenia. *The Journal of Clinical Psychiatry, 71*(04), 411–418. doi: 10.4088/jcp.08r04808yel.

Dodgson, G., Ross, L., Tiffin, P., Mitford, E. & Brabban, A. (2012) Outcomes post-discharge from an early intervention in psychosis service. *Early Intervention Psychiatry, 6*(4), 465–468. doi: 10.1111/j.1751-7893.2012.00349.x.

Doll, R. (2004) Mortality in relation to smoking: 50 years' observations on male British doctors. *British Medical Journal, 328*(7455), 1519–1520. doi: 10.1136/bmj.38142.554479.ae.

Dominguez, M., Fisher, H., Johnson, S. & Hodes, M. (2014) EPA-1641 – The influence of age and family factors in shaping pathways to care in first episode psychosis. *European Psychiatry, 29*, 1. doi: 10.1016/s0924-9338(14)78789-9.

Dominguez, M. D., Wichers, M., Lieb, R., Wittchen, H. U. & van Os, J. (2011) Evidence that onset of clinical psychosis is an outcome of progressively more persistent subclinical psychotic experiences: An 8-n year cohort study. *Schizophrenia Bulletin, 37*(1), 84–93.

Domínguez-Martínez, T., Medina-Pradas, C., Kwapil, T. & Barrantes-Vidal, N. (2017) Relatives' expressed emotion, distress and attributions in clinical high-risk and recent onset of psychosis. *Psychiatry Research, 247*, 323–329. doi: 10.1016/j.psychres.2016.11.048.

Dossenbach, M., Hodge, A., Anders, M., Molnár, B., Peciukaitiene, D., Krupka-Matuszczyk, I., et al. (2005) Prevalence of sexual dysfunction in patients with schizophrenia: international variation and underestimation. *The International Journal of Neuropsychopharmacology, 8*(2), 195–201. doi: 10.1017/s1461145704005012.

Doucet, S., Letourneau, N. & Blackmore, E. (2012) Support needs of mothers who experience postpartum psychosis and their partners. *Journal of Obstetric, Gynecologic and Neonatal Nursing, 41*(2), 236–245. doi: 10.1111/j.1552-6909.2011.01329.x.

Doyle, R., Behan, C., O'Keeffe, D., Masterson, S., Kinsella, A. Kelly, A., et al. (2017) Clozapine use in a cohort of first-episode psychosis. *Journal Of Clinical Psychopharmacology, 37*(5), 512–517. doi: 10.1097/jcp.0000000000000734.

Doyle, R., Turner, N., Fanning, F., Brennan, D., Renwick, L., Lawlor, E. & Clarkem, M. (2014) First-episode psychosis and disengagement from treatment: A systematic review. *Psychiatric Services, 65*(5), 603–611.

Drake, R. E., Bond, G. R. & Becker, D. R. (2012) *Individual placement and support: An evidence-based approach to supported employment.* Oxford: Oxford University Press.

Drayton, M., Birchwood, M. & Trower, P. (1998) Early attachment experiences and recovery from psychosis. *British Journal of Clinical Psychology, 37*, 269–284.

Drugs A–Z|FRANK. (2018). Talktofrank.com. Retrieved 25 April 2018, from www.talktofrank.com/drugs-a-z

Drummond, C., Day, E. & Strang, J. (2018). Return failing drug and alcohol detoxification services to NHS control – The BMJ. Blogs.bmj.com. Retrieved 25 April 2018, from http://blogs.bmj.com/bmj/2017/11/30/return-failing-drug-and-alcohol-detoxification-services-to-nhs-control/.

Duggan, A., Warner, J., Knapp, M., et al. (2003) Modelling the impact of clozapine on suicide in patients with treatment-resistant schizophrenia in the UK. *British Journal of Psychiatry, 182*, 505–508.

Dunkley, J. & Bates, G. (2015) Recovery and adaptation after first-episode psychosis: The relevance of posttraumatic growth. *Psychosis, 7*(2), 130–140.

Dunkley, J. E., Bates, G. W. & Findlay, B. M. (2015) Understanding the trauma of first-episode psychosis. *Early Intervention in Psychosis, 9*(3), 211–220. doi: 10.1111/eip.12103.

Durie, M. (1994). *Whaiora, Maori health development.* Auckland: Oxford University Press.

Durmaz, H. & Okanli, A. (2014) Investigation of the effect of self-efficacy levels of caregiver family members of the individuals with schizophrenia on burden of care. *Archives of Psychiatric Nursing, 28*(4), 290–294. doi: 10.1016/j.apnu.2014.04.004.

Dutta, R., Murray, R. M., Hotopf, M., Allardyce, J., Jones, P. B., & Boydell, J. (2010) Reassessing the long-term risk of suicide after a first episode of psychosis. *Archive of General Psychiatry, 67(12),* 1230–1237. doi: 10.1001/archgenpsychiatry.2010.157.

Dutta, R., Greene, T., Addington, J., McKenzie, K., Phillips, M. & Murray, R. M. (2007) Biological, life course, and cross-cultural studies all point toward the value of dimensional and developmental ratings in the classification of psychosis. *Schizophrenia Bulletin, 33*(4), 868–876.

Edgcumbe, D. (2010) But there are no QOF points for Balint work!: Its place in modern practice. *British Journal of General Practice, 60*(580), 858–859. doi: 10.3399/bjgp10x539380.

Ediriweera, H., Fernando, S. & Pai, N. (2012) Mental health literacy survey among Sri Lankan carers of patients with schizophrenia and depression. *Asian Journal of Psychiatry, 5*(3), 246–250. doi: 10.1016/j.ajp.2012.02.016.

Egerton, A., Valmaggia, L., Howes, O., Day, F., Chaddock, C., Allen, P., et al. (2016) Adversity in childhood linked to elevated striatal dopamine function in adulthood. *Schizophrenia Research, 176*(2–3), 171–176. doi: 10.1016/j.schres.2016.06.005.

Ehlers, A. & Clark, D. M. (2000) A cognitive model of posttraumatic stress disorder. *Behaviour Research and Therapy, 38*, 319–345.

Eisenstadt, P., Monteiro, V. B., Diniz, M. J. & Chaves, A. C. (2012) Experience of recovery from a first-episode psychosis. *Early Intervention Psychiatry, 6*(4), 476–480. doi: 10.1111/j.1751-7893.2012.00353.x.

Eisner, E., Barrowclough, C., Lobban, F. & Drake, R. (2014) Qualitative investigation of targets for and barriers to interventions to prevent psychosis relapse. *BMC Psychiatry, 14*, 201.

Eisner, E., Drake, R. & Barrowclough, C. (2013) Assessing early signs of relapse in psychosis: review and future directions. *Clinical Psychology Review, 33*(5), 637–653.

Eisner, E., Drake, R., Lobban, F., Bucci, S., Emsley, R. & Barrowclough, C. (2018) Comparing early signs and basic symptoms as methods for predicting psychotic relapse in clinical practice. *Schizophrenia Research, 192*, 124–130.

Elis, O. & Caponigro, J. M. & Kring, A. M. (2013) Psychosocial treatments for negative symptoms in schizophrenia: Current practices and future directions. *Clinical Psychology Review, 33*, 914–928. doi: 10.1016/j.cpr.2013.07.001.

Ellett, L. (2013) Person-based cognitive therapy for distressing psychosis. In E. Morris, L. Johns & J. Oliver (eds.) *Acceptance and commitment therapy and mindfulness for psychosis*. Chichester: John Wiley & Sons Ltd.

El-Mallakh, P. & Findlay, J. (2015) Strategies to improve medication adherence in patients with schizophrenia: the role of support services. *Neuropsychiatric Disease and Treatment, 1077*. doi: 10.2147/ndt.s56107.

Emsley, R. (2006) Time course for antipsychotic treatment response in first-episode schizophrenia. *The American Journal of Psychiatry, 163*(4), 743. doi: 10.1176/appi.ajp.163.4.743.

Emsley, R., Oosthuizen, P. P., Kidd, M., Koen, L., Niehaus, D. J. & Turner, H. J. (2006) Remission in first-episode psychosis: predictor variables and symptom improvement patterns. *Journal of Clinical Psychiatry, 67*(11), 1707–1712.

Emsley, R., Oosthuizen, P., Niehaus, D. & Koen, L. (2008) Time course of early treatment response and its relationship to remission in first episode schizophrenia. *Schizophrenia Research, 102*(1–3), 37. doi: 10.1016/s0920-9964(08)70118-x.

Engur, B. (2017) Parents with psychosis: Impact on parenting and parent-child relationship. *Journal of Child and Adolescent Behaviour, 5*(1), 327. doi: 10.4172/2375-4494.1000327.

Erickson, D. H., Beiser, M. & Iacono, W. G. (1998) Social support predicts 5-year outcome in first-episode schizophrenia. *Journal of Abnormal Psychology, 107*, 681–685.

Evans-Lacko, S., Brohan, E., Mojtabai, R. & Thornicroft, G. (2012) Associations between public views of mental illness and self-stigma among individuals with mental illness in 14 European countries. *Psychological Medicine, 42*(8), 1741–1752. doi: 10.1017/S00332917110025858.

Evans-Lacko, S., Kohrt, B., Henderson, C. & Thornicroft, G. (2018) Public anti-stigma programmes might improve help seeking. *The British Journal of Psychiatry, 211*, 182–184. doi: 10.1192/bjp.211.3.182.

Evensen, J., Røssberg, J. I., Barder, H., Haahr, U., ten Velden Hegelstad, W., Joa, I., et al. (2012a) Apathy in first episode psychosis patients: A ten year longitudinal follow-up study. *Schizophrenia Research, 136*, 19–24.

Evensen, J., Røssberg, J. I., Batrowerrder, H., Haahr, U., ten Velden Hegelstad, W., Joa, I., et al. (2012b) Flat affect and social functioning: a 10 year follow-up study of first episode psychosis patients. *Schizophrenia Research, 139*, 99–104.

Evenson, E., Rhodes, J., Feigenbaum, J. & Solly, A. (2008) The experiences of fathers with psychosis. *Journal of Mental Health, 17*(6), 629–642. doi: 10.1080/09638230701506259.

Evert, H., Harvey, C., Trauer, T. & Herrman, H. (2003) The relationship between social networks and occupational and self-care functioning in people with psychosis. *Social Psychiatry and Psychiatric Epidemiology, 38*(4), 180–188.

Fadden, G., Heelis, R. & Bisnauth, R. (2010) Training mental health care professionals in behavioural family therapy: an audit of trainers' experiences in the West Midlands. *The Journal of Mental Health Training, Education and Practice, 5*(2), 27–35. doi: 10.5042/jmhtep.2010.0363.

Falloon, I. (1984) Relapse: A reappraisal of assessment of outcome in schizophrenia. *Schizophrenia Bulletin, 10*(2), 293–299. doi: 10.1093/schbul/10.2.293.

Falloon, I. & Liberman, R. (1983) Behavioral family interventions in the management of chronic schizophrenia. In W. McFarlane & C. Beets, *Family therapy of schizophrenia.* New York: Guildford Press.

Fan, X., Borba, C., Copeland, P., Hayden, D., Freudenreich, O., Goff, D., et al. (2012) Metabolic effects of adjunctive aripiprazole in clozapine-treated patients with schizophrenia. *Acta Psychiatrica Scandinavica, 127*(3), 217–226. doi: 10.1111/acps.12009.

Fearon, P. (2013) Can early intervention services modify pathways into care? *British Journal Psychiatry, 202*(4), 249–250. doi: 10.1192/bjp.bp.112.111930.

Fearon, P., Kirkbride, J. B., Morgan, C., Dazzan, P., Morgan, K., AESOP Study Group, et al. (2006) Incidence of schizophrenia and other psychoses in ethnic minority groups: Results from the MRC AESOP Study. *Psychological Medicine, 36*(11), 1541–1550. doi: 10.1017/S0033291706008774.

Fedyszyn, I. E., Harris, M. G., Robinson, J., Edwards, J. & Paxton, S. J. (2011) Characteristics of suicide attempts in young people undergoing treatment for first episode psychosis. *Australian and New Zealand Journal of Psychiatry, 45*(10), 838–845.

Ferdinand, R., Sondeijker, F., van der Ende, J., Selten, J., Huizink, A. & Verhulst, F. (2005). Cannabis use predicts future psychotic symptoms, and vice versa. *Addiction, 100*(5), 612–618. http://dx.doi.org/10.1111/j.1360-0443.2005.01070.x

Fernando, S., Deane, F., McLeod, H. & Davis, E. (2017) A carer burden and stigma in schizophrenia and affective disorders: Experiences from Sri Lanka. *Asian Journal of Psychiatry, 26*, 77–81. doi: 10.1016/j.ajp.2017.01.023.

Fett, A. K. J., Viechtbauer, W., Penn, D. L., van Os, J. & Krabbendam, L. (2011) The relationship between neurocognition and social cognition with functional outcomes in schizophrenia: a meta-analysis. *Neuroscience & Biobehavioral Reviews, 35*, 573–588.

Fine, C., Gardner, M., Craigie, J. & Gold, I. (2007) Hopping, skipping or jumping to conclusions? Clarifying the role of the JTC bias in delusions. *Cognitive Neuropsychiatry, 12*(1), 46–77. doi: https://doi.org/10.1080/13546800600750597.

Finnema, E. J., Louwerens, J. W., Slooff, C. J. & Bosch, R. J. (1996) Expressed emotion on long-stay wards. *Journal of Advanced Nursing, 24*, 473–478.

Firth, J., Carney, R., French, P., Elliott, R., Cotter, J. & Young, A. (2016a) Long-term maintenance and effects of exercise in early psychosis. *Early Intervention in Psychiatry*. doi: 10.1111/eip.12365.

Firth, J., Carney, R., Jerome, L., Elliott, R., French, P. & Yung, A. R. (2016b) The effects and determinants of exercise participation in first-episode psychosis: a qualitative study. *BMC Psychiatry, 16*.

Flavell, J. H. (1979) Metacognition and cognitive monitoring: A new area of cognitive–developmental inquiry. *American Psychologist, 34*(10), 906–911.

Floyd, D., Gemmell, E., and Brown, J. (2014) Quality of life elements in schizophrenia for patients and carers offer challenges to and opportunities for intervention. *Value in Health, 17*(7), 572–573. doi: 10.1016/j.jval.2014.08.1919.

Fowler, D., Freeman, D., Smith, B., Kuipers, E., Bebbington, P., Bashforth, H., et al. (2006) The Brief Core Schema Scales (BCSS): Psychometric properties and associations with paranoia and grandiosity in non-clinical and psychosis samples. *Psychological Medicine, 36*(6), 749–759. doi: 10.1017/S0033291706007355.

Fowler, D., French, P., Hodgekins, J., Lower, R., Turner, R., Burton, S. & Wilson, J. (2013) CBT to address and prevent social disability in early and emerging psychosis. In C. Steel (ed.) *CBT for schizophrenia: evidence-based interventions and future directions.* (pp. 143–167). Chichester: John Wiley & Sons, Ltd.

Fowler, D., Hodgekins, J., French, P., Marshall, M., Freemantle, N., McCrone, P., et al. (2018) Social recovery therapy in combination with early intervention services for enhancement of social recovery in patients with first-episode psychosis (SUPER-EDEN3): A single-blind, randomised controlled trial. *Lancet Psychiatry, 5*(1), 41–50. doi: 10.1016/S2215-0366(17)30476-5.

Fowler, D., Hodgekins, J., Howells, L., Millward, M., Ivins, A., Taylor, G., et al. (2009a) Can targeted early intervention improve functional recovery in psychosis? A historical control evaluation of the effectiveness of different models of early intervention service provision in Norfolk 1998–2007. *Early Intervention in Psychiatry, 3*, 282–288.

Fowler, D., Hodgekins, J., Painter, M., Reilly, T., Crane, C., Macmillan, I., et al. (2009b) Cognitive behaviour therapy for improving social recovery in psychosis: a report from the ISREP MRC Trial Platform study (Improving Social Recovery in Early Psychosis). *Psychological Medicine, 39*, 1627–1636.

Francey, S., Jovev, M., Phassouliotis, C., Cotton, S. & Chanen, A. (2017) Does co-occurring borderline personality disorder influence acute phase treatment for first-episode psychosis? *Early Intervention in Psychiatry.* http://dx.doi.org/10.1111/eip.12435.

Franz, L., Carter, T., Leiner, A., Bergner, E., Thompson, N. & Compton, M. (2010) Stigma and treatment delay in first-episode psychosis: A grounded theory study. *Early Intervention in Psychiatry, 4*(1), 47–56. doi: 10.1111/j.1751-7893.2009.00155.x.

Freeman, D. (2011) Improving cognitive treatments for delusional. *Schizophrenia Research, 132*, 135–139.

Freeman, D. (2016) Persecutory delusions: a cognitive perspective on understanding and treatment. *The Lancet Psychiatry, 3*(7), 685–692. doi: 10.1016/S2215-0366(16)00666-3.

Freeman, D., Bradley, J., Waite, F., Sheaves, B., DeWeever, N., Bourke, E., et al. (2016) Targeting recovery in persistent delusions: A proof of principle study of a new translational psychological treatment (the Feeling Safe Programme). *Behavioural and Cognitive Psychotherapy, 44*, 539–552. doi: 10.1017/s135246816000060.

Freeman, D,. Dunn, G., Startup, H., Pugh, K., Cordwell, J., Mander, H., et al. (2015). Effects of cognitive behaviour therapy for worry on persecutory delusions in patients with psychosis (WIT): A parallel, single-blind, randomised controlled trial with a mediation analysis. *Lancet Psychiatry, 2(4)*, 305–313. doi: 10.1016/S2215-0366(15)00039-5.

Freeman, D. & Garety, P. A. (2003) Connecting neurosis and psychosis: the direct influence of emotion on delusions and hallucinations. *Behaviour Research and Therapy, 41*, 923–947.

Freeman, D. & Garety, P. A. (2014). Advances in understanding and treating persecutory delusions: a review. *Social Psychiatry Psychiatric Epidemiology, 49* (8), 1179–1189. doi: 10.1077/s00127-014-0927-7.

French, P., Morrison, A. P. (2004) *Early detection and cognitive therapy for people at high risk of developing psychosis: A treatment approach.* Chichester: Wiley.

French, P., Smith, J., Shiers, D., Reed, M. & Rayne, M. (2010) *Promoting recovery in early psychosis.* Chichester: Wiley-Blackwell.

Frith, U. & Happé, F. (1994) Autism: beyond 'theory of mind'. *Cognition, 50*(1–3), 115–132. http://dx.doi.org/10.1016/0010-0277(94)90024-8.

Fu, D., Turkoz, I., Walling, D., Lindenmayer, J., Schooler, N. & Alphs, L. (2018) Paliperidone palmitate once-monthly maintains improvement in functioning domains of the Personal and Social Performance scale compared with placebo in subjects with schizoaffective disorder. *Schizophrenia Research, 192,* 185–193. doi: 10.1016/j.schres.2017.04.004.

Fusar-Poli, P., Bonoldi, I., Yung, A. R., Borgwardt, S., Kempton, M. J., Valmaggia, L., et al. (2012) Predicting psychosis: Meta-analysis of transition outcomes in individuals at high clinical risk. *Archives of General Psychiatry, 69*(3), 220–229. doi: 10.1001/archgenpsychiatry.2011.1472.

Fusar-Poli, P., McGorry, P. D. & Kane, J. M. (2017) Improving outcomes of first-episode psychosis: an overview. *World Psychiatry, 16,* 251–265.

Fusar-Poli, P., Papanastasiou, E., Stahl, D., Rocchetti, M., Carpenter, W., Shergill, S. & McGuire, P. (2014) Treatments of negative symptoms in schizophrenia: Meta-analysis of 168 randomized placebo-controlled trials. *Schizophrenia Bulletin, 41*(4), 892–899. doi: 10.1093/schbul/sbu170.

Fusar-Poli, P., Rocchetti, M., Sardella, A., Avila, A., Brandizzi, M., Caverzasi, E., et al. (2015) Disorder, not just state of risk: meta-analysis of functioning and quality of life in people at high risk of psychosis. *British Journal of Psychiatry, 207*(3), 198–206. doi: 10.1192/bjp.bp.114.157115.

Fusar-Poli, P., Smieskova, R., Kempton, M., Ho, B., Andreasen, N. & Borgwardt, S. (2013) Progressive brain changes in schizophrenia related to antipsychotic treatment? A meta-analysis of longitudinal MRI studies. *Neuroscience & Biobehavioral Reviews, 37*(8), 1680–1691. doi: 10.1016/j.neubiorev.2013.06.001.

Gaebel, W. (1995) Is intermittent, early intervention medication an alternative for neuroleptic maintenance treatment? *International Clinical Psychopharmacology, 9,* 11–16. doi: 10.1097/00004850-199501005-00003.

Gaebel, W. & Riesbeck, M. (2014) Are there clinically useful predictors and early warnings signs of impending relapse? *Schizophrenia Research, 152,* 469–477.

Gajwani, R., Larkin, M. & Jackson, C. (2018) 'What is the point of life?': An interpretative phenomenological analysis of suicide in young men with first-episode psychosis. *Early Intervention Psychiatry, 12*(6), 1120–1127 doi: 10.1111/eip.12425.

Galderisi, S., Davidson, M., Kahn, R. S., Mucci, A., Boter, H., EUFEST Group et al. (2009) Correlates of cognitive impairment in first episode schizophrenia: the EUFEST study. *Schizophrenia Research, 115*(2–3), 104–114.

Galderisi, S., Mucci, A., Bitter, I., Libiger, J., Bucci, P., EUFEST Study Group et al. (2013) Persistent negative symptoms in first episode patients with schizophrenia: results from the European First Episode Schizophrenia Trial. *European Neuropsychopharmacology, 23*(3), 196–204.

Garcia, I., Vasiliou, C. & Penketh, K. (2007) *Listen up! Person-centred approaches to help young people experiencing mental health and emotional problems.* London: Mental Health Foundation.

Gard, D. E., Kring, A. M., Gard, M. G., Horan, W. P. & Green, M. F. (2007) Anhedonia in schizophrenia: Distinctions between anticipatory and consummatory pleasure. *Schizophrenia Research, 93*, 253–260.

Garety, P. A., Fowler, D., Freeman, D., Bebbington, P., Dunn, G. & Kuipers, E. (2008) Cognitive-behavioural therapy and family intervention for relapse prevention and symptom reduction in psychosis: Randomised controlled trial. *British Journal of Psychiatry, 192*(6), 412–423. doi: 10.1192/bjp.bp.107.043570.

Garety, P. A. & Freeman, D. (2013) The past and future of delusions research: From the inexplicable to the treatable. *British Journal of Psychiatry, 203*, 327–333.

Garety, P. A., Freeman, D., Jolley, S., Ross, K., Waller, H. & Dunn, G. (2011) Jumping to conclusions: The psychology of delusional reasoning. *Advances in Psychiatric Treatment, 17*, 332–339.

Garety, P. A., Kuipers, E., Fowler, D., Freeman, D. & Bebbington, P. (2001) A cognitive model of the positive symptoms of psychosis. *Psychological Medicine, 31*(2), 189–195. doi: https://doi.org/10.1017/S0033291701003312.

Gasquet, I., Haro, J. M., Tcherny-Lessenot, S., Chartier, F. & Lépine, J. P. (2008) Remission in the outpatient care of schizophrenia: 3-year results from the Schizophrenia Outpatients Health Outcomes (SOHO) study in France. *European Psychiatry, 23(7)*, 491–496. doi: 10.1016/j.eurpsy.2008.03.012.

Gaudiano, B. A. (ed.) (2015) *Incorporating acceptance and mindfulness into the treatment of psychosis: Current trends and future directions*. New York: Oxford University Press.

Gaudiano, B. A., Herbert, J. D. & Hayes, S. C. (2010) Is it the symptom or the relation to it? Investigating potential mediators of change in acceptance and commitment therapy for psychosis. *Behavior Therapy, 41*, 543–554.

Gaynor, K., Dooley, B., Lawlor, E., Lawoyin, R. & O'Callaghan, E. (2011) Group cognitive behavioural therapy as a treatment for negative symptoms in first-episode psychosis. *Early Intervention in Psychiatry, 5*, 168–173.

Geddes, J., Freemantle, N., Harrison, P. & Bebbington, P. (2000) Atypical antipsychotics in the treatment of schizophrenia: systematic overview and meta-regression analysis. *British Medical Journal, 321*(7273), 1371–1376. doi: 10.1136/bmj.321.7273.1371.

Geddes, J. R., Barbui, C. & Cipriani, A. (2009) Risk of suicidal behaviour in adults taking antidepressants. *British Medical Journal, 339*, doi: 10.1136/bmj.b3066.

Gee, B., Hodgekins, J., Fowler, D., Marshall, M., Everard, L., Lester, H., et al. (2016a) The course of negative symptom in first episode psychosis and the relationship with SR. *Schizophrenia Research, 174*, 165–171.

Gee, B., Notley, C., Byrne, R., Clarke, T., Hodgekins, J., French, P., et al. (2016b) Young people's experiences of Social Recovery Cognitive Behavioural Therapy and treatment as usual in the PRODIGY trial. *Early Intervention in Psychiatry, 12*(5), 879–885.

Geschwind, N., Peeters, F., Jacobs, N., Delespaul, P., Derom, C., Thiery, E., Wichers, M., et al. (2010). Meeting risk with resilience: Hhigh daily life reward experience preserves mental health. *Acta Psychiatrica Scandinavica, 122*, 129–138.

Giffort, D., Schmook, A., Woody, C., Vollendorf, C. & Gervain, M. (1995) *Construction of a scale to measure consumer recovery*. Springfield, IL, Illinois Office of Mental Health.

Giggs, J. A. (1986) Mental disorders and ecological structure in Nottingham. *Social Science and Medicine, 23*(10), 945–961. doi: 10.1016/0277-9536(86)90252-2.

Gilbert, P. (2003) Evolution, social roles, and the differences in shame and guilt. *Social Research: An International Quarterly of the Social Sciences, 70*, 1205–1230.

Gilbert, P. (2010) *Compassion focused therapy: distinctive features.* London: Routledge.

Gilbert. P. & Allan, S. (1998) The role of defeat and entrapment (arrested flight) in depression: An exploration of an evolutionary view. *Psychological Medicine, 28(3)*: 585–598.

Gilbert, P., Clarke, M., Hempel, S., Miles, J. N. V. & Irons, C. (2004) Criticizing and reassuring oneself: An exploration of forms, styles, and reasons in female students. *British Journal of Clinical Psychology, 43*, 31–50. doi: 10.1348/014466504772812959.

Girgis, R., Phillips, M., Li, X., Li, K., Jiang, H. Wu, C., et al. (2011) Clozapine v. chlorpromazine in treatment-naive, first-episode schizophrenia: 9-year outcomes of a randomised clinical trial. *The British Journal of Psychiatry, 199*(4), 281–288. doi: 10.1192/bjp.bp.110.081471.

Gleeson, J., Álvarez-Jiménez, M., Cotton, S. M., Parker, A. G. & Hetrick, S. (2010) A systematic review of relapse measurement in randomized controlled trials of relapse prevention in first-episode psychosis. *Schizophrenia Research, 119*(1–3), 79–88. doi: 10.1016/j.schres.2010.02.1073.

Gleeson, J., Chanen, A., Cotton, S., Pearce, T., Newman, B. & McCutcheon, L. (2011) Treating co-occurring first-episode psychosis and borderline personality: A pilot randomized controlled trial. *Early Intervention in Psychiatry, 6*(1), 21–29. http://dx.doi.org/10.1111/j.1751-7893.2011.00306.x

Gleeson, J., Cotton, S., Álvarez-Jiménez, M., Wade, D., Gee, D., Crisp, K., et al. (2013) A randomized controlled trial of relapse prevention therapy for first-episode psychosis patients: Outcome at 30-month follow-up. *Schizophrenia Bulletin, 39*(2), 436–448. doi: 10.1093/schbul/sbr165.

Gleeson, J., Lederman, R., Herrman, H., Koval, P., Eleftheriadis, D., Bendall, S et al. (2017) Moderated online social therapy for carers of young people recovering from first-episode psychosis: Study protocol for a randomised controlled trial. *Trials, 18*(1). doi: 10.1186/s13063-016-1775-5.

Glick, I., Correll, C., Altamura, A., Marder, S., Csernansky, J., Weiden, P., et al. (2011) Mid-term and long-term efficacy and effectiveness of antipsychotic medications for schizophrenia. *The Journal of Clinical Psychiatry, 72*(12), 1616–1627. doi: 10.4088/jcp.11r06927.

Goff, D. (2015) Drug development in schizophrenia. *Current Opinion in Psychiatry, 28*(3), 207–215. doi: 10.1097/yco.0000000000000152.

Goldman, H. H., Skodol, A. E. & Lave, T. R. (1992) Revising axis V for DSM-IV: A review of measures of social functioning. *The American Journal of Psychiatry, 149*(9).

Goldney, R. D. (2011) Antidepressants and suicidal prevention. In R. O'Connor, S. Platt & J. Gordon (eds) *International handbook of suicide prevention: Research, policy and practice.* Chichester: Wiley-Blackwell.

González-Blanch, C., Gleeson, J., Cotton, S., Crisp, K., McGorry, P. & Álvarez-Jiménez, M. (2015) Longitudinal relationship between expressed emotion and cannabis misuse in young people with first-episode psychosis. *European Psychiatry, 30*(1): 20–25. doi: 10.1016/j.eurpsy.2014.07.002.

González-Blanch, C., Perez-Iglesias, R., Pardo-Garcia, G., Rodriguez-Sanchez, J. M., Martinez-Garcia, O., Vazquez-Barquero, J. L., et al. (2010) Prognostic value of cognitive functioning for global functional recovery in first-episode schizophrenia. *Psychological Medicine, 40*, 935–944.

Gooding, P. A., Littlewood, D., Owen, R., Johnson, J. & Tarrier, N. (2017) Psychological resilience in people experiencing schizophrenia and suicidal thoughts and behaviours. *Journal of Mental Health, 28*, 1–7.

Goodman, W. K., Lawrence, M. D., Price, H., Rasmussen, S. A., Mazure, C., Fleischmann, R. L., et al. (1989) The Yale-Brown Obsessive-Compulsive Scale. *Archives of General Psychiatry, 48*, 1006–1016.

Goss, K., Gilbert, P. & Allan, S. (1994) An exploration of shame measures: 1: The other as shamer scale. *Personality and Individual Differences, 17*, 713–717. doi: 10.1016/0191-8869(94)90150-3.

Gottlieb, J., Harper Romeo, K., Penn, D., Mueser, K. & Chiko, B. (2013) Web-based cognitive-behavioural therapy for auditory hallucinations in persons with psychosis: a pilot study. *Schizophrenia Research, 145*, 82–87.

GOV.UK. (2015) E-cigarettes: an evidence update Retrieved from www.gov.uk/government/publications/e-cigarettes-an-evidence-update.

Graeber, D. A., Moyers, T. B., Griffith, G., Guajardo, E. & Tonigan, S. (2003) A pilot study comparing motivational interviewing and an educational intervention in patients with schizophrenia and alcohol use disorders. *Community Mental Health Journal, 39*, 189–202.

Granholm, E., Ben-Zeev, D. & Link, P. C. (2009) Social disinterest attitudes and group cognitive-behavioral social skills training for functional disability in schizophrenia. *Schizophrenia Bulletin, 35*, 874–883.

Granholm, E., Holden, J., Link, P. C., McQuaid, J. R. & Jeste, D. V. (2013) Randomized controlled trial of cognitive behavioral social skills training for older consumers with schizophrenia: defeatist performance attitudes and functional outcome. *The American Journal of Geriatric Psychiatry, 21*, 251–262.

Grant, P. M. & Beck, A. T. (2009) Defeatist beliefs as a mediator of cognitive impairment, negative symptoms, and functioning in schizophrenia. *Schizophrenia Bulletin, 35,* 798–806.

Grant, P. M., Huh, G. A., Perivoliotis, D., Stolar, N. & Beck, A. T. (2012) Randomised trial to evaluate the efficacy of cognitive therapy for low-functioning patients with schizophrenia. *Archives of General Psychiatry, 69*(2), 121–127.

Gras, A., Amad, A., Thomas, P. & Jardri, R. (2014) Hallucinations et trouble de personnalité borderline: une revue de littérature. *L'encéphale, 40*(6), 431–438. http://dx.doi.org/10.1016/j.encep.2014.07.002.

Grealish, A., Tai, S., Hunter, A. & Morrison, A. (2013) Qualitative exploration of empowerment from the perspective of young people with psychosis. *Clinical Psychology and Psychotherapy, 20*(2), 136–148.

Green, M. (2016) Impact of cognitive and social cognitive impairment on functional outcomes in patients with schizophrenia. *The Journal of Clinical Psychiatry, 2,* 8–11. doi: 10.4088/jcp.14074su1c.02.

Green, M. F. (1996) What are the functional consequences of neurocognitive deficits in schizophrenia? *The American Journal of Psychiatry, 153*, 321.

Greenwood, K., Sweeney, A., Williams, S., Garety, P., Kuipers, E., Scott, J. & Peters, E. (2010) Choice of Outcome In CBT for psychosEs (CHOICE): The development of a new service user–led outcome measure of CBT for psychosis. *Schizophrenia Bulletin, 36*(1), 126–135.

Greenwood, P. & Shiers, D. (2016) Don't just screen intervene; a quality improvement initiative to improve physical health screening of young people experiencing severe mental illness. *Mental Health Review Journal, 21*(1), 48–60. doi: 10.1108/mhrj-01-2015-0003.

Gregory, A., Mallikarjun, P. & Upthegrove, R. (2017) Treatment of depression in schizophrenia: Systematic review and meta-analysis. *British Journal of Psychiatry, 211*(4), 198–204. doi: 10.1192/bjp.bp.116.190520.

Gregory, M. (2009) Why are family interventions important? A family member perspective. In F. Lobban & C. Barrowclough, *A casebook of family interventions for psychosis*, Chichester: Wiley.

Griffiths, S. L., Wood, S. J. & Birchwood, M. (2018) Vulnerability to psychosocial disability in psychosis. *Epidemiology and Psychiatric Sciences*, 1–6.

Gross, J. J. & John, O. P. (2003) Individual differences in two emotion regulation processes: Implications for affect, relationships and well-being. *Journal of Personality and Social Psychology, 85*, 348–362.

Grubaugh, A. L., Zinzow, H. M., Paul, P., Egede, L. E. & Freuh, C. (2011) Trauma exposure and posttraumatic stress disorder in adults with severe mental illness: A critical review. *Clinical Psychology Review, 31*(6), 883–899. doi: 10.1016/j.cpr.2011.04.003.

Gucci, F. & Marmo, F. (2016) A study on the effectiveness of E-Mental Health in the treatment of psychosis: Looking to recovery. *European Psychiatry, 33*, 27–28.

Guloksuz, S. & Van Os, J. (2018) The slow death of the concept of schizophrenia and the painful birth of the psychosis spectrum. *Psychological Medicine, 48*(2), 229–244. doi: 10.1017/S0033291717001775.

Gumley, A. & Clark, S. (2012) Risk of arrested recovery following first episode psychosis: An integrative approach to psychotherapy. *Journal of Psychotherapy Integration, 22*(4), 298–313.

Gumley, A. & Park, P. (2010) Relapse prevention in early psychosis. In P. French, J. Smith, D. Shiers, M. Reid & M. Rayne. *Promoting recovery in early psychosis: A practice manual*. Chichester, Wiley-Blackwell.

Gumley, A., Braehler, C., Laithwaite, H., MacBeth, A. & Gilbert, P. (2010) A compassion focused model of recovery after psychosis. *International Journal of Cognitive Therapy, 3*(2), 186–201. doi: 10.1521/ijct.2010.3.2.186.

Gumley, A. & Schwannauer, M. (2006) *Staying well after psychosis: A cognitive interpersonal approach to recovery and relapse prevention.* Chichester: John Wiley & Sons.

Gunderson, J. (2010) Borderline personality disorder: Ontogeny of a diagnosis. *FOCUS, 8*(2), 230–239. http://dx.doi.org/10.1176/foc.8.2.foc230.

Gupta, S., Lakshmanan, D., Khastgir, U. & Nair, R. (2017) Management of antipsychotic-induced hyperprolactinaemia. *British Journal of Psychiatry Advances, 23*(4), 278–286.

Gureje, O., Harvey, C. & Herrman, H. (2004) Self-esteem in patients who have recovered from psychosis: profile and relationship to quality of life. *Australian and New Zealand Journal of Psychiatry, 38*, 334–338.

Haddock, G., Eisner, E., Davies, G., Coupe, N. & Barrowclough, C. (2013) Psychotic symptoms, self-harm and violence in individuals with schizophrenia and substance misuse problems. *Schizophrenia Research, 151*(1–3), 215–220. doi: 10.1016/j.schres.2013.10.031.

Haddock, G., McCarron, J., Tarrier, N. & Faragher, E. B. (1999) Scales to measure dimensions of hallucinations and delusions: The psychotic symptom rating scales (PSYRATS). *Psychological Medicine, 29*(4), 879–889.

Haddock, G., Wood, L., Watts, R., Dunn, G., Morrison, A. & Price, J. (2011) The Subjective Experiences of Psychosis Scale (SEPS): Psychometric evaluation of a scale to assess outcome in psychosis. *Schizophrenia Research, 133*(1–3), 244–249.

Häfner, H. & an der Heiden, W. (1999) The course of schizophrenia in the light of modern follow-up studies: the ABC and WHO studies. *European Archives of Psychiatry and Clinical Neuroscience, 249*(4), 14–26.

Häfner, H., Löffler, W., Maurer, K., Hambrecht, M. & Heiden, W. (1999) Depression, negative symptoms, social stagnation and social decline in the early course of schizophrenia. *Acta Psychiatrica Scandinavica, 100,* 105–118.

Hagen, B. & Nixon, G. (2010) Psychosis as a potentially transformative experience: implications for psychologists and counsellors. *Procedia – Social and Behavioural Sciences, 5,* 722–726.

Hagen, K., Hansen, B., Inge, J & Larsen, T. K. (2013) Prevalence and clinical characteristics of patients with obsessive-compulsive disorder in FEP. *BMC Psychiatry, 13*(156). doi: 10.1186/1471-244X-13-156.

Hahlweg, K., Nuechterlein, K., Goldstein, M., Magana, A., Doane, J. & Snyder, K. (1987) Parental expressed emotion attitudes and intrafamilial communication behavior. In K. Hahlweg & M. Goldstein, *Understanding major mental disorders: The contribution of family interaction research* (pp. 156–175). New York: Family Process Press.

Hall, R. C. (1995) Global assessment of functioning: A modified scale. *Psychosomatics, 36,* 267–275.

Halperin, S., Nathan, P., Drummon, P. & Castle, D. (2000) A cognitive-behavioural group based intervention for social anxiety in schizophrenia. *Australia and New Zealand Journal of Psychiatry, 34,* 809–813. doi: 10.1080/j.1440-1614.2000.00820.

Hamm, J., Hasson-Ohayon, I., Kukla, M. & Lysaker, P. (2013) Individual psychotherapy for schizophrenia: trends and developments in the wake of the recovery movement. *Psychology Research and Behaviour Management, 6,* 45–54.

Harrigan, S. M., McGorry, P. D. & Krstev, H. (2003) Does treatment delay in first-episode psychosis really matter? *Psychological Medicine, 33,* 97–110.

Harris, K., Collinson, C. & das Nair, R. (2012) Service-users' experiences of an early intervention in psychosis service: An interpretative phenomenological analysis. *Psychology and Psychotherapy, 85*(4), 456–469. doi: 10.1111/j.2044-8341.2011.02043.x.

Harris, M. G., Henry, L. P., Harrigan, S. M., Purcell, R., Schwartz, O. S., Farrelly, S. E., et al. (2005) The relationship between duration of untreated psychosis and outcome: an eight-year prospective study. *Schizophrenia Research, 79*(1), 85–93.

Harrop, C. & Trower, P. (2001) Why does schizophrenia develop at late adolescence? *Clinical Psychology Review, 21,* 241–265.

Hartley, S., Barrowclough, G. & Haddock, G. (2013) Anxiety and depression in psychosis: A systematic review of associations with positive psychotic symptoms. *Acta Psychiatrica Scandinavica, 128,* 327–346. doi: 10.1111/acps.12080.

Harvey, P. D. & Bellack, A. S. (2009) Toward a terminology for functional recovery in schizophrenia: is functional remission a viable concept? *Schizophrenia Bulletin, 35,* 300–306.

Hasson-Ohayon, I., Arnon-Ribenfeld, N., Hamm, J. A. & Lysaker, P. H. (2017) Agency before action: The application of behavioral activation in psychotherapy with persons with psychosis. *Psychotherapy, 54,* 245.

Haw, C., Hawton, K., Sutton, L., Sinclair, J. & Deeks, J. (2005) Schizophrenia and deliberate self-harm: A systematic review of risk factors. *Suicide Life Threatening Behaviour, 35*(1), 50–62.

Hawton, K. & van Heeringen, K. (2009) Suicide. *The Lancet, 373*(9672), 1372–1381. doi: 10.1016/S0140-6736(09)60372-X.

Hayes, C. & Hofmann, S. (2017) The third wave of cognitive behavioural therapy and the rise of process-based care. *World Psychiatry, 16*(3), 245–246.

Hayes, S. C., Strosahl, K. & Wilson, K. G. (1999) *Acceptance and Commitment Therapy: An experiential approach to behavior change.* New York, The Guilford Press.

Hazell, C. M., Hayward, M., Cavanagh, K. & Strauss, C. (2016) Systematic review and meta-analysis of low intensity CBT for psychosis. *Clinical Psychology Review, 45*, 183–193.

Heelis, R., Graham, H. & Jackson, C. (2016) A preliminary test of the interpersonal psychological theory of suicidal behavior in young people with a first episode of psychosis. *British Journal of Clinical Psychology, 72(*1), 79–87. doi: 10.1002/jclp. 22233.

Heinrichs, D. W., Hanlon, T. E. & Carpenter, W. T. Jr. (1984) The Quality of Life Scale: an instrument for rating the schizophrenic deficit syndrome. *Schizophrenia Bulletin, 10(3)*, 388–398.

Heinz, A., Deserno, L. & Reininghaus, U. (2013) Urbanicity, social adversity and psychosis. *World Psychiatry, 12*(3), 187–197.

Helfer, B., Samara, M., Huhn, M., Klupp, E., Leucht, C., Zhu, Y., et al. (2016) Efficacy and safety of antidepressants added to antipsychotics for schizophrenia: A systematic review and meta-analysis. *The American Journal of Psychiatry, 173*(9), 876–886. doi: 10.1176/appi.ajp.2016.15081035.

Helle, S., Ringen, P., Melle, I., Larsen, T., Gjestad, R., Johnsen, E., et al. (2016) Cannabis use is associated with 3 years earlier onset of schizophrenia spectrum disorder in a naturalistic, multi-site sample (N = 1119). *Schizophrenia Research, 170*(1), 217–221.

Henderson, C. Robinson, E., Evans-Lacko, S. & Thornicroft, G. (2017) Relationships between anti-stigma programmes awareness, disclosure comfort and intended help seeking regarding a mental health problem. *The British Journal of Psychiatry, 211*, 316–322. doi: 10.1192/bjp.bp:116.195867.

Hennekens, C., Hennekens, A., Hollar, D. & Casey, D. (2005) Schizophrenia and increased risks of cardiovascular disease. *American Heart Journal, 150*(6), 1115–1121. doi: 10.1016/j.ahj.2005.02.007.

Hennen, J., Baldessarini, R. J. (2005) Suicidal risk during treatment with clozapine: a meta-analysis. *Schizophrenia Research, 73*(2–3), 139–145. doi: 10.1016/j.schres. 2004.05.015.

Henriksen, M. G., Nordgaard, J. & Jansson, L. B. (2017) Genetics of schizophrenia: Overview of methods, findings and limitations. *Frontiers in Human Neuroscience, 11*, 322. doi: http://doi.org/10.3389/fnhum.2017.00322.

Herz, M. & Melville, C. (1980) Relapse in schizophrenia. *The American Journal of Psychiatry, 137*, 801–812.

Heslin, M., Lomas, B., Lappin, J. M., Donoghue, K., Reininghaus, U., Onyejiaka, A., et al. (2015) Diagnostic change 10 years after a first episode of psychosis. *Psychological Medicine, 45*(13), 2757–2769. doi: 10.1017/S0033291715000720.

Hickling, L., Perez-Iglesias, R., Ortiz-García de la Foz, V., Balanzá-Martínez, V., McGuire, P., Crespo-Facorro, B., et al. (2017) Tobacco smoking and its association with cognition in first episode psychosis patients. *Schizophrenia Research, 192*, 269–273. doi: 10.1016/j.schres.2017.04.018.

Hirsch, S., Bowen, J., Emami, J., Cramer, P., Jolley, A., Haw, C. & Dickinson, M. (1996) A one-year prospective study of the effect of life events and medication in the aetiology of schizophrenic relapse. *British Journal of Psychiatry, 168*, 49–56. doi: 10.1192/bjp. 168.1.49.

Ho, R., Lo, P., Chan, C. & Chen, E. (2014) EPA-0752 – Spirituality in schizophrenia: do patients and healthcare professionals have similar understanding? *European Psychiatry, 29*(1).

Ho, W. H., Chang, W. C., Tang, Y. M., Hui, L. M. & Chan, K. W. (2018) 3-year negative symptom trajectory and its relationship with symptom and functional outcomes in first episode non-affective psychosis: A prospective 13-year follow-up study. *Schizophrenia Bulletin, 44*(1), 372–373. doi: 10.1093/schbul/sby018.909.

Hodgekins, J., Birchwood, M., Christopher, R., Marshall, M., Coker, S., Everard, L., et al. (2015a) Investigating trajectories of SR in individuals with first-episode psychosis: A latent class growth analysis. *The British Journal of Psychiatry, 207*, 536–543.

Hodgekins, J. & Fowler, D. (2010) CBT and recovery from psychosis in the ISREP trial: Mediating effects of hope and positive beliefs on activity. *Psychiatric Services, 61*, 321–324.

Hodgekins, J., French, P., Birchwood, M., Mugford, M., Christopher, R., Marshall, M., et al. (2015b) Comparing time use in individuals at different stages of psychosis and a non-clinical comparison group. *Schizophrenia Research, 161*, 188–193.

Hofmann, S. G., Sawyer, A. T., Witt, A. A. & Oh, D. (2010) The effect of mindfulness-based therapy on anxiety and depression: A meta-analytic review. *Journal of Consulting and Clinical Psychology, 78*(2), 169–183.

Hogarty, G. E., Flesher, S., Ulrich, R., Carter, M., Greenwald, D., Pogue-Geile, M., et al. (2004) Cognitive enhancement therapy for schizophrenia: Effects of a 2-year randomized trial on cognition and behavior. *Archives of General Psychiatry, 61*, 866–876.

Hogarty, G. E., Kornblith, S. J., Greenwald, D., DiBarry, A. L., Cooley, S., Ulrich, R. F., et al. (1997) Three-year trials of personal therapy among schizophrenic patients living with or independent of family I: Description of study and effects on relapse rates. *The American Journal of Psychiatry, 154*, 1504–1513.

Hogins, S. & Klein, S. (2017) New clinically relevant findings about violence by people with schizophrenia. *Canadian Journal of Psychiatry, 62*(2), 86–93. doi: 10.1177/070 6743716648300.

Holt, R. & Peveler, R. (2010) Antipsychotics and hyperprolactinaemia: mechanisms, consequences and management. *Clinical Endocrinology, 74*(2), 141–147. doi: 10.1111/ j.1365-2265.2010.03814.x.

Hooley, J. (1987) The nature and origins of expressed emotion. In K. Hahlweg & M. Goldstein, *Understanding major mental disorder: The contribution of family interaction research* (pp. 176–194). New York: Family Process Press.

Horan, W. P., Ventura, J., Nuechterlein, K. H., Subotnik, K. L., Hwang, S. S. & Mintz, J. (2005) Stressful life events in recent-onset schizophrenia: Reduced frequencies and altered subjective appraisals. *Schizophrenia Research, 75*(2–3), 363–374. doi: 10.1016/ j.schres.2004.07.019.

Howard, L., Leese, M. & Thornicroft, G. (2000) Social networks and functional status in patients with psychosis. *Acta Psychiatrica Scandinavica, 102*, 376–385.

Howes, O., McCutcheon, R., Owen, M. & Murray, R. (2017) The role of genes, stress, and dopamine in the development of schizophrenia. *Biological Psychiatry, 81*(1) 9–20.

Howes, O. D. & Kapur, S. (2009) The dopamine hypothesis of schizophrenia: version III–the final common pathway. *Schizophrenia Bulletin, 35*(3), 549–562.

Huber, G. & Gross, G. (1989) The concept of basic symptoms in schizophrenic and schizoaffective psychoses. *Recent Progress in Medicine, 80*(12), 646–652.

Huguelet, P., Mohr, S., Jung, V., Gillieron, C., Brandt, P. Y. & Borras, L. (2007) Effect of religion on suicide attempts in outpatients with schizophrenia or schizo-affective disorders compared with inpatients with non-psychotic disorders. *European Psychiatry, 22*(3), 188–194.

Hunt, I. M., Robinson, J., Bickley, H., Meehan, J., Parsons, R., McCann, K., et al. (2003) Suicides in ethnic minorities within 12 months of contact with mental health services. National clinical survey. *British Journal of Psychiatry, 183,* 155–160.

IRIS (2000) Early intervention in psychosis: Clinical guidelines and service frameworks. Retrieved from Kaleidoscope nsf.

Islam, Z. Rabiee, F. & Singh, S. (2015) Black and minority ethnic groups perception and experience of early intervention in psychosis services in the United Kingdom. *Journal of Cross-Cultural Psychology,* 1–17.

Isvoranu, A.-M., van Borkulo, C. D., Boyette, L. L., Wigman, J. T. W., Vinkers, C. H., Borsboom, D. & Group Investigators. (2017) A network approach to psychosis: Pathways between childhood trauma and psychotic symptoms. *Schizophrenia Bulletin, 43*(1), 187–196. doi: http://doi.org/10.1093/schbul/sbw055.

Iuvone, T., Esposito, G., De Filippis, D., Scuderi, C. & Steardo, L. (2009) Cannabidiol: a promising drug for neurodegenerative disorders? *CNS Neuroscience Therapy, 15*(1), 65–75. doi: 10.1111/j.1755-5949.2008.00065.x.

Iyer, S. N., Mangala, R., Anitha, J., Thara, R. & Malla, A. K. (2011) An examination of patient-identified goals for treatment in a first-episode programme in Chennai, India. *Early Intervention in Psychiatry, 5,* 360–365.

Jääskeläinen, E., Juola, P., Hirvonen, N., McGrath, J. J., Saha, S., Isohanni, M., Veijola, J. & Miettunen, J. (2013) A systematic review and meta-analysis of recovery in schizophrenia. *Schizophrenia Bulletin, 39*(6), 1296–1306.

Jackson, C., Bernard, M. & Birchwood, M. (2011) The efficacy of psychotherapy in reducing post-psychotic trauma. *Epidemiologic e Psychiatric Sociale (EPS), 20*(2), 127–131.

Jackson, C. & Birchwood, M. (1996) Early intervention in psychosis: Opportunities for secondary prevention. *British Journal of Clinical Psychology, 35,* 487–502. doi: 10.1111/j.2044-8260.1996.tb01206.x.

Jackson, C., Birchwood, M. & the UK NEDEN group (2012) Suicidality during the first year of early intervention. Paper presented to the 8th IEPA Conference, San Francisco, USA, October 11th–13th.

Jackson, C., Knott, C., Skeate, A. & Birchwood, M. (2005) The trauma of FEP. *Australian and New Zealand Journal of Psychiatry, 38,* 327–333.

Jackson, C., Trower, P., Reid, I., Smith, J., Townend, M., Barton, K., et al. (2009) Improving psychological adjustment following a first episode of psychosis: A randomised control trial of cognitive therapy to reduce post psychotic trauma symptoms. *Behaviour Research and Therapy, 47,* 454–462. doi: 10.1016/j.brat.2009.02.009.

Jacobson, N. & Greenley, D. (2001) What is recovery? A conceptual model and explication. *Psychiatric Services, 52*(4), 482–485.

Jagannathan, A., Thirthalli, J., Hamza, A., Nagendra, H. & Gangadhar, B. (2014) Predictors of family caregiver burden in schizophrenia: Study from an in-patient tertiary care hospital in India. *Asian Journal of Psychiatry, 8,* 94–98. doi: 10.1016/j.ajp.2013.12.018.

Jansen, J., Haahr, U., Lyse, H., Pedersen, M., Trauelsen, A. & Simonsen, E. (2017) Psychological flexibility as a buffer against caregiver distress in families with psychosis. *Frontiers in Psychology, 8.* doi: 10.3389/fpsyg.2017.01625.

Janssen, I., Hanssen, M., Bak, M., Bijl, R. V., de Graaf, R., Vollebergh, W., McKenzie, K. & van Os, J. (2003) Discrimination and delusional ideation. *British Journal of Psychiatry, 182*(1), 71–76. doi: 10.1192/bjp.182.1.71.

Jauhar, S., McKenna, P. J., Radua, J., Fung, E., Salvador, R. & Laws, K. R. (2015) Cognitive behavioural therapy for the symptoms of schizophrenia: Systematic review and meta-analysis with examination of potential bias. *British Journal of Psychiatry, 204*, 20–29. doi: 10.1192/bjp.bp.112.116285.

Jee, C. (2017) NHS 'Silver Linings' app to help young people manage mental health. Retrieved from www.techworld.com/news/apps-wearables/nhs-silver-linings-app-help-young-people-manage-mental-health-3597926/.

Jerrell, J. M., Cousins, V. C. & Roberts, K. M. (2006) Psychometrics of the recovery process inventory. *Journal of Behavioral Health Services & Research, 33*, 464–473.

Johansen, K. (1999) Efficacy of metformin in the treatment of NIDDM. Meta-analysis. *Diabetes Care, 22*(1), 33–37. doi: 10.2337/diacare.22.1.33.

Johns, L. C., van Os, J. (2001) The continuity of psychotic experiences in the general population. *Clinical Psychology Review, 21*(8), 1125–1141. doi: https://doi.org/10.1016/S0272-7358(01)00103-9.

Johnson, D., Penn, D., Fredrickson, B., Kring, A., Myer, P., Catalino, L. & Brantley, M. (2011) A pilot study of loving-kindness meditation for the negative symptoms of schizophrenia. *Schizophrenia Research, 129*(2–3), 137–140.

Johnson, J., Jones, C., Lin, A., Wood, S., Heinze, K. & Jackson, C. (2014) Shame amplifies the association between stressful life events and paranoia amongst young adults using mental health services: Implications for understanding risk and psychological resilience. *Psychiatry Research, 220*(1–2), 217–225. doi: 10.1016/j.psychres.2014.07.022.

Johnson, J., Wood, A., Gooding, P., Taylor, P. & Tarrier, N. (2011) Resilience to suicidality: The buffering hypothesis. *Clinical Psychology Review, 31*(4), 563–591.

Johnson S, Sheridan Rains L, Marwaha S, Strang J, Craig T, Weaver T., et al. (2016) A randomised controlled trial of the clinical and cost-effectiveness of a contingency management intervention compared to treatment as usual for reduction of cannabis use and of relapse in early psychosis (CIRCLE): *A study protocol for a randomised controlled trial.* Trials, 17(1), 515.

Joiner, T. (2005) Why people die by suicide. Cambridge, MA: Harvard University Press.

Jones, H. (2002) Dopamine and antipsychotic drug action revisited. *The British Journal of Psychiatry, 181*(4), 271–275. doi: 10.1192/bjp.181.4.271.

Jones, N., Godzikovskaya, J., Zhao, Z., Vasquez, A., Gilbert, A. & Davidson, L. (2017) Intersecting disadvantage: Unpacking poor outcomes within early intervention in psychosis services. *Early Intervention Psychiatry, 27*. doi: 10.1111/eip.12508.

Jones, P., Barnes, T., Davies, L., Dunn, G., Lloyd, H., Hayhurst, K. P. et al. (2006) Randomized controlled trial of the effect on quality of life of second- vs. first-generation antipsychotic drugs in schizophrenia. *Archives of General Psychiatry, 63*(10), 1079–1087. doi: 10.1001/archpsyc.63.10.1079.

Jordan, G., MacDonald, K., Pope, M., Schorr, E., Malla, A. & Iyer, S. (2018) Positive changes experienced after a first episode of psychosis: A systematic review. *Psychiatric Services, 69*(1), 84–99.

Jordan, G., Pope, M., Lambrou, A., Malla, A. & Iyer, S. (2016) Post-traumatic growth following a first episode of psychosis: A scoping review. *Early Intervention in Psychiatry, 11*(3), 187–199. doi: 10.1111/eip.12349.

Jørgensen, R., Zoffmann, V., Munk-Jørgensen, P., Buck, K., Jensen, S., Hansson, L., et al. (2015) Relationships over time of subjective and objective elements of recovery in persons with schizophrenia. *Psychiatry Research, 228*(1), 14–19.

Joseph, J., Kremen, W. S., Franz, C. E., Glatt, S. J., van de Leemput, J., Chandler, S. D., et al. (2017) Predictors of current functioning and functional decline in schizophrenia. *Schizophrenia Research, 188*, 158–164.

Kahn, R. & Fleischhacker, W. (2008) Lessons from schizophrenia study: EUFEST. *European Psychiatry, 23*, 6–7. doi: 10.1016/j.eurpsy.2008.01.025.

Kahn, R., Fleischhacker, W., Boter, H., Davidson, M., Vergouwe, Y., EUFEST Study Group et al. (2008) Effectiveness of antipsychotic drugs in first-episode schizophrenia and schizophreniform disorder: An open randomised clinical trial. *The Lancet, 371*(9618), 1085–1097. doi: 10.1016/s0140-6736(08)60486-9.

Kallivayalil, R. (2008) Are we over-dependent on pharmacotherapy? *Indian Journal of Psychiatry, 50*(1), 7. doi: 10.4103/0019-5545.39750.

Kam, S. M., Singh, S. P. & Upthegrove, R. (2015) What needs to follow early intervention? Predictors of relapse and functional recovery following first-episode psychosis. *Early Intervention in Psychiatry, 9*, 279–283.

Kane, J. (1988) Clozapine for the treatment resistant schizophrenic. *Archives of General Psychiatry, 15*(9), 789. doi: 10.1001/archpsych.1988.01800330013001.

Kane, J., Robinson, D., Schooler, N., Mueser, K., Penn, D., Rosenheck, R., et al. (2016) Comprehensive versus usual community care for first-episode psychosis: 2-year outcomes from the NIMH RAISE Early Treatment Program. *The American Journal of Psychiatry, 173*(4), 362–372. doi: 10.1176/appi.ajp.2015.15050632.

Kanter, J. W., Manos, R. C., Bowe, W. M., Baruch, D. E., Busch, A. M. & Rusch, L. C. (2010) What is behavioral activation? A review of the empirical literature. *Clinical Psychology Review, 30*, 608–620.

Kantrowitz, J. & Javitt, D. (2010) Thinking glutamatergically: Changing concepts of schizophrenia based upon changing neurochemical models. *Clinical Schizophrenia & Related Psychoses, 4*(3), 189–200. doi: 10.3371/csrp.4.3.6.

Kapur, S. (2004) Psychosis as a state of aberrant salience: A framework linking biology, phenomenology, and pharmacology in schizophrenia. *The American Journal of Psychiatry, 160*(1), 13–23. doi: 10.1176/appi.ajp.160.1.13.

Kapur, S., Arenovich, T., Agid, O., Zipursky, R., Lindborg, S. & Jones, B. (2005) Evidence for onset of antipsychotic effects within the first 24 hours of treatment. *The American Journal of Psychiatry, 162*(5), 939–946. doi: 10.1176/appi.ajp.162.5.939.

Kapur, S., Mizrahi, R. & Li, M. (2005) From dopamine to salience to psychosis—linking biology, pharmacology and phenomenology of psychosis. *Schizophrenia Research, 79*(1), 59–68. doi: 10.1016/j.schres.2005.01.003.

Kapur, S., Remington, G. & Jones, C. (1999) Does dopamine receptor occupancy predict antipsychotic response and side effects? A randomised double-blind test of hypothesis. *Schizophrenia Research, 36*, 242.

Kate, N., Grover, S., Kulhara, P. & Nehra, R. (2013a) Caregiving appraisal in schizophrenia: A study from India. *Social Science and Medicine, 98*, 135–140. doi: 10.1016/j.socscimed.2013.09.005.

Kate, N., Grover, S., Kulhara, P. & Nehra, R. (2013b) Relationship of caregiver burden with coping strategies, social support, psychological morbidity, and quality of life in the caregivers of schizophrenia. *Asian Journal of Psychiatry, 6*(5), 380–388. doi: 10.1016/j.ajp.2013.03.014.

Kate, N., Grover, S., Kulhara, P. & Nehra, R. (2014) Relationship of quality of life with coping and burden in primary caregivers of patients with schizophrenia. *International Journal of Social Psychiatry, 60*(2), 107–116. doi: 10.1177/0020764012467598.

Kay, S.R., Fiszbein, A. & Opler, L.A. (1987) The positive and negative syndrome scale (PANSS) for schizophrenia. *Schizophrenia Bulletin, 13*(2), 261–276.

Kaya, Y. & Oz, F. (2015) The social functionality of schizophrenic patients and the burden experienced by their caregivers. *European Psychiatry, 30*, 1687. doi: 10.1016/s0924-9338(15)31293-1.

Kaymaz, N., Drukker, M., Lieb, R., Wittchen, H., Werbeloff, N., Weiser, M., et al. (2012) Do subthreshold psychotic experiences predict clinical outcomes in unselected non-help-seeking population-based samples? A systematic review and meta-analysis, enriched with new results. *Psychological Medicine, 42*(11), 2239–2253. doi: 10.1017/S0033291711002911.

Keen, N., George, D., Scragg, P. & Petters, E. (2017a) The role of shame in people with a diagnosis of schizophrenia. *The British Journal of Clinical Psychology, 56*(2), 115–129. doi: https://doi.org/10.1111/bjc.12125.

Keen, N., Hunter, E. C. M. & Peters, E. (2017b) Integrated trauma-focused cognitive-behavioural therapy for post-traumatic stress and psychotic symptoms: A case series study using imaginal reprocessing strategies. *Frontiers in Psychiatry, 8*, 92. doi: 10.3389/fpsyt.2017.00092.

Kelleher, I. & Cannon, M. (2014) Whither the psychosis-neurosis borderline? *Schizophrenia Bulletin, 40*(2), 266–268. http://dx.doi.org/10.1093/schbul/sbt230.

Kelly, C. (2000) Cigarette smoking and schizophrenia. *Advances in Psychiatric Treatment, 6*(5), 327–331. doi: 10.1192/apt.6.5.327.

Kelly, J., Brown, S., Abrantes, A., Kahler, C. & Myers, M. (2008) Social recovery model: An 8-year investigation of adolescent 12-step group involvement following inpatient treatment. *Alcoholism: Clinical and Experimental Research, 32*(8), 1468–1478. http://dx.doi.org/10.1111/j.1530-0277.2008.00712.x

Kelly, S. (2011) *Carers need recovery too: An evaluation of the use of wellness recovery action planning and its effectiveness for carers.* Edinburgh: Edinburgh Carers' Council.

Kemp, R., Hayward, P., Applewhaite, G., Everitt, B. & David, A. (1996) Compliance therapy in psychotic patients: randomised controlled trial. *British Medical Journal, 312*, 345–349.

Kendall, T. (2012) Treating negative symptoms of schizophrenia. *British Medical Journal, 344*, 664. doi: 10.1136/bmj.e664.

Kennard, L. & O'Shaughnessy, K. (2016) Treating hypertension in patients with medical comorbidities. *British Medical Journal, 101*. doi: 10.1136/bmj.i101.

Keown, P., French, J., Gibson, G., Newton, E., Cull, S., Brown, P., et al. (2016) Too much detention? Street triage and detentions under Section 136 Mental Health Act in the North-East of England: A descriptive study of the effects of a Street Triage intervention. *British Medical Journal.* doi: 10.1136/bmjopen-2016-011837.

Keshavan, M. S., Haas, G., Miewald, J., Montrose, D. M., Reddy, R., Schooler, N. R., et al. (2003) Prolonged untreated illness duration from prodromal onset predicts outcome in first episode psychoses. *Schizophrenia Bulletin, 29*, 757.

Khandaker, G., Cousins, L., Deakin, J., Lennox, B., Yolken, R. & Jones, P. (2015) Inflammation and immunity in schizophrenia: Implications for pathophysiology and treatment. *The Lancet Psychiatry, 2*(3), 258–270. doi: 10.1016/s2215-0366(14)00122-9.

Khoury, B. & Lecomte, T. (2012) Emotional regulation and schizophrenia. *International Journal of Cognitive Therapy, 51*(1), 67–76.

Khoury, B., Lecomte, T., Gaudiano, B. & Paquin, K. (2013) Mindfulness interventions for psychosis: A meta-analysis. *Schizophrenia Research, 150*(1), 176–184.

Khunti, K. (2005) Metabolic syndrome. *British Medical Journal, 331*(7526), 1153–1154. doi: 10.1136/bmj.331.7526.1153.

Killackey, E., Allott, K., Jackson, H. J., Scutella, R., Tseng, Y. P., Borland, J., et al. (2018) Individual placement and support for vocational recovery in first-episode psychosis: randomised controlled trial. *The British Journal of Psychiatry, 214*, 1–7.

Kincaid, D., Doris, M., Shannon, C. & Mulholland, C. (2017) What is the prevalence of autism spectrum disorder and ASD traits in psychosis? A systematic review. *Psychiatry Research, 250*, 99–105. http://dx.doi.org/10.1016/j.psychres.2017.01.017.

Kinderman, P. (2005) A psychological model of mental disorder. *Harvard Review of Psychiatry, 13*, 206–217.

King, B. & Lord, C. (2011) Is schizophrenia on the autism spectrum? *Brain Research, 1380*, 34–41. http://dx.doi.org/10.1016/j.brainres.2010.11.031.

Kingdon, D., Ashcroft, K., Bhandari, B., Gleeson, S., Warikoo, N., Symons, M., et al. (2010) Schizophrenia and borderline personality disorder. *The Journal Of Nervous and Mental Disease, 198*(6), 399–403. http://dx.doi.org/10.1097/nmd.0b013e3181e08c27.

Kingsep, P., Nathan, P. & Castle, D. (2003) Cognitive behavioural group treatment for social anxiety in schizophrenia. *Schizophrenia Research, 63*, 121–120. doi: 10.1016/S0920-9964(02)00376-6.

Kirkbride, J. B., Barker, D., Cowden, F., Stamps, R., Yang, M., Jones, P. B., et al. (2008) Psychoses, ethnicity and socio-economic status. *The British Journal of Psychiatry, 193*(1), 18–24. doi: 10.1192/bjp.bp.107.041566.

Kirkbride, J. B., Errazuriz, A., Croudace, T. J., Morgan, C., Jackson, D., Boydell, J., et al. (2012a) Incidence of schizophrenia and other psychoses in England, 1950–2009: A systematic review and meta-analyses. *PLoS ONE, 7*(3). doi: http://doi.org/10.1371/journal.pone.0031660.

Kirkbride, J. B., Hameed, Y., Ioannidis, K., Ankireddypalli, G., Crane, C. M., Nasir, M., et al. (2017) Ethnic minority status, age-at-immigration and psychosis risk in rural environments: Evidence from the SEPEA study. *Schizophrenia Bulletin, 43*(6), 1251–1261. doi: 10.1093/schbul/sbx010.

Kirkbride, J. B., Stubbins, C. & Jones, P. B. (2012b) Psychosis incidence through the prism of early intervention services. *The British Journal of Psychiatry, 200*(2), 156–157. doi: 10.1192/bjp.bp.111.094896.

Kishimoto, T., De Hert, M., Carlson, H., Manu, P. & Correll, C. (2012) Osteoporosis and fracture risk in people with schizophrenia. *Current Opinion in Psychiatry, 25*(5), 415–429. doi: 10.1097/yco.0b013e328355e1ac.

Kissling, W. (1991) Duration of neuroleptic maintenance treatment. *Guidelines for Neuroleptic Relapse Prevention in Schizophrenia*, 94–112. doi: 10.1007/978-3-642-86922-8_17.

Klapheck, K., Lincoln, T. & Bock, T. (2014) Meaning of psychoses as perceived by patients, their relatives and clinicians. *Psychiatry Research, 215*(3), 760–765. doi: 10.1016/j.psychres.2014.01.017.

Kline, E. & Thomas, L. (2018) Cultural factors in first episode psychosis treatment engagement. *Schizophrenia Research, 195*, 74–75. doi: 10.1016/j.schres.2017.08.035.

Kobayashi, M., Ito, H., Okumura, Y., Mayahara, K., Matsumoto, Y. & Hirakawa, J. (2010) Hospital readmission in first-time admitted patients with schizophrenia: Smoking patients had higher hospital readmission rate than non-smoking patients. *The International Journal of Psychiatry in Medicine, 40*(3), 247–257. doi: 10.2190/pm.40.3.b.

Koschorke, M., Padmavati, R., Kumar, S., Cohen, A., Weiss, H., Chatterjee, S., et al. (2017) Experiences of stigma and discrimination faced by family caregivers of people with schizophrenia in India. *Social Science and Medicine, 178*, 66–77. doi: 10.1016/j.socscimed.2017.01.061.

Køster, A., Lajer, M., Lindhardt, A. & Rosenbaum, B. (2008) Gender differences in first episode psychosis. *Social Psychiatry & Psychiatric Epidemiology, 43*, 940–946.

Koutra, K., Simos, P., Triliva, S., Lionis, C. & Vgontzas, A. (2016) Linking family cohesion and flexibility with expressed emotion, family burden and psychological distress in caregivers of patients with psychosis: A path analytic model. *Psychiatry Research, 240*, 66–75. doi: 10.1016/j.psychres.2016.04.017.

Koutra, K., Triliva, S., Roumeliotaki, T., Basta, M., Simos, P., Lionis, C., et al. (2015) Impaired family functioning in psychosis and its relevance to relapse: a two-year follow-up study. *Comprehensive* Psychiatry, 62, 1–12. doi: 10.1016/j.comppsych.2015.06.006.

Koutra, K., Vgontzas, A., Lionis, C. & Triliva, S. (2014) Family functioning in first-episode psychosis: A systematic review of the literature. *Social Psychiatry and Psychiatric Epidemiology, 49*(7), 1023–1036. doi: 10.1007/s00127-013-0816-6.

Koyama, T., Kamio, Y., Inada, N. & Kurita, H. (2008) Sex differences in WISC-III profiles of children with high-functioning pervasive developmental disorders. *Journal of Autism and Developmental Disorders, 39*(1), 135–141. http://dx.doi.org/10.1007/s10803-008-0610-6.

Kozhyna, G., Korostiy, V. & Gaichuk, L. (2013) 1974 – Integrative model of psychoeducation in the treatment of patients with schizophrenia. *European Psychiatry, 28*, 1. doi: 10.1016/s0924-9338(13)76913-x.

Kråkvik, B., Larøi, F., Kalhovde, A., Hugdahl, K., Kompus, K. & Salvesen, Ø., et al. (2015) Prevalence of auditory verbal hallucinations in a general population: A group comparison study. *Scandinavian Journal of Psychology, 56*(5), 508–515. http://dx.doi.org/10.1111/sjop.12236.

Kretchy, I., Osafo, J., Agyemang, S., Appiah, B. & Nonvignon, J. (2018) Psychological burden and caregiver-reported non-adherence to psychotropic medications among patients with schizophrenia. *Psychiatry Research, 259*, 289–294. doi: 10.1016/j.psychres.2017.10.034.

Kreyenbuhl, J., Buchanan, R. W., Dickerson, F. B., Dixon, L. B. & Schizophrenia Patient Outcomes Team (2010) The Schizophrenia Patient Outcomes Research Team (PORT). Updated treatment recommendations 2009. *Schizophrenia Bulletin, 26*, 94–103. doi: 10.1093/schbul/sbp130.

Krystal, A., Goforth, H. & Roth, T. (2008) Effects of antipsychotic medications on sleep in schizophrenia. *International Clinical Psychopharmacology, 23*(3), 150–160. doi: 10.1097/yic.0b013e3282f39703.

Kuipers, E. (2008) The case for early, medium and late intervention in psychosis. *World Psychiatry, 7*(3), 158–159. doi: 10.1002/j.2051-5545.2008.tb00184.x.

Kuipers, E., Onwumere, J. & Bebbington, P. (2010) Cognitive model of caregiving in psychosis. *British Journal f Psychiatry, 196*(4), 259–265. doi: 10.1192/bjp.bp.109.070466.

Kuipers, L. & Bebbington, P. (1988) Expressed emotion research in schizophrenia: theoretical and clinical implications. *Psychological Medicine, 18*(4), 893. doi: 10.1017/s0033291700009831.

Kukla, M., Lysaker, P. & Salyers, M. (2013) Do persons with schizophrenia who have better metacognitive capacity also have a stronger subjective experience of recovery? *Psychiatry Research, 209*(3), 381–385.

Kurihara, T, Kato, M., Reverger, R. & Tirta I.G. (2011) Seventeen-year clinical outcome of schizophrenia in Bali. *European Psychiatry, 26*(5): 333–338. doi: 10.1016/j.eurpsy.2011.04.003.

Ladea, M., Bran, M. & Claudiu, S. M. (2016) Online destigmatization of schizophrenia: A Romanian experience. *European Psychiatry, 33*, 276.

Lafond, V. (2009) Coming to terms with mental illness in the family – working constructively through its grief. In F. Lobban & C. Barrowclough (eds) *A casebook of family interventions for psychosis* (pp. 167–184). Chichester: Wiley-Blackwell.

Lako, I. M., Bruggerman, R., Knegtering, H., Wiersma, D., Schoevers, R. A., Sloof, C. J., et al. (2012a) A systematic review of instruments to measure depression in patients with schizophrenia. *Journal of Affective Disorders, 140*(1), 38–47. doi: 10.1016/j.jad.2011.10.014.

Lako, I. M., Taxis, K., Bruggeman, R., Richard, K. H., Burger, H., Wiersma, D., et al. (2012b) The course of depressive symptoms and prescribing patterns of antidepressants in schizophrenia in a one year follow-up study. *European Psychiatry, 27*, 240–244. doi: 10.1016/j.eurpsy.2010.10.007.

Lal, S. & Malla, A. (2015) Service engagement in first episode psychosis: Current issues and future directions. *Canadian Journal of Psychiatry, 60*(8), 341–345.

Lally, J., Ajnakina, O., Di Forti, M., Trotta, A., Demjaha, A., Kolliakou, A., et al. (2016) Two distinct patterns of treatment resistance: clinical predictors of treatment resistance in first-episode schizophrenia spectrum psychoses. *Psychological Medicine, 46*(15), 3231–3240.

Lally, J., Ajnakina, O., Stubbs, B., Cullinane, M., Murphy, K. C., Gaughran, F. & Murray, R. M. (2017) Remission and recovery from first-episode psychosis in adults: Systematic review and meta-analysis of long-term outcome studies. *The British Journal of Psychiatry, 211*, 350–358.

Lam, M. M., Pearson, V., Ng, R. M., Chiu, C. P., Law, C. W. & Chen, E. Y. (2011) What does recovery from psychosis mean? Perceptions of young first-episode patients. *The International Journal of Social Psychiatry, 57*(6), 580–587. doi: 10.1177/0020764010374418.

Lambert, M., Conus, P., Cotton, S., Robinson, J., McGorry, P. & Schimmelmann, B. (2010a) Prevalence, predictors, and consequences of long-term refusal of antipsychotic treatment in first-episode psychosis. *Journal of Clinical Psychopharmacology, 30*(5), 565–572. doi: 10.1097/jcp.0b013e3181f058a0.

Lambert, M., Conus, P., Lubman, D. I., Wade, D., Yuen, H., Moritz, S., et al. (2005) The impact of substance use disorders on clinical outcome in 643 patients with first-episode psychosis. *Acta Psychiatria Scandinavica, 112*(2), 141–148.

Lambert, M., Karow, A., Leucht, S., Schimmelmann, B. G. & Naber, D. (2010b) Remission in schizophrenia: validity, frequency, predictors, and patients' perspective 5 years later. *Dialogues in Clinical Neuroscience, 12*(3), 393–407.

Lambert, M., Naber, D., Schacht, A., Wagner, T., Hundemer, H., Karow, A., et al. (2008) Rates and predictors of remission and recovery during 3 years in 392 never-treated patients with schizophrenia. *Acta Psychiatrica Scandinavica, 118*(3), 220–229. doi: 10.1111/j.1600-0447.2008.01213.

Lappin, J. M., Heslin, M., Lomas, B., Jones, P. B., Doody, G. A., Reininghaus, U. A., et al. (2018) Early sustained recovery following first episode psychosis: Evidence from the AESOP10 follow-up study. *Schizophrenia Research.* doi: 10.1016/j.schres.2018.03.014.

Lardinois, M., Lataster, T., Mengelers, R., Van Os, J. & Myin-Germeys, I. (2011) Childhood trauma and increased stress sensitivity in psychosis. *Psychiatrica Scandinavica, 123*, 28–35.

Large, M., Sharma, S., Compton, M., Slade, T. & Nielssen, O. (2011) Cannabis use and earlier onset of psychosis. *Archives of General Psychiatry, 68*(6), 555. http://dx.doi. org/10.1001/archgenpsychiatry.2011.

Lasalvia, A., Bonetto, C., Tosato, S., Zanatta, G., Cristofalo, D., PICOS-Veneto Group et al. (2014) First-contact incidence of psychosis in north-eastern Italy: Influence of age, gender, immigration and socioeconomic deprivation. *The British Journal of Psychiatry, 205*(2), 127–134. doi: 10.1192/bjp.bp.113.134445.

Laursen, T., Nordentoft, M. & Mortensen, P. (2014) Excess early mortality in schizophrenia. *Annual Review of Clinical Psychology, 10*(1), 425–448. doi: 10.1146/annurev-clinpsy-032813-153657.

Lavis, A., Lester, H., Everard, L., Freemantle, N., Amos, T., Fowler, D., et al. (2015) Layers of listening: Qualitative analysis of the impact of early intervention services for first-episode psychosis on carers' experiences. *British Journal of Psychiatry, 207*(02), 135–142. doi: 10.1192/bjp.bp.114.146415.

Law, D. & Jacob, J. (2015) *Goals and goal based outcomes (GBOs): Some useful information* (3rd ed.). London: CAMHS Press.

Law, H. & Morrison, A. P. (2014) Recovery in psychosis: A Delphi study with experts by experience. *Schizophrenia Bulletin, 40*(6), 1347–1355. doi: 10.1093/schbul/sbu047.

Law, H., Morrison, A., Byrne, R. & Hoson, E. (2012) Recovery from psychosis: a user informed review of self-report instruments for measuring recovery. *Journal of Mental Health, 21*(2), 192–207.

Lean, M., Leslie, W., Barnes, A., Brosnahan, N., Thom, G., McCombie, L., et al. (2017) Primary care-led weight management for remission of type 2 diabetes (DiRECT): An open-label, cluster-randomised trial. *The Lancet*. doi: 10.1016/s0140-6736(17)33102-1.

Leclerc, E., Noto, C., Bressan, R. & Brietzke, E. (2015) Determinants of adherence to treatment in first episode psychosis: A comprehensive review. *Revista Brasileira de Psiquitra, 37*, 168–176. doi: 10.1590/1516-4446.2014.1539.

Lecomte, T., Corbière, M., Ehmann, T., Addington, J., Abdel-Baki, A. & Macewan, B. (2014a) Development and preliminary validation of the First Episode Social Functioning Scale for early psychosis. *Psychiatric Research, 216*(3), 412–417. doi: 10.1016/j. psychres.2014.01.044.

Lecomte, T., Corbiere, M., Simard, S. & Leclerc, C. (2014b) Merging evidence based psycho-social interventions in schizophrenia. *Behavioural Science, 4*, 437–447. doi: 10.3390/bs4040437.

Lee, D. A. & James, S. (2011) *The compassionate-mind guide to recovering from trauma and PTSD: Using compassion focused therapy to overcome flashbacks, shame, guilt, and fear*. Oakland, CA: New Harbinger Publications, Inc.

Lee, D. A., Scragg, P. & Turner, S. W. (2001) The role of shame and guilt in reactions to traumatic events: A clinical formulation of shame-based and guilt-based PTSD. *The British Journal of Medical Psychology, 74*, 451–466.

Lee, J., Rekhi, G., Mitter, N., Bong, Y. L., Kraus, M. S., Lam, M., et al. (2013) The Longitudinal Youth at Risk Study (LYRIKS): An Asian UHR perspective. *Schizophrenia Research, 151*(1–3), 279–283. doi: 10.1016/j.schres.2013.09.025.

Lee, M. (1999) A comparison of the effect of clozapine with typical neuroleptics on cognitive function in neuroleptic-responsive schizophrenia. *Schizophrenia Research, 37*(1), 1–11. doi: 10.1016/s0920-9964(98)00145-5.

Lee, R. S. C., Redoblado-Hodge, M. A., Naismith, S. L., Hermens, D. F., Porter, M. A. & Hickie, I. B. (2013) Cognitive remediation improves memory and psychosocial functioning in first-episode psychiatric out-patients. *Psychological Medicine*, 43, 1161–1173.

Leenhardt, A., Glaser, E., Burguera, M., Nurnberg, M., Maison-Blanche, P. & Coumel, P. (1994) Short-coupled variant of torsade de pointes. A new electrocardiographic entity in the spectrum of idiopathic ventricular tachyarrhythmias. *Circulation, 89*(1), 206–215. doi: 10.1161/01.cir.89.1.206.

Leeson, V. C., Barnes, T. R., Hutton, S. B., Ron, M. A. & Joyce, E. M. (2009) IQ as a predictor of functional outcome in schizophrenia: A longitudinal, four-year study of first-episode psychosis. *Schizophrenia Research, 107*, 55–60.

L eff, J. & Vaughn, C. (1985) *Expressed emotion in families*. New York: The Guilford Press.

Leggatt, M. (2012) *Training family peer support workers in an early intervention mental health service*. Orygen: Youth Health Research Centre.

Leggatt, M. & Woodhead, G. (2015) Family peer support work in an early intervention youth mental health service. *Early Intervention in Psychiatry, 10*(5), 446–451. doi: 10.1111/eip.12257.

Lennox, B., Palmer-Cooper, E., Pollak, T., Hainsworth, J., Marks, J., PPiP study team et al. (2017) Prevalence and clinical characteristics of serum neuronal cell surface antibodies in first-episode psychosis: A case-control study. *The Lancet Psychiatry, 4*(1), 42–48. doi: 10.1016/s2215-0366(16)30375-3.

Lenior, M. E., Dingemans, P. M., Linszen, D. H., De Haan, L. & Schene, A. H. (2001) Social functioning and the course of early-onset schizophrenia: Five-year follow-up of a psychosocial intervention. *The British Journal of Psychiatry, 179*(1), 53–58.

Lepore, S. J. & Revenson, T. A. (2006) Resilience and posttraumatic growth: Recovery, resistance, and reconfiguration. In L. G. Calhoun & R. G. Tedeschi (eds) *Handbook of posttraumatic growth, research and practice* (pp. 24–46). Mahwah, NJ: Routledge.

Lester, H. (2013) The James Mackenzie Lecture 2012: Bothering about Billy. *British Journal of General Practice, 63*(608), 232–234. doi: 10.3399/bjgp13x664414.

Lester, H., Khan, N., Jones, P, Marshall, M, Fowler, D., Amos, T., et al. (2012) Service users' views of moving on from early intervention services for psychosis: A longitudinal study in primary care. *British Journal of General Practice, 62*(596), 183–190.

Lester, H., Marshall, M., Jones, P., Fowler, D., Amos, T., Khan, N., et al. (2011) Views of young people in early intervention services for first-episode psychosis in England. *Psychiatric Services, 62*(8), 882–887. doi: 10.1176/ps.62.8.pss6208_0882.

Leucht, S. (2012) Meta-analysis on relapse prevention with anti-psychotic drugs compared to placebo in. *Schizophrenia Research, 136*, 58. doi: 10.1016/s0920-9964(12)70210-4.

Leucht, S., Arbter, D., Engel, R. R., Kissling, W. & Davis, J. M. (2009) How effective are second generation anti-psychotic drugs? A meta-analysis of placebo controlled trials. *Molecular Psychiatry, 14*, 429–447. doi: 10.1038/sj.mp.4002136.

Leucht, S., Busch, R., Hamann, J., Kissling, W. & Kane, J. (2005) Early-onset hypothesis of antipsychotic drug action: A hypothesis tested, confirmed and extended. *Biological Psychiatry, 57*(12), 1543–1549. doi: 10.1016/j.biopsych.2005.02.023.

Leucht, S., Corves, C., Arbter, D., Engel, R., Li, C. & Davis, J. (2009) Second-generation versus first-generation antipsychotic drugs for schizophrenia: A meta-analysis. *The Lancet, 373*(9657), 31–41. doi: 10.1016/s0140-6736(08)61764-x.

Leucht, S. & Heres, S. (2006) Epidemiology, clinical consequences, and psychosocial treatment of nonadherence in schizophrenia; *Journal of Clinical Psychiatry, 67*(5): 3–8.

Leucht, S., Pitschel-Walz, G., Abraham, D. & Kissling, W. (1999) Efficacy and extra-pyramidal side-effects of the new antipsychotics olanzapine, quetiapine, risperidone, and sertindole compared to conventional antipsychotics and placebo. A meta-analysis of randomized controlled trials. *Schizophrenia Research, 35,* 51–68.

Leucht, S., Tardy, M., Komossa, K., Heres, S., Kissling, W., Salanti, G. & Davis, J. (2012) Antipsychotic drugs versus placebo for relapse prevention in schizophrenia: A systematic review and meta-analysis. *The Lancet, 379*(9831), 2063–2071. doi: 10.1016/s0140-6736(12)60239-6.

Levine, S. Z., Bakst, S., Rabinowitz, J. (2010) Suicide attempts at the time of first admission and during early course schizophrenia: A population-based study. *Psychiatry Research, 177*(1–2), 55–59.

Levkovitz, Y., Mendlovich, S., Riwkes, S., Braw, Y., Levkovitch-Verbin, H., Gal, G., et al. (2009) A double-blind, randomized study of minocycline for the treatment of negative and cognitive symptoms in early-phase schizophrenia. *The Journal of Clinical Psychiatry, 71*(2), 138–149. doi: 10.4088/jcp.08m04666yel.

Lewis, C., Takala, C., Qaadir, A., Cowan, K., Borreggine, K. & Rackley, S. (2017) Jinn and psychosis: Providing culturally informed care to Muslim adolescents and families. *Journal of the American Academy of Child and Adolescent Psychiatry, 56*(6), 455–457. doi: 10.1016/j.jaac.2017.03.009.

Lewis, S., Barnes, T., Davies, L., Murray, R. M., Dunn, G., Hayhurst, K., et al. (2005) Randomized controlled trial of effect of prescription of clozapine versus other second-generation antipsychotic drugs in resistant schizophrenia. *Schizophrenia Bulletin, 32*(4), 715–723. doi: 10.1093/schbul/sbj067.

Li, X., Tang, Y. & Wang, C. (2013) Adjunctive aripiprazole versus placebo for antipsychotic-induced hyperprolactinemia: Meta-analysis of randomized controlled trials. *Plos ONE, 8*(8). doi: 10.1371/journal.pone.0070179.

Liberman, R. P. & Kopelowicz, A. (2005) Recovery from schizophrenia: A concept in search of research. *Psychiatric Services, 56*(6), 735–742.

Lieberman, J. A. (2015) *Shrinks: The untold story of psychiatry.* London: Weidenfeld and Nicolson.

Lieberman, J., Phillips, M., Gu, H., Stroup, S., Zhang, P., Kong, L., et al. (2002) Atypical and conventional antipsychotic drugs in treatment-naive first-episode schizophrenia: A 52-week randomized trial of clozapine vs. chlorpromazine. *Neuropsychopharmacology.* doi: 10.1038/sj.npp.1300157.

Lieberman, J. A., Stroup, T. S., McEvoy, J. P., Swartz, M. S., Rosenheck, R. A., (CATIE) investigators, et al. (2005) Effectiveness of antipsychotic drugs in patients with chronic schizophrenia. *New England Journal of Medicine, 353*(12), 1209–1223. doi: 10.1056/nejmoa051688.

Liemburg, E., Castelein, S., Stewart, R., van der Gaag, M., Aleman, A., Knegtering, H. & Outcome of Psychosis (GROUP) Investigators (2013) Two subdomains of negative symptoms in psychotic disorders: Established and confirmed in two large cohorts. *Journal of Psychiatric Research, 47,* 718–725.

Lincoln, T., Mehl, S., Ziegler, M., Kesting, M., Exner, C. & Rief, W. (2010) Is fear of others linked to an uncertain sense of self? The relevance of self-worth, interpersonal self-concepts, and dysfunctional beliefs to paranoia. *Behaviour Therapy, 41,* 187–197.

Lindenmayer, J., Nasrallah, H., Pucci, M., James, S. & Citrome, L. (2013) A systematic review of psychostimulant treatment of negative symptoms of schizophrenia: Challenges and therapeutic opportunities. *Schizophrenia Research, 147*(2–3), 241–252. doi: 10.1016/j.schres.2013.03.019.

Lindsey, M. A., Brandt, N. E., Becker, K. D., Becker, K. B., Lee, B. R., Barth, R. P., et al. (2014) Identifying the common elements of treatment engagement interventions in children's mental health services. *Clinical Child and Family Psychology Review, 17*(3), 283–298. doi: 10.1007/s10567-013-0163.

Lisiecka, D. M., Suckling, J., Barnes, T. R., Chaudhry, I. B., Dazzan, P., Husain, N., et al. (2015) The benefit of minocycline on negative symptoms in early-phase psychosis in addition to standard care-extent and mechanism (BeneMin): study protocol for a randomised controlled trial. *Trials, 16*, 71.

Lobban, F. & Barrowclough, C. (2009) *A casebook of family interventions for psychosis.* Chichester: Wiley-Blackwell.

Lobban, F. & Barrowclough, C. (2016) An interpersonal CBT framework for involving relatives in interventions for psychosis: Evidence base and clinical implications. *Cognitive Therapy and Research, 40*(2), 198–215. doi: 10.1007/s10608-015-9731-3.

Lobban, F., Postlethwaite, A., Glentworth, D., Pinfold, V., Wainwright, L., Dunn, G., et al. (2013) A systematic review of randomised controlled trials of interventions reporting outcomes for relatives of people with psychosis. *Clinical Psychology Review, 33*(3), 372–382. doi: 10.1016/j.cpr.2012.12.004.

Lofors, J. & Sundquist, K. (2007) Low-linking social capital as a predictor of mental disorders: A cohort study of 4.5 million Swedes. *Social Science and Medicine, 64*(1), 21–34. doi: 10.1016/j.socscimed.2006.08.024.

Longden, E., Sampson, M. & Read, J. (2016) Childhood adversity and psychosis: Generalised or specific effects? *Epidemiology and Psychiatric Sciences, 25*(4), 349–359. doi: 10.1017/S204579601500044X.

Lu, W., Mueser, K. T., Rosenberg, S. D., Yanos, P. T. & Mahmoud, N. (2017) Posttraumatic reactions to psychosis: A qualitative analysis. *Frontiers in Psychiatry, 8.* doi: 10.3389/fpsyt.2017.00129.

Lucas, S., Redoblado-Hodge, M. A., Shores, A., Brennan, J. & Harris, A. (2008) Predictors of outcome three years after diagnosis of first episode psychosis. *Psychiatry Research, 161*, 11–18.

Lucksted, A., Essock, S. M., Stevenson, J., Mendon, S. J., Nossel, I. R., Goldman, H. H. & Dixon, L. B. (2015) Client views of engagement in the RAISE connection early psychosis recovery program. *Psychiatric Services, 66*(7), 699–704. doi: http://doi.org/10.1176/appi.ps.201400475.

Lutgens, D., Gariepy, G. & Malla, A. (2017) Psychological and psychosocial interventions for negative symptoms in psychosis: Systematic review and meta-analysis. *The British Journal of Psychiatry, 210*(5), 324–332. doi: 10.1192/bjp.bp.116.197103.

Lutgens, D., Iyer, S., Joober, R., Brown, T. G., Norman, R., Latimer, E., et al. (2015) A five-year randomized parallel and blinded clinical trial of an extended specialized early intervention vs. regular care in the early phase of psychotic disorders: Study protocol. *BMC Psychiatry, 15*(1), 22. doi: 10.1186/s12888-015-0404-2.

Lynch, D., Laws, K. R. & McKenna, P. J. (2010) Cognitive behaviour therapy for major psychiatric disorder: does it really work? A meta-analytical review of well controlled trials. *Psychological Medicine, 40*, 9–24.

Lysaker, P., Buck, K., Taylor, A. & Roe, D. (2008) Associations of metacognition and internalized stigma with quantitative assessments of self-experience in narratives of schizophrenia. *Psychiatry Research, 157*(1–3), 31–38.

Lysaker, P., Hamm, J., Hasson-Ohayon, I., Pattison, M. & Leonhardt, B. (2018) Promoting recovery from severe mental illness: Implications from research on metacognition and metacognitive reflection and insight therapy. *World Journal of Psychiatry, 8*(1), 1–11.

Lysaker, P. H., Meyer, P. S., Evans, J. D., Clements, C. A. & Marks, K. A. (2001) Childhood sexual trauma and psycho-social functioning in adults with schizophrenia. *Psychiatric Services, 52*, 1485–1488.

Ma, C. F, Chien, W. T. & Bressington, D. T. (2017) Family intervention for caregivers of people with recent-onset psychosis: A systematic review and meta-analysis. *Early Intervention Psychiatry*. doi: 10.1111/eip.12494.

MacBeth, A. & Gumley, A. (2008) Premorbid adjustment, symptom development and quality of life in first episode psychosis: A systematic review and critical reappraisal. *Acta Psychiatrica Scandinavica, 117*, 85–99.

MacBeth, A., Gumley, A., Schwannauer, M. & Fisher, R. (2011) Attachment states of mind, mentalization, and their correlates in a first-episode psychosis sample. *Psychology and Psychotherapy: Theory, Research and Practice, 84*, 42–57.

MacDougall, A. G., Vandermeer, M. R. J. & Norman, R. M. G. (2017) Determinants of self-esteem in early psychosis: The role of perceived social dominance. *Psychiatry Research, 258*, 583–586. doi: 10.1016/j.psychres.2016.05.050.

MacKeith, J., Burns, S. & Graham, K. (2008) *The outcome star*. London: London Housing Foundation and Triangle Consulting.

Mackin, P. (2007) Cardiac side effects of psychiatric drugs. *Human Psychopharmacology: Clinical and Experimental, 23*(1), 3–14. doi: 10.1002/hup.915.

Macmillan, I., Howells, L., Kale, K., Hackmann, C., Taylor, G., Hill, K., Bradford, S. & Fowler, D. (2007) Social and symptomatic outcomes of first-episode bipolar psychoses in an early intervention service. *Early Intervention in Psychiatry, 1*, 79–87.

Madras, B. (2013) History of the discovery of the antipsychotic dopamine D2 receptor: A basis for the dopamine hypothesis of schizophrenia. *Journal of the History of the Neurosciences, 22*(1), 62–78. doi: 10.1080/0964704x.2012.678199.

Madsen, T., Karstoft, K. I., Secher, R. G., Austin, S. F. & Nordentoft, M. (2016) Trajectories of suicidal ideation in patients with first-episode psychosis: secondary analysis of data from the OPUS trial. *The Lancet Psychiatry, 3*(5), 443–450. doi: https://doi.org/10.1016/S2215-0366(15)00518-0.

Mahmoud, A., Hayhurst, K., Drake, R. & Lewis, S. (2011) Second generation antipsychotics improve sexual dysfunction in schizophrenia: A randomised controlled trial. *Schizophrenia Research and Treatment, 2011*, 1–6. doi: 10.1155/2011/596898.

Mailman, R. & Murthy, V. (2010) Third generation antipsychotic drugs: Partial agonism or receptor functional selectivity? *Current Pharmaceutical Design, 16*(5), 488–501. doi: 10.2174/138161210790361461.

Malla, A., Joober, D., Iyer, S., Norman, R., Schmitz, N., Brown, T., et al. (2017) Comparing three year extension of early intervention services to regular care following two years of early intervention in first episode psychosis: a randomised single blind clinical trial. *World Psychiatry, 16*, 278–286.

Malla, A., McLean, T. & Norman, R. (2004) A group psychotherapeutic intervention during recovery from first-episode psychosis. In J. Gleeson & P. McGorry (eds) *Psychological interventions in early psychosis: A treatment handbook*. Chichester, John Wiley & Sons Ltd.

Malla, A., Norman, R. M. B., Jakhar, J. & Ahmed, R. (2002) Negative symptoms in first episode non-affective psychosis. *Acta Psychiatrica Scandinavica, 105*(6), 431–439. doi: 10.1034/j.1600-0447.2062.02139.

Malla, A. & Payne, J. (2005) First-episode psychosis: psychopathology, quality of life, and functional outcome. *Schizophrenia Bulletin, 31*, 650–671.

Malla, A., Shah, J & Lal, S. (2017) Advances and challenges in early intervention in psychosis. *World Psychiatry, 16*(3), 274–275.

Mander, H. & Kingdon, D. (2015) The evolution of cognitive–behavioral therapy for psychosis. *Psychology Research and Behavior Management, 8*, 63.

Mann, F., Fisher, H., Major, B., Lawrence, J., Tapfumaneyi, A., MiData Consortium et al. (2014) Ethnic variation in compulsory detention and hospital admission for psychosis across four UK Early Intervention Services. *BMC Psychiatry, 14*, 256. doi: www.biomedcentral.com/1471-244X/14/256.

Mansueto, G. & Faravelli, C. (2017) Recent life events and psychosis: The role of childhood adversities. *Psychiatry Research, 256*, 111–117. doi: 10.1016/j.psychres.2017.06.042.

Marcus, M., Westra, H., Angus, L. & Kertes, A. (2011) Client experiences of motivational interviewing for generalized anxiety disorder: A qualitative analysis. *Psychotherapy Research, 21*, 447–461.

Marshall, M., Lewis, S., Lockwood, A., Drake, R., Jones, P. & Croudace, T. (2005) Association between duration of untreated psychosis and outcome in cohorts of first-episode patients: a systematic review. *Archives of General Psychiatry, 62*, 975–983.

Martindale, B. & Summers, A (2013) The psychodynamics of psychosis. *Advances in Psychiatric Treatment, 19*, 124–131.

Marwaha, S., Balachandra, S. & Johnson, S. (2009) Clinicians' attitudes to the employment of people with psychosis. *Social Psychiatry and Psychiatric Epidemiology, 44*, 349.

Marwaha, S., Thompson, A., Upthegrove, R. & Broome, M. R. (2016) Fifteen years on – early intervention for a new generation. *The British Journal of Psychiatry, 209*(3), 186–188. doi: 10.1192/bjp.bp.115.170035.

Matheson, C. (2016) A new diagnosis of complex Post-traumatic Stress Disorder, PTSD – a window of opportunity for the treatment of patients in the NHS? *Psychoanalytic Psychotherapy, 30:4*, 329–344. doi 10.1080/02668734.2016.1252943.

Maura, J. & Weisman de Mamani, A. (2017) Culturally adapted psychosocial interventions for schizophrenia: A review. *Cognitive and Behavioral Practice, 24*(4), 445–458. doi: 10.1016/j.cbpra.2017.01.004.

May, R. (2004) Making sense of psychotic experience and working towards recovery. In J. Gleeson & P. McGorry (eds) *Psychological interventions in early psychosis: A treatment handbook*. Chichester: John Wiley & Sons Ltd.

Mayhew, S. (2015) Compassion focused therapy for people experiencing psychosis. In A. Meaden & A. Fox (eds) *Innovations in psychosocial interventions for psychosis: Working with the hard to reach*. New York: Brunner-Routledge.

Mayoral-van Son, J., de la Foz, V., Martinez-Garcia, O., Moreno, T., Parrilla-Escobar, M., et al. (2015) Clinical outcome after antipsychotic treatment discontinuation in functionally recovered first-episode nonaffective psychosis individuals. *The Journal of Clinical Psychiatry*, 492–500. doi: 10.4088/jcp.14m09540.

Mazor, Y., Gelkopf, M., Mueser, K. & Roe, D. (2016) Posttraumatic growth in psychosis. *Frontiers in Psychiatry, 7*, 202.

McCaffrey, T., Carr, C., Petter Solli, H. & Hense, C. (2018) Music therapy and recovery in mental health: Seeking a way forward. *Voices: A World Forum for Music Therapy, 18*(1).

McCann, T., Cotton, S. & Lubman, D. (2017) Social problem solving in carers of young people with a first episode of psychosis: a randomized controlled trial. *Early Intervention in Psychiatry, 11*(4), 346–350. doi: 10.1111/eip.12301.

McCann, T., Lubman, D. & Clark, E. (2011) Responding to stigma: First-time caregivers of young people with first-episode psychosis. *Psychiatric Services, 62*(5), 548–550. doi: 10.1176/ps.62.5.pss6205_0548.

McCann, T., Lubman, D., Cotton, S., Murphy, B., Crisp, K., Catania, L., et al. (2013) A randomized controlled trial of bibliotherapy for carers of young people with first-episode psychosis. *Schizophrenia Bulletin, 39*(6), 1307–1317. doi: 10.1093/schbul/sbs121.

McCrone, P., Singh, S., Knapp, M., Smith, J., Clark, M., Shiers, D., et al. (2013) The economic impact of early intervention in psychosis services for children and adolescents. *Early Intervention in Psychiatry, 7*(4), 368–373. doi: 10.1111/eip.12024.

McEvoy, J. (2006) Effectiveness of clozapine versus olanzapine, quetiapine and risperidone in patients with chronic schizophrenia who did not respond to prior atypical antipsychotic treatment. *The American Journal of Psychiatry, 163*(4), 600. doi: 10.1176/appi.ajp.163.4.600.

McGinty, J., Sayeed Haque, M. & Upthegrove, R. (2018) Depression during first episode psychosis and subsequent suicide risk: A systematic review and meta-analysis of longitudinal studies. *Schizophrenia Research, 195*, 58–66. doi: 10.1016/j.schres.2017.09.040.

McGlashan, T. (1987) Recovery style from mental illness and long-term outcome. *The Journal of Nervous and Mental Disease, 175*, 681–685.

McGlashan, T. (1988) A selective review of recent North American long-term follow-up studies of schizophrenia. *Schizophrenia Bulletin, 14*(4), 515–542.

McGorry, P. D. (2011) Pre-emptive intervention in psychosis: Agnostic rather than diagnostic. *Australian & New Zealand Journal of Psychiatry, 45*, 515–519.

McGorry, P. D. (2015) Early intervention in psychosis: obvious, effective, overdue. *The Journal of Nervous and Mental Disease, 203*(5), 310–318.

McGorry, P. D., Bates, T. & Birchwood, M. (2013) Designing youth mental health services for the 21st century: Examples from Australia, Ireland and the UK. *British Journal of Psychiatry, 54*, 30–5. doi: 10.1192/bjp.bp.112.119214.

McGorry, P. D., Cocks, J., Power, P., Burnett, P., Harrigan, S. & Lambert, T. (2011) Very low-dose risperidone in first-episode psychosis: A safe and effective way to initiate treatment. *Schizophrenia Research.* doi: http://dx.doi.org/10.1155/2011/631690.

McGorry, P. D., Edwards, J., Mihalopoulos, C., Harrigan, S. & Jackson, H. (1996) EPPIC: An evolving system of early detection and optimal management. *Schizophrenia Bulletin, 22*, 305–326.

McGorry, P. D., Hickie, I. B., Yung, A. R., Pantelis, C. & Jackson, H. J. (2006) Clinical staging of psychiatric disorders: A heuristic framework for choosing earlier, safe, and more effective interventions. *Australian and New Zealand Journal of Psychiatry, 40*, 616–622.

McGorry, P. D., Killackey, E. & Yung, A. (2008) Early intervention in psychosis: Concepts, evidence and future directions *World Psychiatry, 7*(3), 148–156.

McGrath, J., Saha, S., Chant, D. & Welham, J. (2008) Schizophrenia: A concise overview of incidence, prevalence, and mortality, *Epidemiologic Reviews, 30*(1), 67–76 doi: https://doi.org/10.1093/epirev/mxn001.

McGurk, S. R. & Mueser, K. T. (2004) Cognitive functioning, symptoms, and work in supported employment: A review and heuristic model. *Schizophrenia Research, 70*, 147–173.

Mead, S. (2014) *Intentional peer support: An alternative approach.* Vermont, US, Intentional Peer Support.

Mead, S. & Copeland, M. E. (2000) What recovery means to us: Consumers' perspectives. *Community Mental Health Journal, 36,* 315–328.

Meaden, A. & Hacker, D. (2011) *Problematic and risk behaviours in psychosis: A shared formulation approach.* London: Routledge.

Melau, M., Albert, N. & Nordentoft, M. (2017) Development of a fidelity scale for Danish specialized early interventions service. *Early Intervention in Psychiatry.* doi: 10.1111/eip.12523.

Mellor, D., Carne, L., Shen, Y., McCabe, M. & Wang, L. (2013) Stigma toward mental illness. *Journal of Cross-Cultural Psychology, 44*(3), 352–364. doi: 10.1177/0022022112451052.

Meltzer, H. & McGurk, S. (1999) The effects of clozapine, risperidone, and olanzapine on cognitive function in schizophrenia. *Schizophrenia Bulletin, 25*(2), 233–256. doi: 10.1093/oxfordjournals.schbul.a033376.

Meng, H., Schimmelmann, B. G., Mohler, B., Lambert, M., Branik, E., Koch, E., et al. (2006) Pre-treatment social functioning predicts 1-year outcome in early onset psychosis. *Acta Psychiatrica Scandinavica, 114,* 249–256.

Menon, M., Mizrahi, R. & Kapur, S. (2008) 'Jumping to conclusions' and delusions in psychosis: Relationship and response to treatment. *Schizophrenia Research, 98*(1–3), 225–231. doi: 10.1016/j.schres.2007.08.021.

Merrett, Z., Rossell, S. & Castle, D. (2016) Comparing the experience of voices in borderline personality disorder with the experience of voices in a psychotic disorder: A systematic review. *Australian & New Zealand Journal of Psychiatry, 50*(7), 640–648. http://dx.doi.org/10.1177/0004867416632595.

Mersh, L., Jones, F. & Oliver, J. (2015) Mindfulness, self-stigma and social functioning in first episode psychosis: A brief report. *Psychosis, 7*(3), 261–264.

Mewton, L. & Andrews, G. (2016) Cognitive behavioral therapy for suicidal behaviors: improving patient outcomes. *Psychology Research and Behavior Management, 9,* 21–29. doi: http://doi.org/10.2147/PRBM.S84589.

Michail, M. (2013) Social anxiety disorders in psychosis: A critical review. In F. Durbano (ed.), *New insights into anxiety disorders* Rijeck, Croatia: Intech. doi: Org/105772/53053.

Michail, M. & Birchwood, M. (2012) Social anxiety disorder and shame cognitions in psychosis. *Psychological Medicine, 43*(01), 133–142. doi: 10.1017/s0033291712001146.

Michail, M. & Birchwood, M. (2014) Social anxiety in FEP: The role of childhood trauma and adult attachment. *Journal of Affective Disorders, 163,* 102–109. doi: 10.1016/j/jad2014.03.033.

Michail, M., Birchwood, M. & Tait, L. (2017) Systematic review of CBT for social anxiety in psychosis. *Brain Sciences, 25*(5). doi: 10.3390/brainsci.

Milev, P., Ho, B. C., Arndt, S. & Andreasen, N. C. (2005) Predictive values of neurocognition and negative symptoms on functional outcome in schizophrenia: A longitudinal first-episode study with 7-year follow-up. *The American Journal of Psychiatry, 162,* 495–506.

Miller, B., Bodenheimer, C. & Crittenden, K. (2011) Second-generation antipsychotic discontinuation in first episode psychosis: An updated review. *Clinical Psychopharmacology and Neuroscience, 9*(2), 45–53. doi: 10.9758/cpn.2011.9.2.45.

Miller, J. L. & Vaillancourt, T. (2007) Relation between childhood peer victimization and adult perfectionism: Are victims of indirect aggression more perfectionistic? *Aggressive Behaviour, 33,* 230–241. doi: 10.1002/ab.20183.

Miller, W. R., C'de Baca, J., Matthews, D. B. & Wilbourne, P. L. (2001) *Personal values card sort.* Albuquerque, NM: University of New Mexico.

Millman, Z. B., Pitts, S. C., Thompson, E., Kline, E. R., Demro, C., Weintraub, M. J., et al. (2017) Perceived social stress and symptom severity among help-seeking adolescents with versus without clinical high-risk for psychosis. *Schizophrenia Research, 192*, 364–370. doi: 10.1016/j.schres.2017.06.002.

Minor, K. S., Friedman-Yakoobian, M., Leung, Y. J., Meyer, E. C., Zimmet, S. V., Caplan, B., et al. (2015) The impact of premorbid adjustment, neurocognition, and depression on social and role functioning in patients in an early psychosis treatment program. *Australian & New Zealand Journal of Psychiatry, 49*, 444–452.

Mitchell, A., Delaffon, V., Vancampfort, D., Correll, C. & De Hert, M. (2011) Guideline concordant monitoring of metabolic risk in people treated with antipsychotic medication: Systematic review and meta-analysis of screening practices. *Psychological Medicine, 42*(1), 125–147. doi: 10.1017/s003329171100105x.

Mitter, N., Subramaniam, M., Abdin, E., Poon, L. & Verma, S. (2013) Predictors of suicide in Asian patients with first episode psychosis. *Schizophrenia Research, 151*(1–3), 274–278. doi: 10.1016/j.schres.2013.10.006.

Miyamoto, B., Galecki, M. & Francois, D. (2015) Guidelines for antipsychotic-induced hyperprolactinemia. *Psychiatric Annals, 45*(5), 266–272. doi: 10.3928/00485713-20150501-09.

Mizuno, E., Takataya, K., Kamizawa, N., Sakai, I. & Yamazaki, Y. (2013) Female families' experiences of caring for persons with schizophrenia. *Archives of Psychiatric Nursing, 27*(2), 72–77. doi: 10.1016/j.apnu.2012.10.007.

Mizuno, Y., Suzuki, T., Nakagawa, A., Yoshida, K., Mimura, M., Fleischhacker, W. & Uchida, H. (2014) Pharmacological strategies to counteract antipsychotic-induced weight gain and metabolic adverse effects in schizophrenia: A systematic review and meta-analysis. *Schizophrenia Bulletin, 40*(6), 1385–1403. doi: 10.1093/schbul/sbu030.

Moghaddam, B. & Javitt, D. (2012) From revolution to evolution: The glutamate hypothesis of schizophrenia and its implication for treatment. *Neuropsychopharmacology, 37*(1), 4–15. doi: 10.1038/npp.2011.181.

Molavi, P., Karimollahi, M., Sadeghie-Ahary, S., Taghizadeh, E. & Elhameh, N. (2015) Social deprivation in family members of patients with schizophrenia. *European Psychiatry, 30*, 1710. doi: 10.1016/s0924-9338(15)31313-4.

Moncrieff, J. (2014) The nature of mental disorder: Disease, distress, or personal tendency? *Philosophy, Psychiatry & Psychology, 21*(3), 257–260. doi: 10.1353/ppp.2014.0028.

Montastruc, J., Laborie, I., Bagheri, H. & Senard, J. (1997) Drug-induced orthostatic hypotension. *Clinical Drug Investigation, 14*(1), 61–65. doi: 10.2165/00044011-199714010-00008.

Morera, T., Pratt, D. & Bucci, S. (2017) Staff views about psychosocial aspects of recovery in psychosis: A systematic review. *Psychology Psychotherapy, 90(1)*, 1–24. doi: 10.1111/papt.12092.

Morgan, C., Charalambides, M., Hutchinson, G. & Murray, R (2010) Migration, ethnicity and psychosis: Toward a socio-developmental model. *Schizophrenia Bulletin, 36*, 655–664.

Morgan, C., Fearon, P., Lappin, J., Heslin, M., Donoghue, K., Lomas, B., et al. (2017) Ethnicity and long-term course and outcome of psychotic disorders in a UK sample: The AESOP-10 study. *The British Journal of Psychiatry, 211*, 88–94. doi: 10.1192/bjp.bp.116.193342.

Morgan, C., Lappin, J., Heslin, M., Donoghue, K., Lomas, B., Reininghaus, U., et al. (2014) Reappraising the long-term course and outcome of psychotic disorders: The AESOP-10 study. *Psychology Medicine, 44(13),* 2713–2726. doi: 10.1017/S0033291714000282.

Morgan, V. A., Castle, D. J. & Jablensky, A. V. (2008) Do women express and experience psychosis differently from men? Epidemiological evidence from the Australian National Study of Low Prevalence (Psychotic) Disorders. *Australian & New Zealand Journal of Psychiatry, 42,* 74–82.

Morin, M. & St-Onge, M. (2015) Factors predicting parents' adaptation when supporting their young adult during a first-episode psychosis. *Early Intervention in Psychiatry, 11*(6), 488–497. doi: 10.1111/eip.12263.

Morosini, P. L., Magliano, L., Brambilla, L., Ugolini, S. & Pioli, R. (2000) Development, reliability and acceptability of a new version of the DSM-IV Social and Occupational Functioning Assessment Scale (SOFAS) to assess routine social functioning. *Acta Psychiatrica Scandinavica, 101,* 323–329.

Morris, E., Johns, L. & Oliver, J. (eds). (2013) *Acceptance and commitment therapy and mindfulness for psychosis.* Chichester: Wiley-Blackwell.

Morrison, A. (2017) A manualised treatment protocol to guide delivery of evidence-based cognitive therapy for people with distressing psychosis: Learning from clinical trials. *Psychosis: Psychological, Social and Integrative Approaches, 9*(3), 271–281. doi: http://dx.doi.org/10.1080/17522439.2017.1295098.

Morrison, A. P., Frame, L. & Larkin, W. (2003) Relationships between trauma and psychosis: A review and integration. *British Journal of Clinical Psychology, 42,* 331–353.

Morrison, A. P., Shryane, N., Beck, R., Heffernan, S., Law, H., McCusker, M., et al. (2013) Psychosocial and neuropsychiatric predictors of subjective recovery from psychosis. *Psychiatry Research, 208*(3), 203–209. doi: 10.1016/j.psychres.2013.05.008.

Mossaheb, N. (2012) Role of aripiprazole in treatment-resistant schizophrenia. *Neuropsychiatric Disease and Treatment, 235.* doi: 10.2147/ndt.s13830.

Mo'tamedi, H., Rezaiemaram, P., Aguilar-Vafaie, M., Tavallaie, A., Azimian, M. & Shemshadi, H. (2014) The relationship between family resiliency factors and caregiver-perceived duration of untreated psychosis in persons with first-episode psychosis. *Psychiatry Research, 219*(3), 497–505.

Mottaghipour, Y. & Bickerton, A. (2005) The pyramid of family care: A framework for family involvement with adult mental health services. *Australian E-Journal for the Advancement of Mental Health, 4*(3), 210–217. doi: 10.5172/jamh.4.3.210.

Mouridsen, S., Rich, B., Isager, T. & Nedergaard, N. (2008) Psychiatric disorders in individuals diagnosed with infantile autism as children: A case control study. *Journal of Psychiatric Practice, 14*(1), 5–12. http://dx.doi.org/10.1097/01.pra.0000308490.47262.e0.

Moyers, T. B. & Martino, S. (2006) What's important in my life. The personal goals and values card sorting task for individuals with schizophrenia. PowerPoint presentation. Retrieved from attcnetwork.org/media/132.

Mueser, K. T., Aalto, S., Becker, D. R., Ogden, J. S., Wolfe, R. S., Schiavo, D., et al. (2005) The effectiveness of skills training for improving outcomes in supported employment. *Psychiatric Services, 56,* 1254–1260.

Mueser, K. T., Bellack, A. S., Morrison, R. L. & Wixted, J. T. (1990) Social competence in schizophrenia: Premorbid adjustment, social skill, and domains of functioning. *Journal of Psychiatric Research, 24,* 51–63.

Mueser, K. T., Deavers, F., Penn, D. L. & Cassisi, J. E. (2013) Psychosocial treatments for schizophrenia. *Annual Review of Clinical Psychology, 9*, 465–497. doi: org/10.1146. annurev-clinpsy-050212-185620.

Mueser, K. T., Gingerich, S., Salyers, M. P., McGuire, A. B., Reyes, R. U. & Cunningham, H. (2005) Illness Management and Recovery (IMR) scales, in measuring the promise. In T. Campbell-Orde, J. Chamberlin, J. Carpenter & H. S. Leff (eds) *A compendium of recovery measures*. Cambridge, MA: Evaluation Center and Human Services Research Institute.

Mueser, K. T. & Glynn, S. M. (2014) Have the potential benefits of CBT for severe mental disorders been undersold? *World Psychiatry, 13*, 253–256. doi: 10.1002/wps.20160.

Mueser, K. T., Glynn, S. M., Cather, C., Zarate, R., Fox, L., Feldman, J., et al. (2009) Family intervention for co-occurring substance use and severe psychiatric disorders: Participant characteristics and correlates of initial engagement and more extended exposure in a randomized controlled trial. *Addictive Behaviors, 34*(10), 867–877.

Mueser, K. T., Glynn, S. M. & Meyer-Kalos, P. S. (2017) What are the key ingredients of optimal psychosocial treatment for persons recovering from a first episode of psychosis? *World Psychiatry, 16*, 266–267.

Mueser, K. T., Lu, W., Rosenberg, S. D. & Wolfe, R. (2010) The trauma of psychosis: Posttraumatic stress disorder and recent onset psychosis. *Schizophrenia Research, 116*, 217–227. doi: 10.1016/j.schres.2009.10.025.

Mueser, K. T., Penn, D., Addington, J., Brunette, M., Gingerich, S., Glynn, S., et al. (2015) The NAVIGATE program for first-episode psychosis: Rationale, overview, and description of psychosocial components. *Psychiatric Services, 66*(7), 680–690.

Mueser, K. T., Salyers, M. P. & Mueser, P. R. (2001) A prospective analysis of work in schizophrenia. *Schizophrenia Bulletin, 27*(2), 281–296.

Mueser, K. T. & Tarrier, N. (eds) (1998) *Handbook of social functioning in schizophrenia*. Needham Heights, MA: Allyn & Bacon.

Mulder, S. & Lines, E. (2005) *A siblings guide to psychosis*. Toronto: Canadian Mental Health Association.

Müller, H., de Millas, W., Gaebel, W., Herrlich, J., Hasan, A., Janssen, B., et al. (2017) Negative schemata about the self and others and paranoid ideation in at-risk states and those with persisting positive symptoms. *Early Intervention Psychiatry, 19*. doi: 10.1111/eip.12433.

Mulligan, J., Sellwood, W., Reid, G., Riddell, S. & Andy, N. (2012) Informal caregivers in early psychosis: evaluation of need for psychosocial intervention and unresolved grief. *Early Intervention in Psychiatry, 7*(3), 291–299. doi: 10.1111/j.1751-7893.2012.00369.x.

Mundt, J. C., Marks, I. M., Shear, M. K. & Greist, J. M. (2002) The Work and Social Adjustment Scale: A simple measure of impairment in functioning. *The British Journal of Psychiatry, 180*(5), 461–464.

Murphy, C., Wilson, C., Robertson, D., Ecker, C., Daly, E. & Hammond, N., et al. (2016) Autism spectrum disorder in adults: Diagnosis, management, and health services development. *Neuropsychiatric Disease and Treatment, 12*, 1669–1686. http://dx.doi.org/10.2147/ndt.s65455.

Murray, R., Quattrone, D., Natesan, S., van Os, J., Nordentoft, M. & Howes, O., et al. (2016) Should psychiatrists be more cautious about the long-term prophylactic use of antipsychotics? *The British Journal of Psychiatry, 209*(5), 361–365. doi: 10.1192/bjp.bp.116.182683.

Murray, R., Quigley, H., Quattrone, D., Englund, A. & Di Forti, M. (2016) Traditional marijuana, high-potency cannabis and synthetic cannabinoids: increasing risk for psychosis. *World Psychiatry, 15*(3), 195–204. http://dx.doi.org/10.1002/wps.20341.

Murri, M. B., Respino, M., Innamorati, M., Cervetti, A., Calcagno, P., Pompili, P., et al. (2015) Is good insight associated with depression among patients with schizophrenia? Systematic review and meta-analysis. *Schizophrenia Research, 162*, 234–247. doi. org/10.1016/j.schres.2015.01.003.

Myin-Germeys I, van Os J. (2007) Stress-reactivity in psychosis: Evidence for an affective pathway to psychosis. *Clinical Psychology Review, 27*(4), 409–424. doi: 10.1016/j. cpr.2006.09.005.

Myles, H., Myles, N. & Large, M. (2015) Cannabis use in first episode psychosis: Meta-analysis of prevalence, and the time course of initiation and continued use. *Australian & New Zealand Journal of Psychiatry, 50*(3), 208–219. http://dx.doi.org/10.1177/000486 7415599846.

Myles, N., Newall, H., Curtis, J., Nielssen, O., Shiers, D. & Large, M. (2012) Tobacco use before, at, and after first-episode psychosis. *The Journal of Clinical Psychiatry, 73*(4), 468–475. doi: 10.4088/jcp.11r07222.

Nahum, M., Fisher, M., Loewy, R., Poelke, G., Ventura, J., Nuechterlein, K., et al. (2014) A novel, online social cognitive training program for young adults with schizophrenia: A pilot study. *Schizophrenia Research Cognition, 1*(1), 11–19.

Napa, W., Tungpunkom, P. & Pothimas, N. (2017) Effectiveness of family interventions on psychological distress and expressed emotion in family members of individuals diagnosed with first-episode psychosis: a systematic review. *JBI Database of Systematic Reviews and Implementation Reports, 15(4)*, 1057–1079. doi: 10.11124/ JBISRIR-2017-003361.

Nasser, M. (1995) The rise and fall of anti-psychiatry. *Psychiatric Bulletin, 19*(12), 743–746. doi: 10.1192/pb.19.12.743.

Naz, B., Craig, T. J., Bromet, E. J., Finch, S. J., Fochtmann, L. J. & Carlson, G. A. (2007) Remission and relapse after the first hospital admission in psychotic depression: A 4-year naturalistic follow-up. *Psychology Medicine, 37*(8), 1173–1181.

Neil, S., Kilbride, M., Pitt, L., Nothard, S., Welford, M., Sellwood, W., et al. (2009) The questionnaire about the process of recovery (QPR): A measurement tool developed in collaboration with service users, *Psychosis, 1*(2), 145–155.

Nelson, H. E. (2005) *Cognitive-behaviour therapy for delusions and hallucinations: A practice manual* (2nd edn). Cheltenham: Nelson Thornes Ltd.

Ngoc, T., Weiss, B. & Trung, L. (2016) Effects of the family schizophrenia psychoeducation program for individuals with recent onset schizophrenia in Vietnam. *Asian Journal of Psychiatry, 22*, 162–166. doi: 10.1016/j.ajp.2016.06.001.

NHS. (2014) *National audit of schizophrenia*, 2nd edn. London: Department of Health.

NHS England. (2016) *The five year forward view for mental health*. London: Department of Health.

NICE. (2009) *Psychosis and schizophrenia in adults: Treatments and management*. London: National Institute for Health and Care Excellence.

NICE. (2011) *Coexisting severe mental illness (psychosis) and substance misuse: assessment and management in healthcare settings*. London: NICE.

NICE. (2014) *Psychosis and schizophrenia in adults: Treatments and management*. NICE Clinical Guideline CG178. London: National Institute for Health and Care Excellence.

NICE. (2016) *Implementing the early intervention in psychosis access and waiting time standard: Guidance*. London: NHS England Publications.

NICE. (2017) *Type 2 diabetes: prevention in people at high risk. Guidance and guidelines.* Retrieved from www.nice.org.uk/guidance/ph38/chapter/glossary.

Nielsen, J., Graff, C., Kanters, J., Toft, E., Taylor, D. & Meyer, J. (2011) Assessing QT interval prolongation and its associated risks with antipsychotics. *CNS Drugs, 25*(6), 473–490. doi: 10.2165/11587800-000000000-00000.

Nielssen, O. & Large, M. (2008) Rates of homicide during the first episode of psychosis and after treatment: A systematic review and meta-analysis. *Schizophrenia Bulletin, 36*(4), 702–712. doi: 10.1093/schbul/sbn144.

Niemantsverdriet, M., Slotema, C., Blom, J., Franken, I., Hoek, H., Sommer, I., et al. (2017) Hallucinations in borderline personality disorder: Prevalence, characteristics and associations with comorbid symptoms and disorders. *Scientific Reports, 7*(1). http://dx.doi.org/10.1038/s41598-017-13108-6.

Nilsen, L., Frich, J., Friis, S., Norheim, I. & Røssberg, J. (2016) Participants' perceived benefits of family intervention following a first episode of psychosis: A qualitative study. *Early Intervention in Psychiatry, 10*(2), 152–159. doi: 10.1111/eip.12153.

Nordentoft, M., Jeppesen, P., Abel, M., Kassow, P., Petersen, L., Thorup, A., et al. (2002) OPUS study: Suicidal behaviour, suicidal ideation and hopelessness among patients with first-episode psychosis: One-year follow-up of a randomised controlled trial. *British Journal of Psychiatry Supplement, 43,* s98–s106.

Nordentoft, M., Laursen, T. M., Agerbo, E., Qin, P., Høyer, E. H. & Mortensen, P. B. (2004) Change in suicide rates for patients with schizophrenia in Denmark, 1981–97: Nested case-control study. *British Medical Journal, 329*(7460), 261. http://doi.org/10.1136/bmj.38133.622488.63.

Norman, R., Anderson, K., MacDougall, A., Manchanda, R., Harricharan, R., Subramanian, P., et al. (2017) Stability of outcomes after 5 years of treatment in an early intervention programme. *Early Intervention in Psychiatry.* doi: 10.1111/eip.12450.

Norman, R., Mallal, A. K., Manchanda, R., Jääskeläinen, D., Harricharan, R., Takhar, J. & Northcott, S. (2007) Does treatment delay predict occupational functioning in first-episode psychosis? *Schizophrenia Research, 91,* 259–262.

Norman, R., MacDougall, A., Manchanda, R., Harricharan, R. (2018) An examination of components of recovery after five years of treatment in an early intervention program for psychosis *Schizophrenia Research, 195,* 469–474. doi: 10.1016/j.schres.2017.08.054.

Norman, R., Windell, D., Lynch, J. & Manchanda, R. (2012) Perceived relational evaluation as a predictor of self-esteem and mood in people with a psychotic disorder. *The Canadian Journal of Psychiatry, 57*(5), 309–316. doi: 10.1177/070674371205700506.

Northumberland, Tyne and Wear NHS Foundation Trust. (2016) *Commonsense confidentiality: Information leaflet.* Patient Information Centre.

Notley, C., Christopher, R., Hodgekins, J., Byrne, R., French, P. & Fowler, D. (2015) Participant views on involvement in a trial of SR cognitive–behavioural therapy. *The British Journal of Psychiatry, 206,* 122–127.

Nuechterlein, K. H. & Dawson, M. E. (1984) A heuristic vulnerability/stress model of schizophrenic episodes. *Schizophrenia Bulletin, 10*(2), 300–312.

Nuechterlein, K. H., Subotnik, K. L., Turner, L. R., Ventura, J., Becker, D. R. & Drake, R. E. (2008) Individual placement and support for individuals with recent-onset schizophrenia: Integrating supported education and supported employment. *Psychiatric Rehabilitation Journal, 31,* 340.

Nuechterlein, K. H., Ventura, J., McEwen, S. C., Gretchen-Doorly, D., Vinogradov, S. & Subotnik, K. L. (2016) Enhancing cognitive training through aerobic exercise after a first schizophrenia episode: Theoretical conception and pilot study. *Schizophrenia Bulletin, 42*, 44–52.

O'Brien, A., Fahmy, R. & Singh, S. P. (2009) Disengagement from mental health services: A literature review. *Social Psychiatry and Psychiatric Epidemiology, 44*, 558–568.

O'Connell, M. J. & Stein, C. H. (2011) The relationship between case manager expectations and outcomes of persons diagnosed with schizophrenia. *Community Mental Health Journal, 47*, 424–435.

O'Connor, R. C. (2011) Towards an integrated motivational-volitional model of suicidal behaviour. In R. O'Connor, S. Platt, & J. Gordon (eds) *International handbook of suicide prevention: Research, policy and practice.* Chichester: Wiley-Blackwell.

O'Donnell, B. F. & Martin, A. M. S. (2016) Emerging behavioural and psychotherapeutic interventions for schizophrenia. *Dusenen Adam: The Journal of Psychiatry and Neurological Sciences, 29*, 189–201. doi: 10.5350/DAJPN20162903001.

O'Donoghue, E., Morris, E., Oliver, J., Johns, L. & Jolley, S. (2018) Adapting ACT workshops for caregivers of psychosis. In E. O'Donoghue, E. Morris, J. Oliver & L. Johns, *ACT for psychosis recovery: A practical manual for group-based interventions using acceptance and commitment therapy.* Oakland, CA, Context Press, New Harbinger.

Office of National Statistics. (2017) NEET. Retrieved 8 March 2019 from www.ons.gov.uk.

O'Keane, V. (2008) Antipsychotic-induced hyperprolactinaemia, hypogonadism and osteoporosis in the treatment of schizophrenia. *Journal of Psychopharmacology, 22*, 70–75. doi: 10.1177/0269881107088439.

O'Keeffe, D., Sheridan, A., Kelly, A., Doyle, R., Madigan, K., Lawlor, E., et al. (2018) 'Recovery' in the real world: Service user experiences of mental health service use and recommendations for change 20 years on from a first episode psychosis. *Administration and Policy in Mental Health and Mental Health Services Research.* doi: https://doi.org/10.1007/s10488-018-0851-4.

Oliva, F., Dalmotto, M., Pirfo, E., Furlan, P. & Picci, R. (2014) A comparison of thought and perception disorders in borderline personality disorder and schizophrenia: Psychotic experiences as a reaction to impaired social functioning. *BMC Psychiatry, 14*(1). http://dx.doi.org/10.1186/s12888-014-0239-2

Oliver, D., Davies, C., Grossland, G., Lim, S., Gifford, G., McGuire, P. & Fusar-Poli, P. (2018) Can we reduce the duration of untreated psychosis? *Schizophrenia Bulletin, 44*(1). doi: 10.1093/schbul/sby.017.787.

Olwit, C., Musisi, S., Leshabari, S. & Sanyu, I. (2015) Chronic sorrow: Lived experiences of caregivers of patients diagnosed with schizophrenia in Butabika Mental Hospital, Kampala, Uganda. *Archives of Psychiatric Nursing, 29*(1), 43–48. doi: 10.1016/j.apnu.2014.09.007.

Onwumere, J., Grice, S. & Kuipers, E. (2016) Delivering cognitive-behavioural family interventions for schizophrenia. *Australian Psychologist, 51*, 52–61.

Onwumere, J., Jansen, J. E & Kuipers, E. (2018) Editorial: Family interventions in psychosis change outcomes in early intervention settings – how much does the evidence support this? *Frontiers in Psychology, 9*, 406. doi: 10.3389/fpsyg.2018.00406.

Oorschot, M., Lataster, T., Thewissen, V., Lardinois, M., Wichers, M., van Os, J., et al. (2011) Emotional experience in negative symptoms of schizophrenia – no evidence for a generalized hedonic deficit. *Schizophrenia Bulletin, 39*, 217–225.

Owen, M. J., Sawa, A. & Mortensen, P. B. (2016) Schizophrenia. *The Lancet, 388*(10039), 86–97. doi: http://doi.org/10.1016/S0140-6736(15)01121-6.

Padwal, R., Kezouh, A., Levine, M. & Etminan, M. (2007) Long-term persistence with orlistat and sibutramine in a population-based cohort. *International Journal of Obesity, 31*(10), 1567–1570. doi: 10.1038/sj.ijo.0803631.

Pallin, S. (2004) Supporting staff and patients after a suicide. In D. Duffy & T. Ryan (eds) *New approaches to prevention suicide: A manual for practitioners.* London: Jessica Kingsley Publishers.

Palmer, B. A., Pankratz, V. S. & Bostwick, J. M. (2005) The lifetime risk of suicide in schizophrenia: A re-examination. *Archives of General Psychiatry, 62* (3), pp. 247–253.

Paolini, E., Moretti, P., Compton, M. T. (2016) Delusions in first-episode psychosis: Principal component analysis of twelve types of delusions and demographic and clinical correlates of resulting domains. *Psychiatry Research, 243,* 5–13. doi: 10.1016/j.psychres.2016.06.002.

Park, Y., Kim, Y. & Lee, J. (2012) Antipsychotic-induced sexual dysfunction and its management. *The World Journal of Men's* Health, *30*(3), 153. doi: 10.5534/wjmh.2012.30.3.153.

Parkinson, S. & Whiter, C. (2016) Exploring art therapy group practice in early intervention psychosis. *International Journal of Art Therapy, 21*(3), 116–127.

Patel, R., Wilson, R., Jackson, R., Ball, M., Shetty, H. & Broadbent, M., et al. (2016). Association of cannabis use with hospital admission and antipsychotic treatment failure in first episode psychosis: An observational study. *BMJ Open, 6*(3), e009888. http://dx.doi.org/10.1136/bmjopen-2015-009888

Patterson, P., Birchwood, M. & Cochrane, R. (2000) Preventing the entrenchment of high expressed emotion in first episode psychosis: Early developmental attachment pathways. *Australian and New Zealand Journal of Psychiatry, 34,* 191–197. doi: 10.1177/000486740003401s29.

Patterson, P., Birchwood, M. & Cochrane, R. (2005) Expressed emotion as an adaptation to loss: prospective study in first-episode psychosis. *British Journal of Psychiatry, 187*(48), 59–64. doi: 10.1192/bjp.187.48.s59.

Pelayo-Terán, J. M., Gajardo-Galán, V., Gómez-Revuelta, M., de la Foz, V. O. G., Ayesa-Arriola, R., Tabarés-Seisdedos, R., et al. (2018) Duration of active psychosis and functional outcomes in first-episode non-affective psychosis. *European Psychiatry, 52,* 29–37.

Pelayo-Terán, J., Galán, V., de la Foz, V., Martínez-García, O., Tabarés-Seisdedos, R., Crespo-Facorro, B., et al. (2017) Rates and predictors of relapse in first-episode non-affective psychosis: A 3-year longitudinal study in a specialized intervention program (PAFIP). *European Archives of Psychiatry and Clinical Neuroscience, 267*(4), 315–323.

Penn, D. L., Uzenoff, S. R., Perkins, D., Mueser, K. T., Hamer, R., Waldheter, E., et al. (2011) A pilot investigation of the Graduated Recovery Intervention Program (GRIP) for first episode psychosis. *Schizophrenia Research, 125,* 247–256.

Penn, D. L., Waldheter, E. J., Perkins, D. O., Mueser, K. T. & Lieberman, J. A. (2005) Psychosocial treatment for first-episode psychosis: A research update. *The American Journal of Psychiatry, 162,* 2220–2220.

Penttilä, M., Jääskeläinen, E., Hirvonen, N., Isohanni, M. & Miettunen, J. (2014) Duration of untreated psychosis as predictor of long-term outcome in schizophrenia: Systematic review and meta-analysis. *The British Journal of Psychiatry, 205*(2), 88–94.

Perälä, J., Suvisaari, J., Saarni. S. I., Kuoppasalmi, K., Isometsä, E., Pirkola, S., et al. (2007) Lifetime prevalence of psychotic and bipolar I disorders in a general population. *Archive of General Psychiatry, 64*(1), 19–28. doi: 10.1001/archpsyc.64.1.19.

Perivoliotis, D. & Cather, C. (2009) Cognitive behavioural therapy of negative symptoms. *Journal of Clinical Psychology, 65*(8), 815–830.

Perkins, R. & Slade, M. (2012) Recovery in England: Transforming statutory services? *International Review of Psychiatry, 24*(1), 29–39. doi: 10.3109/09540261.2011.645025.

Perry, B. & Singh, S. (2017) First-episode psychosis and abnormal glycaemic control – Authors' reply. *The Lancet Psychiatry, 4*(1), 24. doi: 10.1016/s2215-0366(16)30411-4.

Peters, E. (2014) An oversimplification of psychosis, its treatment, and outcomes? *The British Journal of Psychiatry, 205,* 159–160.

Peters, E., Crombie, T., Agbedjro, D., Johns, L. C., Stahl, D., Greenwood, K., et al. (2015) The long-term effectiveness of cognitive behaviour therapy for psychosis within a routine psychological therapies service. *Frontiers in Psychology, 6,* 1658. doi: 10.3389/fpsyg.2015.01658.

Peters, E., Joseph, S., Day, S. & Garety, P. (2004) Measuring delusional ideation: The 21-item Peters et al. Delusions Inventory (PDI). *Schizophrenia Bulletin, 30*(4), 1005–1022.

Peters, E., Moritz, S., Schwannauer, M., Wiseman, Z., Greenwood, K. E., Scott, J., et al. (2013) Cognitive biases questionnaire for psychosis. *Schizophrenia Bulletin.* doi: http://dx.doi.org/10.1093/schbul/sbs199.

Petersen, L., Jeppesen, P., Thorup, A., Abel, M., Øhlenschlæger, J., Christensen, T., et al. (2005) A randomised multicentre trial of integrated versus standard treatment for patients with a first episode of psychotic illness. *British Medical Journal, 331*(7517), 602. doi: 10.1136/bmj.38565.415000.e01.

Petrakis, M. & Laxton, S. (2017) Intervening early with family members during first-episode psychosis: An evaluation of mental health nursing psychoeducation within an inpatient unit. *Archives of Psychiatric Nursing, 31*(1), 48–54. doi: 10.1016/j.apnu. 2016.07.015.

Petrakis, M., Oxley, J. & Bloom, H. (2013) Carer psychoeducation in first-episode psychosis: Evaluation outcomes from a structured group programme. *International Journal of Social Psychiatry, 59*(4), 391–397. doi: 10.1177/0020764012438476.

Pfammatter, M., Junghan, U. M. & Brenner, H. D. (2006) Efficacy of psychological therapy in schizophrenia: Conclusions from meta-analyses. *Schizophrenia Bulletin, 32,* 64–80.

Pharoah, F., Mari, J., Rathbone, J. & Wong, W. (2010) Family intervention for schizophrenia. *The Cochrane Database of Systematic Reviews, 12.* doi: 10.1002/14651858. CD000088.pub2.

Pietruch, M. & Jobson, L. (2012) Posttraumatic growth and recovery in people with first episode psychosis: An investigation into the role of self-disclosure. *Psychosis, 4*(3), 213–223.

Pitt, L., Kilbride, M., Nothard, S., Welford, M. & Morrison, T. (2007) Researching recovery from psychosis: A user led project. *Psychiatric Bulletin, 31.* 55–60.

Pompili, M., Baldessarini, R. J., Forte, A., Erbuto, D., Serafini, G., Fiorillo, A., et al. (2016) Do atypical antipsychotics have antisuicidal effects? A hypothesis-generating overview. *The International Journal of Molecular Sciences, 17*(10).

Pompili, M., Serafini, G., Innamorati, M., Lester, D., Shrivastava, A., Giradi, P., et al. (2011) Suicide risk in first episode psychosis: A selective review of the current literature. *Schizophrenia Research, 129,* 1–11.

Power, P. (2017) Outcome and recovery in first-episode psychosis. *The British Journal of Psychiatry, 211*(6), 331–333. doi: 10.1192/bjp.bp.117.205492.

Power, P. & McGowan, S. (2011) *Suicide risk management in early intervention.* London: The National Mental Health Development Unit.

Power, P. J. R., Bell, R. J., Mills, R., Herrma-Doig, T., Davern, M., Henry, L., et al. (2003) Suicide prevention in first episode psychosis: The development of a randomised controlled trial of cognitive therapy for acutely suicidal patients with early psychosis. *Australian and New Zealand Journal of Psychiatry, 37*(4), 414–420. doi: 10.1046/j.1440-1614.2003.01209.x.

Pradhan, B . & Pinninti, N. R. (2016) Yoga and mindfulness-based cognitive therapy for psychosis (*Y-MBCTp*©): A pilot study on its efficacy as brief therapy. In: B. Pradhan, N. Pinninti, & S. Rathod (eds) *Brief interventions for psychosis*. New York: Springer.

Praharaj, S., Jana, A., Goyal, N. & Sinha, V. (2011) Metformin for olanzapine-induced weight gain: a systematic review and meta-analysis. *British Journal of Clinical Pharmacology, 71*(3), 377–382. doi: 10.1111/j.1365-2125.2010.03783.x.

Priebe, S. (2007) Social outcomes in schizophrenia. *The British Journal of Psychiatry, 191*, 15–20.

Priebe, S., McCabe, R., Ballenkamp, L., Hansson, L., Martinez-Leal, R., Rössler, W., et al. (2007) Structured patient-clinician communication and 1-year outcomes in community mental health care. *The British Journal of Psychiatry, 191*, 420–246. doi: 10.1192.bjp.bp.107.036939.

Putnam, R. & Goss, K. A. (2002) 'Introduction' In R. Putnam (ed.) *Democracies in flux: The evolution of social capital in contemporary society*. Oxford: Oxford University Press.

Rabinovitch, M., Cassidy, C., Schmitz, N., Joober, R. & Malla, A. (2013) The influence of perceived social support on medication adherence in first-episode psychosis. *The Canadian Journal of Psychiatry, 58*(1), 59–65. doi: 10.1177/070674371305800111.

Radhakrishnan, M., McCrone, P., Lafortune, L., Everard, L., Fowler, D., Amos, T., et al. (2017) Cost-effectiveness of early intervention services for psychosis and fidelity to national policy implementation guidance. *Early Intervention Psychiatry, 12*(4), 747–756. doi: 10.1111/eip.12481.

Radhakrishnan, R., Wilkinson, S. T. & D'Souza, D. C. (2014) Gone to pot – a review of the association between cannabis and psychosis. *Frontiers in Psychiatry, 5*, 54. doi: http://doi.org/10.3389/fpsyt.2014.00054.

Rajapakse, T., Garcia-Rosales, A. G., Weerawardene, S., Cotton, S. & Fraser, R. (2011) Themes of delusions and hallucinations in first episode psychosis. *Early Intervention in Psychosis, 5*, 254–258.

Randal, C., Bucci, S., Morera, T., Barrett, M. & Pratt, D. (2016) Mindfulness-based cognitive therapy for psychosis: Measuring psychological change using repertory grids. *Clinical Psychology and Psychotherapy, 23*(6), 496–508.

Randolph, E. T. (1998) Social networks and schizophrenia. In K. T. Mueser and N. Tarrier (eds) *Handbook of social functioning in schizophrenia* (pp. 238–246). London: Pearson.

Rapado-Castro, M., McGorry, P. D., Yung, A., Calvo, A. & Nelson, B. (2015) Sources of clinical distress in young people at ultra high risk of psychosis. *Schizophrenia Research, 165*(1), 15–21. doi: 10.1016/j.schres.2015.03.022.

Read, J. & Gumley, A. (2008) Can attachment theory help explain the relationship between childhood adversity and psychosis? *Attachment: New Directions in Psychotherapy and Relational Psychoanalysis, 2*, 1–35.

Read, J., Hammersley, P. & Rudegeair, T. (2007) Why, when and how to ask about childhood abuse. *Advances in Psychiatric Treatment, 13*, 101–110.

Read, J., Van Os, J., Morrison, A. P. & Ross, C. A. (2005) Childhood trauma, psychosis and schizophrenia: A literature review with theoretical and clinical implications. *Acta Psychiatrica Scandinavica, 112*, 330–350. doi: 10.1111/.1600-0447.2005.66634.

Rector, N. A., Beck, A. & Stolar, N. (2005) Negative symptoms of schizophrenia: A cognitive perspective. *Canadian Journal of Psychiatry, 50*(5), 247–57. doi: 1177/070674 37505000503.

Reeder, C., Newton, E., Frangou, S. & Wykes, T. (2004) Which executive skills should we target to affect social functioning and symptom change? A study of a cognitive remediation therapy program. *Schizophrenia Bulletin, 30*(1), 87.

Reininghaus, U., Dutta, R., Dazzan, P., Doody, G., Fearon, P., Lappin, J., et al. (2014) Mortality in schizophrenia and other psychoses: A 10-year follow-up of the ÆSOP first-episode cohort. *Schizophrenia Bulletin, 41*(3), 664–673. doi: 10.1093/schbul/sbu138.

Reininghaus, U., Kempton, M. J., Valmaggia, L., Craig, T. K., Garety, P., Onyejiaka, A., et al. (2016) Stress sensitivity, aberrant salience, and threat anticipation in early psychosis: An experience sampling study. *Schizophrenia Bulletin, 42*(3), 712–722. doi: 10.1093/schbul/sbv190.

Remington, G., Foussias, G., Fervaha, G., Agid, O., Takeuchi, H., Lee, J., et al. (2016) Treating negative symptoms in schizophrenia: An update. *Current Treatment Options in Psychiatry, 3*(2), 133–150. doi: 10.1007/s40501-016-0075-8.

Renner, K. A., Valentiner, D. P. & Holzman, J. B. (2017) Focus-of-attention behavioral experiment: An examination of a therapeutic procedure to reduce social anxiety. *Cognitive Behaviour Therapy, 46*(1), 60–74.

Repper, J., with contributions from Aldridge, B., Gilfoyle, S., Gillard, S., Perkins, R. & Rennison, J. (2013) *Peer support workers: Theory and practice.* ImROC briefing, Centre for Mental Health and Mental Health Network, NHS Confederation.

Rethink Mental Illness (2014) *Lost generation: Why young people with psychosis are being left behind, and what needs to change.* London: Rethink Mental Illness.

Revell, E. R., Neill, J. C., Harte, M., Khan, Z. & Drake, R. J. (2015) A systematic review and meta-analysis of cognitive remediation in early schizophrenia. *Schizophrenia Research, 168*, 213–222.

Reveulta, M. G., Galan, V. G., Ruiz, M. J., Olivares, O. P., Rodriguez, R. L., De Santayana Jenaro, G. P., et al. (2017) Anticipating outcome: Predictors of first and subsequent relapses in schizophrenia: A 3 year follow up. *European Psychiatry, 41*, 97. doi: 10.1016/j.eurpsy.2017.01.301.

Rhodes, J. & Jakes, S. (2009) *Narrative CBT for psychosis.* New York: Routledge.

Riblet, N. B. V., Shiner, B., Young-Xu, Y. & Watts, B. V. (2017) Strategies to prevent death by suicide: Meta-analysis of randomised controlled trials. *The British Journal of Psychiatry, 210*(6), 396–402. doi: 10.1192/bjp.bp.116.187799.

Rigucci, S., Marques, T. R., Di Forti, M., Taylor, H., Dell'Acqua, F., Mondelli, V., et al. (2015) Effect of high-potency cannabis on corpus callosum microstructure. *Psychological Medicine, 46*(4), 841–854.

Riley, G., Gregory, N., Bellinger, J., Davies, N., Mabbott, G. & Sabourin, R. (2011) Carer's education groups for relatives with a first episode of psychosis: An evaluation of an eight-week education group. *Early Intervention in Psychiatry, 5*(1), 57–63. doi: 10.1111/j.1751-7893.2010.00195.x.

Rinaldi, M., Killackey, E., Smith, J., Shepherd, G., Singh, S. P. & Craig, T. (2010) First episode psychosis and employment: A review. *International Review of Psychiatry, 22*, 148–162.

Ringbäck Weitoft, G., Berglund, M., Lindström, E. A., Nilsson, M., Salmi, P. & Rosén, M. (2014) Mortality, attempted suicide, re-hospitalisation and prescription refill for clozapine and other antipsychotics in Sweden: A register-based study. *Pharmacoepidemiology & Drug Safety, 23*, 290–298. doi: 10.1002/pds.3567.

Roberts, G. (2009) *Putting recovery at the heart of all we do.* www.iris-initiative.org.uk.

Roberts, G. & Wolfson, P. (2004) The rediscovery of recovery: Open to all. *Advances in Psychiatric Treatment, 10*, 37–48.

Robins, E. & Guze, S. B. (1970) Establishment of diagnostic validity in psychiatric illness: Its application to schizophrenia. *The American Journal of Psychiatry. 126*(7), 983–987. doi: https://doi.org/10.1176/ajp.126.7.983.

Robinson, D., Woerner, M., Alvir, J., Bilder, R., Goldman, R. & Geisler, S., et al. (1999) Predictors of relapse following response from a first episode of schizophrenia or schizoaffective disorder. *Archives of General Psychiatry, 56*(3), 241. doi: 10.1001/archpsyc.56.3.241.

Robinson, D., Woerner, M. G., McMeniman, M., Mendelowitz, A. & Bilder, R. M. (2004) Symptomatic and functional recovery from a first episode of schizophrenia or schizoaffective disorder. *The American Journal of Psychiatry, 161*, 473–479.

Robinson, J., Cotton, S. M., Conus, P., Schimmelmann, B., McGorry, P. D. & Lambert, M. (2009) Prevalence and predictors of suicide attempt in an incidence cohort of 661 young people with first episode psychosis. *Australian and New Zealand Journal of Psychiatry, 43*(2), 149–157.

Robinson, J., Harris, M. G., Harrigan, S. M., Henry, L. P., Farelly, S., Prosser, A., et al. (2010) Suicide attempt in first-episode psychosis: A 7.4 year follow up study. *Schizophrenia Research, 116*(1), 1–8.

Rodrigues, R. & Anderson, K. K. (2017) The traumatic experience of first-episode psychosis: A systematic review and meta-analysis. *Schizophrenia Research.* doi: https://doi.org/10.1016/j.schres.2017.01.045.

Rolland, B., Jardri, R., Amad, A., Thomas, P., Cottencin, O. & Bordet, R. (2014) Pharmacology of hallucinations: Several mechanisms for one single symptom? *Biomedical Research International*, 1–9. doi: 10.1155/2014/307106.

Rollnick, S. & Miller, W. R. (1995) What is motivational interviewing? *Behavioural and Cognitive Psychotherapy, 23*, 325–334.

Rollnick, S., Miller, W., Butler, C. & Aloia, M. (2008) Motivational interviewing in health care: Helping patients change behavior. *COPD: Journal of Chronic Obstructive Pulmonary Disease, 5*(3), 203. http://dx.doi.org/10.1080/15412550802093108.

Romm, K. L., Rossberg, J. I., Hansen, C. F., Haug, E., Andreassen, O. A. & Melle, I. (2011) Self-esteem is associated with premorbid adjustment and positive psychotic symptoms in early psychosis. *BMC Psychiatry, 11*, 136.

Rooke, O. & Birchwood, M. (1998) Loss, humiliation and entrapment as appraisals of schizophrenic illness: A prospective study of depressed and non-depressed patients. *British Journal of Clinical Psychology, 37*, 259–268.

Rosen, P. & Garety, P. A. (2005) Predicting recovery from schizophrenia. *Schizophrenia Bulletin, 31*, 735–750.

Rosenfarb, I., Bellack, A., Aziz, N., Kratz, K. & Sayers, S. (2004) Race, family interactions, and patient stabilization in schizophrenia. *Journal of Abnormal Psychology, 113*, 109–115.

Rosenheck, R., Estroff, S. E., Sint, K., Lin, H., Mueser, K. T., RAISE-ETP Investigators, et al. (2017a) Incomes and outcomes: Social Security disability benefits in first-episode psychosis. *The American Journal of Psychiatry, 174*, 886–894.

Rosenheck, R., Leslie, D., Keefe, R., McEvoy, J., Swartz, M., CATIE Study Investigators Group, et al. (2006) Barriers to employment for people with schizophrenia. *The American Journal of Psychiatry, 163*, 411–417.

Rosenheck, R., Mueser, K. T., Sint, K., Lin, H., Lynde, D. W., Glynn, S. M., et al. (2017b) Supported employment and education in comprehensive, integrated care for first episode psychosis: Effects on work, school, and disability income. *Schizophrenia Research, 182*, 120–128.

Rossi, A., Amore, M., Galderisi, S., Rocca, P., Bertolino, A., Italian Network of Research on Psychoses et al. (2017) The complex relationship between self-reported 'personal recovery' and clinical recovery in schizophrenia. *Schizophrenia Research, 192*, 108–112.

Royal College of Psychiatrists (2018) *Early Intervention in Psychosis Network (EIPN) self-assessment.* London: Royal College of Psychiatrists.

Royal College of Psychiatrists, Care Services Improvement Partnership and Social Care Institute for Excellence. (2007) *A common purpose: Recovery in future mental health services.* Royal College of Psychiatrists.

Ruby, E., Polito, S., McMahon, K., Gorovitz, M., Corcoran, C. & Malaspina, D. (2014) Pathways associating childhood trauma to the neurobiology of schizophrenia. *Frontiers in Psychological and Behavioral Science, 3*(1), 1–17.

Ruggeri, M., Bonetto, C., Lasalvia, A., Fioritti, A., De Girolamo, G., GET UP Group, et al. (2015) Feasibility and effectiveness of a multi-element psychosocial intervention for first-episode psychosis: results from the cluster-randomized controlled GET UP PIANO trial in a catchment area of 10 million inhabitants. *Schizophrenia Bulletin, 41*, 1192–1203.

Rummel-Kluge, C., Komossa, K., Schwarz, S., Hunger, H., Schmid, F. & Kissling, W., et al. (2010) Second-generation antipsychotic drugs and extrapyramidal side effects: A systematic review and meta-analysis of head-to-head comparisons. *Schizophrenia Bulletin, 38*(1), 167–177. doi: 10.1093/schbul/sbq042.

Russell, D., Peplau, L. A. & Cutrona, C. E. (1980) The revised UCLA Loneliness Scale: concurrent and discriminant validity evidence. *Journal of Personality and Social Psychology, 39*(3), 472–480.

Rutten, B. P., Hammels, C., Geschwind, N., Menne-Lothmann, C., Pishva, E., Schruers, K., et al. (2013) Resilience in mental health: Linking psychological and neurobiological perspectives. *Acta Psychiatrica Scandinavica, 128*, 3–20.

Ryrie, I., Hellard, L., Kearns, C., Robinson, D., Pathmanathan, I. & O'Sullivan, D. (1997) Zoning: A system for managing case work and targeting resources in community mental health teams. *Journal of Mental Health, 6*(5), 515–523. doi: http://dx.doi.org/10.1080/09638239718608.

Sabbioni, D., Feehan, S., Nicholis, C., Soong, W., Rigoli, D., Follett, D., et al. (2018) Providing culturally informed mental health services to Aboriginal youth: the Youth-Link model in Western Australia. *Early Intervention in Psychiatry, 12*(5), 987–994.

Sadath, A., Muralidhar, D., Varambally, S., Gangadhar, B. & Jose, J. (2017) Do stress and support matter for caring? The role of perceived stress and social support on expressed emotion of carers of persons with first episode psychosis. *Asian Journal of Psychiatry, 25*, 163–168. doi: 10.1016/j.ajp.2016.10.023.

Sadath, A., Muralidhar, D., Varambally, S., Jose, J. & Gangadhar, B. (2015) Family intervention in first-episode psychosis. *SAGE Open, 5*(4). doi: 10.1177/2158244015613108.

Sagut, P. & Duman, Z. (2016) Comparison of caregiver burden in first episode versus chronic psychosis. *Archives of Psychiatric Nursing, 30*(6), 768–773. doi: 10.1016/j.apnu.2016.07.011.

Samara, M., Leucht, C., Leeflang, M., Anghelescu, I., Chung, Y. & Crespo-Facorro, B. et al. (2015) Early improvement as a predictor of later response to antipsychotics in schizophrenia: A diagnostic test review. *The American Journal of Psychiatry, 172*(7), 617–129.

Sampson, S., Mansour, M., Maayan, N., Soares-Weiser, K. & Adams, C. (2013) Intermittent drug techniques for schizophrenia. *Cochrane Database of Systematic Reviews*. doi: 10.1002/14651858.cd006196.pub2.

Sandhu, A., Ives, J., Birchwood, M. & Upthegrove, R. (2013) The subjective experience and phenomenology of depression following FEP: A qualitative study using photo elicitation. *Journal of Affective Disorders, 149*, 166–174. doi: 10.1016/j.jad.2013.01.018.

Santesteban-Echarri, O., Paino, M., Rice, S., González-Blanch, C., McGorry, P., Gleeson, J., et al. (2017). Predictors of functional recovery in first-episode psychosis: A systematic review and meta-analysis of longitudinal studies. *Clinical Psychology Review, 58*, 59–75.

Saravanan, B., Jacob, K. S., Johnson, S., Prince, M., Bhugra, D. & David, A. S. (2010) Outcome of first-episode schizophrenia in India: Longitudinal study of effect of insight and psychopathology. *The British Journal of Psychiatry, 196*, 454–459.

Schizophrenia Commission (2012) *The abandoned illness: A report from the Schizophrenia Commission*. London: Rethink Mental Illness.

Schmidt, S. J., Mueller, D. R. & Roder, V. (2011) Social cognition as a mediator variable between neurocognition and functional outcome in schizophrenia: Empirical review and new results by structural equation modeling. *Schizophrenia Bulletin, 37*, 41–54.

Schoeler, T., Monk, A., Sami, M. B., Klamerus, E., Foglia, E., Brown, R., et al. (2016) Continued versus discontinued cannabis use in patients with psychosis: A systematic review and meta-analysis. *The Lancet. Psychiatry, 3*(3), 215–225. doi: 10.1016/S2215-0366(15)00363-6.

Schoeler, T., Petros, N., Di Forti, M., Pingault, J., Klamerus, E. & Foglia, E., et al. (2016). Association between continued cannabis use and risk of relapse in first-episode psychosis. *JAMA Psychiatry, 73*(11), 1173. http://dx.doi.org/10.1001/jamapsychiatry.2016.2427.

Schooler, N. H., Weissman, G., Hogarty, G., Hargreaves, W. A., Attkisson, C. C. & Sorenson, J. (1979) *Resource materials for community mental health program evaluators*. Rockville, MD: National Institute of Mental Health.

Schroeder, K., Fisher, H. & Schäfer, I. (2013) Psychotic symptoms in patients with borderline personality disorder. *Current Opinion in Psychiatry, 26*(1), 113–119. http://dx.doi.org/10.1097/yco.0b013e32835a2ae7.

Schulz, S. & Murray, A. (2016) Assessing cognitive impairment in patients with schizophrenia. *The Journal of Clinical Psychiatry, 77*, 3–7. doi: 10.4088/jcp.14074su1c.01.

Secher, R. G., Hjorthøj, C. R., Austin, S. F., Thorup, A., Jeppesen, P., Mors, O. & Nordentoft, M. (2015) Ten-year follow-up of the OPUS specialized early intervention trial for patients with a first episode of psychosis. *Schizophrenia Bulletin, 41*(3), 617–26. doi: 10.1093/schbul/sbu155.

Seddon, J., Birchwood, M., Copello, A., Everard, L., Jones, P. & Fowler, D., et al. (2015) Cannabis use is associated with increased psychotic symptoms and poorer psychosocial functioning in first-episode psychosis: A report from the UK National EDEN Study. *Schizophrenia Bulletin, 42*(3), 619–625. http://dx.doi.org/10.1093/schbul/sbv154.

Segal, Z. V., Williams, J. M. G. & Teasdale, J. D. (2002) *Mindfulness-based cognitive therapy for depression: A new approach to preventing relapse*. New York, Guilford.

Sehlo, M., Youssef, U., Hussein, R. & Elgohary, H. (2015) The relationship of perceived family criticism and other risk factors to violence among patients with schizophrenia. *Middle East Current Psychiatry, 22*(2), 70–75. doi: 10.1097/01.xme.0000461768. 22702.35.

Seikkula, J., Aaltonen, J., Alakare, B., Haarakangas, K., Keränen, J. & Lehtinen, K. (2006) Five-year experience of first-episode nonaffective psychosis in open-dialogue approach: Treatment principles, follow-up outcomes, and two case studies. *Psychotherapy Research, 16*(2), 214–228.

Selick, A., Durbin, J., Vu, N., O'Connor, K., Volpe, T. & Lin, E. (2017) Barriers and facilitators to implementing family support and education in Early Psychosis Intervention programmes: A systematic review. *Early Intervention in Psychiatry, 11*(5), 365–374. doi: 10.1111/eip. 12400.

Selten, J., van Os, J. & Cantor-Graae, E. (2016) The social defeat hypothesis of schizophrenia: Issues of measurement and reverse causality. *World Psychiatry, 15*(3), 294–295. doi: http://doi.org/10.1002/wps.20369.

Selten, J. P., Wiersma, D. & van den Bosch, R. J. (2000) Distress attributed to negative symptoms in schizophrenia. *Schizophrenia Bulletin, 26,* 737.

Sharma, T., Guski, L. S., Freund, N. & Gøtzsche, P. C. (2016) Suicidality and aggression during antidepressant treatment: Systematic review and meta-analyses based on clinical study reports. *British Medical Journal.* doi: https://doi.org/10.1136/bmj.i65.

Shawyer, R., Ratcliff, K., Mackinnon, A., Farhall, J., Hayes, S. & Copolov, D. (2007) The voices acceptance and action scale (VAAS): Pilot data. *Journal of Clinical Psychology, 63*(6), 593–606.

Shen, L., Liao, M. & Tseng, Y. (2012) Recent advances in imaging of dopaminergic neurons for evaluation of neuropsychiatric disorders. *Journal of Biomedicine and Biotechnology,* 1–14. doi: 10.1155/2012/259349.

Shiers, D., Bradshaw, T. & Campion, J. (2015) Health inequalities and psychosis: Time for action. *The British Journal of Psychiatry, 207*(6), 471–473. doi: 10.1192/bjp.bp. 114.152595.

Short, S. (2006) *Review of the UK 2000 Time Use Survey.* London: Office for National Statistics, 11.

Shrivastava, A., Johnston, M., Thakar, M., Stitt, L. & Shah, N. (2011) Social outcome in clinically recovered first-episode schizophrenia in a naturalistic, ten-year, follow-up study in India. *Clinical Schizophrenia and Related Psychoses, 5*(2).

Siegel, S. J., Irani, F., Brensinger, C. M., Kohler, C. G., Bilker, W. B., Ragland, J. D., et al. (2006). Prognostic variables at intake and long-term level of function in schizophrenia. *American Journal of Psychiatry, 163*(3), 433–441.

Silverstein, S. M. & Bellack, A. S. (2008) A scientific agenda for the concept of recovery as it applies to schizophrenia. *Clinical Psychology Review, 28,* 1108–1124.

Silverstein, S. M., Spaulding, W. D., Menditto, A. A., Savitz, A., Liberman, R. P., Berten, S., et al. (2008) Attention shaping: A reward-based learning method to enhance skills training outcomes in schizophrenia. *Schizophrenia Bulletin, 35,* 222–232.

Simonsen, C., Faerden, A., Romm, K. L., Berg, A. O., Bjella, T., Sundet, K., et al. (2017) Early clinical recovery in first-episode psychosis: Symptomatic remission and its correlates at 1-year follow-up. *Psychiatry Research, 254,* 118–125. doi: 10.1016/j. psychres.2017.04.050.

Simonsen, E., Friis, S., Haahr, U., Johannessen, J. O., Larsen, T. K., Melle, I., et al. (2007) Clinical epidemiologic first-episode psychosis: 1-year outcome and predictors. *Acta Psychiatrica Scandinavica, 116,* 54–61.

Sin, J., Gillard, S., Spain, D., Cornelius, V., Chen, T. & Henderson, C. (2017) Effectiveness of psychoeducational interventions for family carers of people with psychosis: A systematic review and meta-analysis. *Clinical Psychology Review, 56*, 13–24. doi: 10.1016/j.cpr.2017.05.002.

Sin, J., Henderson, C., Pinfold, V. & Norman, I. (2013) The E Sibling Project – exploratory randomised controlled trial of an online multi-component psychoeducational intervention for siblings of individuals with first episode psychosis. *BMC Psychiatry, 13*(1). doi: 10.1186/1471-244x-13-123.

Singh, J., Kour, K. & Jayaram, M. (2012) Acetylcholinesterase inhibitors for schizophrenia. *Cochrane Database of Systematic Reviews*. doi: 10.1002/14651858.cd007967.pub2.

Singh, S., Singh, V., Kar, N. & Chan, K. (2010) Efficacy of antidepressants in treating the negative symptoms of chronic schizophrenia: meta-analysis. *The British Journal of Psychiatry, 197*(3), 174–179. doi: 10.1192/bjp.bp.109.067710.

Singh, S. P., Brown, L. J., Winsper, C., Gajwani, R., Islam, Z, Jasani, R., et al. (2015) Ethnicity and pathways to care during first episode psychosis: The role of cultural illness attributions. *BMC Psychiatry, 15*(1).

Singh, S. P., Islam, Z., Brown, L. J., Gajwani, R., Jasani, R., Rabiee, F., et al. (2013) *Ethnicity, detention and early intervention: Reducing inequalities and improving outcomes for black and minority ethnic patients: the ENRICH programme, a mixed-methods study.* Southampton, UK: NIHR Journals Library; Programme Grants for Applied Research.

Sitko, K., Bentall, R. P., Shevlin, M., O'Sullivan, N. & Sellwood, W. (2014) Associations between specific psychotic symptoms and specific childhood adversities are medicated by attachment styles: An analysis of the National Comorbidity Survey. *Psychiatry Research, 217*, 202–209. doi: 10.1016/j.psychres.2014.03.019.

Slade, M. (2009a) *100 Ways to Support Recovery: A Guide for Mental Health Professionals.* London: Rethink.

Slade, M. (2009b) *Personal recovery and mental illness: A guide for mental health professionals. (values-based practice).* Cambridge: Cambridge University Press.

Slade, M., Amering, M. & Oades, L. (2008) Recovery: An international perspective. *Epidemiologia e Psichiatria Sociale, 17*(2), 128–137.

Slade, M. & Hayward, M. (2017) Recovery, psychosis and psychiatry: Research is better than rhetoric. *Acta Psychiatrica Scandinavica, 116*(2), 81–83.

Sledge, W. H., Lawless, M., Sells, D., Wieland, M., O'Connell, M. J. & Davidson, L. (2011) Effectiveness of peer support in reducing readmissions of persons with multiple psychiatric hospitalizations. *Psychiatric Services, 62*, 541–544.

Smailes, D, Alderson-Day, B., Fernyhough, C., McCarthy-Jones, S., Dodgson, G. (2015) Tailoring cognitive behavioral therapy to subtypes of voice-hearing. *Frontier in Psychology, 6*(1933). doi: 10.3389/fpsyg.2015.01933.

Smallwood, J., Jolley, S., Makhijani, J., Grice, S., O'Donoghue, E., Bendon, P., et al. (2016) Implementing specialist psychological support for caregivers in psychosis services: A preliminary report. *Psychosis, 9*(2), 119–128. doi: 10.1080/17522439.2016.1259647.

Smith, J., Fadden, G. & Taylor, L. (2010) The needs of siblings in first episode psychosis. In P. French, M. Reed, J. Smith, M. Rayne & D. Shiers, *Early intervention in psychosis: Promoting recovery.* Oxford: Blackwell.

Smith, T. E, Easter, A., Pollock, M., Pope, L. G. & Wisdom, J. P. (2013) Disengagement from care: Perspectives of individuals with serious mental illness and of service providers. *Psychiatric Services, 64*(8), 770–775.

Smith, T. E., Hull, J. W., Goodman, M., Hedayat-Harris, A., Willson, D. F., Israel, L. M. & Munich, R. L. (1999) The relative influences of symptoms, insight, and neurocognition on social adjustment in schizophrenia and schizoaffective disorder. *The Journal of Nervous and Mental Disease, 187*, 102–108.

Soares, B. & Silva de Lima, M. (2006) Penfluridol for schizophrenia. *Cochrane Database of Systematic Reviews.* doi: 10.1002/14651858.cd002923.pub2.

Sonmez, N., Romm, K. L., Andreassen, O. A., Melle, I & Rossberg, J. I. (2013) Depressive symptoms in FEP: A one year follow-up study. *BMC Psychiatry, 13*, 106. doi: 10.1186/1471-244X-13-106.

Speckens, A. E. & Hawton, K. (2005) Social problem solving in adolescents with suicidal behavior: A systematic review. *Suicide and Life Threatening Behaviour, 35*(4), 365–387.

Spitzer, R. L, Andreasen, N. C. & Endicott, J. (1978) Schizophrenia and other psychotic disorders in DSM-III. *Schizophrenia Bulletin, 4*(4), 489–510.

Spivak, B., Mester, R., Wittenberg, N., Maman, Z. & Weizman, A. (1997) Reduction of aggressiveness and impulsiveness during clozapine treatment in chronic neuroleptic-resistant schizophrenic patients. *Clinical Neuropharmacology, 20*(5), 442–446. doi: 10.1097/00002826-199710000-00009.

Srihari, V., Tek, C., Kucukgoncu, S., Phutane, V., Breitborde, N., Pollard, J., et al. (2015) First-episode services for psychotic disorders in the U.S. public sector: A pragmatic randomized controlled trial. *Psychiatric Services, 66*(7), 705–712.

Stack, S. & Kposowa, A. J. (2011) Religion and suicide acceptability: a cross-national analysis. *Journal for the Scientific Study of Religion, 50*(2), 89–306. doi: 10.1111/j.1468-5906.2011.01568.x.

Stahlberg, O., Anckarsäter, H., Rastam, M. & Gillberg, C. (2004) Bipolar disorder, schizophrenia, and other psychotic disorders in adults with childhood onset AD/HD and/or autism spectrum disorders. *Journal of Neural Transmission, 111*(7), 891–902.

Stain, H. J., Brønnick, K., Hegelstad, W. T., Joa, I., Johannessen, J. O., Langeveld, J., et al. (2013) Impact of interpersonal trauma on the social functioning of adults with first-episode psychosis. *Schizophrenia Bulletin, 40*(6), 1491–1498.

Stain, H. J., Bucci, S., Baker, A. L., Carr, V., Emsley, R., Halpin, S., et al. (2016) A randomised controlled trial of cognitive behaviour therapy versus non-directive reflective listening for young people at ultra high risk of developing psychosis: The detection and evaluation of psychological therapy (DEPTh) trial. *Schizophrenia Research, 176*(2–3), 212–219. doi: 10.1016/j.schres.2016.08.008.

Staring, A. B., TerHuurne, M. A. & van Der Gaag, M. (2013) Cognitive behaviour therapy of negative symptoms (CBTn) in psychotic disorders: A pilot study. *Journal of Behaviour Therapy and Experimental Psychiatry, 44*, 300–306.

Staring, A. B., Van der Gaag, M., Koopmans, G. T., Selten, J. P., Van Beveren, J., Hengeveld, M., et al. (2010) Treatment adherence therapy in people with psychotic disorders: Randomised controlled trial. *British Journal of Psychiatry, 197*(6), 448–455. doi: 10.1192/bjp.bp.110.077289.

Statistics on Drug Misuse, England. (2017) GOV.UK. Retrieved 25 April 2018, from www.gov.uk/government/statistics/statistics-on-drug-misuse-england-2017.

Statistics on Smoking, England. (2017) [PAS]. Retrieved from http://digital.nhs.uk/pubs/smoking17.

Sterk, B., van Rossum, I. W., Muis, M. & De Haan, L. (2013) Priorities, satisfaction and treatment goals in psychosis patients: An online consumer's survey. *Pharmacopsychiatry, 46*, 88–93.

Stober, J. (1998b) The Frost Multidimensional Perfectionism Scale: More perfect with four (instead of six) dimensions. *Personality and Individual Differences, 24*, 481–491.

Stowkowy, J., Addington, D., Liu, L., Hollowell, B. & Addington, J. (2012) Predictors of disengagement from treatment in an early psychosis program. *Schizophrenia Research, 136*(1–3), 7–12. doi: 10.1016/j.schres.2012.01.027.

Strauss, C. & Hayward, M. (2013) Group person-based cognitive therapy for distressing psychosis. In E. Morris, L. Johns & J. Oliver (eds) *Acceptance and commitment therapy and mindfulness for psychosis*. Chichester: Wiley.

Strauss, C., Hugdahl, K., Waters, F. Hayward, M., Bless, J. J., Falkenberg, L. E., et al. (2018) The Beliefs about Voices Questionnaire-Revised: A factor analysis form 450 participants. *Psychiatry Research, 259*, 95–103.

Strauss, J. S. & Carpenter, W. T. (1974) The prediction of outcome in schizophrenia: II. Relationships between predictor and outcome variables: A report from the WHO International Pilot Study of Schizophrenia. *Archives of General Psychiatry, 31*, 7–42.

Strauss, J. S. & Carpenter, W. T. (1977) Prediction of outcome in Schizophrenia: III. Five-year outcome and its predictors. *Archives of General Psychiatry, 34*, 159–163.

Stroup, T., Lieberman, J., McEvoy, J., Davis, S., Swartz, M.; CATIE Investigators, et al. (2009) Results of phase 3 of the CATIE schizophrenia trial. *Schizophrenia Research, 107*(1), 1–12. doi: 10.1016/j.schres.2008.10.011.

Subandi, M. (2011) *The role of family empowerment and family resilience on recovery from psychosis*. Yogyakarta, Indonesia: Gadjah Mada University.

Subandi, M. (2015) Bangkit: The processes of recovery from first episode psychosis in Java. *Culture, Medicine, and Psychiatry, 39*(4), 597–613.

Sullivan, S., Northstone, K., Gadd, C., Walker, J., Margelyte, R., Richards, A., et al. (2017) Models to predict relapse in psychosis: A systematic review. *PLoS One, 12*(9). doi: 0.1371/journal.pone.0183998.

Summers, A. (2006) Psychological formulations in psychiatric care: Staff views on their impact. *The Psychiatrist, 30*, 341–343.

Swan, S., Keen, N., Reynolds & Onwumere, J. (2017) Psychological interventions for post-traumatic stress symptoms in psychosis: A systematic review of outcomes. *Frontiers in Psychology, 8*, 341. doi: 10.3389/fpsyg.2017.00341.

Swartz, M. S., Perkins, D. O., Stroup, T. S., Davis, S. M., Capuano, G. CATIE Investigators, et al. (2007) Effects of antipsychotic medications on psychosocial functioning in patients with chronic schizophrenia: Findings from the NIMH CATIE study. *The American Journal of Psychiatry, 164*, 428–436.

Szasz, T. (1974) *The myth of mental illness*. New York: Perennial.

Tait, L., Birchwood, M. & Trower, P. (2003) Predicting engagement with services for psychosis: Insight, symptoms and recovery style. *British Journal of Psychiatry, 182*(2), 123–128.

Tait, L., Birchwood, M. & Trower, P. (2004) Adapting to the challenge of psychosis: personal resilience and the use of sealing-over (avoidant) coping strategies. *British Journal of Psychiatry, 185*(5), 410–415.

Tait, L., Ryles, D & Sidwell, A. (2010) Strategies for engagement. In P. French, M. Reed, J. Smith, M. Rayne & D. Shiers (eds) *Early intervention in psychosis: Promoting recovery*. Oxford: Blackwell Publishing Ltd.

Takahashi, H., Ideno, T., Okubo, S., Matsui, H., Takemura, K., Matsuura, M., et al. (2009) Impact of changing the Japanese term for 'schizophrenia' for reasons of stereotypical beliefs of schizophrenia in Japanese youth. *Schizophrenia Research, 112*(1–3), 149–152. doi: 10.1016/j.schres.2009.03.037.

Tan, R., Gould, R., Combes, H. & Lehmann, S. (2014) Distress, trauma, and recovery: Adjustment to first episode psychosis. *Psychology and Psychotherapy: Theory, Research and Practice, 87*(1), 80–95.

Tandberg, M., Ueland, T., Andreassen, O. A., Sundet, K. & Melle, I. (2012) Factors associated with occupational and academic status in patients with first-episode psychosis with a particular focus on neurocognition. *Social Psychiatry & Psychiatric Epidemiology, 47*, 1763–1773.

Tang, C., Subramaniam, M., Ng, B., Abdin, E., Poon, L. & Verma, S. (2016) Clozapine use in first-episode psychosis. *The Journal of Clinical Psychiatry, 77*(11), 1447–1453. doi: 10.4088/jcp.15m10063.

Tantirangsee, N., Assanangkornchai, S. & Marsden, J. (2015) Effects of a brief intervention for substance use on tobacco smoking and family relationship functioning in schizophrenia and related psychoses: A randomised controlled trial. *Journal of Substance Abuse Treatment, 51*, 30–37. doi: 10.1016/j.jsat.2014.10.011.

Tapfumaneyi, A., Johnson, S., Joyce, J., Major, B., Lawrence, J., MiData Consortium, et al. (2015) Predictors of vocational activity over the first year in inner-city early intervention in psychosis services. *Early Intervention Psychiatry, 9*(6), 447–458. doi: 10.1111/eip.12125.

Tarricone, I., Ferrari Gozzi, B., Serretti, A., Grieco, D. & Berardi, D. (2009) Weight gain in antipsychotic-naive patients: A review and meta-analysis. *Psychological Medicine, 40*(2), 187. doi: 10.1017/s0033291709990407.

Tarrier, N. (2014) CBT for psychosis: Effectiveness, diversity, dissemination, politics, the future and technology. *World Psychiatry, 13*(3), 256–257. doi.10.1002/wps.20161.

Tarrier, N., Gooding, P., Pratt, D., Kelly, J., Maxwell, J. & Awenet, Y. (2013) *Cognitive behavioural prevention of suicide in psychosis: A treatment manual.* London: Routledge.

Tarrier, N., Kelly, J., Maqsood, S., Snelson, N., Maxwell, J., Law, H., Dunn, G. & Gooding, P. (2014) The cognitive behavioural prevention of suicide in psychosis: a clinical trial. *Schizophrenia Research. 156*(2–3), 204–210. doi: 10.1016/j.schres.2014.04.029.

Tarrier, N., Khan, S., Cater, J. & Picken, A. (2007) The subjective consequences of suffering a first episode psychosis: trauma and suicide behaviour. *Social Psychiatry and Psychiatric Epidemiology, 42*(1), 29–35.

Tas, C., Danaci, A., Cubukcuoglu, Z. & Brüne, M. (2012) Impact of family involvement on social cognition training in clinically stable outpatients with schizophrenia: A randomized pilot study. *Psychiatry Research, 195*(1–2), 32–38. doi: 10.1016/j.psychres.2011.07.031.

Tek, C., Kucukgoncu, S., Guloksuz, S., Woods, S., Srihari, V. & Annamalai, A. (2015) Antipsychotic-induced weight gain in first-episode psychosis patients: A meta-analysis of differential effects of antipsychotic medications. *Early Intervention in Psychiatry, 10*(3), pp. 193–202. doi: 10.1111/eip.12251.

Tennakoon, L., Fannon, D., Doku, V., O'Ceallaigh, S., Soni, W., Santamaria, M., et al. (2000) Experience of caregiving: Relatives of people experiencing a first episode of psychosis. *British Journal of Psychiatry, 177*(6), 529–533. doi: 10.1192/bjp.177.6.529.

Tessier, A., Boyer, L., Husky, M., Baylé, F., Llorca, P. & Misdrahi, D. (2017) Medication adherence in schizophrenia: The role of insight, therapeutic alliance and perceived trauma associated with psychiatric care. *Psychiatry Research, 257*, 315–321. doi: 10.1016/j.psychres.2017.07.063.

Thomas, N. (2015) What's really wrong with cognitive behavioral therapy for psychosis? *Frontiers in Psychology, 6*, 323.

Thomas, N., Farhall, J., Foley, F., Leitan, N., Villagonzalo, K. A., Ladd, E., et al. (2016) Promoting personal recovery in people with persisting psychotic disorders: Development and pilot study of a novel digital intervention. *Frontiers in Psychiatry, 7*, 196.

Thomas, N., Hayward, M., Peters, E., van der Gaag, M., Bentall, R. P., Jenner, J., et al. (2014) Psychological therapies for auditory hallucinations. Current status and key research directions. *Schizophrenia Bulletin, 40*, 202–212.

Thompson, K., McGorry, P. & Harrigan, S. (2003) Recovery style and outcome in first-episode psychosis. *Schizophrenia Research, 62*(1–2), 31–36.

Thorup, A., Petersen, L., Jeppesen, P., Øhlenschlæger, J., Christensen, T., Krarup, G., et al. (2006) Social network among young adults with first-episode schizophrenia spectrum disorders. *Social Psychiatry and Psychiatric Epidemiology, 41*, 761–770.

Thorup, A., Petersen, L., Jeppesen, P., Øhlenschlæger, J., Christensen, T., Krarup, G., et al. (2007) Gender differences in young adults with first-episode schizophrenia spectrum disorders at baseline in the Danish OPUS study. *The Journal of Nervous and Mental Disease, 195*, 396–405.

Tiihonen, J. (2006) Effectiveness of antipsychotic treatments in a nationwide cohort of patients in community care after first hospitalisation due to schizophrenia and schizoaffective disorder: Observational follow-up study. *British Medical Journal, 333*(7561), 224–230. doi: 10.1136/bmj.38881.382755.2f.

Tiihonen, J., Mittendorfer-Rutz, E., Majak, M., Mehtälä, J., Hoti, F., Jedenius, E., et al. (2017) Real-world effectiveness of antipsychotic treatments in a nationwide cohort of 29 823 patients with schizophrenia. *JAMA Psychiatry, 74*(7), 686. doi: 10.1001/jamapsychiatry.2017.1322.

Time to Change. (2016) *300 Voices Toolkit.* London. Retrieved from: www.time-change.org.uk/resources/guides-toolkits.

Tindall, R., Francey, S. & Hamilton, B. (2015) Factors influencing engagement with case managers: Perspectives of young people with a diagnosis of first episode psychosis. *International Journal of Mental Health Nursing, 24*(4), 295–303.

Tindall, R., Simmons, M. B., Allott, K. & Hamilton, B. E. (2018) Essential ingredients of engagement when working alongside people after their first episode of psychosis: A qualitative meta-analysis. *Early Intervention in Psychiatry.* doi: https://doi.org/10.1111/eip.12566.

Tohen, M., Khalsa, H. K., Salvatore, P., Vieta, E., Ravichandran, C. & Baldessarini, R. J. (2012) Two-year outcomes in first-episode psychotic depression The McLean-Harvard First-Episode Project. *Journal of Affective Disorders, 136(1–2)*, 1–8. doi: 10.1016/j.jad.2011.08.028.

Tomassi, S., Tosato, S., Mondelli, V, Faravelli, C., Lasalvia, A., GET UP Group, et al. (2017) Influence of childhood trauma on diagnosis and substance misuse in FEP. *The British Journal of Psychiatry, 211*, 151–156. doi: 10.1192/bjp.bp.116.194019.

Tonarelli, S. B., Pasillas, R., Alvarado, L., Dwivedi, A. & Cancellare, A. (2016) Acceptance and Commitment Therapy compared to treatment as usual in psychosis: A systematic review and meta-analysis. *Journal of Psychiatry, 19*, 366.

Torgersen, S., Kringlen, E. & Cramer, V. (2001) The prevalence of personality disorders in a community sample. *Archives of General Psychiatry, 58*(6), 590. http://dx.doi.org/10.1001/archpsyc.58.6.590.

Torrey, W. C., Mueser, K. T., McHugo, G. H. & Drake, R. E. (2000) Self-esteem as an outcome measure in studies of vocational rehabilitation for adults with severe mental illness. *Psychiatric Services, 51*, 229–233.

Tortelli, A., Errazuriz, A., Croudace, T., Morgan, C., Murray, R. M., Jones, P. B., et al. (2015) Schizophrenia and other psychotic disorders in Caribbean-born migrants and their descendants in England: Systematic review and meta-analysis of incidence rates, 1950–2013. *Social Psychiatry and Psychiatric Epidemiology, 50*(7), 1039–1055. doi: http://doi.org/10.1007/s00127-015-1021-6.

Treynor, W., Gonzalez, R. & Nolen-Hoeksema, S. (2003) Rumination reconsidered: A psychometric analysis. *Cognitive Therapy and Research, 27(3)*, 247–259.

Trower, P., Birchwood, M., Meaden, A., Byrne, S., Nelson, A. & Ross, K. (2004) Cognitive therapy for command hallucinations: Randomised controlled trial. *The British Journal of Psychiatry, 184*, 312–320.

Tschöke, S., Steinert, T., Flammer, E. & Uhlmann, C. (2014) Similarities and differences in borderline personality disorder and schizophrenia with voice hearing. *The Journal of Nervous and Mental Disease, 202*(7), 544–549. http://dx.doi.org/10.1097/nmd. 0000000000000159.

Tschöke, S., Uhlmann, C. & Steinert, T. (2011) Schizophrenia or trauma-related psychosis? Schneiderian first rank symptoms as a challenge for differential diagnosis. *Neuropsychiatry, 1*(4), 349–360. http://dx.doi.org/10.2217/npy.11.27.

Tsuda, Y., Saruwatari, J. & Yasui-Furukori, N. (2014) Meta-analysis: The effects of smoking on the disposition of two commonly used antipsychotic agents, olanzapine and clozapine. *British Medical Journal, 4*(3), doi: 10.1136/bmjopen-2013-004216.

Tungaraza, T. & Farooq, S. (2015) Clozapine prescribing in the UK: Views and experience of consultant psychiatrists. *Therapeutic Advances in Psychopharmacology, 5*(2), 88–96. doi: 10.1177/2045125314566808.

Turner, D. T., McGlanaghy, E., Cuijpers, P., van der Gaag, M., Karyotaki, E. & MacBeth, A. (2018) A meta-analysis of social skills training and related interventions for psychosis. *Schizophrenia Bulletin, 44*(3), 475–491.

Turner, D. T., van der Gaag, M., Karyotaki, E. & Cuijpers, P. (2014) Psychological interventions for psychosis: A meta-analysis of comparative outcome studies. *The American Journal of Psychiatry, 171*(5), 523–538. doi: 10.1176/appi.ajp.2013.13081159.

Turner, M., Bernard, M., Birchwood, M., Jackson, C. & Jones, C. (2013) The relationship between shame and post-psychotic trauma. *British Journal of Clinical Psychology, 52*, 1623–1682. doi: 10.1111/bjc.12007.

Tyrer, P. & Kendall, T. (2009) The spurious advance of antipsychotic drug therapy. *The Lancet, 373*(9657), 4–5. doi: 10.1016/s0140-6736(08)61765-1.

Uher, R. (2014) Gene–environment interactions in severe mental illness. *Frontiers in Psychiatry, 5*, 48. doi: http://doi.org/10.3389/fpsyt.2014.00048.

United Nations Office on Drugs and Crime. (2016) *World drug report*. New York: United Nations.

Upthegrove, R. (2009) Depression in schizophrenia and early psychosis: Implications for assessment and treatment. *Advances in Psychiatric Treatment, 15*, 372–379.

Upthegrove, R., Birchwood, M., Ross, K., Brunett, K., McCallum, R. & Jones, L. (2010) The evolution of depression and suicidality in first episode psychosis. *Acta Psychiatrica Scandinavica, 122*, 211–218. doi:/10.1016/j.psychres.2014.03.023.

Upthegrove, R., Ross, K., Brunet, K., McCollum, R. & Jones, L. (2014) Depression in FEP: The role of subordination and shame. *Psychiatry Research, 217*, pp. 177–184.

Valencia, M. Caraveo, J., Colin, R., Verduzco, W. & Corona, F. (2014) Symptomatic remission and functional recovery in patients with schizophrenia. *Salud Mental, 37*, 59–74.

Vancampfort, D., Madou, T., Moens, H., De Backer, T., Vanhalst, P., Helon, C., et al. (2015a) Could autonomous motivation hold the key to successfully implementing life-style changes in affective disorders? A multi-centre cross sectional study. *Psychiatry Research, 228*, 100–106.

Vancampfort, D., Stubbs, B., Mitchell, A., De Hert, M., Wampers, M., Ward, P. B., et al. (2015b) Risk of metabolic syndrome and its components in people with schizophrenia and related psychotic disorders, bipolar disorder and major depressive disorder: A systematic review and meta-analysis. *World Psychiatry, 14*(3), 339–347. doi: 10.1002/wps.2025.

Van den Berg, D. P. G., de Bont, P. A. J. M, van Der Vleugel, B. M., de Roos, C., de Jongh, A. Van Minnen, A., et al. (2015) Prolonged exposure vs. eye movement desensitisation and reprocessing vs. waiting list for posttraumatic stress disorder in patients with a psychotic disorder: A randomised clinical trial. *JAMA Psychiatry, 72*, 259–267. doi: 10.1001/jamapsychiatry.2014.2637.

Van der Gaag, M., Smit, F., Bechdolf, A., French, P., Linszen, D. H., Yung, A. R., et al. (2013) Preventing a first episode of psychosis: Meta-analysis of randomized controlled prevention trials of 12 month and longer-term follow-ups. *Schizophrenia Research, 149*(1–3), 56–62. doi: 10.1016/j.schres.2013.07.004.

Van der Gaag, M., Valmaggia, L. R. & Smit, F. (2014) Effects of individually tailored formulation-based cognitive behavioural therapy in auditory hallucinations and delusions: A meta-analysis. *Schizophrenia Research, 156*, 30–37.

Van der Werf, M., Hanssen, M., Köhler, S., Verkaaik, M., Verhey, F., Van Winkel, R., et al. (2014) Systematic review and collaborative recalculation of 133 693 incident cases of schizophrenia. *Psychological Medicine, 44*(1), 9–16. doi: 10.1017/S00332917 12002796.

Van Eck, R. M, Burger, T. J., Vellinga, A, Schirmbeck, F. & de Haan, L. (2018) The relationship between clinical and personal recovery in patients with schizophrenia spectrum disorders: A systematic review and meta-analysis. *Schizophrenia Bulletin, 44*(3), 631–642. doi: 10.1093/schbul/sbx088.

Van Heeringen, K., and Mann, J. J. (2014) The neurobiology of suicide. *Lancet Psychiatry, 1*(1), pp. 63–72. doi: 10.1016/S2215-0366(14)70220-2.

Van Humbeeck, G., Van Audenhove, C., Pieters, G., De Hert, M., Storms, G., Vertommen, H., et al. (2002) Expressed emotion in the client-professional caregiver dyad: Are symptoms, coping strategies and personality related? *Social Psychiatry and Psychiatric Epidemiology, 37*, 364–371.

Van Meijel, B, van der Gaag, M., Kahn, R. S. & Grypdonck, M. H. (2004) Recognition of early signs in patients with schizophrenia: A review of the literature. *International Journal of Mental Health Nursing, 13*, 107–116.

Van Orden, K. A., Cukrowicz, K. C., Witte, T. K. & Joiner, T. E. (2012) Thwarted belongingness and perceived burdensomeness: Construct validity and psychometric properties of the Interpersonal Needs Questionnaire. *Psychological Assessment, 24*(1), 197–215. doi: 10.1037/a0025358.

Van Os, J. & Guloksuz, S. (2017) A critique of the 'ultra-high risk' and 'transition' paradigm. *World Psychiatry, 16*(2), 200–206. doi: 10.1002/wps.20423.

Van Os, J. & Kapur, S. (2009) Schizophrenia. *Lancet, 374*(9690), 635–645. doi: 10.1016/S0140-6736(09)60995-8.

Van Os, J., Kenis, G. & Rutten, B. P. (2010) The environment and schizophrenia. *Nature, 468*(7321), 203–212. doi: 10.1038/nature09563.

Van Rooijen, G., Vermeulen, J. M., Ruhe, H. G. & de Haan, L. (2017) Treating depressive episodes or symptoms in patients with schizophrenia. *CNS Spectrum*, 1–10. doi: http://doi.org/10.1017/S1092852917000554.

Van Winkel, R., Van Nierop, M., Myin-Germeys, I. & van Os, J. (2013) Childhood trauma as a cause of psychosis: Linking genes, psychology, and biology. *The Canadian Journal of Psychiatry*, *58*(1), 44–51. doi: 10.1177/070674371305800109.

Varese, F., Smeets, F., Drukker, M., Lieverse, R., Lataster, T., Viechtbauer, W., et al. (2012) Childhood adversities increase the risk of psychosis: A meta-analysis of patient-control, prospective- and cross-sectional cohort studies. *Schizophrenia Bulletin*, *38*(4), 661–671. doi: 10.1093/schbul/sbs050.

Vass, V., Morrison, A. P., Law, H., Dudley, J., Taylor, P., Bennett, K. M., et al. (2015) How stigma impacts on people with psychosis: The mediating effect of self-esteem and hopelessness on subjective recovery and psychotic experiences. *Psychiatry Research*, *230*, 487–495. doi: 10.1016/j.psychres,2015.09.042.

Vassos, E., Pedersen, C. B., Murray, R. M., Collier, D. A. & Lewis, C. M. (2012) Meta-analysis of the association of urbanicity with schizophrenia. *Schizophrenia Bulletin*, *38*(6), 1118–1123. doi: http://doi.org/10.1093/schbul/sbs096.

Vaughn, C. (1986) Patterns of emotional response in the families of schizophrenic patients. In M. Goldstein, I. Hand & K. Halweg, *Treatment of schizophrenia* (pp. 97–106). New York: Springer-Verlag.

Veale, D. (2001) Cognitive behaviour therapy for body dysmorphia disorder. *Advances in Psychiatric Treatment*, *7*, 125–132.

Velligan, D. I., Kern, R. S. & Gold, J. M. (2006) Cognitive rehabilitation for schizophrenia and the putative role of motivation and expectancies. *Schizophrenia Bulletin*, *32*, 474–485.

Velthorst, E., Koeter, M., van der Gaag, M., Nieman, D. H., Fett, A. K., Smit, F., et al. (2015) Adapted cognitive–behavioural therapy required for targeting negative symptoms in schizophrenia: Meta-analysis and meta-regression. *Psychological Medicine*, *45*, 453–465. doi: 10.1017/S003329174001147.

Venkatasubramanian, G. & Amaresha, A. (2012) Expressed emotion in schizophrenia: An overview. *Indian Journal of Psychological Medicine*, *34*(1), 12. doi: 10.4103/0253-7176.96149.

Ventura, J., Hellemann, G. S., Thames, A. D., Koellner, V. & Nuechterlein, K. H. (2009) Symptoms as mediators of the relationship between neurocognition and functional outcome in schizophrenia: A meta-analysis. *Schizophrenia Research*, *113*, 189–199.

Ventura, J., Subotnik, K. L., Gretchen-Doorly, D., Casaus, L., Boucher, M., Hellemann, G. S., et al. (2017) Cognitive remediation can improve negative symptoms and social functioning in first-episode schizophrenia: A randomized controlled trial. *Schizophrenia Research*, doi: 10.1016/j.schres.2017.10.005.

Verma, S., Subramaniam, M., Abdin, E., Poon, L. Y. & Chong, S. A. (2012) Symptomatic and functional remission in patients with first-episode psychosis. *Acta Psychiatrica Scandinavica*, *126*, 282–289.

Vidal, C., Reese, C., Fischer, B., Chiapelli, J. & Himelhoch, S. (2015) Meta-analysis of efficacy of mirtazapine as an adjunctive treatment of negative symptoms in schizophrenia. *Clinical Schizophrenia & Related Psychoses*, *9*(2), 88–95. doi: 10.3371/csrp.vire.030813.

Vieweg, W. (2003) New generation antipsychotic drugs and QTc interval prolongation. *The Primary Care Companion to the Journal of Clinical Psychiatry*, *5*(5), 205–215. doi: 10.4088/pcc.v05n0504.

Volden, J. & Lord, C. (1991) Neologisms and idiosyncratic language in autistic speakers. *Journal of Autism and Developmental Disorders, 21*(2), 109–130. http://dx.doi.org/10.1007/bf02284755.

Waghorn, G., Hielscher, E., Saha, S. & McGrath, J. J. (2016) Cognitive and clinical indicators of employment assistance needs from a national survey of individuals living with psychosis. *Psychiatric Rehabilitation Journal, 39*, 112.

Wahlbeck, K., Cheine, M. & Essali, A. (1999) Clozapine versus typical neuroleptic medication for schizophrenia. *Cochrane Database of Systematic Reviews*. doi: 10.1002/14651858.cd000059.

Waldheter, E. J., Penn, D. L., Perkins, D. O., Mueser, K. T., Owens, L. W. & Cook, E. (2008) The graduated recovery intervention program for first episode psychosis: Treatment development and preliminary data. *Community Mental Health Journal, 44*, 443.

Walker, A., Lanza, L., Arellano, F. & Rothman, K. (1997) Mortality in current and former users of clozapine. *Epidemiology, 8*(6), 671. doi: 10.1097/00001648-199710000-00010.

Walker, A., Spring, J. & Travis, M. (2017) Addressing cognitive deficits in schizophrenia: Toward a neurobiologically informed approach. *Biological Psychiatry, 81*(1), 1–3. doi: 10.1016/j.biopsych.2016.10.023.

Warner, R. (2009) Recovery from schizophrenia: The recovery model. *Current Opinion in Psychiatry, 22*(4), 374–380. doi: 10.1097/YCO.0b013e32832c920b.

Wciórka, J., Switaj, P. & Anczewska, M. (2015) The stages of recovery in relation to the other subjective and objective aspects of psychosis. *Psychiatry Research, 225*, 613–618.

Weeraskera, P. (1993) Formulation: A multiperspective model. *The Canadian Journal of Psychiatry, 38*(5), 351–358.

Weiden, P., Mackell, J. & McDonnell, D. (2004) Obesity as a risk factor for antipsychotic noncompliance. *Schizophrenia Research, 66*(1), 51–57. doi: 10.1016/s0920-9964(02)00498-x.

Weisman, A. G., Nuechterlein, K. H., Goldstein, M. J. & Snyder, K. (1998) Expressed emotion, attributions, and schizophrenia symptom dimensions. *Journal of Abnormal Psychology, 107*, 355.

Weiss, D. S. & Marmar, C. R. (1997) The Impact of Event Scale-Revised. In J. P. Wilson & T. M. Keane (eds), *Assessing psychological trauma and PTSD: A handbook for practitioners* (pp. 399–411). New York: Guilford Press.

Westra, H. A., Aviram, A. & Doell, F. K. (2011) Extending motivational interviewing to the treatment of major mental health problems: Current directions and evidence. *The Canadian Journal of Psychiatry, 56*, 643–650.

Whale, R., Harris, M., Kavanagh, G., Wickramasinghe, V., Jones, C. & Marwaha, S., et al., (2016) Effectiveness of antipsychotics used in first-episode psychosis: A naturalistic cohort study. *British Journal of Psychiatry, 2*(5), 323–329. doi: 10.1192/bjpo.bp.116.002766.

Whaley, A. & Geller, P. (2003) Ethnic/racial differences in psychiatric disorders: A test of four hypotheses. *Ethnicity & Disease, 13*, 499–512.

White, H., Price, L. & Barker, T. (2017) Exploring the impact of peer support in early intervention in psychosis. *Mental Health and Social Inclusion, 21*(2), 102–109.

Whitehead, C., Moss, S., Cardno, A. & Lewis, G. (2003) Anti-depressants for the treatment of depression in people with schizophrenia: A systematic review. *Psychological Medicine, 33*(4), 589–599.

Whitty, P., Clarke, M., McTigue, O., Browne, S., Kamali, M., Kinsella, A., et al. (2008) Predictors of outcome in first-episode schizophrenia over the first 4 years of illness. *Psychological Medicine, 38(8)*, 1141–1146. doi: 10.1017/S003329170800336X.

Wiersma, D., Wanderling, J., Dragomirecka, E., Ganev, K., Harrison, G., An Der Heiden, W. A., et al. (2000) Social disability in schizophrenia: Its development and prediction over 15 years in incidence cohorts in six European centres. *Psychological Medicine, 30*, 1155–1167.

Wiersma, D., Wunderink, A., Nienhuis, F. & Sytema, S. (2007) The MESIFOS-trial: Treatment strategies in remitted first episode psychosis. *European Psychiatry, 22*, 76–77. doi: 10.1016/j.eurpsy.2007.01.294.

Wiguna, T., Ismail, R., Noorhana, S., Kaligis, F., Aji, A. & Belfer, M. (2015) Family responses to a child with schizophrenia: An Indonesian experience. *Asian Journal of Psychiatry, 18*, 66–69. doi: 10.1016/j.ajp.2015.09.009.

Willetts, L. & Leff, J. (2003) Improving the knowledge and skills of psychiatric nurses: efficacy of a staff training programme. *Journal of Advanced Nursing, 42*, 237–243.

Williams, J., Leamy, M., Pesola, F., Bird, V., Le Boutiller, C. & Slade, M. (2015) Psychometric evaluation of the questionnaire about the process of recovery (QPR). *The British Journal of Psychiatry, 207*, 551–555.

Williams, J. M. G., Barnhofer, T., Crane, C. & Beck, A. T. (2005) Problem solving deteriorates following mood challenge in formerly depressed patients with a history of suicidal ideation. *Journal of Abnormal Psychology, 114*, 421–431. doi: 10.1037/0021-843X.114.3.421.

Williams, S. (2015) *Recovering from psychosis: Empirical evidence and lived experience.* London: Routledge.

Wimberley, T., Støvring, H., Sørensen, H., Horsdal, H., MacCabe, J. & Gasse, C. (2016) Predictors of treatment resistance in patients with schizophrenia: A population-based cohort study. *The Lancet Psychiatry, 3*(4), 358–366. doi: 10.1016/s2215-0366(15)00575-1.

Windell, D. & Norman, R. M. (2013) A qualitative analysis of influences on recovery following a first episode of psychosis. *The International Journal of Social Psychiatry, 59*(5), 493–500. doi: 10.1177/0020764012443751.

Windell, D. L., Norman, R., Lal, S. & Malla, A. (2015) Subjective experiences of illness recovery in individuals treated for first-episode psychosis. *Social Psychiatry and Psychiatric Epidemiology, 50*(7), 1069–77. doi: 10.1007/s00127-014-1006-x.

Windell, D., Norman, R. & Mall, A. K. (2012) The personal meaning of recovery among individuals treated for a first episode of psychosis. *Psychiatric Services, 63*, 548–553.

Wing, J. K., Curtis, R. H. & Beevor, A. S. (1996) *HoNOS: Health of the Nation Outcome Scales: Report on research and development July 1993–December 1995.* London: Royal College of Psychiatrists.

Winton-Brown, T., Elanjithara, T., Power, P., Coentre, R., Blanco-Polaina, P. & McGuire, P. (2017) Five-fold increased risk of relapse following breaks in antipsychotic treatment of first episode psychosis. *Schizophrenia Research, 179*, 50–56. doi: 10.1016/j.schres.2016.09.029.

Wisdom, J., Manuel, J. & Drake, R. (2011) Substance use disorder among people with first-episode psychosis: A systematic review of course and treatment. *Psychiatric Services, 62*(9). http://dx.doi.org/10.1176/appi.ps.62.9.1007.

Wium-Andersen, M., Orsted, D. & Nordestgaard, B. (2015) Tobacco smoking is causally associated with antipsychotic medication use and schizophrenia, but not with antidepressant medication use or depression. *International Journal of Epidemiology, 44*(2), 566–577. doi: 10.1093/ije/dyv090.

Wobrock, T., Guse, B., Cordes, J., Wölwer, W., Winterer, G. & Gaebel, W., et al. (2015) Left prefrontal high-frequency repetitive transcranial magnetic stimulation for the treatment of schizophrenia with predominant negative symptoms: A sham-controlled, randomized multicenter trial. *Biological Psychiatry, 77*(11), 979–988. doi: 10.1016/j. biopsych.2014.10.009.

Wong, C., Davidson, L., Anglin, D., Link, B., Gerson, R., Malaspina, D., et al. (2009) Stigma in families of individuals in early stages of psychotic illness: family stigma and early psychosis. *Early Intervention in Psychiatry, 3*(2), 108–115. doi: 10.1111/j.1751-7893. 2009.00116.x.

Wood, L. & Alsawy, S. (2017) Recovery in psychosis from a service user perspective: A systematic review and thematic synthesis of current qualitative evidence. *Community Mental Health Journal.* doi: 10.1007/s10597-017-0185-9.

Woods, A., Jones, N., Alderson-Day, B., Callard, F. & Fernyhough, C. (2015) Experiences of hearing voices: Analysis of a novel phenomenological survey. *The Lancet Psychiatry, 2*(4), 323–331. http://dx.doi.org/10.1016/s2215-0366(15)00006-1.

World Health Organisation. (2001) *International classification of functioning, disability and health: ICF.* Geneva: World Health Organization.

World Health Organisation. (2012) *Resources for the prevention and treatment of substance use disorders.* Geneva: WHO.

Worthington, A., Rooney, P. & Hannan, R. (2013) *The triangle of care – carers included: A guide to best practice in mental health care in England* (2nd edn). London: Carers Trust.

Wright, B., Williams. C. & Garland, A. (2002) Using the 5-area approach with psychiatric patients. *Advances in Psychiatric Treatment,* 8, 307–315.

Wright, N. P., Turkington, D., Kelly, O. P., Davies, D., Jacobs, A. M. & Hopton, J. (2014) *Treating psychosis: A clinician's guide to integrating acceptance and commitment therapy, compassion-focused therapy, and mindfulness approaches within the cognitive behavioural therapy tradition.* Oakland, CA: New Harbinger Publications.

Wunderink, A., Nienhuis, F., Sytema, S., Slooff, C., Knegtering, R. & Wiersma, D. (2008) Guided discontinuation versus maintenance treatment in remitted first episode psychosis: Relapse rates and functional outcome. *Schizophrenia Research, 102*(1–3), 52–53. doi: 10.1016/s0920-9964(08)70166-x.

Wunderink, L., Nieboer, R. M., Wiersma, D., Sytema, S. & Nienhuis, F. J. (2013) Recovery in remitted first-episode psychosis at 7 years of follow-up of an early dose reduction/discontinuation or maintenance treatment strategy: long-term follow-up of a 2-year randomized clinical trial. *JAMA Psychiatry, 70*, 913–920.

Wunderink, L., Sytema, S., Nienhuis, F. J. & Wiersma, D. (2009) Clinical recovery in first-episode psychosis. *Schizophrenia Bulletin, 35*, 362–369.

Wüsten, C. & Lincoln, T. (2017) The association of family functioning and psychosis proneness in five countries that differ in cultural values and family structures. *Psychiatry Research, 253*, 158–164. doi: 10.1016/j.psychres.2017.03.041.

Wutke, K. (2013) Relatives of people with psychosis: Experiences of caregiving and interventions (DClinPsych). University of Warwick.

Wyatt, R. (1991) Neuroleptics and the natural course of schizophrenia. *Schizophrenia Bulletin, 17*(2), 325–351. doi: 10.1093/schbul/17.2.325.

Wykes, T., Huddy, V., Cellard, C., McGurk, S. R. & Czobor, P. (2011) A meta-analysis of cognitive remediation for schizophrenia: Methodology and effect sizes. *The American Journal Psychiatry, 168*(5), 472–485.

Wykes, T. & Reeder, C. (2005) *Cognitive remediation therapy for schizophrenia: An introduction.* New York: Brunner-Routledge.

Wykes, T., Reeder, C., Huddy, V., Taylor, R., Wood, H., Ghirasim, N., et al. (2012) Developing models of how cognitive improvements change functioning: mediation, moderation and moderated mediation. *Schizophrenia Research, 138*, 88–93.

Wykes, T., Steel, C., Everitt, B. & Tarrier, N. (2008) Cognitive behavior therapy for schizophrenia: Effect sizes, clinical models, and methodological rigor. *Schizophrenia Bulletin, 34*, 523–537.

Yalom, I. & Leszcz, M. (2008) *The theory and practice of group psychotherapy.* London: Hachette.

Yamazawa, R., Nemoto, T., Kobayashi, H., Chino, B., Kashima, H. & Mizuno, M. (2008) Association between duration of untreated psychosis, premorbid functioning, and cognitive performance and the outcome of first-episode schizophrenia in Japanese patients: Prospective study. *Australian & New Zealand Journal of Psychiatry, 42*, 159–165.

Yanos, P. T., Roe, D., Markus, K. & Lysaker, P. H. (2008) Pathways between internalized stigma and outcomes related to recovery in schizophrenia spectrum disorders. *Psychiatric Services, 59*, 1437–1442.

Yoshimura, B., Yada, Y., So, R., Takaki, M. & Yamada, N. (2017) The critical treatment window of clozapine in treatment-resistant schizophrenia: Secondary analysis of an observational study. *Psychiatry Research, 250*, 65–70. doi: 10.1016/j.psychres.2017.01.064.

Young, D. (2015) Positive effects of spirituality in facilitating recovery for people with severe mental illness. *International Journal of Psychosocial Rehabilitation, 19*(1), 5–12.

Yung, A. R. (2017) Treatment of people at ultra-high risk for psychosis. *World Psychiatry, 16*, 207–208. doi: 10.1002/wps.20424.

Yung, A., Nelson, B., Baker, K., Buckby, J., Baksheev, G. & Cosgrave, E. (2009) Psychotic-like experiences in a community sample of adolescents: Implications for the continuum model of psychosis and prediction of schizophrenia. *Australian & New Zealand Journal of Psychiatry, 43*(2), 118–128. http://dx.doi.org/10.1080/00048670802607188

Yung, A., Stanford, C., Cosgrave, E., Killackey, E., Phillips, L., Nelson, B., et al. (2006) Testing the Ultra High Risk (prodromal) criteria for the prediction of psychosis in a clinical sample of young people. *Schizophrenia Research, 84*(1), 57–66.

Yu Zheng, C. (2016) Time to re-evaluate clozapine practices. *Acta Psychopathologica, 2*(6). doi: 10.4172/2469-6676.100070.

Zhang, J., Gallego, J., Robinson, D., Malhotra, A., Kane, J. & Correll, C. (2012) Efficacy and safety of individual second-generation vs. first-generation antipsychotics in first-episode psychosis: A systematic review and meta-analysis. *The International Journal of Neuropsychopharmacology, 16*(6), 1205–1218. doi: 10.1017/s1461145712001277.

Zhou, Y., Ning, Y., Rosenheck, R., Sun, B., Zhang, J., Ou, Y., et al. (2016) Effect of living with patients on caregiver burden of individual with schizophrenia in China. *Psychiatry Research, 245*, 230–237. doi: 10.1016/j.psychres.2016.08.046.

Zhu, Y., Krause, M., Huhn, M., Rothe, P., Schneider-Thoma, J., Chaimani, A., et al. (2017) Antipsychotic drugs for the acute treatment of patients with a first episode of schizophrenia: A systematic review with pairwise and network meta-analyses. *The Lancet Psychiatry, 4*(9), 694–705.

Zimmerman, M. (1994) Diagnosing personality disorders. *Archives of General Psychiatry, 51*(3), 225. http://dx.doi.org/10.1001/archpsyc.1994.03950030061006.

Zou, H., Li, Z., Nolan, M., Wang, H. & Hu, L. (2013) Self-management among Chinese people with schizophrenia and their caregivers: A qualitative study. *Archives of Psychiatric Nursing, 27*(1), 42–53. doi: 10.1016/j.apnu.2012.10.002.

Index

Printed in Great Britain
by Amazon